KU-009-335

Dear Reader,

Thank you for choosing *Mastering AutoCAD 2015 and AutoCAD LT 2015*. This book is part of a family of premium-quality Sybex books, all of which are written by outstanding authors who combine practical experience with a gift for teaching.

Sybex was founded in 1976. More than 30 years later, we're still committed to producing consistently exceptional books. With each of our titles, we're working hard to set a new standard for the industry. From the paper we print on, to the authors we work with, our goal is to bring you the best books available.

I hope you see all that reflected in these pages. I'd be very interested to hear your comments and get your feedback on how we're doing. Feel free to let me know what you think about this or any other Sybex book by sending me an email at contactus@sybex.com. If you think you've found a technical error in this book, please visit http://sybex.custhelp.com. Customer feedback is critical to our efforts at Sybex.

Best regards,

Chris Webb
Associate Publisher
Sybex, an Imprint of Wiley

To the memory of my brother
Masayuki Omura: 1939–2014.
—G.O.

3230328631

# Mastering
## AutoCAD® 2015 and
## AutoCAD LT® 2015

George Omura

with Brian Benton

CITY OF GLASGOW COLLEGE
North Hanover Street Library
60 North Hanover Street
G1 2EP
066 4132

AUTODESK®
Official Press

SYBEX®
A Wiley Brand

Senior Acquisitions Editor: Willem Knibbe

Development Editor: Stephanie Barton

Technical Editor: Richard Hawley

Production Editor: Dassi Zeidel

Copy Editor: Liz Welch

Editorial Manager: Pete Gaughan

Vice President and Executive Group Publisher: Richard Swadley

Associate Publisher: Chris Webb

Book Designers: Maureen Forys, Happenstance Type-O-Rama; Judy Fung

Compositor: Craig Woods, Happenstance Type-O-Rama

Proofreader: Amy J. Schneider

Indexer: Ted Laux

Project Coordinator, Cover: Todd Klemme

Cover Designer: Wiley

Cover Image: ©iStock.com/pawel.gaul

Copyright © 2014 by John Wiley & Sons, Inc., Indianapolis, Indiana

Published simultaneously in Canada

ISBN: 978-1-118-86208-7

ISBN: 978-1-118-93246-9 (ebk)

ISBN: 978-1-118-86222-3 (ebk)

No part of this publication may be reproduced, stored in a retrieval system or transmitted in any form or by any means, electronic, mechanical, photocopying, recording, scanning or otherwise, except as permitted under Sections 107 or 108 of the 1976 United States Copyright Act, without either the prior written permission of the Publisher, or authorization through payment of the appropriate per-copy fee to the Copyright Clearance Center, 222 Rosewood Drive, Danvers, MA 01923, (978) 750-8400, fax (978) 646-8600. Requests to the Publisher for permission should be addressed to the Permissions Department, John Wiley & Sons, Inc., 111 River Street, Hoboken, NJ 07030, (201) 748-6011, fax (201) 748-6008, or online at http://www.wiley.com/go/permissions.

Limit of Liability/Disclaimer of Warranty: The publisher and the author make no representations or warranties with respect to the accuracy or completeness of the contents of this work and specifically disclaim all warranties, including without limitation warranties of fitness for a particular purpose. No warranty may be created or extended by sales or promotional materials. The advice and strategies contained herein may not be suitable for every situation. This work is sold with the understanding that the publisher is not engaged in rendering legal, accounting, or other professional services. If professional assistance is required, the services of a competent professional person should be sought. Neither the publisher nor the author shall be liable for damages arising herefrom. The fact that an organization or Web site is referred to in this work as a citation and/or a potential source of further information does not mean that the author or the publisher endorses the information the organization or Web site may provide or recommendations it may make. Further, readers should be aware that Internet Web sites listed in this work may have changed or disappeared between when this work was written and when it is read.

For general information on our other products and services or to obtain technical support, please contact our Customer Care Department within the U.S. at (877) 762-2974, outside the U.S. at (317) 572-3993 or fax (317) 572-4002.

Wiley publishes in a variety of print and electronic formats and by print-on-demand. Some material included with standard print versions of this book may not be included in e-books or in print-on-demand. If this book refers to media such as a CD or DVD that is not included in the version you purchased, you may download this material at http://booksupport.wiley.com. For more information about Wiley products, visit www.wiley.com.

Library of Congress Control Number: 2014931926

TRADEMARKS: Wiley and the Sybex logo are trademarks or registered trademarks of John Wiley & Sons, Inc. and/or its affiliates, in the United States and other countries, and may not be used without written permission. AutoCAD and AutoCAD LT are registered trademarks of Autodesk, Inc. All other trademarks are the property of their respective owners. John Wiley & Sons, Inc. is not associated with any product or vendor mentioned in this book.

10 9 8 7 6 5 4 3 2

# Acknowledgments

Many talented and hardworking folks gave their best effort to produce *Mastering AutoCAD 2015 and AutoCAD LT 2015*. I offer my sincerest gratitude to those people who helped bring this book to you.

Heartfelt thanks go to the editorial and production teams at Sybex for their efforts. Willem Knibbe and Pete Gaughan made sure things got off to a great start and were there for support at all times. Steph Barton kept a watchful eye on the progress of the book. Richard Hawley did an excellent job of ensuring that I didn't make any glaring mistakes and offered many great suggestions. On the production side, Dassi Zeidel kept the workflow going and answered my dumb questions during the review process, and Liz Welch made sure I wasn't trying out new uses of the English language.

Thanks also go to Denis Cadu, who has always given his steadfast support to my efforts over many projects. Jim Quanci always gives his generous and thoughtful assistance to us author types—I'd be lost without your help, Jim. Thanks to Barbara Vezos for her support. Finally, as always, a big thanks to Shaan Hurley, Lisa Crounse, and the Autodesk beta team for generously allowing us to have a look at the prerelease software.

And a great big thank-you to my family and friends, who have been there for me through thick and thin.

# About the Authors

**George Omura** is a licensed architect, Autodesk Authorized Author, and CAD specialist with more than 27 years of experience in AutoCAD and over 35 years of experience in architecture. He has worked on design projects ranging from resort hotels to metropolitan transit systems. George has written numerous other AutoCAD books for Sybex, including *Introducing AutoCAD 2010 and AutoCAD LT 2010* and *Mastering AutoCAD 2012 and AutoCAD LT 2012*.

**Brian C. Benton** is a senior engineering technician, CAD service provider, technical writer, and blogger. He has over 20 years of experience in various design fields (mechanical, structural, civil, survey, marine, environmental) and is well versed in many design software packages (CAD, GIS, graphics). He is *Cadalyst* magazine's Tip Patroller, AUGI HotNews production manager, and Infinite Skills' AutoCAD training video author.

# Contents at a Glance

# Contents

# Introduction

Welcome to *Mastering AutoCAD 2015 and AutoCAD LT 2015*. As many readers have already discovered, this book is a unique blend of tutorial and reference that includes everything you need to get started and stay ahead with Autodesk® AutoCAD® software. With this edition, you get coverage of the latest features of both AutoCAD 2015 and AutoCAD LT® 2015 software along with detailed information on existing features.

## How to Use This Book

Rather than just showing you how each command works, this book shows you AutoCAD 2015 in the context of a meaningful activity. You'll learn how to use commands while working on an actual project and progressing toward a goal. This book also provides a foundation on which you can build your own methods for using AutoCAD and become an AutoCAD expert. For this reason, we haven't covered every single command or every permutation of a command response. You should think of this book as a way to get a detailed look at AutoCAD as it's used on a real project. As you follow the exercises, we also encourage you to explore AutoCAD on your own, applying the techniques you learn to your own work.

Both experienced and beginning AutoCAD users will find this book useful. If you aren't an experienced user, the way to get the most out of this book is to approach it as a tutorial—chapter by chapter, at least for the first two parts of the book. You'll find that each chapter builds on the skills and information you learned in the previous one. To help you navigate, the exercises are shown in numbered steps. To address the needs of all readers worldwide, the exercises provide both Imperial (feet/inches) and metric measurements. Some exercises use generic units of measurement or, if the focus of the exercise is not dependent on the measurement system, Imperial is used.

After you've mastered the material in Parts 1 and 2, you can follow your interests and explore other parts of the book in whatever order you choose. Part 3 takes you to a more advanced skill level. There you'll learn more about storing and sharing drawing data and how to create more complex drawings. If you're interested in 3D, check out Part 4. If you want to start customizing right away, go to Part 5. You can check out Chapter 25 at any time because it gives you general information about sharing AutoCAD files with your coworkers and consultants. You can also use this book as a ready reference for your day-to-day problems and questions about commands. The Bottom Line section at the end of each chapter will help you review and look at different ways to apply the information you've learned. Experienced users will also find this book a handy reference tool.

Finally, you can learn more about AutoCAD through the author-supplied bonus chapters found at www.omura.com/chapters. For example, if you run into problems using AutoCAD, see the section "When Things Go Wrong" in the bonus chapter "Hardware and Software Tips." To delve into the details of printers and plotting, check out the bonus chapter "Understanding Plot Styles."

## AutoCAD 2015 and AutoCAD LT 2015

Autodesk has released both AutoCAD 2015 and AutoCAD LT 2015 simultaneously. Not surprisingly, they're nearly identical in the way they look and work. You can share files between the two programs with complete confidence that you won't lose data or corrupt files. The main differences are that AutoCAD LT doesn't support all the 3D functions of AutoCAD 2015, nor does it support the customization tools of AutoLISP® or the .NET Framework. But AutoCAD LT still has plenty to offer in both the productivity and customization areas. Because they're so similar, we can present material for both programs with only minor adjustments.

When a feature is discussed that is available only in AutoCAD 2015, you'll see the AutoCAD Only icon.

For the purposes of this publication, the "ACAD only" icon means the relevant (or adjacent) content applies only to AutoCAD software and not to AutoCAD LT software.

You'll also see warning messages when tutorials vary between AutoCAD 2015 and AutoCAD LT. If only minor differences occur, you'll see either a warning message or directions embedded in the tutorial indicating the differences between the two programs.

We've also provided workaround instructions wherever possible when AutoCAD LT doesn't offer a feature found in AutoCAD 2015.

## Getting Information Fast

In each chapter, you'll find extensive tips and discussions in the form of sidebars set off from the main text. These provide a wealth of information we have gathered over years of using AutoCAD on a variety of projects in different office environments. You may want to browse through the book and read these boxes just to get an idea of how they might be useful to you.

Another available quick reference is the online bonus chapter "System Variables and Dimension Styles." It contains descriptions of all the dimension settings with comments on their uses. If you experience any problems, you can consult the section "When Things Go Wrong" in the online bonus chapter "Hardware and Software Tips."

## The Mastering Series

The *Mastering* series from Sybex provides outstanding instruction for readers with intermediate and advanced skills in the form of top-notch training and development for those already working in their field, and clear, serious education for those aspiring to become pros. Every *Mastering* book includes the following:

♦ Skill-based instruction, with chapters organized around real tasks rather than abstract concepts or subjects

♦ Self-review test questions, so you can be certain you're equipped to do the job right

# What to Expect

*Mastering AutoCAD 2015 and AutoCAD LT 2015* is divided into five parts, each representing a milestone in your progress toward becoming an expert AutoCAD user. Here is a description of those parts and what they will show you.

## Part 1: The Basics

As with any major endeavor, you must begin by tackling small, manageable tasks. In this first part, you'll become familiar with the way AutoCAD looks and feels.

♦ Chapter 1, "Exploring the Interface," shows you how to get around in AutoCAD.

♦ Chapter 2, "Creating Your First Drawing," details how to start and exit the program and how to respond to AutoCAD commands.

♦ Chapter 3, "Setting Up and Using the Drafting Tools," tells you how to set up a work area, edit objects, and lay out a drawing.

♦ Chapter 4, "Organizing Objects with Blocks and Groups," explores some tools unique to CAD: symbols, blocks, and layers. As you're introduced to AutoCAD, you'll also get a chance to make some drawings that you can use later in the book and perhaps even in future projects of your own.

♦ Chapter 5, "Keeping Track of Layers and Blocks," shows you how to use layers to keep similar information together and object properties such as linetypes to organize things visually.

## Part 2: Mastering Intermediate Skills

After you have the basics down, you'll begin to explore some of the more subtle qualities of AutoCAD.

♦ Chapter 6, "Editing and Reusing Data to Work Efficiently," tells you how to reuse drawing setup information and parts of an existing drawing.

♦ Chapter 7, "Mastering Viewing Tools, Hatches, and External References," details how to use viewing tools and hatches and how to assemble and edit a large drawing file.

♦ Chapter 8, "Introducing Printing, Plotting, and Layouts," shows you how to get your drawing onto hard copy.

♦ Chapter 9, "Adding Text to Drawings," tells you how to annotate your drawing and edit your notes.

♦ Chapter 10, "Using Fields and Tables," shows you how to add spreadsheet functionality to your drawings.

♦ Chapter 11, "Using Dimensions," gives you practice in using automatic dimensioning (another unique CAD capability).

## Part 3: Mastering Advanced Skills

At this point, you'll be on the verge of becoming a real AutoCAD expert. Part 3 is designed to help you polish your existing skills and give you a few new ones.

♦ Chapter 12, "Using Attributes," tells you how to attach information to drawing objects and how to export that information to database and spreadsheet files.

♦ Chapter 13, "Copying Existing Drawings from Other Sources," details techniques for transferring paper drawings to AutoCAD. You'll also learn how to include aerial and map views in your drawings.

♦ Chapter 14, "Advanced Editing and Organizing," is where you'll complete the apartment building tutorial. During this process you'll learn how to integrate what you've learned so far and gain some tips on working in groups.

♦ Chapter 15, "Laying Out Your Printer Output," shows you the tools that let you display your drawing in an organized fashion.

♦ Chapter 16, "Making 'Smart' Drawings with Parametric Tools," introduces you to parametric drawing. This feature lets you quickly modify a drawing by changing a few parameters.

♦ Chapter 17, "Using Dynamic Blocks," shows you how you can create blocks that can be edited with grips without having to redefine them.

♦ Chapter 18, "Drawing Curves," gives you an in-depth look at some special drawing objects, such as splines and fitted curves.

♦ Chapter 19, "Getting and Exchanging Data from Drawings," is where you'll practice getting information about a drawing and learn how AutoCAD can interact with other applications, such as spreadsheets and page layout programs. You'll also learn how to copy and paste data.

## Part 4: 3D Modeling and Imaging

Although 2D drafting is the workhorse application in AutoCAD, its 3D capabilities give you a chance to expand your ideas and look at them in a new light.

♦ Chapter 20, "Creating 3D Drawings," covers basic features for creating three-dimensional drawings.

♦ Chapter 21, "Using Advanced 3D Features," introduces you to some of the program's more powerful 3D capabilities.

♦ Chapter 22, "Editing and Visualizing 3D Solids," takes a closer look at 3D solids and how they can be created, edited, and displayed in AutoCAD 2015.

♦ Chapter 23, "Exploring 3D Mesh and Surface Modeling," introduces you to free-form 3D modeling using mesh and surface objects. With this latest addition to AutoCAD, there isn't anything you can't model in 3D.

## Part 5: Customization and Integration

One of the greatest strengths of AutoCAD is its openness to customization, which you'll explore in this section.

♦ Chapter 24, "Customizing Toolbars, Menus, Linetypes, and Hatch Patterns," shows you how to use workspaces, customize the user interface, and create custom linetypes and hatch patterns. You'll also be introduced to the DIESEL macro language.

♦ Chapter 25, "Managing and Sharing Your Drawings," shows you how to adapt AutoCAD to your own work style. You'll learn about the tools that help you exchange drawings with others and how to secure your drawings to prevent tampering.

## The Appendices

Finally, this book has several appendices.

♦ Appendix A, "The Bottom Line," contains the solutions to the book's Master It review questions.

♦ Appendix B, "Installing and Setting Up AutoCAD," contains an installation and configuration tutorial. If AutoCAD isn't already installed on your system, follow the steps in this tutorial before starting Chapter 1.

♦ Appendix C, "The Autodesk AutoCAD 2015 Certification," shows you where in the book the learning objectives are covered for the Certified User, Certified Associate, and Certified Professional Exams. If you want to get certified, this information will be very useful.

# Where to Get the Tutorial Files and Bonus Chapters

Many of the exercises in this book make use of sample files that you can download from the following website: www.sybex.com/go/masteringautocad2015. With these files, you can pick up an exercise anywhere you like without having to work through the book from front to back. You can also use these sample files to repeat exercises or to just explore how files are organized and put together. You can also download additional bonus chapters that cover other AutoCAD features from www.omura.com/chapters. The bonus chapters are:

♦ "Using the Express Tools" gives you a gentle introduction to the world of AutoCAD customization. You'll learn how to load and use existing Express tools that expand the software's functionality, and you'll be introduced to AutoLISP as a tool to create macros.

♦ "Exploring AutoLISP" is a primer to this popular macro language found in AutoCAD. You'll learn how you can create custom commands built on existing ones and how you can retrieve and store locations and other data.

♦ "Hardware and Software Tips" provides information about hardware related to AutoCAD. It also offers tips on improving the performance of AutoCAD and troubleshooting and provides more detailed information on setting up the plotting feature.

♦ "System Variables and Dimension Styles" provides a reference to dimension style settings.

- ◆ "Understanding Plot Styles" discusses methods for controlling lineweights and shading in your printer output.

- ◆ "Rendering 3D Drawings" shows how you can use AutoCAD to produce lifelike views of your 3D drawings.

- ◆ "Keeping a Project Organized with Sheet Sets" shows you how to use the Sheet Set Manager to simplify your file management. By using the Sheet Set Manager, you can automate some of the tedious drawing coordination tasks.

---

### THE AUTOCAD FREE TRIAL

If you don't have AutoCAD, you can download and install a trial version from the Autodesk website (www.autodesk.com). Be aware that the trial is good for only 30 days and cannot be reinstalled to add time to the trial period—don't start to use it until you're certain you'll have plenty of free time to practice using AutoCAD.

---

### FREE AUTODESK SOFTWARE FOR STUDENTS AND EDUCATORS

The Autodesk Education Community is an online resource with more than 5 million members that enables educators and students to download—for free (see website for terms and conditions)—the same software used by professionals worldwide. You can also access additional tools and materials to help you design, visualize, and simulate ideas. Connect with other learners to stay current with the latest industry trends and get the most out of your designs. Get started today at www.autodesk.com/joinedu.

---

## The Minimum System Requirements

This book assumes you have a Windows-based PC with at least a dual-core processor or equivalent CPU. Your computer should have at least one DVD drive and a hard disk with 2 GB or more of free space for the AutoCAD program files and about 120 MB of additional space for sample files and the workspace. In addition to these requirements, you should have enough free disk space to allow for a Windows virtual memory page file that is about 1.5 times the amount of installed RAM. Consult your Windows manual or the online bonus chapter "Hardware and Software Tips," available at www.omura.com/chapters, for more on virtual memory.

AutoCAD 2015 runs best on systems with at least 2 GB or more of RAM. Your computer should also have a high-resolution monitor and an up-to-date display card. An SVGA display with a resolution of 1024×768 or greater will work fine with AutoCAD, but if you want to take full advantage of the 3D features, you should have a 128 MB or greater, OpenGL-capable, workstation-class graphics card. If you intend to use a digitizer tablet, you'll need one free USB port available. We also assume you're using a mouse and have the use of a printer or a plotter. Finally, you'll need an Internet connection to take full advantage of the support offerings from Autodesk.

If you want a more detailed explanation of hardware options with AutoCAD, see the online bonus chapter "Hardware and Software Tips." You'll find a general description of the available hardware options and their significance to AutoCAD.

## Doing Things in Style

Much care has been taken to see that the stylistic conventions in this book—the use of uppercase or lowercase letters, italic or boldface type, and so on—are the ones most likely to help you learn AutoCAD. On the whole, their effect should be subliminal. However, you may find it useful to be conscious of the following rules:

◆ Menu selections are shown by a series of options separated by the ➢ symbol (for example, choose File ➢ New). These are typically used to show selections from a context menu or the Application menu, which you will learn about in Chapter 1.

◆ Keyboard entries are shown in boldface (for example, enter **Rotate↵**).

◆ Command-line prompts are shown in a monospaced font (for example, `Select objects:`).

For most functions, this book describes how to select options from Ribbon panels and the Application menu. In addition, where applicable, we include related keyboard shortcuts and command names in parentheses. These command names provide continuity for readers who are accustomed to working at the Command prompt.

## New Features of AutoCAD 2015

AutoCAD 2015 has a long list of new features, many of which are aimed at making your work easier and faster. Some features like Autodesk 360® and Autodesk Exchange are web tools that help you share your work, keep up with the latest on AutoCAD, and discuss issues you may be having. Here are some of the new features we cover in this book:

◆ Improved online help and collaboration tools

◆ Updated color scheme

◆ Improved visual feedback

◆ Quicker access to blocks

◆ Streamlined status bar

◆ Lasso selection

◆ Viewport enhancements

◆ Easy-to-use text columns

## Contact the Authors

We hope that *Mastering AutoCAD 2015 and AutoCAD LT 2015* will be of benefit to you and that, after you've completed the tutorials, you'll continue to use the book as a reference. If you have comments, criticism, or ideas about how the book can be improved, you can email us at the following addresses:

George Omura: george.omura@gmail.com

Brian C. Benton: bbenton@cad-a-blog.com

If you find errors, please let our publisher know. Visit the book's web page, www.sybex.com/go/masteringautocad2015, and click the Errata link to find a form to use to identify the problem.

And thanks for choosing *Mastering AutoCAD 2015 and AutoCAD LT 2015*.

# Part 1

# The Basics

# Chapter 1

# Exploring the Interface

Before you can start to use the new capabilities of the AutoCAD® 2015 software, you must become familiar with the basics. If you're completely new to AutoCAD, you'll want to read this first chapter carefully. It introduces you to many basic operations of AutoCAD, such as opening and closing files, getting a close-up look at part of a drawing, and changing a drawing. If you're familiar with earlier versions of AutoCAD, you should review this chapter anyway to get acquainted with the features you haven't already used.

Autodesk releases new versions of AutoCAD every year. Part of this strategy is to introduce improvements that focus on a particular category of features. This latest version, AutoCAD 2015, offers interface enhancements to make working with AutoCAD easier.

In previous versions, AutoCAD would open directly into a new, blank drawing. AutoCAD now opens to the *Dashboard*, a feature that enables you to quickly create a new drawing or open a previously opened drawing. Recently opened drawings are shown as thumbnails in the Dashboard.

Other new features can be found when you start to draw. If you've used earlier versions of AutoCAD, you'll notice a new "dark" color scheme. Line work looks smoother with a new anti-aliasing feature. Other visual effects have been added to help you select objects and to give you better feedback as you perform common tasks.

Before you begin the exercises in this chapter, make sure that you have loaded the sample files from this book's web page at www.sybex.com/go/masteringautocad2015. See the introduction for details. If you have purchased the e-book version, please see the introduction for instructions on how to download the sample files.

In this chapter, you will learn to

♦ Use the AutoCAD window

♦ Get a closer look with the Zoom command

♦ Save a file as you work

♦ Make changes and open multiple files

## Taking a Guided Tour

First, you'll get a chance to familiarize yourself with the AutoCAD screen and how you communicate with AutoCAD. As you do the exercises in this chapter, you'll also get a feel for how to work with this book. Don't worry about understanding or remembering everything you see in this chapter. You'll get plenty of opportunities to probe the finer details of the program as you work through the later chapters. To help you remember the material, we have included a brief set of questions at the end of each chapter. For now, just enjoy your first excursion into AutoCAD.

**ACAD only**

### AutoCAD References in This Book

In this chapter and throughout the rest of the book, when we say AutoCAD, we mean both AutoCAD and AutoCAD LT®. Some topics apply only to AutoCAD. In those situations, you'll see an icon indicating that the topic applies only to AutoCAD and not to AutoCAD LT. If you're using AutoCAD LT 2015, these icons can help you focus on the topics that are more relevant to your work by letting you skim over items that do not apply.

AutoCAD 2015 is designed to run on Windows 7 and Windows 8. This book was written using AutoCAD 2015 running Windows 7 Professional.

## Launching AutoCAD

If you've already installed AutoCAD (see Appendix B, "Installing and Setting Up AutoCAD") and are ready to jump in and take a look, proceed with the following steps to launch the program:

1. Choose Start ➢ All Programs ➢ Autodesk ➢ AutoCAD 2015 ➢ AutoCAD 2015. You can also double-click the AutoCAD 2015 icon on your Windows Desktop. AutoCAD LT users will use AutoCAD LT 2015 in place of AutoCAD 2015.

2. The AutoCAD Dashboard appears, offering options to open existing drawings or to create a new drawing. You may also see the Design Feed panel, which allows you to use a cloud-based collaboration feature. Click the Start Drawing thumbnail in the left side of the view under "Get Started" (see Figure 1.1).

3. The AutoCAD window displays a blank default document named Drawing1.dwg. Users may see the Sheet Set Manager palette to the left of the AutoCAD window. AutoCAD LT users may see the Info palette to the left of the AutoCAD window.

**FIGURE 1.1**
The Dashboard offers easy access to previous work.

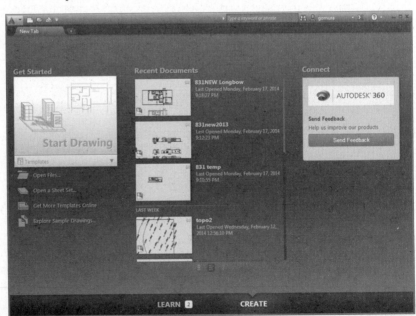

If you're using the trial version, you'll see the Product License Activation window before step 2. This window shows you the number of days you have left in the trial version. You can also activate the product here if you purchase a license. Click the Try button to continue opening the program. Now let's look at the AutoCAD window in detail. Don't worry if it seems like a lot of information. You don't have to memorize it, but by looking at all the parts, you'll be aware of what is available in a general way.

## The AutoCAD Window

**CERT OBJECTIVE**

The AutoCAD program window is divided into several parts:

◆ Application menu

◆ Quick Access toolbar

◆ InfoCenter

◆ Ribbon

◆ Drawing tabs

◆ Drawing area

◆ UCS icon (User Coordinate System icon)

◆ Viewport Controls

◆ ViewCube®

◆ Navigation bar

◆ Command window

◆ Status bar

Figure 1.2 shows a typical layout of the AutoCAD program window. You can organize the AutoCAD window into any arrangement you want and save it as a *workspace*. You can save and recall a workspace at any time using the Workspace Switching tool in the Quick Access toolbar. (You'll learn more about this tool in the next chapter.) The default workspace in Figure 1.2 is called the Drafting & Annotation workspace and is one of several workspaces built into AutoCAD.

---

### AutoCAD for 3D

For 3D modeling work, AutoCAD offers the 3D Modeling workspace and 3D drawing templates. The combination of these two features can make AutoCAD look like a very different program, but beneath the different appearance the underlying program is the same. You'll learn more about workspaces and templates later in this chapter and in Chapter 24, "Customizing Toolbars, Menus, Linetypes, and Hatch Patterns." Part 4 of this book shows you the 3D features and tools of AutoCAD in more detail.

**FIGURE 1.2**

A typical arrangement of the elements in the AutoCAD window

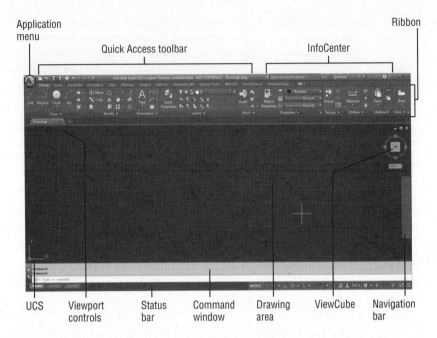

Application menu · Quick Access toolbar · InfoCenter · Ribbon

UCS · Viewport controls · Status bar · Command window · Drawing area · ViewCube · Navigation bar

In the upper-left corner of the AutoCAD program window, the red AutoCAD icon displays the Application menu, which offers a set of options not directly related to drawing; we'll elaborate on this menu in the next section. The Quick Access toolbar at the top of the drawing area (shown in Figure 1.3) includes the basic file-handling functions you find in nearly all Windows programs. The InfoCenter is the AutoCAD online help facility; you'll learn more about it in Chapter 2, "Creating Your First Drawing." The Ribbon uses icons to provide nearly all the commands you'll need; you'll learn more about it in the section "Using the Ribbon" later in this chapter.

**FIGURE 1.3**

The Quick Access toolbar, featuring basic Windows file-handling functions, appears above the Ribbon.

Quick Access toolbar · InfoCenter

Ribbon tabs · Ribbon panels

Ribbon panel title bars

The drawing area occupies most of the screen. Everything you draw appears in this area. As you move your mouse around, crosshairs appear to move within the drawing area. This is the drawing cursor that lets you point to locations in the drawing area. You'll get your first chance to work with the drawing area later, in the section "Picking Points in the Drawing Area."

Just above the drawing area are the Drawing tabs that let you create new drawings or switch between open drawings in a way similar to popular web browsers. Notice the "x" in the current tab that lets you close the current drawing, and the plus icon just to the right of the tab that lets you create a new drawing or open an existing one. When you click the plus icon, the Dashboard appears, allowing you to start a new drawing or open an existing one. Right-click on the plus icon, and a context menu opens that offers you the option to open an existing drawing, to save all of the currently open drawings, or to close all of the drawings.

If you hover over the Drawing tab, you'll see preview images of the model and layouts of the drawing. You'll learn more about model and layout spaces later in this chapter.

Within the drawing area, you see several items along the side and in the corners. The UCS icon appears in the lower-left corner. You'll learn more about the UCS icon in a moment. In the upper-right corner, you see the ViewCube. The ViewCube is primarily for 3D modeling, and we look at those techniques in Chapter 20, "Creating 3D Drawings." You'll also see a Navigation bar along the right edge of the AutoCAD window. This bar offers tools you can use to get around in your drawing. Basic tools like Zoom and Pan can be found here as well as some advanced tools for viewing 3D models.

The Viewport controls in the upper-left corner of the drawing area offer menu options to control 3D and 2D views and visual styles and duplicate some of the functions of the ViewCube. You'll explore the Viewport controls when you delve into 3D modeling in Chapter 23, "Exploring 3D Mesh and Surface Modeling."

Just below the drawing area in the lower-left corner are the Model and Layout tabs. These tabs enable you to switch quickly between different types of views called the *model* and *layout* views. You'll get to see firsthand how these work in a section called "Working with AutoCAD" later in this chapter.

The Command window, located just below the drawing area, gives you feedback about the AutoCAD commands as you use them. You can move and resize this window just as you move and resize other display components. By default, the Command window is in its undocked position, as shown in Figure 1.4. We'll elaborate on the Command window in the section "Working in the Command Window" later in this chapter.

**FIGURE 1.4**
The Command window and the status bar

Below the Command window is the status bar (also shown in Figure 1.4). The status bar gives you information at a glance about the state of the drawing. The tools in the status bar offer aids to the drafting process.

## Using the Application Menu

The Application menu offers tools to help you manage your AutoCAD files. It is basically the File pull-down menu from previous versions of AutoCAD. Try it out to see how it works:

1. Click the Application menu icon in the upper-left corner of the AutoCAD window. A list of options appears.

2. Move the cursor slowly down the list of options in the left column. As you highlight the options, additional options appear in a column to the right.

3. Highlight the Export option to see the various formats available for export (see Figure 1.5).

**FIGURE 1.5**
The Export option in the Application menu showing the list of export options

The Application menu also gives you a convenient way to find recently used files or to get to a file you already have open. If you move your cursor away from the list of options to the left in the Application menu, you'll see Recent Documents in the upper-left portion of the menu. You'll also see two icon tools, named Open Documents and Recent Documents (see Figure 1.6).

**FIGURE 1.6**
The Open Documents and Recent Documents tools

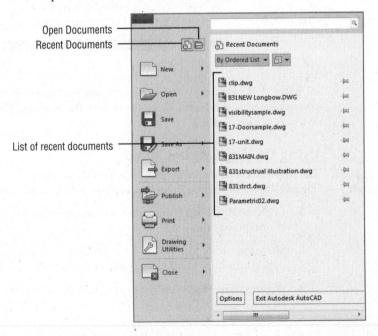

The Open Documents option lets you quickly change from one open file to another when you are viewing your files full-screen. The Recent Documents option displays a list of documents on which you've recently worked.

You can use the View tool in the upper-right portion of the Application menu to select the way the list of files is displayed in a manner similar to the way you would use the Windows Explorer View option. You can click this icon and select Small Images to have the list display the files with thumbnail images of their content. Hover over a filename and you will see a tool tip that displays a larger thumbnail of the drawing.

## Using the Ribbon

**CERT OBJECTIVE**

The most prominent feature in the AutoCAD window, besides the drawing area, is the Ribbon (see Figure 1.7). This is where you'll be selecting tools to draw, edit, or perform other functions. The Ribbon contains a set of panels representing groups of tools and features. The name of each Ribbon panel is found in its title bar at the bottom of the panel. Ribbon panels are further organized by the tabs that appear above them. Each tool in the Ribbon offers a tool tip and cue card that provides a short description to help you understand what the tool icon represents.

**FIGURE 1.7**

A typical cue card from a Ribbon panel tool

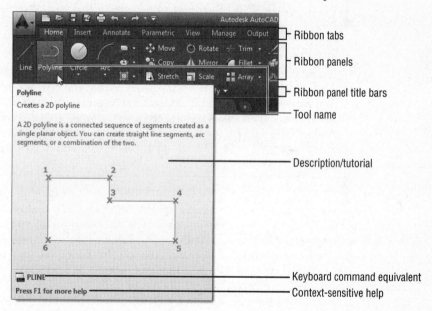

If you see only the Ribbon tabs, click the arrowhead button in the Ribbon Control tool. If you

don't even see the tabs, type **Ribbon↵**.

Move the arrow cursor onto one of the Ribbon panel tools and leave it there for a moment; you'll see a tool tip appear just below the cursor. Hold the cursor there a bit longer and the tool tip changes to give you even more information about the tool.

In most cases, you'll be able to guess what each tool does by looking at its icon. The icon with an arc in the Draw Ribbon panel, for instance, indicates that the tool draws arcs; the one with the circle shows that the tool draws circles; and so on. For further clarification, the tool tip gives you the name of the tool.

## COMMUNICATING WITH THE COMMAND WINDOW AND DYNAMIC INPUT DISPLAY

AutoCAD is the perfect servant: It does everything you tell it to do and no more. You communicate with AutoCAD by using tools and menu options, which invoke AutoCAD commands. A *command* is a single-word instruction you give to AutoCAD telling it to do something, such as draw a line (the Line tool in the Draw Ribbon panel) or erase an object (the Erase tool in the Modify Ribbon panel). Whenever you invoke a command, either by typing it or by selecting an option or tool, AutoCAD responds by presenting messages to you in the Command window and the Dynamic Input display or by displaying a dialog box. The Dynamic Input display is the display of information that appears at the cursor and consists of messages, dimensions, and coordinates.

The messages in the Command window, or in the Dynamic Input display, often tell you what to do next, or they may display a list of available options. A single command often presents a series of messages that you answer to complete the command. These messages serve as an aid to new users who need a little help. If you ever get lost while using a command or forget what you're supposed to do, look at the Command window for clues. As you become more comfortable with AutoCAD, you'll find that you won't need to refer to these messages as frequently.

You can also right-click to display a set of options that relate directly to your current activity. For example, if you right-click before picking the first point for the Rectangle command, a set of options appears displaying the same options that are listed in the Command prompt along with some additional options.

Finally, the Dynamic Input display allows you to enter dimensional data of objects as you draw them. Besides echoing the command-line messages, the Dynamic Input display shows temporary dimensions, coordinates, and angles of objects you're drawing and editing. As you enter coordinate or angle values through the keyboard, they appear in the Dynamic Input display. You can easily turn the Dynamic Input display on or off by clicking the Dynamic Input tool in the status bar. When the Dynamic Input display is turned off, your keyboard input appears only in the Command window.

---

As a new user, you'll find these tool tips helpful because they show you the name of the tool and a brief description of how to use it. Typically, when we ask you to select a tool we'll use the name shown in the tool tip to help you identify the tool. In the case of a tool with flyouts, the tool name changes under different conditions. For those tools, we'll use a general description to identify the tool. You'll learn more about flyouts a bit later in this chapter (see the section "Understanding Flyouts").

As you work through this book, we'll ask you to select tools from the Ribbon panels. You'll often be asked to switch between different tabs to select tools from other sets of panels. To make the process simpler to read, we'll use a somewhat abbreviated description of a tool's location. For example, for the Line tool we'll say, "Click the Line tool in the Home tab's Draw panel." For the Move tool, we'll say, "Click the Move tool in the Home tab's Modify panel."

### EXPANDING HIDDEN PANELS

In addition to the visible tools, some buttons are hidden from view. You can expand many of the Ribbon panels to select more of them. If you see an arrowhead to the right of a panel's title bar, you can click the title bar to expand the panel (see Figure 1.8). The panel expands to reveal additional tools. If you move the cursor to the drawing area, the expanded panel shrinks to its original size. You can also click the pushpin icon in the expanded panel title bar to lock the panel in its open position.

**FIGURE 1.8**
The arrowhead in the panel title bar tells you that additional tools are available.

Click the title bar to expand the panel.

Pushpin icon

From now on, we'll refer to the location of additional tools as the expanded panel. For example, we'll say, "Click the Ray tool in the expanded Draw panel" when we want you to select the Ray tool.

If you are working on a smaller screen with low resolution, some of the Ribbon panels to the far right may look different from what you are shown in this book. On a low-resolution screen, AutoCAD will automatically reduce the size of the panels to the right of the Ribbon so that they show only their title (see Figure 1.9).

**FIGURE 1.9**
The Properties, Groups, Utilities, and View panels are reduced to single icons with a smaller AutoCAD window.

To see the tools, hover over the panel (see Figure 1.10).

Finally, the Workspace drop-down menu in the Quick Access toolbar may be hidden from view in a low-resolution display. If you don't see these options in your AutoCAD window, click the double arrowhead icon to the far right of the Quick Access toolbar to reveal it.

## UNDERSTANDING FLYOUTS

The *flyouts* are one more feature you'll want to know about. Flyouts are similar to expanded panels because you can click an arrowhead to gain access to additional tools. Unlike a whole panel, however, flyouts give you access to different methods for using a particular tool. For example, AutoCAD lets you draw circles in several ways, so it offers a flyout for the Circle tool in the Home tab's Draw panel. If you click the arrowhead below the Circle icon in the Draw panel, you'll see additional tools for drawing circles (see Figure 1.11).

**FIGURE 1.10**
Hover over the
panel to see
the tools.

**FIGURE 1.11**
Flyouts

Click the flyout
arrowhead to display
additional tools.

If you select a tool option from a flyout, that option becomes the default tool for the icon you chose. For example, when you hover your cursor over the Circle icon in the Draw panel, the tool tip shows "Center, Radius" for the tool's name. If you click the arrowhead below the Center, Radius tool and select 2-Point, then 2-Point becomes the default tool and you'll see "2-Point" for the name of the tool in the tool tip (see Figure 1.12).

**FIGURE 1.12**
The tool with a fly-
out will change to
the last tool used.

The Circle tool starts out
as Center, Radius…

Select 2-Point from the
flyout and the default Circle
tool becomes 2-Point.

## GENERAL TOOL NAMES VS. TOOL TIP NAMES

Because the tool tip for tools with flyouts can change, describing them by name can be a bit problematic. The name may have changed based on the last tool you used from a flyout. For this reason, if a tool has a flyout we'll refer to it by a general name that is related to the set of tools contained within it rather than by the tool tip name. For example, we'll call the circle icon tool the Circle tool rather than the Center, Radius tool.

## TOOLS VS. THE KEYBOARD

Throughout this book, you'll be told to select tools from the Ribbon panels to invoke commands. For new and experienced users alike, the Ribbon panels offer an easy-to-remember method for accessing commands. If you're an experienced AutoCAD user, you can type commands directly from the keyboard. Most of the keyboard commands you know and love still work as they did before.

Many tools and commands have *aliases*. Aliases are one-, two-, or three-letter abbreviations of a command name. As you become more proficient with AutoCAD, you may find these aliases helpful. As you work through this book, the shortcuts will be identified for your reference.

Finally, if you're feeling adventurous you can create your own aliases and keyboard shortcuts for executing commands by adding them to the AutoCAD support files. Chapter 24 discusses how to customize menus, Ribbon panels, toolbars, and keyboard shortcuts.

## Picking Points in the Drawing Area

Now that you've seen the general layout of AutoCAD, take a look at the coordinate readout and the drawing cursor to get a sense of how the parts of the AutoCAD screen work together:

1. Move the cursor around in the drawing area. As you move it, notice how the coordinate readout changes to tell you the cursor's location. It shows the coordinates in an X, Y, Z format.

2. Place the cursor in the middle of the drawing area and click the left mouse button. Move the cursor and a rectangle follows. This is a *window selection*; you'll learn more about this window in Chapter 2. You also see a coordinate readout following the cursor and the message Specify opposite corner or. This display at the cursor is called the *Dynamic Input display*. You'll learn more about it a little later in this chapter (see Figure 1.13).

**FIGURE 1.13**

The Dynamic Input
display cursor

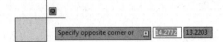

3. Move the cursor a bit in any direction; then, click the left mouse button again. Notice that the window selection disappears as does the Dynamic Input display.

4. Try picking several more points in the drawing area. Notice that, as you click, you alternately start and end a window selection.

If you happen to click the right mouse button, a context menu appears. A right-click frequently opens a menu containing options that are *context sensitive*. This means the contents of the menu depend on the location where you right-click as well as the command that is active at the time. If there are no appropriate options at the time of the right-click, AutoCAD treats the right-click as an Enter (⏎) keystroke. You'll learn more about these options as you progress through the book. For now, if you happen to open this menu by accident press the Esc key to close it.

## Using the UCS Icon

In the lower-left corner of the drawing area, you see an L-shaped line. This is the *User Coordinate System (UCS)* icon, which tells you your orientation in the drawing. This icon becomes helpful as you start to work with complex 2D drawings and 3D models. The X and Y indicate the x- and y-axes of your drawing. Chapter 21, "Using Advanced 3D Features," discusses this icon in detail. For now, you can use it as a reference to tell you the direction of the axes.

---

### IF YOU CAN'T FIND THE UCS ICON

The UCS icon can be turned on and off, so if you're on someone else's system and you don't see the icon or it doesn't look as it does in this chapter, don't panic. See Chapter 21 for more information.

---

## Working in the Command Window

As mentioned, at the bottom of the screen, just above the status bar, is a small horizontal window called the *Command window*. Here, AutoCAD displays responses to your input while you're using a command. By default, it shows one line of text. This line shows the current responses to your command input as well as command options. As you work through a command, you'll see more responses, with earlier responses scrolling upward in faded text. You can view text that has scrolled out of sight by clicking the up-pointing arrowhead at the far right of the Command window. Right now, the command line displays the words "Type a command" in a box (see Figure 1.4, earlier in this chapter). This tells you that AutoCAD is waiting for a command. When you click a point in the drawing area, you see the message Specify opposite corner:. At the same time, the cursor starts to draw a window selection that disappears when you click another point. The same message appears in the Dynamic Input display at the cursor.

As a new user, pay special attention to messages displayed in the Command window and the Dynamic Input display because this is how AutoCAD communicates with you. Besides giving you messages, the Command window records your activity within AutoCAD. You can use the scroll bar to the right of the Command window to review previous messages. You can also enlarge the window for a better view. (Chapter 2 discusses these components in more detail.)

Now, let's look at the AutoCAD window components in detail.

---

**THE COMMAND WINDOW AND DYNAMIC INPUT DISPLAY**

The Command window and the Dynamic Input display allow AutoCAD to provide text feedback on your actions. You can think of these features as a chat window for communicating with AutoCAD—as you enter commands, AutoCAD responds with messages. As you become more familiar with AutoCAD, you may find that you don't need to rely on the Command window and Dynamic Input display as much. For new and casual users, however, the Command window and Dynamic Input display can be helpful in understanding what steps to take as you work.

---

## Working with AutoCAD

Now that you've been introduced to the AutoCAD window, you're ready to try using a few AutoCAD commands. First you'll open a sample file and make a few modifications to it. In the process, you'll become familiar with common methods of operation in AutoCAD.

### Opening an Existing File

In this exercise, you'll get a chance to see and use a typical Select File dialog box.

Before you start, make sure you have installed the sample files for this book from the book's web page. See the introduction for instructions on how to find the sample files.

To start, you'll open an existing file:

1. In the Drawing tab at the top-left of the drawing area, click the Close icon to the far right of the tab. It looks like an X.

   A message appears, asking whether you want to save the changes you've made to the current drawing. Click No.

2. In the Dashboard, click the Open Files option just below the Start Drawing icon in the left column. The Select File dialog box opens. This is a typical Windows file dialog box with an added twist: In the large Preview box on the right, you can preview a drawing before you open it, thereby saving time while searching for files. To the left is a panel known as the Places list, in which you can find frequently used locations on your computer or the Internet (see Figure 1.14).

**FIGURE 1.14**
The Select File
dialog box

If you don't see a Preview box in the Select File dialog box, click the word *Views* in the upper-right corner and select Preview from the list that appears.

**3.** In the Select File dialog box, open the Look In drop-down list and locate the Chapter 01 folder of the Mastering AutoCAD 2015 sample files. (You may need to explore the list to find it.)

**4.** Move the arrow cursor to the clip.dwg file and click it. Notice that the clip.dwg file-name now appears in the File Name input box below the file list. The Preview box also now shows a thumbnail image of the file. Be aware that a thumbnail may not show for files from older versions of AutoCAD.

**5.** Click the Open button at the bottom of the Select File dialog box. AutoCAD opens the clip.dwg file, as shown in Figure 1.15.

**FIGURE 1.15**
The Layout1 view of
the clip.dwg file

The clip.dwg file opens to display a *layout* view of the drawing. A layout is a type of view in which you lay out different views of your drawing in preparation for printing. You can tell you are in a layout view by the white area over the gray background. This white area represents your drawing on a printed page. This view is like a print preview.

Also note that the AutoCAD window's title bar displays the name of the drawing. The name is also displayed in the Drawing tab. This offers easy identification of the file.

This particular file contains both 2D drawings and a 3D model of a typical locking clip. The layout view shows top, front, and right-side views as well as an isometric view.

## Getting a Closer Look

One of the most frequently used commands is Zoom, which gives you a closer look at part of your drawing. This command offers a variety of ways to control your view. In this section, you'll enlarge a portion of the clip drawing to get a more detailed look. You use a *zoom window* to tell AutoCAD which area you want to enlarge.

You'll start by switching to a Model Space view of the drawing. The Model Space view places you in a workspace where you do most of your drawing creation and editing. Follow these steps:

1. Hover over the Clip tab at the top left of the drawing area (see the left panel in Figure 1.16). You'll see two preview icons showing the Model Space on the left and the layout on the right. If you hover over the Model Space image, the drawing area will temporarily change to show you the full view of the Model Space.

2. Click the image on the left showing the Model Space (see Figure 1.16).

**FIGURE 1.16**
Hover over the Drawing tab and click the Model Space image (left) or click the Model tab in the lower-left corner of the drawing area (right).

Your view changes to show the full 3D model with the 2D representations of the model (see Figure 1.17). You can also click the Model tab below the drawing area (see the right panel in Figure 1.16) to accomplish the same change from the layout to Model Space. Note that when you hover over the Model tab, you see a preview image of the Model Space.

3. Type **PLAN**↵↵. Your display changes to a two-dimensional view looking down on the drawing, as shown in Figure 1.18.

4. Click the Zoom Window tool from the Zoom flyout in the Navigation bar (see Figure 1.19). Remember that to open the flyout, you need to click the arrowhead next to or below the tool.

You can also click the Window tool from the Zoom flyout in the View tab's Navigate panel (see Figure 1.20) or type the command **Z**↵**W**↵. If you don't see the Navigate panel, right click in the ribbon and choose Show Panels ➤ Navigate.

**FIGURE 1.17**
3D model with 2D
representations of
the model

**FIGURE 1.18**
Placing the zoom
window around
the clip

First click here …                    and then click here.

**FIGURE 1.19**
Choosing the Zoom
Window tool from
the Zoom flyout in
the Navigation bar

Flyout arrowhead

**FIGURE 1.20**
The Zoom flyout and Window tool in the View tab's Navigate panel

Click the flyout arrowhead.

Select Window.

5. The Dynamic Input display shows the `Specify first corner:` prompt. Look at the image in Figure 1.18. Move the crosshair cursor to a location similar to the one shown in the figure labeled "First click here"; then, left-click. Move the cursor and the rectangle appears with one corner fixed on the point you just picked; the other corner follows the cursor.

6. The Dynamic Input display now shows the `Specify opposite corner:` prompt. Position the other corner of the zoom window so it encloses the lower image of the clip, as shown in Figure 1.18, and left-click the mouse again. The clip enlarges to fill the screen.

In this exercise, you used the Window option of the Zoom command to define an area to enlarge for your close-up view. You saw how AutoCAD prompts you to indicate first one corner of the window selection and then the other. These messages are helpful for first-time users of AutoCAD. You'll use the Window option frequently—not just to define views but also to select objects for editing.

Getting a close-up view of your drawing is crucial to working accurately, but you'll often want to return to a previous view to get the overall picture. To do so, choose Zoom Previous from the Zoom flyout in the Navigation bar (see Figure 1.21). You may also type **Z↵P↵**.

**FIGURE 1.21**
The Zoom Previous option

Zoom Extents
Zoom Window
Zoom Previous
Zoom Realtime

Do this now and the previous view appears. Click Zoom Previous again and the view showing the entire clip returns to the screen.

You can quickly enlarge or reduce your view by using the Zoom Realtime option of the Zoom command. Follow these steps to change your view with Zoom Realtime:

Zoom Realtime

1. Click the Zoom Realtime option from the Navigation bar's Zoom flyout. You can also type **Z↵↵**.

2. Place the Zoom Realtime cursor slightly above the center of the drawing area, and then click and drag downward. Your view zooms out to show more of the drawing.

3. While still holding the left mouse button, move the cursor upward. Your view zooms in and enlarges. When you have a view similar to the one shown in Figure 1.22, release the mouse button. (Don't worry if you don't get *exactly* the same view as the figure. This is just for practice.)

**FIGURE 1.22**
The final view you want to achieve in step 3 of the exercise

4. You're still in Zoom Realtime mode. Click and drag the mouse again to see how you can further adjust your view. To exit, you can select another command besides Zoom or Pan, or press the Esc key.

5. Press the Esc key twice to exit the Zoom Realtime command.

If you prefer, you can use the wheel on your mouse to zoom and pan over your view. Roll the wheel to zoom in and out or click and drag the wheel to pan. Be aware that Zoom Realtime offers finer control over the amount of magnification than the mouse wheel does.

As you can see from this exercise, you have a wide range of options for viewing your drawings just by using a few tools. These tools are all you need to control the display of 2D drawings.

## Saving a File as You Work

It's a good idea to save your file periodically as you work on it. As with any Windows program, you can save it under its original name (click the Save tool on the Quick Access toolbar) or under a different name (choose Save As from the Application menu or the Quick Access toolbar), thereby creating a new file.

By default, AutoCAD automatically saves your work at 10-minute intervals under a name that is a combination of the current filename plus a number and that ends with the .sv$ filename extension; this is known as the *Automatic Save* feature. Using settings in the Options dialog box or system variables, you can change the name of the autosaved file and control the time between autosaves. See "The Open and Save Tab" in Appendix B for details.

---

**"I CAN'T FIND MY AUTOMATIC SAVES!"**

As an IT manager at ELS Architecture and Urban Planning, this author (George) is often asked, "Where does AutoCAD put the Automatic Save files?" By default, in Windows 7, the Automatic Save file is stored in C:\Users\\*User Name*\appdata\local\temp\. You can find the exact location for your system by typing **Savefilepath↵** at the Command prompt. This file location is often set as a hidden folder, so you may need to set up Windows Explorer to display hidden folders before you can get to the Automatic Save file. You can also specify a different location for the Automatic Save files. See Appendix B for information on how to locate hidden files and specify a location for your files.

## Making Changes

You'll frequently make changes to your drawings. One of the primary advantages of AutoCAD is the ease with which you can make modifications. The following exercise shows you a typical sequence of operations involved in changing a drawing:

1. Use the Save As option in the Application menu to save the current `clip.dwg` file under the name **MyFirst**. For convenience, you can save your files in the `My Documents` folder.

2. From the Home tab's Modify panel, click the Erase tool.

   Notice that the cursor has turned into a small square. This square is called the *pickbox*. You also see `Select objects:` in the Command window and the Dynamic Input display. This message helps remind new users what to do.

3. Move the pickbox over the drawing, placing it on various parts of the clip. Don't click anything yet. Notice that as you hover your cursor over objects with the pickbox, they're highlighted. This helps you see the objects that the pickbox is likely to select should you click the left mouse button.

4. Place the pickbox on the crosshatch pattern of the clip (see Figure 1.23), and click. The crosshatch becomes highlighted. The pickbox and the `Select objects:` prompt remain, indicating that you can continue to select objects.

**FIGURE 1.23**
Erasing a portion of the clip

Click here.

5. Press ↵. The crosshatch disappears. You've just erased a part of the drawing.

In this exercise, first you issued the Erase command and then you selected an object by using a pickbox to click it. The pickbox tells you that you must select items on the screen, and it shows you what you're about to select by highlighting objects as you hover the cursor over them. Once you've clicked an object or a set of objects, press ↵ to move on to the next step. This sequence of steps is common to many of the commands you'll work with in AutoCAD.

You can also click an object or a set of objects and then press the Delete key.

## Working with Multiple Files

You can have multiple documents open at the same time in AutoCAD. This feature can be especially helpful if you want to exchange parts of drawings between files or if you want another file open for reference. Try the following exercise to see how multiple documents work in AutoCAD:

1. Click the plus icon to the right of the MyFirst tab at the top of the drawing area.

2. In the Dashboard, locate the Templates option at the bottom of the Start Drawing icon and click it (Figure 1.24).

CITY OF GLASGOW COLLEGE
North Hanover Street Library
60 North Hanover Street

**FIGURE 1.24**
Click the Templates
option below the
Start Drawing icon.

3. Select acad.dwt from the drop-down list.

4. Go to the Ribbon and in the View tab's User Interface panel, click Tile Vertically to get a view of both drawing files.

When you create a new file in AutoCAD, you're actually opening a copy of a *template file*, as you saw in step 1. A template file is a blank file that is set up for specific drawing types. The acad.dwt file is a generic template set up for Imperial measurements. Another template file, called acadiso.dwt, is a generic template useful for metric measurements. Other templates are set up for specific drawing-sheet sizes and measurement systems. You'll learn more about templates in Chapter 6, "Editing and Reusing Data to Work Efficiently."

Next, let's try drawing a rectangle to see how AutoCAD behaves while drawing objects:

1. Click the Rectangle tool in the Home tab's Draw panel, as shown in Figure 1.25.

**FIGURE 1.25**
Click the Rectangle
tool in the Draw
panel.

Notice that the Command window now shows the following prompt:

```
Specify first corner point or
[Chamfer/Elevation/Fillet/Thickness/Width]:
```

AutoCAD is asking you to select the first corner for the rectangle, and in brackets, it's offering a few options you can take advantage of at this point in the command. Don't worry about those options right now. You'll have an opportunity to learn about command options in Chapter 2. You also see the same prompt, minus the bracketed options, in the Dynamic Input display at the cursor. You can view the command options at the cursor by pressing the down arrow key on your keyboard.

2. Click a point roughly in the lower-left corner of the drawing area, as shown in Figure 1.26. Now as you move your mouse, a rectangle follows the cursor, with one corner fixed at the position you just selected. You also see the following prompt in the Command window, with a similar prompt in the Dynamic Input display:

```
Specify other corner point or [Area/Dimensions/Rotation]:
```

**FIGURE 1.26**
Selecting the first point of a rectangle

Click here to start the rectangle.

**3.** Click another point anywhere in the upper-right region of the drawing area (see Figure 1.27). A rectangle appears. You'll learn more about the different cursor shapes and what they mean in Chapter 2.

**FIGURE 1.27**
After you've selected the first point of the rect-angle, you'll see a rectangle follow the motion of your mouse.

**4.** Let's try copying objects between these two files. Click in the window with the clip drawing to make it active.

**5.** Click Zoom All from the Zoom flyout of the Navigation bar to get an overall view of the drawing (see Figure 1.28). You can also type **Z↵A↵**.

**FIGURE 1.28**
The Zoom All option gives you an overall view of your drawing.

6. Click the 2D version of the clip at the bottom of the drawing to select it. A dot appears at the center of the clip and a rectangle encloses it. The dot is called a *grip*; you'll learn more about grips in the next chapter (see Figure 1.29).

**FIGURE 1.29**

Grip shown in the 2D drawing

Select this part
of the drawing.

7. Right-click and select Clipboard and then Copy. You can also press Ctrl+C to invoke the Windows Copy To Clipboard shortcut.

8. Click inside the other drawing window to make it active.

9. Right-click and select Clipboard and then Paste. You can also press Ctrl+V to invoke the Windows Paste From Clipboard shortcut. The Specify Insertion Point prompt appears.

10. Click inside the rectangle. The clip appears at the cursor in the new drawing.

11. This ends the exercises for this chapter. Save your myfirst.dwg file for future reference.

---

**LOSE THE NAVIGATION BAR?**

If for some reason the Navigation bar is not visible, you can use the User Interface tool found in the User Interface panel of the View tab on the Ribbon to open it again. Click the User Interface tool and select Navigation Bar from the menu.

---

Note that you've had two files open at once. You can have as many files open as you want as long as your computer has adequate memory to accommodate them. You can control the individual document windows as you would any window, using the window control buttons in the upper-right corner of the drawing area.

## Adding a Predrawn Symbol with the Tool Palettes

In the preceding exercise, you saw how you can easily copy an object from one file to another by using the standard Windows Cut and Paste feature. AutoCAD offers several tool palettes that enable you to click and drag predrawn objects into your drawing.

You can open the tool palettes by clicking the Tool Palettes tool in the Interface tab's Palettes panel, as shown in Figure 1.30.

**FIGURE 1.30**

Open the Tool Palettes tool from the View tab.

View tab

Tool Palettes tool in the Palettes panel

Once the tool palettes are open, you can select a tab containing the predrawn objects you want to use and then click the specific object you want to add. The object appears at the cursor, ready for you to select a location (see Figure 1.31).

In addition to predrawn objects, the tool palettes offer a way to add hatch patterns and other components quickly to your drawing. They're great tools to help you manage your library of custom, predrawn symbols. Chapter 25, "Managing and Sharing Your Drawings," shows you how to use and customize the tool palettes.

**FIGURE 1.31**

The tool palettes offer predrawn symbols that you can easily place in your drawings.

Select a tab containing predrawn symbols you want to use.

Click on a symbol.

The symbol appears at the cursor ready to be placed in the drawing.

# The Bottom Line

**Use the AutoCAD window.**   AutoCAD is a typical Windows graphics program that makes use of menus, toolbars, Ribbon panels, and palettes. If you've used other graphics programs, you'll see at least a few familiar tools.

**Master It**   Name the components of the AutoCAD window you can use to select a function.

**Get a closer look with the Zoom command.**   One of the first things you'll want to learn is how to manipulate your views. The Zoom command is a common tool in graphics programs.

**Master It**   Name at least two ways of zooming into a view.

**Save a file as you work.**   Nothing is more frustrating than having a power failure that causes you to lose hours of work. It's a good idea to save your work frequently. AutoCAD offers an Automatic Save feature that can be a lifesaver if you happen to forget to save your files.

**Master It**   How often does the AutoCAD Automatic Save feature save your drawing?

**Make changes and open multiple files.**   As with other Windows programs, you can have multiple files open and exchange data between them.

**Master It**   With two drawings open, how can you copy parts of one drawing into the other?

# Chapter 2

# Creating Your First Drawing

This chapter examines some of the basic functions of the AutoCAD® software. You'll get a chance to practice with the drawing editor by building a simple drawing to use in later exercises. You'll learn how to give input to AutoCAD, interpret prompts, and get help when you need it. This chapter also covers the use of coordinate systems to give AutoCAD exact measurements for objects. You'll see how to select objects you've drawn and how to specify base points for moving and copying.

If you're not a beginning AutoCAD user, you may want to move on to the more complex material in Chapter 3, "Setting Up and Using the Drafting Tools." You can use the files supplied at the book's web page (www.sybex.com/go/masteringautocad2015) to continue the tutorials at that point.

Beginning in this chapter, we'll be using a setup that displays a white drawing background instead of the dark gray background you see on your screen. We do this to keep the figures legible in the printed version of this book, but the difference should not hinder your understanding of the figures. If you like, you can set up your screen with a white background by following the instructions in Appendix B, "Installing and Setting Up AutoCAD," in the section "Set Up AutoCAD with a White Background."

In this chapter, you will learn to:

♦ Specify distances with coordinates

♦ Interpret the cursor modes and understand prompts

♦ Select objects and edit with grips

♦ Use dynamic input

♦ Display data in a text window

♦ Display the properties of an object

♦ Get help

## Getting to Know the Home Tab's Draw and Modify Panels

Your first task in learning how to draw in AutoCAD software is simply to draw a line. Since AutoCAD is designed as a precision drawing tool, you'll be introduced to methods that allow you to input exact distances. But before you begin drawing, take a moment to familiarize yourself with the features you'll be using more than any other to create objects with AutoCAD: the Draw and Modify panels. Try these steps:

1.  Start AutoCAD just as you did in Chapter 1, "Exploring the Interface," by choosing Start ➢ All Programs ➢ Autodesk ➢ AutoCAD 2015 ➢ AutoCAD 2015.

2.  Click the Templates drop-down arrowhead in the Dashboard and select `acad.dwt` (Figure 2.1). Metric users should use the `acadiso.dwt` template. You could also click the Start Drawing icon, but I ask you to use the `acad.dwt` or `acadiso.dwt` template to ensure that you are set up with the same defaults as in this exercise.

**FIGURE 2.1**
The Select Template drop-down list

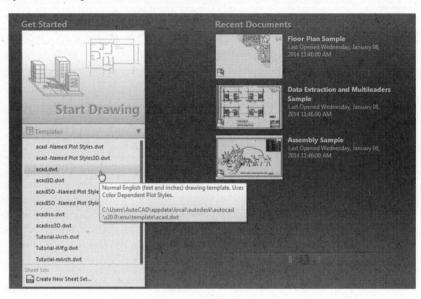

3.  Make sure you are in the Drafting & Annotation workspace. Click the Workspace Switching tool in the Status bar ⚙ ▾ and select Drafting and Annotation.

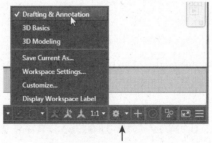

Workspace Switching tool.

4.  Move the arrow cursor to the Line tool in the Home tab's Draw panel at the far upper-left portion of the AutoCAD window, and rest it there so that the tool tip appears. As you hold the cursor over the tool, first one tool tip appears and then another (see Figure 2.2).

**5.** Slowly move the arrow cursor to the right over the other tools in the Home tab's Draw panel and read each tool tip.

**FIGURE 2.2**
The Draw panel

First tool tip

Second tool tip with a more detailed description of the tool

In most cases, you'll be able to guess what each tool does by looking at its icon. The icon with an arc, for instance, indicates that the tool draws arcs; the one with the ellipse signifies that the tool draws ellipses; and so on. If you hover over the tool, you'll see the tool tip name and the keyboard command associated with the tool. Hold the cursor for a bit longer and a cue card appears that gives a brief explanation of how to use the tool.

---

### Don't Get Stuck on the Prompts

In many of the exercises in this book, we'll mention the Command prompt that appears in the Command window. The prompts are shown for your reference, but don't let yourself get too bogged down by them. For example, we'll say, "At the `Specify lower left corner or [ON/OFF] <0.0000,0.0000>:` prompt, press ↵." The important part is to "press ↵." You can skim over the prompt. Just keep in mind that the prompts can offer some direction and show the options for the current command. They can also serve as helpful reminders later when you're working on your own.

---

You see several tools in the Home tab's Draw and Modify panels. In Chapter 1, you saw that if you click the arrow in a panel's title bar, the panel expands to reveal more tools (see Figure 2.3). Once you've selected a tool from the expanded Draw or Modify panel, the expanded panel closes. If you want to keep the expanded panel open, click the pushpin icon at the left end of the expanded panel's title bar.

**FIGURE 2.3**
The Home tab's
Draw and Modify
panel tools

## Starting Your First Drawing

In Chapter 1, you looked at a preexisting sample drawing. This time, you'll begin to draw your own drawing by creating a door that will be used in later exercises. First, though, you must learn how to tell AutoCAD what you want, and even more importantly, you must understand what AutoCAD wants from you.

---

### IMPERIAL AND METRIC

In this chapter, you'll start to see instructions for both Imperial and metric measurements. In general, you'll see the instructions for Imperial measurement first, followed by the metric instructions. You won't be dealing with inches or centimeters yet, however. You're just getting to know the AutoCAD system.

---

You'll start by setting the size of the work area, known as the drawing *limits*. These limits aren't fixed in any way, and you aren't forced to stay within the bounds of the drawing limits unless the Limits command's ON/OFF option is turned on. But limits can help to establish a starting area from which you can expand your drawing.

You currently have a new blank file, but it's a little difficult to tell the size of your drawing area. Let's set up the work area so you have a better idea of the space with which you're working:

1. Enter **Limits**↵.

2. At the Specify lower left corner or [ON/OFF] <0.0000,0.0000>: prompt, press ↵.

**3.** At the Specify upper right corner <12.0000,9.0000>: prompt, metric users should enter **40,30**↵. If you use Imperial units (feet and inches), press ↵ to accept the default of 12.0000,9.0000.

**4.** Type **Z**↵**A**↵ for the Zoom All command. You can also select Zoom All from the Zoom fly-out on the Navigation bar.

In the last step, the All option of the Zoom command uses the limits you set up in steps 2 and 3 to determine the display area. In a drawing that contains objects, the Zoom tool's All option displays the limits plus the area occupied by the objects in the drawing if they happen to fall outside the limits. Now give your file a unique name:

**1.** Choose Save As from the Application menu or type **Saveas**↵ to open the Save Drawing As dialog box.

**2.** Type **Door**. As you type, the name appears in the File Name text box.

**3.** Save your file in the My Documents folder, or if you prefer, save it in another folder of your choosing. Just remember where you put it because you'll use it later.

**4.** Click Save. You now have a file called Door.dwg, located in the My Documents folder. Of course, your drawing doesn't contain anything yet. You'll take care of that next.

---

### UNDERSTANDING THE DRAWING AREA

The new file shows a drawing area roughly 12 inches wide by 9 inches high. Metric users have a file that shows an area roughly 40 millimeters (mm) wide by 30 mm high. This is just the area you're given to start with, but you're not limited to it in any way. No visual clues indicate the size of the area. To check the area size for yourself, move the crosshair cursor to the upper-right corner of the drawing area and observe the value in the coordinate readout in the lower-left corner. The coordinate readout won't show exactly 12×9 inches, or 40×30 mm for metric, because the proportions of your drawing area aren't likely to be exactly 12×9 or 40×30. AutoCAD does try to optimize the display for the drawing area when you choose the All option of the Zoom command.

---

Now you can start to explore the drawing process. To begin a drawing, follow these steps:

**1.** Click the Line tool on the Home tab's Draw panel, or type **L**↵.

You've just issued the Line command. AutoCAD responds in two ways. First, you see the message

```
Specify first point:
```

in the Command prompt, asking you to select a point to begin your line. Also, the cursor changes its appearance; it no longer has a square in the crosshairs. This is a clue telling you to pick a point to start a line.

**2.** Using the left mouse button, select a point on the screen just a little to the left and below the center of the drawing area (Figure 2.4). After you select the point, AutoCAD changes the prompt to this:

```
Specify next point or [Undo]:
```

**FIGURE 2.4**

A rubber-banding line

Now, as you move the mouse around, notice the line with one end fixed on the point you just selected and the other end following the cursor in a *rubber-banding* motion (see the first image in Figure 2.4). You also see a message asking you to Specify next point or.

**3.** Move the cursor to a location directly to the left or right of the point you clicked, and you'll see a dashed horizontal line appear along with a different message at the cursor. This action also occurs when you point directly up or down. Your cursor seems to jump to a horizontal or vertical position.

This feature is called *Polar Tracking*. Like a T square or triangle, it helps to restrict your line to an exact horizontal or vertical direction. You can turn Polar Tracking on or off by clicking the Polar Tracking tool in the status bar. You'll learn more about this tool in Chapter 3.

4. Continue with the Line command. Move the cursor to a point below and to the right of the first point you selected and click again. You've just drawn a line segment, and a second rubber-banding line appears (see the second image in Figure 2.4).

5. If the line you drew isn't the exact length you want, you can back up during the Line command and change it. To do this, type **U**↵. The line you drew previously rubber-bands as if you hadn't selected the second point to fix its length.

6. Right-click and select Enter. This terminates the Line command.

The Undo and Redo tools in the Quick Access toolbar offer Undo and Redo drop-down lists from which you can select the exact command you want to undo or redo. See the sidebar "Getting Out of Trouble" later in this chapter for more information.

You've just drawn, and then undrawn, a line of an arbitrary length. In step 6 of the last exercise, you were asked to terminate the Line command. If you happen to forget that a command is still active, two onscreen clues can remind you of the status of AutoCAD. If you don't see the words Type a Command in the Command window, a command is still active. Also, the cursor is the plain crosshair without the box at its intersection.

Many tools will display a small icon or *badge* next to the cursor. The badge will be similar to the tool's icon in most cases. A red X appears when hovering over an object while using the Erase tool. A question mark appears when using the Measure, ID, or List tool.

From now on, we'll refer to the crosshair cursor without the small box as the Point Selection mode of the cursor. Figure 2.5 shows all the modes of the drawing cursor.

---

## WHY USE THE KEYBOARD COMMANDS?

For many years, Autodesk has been encouraging users to move away from the command line and keyboard method of command entry, but it seems that AutoCAD users will have none of that. Although you would expect "grizzled veteran" users to stick with the keyboard entry method, you might be surprised to find that young "fresh out of school" apprentice architects also prefer the keyboard over the newer palettes and ribbons in AutoCAD.

We made this observation to one of the designers of AutoCAD at a recent Autodesk function. Without hesitation, he answered that "keyboard entry is much faster." In our experience, it isn't just faster. Entering commands via the keyboard gives you a more "connected" feeling with AutoCAD. Work seems to flow much smoother. If you learn the keyboard commands, you'll also find that customizing AutoCAD is much easier. So for these reasons, we encourage you to try both the keyboard and the buttons to see which you prefer. You'll find that, wherever possible, we'll give the keyboard command equivalent to a tool selection in the exercises of this book. Remember that a tool's tool tip will also show its keyboard command.

**FIGURE 2.5**
The drawing
cursor's modes

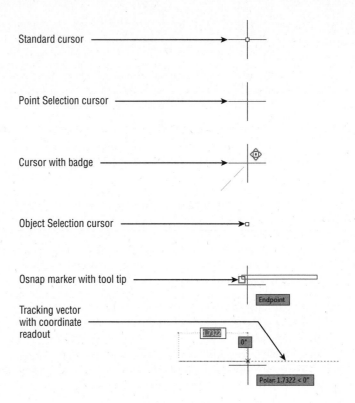

Standard cursor

Point Selection cursor

Cursor with badge

Object Selection cursor

Osnap marker with tool tip

Tracking vector
with coordinate
readout

## Specifying Exact Distances with Coordinates

Next, you'll continue with the Line command to draw a plan view (an overhead view) of a door, to no particular scale. This will give you some practice in drawing objects to exact distances. Later, you'll resize the drawing for use in future exercises. The door will be 3 units long and 0.15 units thick. For metric users, the door will be 9 units long and 0.5 units thick. To specify these exact distances in AutoCAD, you can use either relative polar coordinates or Cartesian coordinates.

### GETTING OUT OF TROUBLE

Beginners and experts alike are bound to make a few mistakes. Before you get too far into the exercise, here are some powerful but easy-to-use tools to help you recover from accidents:

**Backspace**   If you make a typing error, press the Backspace key to back up to your error and then retype your command or response. The Backspace key is in the upper-right corner of the main keyboard area.

**Escape (Esc)**   This is perhaps the single most important key on your keyboard. When you need to exit a command or a dialog box quickly without making changes, press the Esc key in the upper-left corner of your keyboard. In most cases, you need to press Esc only once, although it won't hurt to press it twice. (Press Esc before editing with grips or issuing commands through the keyboard.)

**U** If you accidentally change something in the drawing and want to reverse that change, click the Undo tool in the Quick Access toolbar (the left-pointing curved arrow). You can also type **U↵** at the Command prompt. Each time you do this, AutoCAD undoes one operation at a time, in reverse order. The last command performed is undone first, then the next-to-last command, and so on. The prompt displays the name of the command being undone, and the drawing reverts to its state prior to that command being issued. If you need to, you can undo everything back to the beginning of an editing session. You can also select the exact command to back up to by using the Undo drop-down list in the Quick Access toolbar.

You can open the Undo drop-down list by clicking the down-pointing arrow found to the right of the Undo tool.

**Undo** If you want more control over the way Undo works, you can use the Undo command, which allows you to "bookmark" places in your editing session that you can "undo" to. Type **Undo↵** and you'll see the `Enter the number of operations to undo or [Auto/Control/BEgin/End/Mark/Back] <1>:` prompt. Enter a number indicating the number of steps you want to undo. Use the Mark option to bookmark a location; then use Back to undo your work to that bookmark. You can use Begin and End to mark the beginning and ending of a set of operations that will be undone all at once. Control offers options to control the behavior of the Undo command. Auto is an option that is on by default and causes AutoCAD to undo the action of the whole command rather than the individual actions within a command.

**Redo** If you accidentally undo one too many commands, you can redo the last undone command by clicking the Redo tool (the right-pointing curved arrow) in the Quick Access toolbar, or you can type **Redo↵**. You can redo several operations that you may have undone with the **Undo** command. You can also select the exact command to redo to by using the Redo drop-down list in the Quick Access toolbar.

**Oops**  If you've deleted something and gone on to use other commands, you can restore the last deleted object or objects by using the Oops command. Oops enables you to restore the last deleted set of objects without having to undo a series of commands.

The Imperial and metric distances aren't equivalent in the exercises in this chapter. For example, 3 units in the Imperial-based drawing aren't equal to 9 metric units. These distances are arbitrary and based on how they appear in the figures in this chapter.

## Specifying Polar Coordinates

To enter the exact distance of 3 (or 9 metric) units to the right of the last point you selected, do the following:

1. Click the Line tool on the Home tab's Draw panel, or type **L⏎**.

2. Click a point slightly to the left of the center of the drawing area to select the start point.

3. Type **@3<0**. Metric users should type **@9<0**. As you type, the letters appear at the Command prompt.

4. Press ⏎. A line appears, starting from the first point you picked and ending 3 units to the right of it (see Figure 2.6). You've just entered a relative polar coordinate.

**FIGURE 2.6**
Notice that the rubber-banding line now starts from the last point selected. This indicates that you can continue to add more line segments.

Line segment, 3 units in length or 9 units for metric users          Rubber-banding line

The "at" sign (@) you entered tells AutoCAD that the coordinate you're specifying is from the last point you selected. The 3 (or 9 metric) is the distance, and the less-than symbol (<) tells AutoCAD that you're designating the angle at which the line is to be drawn. The last part is the value for the angle, which in this case is 0 for 0°. This is how to use polar coordinates to communicate distances and directions to AutoCAD.

If you're accustomed to a different method for describing directions, you can set AutoCAD to use a vertical direction or downward direction as 0°. See Chapter 3 for details.

Angles are given based on the system shown in Figure 2.7, in which 0° is a horizontal direction from left to right, 90° is straight up, 180° is horizontal from right to left, and so on. You can specify degrees, minutes, and seconds of arc if you want to be that exact. You can also specify angles using negative values, which would mirror the direction around the x-axis. For example, a minus 45° angle would point in the direction shown as 315° in Figure 2.7. We'll discuss angle formats in more detail in Chapter 3.

**FIGURE 2.7**
AutoCAD default system for specifying angles

## Specifying Relative Cartesian Coordinates

For the next line segment, let's try another method for specifying exact distances:

1. Enter @0,0.15↵. Metric users should enter @0,0.5↵. A short line appears above the endpoint of the last line. Once again, @ tells AutoCAD that the coordinate you specify is from the last point picked. But in this example, you give the distance in X and Y values. The X distance, 0, is given first, followed by a comma, and then the Y distance, 0.15 or 0.5. This is how to specify distances in relative Cartesian coordinates.

---

**COMMAS AND PERIODS**

Step 1 indicates that metric users should enter @0,0.5↵ for the distance. Instead, you could enter @0,.5 (zero comma point five). The leading zero is included for clarity. European metric users should be aware that the comma is used as a separator between the X and Y components of the coordinate. In AutoCAD, commas aren't used for decimal points; you must use a period to denote a decimal point.

---

2. Enter @-3,0↵. Metric users should enter @-9,0↵. This distance is also in X,Y values, but here you use a negative value to specify the X distance. The result is a drawing that looks like Figure 2.8.

**FIGURE 2.8**

These three sides of the door were drawn by using the Line tool. Points are specified by using either relative Cartesian or polar coordinates.

Rubber-banding
line

Positive values in the Cartesian coordinate system are from left to right and from bottom to top (see Figure 2.9). (You may remember this from your high school geometry class!) If you want to draw a line from right to left, you must designate a negative value. It's also helpful to know where the origin of the drawing lies. In a new drawing, the origin—or coordinate 0,0—is in the lower-left corner of the drawing.

**FIGURE 2.9**

Positive and negative Cartesian coordinate directions

**3.** Type **C↵**. This C stands for the Close option. You can also click the Close option in the command line or right-click and select Close from the context menu. A line connecting the first and last points of a sequence of lines is drawn (see Figure 2.10), and the Line command terminates. The rubber-banding line also disappears, telling you that AutoCAD has finished drawing line segments. You can also use the rubber-banding line to indicate direction while simultaneously entering the distance through the keyboard. See the sidebar "Other Ways to Enter Distances" later in this chapter.

**FIGURE 2.10**
Distance and direction input for the door. Distances for metric users are shown in brackets.

To finish drawing a series of lines without closing them, you can press Esc, ↵, or the spacebar.

# Interpreting the Cursor Modes and Understanding Prompts

The key to working with AutoCAD successfully is understanding the way it interacts with you. The following sections will help you become familiar with some of the ways AutoCAD prompts you for input. Understanding the format of the messages in the Command window and recognizing other events on the screen will help you learn the program more easily.

## Understanding Cursor Modes

As the Command window aids you with messages, the cursor gives you clues about what to do. Figure 2.5 earlier illustrates the various modes of the cursor, and it gives a brief description of the role of each mode. Take a moment to study this figure.

**The Standard cursor** tells you that AutoCAD is waiting for instructions. You can also edit objects by using grips when you see this cursor. *Grips* are squares, rectangles, or arrowheads that appear at endpoints and at the midpoint of objects when they're selected. (You might know them as *workpoints* from other graphics programs.)

**The Point Selection cursor** appears whenever AutoCAD expects point input. It can also appear in conjunction with a rubber-banding line. You can either click a point or enter a coordinate through the keyboard.

**The cursor with badge** lets you know at a glance which tool you are using. The badge will be similar to the tool icon currently being used. A red X badge appears when hovering over an object while using the Erase tool. A question mark badge appears when using the Measure, ID, or List tool.

**The Object Selection or Pickbox cursor** tells you that you must select objects—either by clicking them or by using any of the object-selection options available.

**The osnap (object snap) marker** appears along with the Point Selection cursor when you invoke an osnap. Osnaps let you accurately select specific points on an object, such as endpoints or midpoints.

**The tracking vector** appears when you use the Polar Tracking or Object Snap Tracking feature. Polar Tracking aids you in drawing orthogonal lines, and Object Snap Tracking helps you align a point in space relative to the geometry of existing objects. Object Snap Tracking works in conjunction with osnaps. You'll learn more about the tracking vector in Chapter 3.

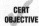

If you're an experienced AutoCAD user, you may prefer to use the old-style crosshair cursor that crosses the entire screen. Choose Options from the bottom of the Application menu to open the Options dialog box, and then click the Display tab. Set the Crosshair Size option near the bottom right of the dialog box to 100. The cursor then appears as it did in previous versions of AutoCAD. As the option name implies, you can set the crosshair size to any percentage of the screen you want. The default is 5 percent.

---

### OTHER WAYS TO ENTER DISTANCES

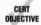

A third method for entering distances is to point in a direction with a rubber-banding line and then enter the distance through the keyboard. For example, to draw a line 3 units long from left to right, click the Line tool on the Home tab's Draw panel, click a start point, and then move the cursor so the rubber-banding line points to the right at some arbitrary distance. With the cursor pointing in the direction you want, type **3**↵. The rubber-banding line becomes a fixed line 3 units long. Using this method, called the Direct Distance method, along with the Ortho mode or Polar Tracking described in Chapter 3, can be a fast way to draw orthogonal lines of specific lengths.

You can also specify an exact angle along with the distance. For example, start the Line command and then pick the first point. Type **3** for the length but don't press ↵. Press the Tab key instead. The line segment will become fixed at 3 units, and as you move the cursor, the segment will rotate freely around the first point. Next, type an angle in degrees, **30**↵ for example, and the line will be drawn at 30 degrees. Or, instead of typing in an angle, just adjust the angle of the line visually until you see the angle you want on the Dynamic Input temporary angle dimension and then click.

If you watch the temporary dimensions as you press the Tab key, you'll see that the Tab key lets you move from the length dimension to the angle dimension and back again. You can press the Tab key at any time to shift back and forth between dimensions. A lock appears next to a dimension that you have entered, telling you that the dimension is "locked" until you tab to it again.

You'll learn more about how to enter values with the Dynamic Input's temporary dimensions later in this chapter.

---

## Choosing Command Options

Many commands in AutoCAD offer several options, which are often presented to you in the Command window in the form of a prompt. This section uses the Arc command to illustrate the format of AutoCAD prompts.

Usually, in a floor-plan drawing in the United States, an arc is drawn to indicate the direction of a door swing. Figure 2.11 shows other standard symbols used in architectural-style drawings.

**FIGURE 2.11**

Samples of standard symbols used in architectural drawings

INCANDESCENT LIGHT    TELEPHONE    OUTLET    TRIPLEX OUTLET

SQUARE LAV    PEDESTAL LAV    KITCHEN SINK    ROUND LAV

BATHTUB    TOILET    URINAL

SINGLE DOOR    DOUBLE DOOR

BIFOLD DOOR    POCKET DOOR

SLIDING DOOR    WINDOW

Next, you'll draw the arc for the door you started in the previous exercise:

1.  Click the 3-Point Arc tool in the Home tab's Draw panel. Click the Arc flyout and select 3-Point. The Specify start point of arc or [Center]: prompt appears in the Command window, and the cursor changes to Point Selection mode. You also see the prompt Specify start point of arc or prompt next to the cursor.

    Examine the Specify start point of arc or [Center]: prompt. The prompt contains two options. The default is stated in the main part of the prompt, which is to specify the start point of the arc. If other options are available, they appear within square brackets. In the Arc command, you see the word Center within brackets telling you that, if you prefer, you can also start your arc by selecting a center point instead of a start point. If multiple options are available, they appear within the brackets and are set off with a slightly darker background. This background tells you that the option is selectable using your cursor and also aids in separating option names. The default is the option AutoCAD assumes you intend to use unless you tell it otherwise.

2. Type **C**↵ to select the Center option or click the word Center in the command line. The Specify center point of arc: prompt appears. Notice that you had to type only the C and not the entire word Center.

   When you see a set of options in the Command window, note their capitalization. If you choose to respond to prompts by using the keyboard, these capitalized letters are all you need to enter to select the option. In some cases, the first two letters are capitalized to differentiate two options that begin with the same letter, such as LAyer and LType. You can also just click the option name in the Command prompt to select the option.

3. Pick a point representing the center of the arc near the upper-left corner of the door (see Figure 2.12). The Specify start point of arc: prompt appears.

4. Type **@3<0**↵. Metric users should type **@9<0**↵. The Specify end point of arc or [Angle chord Length]: prompt appears.

5. Move the mouse and a temporary arc appears, originating from a point 3 units to the right of the center point you selected and rotating about that center, as shown in Figure 2.12. (Metric users will see the temporary arc originating 9 units to the right of the center point.)

   As the prompt indicates, you now have three options. You can enter an angle, a chord length, or the endpoint of the arc. The prompt default, to specify the endpoint of the arc, picks the arc's endpoint. Again, the cursor is in Point Selection mode, telling you it's waiting for point input. To select this default option, you only need to pick a point on the screen indicating where you want the endpoint.

6. Move the cursor so that it points in a vertical direction from the center of the arc. You'll see the Polar Tracking vector snap to a vertical position.

7. Click any location with the Polar Tracking vector in the vertical position. The arc is now fixed in place, as shown in Figure 2.12.

This exercise has given you some practice working with AutoCAD Command window prompts and entering keyboard commands—skills you'll need when you start to use advanced AutoCAD functions.

**FIGURE 2.12**
Using the Arc command

As you can see, AutoCAD has a distinct structure in its prompt messages. You first issue a command, which in turn offers options in the form of a prompt. Depending on the option you select, you get another set of options or you're prompted to take some action, such as picking a point, selecting objects, or entering a value.

As you work through the exercises, you'll become intimately familiar with this routine. After you understand the workings of the Ribbon panels, the Command window prompts, and the dialog boxes, you can almost teach yourself the rest of the program!

---

### USING AUTOCOMPLETE AND AUTOCORRECT

You may have noticed that as you enter a command through the keyboard, the Command window offers suggestions to complete your typing in a way similar to many web browsers. For example, if you type **LI**, a list pops up offering a number of commands that start with *LI*. You can then click the option that you want to use. This feature can be helpful when you forget the full name of a command.

AutoCorrect works in a similar way, but instead of offering a list of commands that start with the letters you type, AutoCAD will try to "correct" a mistyped command. For example, if you type **crl**, AutoCAD will display several commands that come close to what you typed.

You can also control how the AutoComplete and AutoCorrect features work. Right-click in the Command window, and then point to the Input Settings option that appears in the context menu. You can then toggle several options on or off. The options are AutoComplete, AutoCorrect, Search System Variables, Search Content, Mid-string Search, and Delay Time.

---

### SELECTING OPTIONS FROM A CONTEXT MENU

Now you know that you can select command options by typing them. You can also right-click at any time during a command to open a context menu containing those same options. For example, in step 2 in the previous exercise, you typed **C↵** to tell AutoCAD that you wanted to select the center of the arc. Instead of typing, you can also right-click to open a menu of options applicable to the Arc command at that time.

In addition to the options shown in the Command prompt, the context menu shows you a few more: Enter, Cancel, Pan, and Zoom. The Enter option is the same as pressing ↵. Cancel cancels the current command. Pan and Zoom let you adjust your view as you're working through the current command.

The menu is context sensitive, so you see only those options that pertain to the command or activity that is currently in progress. Also, when AutoCAD is expecting a point, an object selection, or a numeric value, right-clicking doesn't display a context menu. Instead, AutoCAD treats a right-click as ↵.

The location of your cursor when you right-click determines the contents of the list of available operations. A right-click in the Command window displays a list of operations you can apply to the command line, such as repeating one of the last several commands you've used or copying the most recent history of command activity to the Clipboard.

A right-click in the drawing area when no command is active displays a set of basic options for editing your file, such as the command most recently used, Undo, Redo, Pan, and Zoom, to name a few (see Figure 2.13). The Cut, Copy, and Paste commands can be found under the Clipboard option.

If you're ever in doubt about what to do in AutoCAD, you can right-click to see a list of options. You'll learn more about these options later in this book. For now, let's move on to the topic of selecting objects.

**FIGURE 2.13**
A set of basic options

### HOW WE'LL SHOW COMMAND OPTIONS

As mentioned earlier, the options in the command line are shown with a slightly darker background color so you can easily determine the name of the options (see Figure 2.14).

**FIGURE 2.14**
The `Angle` and `chord Length` options are separated by a gray background.

Unfortunately, it's a bit more difficult to show the options in the same way in this book, so from now on, when we show the command options, we'll use a forward slash mark to separate the options. For example, in the Arc command options discussed earlier, you saw this command prompt:

```
Specify end point of arc or [Angle chord Length]
```

We'll show it like this, using the / symbol to separate the command options:

```
Specify end point of arc or [Angle/chord Length]
```

Without the / symbol, you might confuse the option names as `Angle chord` and `Length`, or you may even think that there are three options named `Angle`, `chord`, and `Length`. Those of you familiar with older versions of AutoCAD will recognize this use of the / symbol as the way AutoCAD used to separate command options in the command line.

## Selecting Objects

In AutoCAD, you can select objects in many ways. The following sections cover two ways: object-selection methods unique to AutoCAD and the Noun/Verb method, the more common selection method used in most popular graphics programs. Because these two methods play a major role in working with AutoCAD, it's a good idea to familiarize yourself with them early on.

If you need to select objects by their characteristics rather than by their location, see Chapter 14, "Advanced Editing and Organizing," which describes the Quick Select and Object Selection Filters tools. These tools let you easily select a set of objects based on their properties, including object type, color, layer assignment, and so on.

## Selecting Objects in AutoCAD

With many AutoCAD commands, you'll see the `Select objects:` prompt. Along with this prompt, the cursor changes from crosshairs to the Object Selection cursor (look back at Figure 2.5). Whenever you see the `Select objects:` prompt and the square Pickbox cursor, you have several options while making your selection. Often, as you select objects on the screen, you'll change your mind about a selection or accidentally select an object you don't want. Let's look at most of the selection options available in AutoCAD and learn what to do when you make the wrong selection.

Before you continue, you'll turn off two features that, although extremely useful, can be confusing to new users. These features are called Running Osnaps and Osnap Tracking. You'll get a chance to explore these features in depth later in this book, but for now follow these steps to turn them off:

**1.** Check to see if either Object Snap or Object Snap Tracking is turned on in the status bar. If they're turned on, they will be a light blue.

**2.** To turn off Object Snap, click the tool in the status bar. When turned off, it will change to gray.

Now, let's see how to select an object in AutoCAD:

CERT
OBJECTIVE

**1.** Choose Move from the Home tab's Modify panel, or type **M**↵.

**2.** At the `Select objects:` prompt, click each of the two horizontal lines that constitute the door. As you know, whenever AutoCAD wants you to select objects the cursor turns into the small square pickbox. This tells you that you're in Object Selection mode. As you place the cursor over an object, it appears thicker to give you a better idea of what you're about to select. As you click an object, it's highlighted, as shown in Figure 2.15.

If objects don't become "thicker" as you roll over them with your selection cursor, the Selection preview system variable may be turned off. You can turn it back on by entering **selectionpreview**↵**3**↵. This setting can also be found in the Selection tab of the Options dialog box. See Appendix B for more on the Options dialog box, and see Bonus Chapter 4, "System Variables and Dimension Styles," for more on system variables, available at `http://www.omura.com/chapters`.

3. After making your selections, you may decide to deselect some items. Enter **U↵** from the keyboard. Notice that one line is no longer highlighted. When you type **U↵**, objects are deselected, one at a time, in reverse order of selection.

**FIGURE 2.15**
Select the lines of the door and they become highlighted.

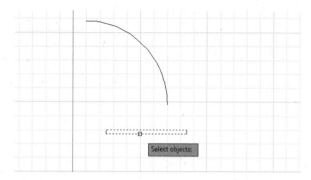

4. You can deselect objects in another way. Hold down the Shift key and click the remaining highlighted line. It reverts to a solid line, showing you that it's no longer selected for editing.

5. By now, you've deselected both lines. Let's try another method for selecting groups of objects. To select objects with a window selection, type **W↵**. The cursor changes to a Point Selection cursor, and the prompt changes to

   `Specify first corner:`

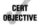

6. Click a point below and to the left of the rectangle representing the door. As you move your cursor across the screen, a selection window appears and stretches across the drawing area. Also notice that the window has a blue tint.

7. After the selection window completely encloses the door but not the arc, click this location to highlight the entire door. This window selects only objects that are completely enclosed by the window, as shown in Figure 2.16.

   Don't confuse the selection window you're creating here with the zoom window you used in Chapter 1, which defines an area of the drawing you want to enlarge. Remember that the Window option works differently under the Zoom command than it does for other editing commands.

8. Press ↵. This tells AutoCAD that you've finished selecting objects. It's important to remember to press ↵ as soon as you finish selecting the objects you want to edit. A new prompt, `Specify base point or [Displacement] <Displacement>:`, appears. The cursor changes to its Point Selection mode.

Now you've seen how the selection process works in AutoCAD—but you're in the middle of the Move command. The next section discusses the prompt that's on your screen and describes how to enter base points and displacement distances.

**FIGURE 2.16**
Selecting the door
in a selection
window

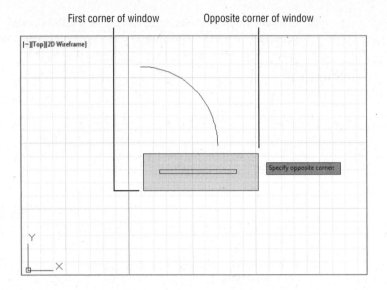

**CONTROLLING THE STATUS BAR DISPLAY**

Toward the right of the status bar, you'll see a tool icon with three horizontal lines. This tool opens a menu that controls the display of the status bar. You use this menu to turn the items in the status bar on or off. A check mark by an item indicates that it's currently on. If for some reason you don't see all the buttons mentioned in the following exercise, check this menu to make sure all the status bar options are turned on. For the items in the left half of the status bar, choose Status Toggles from the menu.

## Providing Base Points

When you move or copy objects, AutoCAD prompts you for a base point, which is a difficult concept to grasp. AutoCAD must be told specifically *from* where and *to* where the move occurs. The *base point* is the exact location from which you determine the distance and direction of the move. After the base point is determined, you can tell AutoCAD where to move the object in relation to that point.

Follow these steps to practice using base points:

**1.** To select a base point, press Shift+right-click. A menu appears, displaying the Object Snap options (see Figure 2.17).

**FIGURE 2.17**

The Object Snap options

When you right-click, make sure the cursor is within the AutoCAD drawing area; otherwise, you won't get the results described in this book.

**2.** Choose Intersection from the Object Snap menu. The Object Snap menu closes.

**3.** Move the cursor to the lower-right corner of the door. Notice that as you approach the corner, a small x-shaped graphic appears on the corner. This is called an *osnap marker*.

**4.** After the x-shaped marker appears, hold the mouse motionless for a second or two. A tool tip appears, telling you the current osnap point AutoCAD has selected.

**5.** Click the left mouse button to select the intersection indicated by the osnap marker. Whenever you see the osnap marker at the point you want to select, you don't have to point exactly at the location with your cursor. Just left-click to select the exact osnap point (see Figure 2.18). In this case, you selected the exact intersection of two lines.

6. At the Specify second point or <use first point as displacement>: prompt, hold down the Shift key and right-click again to open the Object Snap menu.

**FIGURE 2.18**

Using the Point Selection cursor and osnap marker

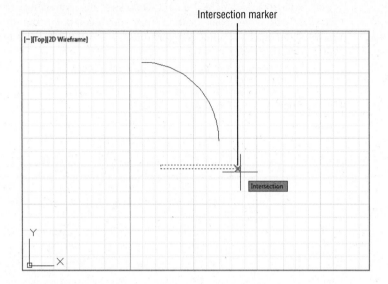

7. This time you'll use the Endpoint osnap, but instead of clicking the option with the mouse, type **E**.

8. Pick the lower-right end of the arc you drew earlier. (Remember that you need to move your cursor close to the endpoint just until the osnap marker appears.) The door moves so that the corner connects exactly with the endpoint of the arc (see Figure 2.19).

**FIGURE 2.19**

Moving the rectangle to its new position using the Endpoint osnap

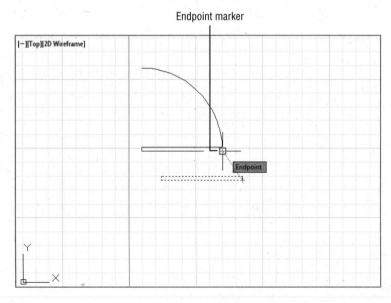

As you can see, the osnap options let you select specific points on an object. You used Endpoint and Intersection in this exercise, but other options are available. Chapter 3 discusses some of the other osnap options. You may have also noticed that the osnap marker is different for each of the options you used. You'll learn more about osnaps in Chapter 3. Now let's continue with our look at point selection.

You may have noticed the statement Use first point as displacement in the prompt in step 6 of the preceding exercise. This means that if you press ↵ instead of clicking a point, the object will move a distance based on the coordinates of the point you selected as a base point. If, for example, the point you click for the base point is at coordinate 2,4, the object will move 2 units in the x-axis and 4 units in the y-axis.

If you want to specify an exact distance and direction by typing a value, select any point on the screen as a base point. As an alternative, you can type @ followed by ↵ at the base point prompt; then, enter the second point's location in relative coordinates. Remember that @ means the last point selected. In the next exercise, you'll try moving the entire door an exact distance of 1 unit at a 45° angle. Metric users will move the door 3 units at a 45° angle. Here are the steps:

1. Click the Move tool on the Home tab's Modify panel.

2. Type **P**↵. The set of objects you selected in the previous exercise is highlighted. P is a selection option that selects the previously selected set of objects.

3. You're still in Object Selection mode, so click the arc to include it in the set of selected objects. The entire door, including the arc, is highlighted.

4. Press ↵ to tell AutoCAD that you've finished your selection. The cursor changes to Point Selection mode.

5. At the Specify base point or [Displacement] <Displacement>: prompt, choose a point on the screen between the door and the left side of the screen (see Figure 2.20).

**FIGURE 2.20**
The highlighted door and the base point just to the left of the door. Note that the base point doesn't need to be on the object that you're moving.

6. Move the cursor around slowly and notice that the door moves as if the base point you selected were attached to it. The door moves with the cursor, at a fixed distance from it. This demonstrates how the base point relates to the objects you select.

7. Type @1<-45↵. (Metric users should type @3<-45↵.) The door moves to a new location on the screen at a distance of 1 unit (3 for metric users) from its previous location and at an angle of minus 45°, which is a direction that is downward at a 45-degree angle.

If AutoCAD is waiting for a command, you can repeat the last command used by pressing the spacebar or pressing ↵. You can also right-click in the drawing area and select the option at the top of the list. If you right-click the Command window, a context menu offers the most recent commands.

This exercise illustrates that the base point doesn't have to be on the object you're manipulating; it can be virtually anywhere on your drawing. You also saw how to reselect a group of objects that were selected previously without having to duplicate the selection process.

## Using Noun/Verb Selection

Nearly all graphics programs today allow the Noun/Verb method for selecting objects. This method requires you to select objects before you issue a command to edit them—that is, you identify the "noun" (the object you want to work on) before the "verb" (the action you want to perform on it). The following exercises show you how to use the Noun/Verb method in AutoCAD.

You've seen that when AutoCAD is waiting for a command, it displays the crosshair cursor with the small square. As mentioned, this square is a pickbox superimposed on the cursor. It indicates that you can select objects even while the Command prompt appears at the bottom of the screen and no command is currently active. The square momentarily disappears when you're in a command that asks you to select points.

### OTHER SELECTION OPTIONS

There are several other selection options you haven't tried yet. You'll see how these options work in exercises later in this book. Or, if you're adventurous, try them now on your own. To use these options, type their keyboard abbreviations (shown in brackets in the following list) at any `Select objects:` prompt:

**Add [A↵]**   Switches from Remove mode to the Add mode. See the description for Remove later in this sidebar.

**All [ALL↵]**   Selects all the objects in a drawing except those in frozen or locked layers. (See Chapter 5, "Keeping Track of Layers and Blocks," for information on layers.)

**Box [B↵]**   Forces the standard selection window so a left-to-right selection uses a standard window and a right-to-left selection uses a crossing window.

**Crossing [C↵]**   Similar to the Window selection option (described later in this sidebar) but selects anything that is entirely within or crosses through the window that you define.

**Crossing Polygon [CP↵]** Acts exactly like Window Polygon (described later in this sidebar), but, like the Crossing selection option, selects anything that crosses through a polygon boundary.

**Fence [F↵]** Selects objects that are crossed by a temporary line called a *fence*. This operation is like using a line to cross out the objects you want to select. After you invoke this option, you can then pick points, as when you're drawing a series of line segments. After you finish drawing the fence, press ↵, and then go on to select other objects or press ↵ again to finish your selection.

Use a Fence selection
to extend a set of
lines to a spline.

Fence          Result

**Group [G↵]** Allows you to select a group by name.

**Last [L↵]** Selects the last object you created.

**Multiple [M↵]** Lets you select several objects first before AutoCAD highlights them. In a large file, selecting objects individually can cause AutoCAD to pause after each selection while it locates and highlights each object. The Multiple option can speed things up: First you select all the objects quickly and then you highlight them all by pressing ↵. This has no menu equivalent.

**Previous [P↵]** Selects the last object or set of objects that was edited or changed.

**Remove [R↵]** Switches to a selection mode whereby the objects you click are removed from the selection set.

**Subobject [SU↵]** Allows selection of faces, edges, and vertices of 3D solid objects. This can also be accomplished by pressing the Ctrl key while picking.

**Object [O↵]** Ends selecting by Subobject and restores normal behavior.

**Undo [U↵]** Removes the most recently added object from the selection set.

**Window [W↵]** Forces a standard window selection. This option is useful when your drawing area is too crowded to use the Autoselect feature to place a window around a set of objects. (See the Auto entry later in this sidebar.) It prevents you from accidentally selecting an object with a single pick when you're placing your window.

**Window Polygon [WP↵]**    Lets you select objects by enclosing them in an irregularly shaped polygon boundary. When you use this option, you see the `First polygon point:` prompt. You then pick points to define the polygon boundary. As you pick points, the `Specify end-point of line or [Undo]:` prompt appears. Select as many points as you need to define the boundary. You can undo boundary line segments as you go by pressing **U↵**. With the boundary defined, press ↵. The bounded objects are highlighted and the `Select objects:` prompt returns, allowing you to use more selection options.

A window polygon selection

The following two selection options are also available but are seldom used. They're intended for use in creating custom menu options or custom tools:

**Auto [AU↵]**    Forces the standard automatic window or crossing window when a point is picked and no object is found. (See the section "Using Autoselect" later in this chapter.) You produce a standard window when you pick the two window corners from left to right, and you produce a crossing window when you pick the two corners from right to left. After you select this option, it remains active for the duration of the current command. Auto is intended for use on systems on which the Autoselect feature has been turned off.

**Single [SI↵]**    Forces the current command to select only a single object. If you use this option, you can pick a single object and the current command acts on that object as if you had pressed ↵ immediately after selecting it. This has no menu equivalent.

In addition to Noun/Verb selection, AutoCAD offers selection options that let you use familiar GUI techniques. See Appendix B to learn how you can control object-selection methods. This appendix also describes how to change the size of the Standard cursor.

Try moving objects by first selecting them and then using the Move command:

1. Press the Esc key twice to make sure AutoCAD isn't in the middle of a command you might have accidentally issued. Then click the arc. The arc is highlighted, and you may also see squares appear at various points on the arc. As stated earlier, these squares are called *grips*. You'll get a chance to work with them later.

2. Choose Move from the Home tab's Modify panel. The cursor changes to Point Selection mode. Notice that the grips on the arc disappear but the arc is still selected.

3. At the `Specify base point or [Displacement] <Displacement>:` prompt, pick any point on the screen. The following prompt appears:

```
Specify second point or
<use first point as displacement>:
```

**4.** Type @1<0↵. Metric users should type @3<0↵. The arc moves to a new location 1 unit (3 units for metric users) to the right.

If this exercise doesn't work as described here, chances are that the Noun/Verb setting has been turned off on your copy of AutoCAD. To turn on the Noun/Verb setting, choose Options from the Application menu to open the Options dialog box and then click the Selection tab. In the Selection Modes group, select the check box next to the Noun/Verb Selection option and click OK.

In this exercise, you picked the arc *before* issuing the Move command. Then, when you clicked the Move tool, you didn't see the `Select objects:` prompt. Instead, AutoCAD assumed you wanted to move the arc that you selected and went directly to the `Specify base point or [Displacement] <Displacement>:` prompt.

## USING AUTOSELECT

Next you'll move the rest of the door in the same direction by using the Autoselect feature:

**1.** Pick a point just above and to the left of the rectangle representing the door. Be sure not to pick the door itself. A selection window appears that you can drag across the screen as you move the cursor. If you move the cursor to the left of the last point selected, the window outline appears dotted and there's a green tint inside the window (see the first image in Figure 2.21). If you move the cursor to the right of that point, the outline appears solid and there's a blue tint inside (see the second image in Figure 2.21).

**2.** Pick a point below and to the right of the door so that the door, but not the arc, is completely enclosed by the window, as shown in the bottom image in Figure 2.21. The door is highlighted (and, again, you may see grips appear at the lines' endpoints and midpoints).

**3.** Click the Move tool again. Just as in the preceding exercise, the `Specify base point or [Displacement] <Displacement>:` prompt appears.

**4.** Pick any point on the screen; then enter @1<0↵. Metric users should enter @3<0↵. The door joins with the arc.

The two selection windows you've just seen—the blue solid one and the dotted green one—represent a standard window and a crossing window. If you use a *standard window*, anything completely within the window is selected. If you use a *crossing window*, anything that crosses through the window is selected. These two types of windows start automatically when you click any blank portion of the drawing area with a Standard cursor or a Point Selection cursor, hence the name *Autoselect*.

Next, you'll select objects with an automatic crossing window:

**1.** Pick a point below and to the right of the door. As you move the cursor left, the crossing (dotted) window appears.

**2.** Select the next point so that the window encloses the door and part of the arc (see Figure 2.22). The entire door, including the arc, is highlighted.

Move **3.** Click the Move tool.

**4.** Pick any point on the screen; then enter @1<180↵. Metric users should type @3<180↵. The door moves back to its original location.

**FIGURE 2.21**
The dotted window (first image) indicates a crossing selection; the solid window (second image) indicates a standard selection window.

Crossing window

Standard window

**FIGURE 2.22**
The door enclosed by a crossing window

You'll find that, in most cases, the Autoselect standard and crossing windows are all you need when selecting objects. They really save you time, so you'll want to become familiar with these features.

**MODIFYING AN AUTOSELECT WINDOW**

Two settings, known as system variables, enable you to use the Autoselect feature in a more flexible way. These two settings, Pickdrag and Pickauto, control the behavior of the Autoselect window, giving you more options to select objects in your drawing.

**Pickdrag**    If you click to start a selection window and then decide you want to use a window polygon, crossing polygon, or fence, you can type **W↵** for a window polygon, **C↵** for a crossing polygon, or **F↵** for a fence. If this does not work, make sure the Pickdrag system variable is set to 2 by typing **PICKDRAG↵2↵**.

**Pickauto**    In a crowded drawing, you may want to use a selection window, but objects close to the cursor may be selected instead. If you set Pickauto to 2 by typing **PICKAUTO↵2↵**, you can click and drag your mouse over an object in a crowded drawing without having the single object selected. AutoCAD will start a selection window instead. You can still use a single click to select a single object.

Before continuing, click the Save tool in the Quick Access toolbar to save the Door.dwg file. You won't want to save the changes you make in the next section, so saving now stores the current condition of the file on your hard disk for safekeeping.

### RESTRICTIONS ON NOUN/VERB OBJECT SELECTION

For many of the modifying or construction-oriented commands, the Noun/Verb selection method is inappropriate because, for those commands, you must select more than one set of objects. You'll know whether a command accepts the Noun/Verb selection method right away. Commands that don't accept the Noun/Verb selection method clear the selection and then ask you to select an object or set of objects.

If you'd like to take a break, now is a good time to do so. If you want, exit AutoCAD, and return to this point in the chapter later. When you return, start AutoCAD and open the Door.dwg file.

**CLICK AND DRAG TO LASSO OBJECTS**

If you need to use an irregular shaped window to select objects, you can use a click-and-drag motion to start a lasso selection. A lasso enables you to draw an irregular "freehand" selection window of any shape. Just as with the rectangular selection window, the direction of the lasso determines the method of selection. A clockwise lasso creates a standard window and a counterclockwise lasso creates a crossing window.

## Editing with Grips

Earlier, when you selected the door, grips appeared at the endpoints, center points, and midpoints of the lines and arcs. You can use grips to make direct changes to the shape of objects or to move and copy them quickly.

If you didn't see grips on the door in the previous exercise, your version of AutoCAD may have the Grips feature turned off. To turn them on, refer to the information on grips in Appendix B.

So far, you've seen how operations in AutoCAD have a discrete beginning and ending. For example, to draw an arc you first issue the Arc command and then go through a series of operations, including answering prompts and picking points. When you're finished, you have an arc and AutoCAD is ready for the next command.

The Grips feature, on the other hand, plays by a different set of rules. Grips offer a small yet powerful set of editing functions that don't conform to the lockstep command/prompt/input routine you've seen so far. As you work through the following exercises, it's helpful to think of grips as a subset of the standard method of operation in AutoCAD.

To practice using the Grips feature, you'll make some temporary modifications to the door drawing.

## Stretching Lines by Using Grips

In this exercise, you'll stretch one corner of the door by grabbing the grip points of two lines:

1. Use the Zoom Realtime tool from the Zoom tool in the View tab's Navigate 2D panel to adjust your view so the size of the door is similar to what is shown in Figure 2.23. You can click and drag the mouse wheel to pan the view if needed.

**FIGURE 2.23**
Stretching lines by using grips. The first image shows the rectangle's corner being stretched upward. The next image shows the new location of the corner at the top of the arc.

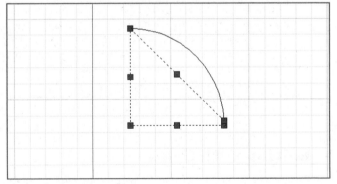

2. Press the Esc key to make sure you're not in the middle of a command. Click a point below and to the left of the door to start a selection window.

3. Click above and to the left of the rectangular part of the door, and then place the selection window around the door rectangle and click to select it.

4. Place the cursor on the lower-left corner grip of the rectangle, *but don't press the mouse button yet*. Notice that the cursor jumps to the grip point and that the grip is highlighted. You also see some dimensions related to the objects associated with the grip.

5. Move the cursor to another grip point. Notice again how the cursor jumps to it. When placed on a grip, the cursor moves to the exact center of the grip point. This means that, for example, if the cursor is placed on an endpoint grip, it's on the exact endpoint of the object.

6. Move the cursor to the upper-left corner grip of the rectangle and click. The grip becomes a solid color and is now a *hot grip*. The prompt displays the following message:

```
**STRETCH**
Specify stretch point or [Base point/Copy/Undo/eXit]:
```

This prompt tells you that Stretch mode is active. Notice the options in the prompt. As you move the cursor, the corner follows, and the lines of the rectangle stretch (see Figure 2.23).

You can control the size and color of grips by using the Selection tab in the Options dialog box; see Appendix B for details.

7. Move the cursor upward toward the top end of the arc and click that point. The rectangle deforms, with the corner placed at your pick point (see Figure 2.23).

Here you saw that a command called Stretch is issued by clicking a grip point. As you'll see in these next steps, a handful of other hot-grip commands are also available:

1. Notice that the grips are still active. Click the grip point that you moved before to make it a hot grip again.

2. Right-click to open a context menu that contains a list of grip-edit options (see Figure 2.24).

**FIGURE 2.24**
A list of grip-edit options

When you click the joining grip point of two contiguous line segments, AutoCAD selects the overlapping grips of two lines. When you stretch the corner away from its original location, the endpoints of both lines follow.

3. Choose Base Point from the list, and then click a point to the right of the hot grip. Now as you move the cursor, the hot grip moves relative to the cursor.

4. Right-click again, choose Copy from the context menu, and enter @1<-30↵. (Metric users should enter @3<-30↵.) Instead of the hot grip moving and the lines changing, copies of the two lines are made with their endpoints 1 unit (or 3 units for metric users) below and to the right of the first set of endpoints.

5. Pick another point just below the last. More copies are made.

6. Press ↵ or enter X↵ to exit Stretch mode. You can also right-click again and choose Exit from the context menu.

In this exercise, you saw that you can select a base point other than the hot grip. You also saw how you can specify relative coordinates to move or copy a hot grip. Finally, you saw that with grips selected on an object, right-clicking opens a context menu that contains grip-edit options.

## Moving and Rotating with Grips

As you've just seen, the Grips feature is an alternative method for editing your drawings. You've already seen how you can stretch endpoints, but you can do much more with grips. The next exercise demonstrates some other options. You'll start by undoing the modifications you made in the preceding exercise:

1. Type U↵. The copies of the stretched lines disappear.

2. Press ↵ again. The deformed door snaps back to its original form.

   Pressing ↵ at the Command prompt causes AutoCAD to repeat the last command entered—in this case, U.

3. You are going to select the entire door. First click a blank area below and to the right of the door.

4. Move the cursor to a location above and to the left of the rectangular portion of the door and click. Because you went from right to left, you created a crossing window. Recall that the crossing window selects anything enclosed and crossing through the window.

5. Click the lower-left grip of the rectangle to turn it into a hot grip. Just as before, as you move your cursor the corner stretches.

6. Right-click and choose Move from the context menu. The Command window displays the following:

```
**MOVE**
Specify move point or [Base point/Copy/Undo/eXit]
```

Now as you move the cursor, the entire door moves with it.

**7.** Position the door near the center of the screen and click. The door moves to the center of the screen. Notice that the Command prompt returns but the door remains highlighted, indicating that it's still selected for the next operation.

**8.** Click the lower-left grip again, right-click, and choose Rotate from the context menu. The Command window displays the following:

```
**ROTATE**
Specify rotation angle or [Base point/Copy/Undo/Reference/eXit]:
```

As you move the cursor, the door rotates about the grip point.

**9.** Position the cursor so that the door rotates approximately 180° (see Figure 2.25). Then Ctrl+click (hold down the Ctrl key and press the left mouse button). A copy of the door appears in the new rotated position, leaving the original door in place.

**FIGURE 2.25**
Rotating and copying the door by using a hot grip. Notice that more than one object is affected by the grip edit, even though only one grip is hot.

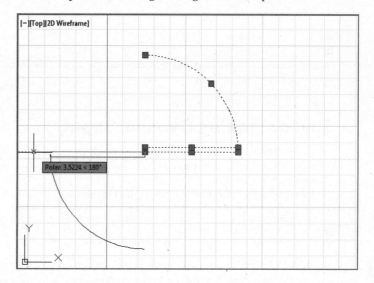

**10.** Press ↵ to exit Grip Edit mode.

You've seen how the Move command is duplicated in a modified way as a hot-grip command. Other hot-grip commands (Stretch, Rotate, Scale, and Mirror) have similar counterparts in the standard set of AutoCAD commands. You'll see how those work in Chapter 11, "Using Dimensions," and Chapter 13, "Copying Existing Drawings from Other Sources."

After you complete any operation by using grips, the objects are still highlighted with their grips active. To clear the grip selection, press the Esc key.

In this exercise, you saw how hot-grip options appear in a context menu. Several other options are available in that menu, including Exit, Base Point, Copy, and Undo.

You can access many of these grip-edit options by pressing the spacebar or ↵ while a grip is selected. With each press, the next option becomes active. The options then repeat if you continue to press ↵. The Ctrl key acts as a shortcut to the Copy option. You have to use it only once; then, each time you click a point, a copy is made.

**SCALING WITH GRIPS**

Grips can be used to scale an object graphically to fit between two other objects. For example, a door can be scaled to fit within a door frame. Place the door so that its hinge side is at the door frame and the door is oriented properly for the frame. With the door selected, click the grip at the hinge side. Right-click and select Scale. Type **R**↵ or select Reference from the command line, and then click the grip at the hinge again. Click the grip at the end of the arc representing the door swing. Finally, click the opposite side of the door frame.

Click the grip at the hinge.    Right-click and select Scale.    Type R↵ and click these grips hinge side first.    Click the endpoint of the frame to scale the door.

# Understanding Dynamic Input

You've seen how AutoCAD displays a lot of information at the cursor through its Dynamic Input display. In this section, you'll now get a chance to explore the Dynamic Input display through grip editing.

You'll start by going back to the original version of the Door.dwg drawing that you saved earlier:

1. Click the Close icon in the Drawing tab of the drawing area.

2. When you're asked if you want to save changes, click No.

3. Click Open from the Quick Access toolbar, and then locate and select the Door.dwg file you saved earlier. You can also open the doorsample.dwg file from the sample files you installed from this book's web page.

   The door appears in the condition in which you left it when you last saved the file.

4. Click the Pan tool in the Navigation bar and click and drag the mouse to pan the view to the center of the drawing area.

5. Right-click and select Exit to exit the Pan tool.

6. Click the arc to expose its grips.

**DON'T SEE THE DYNAMIC INPUT DISPLAY?**

If you don't see the Dynamic Input display at the cursor, type **Dynmode** ↵ ↵ to turn it on. You can also click the Customization tool to the far right end of the status bar and select Dynamic Input to add the Dynamic Input tool to the Status Bar. This tool lets you toggle the Dynamic Input display on and off.

**7.** Place the cursor on the grip at the middle of the arc, but don't click it. (This is called *hovering* over a grip.) You see the dimensions of the arc appear as well as a menu offering two options: Stretch and Radius. The dimensions are useful when you need to check the size of objects you've drawn (see Figure 2.26).

**FIGURE 2.26**
Hovering over
a grip

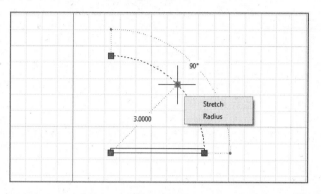

**8.** Click the Radius option in the grip menu. The Command prompt appears at the cursor, and the radius dimension changes to a text box.

**9.** Move the cursor toward the upper-right corner of the drawing area. The radius dimension of the arc changes as you move the cursor.

**10.** Enter 4↵. Metric users enter 12↵. As you type, the new value appears in the radius dimension. When you press ↵, the arc changes to the new radius.

**11.** Click the Undo button to revert to the original arc size.

Here you saw the basic methods for using the Dynamic Input display. You can hover over an object's grip to display its dimensions along with a grip menu. The menu appears for many but not all grips, and the contents of the menu depend on the object selected. Click the grip and, if available, the dimensions can be edited directly through the keyboard. In this example, you were able to change the radius of the arc to an exact value by selecting the Radius option from the grip menu and then entering a value. Depending on the grip you click, you can change a dimension through direct keyboard input. For example, if you want to change the degrees the arc covers instead of its radius, you can hover over the arrow grip at either end of the arc and select Lengthen. The dimensions that appear can then be edited to increase or decrease the length of the arc without affecting its radius.

Next, try Dynamic Input display on a line:

**1.** Click the bottommost line of the door, as shown in Figure 2.27; hover over the rightmost grip on the selected line. Just as you saw with the arc, you can see the dimensions of the line, including its length and directional angle. You also see a menu that offers the Stretch and Lengthen options.

**2.** Click the grip over which you're hovering, and then move the cursor up and to the right. You see two dimensions: One indicates the overall length and the other shows the change in length of the line. You also see the Command prompt at the cursor. Notice that the dimension indicating the change in length is highlighted (see Figure 2.28).

**3.** Type **1** and press the Tab key, not the Enter key, to increase the length of the line by 1 unit. Metric users should enter **3** and press the Tab key. Now, as you move the cursor, the line is locked at a new length that is 1 or 3 units longer than its original length. Also notice that the overall dimension is highlighted. You also see a lock icon on the length dimension (see Figure 2.29).

**FIGURE 2.27**

Selecting a line on the door

**FIGURE 2.28**

The overall length dimension and the change in length dimension

**4.** Press the Tab key again. The angle value is highlighted.

**5.** Type **45** and press the Tab key to lock the angle of the line at 45°.

**FIGURE 2.29**

The line locked at a new length

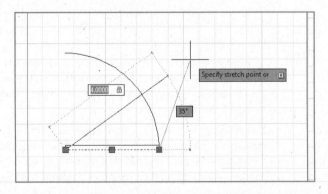

   **6.** Make sure the cursor isn't too close to the locked endpoint of the line and then click the left mouse button. The line is now in its new orientation with a length of 4 (12 for metric users) and an angle of 45°, as shown in Figure 2.30.

**FIGURE 2.30**
The line's new length and orientation

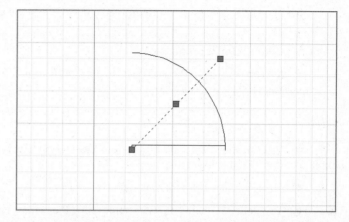

   You can see that the Dynamic Input display lets you enter specific dimensions for the selected object, making possible precise changes in an object's size. Choose Lengthen from the grip menu if you just want to change the length of the line.

   You can also use the Dynamic Input display while using other grip-editing features. Try the following exercise to see how the Dynamic Input display works while moving objects:

   **1.** Click above and to the right of the door drawing to start a crossing selection window.

   **2.** Click below and to the left to select the entire door drawing.

   **3.** Click the middle grip of the arc.

   **4.** Right-click and choose Move. You see the Command prompt at the cursor with the distance value highlighted. As you move the cursor, you can see the distance and angle values in the Dynamic Input display change (see Figure 2.31).

**FIGURE 2.31**
The Dynamic Input display

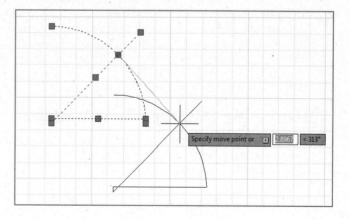

5. Type **4** and then press the Tab key. As you move the cursor, the distance from the original location of the arc's midpoint is locked at 4 (or 12) units. The angle value is now highlighted and available for editing.

6. Type **225** and then press the Tab key to lock the angle at 225°.

7. Click a location away from the door drawing. The door moves to its new location, exactly 4 units from its original location.

As you can see from these exercises, the Dynamic Input display adds some helpful methods for editing objects. To summarize, here is a rundown of the basic Dynamic Input display features:

◆ You can quickly check the dimensions of an object by selecting it and then hovering over a grip.

◆ You can alter an object's dimensions by entering values into the highlighted dimensions of the Dynamic Input display.

◆ To highlight a different dimension, press the Tab key.

◆ To accept any changes you've made using the Dynamic Input display, click at a location away from the grip you're editing. You can also press ↵ or the spacebar.

Not all grips offer dimensions that can be edited. If you click the midpoint grip on the line, for example, you won't see the dimensions of the line, although you'll see the Command prompt and you'll be able to enter a new coordinate for the midpoint.

As you've seen in the arc and line examples, each object offers a different set of dimensions. If you like the way the Dynamic Input display works, you can experiment on other types of objects. AutoCAD offers a number of settings that let you control the behavior of the Dynamic Input display. You'll learn about those settings in Appendix B.

---

**TYPING COORDINATES WITH DYNAMIC INPUT**

When entering coordinates through the keyboard while Dynamic Input is enabled, you have to use a slightly different notation for relative and absolute coordinates. If you're entering relative coordinates, you can leave off the @ sign, so instead of typing **@12,9**↵, you can simply type **12,9**↵. If you are entering absolute coordinates, you need to precede your coordinate list with a # sign. So instead of entering **1,1**↵ to specify a point at coordinate 1,1, you would need to enter **#1,1**↵.

---

# Displaying Data in a Text Window

You may have noticed that as you work in AutoCAD, the activity displayed in the Command window scrolls up. Sometimes, it's helpful to view information that has scrolled past the view shown in the Command window. For example, you can review the command activity from your session to check input values or to recall other data-entry information. Try the following exercise to see how the Text Window works:

CERT
OBJECTIVE

**1.** From the Home tab's expanded Properties panel, click the List tool.

**2.** At the Select objects: prompt, click the arc and press ↵. A text window appears and displays information about the arc (see Figure 2.32). If your command window is undocked, it will expand to display the information. Toward the bottom is the list of the arc's properties. Don't worry if the meaning of some listed properties isn't obvious yet; as you work your way through this book, you'll learn what the properties of an object mean.

**FIGURE 2.32**
The expanded Auto-CAD Command window showing the data displayed by the List tool

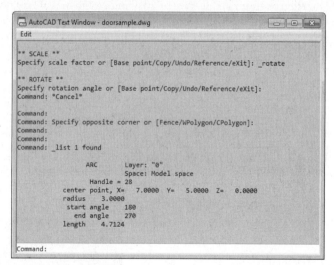

**3.** If your command window is unlocked, you can dismiss the expanded Command window by clicking in the drawing area. To bring it back, press the F2 function key or click the up-pointing arrowhead at the far right of the unlocked Command window.

You can set the number of lines that AutoCAD retains by using the Options dialog box, or you can have AutoCAD record the AutoCAD Text Window information in a text file.

When you have more than one document open, the AutoCAD Command window displays a listing for the drawing that is currently active.

---

**DOCKING THE COMMAND WINDOW**

If you've used AutoCAD before, you may wonder if you can restore the old-style Command window. You can do this by docking the window to the bottom of the AutoCAD window. Once this is done, the Command window behaves the same way as in earlier versions of AutoCAD. You can open a separate Text Window by entering **TEXTSCR↵** or by pressing F2.

---

## Displaying the Properties of an Object

**CERT OBJECTIVE**

While we're on the subject of displaying information, you'll want to know about the Properties palette. In the preceding exercise, you saw how the List command showed some information regarding the properties of an object, such as the location of an arc's center and endpoints. You can also double-click an object to display the Quick Properties palette that shows other basic information about the object. (You might accidentally display the Quick Properties palette from time to time!) The Properties palette provides a more complete view of an object's properties with the additional feature of allowing you to make changes to those properties. The Properties palette is so useful, you may want to consider leaving it open all the time.

To see what the Properties palette is for, try the following exercise:

1. If you haven't done so already, select the arc in the drawing, right-click it, and select Properties to open the Properties palette, which displays a list of the arc's properties. Don't worry if many of the items in this palette are undecipherable; you'll learn more about this palette as you work through the early chapters of this book. For now, just be aware that you can get to this palette with a right-click and that it displays the object's properties. You can also use it to modify many of the properties listed (see Figure 2.33).

2. Click the small Auto-hide box at the top of the Properties palette. It's the icon that looks like a double arrow. The icon changes to a single arrow. The Auto-hide option in the Properties palette lets you keep the palette open without having it take up too much of the drawing area. This can be useful when you need to edit the properties of many objects.

3. Move the cursor away from the Properties palette. The Properties palette collapses so that only the title bar remains.

4. Hover the cursor on the Properties palette title bar. The Properties palette opens to display all the options again.

**5.** Click the Auto-hide box again to restore the "always open" mode of the palette.

**FIGURE 2.33**

Object Properties
palette

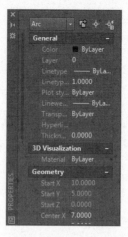

**6.** Close the Properties palette by clicking the X in its upper corner. (The X appears in the upper-left or upper-right corner, depending on the placement of the palette in the AutoCAD window.) You can also right-click the title bar on the side of the Properties palette and then choose Close from the context menu.

**7.** You're finished with the door drawing, so choose Close from the Application menu.

**8.** In the AutoCAD dialog box, click the No button. (You've already saved this file just as you want it, so you don't need to save it again.)

In many cases, you can open the Properties palette by double-clicking an object. Some objects, however, display a dialog box to allow you to edit them.

Another feature related to the Properties palette is the Quick Properties tool and palette. The Quick Properties palette appears whenever you double-click an object or set of objects (Figure 2.34).

**FIGURE 2.34**

The Quick Proper-
ties palette

The Quick Properties palette lets you control just a few properties of an object (color, layer, linetype, and length). When turned on, it pops up every time you select an object, so you may want to limit its use to those times when you are adjusting the color, layer, and linetype of objects in your drawing.

**USING ROTATE REFERENCE TO ALIGN OBJECTS**

You can use the Rotate command's Reference option to align a set of objects graphically to another object. For example, suppose you want to rotate a set of circles inside a hexagon to align with the corner of the hexagon.

To do this, you can use the Reference option as follows:

1. Start the Rotate command, and select the circles.

2. At the `Specify base point:` prompt, use the Center osnap to select the center of the hexagon as represented by the central circle. Once you do this, the objects rotate around the selected point as you move your cursor.

Select the center of the hexagon for the base point.

Type R↵ and select the center of the hexagon again.

Select the center of one of the circles you want to align to a corner.

Select a corner of the hexagon to align the circles to the corners.

3. At the `Specify rotation angle or [Copy/Reference]:` prompt, enter **R**↵.

4. At the `Specify the reference angle <0>:` prompt, use the Center osnap to select the center of the hexagon again. You can also enter **@**↵ since the last point you selected was the center.

5. At the `Specify second point:` prompt, use the Center osnap to select the center of one of the circles you want to align with the hexagon. Now, as you move the cursor, the circle whose center you selected is aligned with the cursor angle.

6. At the `Specify the new angle or [Points]:` prompt, use the Endpoint osnap to select one of the corners of the hexagon. The circles align with the corners.

You can also use grips to align objects. Here's how: Select the object or set of objects and then click a grip. The grip you select becomes the rotation point, so select this first grip carefully. Right-click and select Rotate. Type **R**↵ and select the grip you just selected and another point to determine the reference angle. Finally, select the new angle for the object or set of objects. If you want to rotate about a point other than the first grip, use the Grip Base right-click option. If you'd like to experiment with the Rotate Reference option, we've provided a sample file that you can use called `rotatereference.dwg`.

# Getting Help

Eventually, you'll find yourself somewhere without documentation and you'll have a question about an AutoCAD feature. AutoCAD provides an online help facility that gives you information on nearly any topic related to AutoCAD.

You can open the AutoCAD Help website by clicking the Help tool in the InfoCenter. There you'll find a comprehensive set of help topics and tools including video tutorials and the standard help documentation. As with many other programs, you can obtain context-sensitive help by pressing the F1 function key.

If you're looking for more general information about AutoCAD, the Dashboard offers some introductory videos and links to online training. Click the Learn option at the bottom of the Dashboard to view these resources. Click the Create option at the bottom of the Dashboard to return to the drawing file options.

## Using the InfoCenter

**CERT OBJECTIVE**

If you want to find information about a topic based on a keyword, you can use the InfoCenter in the upper-right corner of the AutoCAD window. Follow these steps:

1. Type **change** in the InfoCenter text box at the top right of the AutoCAD window, and then click the Search tool to the right of the input box.

2. The AutoCAD Help window opens and displays information on the Change command (see Figure 2.35).

**FIGURE 2.35**
The AutoCAD Help window showing information on the Change command

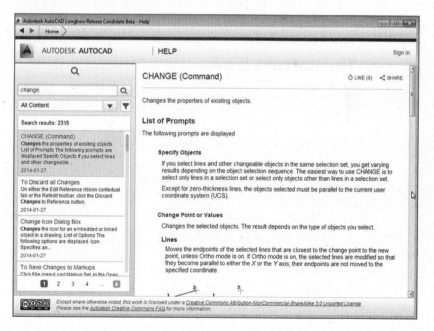

You can use Boolean AND, OR, NEAR, and NOT in conjunction with other keywords to help filter your searches, just as in a typical search engine that you might use in your web browser.

## Finding Additional Sources of Help

The InfoCenter is the main online source for reference material, but you can also find answers to your questions through the other options in the InfoCenter's Help flyout menu. You can open this menu by clicking the arrowhead next to the InfoCenter Help tool. Here is a brief description of them:

**Help**   Opens the AutoCAD 2015 Help website.

**Download Offline Help**   Lets you select and download help files that can be stored locally on your PC. These help files can be useful if you find yourself in a location without Internet access.

**Send Feedback**   Autodesk offers the product feedback web page, which enables you to send comments to Autodesk. The Send Feedback option takes you directly to this page.

**Download Language Packs**   If you need to set up AutoCAD for a language other than English, you can download a language pack using this link.

**Customer Involvement Program**   The Customer Involvement Program is really a way for Autodesk to monitor the condition of AutoCAD by allowing its customers to send comments about program errors or crashes. This voluntary program lets you participate anonymously, or you can provide contact information for follow-up contacts.

**Desktop Analytics**   Autodesk also provides an opt-in for their Desktop Analytics program. This program monitors your AutoCAD activity by collecting use, session length, country location, document type, size, and whether documents are open locally or from Autodesk® 360.

**About Autodesk AutoCAD 2015**   This option provides information about the version of AutoCAD you're using.

# The Bottom Line

**Specify distances with coordinates.**   One of the most basic skills you need to learn is how to indicate exact distances through the keyboard. AutoCAD uses a simple annotation system to indicate distance and direction.

**Master It**   What would you type to indicate a relative distance of 14 units at a 45° angle?

**Interpret the cursor modes and understand prompts.**   The AutoCAD cursor changes its shape depending on the command that is currently active. These different cursor modes can give you a clue regarding what you should be doing.

**Master It**   Describe the Point Selection cursor and the Pickbox cursor.

**Select objects and edit with grips.**   Grips are small squares or arrowheads that appear at key points on the object when they're selected. They offer a powerful way to edit objects.

**Master It**   How do you select multiple grips?

**Understand the AutoCAD Cursor.**   The cursor changes in appearance depending on the tool or command that is being used.

**Master It**   What does the cursor badge look like when using the Erase tool?

**Display data in a text window.**    AutoCAD offers the AutoCAD Text Window, which keeps a running account of the commands you use. This can be helpful in retrieving input that you've entered when constructing your drawing.

**Master It**    Name a command that displays its results in the AutoCAD Text Window.

**Display the properties of an object.**    The Properties palette is one of the most useful sources for drawing information. Not only does it list the properties of an object, it also lets you change the shape, color, and other properties of objects.

**Master It**    How do you open the Properties palette for a particular object?

**Get help.**    The AutoCAD Autodesk Exchange website is thorough in its coverage of AutoCAD features. New and experienced users alike can often find answers to their questions through the Help window, so it pays to become familiar with it.

**Master It**    What keyboard key do you press for context-sensitive help?

# Chapter 3

# Setting Up and Using the Drafting Tools

Chapter 1, "Exploring the Interface," and Chapter 2, "Creating Your First Drawing," covered the basic information you need to understand the workings of the AutoCAD® 2015 software. Now you'll put this knowledge to work. In this architectural tutorial, which begins here and continues through Chapter 14, "Advanced Editing and Organizing," you'll draw an apartment building composed of studios. We'll show you how to use AutoCAD commands and give you a solid understanding of the basic AutoCAD package. With these fundamentals, you can use AutoCAD to its fullest potential regardless of the kinds of drawings you intend to create or the enhancement products you may use in the future.

In this chapter, you'll start drawing an apartment's bathroom fixtures. In the process, you'll learn how to use the basic AutoCAD tools. You'll also be introduced to the concept of drawing scale and how the size of what you draw is translated into a paper sheet size.

In this chapter, you will learn to

♦ Set up a work area

♦ Explore the drawing process

♦ Plan and lay out a drawing

♦ Use the AutoCAD modes as drafting tools

## Setting Up a Work Area

Before beginning most drawings, you should set up your work area. To do this, determine the *measurement system*, the *drawing sheet size*, and the *scale* you want to use. The default work area is roughly 16″×9″ at full scale, given a decimal measurement system in which 1 unit equals 1 inch. Metric users will find that the default area is roughly 550 mm × 300 mm, in which 1 unit equals 1 mm. If these are appropriate settings for your drawing, you don't have to do any setting up. It's more likely, however, that you'll make drawings of various sizes and scales. For example, you might want to create a drawing in a measurement system in which you can specify feet, inches, and fractions of inches at 1′ = 1″ scale and print the drawing on an 8 ½″×11″ sheet of paper.

In this section, you'll learn how to set up a drawing exactly the way you want.

## Specifying Units

You'll start by creating a new file called Bath. Then you'll set up the unit style.

Use these steps to create the file:

1. If you haven't done so already, start AutoCAD. If AutoCAD is already running, click the Templates drop-down list just below the Start Drawing icon in the Dashboard.

2. Select acad.dwt from the list. Metric users should select acadiso.dwt.

3. Type Z⏎A⏎ or select Zoom All from the Zoom flyout in the Navigation bar.

4. Choose Save As from the Application menu.

5. In the Save Drawing As dialog box, enter **Bath** for the filename.

6. Check to make sure you're saving the drawing in the My Documents folder or in the folder where you've chosen to store your exercise files, and then click Save.

---

### USING THE IMPERIAL AND METRIC EXAMPLES

The exercises in this book are shown in both the metric and Imperial measurement systems. Be sure that if you start to work with the Imperial system, you continue with it throughout this book.

The metric settings described in this book are only approximations of their Imperial equivalents. For example, the drawing scale for the metric example is 1:10, which is close to the 1″ = 1′-0″ scale used in the Imperial example. In the grid example, you're asked to use a 30-unit grid, which is close to the 1′ grid of the Imperial example. Dimensions of objects are similar, but not exact. For example, the Imperial version of the tub measures 2′-8″ × 5′-0″ and the metric version of the tub is 81 cm × 152 cm. The actual metric equivalent of 2′-8″ × 5′-0″ is 81.28 cm × 152.4 cm. Measurements in the tub example are rounded to the nearest centimeter.

Metric users should also be aware that AutoCAD uses a period as a decimal point instead of the comma used in most European nations, South Africa, and elsewhere. Commas are used in AutoCAD to separate the X, Y, and Z components of a coordinate.

---

The next thing you want to tell AutoCAD is the *unit style* you intend to use. So far, you've been using the default, which is a generic decimal unit. This unit can be interpreted as inches, centimeters, feet, kilometers, or light-years—whatever you like. When it comes time to print your drawing, you can tell AutoCAD how to convert these units into a meaningful scale.

If you are a U.S. user, decimal units typically represent inches. If you want to be able to enter distances in feet, you must change the unit style to a style that accepts feet as input. In this chapter, you'll do this through the Drawing Units dialog box shown in Figure 3.1.

If you're a civil engineer, you should know that the Engineering unit style lets you enter feet and decimal feet for distances. For example, the equivalent of 12′-6″ is 12.5′. If you use the Engineering unit style, you'll ensure that your drawings conform to the scale of drawings created by your architectural colleagues.

**FIGURE 3.1**

The Drawing Units
dialog box

Follow these steps to set a unit style:

1. Choose Drawing Utilities ➢ Units from the Application menu or type **Un**↵ to open the Drawing Units dialog box. Remember that the Application menu can be opened by clicking the red AutoCAD icon in the upper-left corner of the AutoCAD window.

2. Let's look at a few of the options available. Click the Type drop-down list in the Length group. Notice the unit styles in the list.

3. Click Architectural. The Sample Output group of the dialog box shows you what the Architectural style looks like in AutoCAD. Metric users should keep this setting as Decimal.

---

**SHORTCUT TO SETTING UNITS**

You can also control the Drawing Units settings by using several system variables. To set the unit style, you can type **'lunits**↵ at the Command prompt. (The apostrophe lets you enter this command while in the middle of other commands.) At the Enter new value for LUNITS <2>: prompt, enter **4** for Architectural.

---

4. Click the Precision drop-down list just below the Type list. Notice the options available. You can set the smallest unit AutoCAD will display in this drawing. For now, leave this setting at its default value of 0'-0 1/16". Metric users will keep the setting at 0.0000.

5. Click the drop-down list in the Insertion Scale group. The list shows various units of measure.

6. Click Inches; if you're a metric user, choose Centimeters. This option lets you control how AutoCAD translates drawing scales when you import drawings from outside the

current drawing. You'll learn more about this feature in Chapter 25, "Managing and Sharing Your Drawings."

**7.** Click OK in the Drawing Units dialog box to return to the drawing.

If you use the Imperial system of measurement, you selected Architectural measurement units for this tutorial, but your work may require a different unit style. You saw the unit styles available in the Drawing Units dialog box. Table 3.1 shows examples of how the distance 15.5 is entered in each of these styles.

**TABLE 3.1:**     Measurement systems available in AutoCAD

| MEASUREMENT SYSTEM | DISPLAY OF MEASUREMENT IN AUTOCAD |
|---|---|
| Scientific | 1.55E+01 (inches or metric) |
| Decimal | 15.5000 (inches or metric) |
| Engineering | 1'-3.5" (input as 1'3.5") |
| Architectural | 1'-31/2" (input as 1'3-1/2") |
| Fractional | 151/2" (input as 15-1/2") |

In the previous exercise, you needed to change only two settings. Let's look at the other Drawing Units settings in more detail. As you read, you may want to refer back to Figure 3.1.

## Fine-Tuning the Measurement System

Most of the time you'll be concerned only with the units and angles settings of the Drawing Units dialog box. But as you saw in the preceding exercise, you can control many other settings related to the input and display of units.

---

**TAKING MEASUREMENTS**

To measure the distance between two points, click Distance from the Measure flyout on the Home tab's Utilities panel, or type **Mea⤶D⤶** and then click the two points. (*Mea* is the shortcut for the Measuregeom command.) If this command doesn't give you an accurate distance measurement, examine the Precision option in the Drawing Units dialog box. If it's set too high, the value returned by the Measuregeom command may be rounded to a greater number than your tolerances allow, even though the distance is drawn accurately.

---

The Precision drop-down list in the Length group lets you specify the smallest unit value that you want AutoCAD to display in the status bar and in the prompts. If you choose a measurement system that uses fractions, the Precision list includes fractional units. You can also control this setting with the Luprec system variable.

The Angle group lets you set the style for displaying angles. You have a choice of five angle types: Decimal Degrees, Degrees/Minutes/Seconds, Grads, Radians, and Surveyor's Units. In the Angle group's Precision drop-down list, you can specify the degree of accuracy you want AutoCAD to display for angles. You can also control these settings with the `Aunits` and `Auprec` system variables.

You can find out more about system variables on the AutoCAD 2015 Help website. Select the Command Reference option in the left column of the page and then choose System Variables. Select the first letter of a system variable name from the list.

You can tell AutoCAD which direction is positive, either clockwise or counterclockwise. The default, which is counterclockwise, is used in this book. The Direction Control dialog box lets you set the direction of the 0 base angle. The default base angle (and the one used throughout this book) is a direction from left to right. However, at times you may want to designate another direction as the 0 base angle. You can also control these settings with the `Angbase` and `Angdir` system variables.

The Insertion Scale setting in the Drawing Units dialog box lets you control how blocks from the tool palettes or DesignCenter™ are scaled as they're imported into your current drawing. A *block* is a collection of drawing objects that form a single object. Blocks are frequently used to create standard symbols. You'll learn more about blocks in Chapter 4, "Organizing Objects with Blocks and Groups." The Insertion Scale setting lets you compensate for drawings of different scales by offering an automatic scale translation when importing blocks from an external file. The `Insunits` system variable also controls the Insertion Scale setting. You'll learn more about this setting in Chapter 25.

If you're new to AutoCAD, don't worry about the Insertion Scale setting right now. Make a mental note of it. It may come in handy in your work in the future.

## Setting Up the Drawing Limits

One of the big advantages of using AutoCAD is that you can draw at full scale; you aren't limited to the edges of a piece of paper the way you are in manual drawing. But you may find it difficult to start drawing without knowing the drawing boundaries. You can set up some arbitrary boundaries using the Limits feature.

You'll be drawing a bathroom that is roughly 8' by 5' (230 cm by 150 cm for metric users). You'll want to give yourself some extra room around the bathroom, so your drawing limits should be a bit larger than that actual bathroom size. You'll use an area of 11' by 8'-6" for the limits of your drawing. Metric users will use an area 297 cm by 210 cm. These sizes will accommodate your bathroom with some room to spare.

Now that you know the area you need, you can use the Limits command to set up the area:

1. Type **LIMITS**↵.

2. At the `Specify lower left corner or [ON/OFF] <0'-0",0'-0">:` prompt, specify the lower-left corner of your work area. Press ↵ to accept the default.

3. At the `Specify upper right corner <1'-0",0'-9">:` prompt, you can specify the upper-right corner of your work area. (The default is shown in brackets.) Enter **132,102**. Or if you prefer, you can enter **11',8'6** because you've set up your drawing for Architectural units. Metric users should enter **297,210**.

4. Select Zoom All from the Zoom flyout in the Navigation bar, or type **Z**↵**A**↵. Although it appears that nothing has changed, your drawing area is now set to a size that will enable you to draw your bathroom at full scale.

Zoom All

5. Move the cursor to the upper-right corner of the drawing area and watch the coordinate readout in the bottom-left corner of the AutoCAD window. Notice that now the upper-right corner has a y-coordinate of approximately 8'-6", or 210 for metric users. The x-coordinate depends on the proportion of your AutoCAD window. The coordinate readout also displays distances in feet and inches.

6. Click the Grid Display tool in the status bar to turn off the grid.

---

### THINGS TO WATCH FOR WHEN ENTERING DISTANCES

When you're using Architectural units, you should be aware of two points:

♦ Use hyphens only to distinguish fractions from whole inches.

♦ You can't use spaces while specifying a dimension. For example, you can specify eight feet, four and one-half inches as 8'4-1/2" or 8'4.5, but not as 8'-4 1/2".

These idiosyncrasies are a source of confusion to many architects and engineers new to AutoCAD because the program often displays architectural dimensions in the standard architectural format but doesn't allow you to enter dimensions that way.

Here are some tips for entering distances and angles in unusual situations:

♦ When entering distances in inches and feet, you can omit the inch (") sign. If you're using the Engineering unit style, you can enter decimal feet and forgo the inch sign entirely.

♦ You can enter fractional distances and angles in any format you like, regardless of the current unit style. For example, you can enter a distance as @1/2 <1.5708r, even if your current unit system is set for decimal units and decimal degrees (1.5708r is the radian equivalent of 90°).

♦ If you have your angle units set to degrees, grads, or radians, you don't need to specify g, r, or d after the angle. You do have to specify g, r, or d, however, if you want to use these units when they aren't the current default angle system.

♦ If your current base angle is set to something other than horizontal from left to right, you can use a double less-than symbol (<<) in place of the single less-than symbol (<) to override the current base angle. The << assumes the base angle of 0° to be a direction from left to right and the positive direction to be counterclockwise.

♦ If your current angle system uses a different base angle and direction and you want to specify an angle in the standard base direction, you can use a triple less-than symbol (<<<) to indicate angles. Note that this works only if Dynamic Input is turned off.

♦ You can specify a denominator of any size when specifying fractions. However, be aware that the value you've set for the maximum number of digits to the right of decimal points (under the Precision setting in the Length group of the Drawing Units dialog box) restricts the fractional value AutoCAD reports. For example, if your units are set for a maximum of two digits of decimals and you give a fractional value of 5/32, AutoCAD rounds this value to 3/16. Note that this doesn't affect the accuracy of the actual drawing dimensions.

♦ You can enter decimal feet for distances in the Architectural unit style. For example, you can enter 6'-6" as 6.5'.

In step 5, the coordinate readout shows you that your drawing area is larger than before. The background grid can help you visualize the area in which you're working. You can control the grid using the Grid Display tool in the status bar, which you'll learn about toward the end of this chapter. Grid Display shows a background grid that helps you visualize distances, and it can also show you the limits of your drawing. It can be a bit distracting for a new user, so we've asked you to turn it off for now.

## Looking at an Alternative to Limits

As an alternative to setting up the drawing limits, you can draw a rectangle that outlines the same area used to define the drawing limits. For example, in the previous exercise you could use the Rectangle tool to draw a rectangle that has its lower-left corner at coordinate 0,0 and its upper-right corner at 132,102 (297,210 for metric users). You can set up the rectangle to be visible without printing using the Layer feature. You'll learn more about layers in Chapter 5, "Keeping Track of Layers and Blocks."

---

### COORDINATING WITH PAPER SIZES

At this point, you may have questions about how your full-scale drawing will fit onto standard paper sizes. AutoCAD offers several features that give you precise control over the scale of your drawing. These features offer industry-standard scales to match your drawing with any paper size you need. You'll learn more about these features as you work through the chapters of this book. However, if you're anxious to find out about them, look at the sections on layouts in Chapter 8, "Introducing Printing, Plotting, and Layouts," and Chapter 15, "Laying Out Your Printer Output," and also check out the Annotative Scale feature in Chapter 9, "Adding Text to Drawings."

---

## Understanding Scale Factors

If you've ever had to create a drawing to scale using pencil and paper, you rely on an architect's or engineer's scale to mark off distances on paper. You are working directly with the final media on which the drawing will appear. With a CAD program, you're a few steps removed from the finished product. Because of this, you need a deeper understanding of your drawing scale and how it's derived. In particular, you must understand *scale factors*. For example, one common use of scale factors is translating the size of a graphic symbol, such as a section symbol in an architectural drawing, to the final plotted text size. When you draw manually, you draw your symbol at the size you want. In a CAD drawing, you need to translate the desired final symbol size to the drawing scale.

When you start adding graphic symbols to your drawing (see Chapter 4), you have to specify a symbol height. The scale factor helps you determine the appropriate symbol height for a particular drawing scale. For example, you may want your symbol to appear 1/2" high in your final plot. But if you draw your symbol to 1/2" in your drawing, it appears as a dot when plotted. The symbol has to be scaled up to a size that, when scaled back down at plot time, appears 1/2" high. For a 1/4" scale drawing, you multiply the 1/2" text height by a scale factor of 48 to get 24". Your symbol should be 24" high in the CAD drawing in order to appear 1/2" high in the final plot. Where did the number 48 come from?

The scale factor for fractional inch scales is derived by multiplying the denominator of the scale by 12 and then dividing by the numerator. For example, the scale factor for 1/4″ = 1′-0″ is (4 times 12) / 1, or 48/1. For 3/16″ = 1′-0″ scale, the operation is (16 times 12) / 3, or 64. For whole-foot scales such as 1″= 10′, multiply the feet side of the equation by 12. Metric scales require simple decimal conversions.

You can also use scale factors to determine your drawing limits. For example, if you have a sheet size of 11″ by 17″ and you want to know the equivalent full-scale size for a 1/4″ scale drawing, you multiply the sheet measurements by 48. In this way, 11″ becomes 528″ (48 times 11″), and 17″ becomes 816″ (48 times 17″). Your work area must be 528″ by 816″ if you intend to have a final output of 11″ by 17″ at 1/4″ = 1′. You can divide these inch measurements by 12″ to get 44′ by 68′.

Table 3.2 shows scale factors as they relate to standard drawing scales. These scale factors are the values by which you multiply the desired final printout size to get the equivalent full-scale size. If you're using the metric system, you can use the drawing scale directly as the scale factor. For example, a drawing scale of 1:10 has a scale factor of 10, a drawing scale of 1:50 has a scale factor of 50, and so on. Metric users need to take special care regarding the base unit. Centimeters are used as a base unit in the examples in this book, which means that if you enter a distance as 1, you can assume the distance to be 1 cm.

**TABLE 3.2:** Scale conversion factors

| SCALE FACTORS FOR ENGINEERING DRAWING SCALES | DRAWING SCALE | | | | | | | |
|---|---|---|---|---|---|---|---|---|
| $n = 1″$ | 10′ | 20′ | 30′ | 40′ | 50′ | 60′ | 100′ | 200′ |
| Scale factor | 120 | 240 | 360 | 480 | 600 | 720 | 1200 | 2400 |
| $n = 1′-0″$ | 1/16″ | 1/8″ | 1/4″ | 1/2″ | 3/4″ | 1″ | 1-1/2″ | 3″ |
| Scale factor | 192 | 96 | 48 | 24 | 16 | 12 | 8 | 4 |

In older drawings, scale factors were used to determine text height and dimension settings. Chances are you will eventually have to work with drawings created by older AutoCAD versions, so understanding scale factors will pay off later. Plotting to a particular scale is also easier with an understanding of scale factors.

## Using Polar Tracking

In this section, you'll draw the first item in the bathroom: the toilet. It's composed of a rectangle representing the tank and a truncated ellipse representing the seat. To construct the toilet, you'll use Polar Tracking, which is one of the more versatile drafting tools. Polar Tracking helps you align your cursor to exact horizontal and vertical angles, much like a T-square and triangle.

In this exercise, you'll use Polar Tracking to draw a rectangular box:

1. Start a line at the coordinate 5′-7″, 6′-3″ by entering **L↵5′7″,6′3″↵**. Metric users should enter **L↵171,189↵** as the starting coordinate. This starting point is somewhat arbitrary, but by entering a specific starting location, you're coordinated with the figures and instructions in this book. You can also use the Line tool in the Draw panel to start the line.

**2.** Make sure Polar Tracking is on (the Polar Tracking tool in the status bar should be blue), and then point the cursor directly to the right of the last point. The tracking vector appears at the cursor along with the Polar Tracking readout and dimensions.

**3.** With the cursor pointing directly to the right, enter **1′-10″**⏎. Metric users should enter **56**⏎. You can use the spacebar in place of the ⏎ key when entering distances in this way.

**4.** Point the cursor downward, enter **9**⏎ for 9″, and click this point. Metric users should enter **23**⏎.

**5.** Continue drawing the other two sides of the rectangle by using Polar Tracking. After you've completed the rectangle, press ⏎ or the Esc key to exit the Line tool. You should have a drawing that looks like Figure 3.2.

**FIGURE 3.2**
A plan view of the toilet tank

As you can see from the exercise, you can use Polar Tracking and the tracking vector to restrain your cursor to horizontal and vertical positions, just as you would use a T-square and triangle. Later, you'll learn how you can set up Polar Tracking to set the angle to any value you want in a way similar to an adjustable triangle.

In some situations, you may find that you don't want Polar Tracking on. You can turn it off by clicking the Polar Tracking tool in the status bar. You can also press the F10 function key to turn Polar Tracking on or off.

Although this exercise tells you to use the Line tool to draw the tank, you can also use the Rectangle tool. The Rectangle tool creates what is known as a *polyline*, which is a set of line or arc segments that act like a single object. You'll learn more about polylines in Chapter 18, "Drawing Curves."

By using the Snap modes in conjunction with the coordinate readout and Polar Tracking, you can locate coordinates and measure distances as you draw lines. This is similar to the way you draw when using a scale. The smallest distance registered by the coordinate readout and Polar Tracking readout depends on the area you've displayed on your screen. For example, if you're displaying an area the size of a football field, the smallest distance you can indicate with your cursor may be 6", or 15 cm. On the other hand, if your view is enlarged to show an area of only one square inch or centimeter, you can indicate distances as small as ¹⁄₁₀₀₀ of an inch or centimeter by using your cursor.

### Setting the Polar Tracking Angle

You've seen how Polar Tracking lets you draw exact vertical and horizontal lines. You can also set Polar Tracking to draw lines at other angles, such as 30° or 45°. To change the angle Polar Tracking uses, you use the Polar Tracking tab in the Drafting Settings dialog box (see Figure 3.3).

**FIGURE 3.3**
The Polar Tracking tab in the Drafting Settings dialog box

Right-click the Polar Tracking tool in the status bar, and then choose Settings from the context menu to open the Drafting Settings dialog box. As an alternative, you can type **DS**↵ and then click the Polar Tracking tab.

To change the Polar Tracking angle, enter an angle in the Increment Angle text box or select a predefined angle from the drop-down list. You can set angles on the fly. Just right-click the Polar Tracking tool and select an angle from the drop-down list.

---

#### ORTHO MODE

Besides using Polar Tracking mode, you can restrain the cursor to a vertical or horizontal direction by using Ortho mode. To use Ortho mode, hold down the Shift key while drawing. You can also press F8 or click Ortho Mode in the status bar to keep Ortho mode on while you draw. When you move the cursor around while drawing objects, the rubber-banding line moves only vertically or horizontally. With Ortho mode turned on, Polar Tracking is automatically turned off.

Numerous other settings are available in the Polar Tracking tab. Here is a list of their functions:

**Additional Angles**   This setting lets you enter a specific angle for Polar Tracking. For example, if you want Polar Tracking to snap to 12 degrees, click the New button next to the Additional Angles list box and enter **12**. The value you enter appears in the list box and, when the Additional Angles check box is selected, Polar Tracking snaps to 12°. To delete a value from the list box, highlight it and click the Delete button.

The Additional Angles option differs from the Increment Angle setting in that the latter causes Polar Tracking to snap to every increment of its setting, whereas Additional Angles snaps only to the angle specified. You can enter as many angles as you want in the Additional Angles list box. As a shortcut, you can use the Polarang system variable (**Polarang.**↵) to set the incremental angle without using the dialog box. The Polarmode system variable lets you determine whether Polar Tracking uses the current UCS or a selected object as the basis for the angle.

**Object Snap Tracking Settings**   These settings let you control whether Object Snap Tracking uses strictly orthogonal directions (0°, 90°, 180°, and 270°) or the angles set in the Polar Angle Settings group in this dialog box. (See the section "Aligning Objects by Using Object Snap Tracking" later in this chapter.)

**Polar Angle Measurement**   These radio buttons let you determine the zero angle on which Polar Tracking bases its incremental angles. The Absolute option uses the current AutoCAD setting for the 0° angle. The Relative To Last Segment option uses the last drawn object as the 0° angle. For example, if you draw a line at a 10° angle and the Relative To Last Segment option is selected with Increment Angle set to 90°, Polar Tracking snaps to 10°, 100°, 190°, and 280°, relative to the actual 0° direction.

---

**NUDGING OBJECTS**

If you need to move objects incrementally in an orthogonal direction, you can use the Nudge feature. Select the object or objects, and then hold down the Ctrl key and press an arrow key. Your selection moves in the direction of the arrow key in small increments.

---

# Exploring the Drawing Process

The following sections present some common AutoCAD commands and show you how to use them to complete a simple drawing. As you draw, watch the prompts and notice how your responses affect them. Also notice how you use existing drawing elements as reference points.

While drawing with AutoCAD, you create simple geometric forms to determine the basic shapes of objects, and you can then modify the shapes to fill in detail.

AutoCAD offers a number of basic 2D drawing object types; lines, arcs, circles, text, dimensions, polylines, points, ellipses, elliptical arcs, spline curves, regions, hatches, and multiline text are the most common. All drawings are built on at least some of these objects. In addition, there are several 3D solids and meshes, which are three-dimensional shapes. You're familiar with lines and arcs; these, along with circles, are the most commonly used objects. As you progress through the book, you'll learn about the other objects and how they're used. You'll also learn about 3D objects in the chapters on AutoCAD 3D.

CERT
OBJECTIVE

## Locating an Object in Reference to Others

Continuing to draw the toilet, to define the seat you'll use an ellipse. Follow these steps:

1. Click the Axis, End Ellipse tool from the Ellipse flyout in the Home tab's Draw panel, or type **EL**↵.

2. At the Specify axis endpoint of ellipse or [Arc/Center]: prompt, pick the midpoint of the bottom horizontal line of the rectangle. To do this, Shift+right-click to open the Object Snap context menu and select Midpoint; then move the cursor toward the bottom line. (Remember, Shift+click the right mouse button to open the Object Snap menu.) When you see the Midpoint Osnap marker on the line, click the left mouse button.

3. At the Specify other endpoint of axis: prompt, point the cursor downward and enter **1'-10"**↵. Metric users should enter **55**↵.

4. At the Specify distance to other axis or [Rotation]: prompt, point the cursor horizontally from the center of the ellipse and enter **8"**↵. Metric users should enter **20**↵. Your drawing should look like Figure 3.4.

**FIGURE 3.4**
The ellipse added to
the tank

First axis endpoint

Other axis endpoint

Second axis endpoint

## Getting a Closer Look

During the drawing process, you'll often want to enlarge areas of a drawing to edit its objects. In Chapter 1, you saw how to use the Zoom capability for this purpose. Follow these steps to enlarge the view of the toilet:

1. Click Zoom Window from the Zoom flyout in the Navigation bar, or type **Z**↵**W**↵. Next, you'll place a closely fitting window around your toilet.

2. At the Specify first corner: prompt, pick a point below and to the left of your drawing, at or near coordinate 5'-0",3'-6". Metric users should use the coordinate 150.0000,102.0000.

3. At the Specify opposite corner: prompt, pick a point above and to the right of the drawing, at or near coordinate 8'-3",6'-8" (246.0000,195.0000 for metric users). The toilet

should be completely enclosed by the zoom window. You can also use the Zoom Realtime tool in conjunction with the Pan Realtime tool. The toilet enlarges to fill more of the screen. Your view should look similar to Figure 3.5.

**FIGURE 3.5**
The line
copied down

If you have a mouse with a scroll wheel, you can avoid using the Zoom command altogether. Just place the cursor on the toilet and turn the wheel to zoom into the image.

## Modifying an Object

Now let's see how editing commands are used to construct an object. To define the back edge of the seat, let's put a copy of the line defining the front of the toilet tank 3" (7 cm for metric users) toward the center of the ellipse:

1. Click the Copy tool in the Home tab's Modify panel, or type **CO**↵.

2. At the `Select objects:` prompt, pick the horizontal line that touches the top of the ellipse. The line is highlighted. Press ↵ to complete your selection.

3. At the `Specify base point or [Displacement/mOde] <Displacement>:` prompt, pick a base point near the line. Then point the cursor down and enter **3"**↵, or **7**↵ if you're a metric user.

4. Press ↵ to exit the Copy command. Your drawing should look like Figure 3.5.

Notice that the Copy command acts exactly like the Move command you used in Chapter 2, except that Copy doesn't alter the position of the objects you select and you must press ↵ to exit Copy.

### TRIMMING AN OBJECT

CERT
OBJECTIVE

Now you must delete the part of the ellipse that isn't needed. You'll use the Trim command to trim off part of the ellipse:

1. Click the Trim tool in the Home tab's Modify panel. If you don't see the Trim tool, click the Trim/Extend flyout and select Trim. You'll see this prompt:

```
Current settings: Projection=UCS Edge=None
Select cutting edges ...
Select objects or <select all>:
```

**2.** Click the line you just created—the one that crosses through the ellipse—and press ↵ to finish your selection.

**3.** At the `Select object to trim or shift-select to extend or [Fence/Crossing/ Project/Edge/eRase/Undo]:` prompt, hover over the topmost portion of the ellipse above the line. Notice that you see a preview of how the ellipse will look when trimmed. The top portion of the ellipse becomes lighter. Also notice the red X by the cursor. This indicates that the selected portion of the ellipse will be deleted.

**4.** Click the topmost portion of the ellipse above the line. This trims the ellipse back to the line.

**5.** Press ↵ to exit the Trim command.

In step 1 of the preceding exercise, the Trim command produces two messages in the prompt. The first message, `Select cutting edges...`, tells you that you must first select objects to define *the edge to which you want to trim an object*. In step 3, you're again prompted to select objects, this time to select the *object to trim*. Here you see a preview of how the ellipse will look before you commit to your selection. The red X by the cursor, called a cursor badge, indicates the action that the current command will apply. You will see several cursor badges as you work in AutoCAD, each one offering a hint regarding the current activity.

Trim is one of a handful of AutoCAD commands that asks you to select two sets of objects: The first set defines a boundary, and the second is the set of objects you want to edit. The two sets of objects aren't mutually exclusive. You can, for example, select the cutting-edge objects as objects to trim. The next exercise shows how this works.

First, you'll undo the trim you just did. Then, you'll use the Trim command again in a slightly different way to finish the toilet:

**1.** Click the Undo button in the Quick Access toolbar, or enter **U**↵ at the Command prompt. The top of the ellipse reappears.

**2.** Start the Trim tool again by clicking it in the Modify panel.

**3.** At the `Select objects or <select all>:` prompt, click the ellipse and the line crossing the ellipse. (See the first image in Figure 3.6.)

**4.** Press ↵ to finish your selection.

**5.** At the `Select object to trim or [Fence/Crossing/Project/Edge/eRase/Undo]:` prompt, click the top portion of the ellipse, as you did in the previous exercise. The ellipse trims back.

**6.** Click a point near the left end of the trim line, outside the ellipse. The line trims back to the ellipse.

**7.** Click the other end of the line. The right side of the line trims back to meet the ellipse. Your drawing should look like the second image in Figure 3.6.

**8.** Press ↵ to exit the Trim command.

**9.** Click Save on the Quick Access toolbar to save the file in its current state, but don't exit the file. You may want to get in the habit of doing this every 20 minutes.

**FIGURE 3.6**
Trimming the
ellipse and the line

Here you saw how the ellipse and the line are both used as trim objects as well as the objects to be trimmed. The Trim options you've seen so far—Fence, Crossing, Project, Edge, Erase, and Undo—are described in the next section in this chapter. Also note that by holding down the Shift key, you can change from trimming an object to extending an object.

### EXPLORING THE TRIM OPTIONS

AutoCAD offers six options for the Trim command: Fence, Crossing, Project, Edge, Erase, and Undo. As described in the following list, these options give you a higher degree of control over how objects are trimmed:

**Fence/Crossing [F or C]** Lets you use a fence or crossing window to select objects.

**Project [P]**   Useful when you're working on 3D drawings. It controls how AutoCAD trims objects that aren't coplanar. Project offers three options: None, UCS, and View. The None option causes Trim to ignore objects that are on different planes so that only coplanar objects are trimmed. If you choose UCS, the Trim command trims objects based on a plan view of the current UCS and then disregards whether the objects are coplanar. (See the middle of Figure 3.7.) View is similar to UCS but uses the current view's "line of sight" to determine how non-coplanar objects are trimmed. (See the bottom of Figure 3.7.)

**FIGURE 3.7**
The Trim command's options

With the Extend option, objects will trim even if the trimmed object doesn't actually intersect with the object to be trimmed.

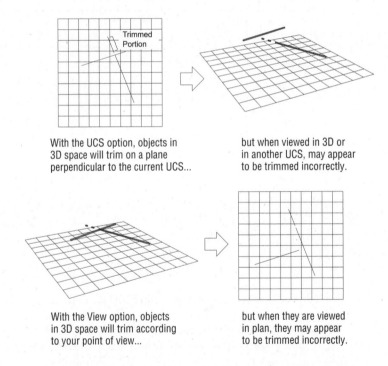

With the UCS option, objects in 3D space will trim on a plane perpendicular to the current UCS...

but when viewed in 3D or in another UCS, may appear to be trimmed incorrectly.

With the View option, objects in 3D space will trim according to your point of view...

but when they are viewed in plan, they may appear to be trimmed incorrectly.

**Edge [E]**   Lets you trim an object to an apparent intersection, even if the cutting-edge object doesn't intersect the object to be trimmed (see the top of Figure 3.7). Edge offers two options: Extend and No Extend. You can also set these options by using the Edgemode system variable.

**Erase [R]**   Allows you to erase an object while remaining in the Trim command.

**Undo [U]**   Causes the last trimmed object to revert to its original length.

You've just seen one way to construct the toilet. However, you can construct objects in many ways. For example, you can trim only the top of the ellipse, as you did in the first trim exercise, and then use the Grips feature to move the endpoints of the line to meet the endpoints of the ellipse. As you become familiar with AutoCAD, you'll start to develop your own ways of working, using the tools best suited to your style.

If you'd like to take a break, now is a good time. You can exit AutoCAD and then come back to the Bath drawing file when you're ready to proceed.

## Planning and Laying Out a Drawing

For the next object, the bathtub, you'll use some new commands to lay out parts of the drawing. This will help you get a feel for the kind of planning you must do to use AutoCAD effectively. You'll begin the bathtub by using the Line command to draw a rectangle 2′-8″ × 5′-0″ (81 cm × 152 cm for metric users) on the left side of the drawing area. For a change this time, you'll use a couple of shortcut methods built into AutoCAD: the Line command's keyboard shortcut and the Direct Distance method for specifying distance and direction.

First, though, you'll go back to the previous view of your drawing and arrange some more room to work. Follow these steps:

1. Return to your previous view, shown in Figure 3.8. A quick way to do this is to type **Z↵P↵**, or if you are returning to the file after closing it, type **Z↵A↵** or use the Zoom All option. Your view returns to the one you had before the last Zoom command.

**FIGURE 3.8**

The view of the finished toilet after using the Zoom Previous tool. You can also obtain this view by using the Zoom All tool from the Zoom flyout.

2. Type **L↵**, and then enter **9,10↵** to start the line at the 0′-9″,0′-10″coordinate. Metric users should enter **24,27↵** for the coordinate 24.0000,27.0000.

3. Place your cursor to the right of the last point selected so that the rubber-banding line is pointing directly to the right, and type **2′8″**. Then press ↵ for the first side of the tub. Metric users should enter **81↵**.

4. Point the rubber-banding line up toward the top of the screen and type **5′**. Then press ↵ for the next side. Metric users should enter **152↵**.

**5.** Point the rubber-banding line directly to the left of the last point and type **2′8″** (**81** for metric users). Then press ↵ for the next side.

**6.** Type **C**↵ to close the rectangle and exit the Line command.

Instead of pressing ↵ during the Direct Distance method, you can press the spacebar, or you can right-click and choose Enter from the context menu.

Now you have the outline of the tub. Notice that you don't have to enter the at sign (@) or angle specification. Instead, you use the Direct Distance method to specify direction and distance. You can use this method for drawing lines or moving and copying objects at right angles. The Direct Distance method is less effective if you want to specify exact angles other than right angles.

---

### BE CAREFUL WITH HYPHENS

When you enter feet and inches in the Command window, you must avoid hyphens or spaces. Thus, 2 feet 8 inches is typed as **2′8″**. But be aware that hyphens are allowed when using the Direct Distance method.

---

The keyboard shortcuts for some of the tools or commands you've used in this chapter are CO (Copy), E (Erase), EL (Ellipse), F (Fillet), M (Move), O (Offset), and TR (Trim). Remember that you can enter keyboard shortcuts and invoke commands only when Type a command is visible in the Command window.

## Making a Preliminary Sketch

In this section, you'll see how planning ahead will make your use of AutoCAD more efficient. When drawing a complex object, you'll often have to do some layout before you do the actual drawing. For those of you who have done manual drafting, this is similar to drawing an accurate pencil sketch using construction lines that you later trace over to produce a finished drawing. The advantage of doing this in AutoCAD is that your drawing doesn't lose any accuracy between the sketch and the final product. Also, AutoCAD enables you to use the geometry of your sketch to aid in drawing. While you're planning your drawing, think about what you want to draw and then decide which drawing elements will help you create that object.

You'll use the Offset command to establish reference lines to help you draw the inside of the tub. This is where the osnap overrides are useful. (See the sidebar "The Osnap Options" later in this chapter.)

You can use the Offset tool on the Home tab's Modify panel to make parallel copies of a set of objects, such as the lines forming the outside of your tub. Offset is different from the Copy command; although Offset allows only one object to be copied at a time, it can remember the distance you specify. The Offset option doesn't work with all types of objects. Only lines, arcs, circles, ellipses, splines, and 2D polylines can be offset.

Standard lines are best suited for the layout of the bathtub in this situation. In Chapter 6, "Editing and Reusing Data to Work Efficiently," you'll learn about two other objects, construction lines and rays, that are specifically designed to help you lay out a drawing. In this exercise, you'll use standard lines:

1. Click the Offset tool in the Home tab's Modify panel, or type **O**↵.

2. At the `Specify offset distance or [Through/Erase/Layer] <Through>:` prompt, enter **3**↵. This specifies the distance of 3″ as the offset distance. Metric users should enter **7** for 7 cm, which is roughly equivalent to 3″.

3. At the `Select object to offset or [Exit/Undo] <Exit>:` prompt, click the bottom line of the rectangle you just drew. Remember that you can click and drag the wheel of your mouse to pan your view while in the middle of a command if needed.

4. At the `Specify point on side to offset or [Exit/Multiple/Undo] <Exit>:` prompt, pick a point inside the rectangle. A copy of the line appears. You don't have to be exact about where you pick the side to offset; AutoCAD only wants to know on which side of the line you want to make the offset copy.

5. The prompt `Select object to offset or [Exit/Undo] <Exit>:` appears again. Click another side to offset. Then click again on a point inside the rectangle.

6. Continue to offset the other two sides. Then offset these four new lines inside the rectangle toward the center. You'll have a drawing that looks like Figure 3.9.

**FIGURE 3.9**
The completed layout

7. When you're done, exit the Offset command by pressing ↵.

## Using the Layout

CERT
OBJECTIVE

In step 4, you may have noticed that a "preview" line appears showing you where the offset line will appear should you select that point. This aids you in determining where to select points while using the Offset command.

Now you'll begin to draw the inside of the tub, starting with the narrow end. You'll use your offset lines as references to construct the arcs that make up the tub. Also in this exercise, you'll set up some of the osnap options to be available automatically whenever AutoCAD expects a point selection. Here are the steps:

1. Right-click the Object Snap tool in the status bar and select Settings from the context menu. You can also type **OS**↵.

2. Click the Clear All button to turn off any options that may be selected.

   Look at the graphic symbols next to each of the osnap options in the Object Snap tab. These are the osnap markers that appear in your drawing as you select osnap points. Each osnap option has its own marker symbol. As you use the osnaps, you'll become more familiar with how they work.

3. Click the Endpoint, Midpoint, and Intersection check boxes so that a check mark appears in each box, and make sure the Object Snap On option is selected. Click OK (see Figure 3.10).

**FIGURE 3.10**

The Object Snap tab in the Drafting Settings dialog box

You've just set up the Endpoint, Midpoint, and Intersection osnaps to be on by default. This is called a *running osnap*; AutoCAD automatically selects the nearest osnap point without your intervention. Now let's see how a running osnap works:

1. Click the 3-Point Arc tool in the Home tab's Draw panel or type **A**↵. See Figure 3.11 for other Arc options available from the Draw panel's Arc flyout.

**FIGURE 3.11**
Examples of how
the Arc flyout
options work

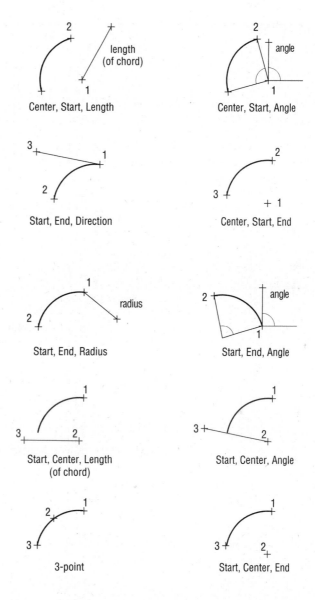

Center, Start, Length

Center, Start, Angle

Start, End, Direction

Center, Start, End

Start, End, Radius

Start, End, Angle

Start, Center, Length
(of chord)

Start, Center, Angle

3-point

Start, Center, End

2. For the first point of the arc, move the cursor toward the intersection of the two lines as indicated in the top image in Figure 3.12. Notice that the Intersection osnap marker appears on the intersection.

**FIGURE 3.12**
Drawing the top, left side, and bottom of the tub

**3.** With the Intersection osnap marker on the desired intersection, click the left mouse button.

**4.** Move the cursor to the midpoint of the second horizontal line near the top. When the Midpoint osnap marker appears at the midpoint of the line, click the left mouse button.

**5.** Use the Intersection osnap marker to locate and select the intersection of the two lines at the upper-left side of the bathtub.

The top image in Figure 3.12 shows the sequence we just described.

If you have several running osnap modes on (Endpoint, Midpoint, and Intersection, for example), pressing the Tab key cycles through those osnap points on the object. This feature can be especially useful in a crowded area of a drawing.

**CERT OBJECTIVE**

### ADJUSTING THE AUTOSNAP FEATURE

When you click the Options button in the Object Snap tab of the Drafting Settings dialog box, you'll see the Drafting tab of the Options dialog box. This tab offers a set of options pertaining to the AutoSnap™ feature. AutoSnap looks at the location of your cursor during osnap selections and locates the osnap point nearest your cursor. AutoSnap then displays a graphic called a *marker* showing you the osnap point it has found. If it's the one you want, left-click your mouse to select it.

The AutoSnap settings enable you to control various features:

**Marker**    Turns the graphic markers on or off.

**Magnet**    Causes the cursor to jump to inferred osnap points.

**Display AutoSnap Tooltip**    Turns the AutoSnap tool tip on or off.

**Display AutoSnap Aperture Box**    Turns the old-style Osnap cursor box on or off.

**Colors**    Controls the color of the AutoSnap marker. This option opens the Drawing Window Colors dialog box, which lets you select a color for your 2D and 3D AutoSnap markers.

**AutoSnap Marker Size**    Controls the size of the graphic marker.

Next, you'll draw an arc for the left side of the tub:

1. Click the Arc tool in the Draw panel again.

2. Type @↵ to select the last point you picked as the start of the next arc.

   It's easy for new users to select points inadvertently. If you accidentally selected additional points after the last exercise and prior to step 1, you may not get the results described here. If this happens, issue the Arc command again; then, use the Endpoint osnap and select the endpoint of the last arc.

3. Type E↵ or select the End option from the command line to tell AutoCAD that you want to specify the other end of the arc instead of the next point. You can also right-click anywhere in the drawing area and choose End from the context menu.

4. At the Specify end point of arc: prompt, use the Intersection osnap to pick the intersection of the two lines in the lower-left corner of the tub. The following image shows a close-up view.

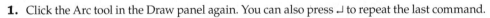

5. Type D↵ or select the Direction option in the command line. You can also right-click anywhere in the drawing area and then choose Direction from the context menu. The arc drags, along with a rubber-banding line from the starting point of the arc, as you move the cursor.

6. Move the cursor to the left of the dragging arc until it touches the middle line on the left side of the tub. Pick that line as shown in the middle image in Figure 3.12. You may need to turn off osnaps temporarily to do this by using a Shift+right-click and selecting None.

In step 5 of the preceding exercise, the rubber-banding line indicates the direction of the arc. Be sure Ortho mode is off because Ortho mode forces the rubber-banding line and the arc in a direction you don't want. Check the status bar; if the Ortho Mode tool is blue (on), press F8 or click the Ortho Mode tool to turn off Ortho mode.

Now, you'll draw the bottom of the tub:

1. Click the Arc tool in the Draw panel again. You can also press ↵ to repeat the last command.

2. Using the Endpoint osnap marker, pick the endpoint of the bottom of the arc just drawn.

3. Using the Midpoint osnap marker, pick the middle horizontal line at the bottom of the tub.

4. Pick the intersection of the two lines in the lower-right corner of the tub. The following image shows a close-up view.

Next, create the right side of the tub by mirroring the left side:

1. Click the Mirror tool on the Home tab's Modify panel. You can also enter **MI**↵ at the Command prompt.

2. At the `Select objects:` prompt, pick the long arc on the left side of the tub to highlight the arc. Press ↵ to indicate that you've finished your selection.

3. At the `Specify first point of mirror line:` prompt, pick the midpoint of the top horizontal line. By now, you should know how to use the automatic osnap modes you set up earlier.

4. At the `Specify second point of mirror line:` prompt, use Polar Tracking mode to pick a point directly below the last point selected.

5. At the `Erase source objects? [Yes/No] <N>:` prompt, press ↵ to accept the Mirror command's default `Erase source objects` option (No) and exit the Mirror command. A mirror image of the arc you picked appears on the right side of the tub. Your drawing should look like Figure 3.13.

**FIGURE 3.13**
The inside of the tub completed with the layout lines still in place

In this exercise, you were able to use osnaps in Running Osnap mode. You'll find that you'll use osnaps constantly as you create your drawings. For this reason, you may want running osnaps on all the time. Even so, at times, running osnaps can get in the way. For example, they may be a nuisance in a crowded drawing when you want to use a zoom window. The osnaps can cause you to select an inappropriate window area by automatically selecting osnap points.

Fortunately, you can toggle Running Osnaps on and off easily by clicking the Object Snap tool in the status bar. If you don't have any running osnaps set, right-click the Object Snap tool and select Settings from the context menu that appears.

## Erasing the Layout Lines

Next, you'll erase the layout lines you created using the Offset command. But this time, you'll try selecting the lines *before* issuing the Erase command.

Follow these steps:

1. Click each internal layout line individually.

   If you have problems selecting just the lines, try using a selection window to select single lines. (Remember, a window selects only objects that are completely within it.)

2. After all the layout lines are highlighted, enter **E↵** to use the keyboard shortcut for the Erase command, or right-click and choose Erase from the context menu. Your drawing will look like Figure 3.14.

**FIGURE 3.14**
The drawing after erasing the layout lines

If you right-clicked to use the context menu in step 2, you'll notice that you have several options besides Erase. You can move, copy, scale, and rotate the objects you selected. These options are similar to the tools on the Home tab's Modify panel in the way they act. But be aware that they act somewhat differently from the hot-grip options described in Chapter 2.

**CERT OBJECTIVE**

### THE OSNAP OPTIONS

Earlier, you made several of the osnap settings automatic so they're available without having to select them from the Osnap context menu. Another way to invoke the osnap options is to type their keyboard equivalents while selecting points or to Shift+right-click and type the capital letter shown in the Osnap context menu for the option you want to use.

The following is a summary (in alphabetic order) of all the available osnap options, including their command line keyboard shortcuts. You can type the command-line keyboard shortcuts to bypass the context menu. You've already used many of these options in this chapter and in the previous one. Pay special attention to those options you haven't yet used in the exercises but may find useful to your style of work. The full name of each option is followed by its keyboard shortcut name in brackets. To use these options, you can enter either the full name or the abbreviation at any point prompt. You can also select these options from the context menu you open by Shift+clicking the right mouse button.

**Apparent Intersection [APP]**  Selects the apparent intersection of two objects. This is useful when you want to select the intersection of two objects that don't actually intersect. You'll be prompted to select the two objects.

**Center [CEN]**  Selects the center of an arc or a circle. You must click the arc or circle itself, not its apparent center.

**Endpoint [ENDP or END]**  Selects the endpoints of lines, polylines, arcs, curves, and 3D Face vertices.

**Extension [EXT]**  Selects a point that is aligned with an imagined extension of a line. For example, you can pick a point in space that is aligned with an existing line but isn't on that line. To use that point, type **ext.⏎** during point selection or select Extension from the Osnap context menu. Then move the cursor to the line whose extension you want to use and hold it there until you see a small, cross-shaped marker on the line. The cursor also displays a tool tip with the word *extension*, letting you know that the Extension osnap is active.

**From [FRO]**  Selects a point relative to a picked point. For example, you can select a point that is 2 units to the left and 4 units above a circle's center. This option is usually used in conjunction with another osnap option, such as From Endpoint or From Midpoint.

**Insert [INS]**  Selects the insertion point of text, blocks, Xrefs, and overlays.

**Intersection [INT]**  Selects the intersection of objects.

**Mid Between 2 Points [M2P]**  Selects a point that is midway between two other points.

**Midpoint [MID]**  Selects the midpoint of a line or an arc. In the case of a polyline, it selects the midpoint of the polyline segment.

**Nearest [NEA]**  Selects a point on an object nearest the pick point.

**Node [NOD]**  Selects a point object.

**None [NON]**  Temporarily turns off Running Osnaps for a single point selection.

**Parallel [PAR]**  Lets you draw a line segment that is parallel to another existing line segment. To use this option, type **par.⏎** during point selection, or select Parallel from the Osnap context menu. Then move the cursor to the line to which you want to be parallel and hold it there until you see a small cross-shaped marker on the line. The cursor also displays a tool tip with the word *parallel*, letting you know that the Parallel osnap is active.

**Perpendicular [PER]**  Selects a position on an object that is perpendicular to the last point selected.

**Point filters** Not really object snaps, but point-selection options that let you filter x-, y-, or z-coordinate values from a selected point. (See Chapter 20, "Creating 3D Drawings," for more on point filters.)

**Quadrant [QUA]** Selects the nearest cardinal (north, south, east, or west) point on an arc or a circle.

**Quick [QUI]** Selects the nearest point, used with other osnap modes.

**Tangent [TAN]** Selects a point on an arc or a circle that represents the tangent from the last point selected.

**Temporary Track Point [TT]** Provides an alternate method for using the Object Snap Tracking feature described later in this chapter.

**3D Osnap** Offers additional osnaps for 3D modeling. With these osnap options, you can select a vector that is perpendicular to a surface or find the midpoint of an edge of a 3D object.

Sometimes you'll want one or more of these osnap options available as the default selection. Remember that you can set Running Osnaps to be on at all times. Type **DS**, and then click the Object Snap tab. You can also right-click the Object Snap tool in the status bar and choose Settings from the context menu to open the Drafting Settings dialog box, or just select osnap options directly from the context menu.

If you need more control over the selection of objects, you'll find the Add/Remove Selection Mode setting useful. This setting lets you deselect a set of objects within a set of objects you've already selected. While in Object Selection mode, enter **R⏎**, then proceed to use a window or other selection tool to remove objects from the selection set. Enter **A⏎** to continue to add options to the selection set. Or, if you need to deselect only a single object, Shift+click it.

## Putting on the Finishing Touches

The inside of the tub still has some sharp corners. To round out these corners, you can use the versatile Fillet tool on the Home tab's Modify panel. Fillet enables you to join lines and arcs end to end, and it can add a radius where they join so there is a smooth transition from arc to arc or line to line. Fillet can join two lines that don't intersect, and it can trim two crossing lines back to their point of intersection.

Another tool, called Chamfer, performs a similar function, but instead of joining lines with an arc, Chamfer joins lines with another line segment. Since they perform similar functions, Fillet and Chamfer occupy the same location on the Modify panel. If you don't see the Fillet tool, click the Chamfer flyout and select Fillet.

Continue with your tutorial by following these steps:

1. Click the Fillet tool on the Home tab's Modify panel, or type **F**↵.

2. At the prompt

   ```
   Current settings: Mode = TRIM, Radius = 0'-0 1/2"
   Select first object or [Undo/Polyline/Radius/Trim/Multiple]:
   ```

   enter **R**↵, or right-click and choose Radius from the context menu. You can also click Radius from the command line.

3. At the `Specify fillet radius <0'-0">:` prompt, enter **4**↵. This tells AutoCAD that you want a 4" radius for your fillet. Metric users should enter **10**↵.

4. Pick two adjacent arcs. The fillet arc joins the two larger arcs.

5. Press ↵ again, and fillet another corner. Repeat until all four corners are filleted. Your drawing should look like Figure 3.15.

**FIGURE 3.15**
A view of the finished toilet and tub with the tub corners filleted

You may have noticed that the Fillet tool offers a preview of the resulting arc. After you click the first of the two lines to be filleted, you can hover over the second line to see a temporary arc appear where the fillet will occur. This feature can help you determine whether the radius of your fillet is really the radius you want.

As you will see in later chapters, the Fillet tool is also used to join two lines quickly end to end to form a corner. You can accomplish this, even if you have the Fillet tool set to join two lines with an arc, by holding down the Shift key while clicking the second line.

## Aligning Objects by Using Object Snap Tracking

CERT
OBJECTIVE

You saw how to use lines to construct an object such as the bathtub. In many situations, using these *construction lines* is the most efficient way to draw, but they can also be a bit cumbersome. AutoCAD offers another tool that helps you align locations in your drawing to existing objects without having to draw intermediate construction lines. The tool is called *Object Snap Tracking*, or *Osnap Tracking*.

Osnap Tracking is like an extension of object snaps that enables you to *align* a point to the geometry of an object instead of just selecting a point on an object. For example, with Osnap Tracking you can select a point that is exactly at the center of a rectangle.

In the following exercises, you'll draw a plan view of a bathroom sink as an introduction to the Osnap Tracking feature. This drawing will be used as a symbol in later chapters.

### GETTING SET UP

First, as a review, you'll open a new file and use the tools you are already familiar with to set up the next drawing.

1. Click the New Tab tool, which is the plus icon to the right of the Drawing tab.

2. In the Select template dialog box, select acad.dwt (metric users select acadiso.dwt) and then click Open.

3. Open the Application menu and select Drawing Utilities ➢ Units. You can also type **UNITS**↵.

4. In the Drawing Units dialog box, select Architectural from the Length type drop-down list and then click OK. Metric users should leave the Length type as Decimal, but should select Centimeters from the Insert Scale drop-down list.

5. Enter **LIMITS**↵, then press ↵ to accept the default lower-left corner coordinates.

6. For the upper-right corner of the limits, enter **48,26**↵. Metric users should enter **122,92**↵.

7. Type **Z**↵**A**↵ to display the overall area of the drawing set by the limits.

8. Choose Save As from the Application menu and save the file under the name **Sink**.

If you find that you use the same drawing setup over and over, you can create template files that are already set up to your own way of working. Templates are discussed in Chapter 6.

### DRAWING THE SINK

You're ready to draw the sink. First, you'll draw the sink countertop. Then you'll make sure Running Osnaps and Osnap Tracking are turned on. Finally, you'll draw the bowl of the sink.

Here are the steps for drawing the outline of the sink countertop:

1. If the grid is on, click the Grid Display tool in the status bar to turn it off.

2. Click the Rectangle tool in the Draw panel, or type **REC**↵.

**3.** At the prompt

```
Specify first corner point or [Chamfer/Elevation/Fillet/Thickness/Width]:
```

enter **0,0**↵. This places one corner of the rectangle in the origin of the drawing.

**4.** At the `Specify other corner point or [Area/Dimensions/Rotation]:` prompt, enter **@2′4,1′6**↵ to place the other corner of the rectangle. Metric users should enter **@71,46**↵. This makes the rectangle 2′-4″ wide and 1′-6″ deep, or 71 cm wide and 46 cm deep for metric users. The rectangle appears in the lower half of the drawing area.

**5.** Choose Zoom Extents from the Zoom flyout on the Navigation bar, or type **Z**↵**E**↵. This enlarges the view of the sink outline so it fits in the drawing area.

**6.** Use the Zoom Realtime tool in the Zoom flyout to adjust your view so it looks similar to the one shown in Figure 3.16. You can also enter **Z**↵↵ to start the real-time zoom feature or just use your scroll wheel.

**FIGURE 3.16**
The view of the sink countertop after making some adjustments

When you draw the bowl of the sink, the bowl will be represented by an ellipse. You want to place the center of the ellipse at the center of the rectangle you've just drawn. To do this, you'll use the midpoint of two adjoining sides of the rectangle as alignment locations. This is where the Osnap Tracking tool will be useful.

You need to make sure the Object Snap tool is turned on and that the Midpoint Object Snap option is also turned on. Then you'll make sure Osnap Tracking is turned on. Use these steps:

**1.** Right-click the Object Snap tool in the status bar and choose Settings from the context menu to open the Drafting Settings dialog box at the Object Snap tab (see Figure 3.17).

**2.** Make sure the Midpoint check box in the Object Snap Modes group is selected.

**3.** Also make sure Object Snap On and Object Snap Tracking On are both selected. Click OK. You'll notice that the Object Snap and Object Snap Tracking buttons in the status bar are now in the on position.

**FIGURE 3.17**
The Object Snap tab
in the Drafting Set-
tings dialog box

Finally, you're ready to draw the ellipse:

1. Click the Center Ellipse tool in the Draw panel, or enter **EL↵C↵**.

2. Move your cursor to the top, horizontal edge of the rectangle until you see the Midpoint tool tip.

3. Move the cursor directly over the Midpoint Osnap marker. Without clicking, hold the cursor there for a second until you see a small cross appear. Look carefully because the cross is small. This is the Object Snap Tracking marker (see Figure 3.18).

You can alternately insert and remove the Object Snap Tracking marker by passing the cursor over the osnap marker.

**FIGURE 3.18**
The Object
Snap Tracking
marker

4.  As you move the cursor downward, a dotted line appears, emanating from the midpoint of the horizontal line. The cursor also shows a small *X* following the dotted line as you move it (see Figure 3.19).

**FIGURE 3.19**
A vertical dotted line appears.

5.  Move the cursor to the midpoint of the left vertical side of the rectangle. Don't click, but hold it there for a second until you see the small cross. Now, as you move the cursor away, a horizontal dotted line appears with an *X* following the cursor (see Figure 3.20).

**FIGURE 3.20**
A horizontal dotted line appears.

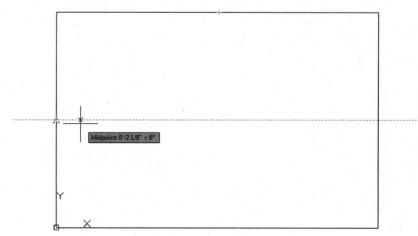

6.  Move the cursor to the center of the rectangle. The two dotted lines appear simultaneously and a small *X* appears at their intersection (see Figure 3.21).

**FIGURE 3.21**
The vertical and horizontal dotted lines appear simultaneously.

7. With the two dotted lines crossing and the X at their intersection, click the left mouse button to select the exact center of the rectangle.

8. Point the cursor to the right, and enter **8**↵ to make the width of the bowl 16″. Metric users should enter **20**↵ for a bowl 40 cm wide.

9. Point the cursor downward, and enter **6**↵ to make the length of the bowl 12″. Metric users should enter **15**↵ for a bowl with a length of 30 cm. The basic symbol for the sink is complete (see Figure 3.22).

**FIGURE 3.22**
The completed bathroom sink

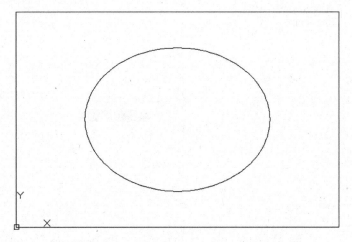

10. Click Save in the Quick Access toolbar and close the current file. You can also save and close the Bath file and exit AutoCAD.

In this exercise, you saw how Object Snap Tracking enables you to align two locations to select a point in space. Although you used only the Midpoint osnap setting in this exercise, you aren't limited to one osnap setting. You can use as many as you need to select the appropriate geometry. You can also use as many alignment points as you need, although in this exercise you used only two. If you like, erase the ellipse and repeat this exercise until you get the hang of using the Object Snap Tracking feature.

As with all the other tools in the status bar, you can turn Object Snap Tracking on or off by clicking the Object Snap Tracking tool.

## Using the AutoCAD Modes as Drafting Tools

Before you finish this chapter, you'll want to know about a few of the other drafting tools that are common to drawing programs. These tools may be compared to a background grid (*Grid mode*) and the ability to "snap" to grid points (*Snap mode*). These drawing modes can be indispensable tools under certain conditions. Their use is fairly straightforward. You can experiment with them on your own using the information in the following sections.

### Using Grid Mode as a Background Grid

Using Grid mode is like having a grid under your drawing to help you with layout, as shown in Figure 3.23. In this figure, the grids are set to a 1' spacing with major grid lines at 5'. The grid also shows, in darker lines, the x- and y-axes that start at the origin of the drawing.

Grids will not print in your final output. They are a visual aid to help you gauge distances. In AutoCAD, Grid mode can also let you see the limits of your drawing because the grid can be set to display only within the limits setting of your drawing. Grid mode can help you visually determine the distances with which you're working in any given view. In this section, you'll learn how to control the grid's appearance. The F7 key toggles Grid mode on and off. You can also click the Grid Display tool in the status bar.

**FIGURE 3.23**
A sample drawing showing the grids turned on

## USING OBJECT SNAP TRACKING AND POLAR TRACKING TOGETHER

In addition to selecting as many tracking points as you need, you can use different angles besides the basic orthogonal angles of 0°, 90°, 180°, and 270°. For example, you can have AutoCAD locate a point that is aligned vertically to the top edge of the sink and at a 45° angle from a corner.

This can be accomplished by using the settings in the Polar Tracking tab of the Drafting Settings dialog box. (See the section "Setting the Polar Tracking Angle" earlier in this chapter.) If you set the increment angle to 45° and turn on the Track Using All Polar Angle Settings option, you'll be able to use 45° in addition to the orthogonal directions. You'll see firsthand how this works in Chapter 6.

To set up the grid spacing, follow these steps:

1. Right-click the Snap Mode tool in the status bar and select Snap Settings (or type **DS↵**) to open the Drafting Settings dialog box showing all the mode settings.

2. Click the Snap And Grid tab if it isn't already selected. You will see six groups: Snap Spacing, Grid Style, Grid Spacing, Polar Spacing, Grid Behavior, and Snap Type. Notice that the Grid X Spacing text box contains a value of 1/2", or 0.5. Metric users see a value of 10 (see Figure 3.24).

3. Enter the grid spacing you want in the Grid X Spacing and Grid Y Spacing input boxes.

4. Click the Grid On check box to make the grid visible. Notice the F7 in parentheses: This tells you that the F7 function key also controls the Grid On/Off function. Click OK to dismiss the Drafting Settings dialog box and save your settings.

If you prefer, you can use the Gridunit system variable to set the grid spacing. Enter **Gridunit↵**, and at the Enter new value for GRIDUNIT <0'-0 1/2",0'-0 1/2">: prompt, enter a grid spacing in x-,y-coordinates. You must enter the Gridunit value as an x-,y-coordinate.

**FIGURE 3.24**

The Snap And Grid tab of the Drafting Settings dialog box

There are several other grid options in the Drafting Settings dialog box. The Grid Style group lets you display the grid as a series of dots instead of the graph-paper-style lines. Place a check mark by the view name where you want to display dots instead of grid lines.

In the Grid Behavior group, the Display Grid Beyond Limits check box lets you determine whether the grid displays outside the limits of the drawing.

The Adaptive Grid option adjusts the grid spacing depending on how much of the view is displayed. If you zoom out to a point where the grid becomes too dense for you to view the drawing, the grid automatically increases its interval. The Major Line Every option in the Grid Spacing group lets you control how frequently the major grid lines (lines that appear darker than the others) appear. The Display Grid Beyond Limits option does what it says—it lets the grid display beyond the drawing limits. Turn this option off to limit the grid display to the drawing limits. The Follow Dynamic UCS option causes the grid to align with the dynamic UCS. See Chapter 20 for more on the Dynamic UCS.

Once you've set up your grid, you can press F7 or click Grid Display in the status bar to turn the grid on and off. (You can also hold down the Ctrl key and press G.)

## Using Snap Modes

The *Snap mode* forces the cursor to move in steps of a specific distance. Snap mode is useful when you want to select points on the screen at a fixed interval. Two snap mode options are available in the Snap And Grid tab's Snap type group: *Grid Snap* and *Polar Snap*. The F9 key toggles Grid Snap mode on and off, or you can click the Snap tool in the status bar. Follow these steps to access the Snap mode:

1. Right-click the Snap Mode tool in the status bar and select Settings (or type **DS.⏎**) to open the Drafting Settings dialog box.

2. In the Snap Spacing group of the dialog box, double-click the Snap X Spacing text box and enter a value for your snap spacing. Then press the Tab key to move to the next option. AutoCAD assumes you want the X and Y snap spacing to be the same unless

you specifically ask for a different Y setting. If you want the X snap spacing to be different from the Y, uncheck the Equal X and Y spacing option.

3. You can click the Snap On check box to turn on Snap mode from this dialog box.

4. Click OK to save your settings and close the dialog box.

---

### CONTROLLING THE COLOR OF GRID LINES

If you find that the colors of the grid lines are too strong and they obscure your drawing, you can set them so they blend into the background. To do this, you use the Options dialog box (see Appendix B, "Installing and Setting Up AutoCAD," for more on this dialog box):

1. Right-click and select Options, or type **Options**↵.

2. Select the Display tab.

3. Click the Colors button in the Window Elements group.

4. Make sure 2D Model Space is selected in the Context list, and then select Grid Minor Lines from the Interface Element list.

5. Select a color for your grid line from the Color drop-down list.

6. Select Grid Major Lines from the Interface Element list and select a color from the Color drop-down list.

7. Click Apply & Close, and then click OK in the Options dialog box.

In steps 5 and 6, you can select from the list of colors or choose the Select Color option at the bottom of the list to select a custom color.

---

With Snap mode on, the cursor seems to move in steps rather than in a smooth motion. The Snap Mode tool in the status bar appears blue, indicating that Snap mode is on. Press F9 or click Snap Mode in the status bar (you can also hold down the Ctrl key and press B) to turn Snap mode on or off.

Note that you can use the Snapunit system variable to set the snap spacing. Enter **Snapunit**↵. Then, at the Enter new value for SNAPUNIT <0'0",0'0">: prompt, enter a snap distance value as an x-,y-coordinate.

Take a moment to look at the Drafting Settings dialog box in Figure 3.24. The other option in the Snap Spacing group enables you to force the X and Y spacing to be equal (Equal X And Y Spacing).

In the Snap Type group, you can change the snap and grid configuration to aid in creating 2D isometric drawings by clicking the Isometric Snap radio button. The PolarSnap option enables you to set a snap distance for the PolarSnap feature. When you click the PolarSnap radio button, the Polar Distance option at the middle left of the dialog box changes from gray to black and white to allow you to enter a Polar Snap distance.

You can also set up the grid to follow the snap spacing automatically. To do this, set Grid X Spacing and Grid Y Spacing to 0.

# The Bottom Line

**Set up a work area.**    A blank AutoCAD drawing offers few clues about the size of the area with which you're working, but you can get a rough idea of the area shown in the AutoCAD window.

**Master It**   Name two ways to set up the area of your work.

**Explore the drawing process.**    To use AutoCAD effectively, you'll want to know how the different tools work together to achieve an effect. The drawing process often involves many cycles of adding objects and then editing them.

**Master It**   Name the tool that causes the cursor to point in an exact horizontal or vertical direction.

**Plan and lay out a drawing.**    If you've ever had to draw a precise sketch with just a pencil and pad, you've probably used a set of lightly drawn guidelines to lay out your drawing first. You do the same thing in AutoCAD, but instead of lightly drawn guidelines, you can use any object you want. In AutoCAD, objects are easily modified or deleted, so you don't have to be as careful when adding guidelines.

**Master It**   What is the name of the feature that lets you select exact locations on objects?

**Use the AutoCAD modes as drafting tools.**    The main reason for using AutoCAD is to produce precision technical drawings. AutoCAD offers many tools to help you produce a drawing with the precision you need.

**Master It**   What dialog box lets you set both the grid and snap spacing?

# Chapter 4

# Organizing Objects with Blocks and Groups

Drawing the tub, toilet, and sink in Chapter 3, "Setting Up and Using the Drafting Tools," may have taken what seemed to you an inordinate amount of time. As you continue to use the AutoCAD® 2015 software, however, you'll learn to draw objects more quickly. You'll also need to draw fewer of them because you can save drawings as symbols and then use those symbols like rubber stamps, duplicating drawings instantaneously wherever they're needed. This saves a lot of time when you're composing drawings.

To make effective use of AutoCAD, begin a *symbol library* of drawings you use frequently. A mechanical designer might have a library of symbols for fasteners, cams, valves, or even complete assemblies used in their application. An electrical engineer might have a symbol library of capacitors, resistors, switches, and the like. A circuit designer will have yet another unique set of frequently used symbols.

In Chapter 3, you drew three objects that architects often use—a bathtub, a toilet, and a sink. In this chapter, you'll see how to create symbols from those drawings.

In this chapter, you will learn to

♦ Create and insert a symbol

♦ Modify a block

♦ Understand the annotation scale

♦ Group objects

## Creating and Using a Symbol

To save a drawing as a symbol, you use the tools in the Home tab's Block panel or the Insert tab's Block Definition panel. In word processors, the term *block* refers to a group of words or sentences selected for moving, saving, or deleting. You can copy a block of text elsewhere within the same file, to other files, or to a separate location on a server or USB storage device for future use. AutoCAD uses blocks in a similar fashion. In a file, you can turn parts of your drawing into blocks that can be saved and recalled at any time. You can also use entire existing files as blocks.

You'll start by opening the file you worked on in the previous chapter and selecting the objects that will become a block:

1. Start AutoCAD, and open the existing Bath file. Use the one you created in Chapter 3, or open the `04-bath.dwg` sample file from this book's web page (`www.sybex.com/go/masteringautocad2015`). Metric users can use the `04-bath-metric.dwg` file. The drawing appears just as you left it in the last session.

2. In the Home tab's Block panel, click the Create tool or type **B⏎**, the keyboard shortcut for the Create tool. This opens the Block Definition dialog box (see Figure 4.1).

**FIGURE 4.1**

The Block Definition dialog box

3. In the Name text box, type **Toilet**.

4. In the Base Point group, click the Pick Point button. This option enables you to select a base point for the block by using your cursor. (The *insertion base point* of a block is a point of reference on the block that is used like a grip.) When you've selected this option, the Block Definition dialog box temporarily closes.

   Notice that the Block Definition dialog box gives you the option to specify the x-, y-, and z-coordinates for the base point instead of selecting a point.

5. Using the Midpoint osnap, pick the midpoint of the back of the toilet as the base point. Remember that you learned how to set up running osnaps in Chapter 3; all you need to do is point to the midpoint of a line to display the Midpoint Osnap marker and then left-click.

After you've selected a point, the Block Definition dialog box reappears. Notice that the X, Y, and Z values in the Base Point group now display the coordinates of the point you picked. For two-dimensional drawings, the z-coordinate should remain at 0.

Next, you need to select the objects you want as part of the block.

6. Click the Select Objects button in the Objects group. Once again, the dialog box momentarily closes. You now see the familiar Select objects: prompt in the Command window, and the cursor becomes a Pickbox cursor. Click a point below and to the left of the toilet. Then use a selection window to select the entire toilet. The toilet is now highlighted.

   Make sure you use the Select Objects option in the Block Definition dialog box to select the objects you want to turn into a block. AutoCAD lets you create a block that contains no objects. If you try to proceed without selecting objects, you'll get a warning message. This can cause confusion and frustration, even for an experienced user.

7. Press ↵ to confirm your selection. The Block Definition dialog box opens again.

8. Select Inches from the Block Unit drop-down list. Metric users should select Centimeters.

9. Click the Description list box, and enter **Standard Toilet**.

10. Make sure the Retain radio button in the Objects group is selected, and then click OK. The toilet drawing is now a block with the name Toilet.

11. Repeat the blocking process for the tub, but this time use the upper-left corner of the tub as the insertion base point and give the block the name Tub. Enter **Standard Tub** for the description.

    You can press ↵ or right-click and choose Repeat BLOCK from the context menu to start the Create Block tool.

When you turn an object into a block, it's stored in the drawing file, ready to be recalled at any time. The block remains part of the drawing file even when you end the editing session. When you open the file again, the block is available for your use. In addition, you can access blocks from other drawings by using the AutoCAD DesignCenter™ and the tool palettes. You'll learn more about the DesignCenter and the tool palettes in Chapter 25, "Managing and Sharing Your Drawings."

A block acts like a single object, even though it's made up of several objects. One unique characteristic of a block is that when you modify it, all instances of it are updated to reflect the modifications. For example, if you insert several copies of the toilet into a drawing and then later decide the toilet needs to be a different shape, you can edit the Toilet block, and all the other copies of the toilet are updated automatically.

You can modify a block in a number of ways after it has been created. In this chapter, you'll learn how to make simple changes to individual blocks by modifying the block's properties. For more detailed changes, you'll learn how to redefine a block after it has been created. Later, in Chapter 17, "Using Dynamic Blocks," you'll learn how to use the Block Editor to make more interactive blocks.

## Understanding the Block Definition Dialog Box

The Block Definition dialog box offers several options that can help make using blocks easier. If you're interested in these options, take a moment to review the Block Definition dialog box as you read the descriptions. If you prefer, you can continue with the tutorial and come back to this section later.

You've already seen how the Name option lets you enter a name for your block. AutoCAD doesn't let you complete the block creation until you enter a name.

You've also seen how to select a base point for your block. The base point is like the grip of the block: It's the reference point you use when you insert the block back into the drawing. In the exercise, you used the Pick Point option to indicate a base point, but you also have the option to enter x-, y-, and z-coordinates just below the Pick Point option. In most cases, however, you'll want to use the Pick Point option to indicate a base point that is on or near the set of objects you're converting to a block.

The Objects group of the Block Definition dialog box lets you select the objects that make up the block. You use the Select Objects button to visually select the objects you want to include in the block you're creating. The QuickSelect button to the right of the Select Objects button lets you filter out objects based on their properties. You'll learn more about QuickSelect in Chapter 14, "Advanced Editing and Organizing." Once you select a set of objects for your block, you'll see a thumbnail preview of the block's contents near the top center of the Block Definition dialog box.

Other options in the Objects group and Settings group let you specify what to do with the objects you're selecting for your block. Table 4.1 shows a list of those other options and what they mean.

**TABLE 4.1:**      The Block Definition dialog box options

| OPTION | PURPOSE |
| --- | --- |
| **Base Point group** | |
| Specify On-Screen | Lets you select the base point for the block after you click OK. |
| Pick Point | Lets you select the base point for the block before you click OK to dismiss the dialog box. |
| X, Y, and Z input boxes | Enables you to enter exact coordinates for the block's base point. |
| **Objects group** | |
| Specify On-Screen | Lets you select the objects for the block after you click OK. |
| Select Objects/QuickSelect | Lets you select the objects for the block before you click OK to dismiss the dialog box. |
| Retain | Keeps the objects you select for your block as they are, or unchanged. |
| Convert To Block | Converts the objects you select into the block you're defining. The block then acts like a single object after you've completed the Create Block command. |
| Delete | Deletes the objects you selected for your block. A warning message appears at the bottom of the Objects group if you haven't selected objects for the block. After you've selected objects, the warning changes to tell you how many objects you've selected. |

| OPTION | PURPOSE |
|---|---|
| **Behavior group** | |
| Annotative | Turns on the Annotation scale feature for blocks. This feature lets you use a single block for different scale views of a drawing. With this feature turned on, AutoCAD can be set to adjust the size of the block to the appropriate scale for the viewport. |
| Match Block Orientation To Layout | With the Annotative option activated, this option is available. This option causes a block to appear always in its normal orientation regardless of the orientation of the layout view. |
| Scale Uniformly | By default, blocks can have a different X, Y, or Z scale. This means they can be stretched in any of the axes. You can lock the X, Y, and Z scales of the block by selecting this option. That way, the block will always be scaled uniformly and can't be stretched in one axis. |
| Allow Exploding | By default, blocks can be exploded or reduced to their component objects. You can lock a block so that it can't be exploded by turning off this option. You can always turn on this option later through the Properties palette if you decide that you need to explode a block. |
| **Settings group** | |
| Block Unit | Lets you determine how the object is to be scaled when it's inserted into the drawing using the DesignCenter feature discussed in Chapter 25. By default, this value is the same as the current drawing's insert value. |
| Hyperlink | Lets you assign a hyperlink to a block. This option opens the Insert Hyperlink dialog box, where you can select a location or file for the hyperlink. |
| **Description and Open In Block Editor** | |
| Description | Lets you include a brief description or keyword for the block. This option is helpful when you need to find a specific block in a set of drawings. You'll learn more about searching for blocks later in this chapter and in Chapter 25. |
| Open In Block Editor | If you turn on this option, the block is created and then opened in the Block Editor, described in Chapter 17. |

## Inserting a Symbol

CERT
OBJECTIVE

You can recall the Tub and Toilet blocks at any time, as many times as you want. You'll draw the interior walls of the bathroom first, and then you'll insert the tub and toilet. Follow these steps to draw the walls:

1. Delete the original tub and toilet drawings. Click the Erase tool in the Modify Ribbon panel, and then enter **All**↵↵ to erase the entire visible contents of the drawing. (Doing so has no effect on the blocks you created previously.)

2. Draw a rectangle 7'-6" by 5'-0". Metric users should draw a 228 cm by 152 cm rectangle. Orient the rectangle so the long sides go from left to right and the lower-left corner is at coordinate 1'-10",1'-10" (or coordinate 56.0000,56.0000 for metric users).

If you use the Rectangle tool to draw the rectangle, make sure you explode it by using the Explode command. This is important for later exercises. (See the section "Unblocking and Redefining a Block" later in this chapter if you aren't familiar with the Explode command.) Your drawing should look like Figure 4.2.

**FIGURE 4.2**

The interior walls of the bathroom

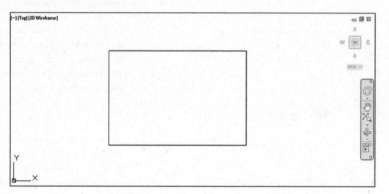

Now you're ready to place your blocks. Start by placing the tub in the drawing. Although there is a fairly simple way to do this, you'll use a dialog box, so you become familiar with some of the options available:

1. In the Block Ribbon panel, click the Insert tool. You'll see a flyout with icons of the blocks you have just created. You could click the icon of the block you want to insert from this flyout, but in this exercise, you'll look at the options available through the Insert dialog box.

2. From the flyout, select More Options. Or instead of clicking the Insert tool, you can type **I**↵ to open the Insert dialog box (see Figure 4.3).

**3.** Click the Name drop-down list to display a list of the available blocks in the current drawing.

**FIGURE 4.3**
The Insert
dialog box

**4.** Click the block named Tub.

**5.** In the Insertion Point and Rotation groups, turn on the Specify On-Screen option. With this option turned on in the Insertion Point group, you're asked to specify an insertion point using your cursor. The Specify On-Screen option in the Rotation group lets you specify the rotation angle of the block graphically as you insert it.

**6.** Click OK and you will see a preview image of the tub attached to the cursor. The upper-left corner you picked for the tub's base point is now on the cursor intersection.

**7.** At the `Specify insertion point or [Basepoint/Scale/X/Y/Z/Rotate]:` prompt, pick the upper-left intersection of the room as your insertion point.

**8.** At the `Specify rotation angle <0>:` prompt, notice that you can rotate the block. This lets you visually specify a rotation angle for the block. You won't use this feature at this time, so press ↵ to accept the default of 0. The tub should look like the one in the top image of Figure 4.4.

**FIGURE 4.4**
The bathroom, first with the tub and then with the toilet inserted

Tub insertion point at corner of room

Tub insertion point at coordinates 5′-8″,6′-10″ (170,208 metric)

You've got the tub in place. Now place the Toilet block in the drawing:

1. Open the Insert dialog box again, but this time select Toilet in the Name drop-down list.

2. Clear the Specify On-Screen check box in the Rotation group.

3. Place the toilet at the midpoint of the line along the top of the rectangle representing the bathroom wall, as shown in the bottom image in Figure 4.4. The toilet appears in the drawing.

You've just used two methods for inserting a block. When you used the Insert dialog box to place the Tub block, you saw a number of options you could use to fine-tune the block while you insert it.

## Scaling and Rotating Blocks

When you insert the tub, you can see it rotate as you move the cursor. You can pick a point to fix the block in place, or you can enter a rotation value. This is the result of selecting the Specify

On-Screen option in the Insert dialog box. You may find that you want the Rotation group's Specify On-Screen option turned on most of the time so you can adjust the rotation angle of the block while you're placing it in the drawing.

The options in the Insert dialog box that you didn't use are the Scale group options. These options let you scale the block to a different size. You can scale the block uniformly, or you can distort the block by individually changing its X, Y, or Z scale factor. With the Specify On-Screen option unchecked, you can enter specific values in the X, Y, and Z text boxes to stretch the block in any direction. If you turn on the Specify On-Screen option, you can visually adjust the X, Y, and Z scale factors in real time. Although these options aren't used often, they can be useful in special situations when a block needs to be stretched one way or another to fit in a drawing.

You aren't limited to scaling or rotating a block when it's being inserted into a drawing. You can always use the Scale or Rotate tool or modify an inserted block's properties to stretch it in one direction or another. The next exercise shows you how this is done:

1. Click the Toilet block to select it.

2. Right-click, and choose Properties from the context menu to open the Properties palette. Take a moment to study the Properties palette. Toward the bottom, under the Geometry heading, you see a set of labels that show *Position* and *Scale*. These labels may appear as *Posi* and *Scal* if the width of the palette is too narrow to show the entire label. Remember that you can click and drag the left or right edge of the palette to change its width. You can also click and drag the border between the columns in the palette.

3. If the first item label under the Geometry heading isn't visible, place the cursor on the label. A tool tip displays the full wording of the item, which is Position X.

4. Move the cursor down one line to display the tool tip for Position Y. This shows how you can view the label even if it isn't fully visible.

5. Continue to move the cursor down to the Scale X label. The tool tip displays the full title and description.

6. Let's try making some changes to the toilet properties. Click the Scale X value in the column just to the right of the Scale X label.

7. Enter **1.5↵**. Notice that the toilet changes in width as you do this.

8. You don't really want to change the width of the toilet, so click the Undo tool in the Quick Access toolbar or enter **U↵**.

9. Close the Properties palette by clicking the X at the top of the Properties palette title bar.

If a block is created with the Scale Uniformly option turned on in the Block Definition dialog box, you can't scale the block in just one axis as shown in the previous exercise. You can only scale the block uniformly in all axes.

**SYMBOLS FOR PROJECTS LARGE AND SMALL**

A symbol library was a crucial part of the production of the San Francisco Main Library construction documents. Shown here is a portion of an AutoCAD floor plan of the library in which some typical symbols were used:

Notice the familiar door symbols, such as the one for the door you created in Chapter 2, "Creating Your First Drawing." And yes, there are even toilets in the lower half of the plan in the public restrooms. Symbol use isn't restricted to building components. Room number labels, diamond-shaped interior elevation reference symbols, and the hexagonal column grid symbols are all common to an architectural drawing, regardless of the project's size. As you work through this chapter, keep in mind that all the symbols used in the library drawing were created using the tools presented here.

You've just seen how you can modify the properties of a block by using the Properties palette. In the exercise, you changed the X scale of the Toilet block, but you could have just as easily changed the Y value. You may have noticed other properties available in the Properties palette. You'll learn more about those properties as you work through this chapter.

You've seen how you can turn a drawing into a symbol, known as a block in AutoCAD. Now let's see how you can use an existing drawing file as a symbol.

CERT
OBJECTIVE

## Using an Existing Drawing as a Symbol

You need a door into the bathroom. Because you've already drawn a door and saved it as a file, you can bring the door into this drawing file and use it as a block:

1. In the Block Ribbon panel, click the Insert tool and select More options. You can also just type **I⏎**.

2. In the Insert dialog box, click the Browse button to open the Select Drawing File dialog box.

3. This is a standard Windows file browser dialog box. Locate the Door.dwg file and double-click it. If you didn't create a door file, you can use the Door.dwg file from the Chapter 04 project files at this book's web page.

   You can also browse your hard disk by looking at thumbnail views of the drawing files in a folder.

**4.** When you return to the Insert dialog box, make sure the Specify On-Screen option is checked in the Insertion Point, Scale, and Rotation groups, and then click OK. As you move the cursor around, notice that the door appears above and to the right of the cursor intersection, as shown in Figure 4.5.

**FIGURE 4.5**
The door drawing being inserted in the Bath file

Door

**5.** At this point, the door looks too small for this bathroom. This is because you drew it 3 units long, which translates to 3″. Metric users drew the door 9 cm long. Pick a point near coordinates 7′-2″,2′-4″ so that the door is placed in the lower-right corner of the room. Metric users should use the coordinates 210,70.

**6.** If you take the default setting for the X scale of the inserted block, the door will remain 3″ long, or 9 cm long for metric users. However, as mentioned earlier, you can specify a smaller or larger size for an inserted object. In this case, you want a 3′ door. Metric users want a 90 cm door. To get that from a 3″ door, you need an X scale factor of 12, or 10 for metric users. (You may want to review "Understanding Scale Factors" in Chapter 3 to see how this is determined.) At the Enter X scale factor, specify opposite corner, or [Corner/XYZ] <1>: prompt, enter **12**⏎. Metric users should enter **10**⏎.

**7.** Press ⏎ twice to accept the default Y = X and the rotation angle of 0°.

The Command prompt appears, but nothing seems to happen to the drawing. This is because when you enlarged the door, you also enlarged the distance between the base point and the object. This raises another issue when you consider using drawings as symbols: All drawings have base points. The default base point is the absolute coordinate 0,0, otherwise known as the *origin*, which is located in the lower-left corner of any new drawing. When you drew the door in Chapter 2, you didn't specify the base point. When you try to bring the door into this drawing, AutoCAD uses the origin of the door drawing as its base point (see Figure 4.6).

AutoCAD also uses the inserted drawing's Insertion scale setting in the Units dialog box to apply the proper scale (see Chapters 3 and 25 for more on the Insert scale setting). This feature is important when the unit type of the inserted drawing differs from the current drawing. For example, you could insert a door drawn in centimeters into a floor plan drawn in feet and inches and as long as the insertion scale is set correctly in the door drawing, the door will appear at the correct size for the floor plan.

**FIGURE 4.6**

By default, a drawing's origin is also its insertion point. You can change a drawing's insertion point by using the Base command.

Origin of door drawing

Because the door appears outside the bathroom, you must first choose All from the Zoom flyout on the View tab's Navigate2D panel to show more of the drawing, and then use the Move command on the Modify panel to move the door to the right-side wall of the bathroom. Let's do so now:

1. Click Zoom All from the Zoom flyout on the Navigation bar. The view of the room shrinks and the door is displayed. Notice that it's now the proper size for your drawing (see Figure 4.7).

**FIGURE 4.7**

The enlarged door

2. Choose the Move tool from the Modify Ribbon panel, or type **M**↵.

3. To pick the door you just inserted, at the `Select objects:` prompt, click a point anywhere on the door and press ↵. Notice that now the entire door is highlighted. This is because a block is treated like a single object, even though it may be made up of several lines, arcs, and so on.

4. At the `Specify base point or [Displacement] <Displacement>:` prompt, turn on Running Osnaps if it isn't already on, and pick the lower-left corner of the door. Remember that pressing the F3 key or clicking Object Snap in the status bar toggles Running Osnaps on or off.

5. At the Specify second point or <use first point as displacement>: prompt, use the Nearest osnap override, and position the door so that your drawing looks like Figure 4.8.

**FIGURE 4.8**
The door on the right-side wall of the bathroom

Because the door is an object that you'll use often, it should be a common size so you don't have to specify an odd value every time you insert it. It would also be helpful if the door's insertion base point were in a more convenient location—that is, a location that would let you place the door accurately within a wall opening. Next, you'll modify the Door block better to suit your needs.

## Modifying a Block

You can modify a block in three ways. One way is to redefine it completely. In earlier versions of AutoCAD, this was the only way to make changes to a block. A second way is to use the Block Editor. A third way is to use the Edit Reference tool on the Insert tab's expanded Reference panel. The Edit Reference tool is also known as the Refedit command.

In the following sections, you'll learn how to redefine a block by making changes to the door symbol. Later, in Chapter 17 you'll see how the Block Editor lets you add adjustability to blocks, and in Chapter 7, "Mastering Viewing Tools, Hatches, and External References," you'll learn about the Edit Reference tool.

Double-clicking most objects displays the Quick Properties palette. Double-clicking a block opens the Edit Block Definition dialog box, which gives you another way to edit blocks. You'll learn more about the Edit Block Definition dialog box in Chapter 17.

### Unblocking and Redefining a Block

One way to modify a block is to break it down into its components, edit them, and then turn them back into a block. This is called *redefining* a block. If you redefine a block that has been inserted in a drawing, each occurrence of that block in the current file changes to reflect the new block definition. You can use this block-redefinition feature to make rapid changes to a design.

To separate a block into its components, use the Explode command:

1. Click Explode from the Home tab's Modify panel. You can also type **X**↵ to start the Explode command.

2. Click the door, and press ↵ to confirm your selection.

   You can simultaneously insert and explode a block by clicking the Explode check box in the lower-left corner of the Insert dialog box.

Now you can edit the individual objects that make up the door, if you desire. In this case, you want to change only the door's insertion point because you've already made it a more convenient size. You'll turn the door back into a block, this time using the door's lower-left corner for its insertion base point:

1. In the Block Ribbon panel, select Create Block, or type **B**↵.

2. In the Block Definition dialog box, select Door from the Name drop-down list.

3. Click the Pick Point button, and pick the lower-left corner of the door.

4. Click the Select Objects button, and select the components of the door, including the small, vertical lines at each end of the door. Press ↵ when you've finished making your selection.

5. Select the Convert To Block option in the Objects group to automatically convert the selected objects in the drawing into a block.

6. Select Inches (or cm for metric users) from the Block Unit drop-down list, and then enter **Standard door** in the Description box.

7. Click OK. You see a warning message that reads, "The block definition has changed. Do you want to redefine it?" You don't want to redefine an existing block accidentally. In this case, you know you want to redefine the door, so click the Redefine button to proceed.

The Select Objects and Pick Point buttons appear in other dialog boxes. Make note of their appearance and remember that when you select them, the dialog box temporarily closes to let you select points or objects and otherwise perform operations that require a clear view of the drawing area.

In step 7, you received a warning message that you were about to redefine the existing Door block. But originally you inserted the door as a file, not as a block. Whenever you insert a drawing file by using the Insert Block tool, the inserted drawing automatically becomes a block in the current drawing. When you redefine a block, however, you don't affect the drawing file you imported. AutoCAD changes only the block in the current file.

You've just redefined the door block. Now place the door in the wall of the room:

1. Choose Erase from the Modify Ribbon panel and then click the door. Notice that the entire door is one object instead of individual lines and an arc. Had you not selected the Convert To Block option in step 5 of the previous exercise, the components of the block would have remained individual objects.

2. Press ↵ to erase the door.

3. Insert the Door block again by using the Insert tool on the Home tab's Block panel. This time, use the Nearest osnap override and pick a point on the right-side wall of the bathroom near coordinate 9'-4",2'-1". Metric users should insert the door near 284,63.4.

4. Use the Grips feature to mirror the door, using the wall as the mirror axis so that the door is inside the room. To mirror an object using grips, select the objects to mirror, click a grip, and right-click. Select Mirror from the context menu; then, indicate a mirror axis with the cursor.

CERT
OBJECTIVE

Your drawing will look like Figure 4.9.

**FIGURE 4.9**
The bathroom floor
plan thus far

Next, you'll see how you can update an external file with a redefined block.

## Saving a Block as a Drawing File

You've seen that, with little effort, you can create a symbol and place it anywhere in a file. Suppose you want to use this symbol in other files. When you create a block by using the Block command, the block exists in the current file only until you specifically instruct AutoCAD to save it as a separate drawing file. When you have an existing drawing that has been brought in and modified, such as the door, the drawing file associated with that door isn't automatically updated. To update the Door file, you must take an extra step and use the Export option on the Application menu. Let's see how this works.

Start by turning the Tub and Toilet blocks into individual files:

1. Press the Esc key to make sure nothing is selected and no command is active.

2. From the Application menu, choose Export ➢ Other Formats to open the Export Data dialog box, which is a simple file dialog box.

3. Open the Files Of Type drop-down list, and select Block (*.dwg).

   If you prefer, you can skip step 3 and instead enter the full filename, including the .dwg extension, as in Tub.dwg.

4. Select the entire contents of the File Name text box and enter **Tub**.

5. Click the Save button to close the Export Data dialog box.

6. At the `[= (block=output file)/* (whole drawing)] <define new drawing>:` prompt, enter the name of the block you want to save to disk as the tub file—in this case, **Tub**↵.

   The Tub block is now saved as a file.

7. Repeat steps 1 through 6 for the Toilet block. Give the file the same name as the block.

---

### OPTIONS FOR SAVING BLOCKS

AutoCAD gives you the option to save a block's file under the same name as the original block or save it with a different name. Usually, you'll want to use the same name, which you can do by entering an equal sign (=) after the prompt.

Normally, AutoCAD saves a preview image with a file. This enables you to preview a drawing file before opening it.

---

## Replacing Existing Files with Blocks

The Wblock command does the same thing as choosing Export ➢ Other Formats, but output is limited to AutoCAD DWG files. Let's try using the Wblock command this time to save the Door block you modified:

1. Issue the Wblock command by typing **Wblock**↵, or use the keyboard shortcut by typing **W**↵. This opens the Write Block dialog box (see Figure 4.10).

**FIGURE 4.10**
The Write Block
dialog box

2. In the Source group, click the Block radio button.

3. Select Door from the drop-down list. You can keep the old name or enter a different name if you prefer.

4. In this case, you want to update the door you drew in Chapter 2. Click the Browse button to the right of the File Name And Path text box in the Destination group.

5. Locate and select the original Door.dwg file that you inserted earlier. Click Save to close the dialog box.

**6.** Click OK. A warning message tells you that the Door.dwg file already exists. Go ahead and click the "Replace the existing…" option to confirm that you want to overwrite the old door drawing with the new door definition.

In this exercise, you typed the Wblock command at the Command prompt instead of choosing Export ➢ Other Formats. The results are the same regardless of which method you use. If you're in a hurry, the Export ➢ Other Formats command is a quick way to save part of your drawing as a file. The Wblock option might be easier for new users because it offers options in a dialog box.

## Understanding the Write Block Dialog Box Options

The Write Block dialog box offers a way to save parts of your current drawing as a file. As you can see from the dialog box shown in the previous exercise, you have several options.

In that exercise, you used the Block option of the Source group to select an existing block as the source object to be exported. You can also export a set of objects by choosing the Objects option. If you choose this option, the Base Point and Objects groups become available. These options work the same way as their counterparts in the Block Definition dialog box, which you saw earlier when you created the Tub and Toilet blocks.

The other option in the Source group, Entire Drawing, lets you export the whole drawing to its own file. This may seem to duplicate the Save As option in the Application menu, but saving the entire drawing from the Write Block dialog box performs some additional operations, such as stripping out unused blocks or other unused components. This has the effect of reducing file size. You'll learn more about this feature later in this chapter.

## Other Uses for Blocks

So far you've used the Block tool to create symbols, and you've used the Export and Wblock commands to save those symbols to disk. As you can see, you can create symbols and save them at any time while you're drawing. You've made the tub and toilet symbols into drawing files that you can see when you check the contents of your current folder.

However, creating symbols isn't the only use for the Block, Export, and Wblock commands. You can use them in any situation that requires grouping objects (though you may prefer to use the more flexible Object Grouping dialog box discussed later in this chapter). You can also use blocks to stretch a set of objects along one axis by using the Properties palette. Export and Wblock also enable you to save a part of a drawing to disk. You'll see instances of these other uses of the Block, Export, and Wblock commands throughout the book.

Block, Export, and Wblock are extremely versatile commands and, if used judiciously, can boost your productivity and simplify your work. If you aren't careful, however, you can get carried away and create more blocks than you can track. Planning your drawings helps you determine which elements will work best as blocks and recognize situations in which other methods of organization are more suitable.

Another way of using symbols is to use the external reference capabilities. External reference files, known as *Xrefs*, are files inserted into a drawing in a way similar to how blocks are inserted. The difference is that Xrefs don't become part of the drawing's database. Instead, they're loaded along with the current file at startup time. It's as if AutoCAD opens several drawings at once: the main file you specify when you start AutoCAD and the Xrefs associated with the main file.

By keeping the Xrefs independent from the current file, you make sure that any changes made to the Xrefs automatically appear in the current file. You don't have to update each inserted copy of an Xref. For example, if you use the Attach tool on the Insert tab's Reference panel (discussed in Chapter 7) to insert the tub drawing and later you make changes to the tub, the next time you open the Bath file, you'll see the new version of the tub. Or if you have both the tub and the referencing drawing open and you change the tub, AutoCAD will notify you that a change has been made to an external reference. You can then update the tub Xref using the External Reference palette.

Xrefs are especially useful in workgroup environments where several people are working on the same project. One person might be updating several files that have been inserted into a variety of other files. Before Xrefs were available, everyone in the workgroup had to be notified of the changes and had to update all the affected blocks in all the drawings that contained them. With Xrefs, the updating is automatic. Many other features are unique to these files. They're discussed in more detail in Chapters 7 and 14.

## Understanding the Annotation Scale

One common use for the AutoCAD block feature is creating *reference symbols*. These are symbols that refer the viewer to other drawings or views in a set of drawings. An example would be a building-section symbol on a floor plan that directs the viewer to look at a location on another sheet to see a cross-sectional view of a building. Such a symbol is typically a circle with two numbers: one is the drawing sheet number and the other is the view number on the sheet (see Figure 4.11).

**FIGURE 4.11**
A single block is used to create building section symbols of different sizes in these layout views. Both views show the same floor plan displayed at different scales.

In the past, AutoCAD users had to insert a reference symbol block multiple times to accommodate different scales of the same view. For example, the same floor plan might be used for a 1/4″ = 1′-0″ scale view and a 1/8″ = 1′-0″ view. An elevation symbol block that works for the 1/4″ = 1′-0″ scale view would be too small for the 1/8″ = 1′-0″ view, so two copies of the same block were inserted, one for each scale. The user then had to place the two blocks on different layers to control their visibility. In addition, if sheet numbers changed, the user had to make sure every copy of the elevation symbol block was updated to reflect the change.

The annotation scale feature does away with this need for redundancy. You can now use a single instance of a block even if it must be displayed in different scale views. To do this, you must take some additional steps when creating and inserting the block. Here's how you do it:

1. Draw your symbol at the size it should appear when plotted. For example, if the symbol is supposed to be a ¼″ circle on a printed sheet, draw the symbol as a ¼″ circle.

2. Open the Block Definition dialog box by choosing the Create Block tool from the Insert tab's Block Definition Ribbon panel.

3. Turn on the Annotative option in the Behavior section of the Block Definition dialog box. You can also turn on the Match Block Orientation To Layout option if you want the symbol to appear always in a vertical orientation (see Figure 4.12).

**FIGURE 4.12**
Select the Annotative option in the Block Definition dialog box.

4. Select the objects that make up the block, and indicate an insertion point as usual.

5. Give the block a name and then click OK.

After you've followed these steps, you need to apply an annotation scale to the newly created block:

1. Click the new block to select it.

2. Right-click and choose Annotative Object Scale ➢ Add/Delete Scales. The Annotation Object Scale dialog box appears (see Figure 4.13).

3. Click the Add button. The Add Scales To Object dialog box appears (see Figure 4.14).

4. Select from the list the scale you'll be using with this block. You can Ctrl+click to select multiple scales. When you've finished selecting scales, click OK. The selected scales appear in the Annotation Object Scale dialog box.

5. Click OK to close the Annotation Object Scale dialog box.

**FIGURE 4.13**
The Annotation
Object Scale
dialog box

**FIGURE 4.14**
The Add Scales To
Object dialog box

At this point, the block is ready to be used in multiple scale views. You need only to select a scale from the model view's Annotation Scale drop-down list or the layout view's Viewport Scale drop-down list, which are both in the lower-right corner of the AutoCAD window (see Figure 4.15). For you to select a scale while in a layout, a viewport border needs to be selected.

**FIGURE 4.15**
The Annotation
Scale and the
layout view's View-
port Scale drop-
down lists

The Annotation Scale drop-down list appears in model view, and the Viewport Scale drop-down list appears in layout view and when a viewport is selected. (See Chapter 15, "Laying Out Your Printer Output," for more about layouts and viewports.) Note that the list has a scroll bar to the right, enabling you to select from a comprehensive list of scales. In layout view, you can set the Viewport Scale value for each individual viewport so the same block can appear at the appropriate size for different scale viewports (see Figure 4.15).

If you want to use several copies of a block that is using multiple annotation scales, you should insert the block and assign the additional annotation scales and then make copies of the block. If you insert a new instance of the block, the block acquires only the annotation scale that is current for the drawing. You'll have to assign additional annotation scales to each new insertion of the block.

If you're uncertain whether an annotation scale has been assigned to a block, you can click the block and you'll see the different scale versions of the block as ghosted images. Also, if you hover over a block triangular symbols appear next to the cursor for blocks that have been assigned annotation scales.

Annotative scale symbol

If you need to change the position of a block for a particular layout viewport scale, go to model view, select the appropriate scale from the Annotation Scale drop-down list, and then adjust the position of the block.

## Grouping Objects

Blocks are extremely useful tools, but for some situations, they're too restrictive. At times, you'll want to group objects so that they're connected but can still be edited individually. For example, consider a space planner who has to place workstations on a floor plan. Although each workstation is basically the same, some slight variations in each station could make the use of blocks unwieldy. For instance, one workstation might need a different configuration to accommodate special equipment, and another workstation might need to be slightly larger than the standard size. You would need to create a block for one workstation and then, for each variation, explode the block, edit it, and create a new block.

A better way is to draw a prototype workstation and turn it into a group. You can copy the group into position and then edit it for each individual situation without losing its identity as a group. AutoCAD LT® offers a different method for grouping objects. If you're using AutoCAD LT, skip this exercise and continue with the following section, "Working with the AutoCAD LT Group Manager."

The following exercise demonstrates how grouping works:

1. Save the Bath file, and then open the drawing Office1.dwg from the sample files at this book's web page. Metric users should open Office1-metric.dwg.

2. Use the Zoom command to enlarge just the view of the workstation, as shown in the first image in Figure 4.16.

**FIGURE 4.16**

A workstation in an office plan

3. Click Group in the Home tab's Groups panel, or type **G**↵ or **Group**↵.

4. Type **N**↵**Station1**↵ or select Name from the Command window and type **Station1**↵ to name your group.

5. At the `Select objects or [Name/Description]:` prompt, use a selection window to select the entire workstation in the lower-left corner of the plan and press ↵. You've just created a group.

Now whenever you want to select the workstation, you can click any part of it to select the entire group. At the same time, you can still modify individual parts of the group—the desk, partition, and so on—without losing the grouping of objects (see the next section, "Modifying Members of a Group").

Another way to create a group is to use the Object Grouping dialog box (see Figure 4.17). Click Group Manager on the Home tab's expanded Groups panel or type **CLASSICGROUP**↵ to open it.

Enter a name for your group in the Group Name text box, and then click the New button. The dialog box will temporarily disappear, allowing you to select the objects for your group. Once you've selected the objects, press ↵ to return to the dialog box. Click OK to complete the creation of the group.

**FIGURE 4.17**
Object Grouping
dialog box

## Modifying Members of a Group

Next you'll make copies of the original group and modify the copies. Figure 4.18 is a sketch of the proposed layout that uses the new workstations. Look carefully and you'll see that some of the workstations in the sketch are missing a few of the standard components that exist in the Station1 group. One pair of stations has a partition removed; another station has one less chair.

**FIGURE 4.18**
A sketch of the new
office layout

The exercises in this section show you how to complete your drawing to reflect the design requirements of the sketch.

Start by making a copy of the workstation:

1. Click Copy on the Modify Ribbon panel or type **Co**↵; then click the Station1 group you just created. Notice that you can click any part of the station to select the entire station. If only a single object is selected, press Shift+Ctrl+A and try clicking another part of the group.

2. Press ↵ to finish your selection.

3. At the `Specify base point or [Displacement/mOde] <Displacement>:` prompt, type **@**↵. Then enter **@8'2"<90** to copy the workstation 8'-2" vertically. Metric users should enter **@249<90**. Press ↵ to exit the Copy command.

   You can also use the Direct Distance method by typing **@**↵ and then pointing the rubber-banding line 90° and typing **8'2"**↵. Metric users should type **249**↵.

4. Issue the Copy command again, but this time click the copy of the workstation you just created. Notice that it too is a group.

5. Copy this workstation 8'-2" (249 cm for the metric users) vertically, just as you did the original workstation. Press ↵ to exit the Copy command.

Next you'll use grips to mirror the first workstation copy:

1. Click the middle workstation to highlight it.

2. Click the grip in the middle of the workstation, as shown in Figure 4.19.

**FIGURE 4.19**
Selecting the grip to mirror the group

Click this grip to begin mirroring the workstation.

3. Right-click and choose Mirror from the context menu. Notice that a temporary mirror image of the workstation follows the movement of your cursor.

4. Turn on Ortho mode, and pick a point directly to the right of the hot grip you picked in step 2. The workstation is mirrored to a new orientation.

5. Press the Esc key twice to clear the grip selection. Also, turn off Ortho mode.

Now that you've got the workstations laid out, you need to remove some of the partitions between the new workstations. If you had used blocks for the workstations, you would first need to explode the workstations that have partitions you want to edit. Groups, however, let you make changes without undoing their grouping.

Use these steps to remove the partitions:

1. Click the Group Select On/Off tool in the Home tab's Groups panel. You can also press Shift+Ctrl+A. Notice that the icon changes from being highlighted to not being highlighted. The Group Select On/Off tool turns groupings on or off so you can select and edit individual objects within a group.

2. Erase the short partition that divides the two workstations, as shown in Figure 4.20. Since you made a mirror copy of the original workstation, you'll need to erase two partitions that are overlapping each other, the original and the copy.

**FIGURE 4.20**
Remove the partitions between the two workstations.

Erase this partition.

3. Press Shift+Ctrl+A again to turn Group back on.

4. To check your workstations, click one of them to see whether all its components are highlighted together.

5. Close the file when you're finished. You don't need to save your changes.

Besides pressing Shift+Ctrl+A to turn groups on and off, you can click the Group Selection On/Off tool in the Home tab's Groups panel. This tool changes the setting for Pickstyle. Pickstyle is a system variable that controls how groups are selected.

## Ungrouping, Adding, and Subtracting from a Group

There are a few other tools in the Groups panel that will come in handy when working with groups (Figure 4.21). The Ungroup tool does exactly what it says: It will "ungroup" a group. Click the Ungroup tool or type **UNGROUP↵**, and then select the group or groups you want to ungroup.

**FIGURE 4.21**
The tools on
the Home tab's
Groups panel

The Group Edit tool enables you to add or subtract objects from a group. You can also rename a group with this tool. Click the Group Edit tool or enter **GROUPEDIT**↵, select the group you want to edit, and then use the Add, Remove, or Rename option from the Dynamic Input menu that appears at the cursor. You can also type **A**↵, **R**↵, or **REN**↵ to add to, remove from, or rename a group, respectively.

The Groups panel can be expanded to display the Group Manager and Group Bounding Box options. The Group Manager tool opens the Object Grouping dialog box. If you've used the Group command in earlier versions of AutoCAD, you'll recognize this as the old Group command. The Group Bounding Box option toggles the way groups are displayed. You can view groups with the grips of all objects displayed, which is how groups were displayed in prior releases of AutoCAD, or you can display groups with a single grip and a bounding box (see Figure 4.22).

**FIGURE 4.22**
Groups in a bound-
ing box (left) and
with all the grips
displayed (right)

## Working with the Object Grouping Dialog Box

Each group has a unique name, and you can also attach a brief description of a group in the Object Grouping dialog box. When you copy a group, AutoCAD assigns an arbitrary name to the newly created group. Copies of groups are considered unnamed, but you can still list them in the Object Grouping dialog box by clicking the Include Unnamed check box. You can click the Rename button in the Object Grouping dialog box to name unnamed groups appropriately (see Figure 4.23). Click the Group Manager tool in the Home tab's Groups panel or type **CLASSICGROUP**↵ to open the Object Grouping dialog box.

Objects in a group aren't bound solely to that group. One object can be a member of several groups, and you can have nested groups (groups within groups).

AutoCAD LT users have a different set of options. See the next section, "Working with the AutoCAD LT Group Manager."

Table 4.2 gives a rundown of the options available in the Object Grouping dialog box.

**FIGURE 4.23**
The Object Grouping dialog box

---

**TABLE 4.2:**      Object Grouping dialog box options

| OPTION | PURPOSE |
|--------|---------|
| Group Name list | Shows the names of groups in the drawing. You can click on the name to edit a group. |
| Group Identification | Identifies your groups with unique elements that let you remember what each group is for. |
| Group Name | Lets you create a new group by naming it first. |
| Description | Lets you include a brief description of the group. |
| Find Name < | Finds the name of a group. The Object Grouping dialog box temporarily closes so you can click a group. |
| Highlight < | Highlights a group that has been selected from the Group Name list. This helps you locate a group in a crowded drawing. |
| Include Unnamed | Determines whether unnamed groups are included in the Group Name list. Check this box to display the names of copies of groups for processing by this dialog box. |
| Create Group | Controls how a group is created. |
| New < | Creates a new group. The Object Grouping dialog box closes temporarily so that you can select objects for grouping. To use this button, you must have either entered a group name or selected the Unnamed check box. |
| Selectable | Lets you control whether the group you create is selectable. See the description of the Selectable button in the Change Group panel later in this table. |

**TABLE 4.2:**     Object Grouping dialog box options   *(continued)*

| OPTION | PURPOSE |
| --- | --- |
| Unnamed | Lets you create a new group without naming it. |
| Change Group | These buttons are available only when a group name is highlighted in the Group Name list at the top of the dialog box. |
| Remove < | Removes objects from a group. |
| Add < | Adds objects to a group. While you're using this option, grouping is temporarily turned off to allow you to select objects from other groups. |
| Rename | Renames a group. |
| Re-Order | Changes the order of objects in a group. The order refers to the order in which you selected the objects to include in the group. You can change this selection order for special purposes such as tool-path machining. |
| Description | Modifies the description of a group. |
| Explode | Separates a group into its individual components. |
| Selectable | Turns individual groupings on and off. When a group is selectable, it can be selected only as a group. When a group isn't selectable, the individual objects in a group can be selected, but not the group. |

If a group is selected, you can remove individual items from the selection with a Shift+click. In this way, you can isolate objects within a group for editing or removal without having to turn off groups temporarily.

## Working with the AutoCAD LT Group Manager

If you're using AutoCAD LT, you use the Group Manager to manage groups. Table 4.3 offers a rundown of the tools that are available in the Group Manager.

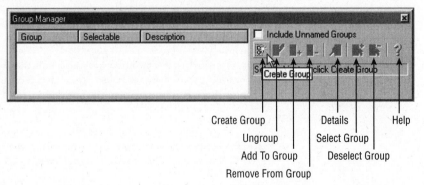

**TABLE 4.3:**     AutoCAD LT 2015 Group Manager options

| OPTION | PURPOSE |
| --- | --- |
| Create Group | Lets you convert a set of objects into a group. Select a set of objects, and then click Create Group. |
| Ungroup | Removes the grouping of an existing group. Select the group name from the list, and then select Ungroup. |
| Add To Group | Lets you add an object to a group. At least one group and one additional object must be selected before this option is available. |
| Remove From Group | Lets you remove one or more objects from a group. To isolate individual objects in a group, first select the group and then Shift+click to remove individual objects from the selection set. After you isolate the object you want to remove, click Remove From Group. |
| Details | Lists detailed information about the group, such as the number of objects in the group and whether it's in Model space or a layout. Select the group name from the group list, and then click Details. |
| Select Group | Lets you select a group by name. Highlight the group name in the group list, and then click Select Group. |
| Deselect Group | Removes a group from the current selection set. Highlight the group name in the group list, and then click Deselect Group. |
| Help | Opens the AutoCAD LT Help website and displays information about the Group Manager. |

You've seen how you can use groups to create an office layout. You can also use groups to help you keep sets of objects temporarily together in a complex drawing. Groups can be especially useful in 3D modeling when you want to organize complex assemblies together for easy selection.

## The Bottom Line

**Create and insert a symbol.**    If you have a symbol that you use often in a drawing, you can draw it once and then turn it into an AutoCAD block. A block can be placed in a drawing multiple times in any location, like a rubber stamp. A block is stored in a drawing as a block definition, which can be called up at any time.

**Master It**   Name the dialog box used to create a block from objects in a drawing, and also name the tool used to open this dialog box.

**Modify a block.** Once you've created a block, it isn't set in stone. One of the features of a block is that you can change the block definition and all the copies of the block are updated to the new definition.

**Master It** What is the name of the tool used to "unblock" a block?

**Understand the annotation scale.** In some cases, you'll want to create a block that is dependent on the drawing scale. You can create a block that adjusts itself to the scale of your drawing through the annotation scale feature. When the annotation scale feature is turned on for a block, the block can be set to appear at the correct size depending on the scale of your drawing.

**Master It** What setting in the Block Definition dialog box turns on the annotation scale feature, and how do you set the annotation scale of a block?

**Group objects.** Blocks can be used as a tool to group objects together, but blocks can be too rigid for some grouping applications. AutoCAD offers groups, which are collections of objects that are similar to blocks but aren't as rigidly defined.

**Master It** How are groups different from blocks?

# Chapter 5

# Keeping Track of Layers and Blocks

Imagine a filing system that has only one category into which you put all your records. For only a handful of documents, such a filing system might work. However, as soon as you start to accumulate more documents you would want to start separating them into meaningful categories, perhaps alphabetically or by their use, so you could find them more easily.

The same is true for drawings. If you have a simple drawing with only a few objects, you can get by without using layers. But as soon as your drawing gets the least bit complicated, you'll want to start sorting your objects into layers to keep track of what's what. Layers don't restrict you when you're editing objects such as blocks or groups, and you can set up layers so that you can easily identify which object belongs to which layer.

In this chapter, you'll learn how to create and use layers to keep your drawings organized. You'll learn how color can play an important role while you're working with layers, and you'll also learn how to include linetypes such as dashes and center lines through the use of layers.

In this chapter, you will learn to

♦ Organize information with layers

♦ Control layer visibility

♦ Keep track of blocks and layers

## Organizing Information with Layers

You can think of layers as overlays on which you keep various types of information (see Figure 5.1). In a floor plan of a building, for example, you want to keep the walls, ceiling, plumbing fixtures, wiring, and furniture separate so that you can display or plot them individually or combine them in different ways. It's also a good idea to keep notes and reference symbols, as well as the drawing's dimensions, on their own layers. As your drawing becomes more complex, you can turn the various layers on and off to allow easier display and modification.

For example, one of your consultants might need a plot of just the dimensions and walls, without all the other information; another consultant might need only a furniture layout. In the days of manual drafting, you would have had to redraw your plan for each consultant or use overlay drafting techniques, which could be cumbersome. With the AutoCAD® 2015 software, you can turn off the layers you don't need and plot a drawing containing only the required information. A carefully planned layering scheme helps you produce a document that combines the types of information needed in each case.

**FIGURE 5.1**

Placing drawing elements on separate layers

Using layers also lets you modify your drawings more easily. For example, suppose you have an architectural drawing with separate layers for the walls, the ceiling plan, and the floor plan. If any change occurs in the wall locations, you can turn on the ceiling plan layer to see where the new wall locations will affect the ceiling, make the proper adjustments, and then turn it off again to see the walls more clearly.

AutoCAD allows an unlimited number of layers, and you can name each layer anything you want, using any characters, with the exception of these: < > / \ " : ; ? * | , = '.

## Creating and Assigning Layers

You'll start your exploration of layers by using a palette to create a new layer, giving your layer a name, and assigning it a color. Then you'll look at alternate ways of creating a layer through the command line. Next you'll assign the new layer to the objects in your drawing. Start by getting familiar with the Layer Properties Manager:

1. Open the Bath file you created in Chapter 4, "Organizing Objects with Blocks and Groups." (If you didn't create one, use either 04b-bath.dwg or 04b-bath-metric.dwg from this book's companion web page, www.sybex.com/go/masteringautocad2015.)

**2.** To display the Layer Properties Manager, click the Layer Properties tool in the Home tab's Layers panel, or type **LA.⏎** to use the keyboard shortcut.

The Layer Properties Manager shows you, at a glance, the status of your layers. Right now, you have only one layer, but as your work expands, so too will the number of layers. You'll then find this palette indispensable.

**3.** Click the New Layer button at the top of the palette. The button has an icon that looks like a star next to a sheet.

A new layer named Layer1 appears in the list box. Notice that the name is highlighted. This tells you that, by typing, you can change the default name to something better suited to your needs.

**4.** Type **Wall**. As you type, your entry replaces the Layer1 name in the list box.

**5.** With the Wall layer name highlighted, click the Color icon in the Wall layer listing to display a dialog box in which you can assign a color to the Wall layer. You will find the Color icon under the Color column; it currently shows White as its value. The icon is just to the left of the word *white*, which doesn't appear in its entirety in the following image.

The Select Color dialog box opens (see Figure 5.2).

**FIGURE 5.2**

The Select Color
dialog box

6. In the row of standard colors next to the ByLayer button, click the green square and then click OK. Notice that the color swatch in the Wall layer listing is now green.

7. Click the X at the top of the Layer Properties Manager's title bar to close it.

From this point on, any object assigned to the Wall layer will appear green, unless the object is specifically assigned a different color.

### USING AUTO-HIDE WITH THE LAYER PROPERTIES MANAGER

The Layer Properties Manager is a non-modal (or modeless) palette, which means that any change you make within the palette will take effect immediately in the drawing. It also means that the palette can stay open even while you perform other operations that aren't layer related. Throughout this chapter, we'll ask you to open or close the Layer Properties Manager, but if you prefer, you can keep it open all the time. If you decide to keep it open, you may want to use the palette's Auto-Hide feature. Click the Auto-Hide icon toward the top of the palette's title bar so that it changes to a single-sided arrowhead.

With Auto-Hide on, the palette will minimize to display only its title bar. To open the palette, click the title bar. To minimize it, point the cursor anywhere outside the palette for a moment. You can also force the palette to the left or right margin of the AutoCAD window. To do this, right-click the palette title bar and select Anchor Left or Anchor Right.

## Using True or PANTONE Colors

In the preceding exercise, you chose a color from the Index Color tab of the Select Color dialog box. Most of the time, you'll find that the Index Color tab includes enough colors to suit your needs. But if you're creating a presentation drawing in which color selection is important, you can choose colors from either the True Color or the Color Books tab of the Select Color dialog box.

The True Color tab offers a full range of colors through a color palette similar to the one found in Adobe Photoshop and other image-editing programs (see Figure 5.3).

**FIGURE 5.3**
The True Color tab

You have the choice of using hue, saturation, and luminance, which is the HSL color model, or you can use the RGB (red, green, blue) color model. You can select HSL or RGB from the Color Model drop-down list in the upper-right corner of the dialog box (see Figure 5.4).

**FIGURE 5.4**
The Color Model
drop-down list

You can also select from DIC, PANTONE, and RAL *color books,* to match those widely used print color systems, by using the Color Books tab (see Figure 5.5).

Let's continue with our look at layers in AutoCAD.

### UNDERSTANDING THE LAYER PROPERTIES MANAGER PALETTE

The Layer Properties Manager conforms to the Windows interface standard. The most prominent feature of this palette is the layer list box, as you saw in the previous exercise. Notice that the bar at the top of the list offers several columns for the various layer properties. Just as in Windows Explorer, you can adjust the width of each column in the list by clicking and dragging either side of the column headings. You can also sort the layer list based on one of these properties by clicking the property name at the top of the list. Also, just as with other Windows list boxes, you can Shift+click to select a block of layer names, or you can Ctrl+click individual names to select multiple layers throughout the list. These features will become helpful as your list of layers grows.

**FIGURE 5.5**

The Color Books tab

Above the layer list, you can see four tool buttons.

You've already seen how the New Layer tool works. The tool next to the New Layer tool, New Layer VP Frozen In All Viewports, looks similar to the New Layer tool and performs a similar function. The main difference is that the New Layer VP Frozen In All Viewports tool freezes the newly created layer. To delete layers, you select a layer or group of layers and then click the Delete Layer tool. Be aware that you can't delete layer 0, locked layers, or layers that contain objects. The Set Current tool enables you to set the current layer, the one on which you want to work. You can also see at a glance which layer is current by the green check mark in the Status column of the layer list.

Another way to create or delete layers is to select a layer or set of layers from the list box and then right-click. A menu appears, which includes the same functions as the tools above the layer list.

You'll also notice another set of three tools farther to the left of the New Layer tool. Those tools offer features to organize your layers in a meaningful way. You'll get a closer look at them a little later in this chapter in the section "Taming an Unwieldy List of Layers."

## CONTROLLING LAYERS THROUGH THE LAYER COMMAND

You've seen how the Layer Properties Manager makes it easy to view and edit layer information and how you can select layer colors from the Select Color dialog box. But you can also control layers through the Command prompt.

Use these steps to control layers via the Command prompt:

1. Press the Esc key to make sure any current command is canceled.

2. At the Command prompt, enter **-Layer**↵. Make sure you include the hyphen in front of the word *Layer*. The following prompt appears:

```
Enter an option
[?/Make/Set/New/Rename/ON/OFF/Color/Ltype/
LWeight/TRansparency/MATerial/VStyle/
Plot/ Freeze/Thaw/LOck/Unlock/stAte/
Description/rEconcile]:
```

You'll learn about many of the options in this prompt as you work through this chapter.

3. Enter **N**↵ to select the New option.

4. At the Enter name list for new layer(s): prompt, enter **Wall2**↵. The [?/Make/Set/ New/Rename/ON/OFF/Color/Ltype/LWeight/TRansparency/MATerial/Plot/PStyle/ Freeze/Thaw/LOck/Unlock/stAte/rEconcile]: prompt appears again.

5. Enter **C**↵.

6. At the New color [Truecolor/COlorbook]: prompt, enter **Yellow**↵. Or, you can enter **2**↵, the numeric equivalent of the color yellow in AutoCAD.

7. At the Enter name list of layer(s) for color 2 (yellow) <0>: prompt, enter **Wall2**↵. The [?/Make/Set/New/Rename/ON/OFF/Color/Ltype/LWeight/TRansparency/ MATerial/Plot/Freeze/Thaw/LOck/Unlock/stAte/rEconcile]: prompt appears again.

8. Press ↵ to exit the Layer command.

Each method of controlling layers has its own advantages. The Layer Properties Manager offers more information about your layers at a glance. On the other hand, the Layer command offers a quick way to control and create layers if you're in a hurry. Also, if you intend to write custom macros, you'll want to know how to use the Layer command, as opposed to using the Layer Properties Manager, because palettes can't be controlled through custom toolbar buttons or scripts.

## ASSIGNING LAYERS TO OBJECTS

CERT
OBJECTIVE

When you create an object, that object is assigned to the current layer. Until now, only one layer has existed—layer 0—and it contains all the objects you've drawn so far. Now that you've created some new layers, you can reassign objects to them by using the Properties palette:

1. Select the four lines that represent the bathroom walls. If you have trouble singling out the wall to the left, use a window to select the wall line.

2. With the cursor in the drawing area, right-click and choose Properties from the context menu to open the Properties palette. This palette lets you modify the properties of an object or a set of objects. (See the upcoming sidebar "Understanding Object Properties.")

3. Click the Layer option on the list in the Properties palette. Notice that an arrow appears in the layer name to the right of the Layer option.

4. Click the down-pointing arrow to the far right of the Layer option to display a list of all the available layers.

5. Select the Wall layer from the list. Notice that the wall lines you selected change to a green color. This tells you that the objects have been assigned to the Wall layer. (Remember that you assigned a green color to the Wall layer.)

6. Close the Properties palette by clicking the X at the top of its title bar.

7. Press the Esc key to clear your selection.

The bathroom walls are now on the new layer called Wall and are green. Layers are more easily distinguished from one another when you use colors to set them apart.

---

### USING THE QUICK PROPERTIES PANEL

CERT
OBJECTIVE

This chapter focuses on the tools in the Ribbon and the Properties palette to set the properties of an object. You can also use the Quick Properties panel to change the color, layer, and linetype of objects. The Quick Properties panel appears when you double-click an object.

---

Next, you'll practice the commands you learned in this section and try some new ones by creating new layers and changing the layer assignments of the rest of the objects in your bathroom:

1. Click the Layer Properties tool in the Home tab's Layers panel to open the Layer Properties Manager. Create a new layer called **Fixture**, and give it the color blue.

You can change the name of a layer in the Layer Properties Manager. Select the layer name that you want to change and click it again so that the name is highlighted, or press the F2 key. You can then rename the layer. This works in the same way as renaming a file or folder in Windows.

2. Press the Esc key to clear any selections and then click the Tub and Toilet blocks.

3. Right-click and choose Properties from the context menu to open the Properties palette.

4. Click Layer in the list of properties, and then select Fixture from the drop-down list to the right of the layer listing.

5. Click the X at the top of the title bar of the Properties palette to dismiss it, and then press the Esc key to clear your selection.

6. Create a new layer for the door, name the layer **Door**, and make it red.

7. Just as you've done with the walls and fixtures, use the Properties palette to assign the door to the Door layer.

8. Use the Layer Properties Manager to create three more layers, one for the ceiling, one for the doorjambs, and one for the floor. Create these layers, and set their colors as indicated (remember that you can open the Select Color dialog box by clicking the color swatch of the layer listing):

| | |
|---|---|
| Ceiling | Magenta (6) |
| Jamb | Green (3) |
| Floor | Cyan (4) |

---

### UNDERSTANDING OBJECT PROPERTIES

It helps to think of the components of an AutoCAD drawing as having properties. For example, a line has geometric properties, such as its length and the coordinates that define its endpoints. An arc has a radius, a center, and beginning and ending coordinates. Even though a layer isn't an object you can grasp and manipulate, it can have properties such as color, linetypes, and lineweights.

By default, objects take on the color, linetype, and lineweight of the layer to which they're assigned, but you can also assign these properties directly to individual objects. These general properties can be manipulated through both the Properties palette and the Home tab's Properties panel.

Although many of the options in the Properties palette may seem cryptic, don't worry about them at this point. As you work with AutoCAD, these properties will become more familiar. You'll find that you won't be too concerned with the geometric properties because you'll be manipulating them with the standard editing tools in the Modify panel. The other properties will be explained in the rest of this chapter and in other chapters.

In step 3 of the previous exercise, you used the Properties palette, which offered several options for modifying the block. The options displayed in the Properties palette depend on the objects you've selected. With only one object selected, AutoCAD displays options that apply specifically to that object. With several objects selected, you'll see a more limited set of options because AutoCAD can change only those properties that are common to all the objects selected.

Note that in a block, you can change the color assignment and linetype of only those objects that are on layer 0. See the sidebar "Controlling Colors and Linetypes of Blocked Objects," in the next section.

## Working on Layers

So far, you've created layers and then assigned objects to them. In this section, you'll learn how to use the layer drop-down list in the Layers panel to assign layers to objects. In the process, you'll make some additions to the drawing.

---

### CONTROLLING COLORS AND LINETYPES OF BLOCKED OBJECTS

Layer 0 has special importance to blocks. When objects assigned to layer 0 are used as parts of a block and that block is inserted on another layer, those objects take on the characteristics of their new layer. However, if those objects are on a layer other than layer 0, they maintain their original layer characteristics even if you insert or change that block to another layer. For example, suppose the tub is drawn on the Door layer instead of on layer 0. If you turn the tub into a block and insert it on the Fixture layer, the objects the tub comprises will maintain their assignment to the Door layer even though the Tub block is assigned to the Fixture layer.

It may help to think of the block function as a clear plastic bag that holds together the objects that make up the tub. The objects inside the bag maintain their assignment to the Door layer even while the bag itself is assigned to the Fixture layer. This concept may be a bit confusing at first, but it should become clearer after you use blocks for a while.

AutoCAD also enables you to have more than one color or linetype on an object. For example, you can use the Color and Linetype drop-down lists in the Properties palette to alter the color or linetype of an object on layer 0. That object then maintains its assigned color and linetype—no matter what its layer assignment. Likewise, objects specifically assigned a color or linetype aren't affected by their inclusion in blocks.

---

The current layer is still layer 0, and unless you change the current layer, every new object you draw will be on layer 0. Here's how to change the current layer:

1. Press the Esc key to clear any selections, and then click the layer drop-down list on the Home tab's Layers panel.

The list shows you all the layers available in the drawing. Notice the icons that appear next to the layer names; they control the status of the layer. You'll learn how to work with these icons later in this chapter. Also notice the box directly to the left of each layer name. This shows you the color of the corresponding layer.

Momentarily placing the cursor on an icon in the layer drop-down list displays a tool tip that describes the icon's purpose.

2. Click the Jamb layer name. The drop-down list closes and the name *Jamb* appears in the panel's layer name box. Jamb is now the current layer.

   You can also use the Layer command to reset the current layer. To do this using the keyboard, enter **-Layer↵S↵** and then type **Jamb↵↵**.

3. Zoom in on the door and draw a 5" line; start at the lower-right corner of the door, and draw toward the right. Metric users should draw a 13 cm line.

4. Draw a similar line from the top-right end of the arc. Your drawing should look like Figure 5.6.

**FIGURE 5.6**
Door at wall with
doorjambs added

Because you assigned the color green to the Jamb layer, on your own screen you'll see that the two lines you just drew to represent the doorjambs are green. This gives you a visual cue about which layer you're on as you draw.

Now you'll use the part of the wall between the jambs as a line representing the door header (the part of the wall above the door). To do this, you'll have to cut the line into three line segments and then change the layer assignment of the segment between the jambs:

CERT
OBJECTIVE

1. Click the Break At Point tool in the Home tab's expanded Modify panel.

2. At the Select object: prompt, click the wall between the two jambs.

3. At the Specify first break point: prompt, use the Endpoint osnap override to pick the endpoint of the door's arc that is touching the wall, as shown previously in Figure 5.6.

4. Click Break At Point on the expanded Modify panel again, and then repeat steps 2 and 3, this time using the jamb near the door hinge location to locate the break point (see Figure 5.6).

Although it may not be obvious, you've just broken the right-side wall line into three line segments: one at the door opening and two more on either side of the jambs. You can also use the Break tool (below the Break At Point tool) to produce a gap in a line segment.

The Break At Point tool won't work on a circle. You can, however, use the Break tool to place a small gap in the circle. If you create a small enough gap, the circle will still look like a full circle.

Next you'll change the Layer property of the line between the two jambs to the Ceiling layer. However, instead of using the Properties palette as you've done in earlier exercises, you'll use a shortcut method:

1. Click the line between the doorjambs to highlight it. Notice that the layer listing in the Layers panel changes to Wall. Whenever you select an object to expose its grips, the Object Color, Linetype, Lineweight, and Plot Style listings in the Properties panel change to reflect those properties of the selected object.

2. Click the layer name in the Layers panel to open the layer drop-down list.

3. Click the Ceiling layer. The list closes and the line you selected changes to the magenta color, showing you that it's now on the Ceiling layer. Also notice that the Object Color list in the Properties panel changes to reflect the new color for the line.

4. Press the Esc key twice to clear the grip selection. Notice that the layer returns to Jamb, the current layer.

5. Click the Zoom Previous tool from the Zoom flyout in the Navigation bar. You can also enter **Z↵P↵**.

In this exercise, you saw that when you select an object with no command active, the object's properties are immediately displayed in the Properties palette under Object Color, Linetype, and Lineweight. Using this method, you can also change an object's color, linetype, and lineweight independent of its layer. Just as with the Properties palette, you can select multiple objects and change their layers through the layer drop-down list. These options in the Home tab's Properties panel offer a quick way to edit some of the properties of objects.

Now, you'll finish the bathroom by adding a sink to a layer named Casework:

1.  Open the Layer Properties Manager, and create a new layer called **Casework**.

2.  With the Casework layer selected in the layer list, click the Set Current button at the top of the palette.

3.  Click the color swatch for the Casework layer listing, and then select Blue from the Select Color dialog box. Click OK to exit the dialog box.

4.  Click X in the Layer Properties Manager palette. Notice that the layer drop-down list in the Layers panel indicates that the current layer is Casework.

    Next you'll add the sink. As you draw, the objects will appear in blue, the color of the Casework layer.

5.  Choose Zoom All from the Zoom flyout on the Navigation bar, or type Z↵A↵.

6.  Click the Insert tool on the Home tab's Block panel, and then click the Browse button in the Insert dialog box to open the Select Drawing File dialog box.

7.  Locate the sink.dwg file from this book's companion web page, and double-click it.

8.  In the Insert dialog box, make sure the Specify On-Screen options in both the Scale and Rotation groups aren't selected; then click OK.

9.  Place the sink roughly in the upper-right corner of the bathroom plan, and then use the Move command to place it accurately in the corner, as shown in Figure 5.7.

**FIGURE 5.7**
The bathroom with sink and counter added

Counter and sink

## Controlling Layer Visibility

We mentioned earlier that you'll sometimes want to display only certain layers to work within a drawing. In this bathroom is a door header that would normally appear only in a reflected ceiling plan. To turn off a layer so that it becomes invisible, you click the lightbulb icon in the Layer Properties Manager, as shown in these steps:

1. Open the Layer Properties Manager by clicking the Layer Properties tool in the Layers panel.

2. Click the Ceiling layer in the layer list.

3. Click the lightbulb icon in the layer list, next to the Ceiling layer name. The lightbulb icon changes from yellow to gray to indicate that the layer is off.

4. Click the X at the top of the Layer Properties Manager's title bar to close it. The door header (the line across the door opening) disappears because you've made it invisible by turning off its layer.

---

### GETTING MULTIPLE USES FROM A DRAWING USING LAYERS

Layering lets you use a single AutoCAD drawing for multiple purposes. A single drawing can show both the general layout of the plan and more detailed information such as the equipment layout and the floor-paving layout.

The following two images are reproductions of the San Francisco Main Library's lower level and show how one floor plan file was used for two purposes. The first view shows the layout of furnishings, and the second view shows a paving layout. In each case, the same floor plan file was used, but in the first panel, the paving information is on a layer that is turned off. Layers also facilitate the use of differing scales in the same drawing. Frequently, a small-scale drawing of an overall plan will contain the same data for an enlarged view of other portions of the plan, such as a stairwell or an elevator core. The detailed information, such as notes and dimensions, might be on a layer that is turned off for the overall plan.

You can also control layer visibility by using the layer drop-down list on the Layers panel:

1. On the Home tab's Layers panel, click the layer drop-down list.

2. Find the Ceiling layer, and note that its lightbulb icon is gray. This tells you that the layer is off and not visible.

3. Click the lightbulb icon to make it yellow; the door header reappears.

4. Click the drawing area to close the layer drop-down list.

Figure 5.8 explains the roles of the other icons in the layer drop-down list. The figure also shows the Freeze Or Thaw In Current Layout Viewport icon, which only appears when you are in a layout. You'll learn more about layouts in Chapter 15, "Laying Out Your Printer Output."

**FIGURE 5.8**
The layer drop-down list icons

When you start to work with layouts in Chapter 8, "Introducing Printing, Plotting, and Layouts," and Chapter 15 you'll learn about *viewports*. A viewport is like a custom view of your drawing. You can have multiple viewports in a layout, each showing a different part of your drawing. Layer properties can be controlled for each viewport independently, so you can set up different linetypes, colors, and layer visibility for each viewport.

## Finding the Layers You Want

With only a handful of layers, it's fairly easy to find the layer you want to turn off. It becomes much more difficult, however, when the number of layers exceeds a couple dozen. The Layer Properties Manager offers some useful tools to help you find the layers you want quickly.

Suppose you have several layers whose names begin with C, such as C-lights, C-header, and C-pattern, and you want to find those layers quickly. You can click the Name button at the top of the layer list to sort the layer names in alphabetic order. (Click the Name button again to reverse the order.) To select those layers for processing, click the first layer name that starts with C, and then scroll down the list until you find the last layer of the group and Shift+click it. All the layers between those layers are selected. If you want to deselect some of those layers, hold down the Ctrl key while clicking the layer names you don't want to include in your selection. Another option is to Ctrl+click the names of other layers you want selected.

The Color and Linetype headings at the top let you sort the list by the color or linetype assignments of the layers. Other columns sort the list by status: On/Off, Freeze/Thaw, Lock/Unlock, and so forth. (See the sidebar "Freeze, Lock, Transparency, and Other Layer Options" later in this chapter.)

Now try changing the layer settings again by turning off all the layers except Wall and Ceiling, leaving just a simple rectangle. In this exercise, you'll get a chance to experiment with the On/Off options of the Layer Properties Manager:

1. Click the Layer Properties tool in the Layers panel.

**2.** Click the top layer name in the list box; then Shift+click the last layer name. All the layer names are highlighted.

Another way to select all the layers at once in the Layer Properties Manager is to right-click the layer list and then choose the Select All option from the context menu. If you want to clear your selections, right-click the layer list and choose Clear All.

**3.** Ctrl+click the Wall and Ceiling layers to deselect them and thus exempt them from your next action.

**4.** Click the lightbulb icon of any of the highlighted layers.

**5.** A message appears, asking if you want the current layer on or off. Select Turn The Current Layer Off in the message box. The lightbulb icons turn gray to show that the selected layers have been turned off.

**6.** Close or minimize the Layer Properties Manager. The drawing now appears with only the Wall and Ceiling layers displayed. It looks like a simple rectangle of the room outline.

**7.** Open the Layer Properties Manager again, select all the layers as you did in step 2, and then click any of the gray lightbulbs to turn on all the layers at once.

**8.** Click the X at the top of the Layer Properties Manager's title bar to close it.

In this exercise, you turned off a set of layers by clicking a lightbulb icon. You can freeze/thaw, lock/unlock, or change the color of a group of layers in a similar manner by clicking the appropriate layer property. For example, clicking a color swatch of one of the selected layers opens the Select Color dialog box, in which you can set the color for all the selected layers.

## Taming an Unwieldy List of Layers

CERT
OBJECTIVE

Chances are you'll eventually end up with a fairly long list of layers. Managing such a list can become a nightmare, but AutoCAD provides some tools to help you organize layers so you can keep track of them more easily.

On the left side of the Layer Properties Manager is a set of tools and a list box designed to help you with your layer-management tasks (see Figure 5.9).

**FIGURE 5.9**

Tools in the Layer Properties Manager that help you manage your layers

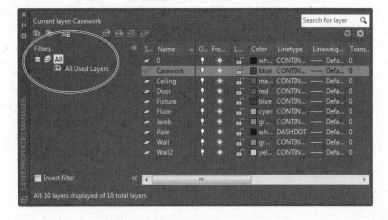

In the upper-left corner of the palette is a toolbar with three tools:

**The New Property Filter Tool**    Lets you filter your list of layers to display only layers with certain properties, such as specific colors or names.

**The New Group Filter Tool**    Lets you create named groups of layers that can be quickly recalled at any time. This tool is helpful if you often work with specific sets of layers. For example, you might have a set of layers in an architectural drawing that pertains to the electrical layout. You could create a group filter called Electrical that filters out all layers except those pertaining to the electrical layout. The filters don't affect the layers in any way; they just limit which layers are displayed in the main layer list.

**The Layer States Manager Tool**    Lets you create sets of layer states. For example, if you want to save the layer settings that have only the Wall and Door layers turned on, you can do so by using this tool.

---

### FREEZE, LOCK, TRANSPARENCY, AND OTHER LAYER OPTIONS

You may have noticed the Freeze and Thaw icons in the Layer Properties Manager. These options are similar to On and Off icons. However, Freeze not only makes layers invisible; it also tells AutoCAD to ignore the contents of those layers when you select the All response at the `Select objects:` prompt. Freezing layers can save time when you issue a command that regenerates a complex drawing. This is because AutoCAD ignores objects on frozen layers during a drawing regen. You'll get firsthand experience with Freeze and Thaw in Chapter 7, "Mastering Viewing Tools, Hatches, and External References."

Another pair of Layer Properties Manager options, Lock and Unlock, offers functionality similar to Freeze and Thaw. If you lock a layer, you can view and snap to objects on that layer, but you can't edit those objects. This feature is useful when you're working on a crowded drawing and you don't want to edit portions of it accidentally. You can lock all the layers except those you intend to edit and then proceed to work without fear of making accidental changes. The expanded Layers Ribbon panel offers a Locked Layer Fading slider that allows you to distinguish locked layers more easily by fading them. The slider does not affect plotter output because it is only a visual aid to use when you are editing your drawings.

Three more options—Lineweight, Plot Style, and Plot—offer control over the appearance of printer or plotter output. Lineweight lets you control the width of lines in a layer. Plot Style lets you assign plotter configurations to specific layers. (You'll learn more about plot styles in the bonus chapter "Understanding Plot Styles," available at `http://www.omura.com/chapters`.) Use the Plot option to specify whether you want a layer to be printed in hard-copy output. This can be useful for setting up layers you may use for layout purposes only. The Linetype option allows you to control line patterns, such as dashed or center lines.

Transparency enables you to make a layer transparent. You can enter a value from 0, which is completely opaque, to 90, which is the maximum transparency allowed. After setting the transparency value, you may need to enter **Re**↵ to see the transparency of the layer.

Finally, you can save layer settings for later recall by using the Layer States Manager tool in the upper-left corner of the Layer Properties Manager. This feature is extremely useful when you want to save different layer combinations. Chapter 14, "Advanced Editing and Organizing," shows you how to use this feature. This option is also accessible from the stAte option in the command-line version of the Layer command.

## FILTERING LAYERS BY THEIR PROPERTIES

Below the New Property Filter, New Group Filter, and Layer States Manager tools is a filter list, which is a hierarchical list displaying the different sets of layer properties and group filters. Right now, you don't have any filters in place, so you see only All and All Used Layers.

In this section, you'll learn how the tools and the filter list box work. You'll start with a look at the New Property Filter tool:

1. Open the Layer Properties Manager by clicking the Layer Properties tool in the Layers panel.

2. Click the New Property Filter tool in the upper-left corner of the Layer Properties Manager to open the Layer Filter Properties dialog box. You see two list boxes. The Filter Definition list box at the top is where you enter your filter criteria. The Filter Preview list box below is a preview of your layer list based on the filter options. Right now, there are no filter options, so the Filter Preview list shows all the layers.

3. In the Filter Definition list box, click the blank box just below the Color label. A button appears in the box (see Figure 5.10).

**FIGURE 5.10**
The Layer Filter Properties dialog box

4. Click in the blank box again; then enter **red**↵. The Filter Preview changes to show only layers that are red. In the current drawing, only one layer has been assigned the color red.

5. Click twice in the blank box below the one you just edited. Again, a button appears.

6. This time, enter **green**↵. The layers that are green appear in the Filter Preview list.

   You can also select a color from the Select Color dialog box by clicking the button that appears in the box.

7. In the Filter Definition list, click in the Name column in the third row down. A cursor appears, followed by an asterisk.

8. Type **F**. Two new layers that have names beginning with *F* are added to the Filter Preview list.

9. In the Filter Name text box at the upper-left corner of the dialog box, change the name Properties Filter1 to **My List**, and then click OK.

Now you see the My List filter in the list box on the left side of the Layer Properties Manager.

The layer list shows only the layers that have properties conforming to those you selected in the Layer Filter Properties dialog box. Notice that My List is highlighted in the filter list to the left. This tells you that My List is the current layer property filter being applied to the layer list to the right.

You can change the layer list display by selecting different options in the filter list. Try these steps:

1. Click the All option in the filter list at the left side of the dialog box. The layer list to the right changes to display all the layers in the drawing. Also note that a brief description of the current layer filter is displayed at the bottom of the dialog box.

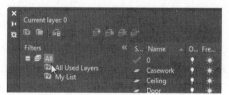

2. Click the All Used Layers option in the filter list. Now all of the layers continue to be displayed.

3. Click My List. The layer list changes back to the limited set of layers from your filter list.

4. Double-click My List. The Layer Filter Properties dialog box opens and displays the list of layer properties you set up earlier for My List. You can edit the criteria for your filter by making modifications in this dialog box.

5. Click Cancel to exit the Layer Filter Properties dialog box.

## CREATING LAYER GROUPS

The preceding exercise shows how you can filter out layer names based on the properties you specify in the Layer Filter Properties dialog box. But suppose you want to create a layer filter list by graphically selecting objects on the screen. You can use the New Group Filter tool to do just that:

1. Click the New Group Filter tool in the upper-left corner of the Layer Properties Manager, and then press ↵ to accept the default name for the group. You see a new listing appear called Group Filter1.

2. Right-click the Group Filter1 listing to the left, and then choose Select Layers ➢ Add from the context menu. Notice that your cursor is now a Pickbox cursor.

3. Click a line representing a wall of the bathroom; then click the door. Press ↵ when you're finished with your selection. The layers of the two objects you selected are displayed in the layer list. Also note that Group Filter1 is highlighted in the filter list to the left.

You may have noticed the Select Layers ➢ Replace option in the context menu in step 2. This option lets you completely replace an existing group filter with a new selection set. It works just like the Select Layers ➢ Add option. You can also click and drag layers from the All layer list to the group filter list name in the left column.

Earlier you saw how you can double-click a properties filter to edit a properties filter list. But group filters work in a slightly different way. If you want to add layers to your group filter, you can click and drag them from the layer list to the group filter name. Here's how it's done:

1. In the Layer Properties Manager, select All from the filter list to the left.

2. Click the Fixture layer in the layer list; then Ctrl+click the Jamb layer in the list. These are the layers you'll add to the Group Filter1 layer group.

3. Click and drag the Fixture and Jamb layers to the Group Filter1 listing in the filter list.

4. To check the addition to Group Filter1, click it in the filter list. The Fixture and Jamb layers have been added to the Group Filter1 list.

If you want to delete a layer from a group filter, you can use the context menu, as shown in these steps:

1. With the Group Filter1 list selected, select the Jamb layer from the layer list and then right-click it.

2. Select Remove From Group Filter from the context menu. (Make sure you don't select Delete Layer.) Jamb is removed from the Group Filter1 list.

You can also convert a layer property filter into a group filter. Select the layer property filter from the filter list, right-click, and then select Convert To Group Filter. The icon for the layer property filter changes to a group filter icon, indicating that it's now a group filter.

You've seen how you can add property and group filters to the Layer Properties Manager by using the tools on the left side of the palette. One tool you haven't explored yet is the Layer

States Manager. To understand how this tool works, you'll need to learn a little more about AutoCAD; look for a discussion of the Layer States Manager in Chapter 14.

Before you move on, you'll want to know about a few other options that appear in the Layer Properties Manager (see Figure 5.11):

**FIGURE 5.11**
Invert Filter, Refresh tool, and Settings button in the Layer Properties Manager

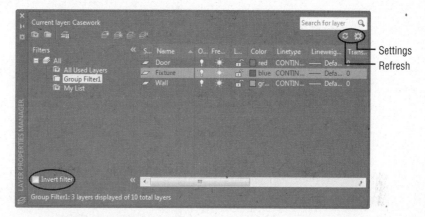

**The Invert Filter Check Box**    Located at the bottom of the Filters list, this option changes the list of layers to show all layers *excluding* those in the selected filter. For example, if the My List filter contains layers that are red and you select Invert Filter, the layer list will display all layers *except* those that are red.

**The Refresh Tool**    Located in the upper-right corner, this tool updates the layer information in the Layer Properties Manager.

**The Settings Button**    Located in the upper-right corner, the Settings button opens the Layer Settings dialog box. This dialog box controls the way you're notified when new layers are added to a drawing (see Figure 5.12).

In the next section, you'll find some tips for how to use layer names so that you can use text filters more effectively.

## NAMING LAYERS TO STAY ORGANIZED

In the previous section, you saw how to create a layer property filter by using the name of a layer. If you name layers carefully, you can use them as a powerful layer-management tool. For example, suppose you have a drawing whose layer names are set up to help you easily identify floor-plan data versus ceiling-plan data, as in the following list:

♦ A-FP-WALL-JAMB

♦ A-FP-WIND-JAMB

♦ A-CP-WIND-HEAD

♦ A-CP-DOOR-HEAD

♦ L-FP-CURB

♦ C-FP-ELEV

**FIGURE 5.12**

The Layer Settings dialog box

The first character in the layer name designates the discipline related to that layer: *A* for architectural, *L* for landscape, and *C* for civil. In this example, layers with names containing the two characters *FP* signify floor-plan layers. *CP* designates ceiling-plan information.

These layer examples are loosely based on a layer-naming convention devised by the American Institute of Architects (AIA). As you can see from this example, careful naming of layers can help you manage them.

If you want to isolate only those layers that have to do with floor plans, regardless of their discipline, enter **??FP\*** in the Name column of the Layer Filter Properties dialog box (see Figure 5.13). You can then give this layer property filter the name Floor Plan by entering **Floor Plan** in the Filter Name text box.

After you've created the Floor Plan layer properties list, you can pick Floor Plan from the filter list on the right side of the Layer Properties Manager and only those layers with names containing the letters *FP* as their third and fourth characters will appear in the list of layers. You can turn off all these layers, change their color assignment, or change other settings quickly without having to wade through layers you don't want to touch. You can create other filter properties to isolate other groups of layers. AutoCAD keeps these filter lists for future use until you delete them by using the Delete option in the context menu. (Right-click the name of the property filter and choose Delete.)

**FIGURE 5.13**
Enter ??FP* in the Name column and Floor Plan in the Filter Name box as shown.

In the ??FP* example, the question marks (??) tell AutoCAD that the first two characters in the layer name can be anything. The *FP* tells AutoCAD that the layer name must contain *F* and *P* in these two places of the name. The asterisk (*) at the end tells AutoCAD that the remaining characters can be anything. The question marks and asterisk are known as *wildcard characters*. They're commonly used filtering tools for the Unix, Linux, and Windows operating systems.

As the number of layers in a drawing grows, you'll find layer filters an indispensable tool. Bear in mind, however, that the successful use of layer filters can depend on a careful layer-naming convention. If you're producing architectural plans, you may want to consider the AIA layer-naming guidelines.

## Assigning Linetypes to Layers

CERT OBJECTIVE

You'll often want to use different linetypes to show hidden lines, center lines, fence lines, or other noncontinuous lines. You can assign a color and a linetype to a layer. You then see International Organization for Standardization (ISO) and complex linetypes, including lines that can be used to illustrate gas and water lines in civil work or batt insulation in a wall cavity.

AutoCAD comes with several linetypes, as shown in Figure 5.14. ISO linetypes are designed to be used with specific plotted line widths and linetype scales. For example, if you're using a pen width of 0.5 mm, set the linetype scale of the drawing to 0.5 as well. (See Chapter 15 for more information on plotting and linetype scale.) You can also create your own linetypes (see Chapter 25, "Managing and Sharing Your Drawings").

**FIGURE 5.14**

Standard, ISO, and complex AutoCAD linetypes

Linetypes that contain text, such as the gas line sample at the bottom of Figure 5.14, use the current text height and font to determine the size and appearance of the text displayed in the line. A text height of 0 displays the text properly in most cases. See Chapter 9, "Adding Text to Drawings," for more on text styles.

AutoCAD stores linetype descriptions in an external file named Acad.lin, or Acadiso.lin for metric users. You can edit this file in a text editor like Notepad to create new linetypes or to modify existing ones. You'll see how this is done in Chapter 24, "Customizing Toolbars, Menus, Linetypes, and Hatch Patterns."

## Adding a Linetype to a Drawing

To see how linetypes work, you'll add a DASHDOT line in the bathroom plan to indicate a shower curtain rod:

1. Open the Layers Properties Manager, and select All from the filter list.

2. Click New Layer, and then type **Pole**⏎ to create a new layer called Pole.

3. Change the color of the Pole layer to Black/White.

   If you're in a hurry, you can simultaneously load a linetype and assign it to a layer by using the Layer command. In this exercise, you enter **-Layer**⏎ at the Command prompt. Then enter **L**⏎, **DASHDOT**⏎, and **Pole**⏎, and press ⏎ to exit the Layer command.

4. In the Pole layer listing, under the Linetype column, click the word *Continuous* to open the Select Linetype dialog box. To find the Linetype column, you may need to scroll the list to the right by using the scroll bar at the bottom of the list (see Figure 5.15).

**FIGURE 5.15**

The Select Linetype
dialog box

The word *Continuous* truncates to *Contin* when the Linetype column is at its default width and the Continuous option is selected.

5. The Select Linetype dialog box offers a list of linetypes from which to choose. In a new file, such as the Bath file, only one linetype is available by default. You must load any additional linetypes you want to use. Click the Load button at the bottom of the dialog box to open the Load Or Reload Linetypes dialog box. Notice that the list of linetype names is similar to the layer drop-down list. You can sort the names alphabetically or by description by clicking the Linetype or Description heading at the top of the list (see Figure 5.16).

**FIGURE 5.16**

The Load Or
Reload Linetypes
dialog box

6. In the Available Linetypes list, scroll down to locate the DASHDOT linetype, click it, and then click OK.

   Notice that the DASHDOT linetype is added to the linetypes available in the Select Linetype dialog box.

7. Click DASHDOT to highlight it; then click OK. DASHDOT appears in the Pole layer listing under Linetype.

8. With the Pole layer still highlighted, click the Set Current button to make the Pole layer current.

9. Exit the Layer Properties Manager.

10. Turn off Object Snap mode; then draw a line across the opening of the tub area, from coordinate 4'-4",1'-10" to coordinate 4'-4",6'-10". Metric users should draw a line from coordinate 133,56 to 133,208.

11. Press ↵ to finish the line.

### CONTROLLING LINETYPE SCALE

Although you've designated this as a DASHDOT line, it appears solid. Zoom in to a small part of the line and you'll see that the line is indeed as you specified.

Because your current drawing is at a scale of 1" = 1', you must adjust the scale of your linetypes accordingly. This too is accomplished in the Linetype Manager dialog box. Here are the steps:

1. Click the Linetype drop-down list in the Home tab's Properties panel and select Other.

2. The Linetype Manager dialog box opens. Click the Show Details button in the upper-right corner of the dialog box. Some additional options appear at the bottom (see Figure 5.17).

**FIGURE 5.17**
The Linetype Manager dialog box

The Linetype Manager dialog box offers Load and Delete buttons that let you load or delete a linetype directly without having to go through a particular layer's linetype setting.

3. Double-click the Global Scale Factor text box, and then type **12**. This is the scale conversion factor for a 1" = 1' scale (see the discussion of scale factors in Chapter 3, "Setting Up and Using the Drafting Tools"). If you are a metric user and the line appears solid, set the Global Scale Factor to 30.

4. Click OK. The drawing regenerates and the shower curtain rod is displayed in the linetype and at the scale you designated.

5. Click the Zoom Previous tool from the Navigation bar or the Previous tool from the View tab's Navigate 2D panel so your drawing looks like Figure 5.18.

**FIGURE 5.18**
The completed bathroom

Shower curtain rod

You can also use the Ltscale system variable to set the linetype scale. Type **LTSCALE⏎**, and at the Enter new linetype scale factor <1.0000>: prompt, enter **12⏎**.

---

**LINETYPES TROUBLESHOOTING**

If you change the linetype of a layer or an object but the object remains a continuous line, check the Ltscale system variable. It should be set to your drawing scale factor. If this doesn't work, set the Viewres system variable to a higher value (see Appendix B, "Installing and Setting Up AutoCAD"). Viewres can also be set by the Arc And Circle Smoothness option in the Display tab of the Options dialog box. The behavior of linetype scales depends on whether you're in Model Space or in a drawing layout. If your efforts to control linetype scale have no effect on your linetype's visibility, you may be in a drawing layout. See Chapter 15 for more on Model Space and layouts.

---

Remember that if you assign a linetype to a layer, everything you draw on that layer will be of that linetype. This includes arcs, polylines, and circles. As explained in the sidebar "Assigning

Colors, Linetypes, and Linetype Scales to Individual Objects" later in this chapter, you can also assign different colors and linetypes to individual objects rather than relying on their layer assignment to define color and linetype. However, you may want to avoid assigning colors and linetypes directly to objects until you have some experience with AutoCAD and a good grasp of your drawing's organization.

In the previous exercise, you changed the global linetype scale setting. This affects all non-continuous linetypes within the current drawing. You can also set the default linetype scale for all new objects with the Current Object Scale option in the Linetype Manager dialog box.

When individual objects are assigned a linetype scale, they're still affected by the global linetype scale set by the Ltscale system variable. For example, say you assign a linetype scale of 2 to the curtain rod in the previous example. This scale is then multiplied by the global linetype scale of 12, for a final linetype scale of 24.

You can also set the default linetype scale for individual objects by using the Celtscale system variable. After it's set, only newly created objects are affected. You must use the Properties palette to change the linetype scale of individual existing objects.

If the objects you draw appear in a different linetype from that of the layer on which they're located, check the default linetype by selecting Other from the Linetype drop-down list on the Home tab's Properties panel. Then, in the Linetype Manager dialog box, highlight ByLayer in the Linetype list and click the Current button. In addition, check the linetype scale of the object itself by using the Properties palette. A different linetype scale can make a line appear to have an assigned linetype that might not be what you expect. (See the sidebar "Assigning Colors, Linetypes, and Linetype Scales to Individual Objects.")

---

**LINETYPES IN LAYOUTS**

A system variable called Psltscale affects how layout viewports display linetypes. When the Psltscale system variable is set to 1, layout viewports display linetypes at the Ltscale setting, which is usually incorrect for the 1-to-1 scale of the layout. When Psltscale is set to 0, linetypes appear in layout viewports in the same way they appear in the Model tab.

---

## ADDING THE FINAL DETAIL

If you're working through the tutorial, your final task is to set up an insertion point for the current drawing to facilitate its insertion into other drawings in the future. Follow these steps:

1. Type **BASE↵**.

2. At the Enter base point <0'-0",0'-0",0'-0">: prompt, use the Endpoint object snap to pick the upper-left corner of the bathroom. The bathroom drawing is complete.

3. Click the Save tool in the Quick Access toolbar to record your work up to now.

## Controlling Lineweights

You may have noticed a Lineweight column in the Layer Properties Manager. If you click this option for a given layer, the Lineweight dialog box opens, which enables you to control the plotted thickness of your lines. Plotted lineweights can also be set through direct object property assignment. You can view lineweights as they will appear in your final plot by making setting changes in the Lineweight Settings dialog box, which you'll learn about in Chapter 15.

With the Lineweight option and Lineweight Settings dialog box, you have greater control over the look of your drawings. This can save time because you don't have to print your drawing just to check for lineweights. You'll be able to see how thick or thin your lines are as you edit your drawing. You'll get a chance to delve into lineweights in Chapter 15.

## Keeping Track of Blocks and Layers

The Insert dialog box and the Layer Properties Manager let you view the blocks and layers available in your drawing by listing them in a window. The Layer Properties Manager also includes information about the status of layers. However, you may forget the layer on which an object resides. You've seen how the Properties option on the context menu shows you the properties of an object. The List tool in the Properties panel also enables you to get information about individual objects.

Use these steps to see an alternate way to view the properties of a block:

1. Click the List tool from the Home tab's expanded Properties panel.

    If you just want to check quickly to see where an object is located, click it. Its layer will appear in the layer drop-down list of the Layers panel.

2. At the Select objects: prompt, click the Tub block and then press ↵ to open the AutoCAD Text Window.

3. The Command window expands to display a list that shows not only the layer on which the tub is located, but also its space, insertion point, name, rotation angle, and scale. If the Command window is in its docked position, the AutoCAD Text Window appears with the list.

The information in the expanded Command window or the AutoCAD Text Window, except the handle listing, is duplicated in the Properties palette. However, having the data in the Command window or Text Window gives you the flexibility to record it in a text file in case you need to store data about parts of your drawing. You can also use the AutoCAD Text Window to access and store other types of data regarding your drawings.

The Space property listed for the Tub block designates whether the object resides in Model Space or Paper Space. You'll learn more about these spaces in Chapter 8 and Chapter 15.

## Getting a Text File List of Layers or Blocks

With complex drawings, it can be helpful to get a text file that lists the layers or blocks in your drawing. You can do this by using the log-file feature in AutoCAD. At the Command prompt, enter **Logfilemode**↵ and then enter **1**↵. Type **-La**↵**?**↵↵ (don't forget the hyphen at the beginning of the La command). If your list of layers is extensive, you may be asked to press ↵ to continue. Do so. Your list of layers appears in the AutoCAD Text Window. For a list of blocks, enter **-Insert**↵**?**↵↵ . When you've obtained your list, close the log-file feature by typing **Logfilemode**↵**0**↵.

---

### ASSIGNING COLORS, LINETYPES, AND LINETYPE SCALES TO INDIVIDUAL OBJECTS

If you prefer, you can set up AutoCAD to assign specific colors and linetypes to objects instead of having objects take on the color and linetype settings of the layer on which they reside. Normally, objects are given a default color and linetype called ByLayer, which means each object takes on the color or linetype of its assigned layer. (You've probably noticed the word *ByLayer* in the Properties panel and in various dialog boxes and tool palettes.)

Use the Properties panel to change the color or linetype of existing objects. This panel lets you set the properties of individual objects. For new objects, use the Object Color drop-down list on the Properties panel to set the current default color to red (for example) instead of ByLayer. Then everything you draw will be red, regardless of the current layer color. The Object Color drop-down list also offers a Select Colors option that opens the Select Color dialog box you saw earlier in this chapter.

For linetypes, you can use the Linetype drop-down list in the Properties panel to select a default linetype for all new objects. The list shows only linetypes that have already been loaded into the drawing, so you must first load a linetype before you can select it.

Another possible color and linetype assignment is ByBlock, which you also set with the Properties panel. ByBlock makes everything you draw white until you turn your drawing into a block and then insert the block on a layer with an assigned color. The objects then take on the color of that layer. This behavior is similar to that of objects drawn on layer 0. The ByBlock linetype works similarly to the ByBlock color.

You can set an object or set of objects to ByLayer or ByBlock using the SETBYLAYER command. Click the Set To ByLayer tool in the Home tab's expanded Modify panel or type **SETBYLAYER**↵, select the objects you want to modify, and follow the prompt.

Finally, if you want to set the linetype scale for each individual object instead of relying on the global linetype scale (the Ltscale system variable), you can use the Properties palette to modify the linetype scale of individual objects. In place of using the Properties palette, you can set the Celtscale system variable to the linetype scale you want for new objects.

As mentioned earlier, stay away from assigning colors and linetypes to individual objects until you're comfortable with AutoCAD; even then, use color and linetype assignments carefully. Other users who work on your drawing may have difficulty understanding your drawing's organization if you assign color and linetype properties indiscriminately.

Once the log-file feature is closed, you can use Windows Notepad to open the AutoCAD log file located in the C:\Users\*User Name*\AppData\Local\Autodesk\AutoCAD 2015\R20.0\ enu\ folder. You'll need to change the Text Document (*.txt) option to All Files. The name of the log file will start with the name of the current drawing, followed by a series of numbers and the .log filename extension, as in 04c-bath-metric_1_1_6500.log.

If you have difficulty finding the log file, enter **(getvar "logfilepath")** at the AutoCAD Command prompt to get a listing of the log-file location. The log file may also be in a hidden folder, so you may have to turn off the hidden folder setting in Windows Explorer. See Appendix B for instructions on how to do this.

With the log-file feature, you can record virtually anything that appears at the Command prompt. You can even record an entire AutoCAD session. The log file can also be helpful in constructing script files to automate tasks. (See Chapter 24 for more information on scripts.) If you want a hard copy of the log file, print it from an application such as Windows Notepad or your favorite word processor.

---

### USING EXCEL TO ANALYZE LARGE LAYER LISTS

You may encounter a drawing that has a very long list of layers. To help you analyze the layers in a drawing, you can copy the layer list into Microsoft Excel by doing the following: Open the Layer Properties Manager and press Ctrl+A to select the entire layer list. Press Ctrl+C to copy the list to the Clipboard, and then open Excel. Press Ctrl+V to paste the list into Excel.

---

## The Bottom Line

**Organize information with layers.**   Layers are perhaps the most powerful feature in AutoCAD. They help to keep drawings well organized, and they give you control over the visibility of objects. They also let you control the appearance of your drawing by setting colors, lineweights, and linetypes.

**Master It**   Describe the process of creating a layer.

**Control layer visibility.**   When a drawing becomes dense with information, it can be difficult to edit. If you've organized your drawing using layers, you can reduce its complexity by turning off layers that aren't important to your current session.

**Master It**   Describe two methods for hiding a layer.

**Keep track of blocks and layers.**   At times, you may want a record of the layers or blocks in your drawing. You can create a list of layers using the log-file feature in AutoCAD.

**Master It**   Where do you go to turn on the log-file feature?

# Part 2

# Mastering Intermediate Skills

# Chapter 6

# Editing and Reusing Data to Work Efficiently

If you're an experienced drafter, you know that you frequently have to draw the same item several times in many drawings. The AutoCAD® 2015 software offers a variety of ways to reuse existing geometry, thereby automating much of the repetitive work usually associated with manual drafting. That's why at least five commands are devoted to duplicating objects— ten if you include the grips options.

In this chapter, as you finish drawing the studio apartment unit, you'll explore some of the ways to exploit existing files and objects while constructing your drawing. For example, you'll use existing files as prototypes for new files, eliminating the need to set up layers, scales, and sheet sizes for similar drawings. With AutoCAD, you can also duplicate objects in multiple arrays. In Chapter 3, "Setting Up and Using the Drafting Tools," you saw how to use the object snap (osnap) overrides on objects to locate points for drawing complex forms. This chapter describes other ways of using lines to aid your drawing.

Because you'll begin to use the Zoom command more in the exercises in this chapter, you'll review this command as you go along. You'll also discover the Pan command—another tool to help you get around in your drawing.

You're already familiar with many of the commands you'll use to draw the apartment unit. So, rather than going through every step of the drawing process, the exercises will sometimes ask you to copy the drawing from a figure and, using notes and dimensions as guides, put objects on the indicated layers. If you have trouble remembering a command you've already learned, go back and review the appropriate section of the book.

In this chapter, you will learn to

♦ Create and use templates

♦ Copy an object multiple times

♦ Develop your drawing

♦ Find an exact distance along a curve

♦ Change the length of objects

♦ Create a new drawing by using parts from another drawing

## Creating and Using Templates

Most programs today include what are called *templates*. A template is a file that is already set up for a specific application. For example, in your word processor you might want to set up a document with a logo, a return address, and a date so you don't have to add these elements each time you create a letter. You might also want to format invoices in a slightly different way. You can set up a template for the needs of each type of document. That way, you don't have to spend time reformatting each new document you create.

Similarly, AutoCAD offers templates, which are drawing files that contain custom settings designed for a particular function. Out of the box, AutoCAD has templates for ISO, ANSI, DIN, GB, and JIS standard drawing formats that include generic title blocks. But you aren't limited to these "canned" templates. You can create your own templates for your particular style and method of drawing.

If you find that you use a particular drawing setup frequently, you can turn one or more of your typical drawings into a template. For example, you might want to create a set of drawings with the same scale and sheet size as an existing drawing. By turning a frequently used drawing into a template, you can save a lot of setup time for subsequent drawings.

### Creating a Template

The following exercise guides you through creating and using a template drawing for your studio's kitchenette. Because the kitchenette will use the same layers, settings, scale, and sheet size as the bathroom drawing, you can use the Bath file as a prototype. Follow these steps:

1. Start AutoCAD in the usual way.

2. Choose Open from the Quick Access toolbar to open the Select File dialog box.

3. Locate the Bath file you created in the previous chapter. You can also use the file 06-bath .dwg from the companion web page at www.sybex.com/go/masteringautocad2015.

4. Click the Erase button on the Home tab's Modify panel, or enter E↵; then type all↵↵. This erases all the objects that make up the bathroom, but other elements, such as layers, linetypes, and stored blocks, remain in the drawing.

5. Choose Save As from the Application menu to open the Save Drawing As dialog box.

6. Open the File Of Type drop-down list, and select AutoCAD Drawing Template (*.dwt). The file list window changes to display the current template files in the \Template\ folder.

7. In the File Name text box, enter the name **Arch8x11h**. If you're a metric user, enter the name **A4plan**.

8. Click Save to open the Template Options dialog box (see Figure 6.1).

9. Enter the following description: **Architectural one inch scale drawing on 8 1/2 by 11 inch media**. Metric users should enter the description **Architectural 1:10 scale drawing on A4 media**.

10. Select English or Metric from the Measurement drop-down list, depending on the unit system you're using.

**FIGURE 6.1**
The Template
Options dialog box

---

### LOCATING THE *TEMPLATE* FOLDER

When you choose the AutoCAD Drawing Template option in the Save Drawing As dialog box, AutoCAD automatically opens the folder containing the template files. The standard AutoCAD installation creates the folder named Template to contain the template files. If you want to place your templates in a different folder, you can change the default template location by using the Options dialog box (choose Options from the bottom of the Application menu). Click the Files tab, double-click to expand Template Settings, and then double-click Drawing Template File Location in the list. Double-click the folder name that appears just below Drawing Template File Location; then select a new location from the Browse For Folder dialog box that appears.

---

**11.** Click the Save All Layers As Reconciled option.

**12.** Click OK to save your new file and create a template. The template file you saved becomes the current file. (As with other Windows programs, choosing File ➤ Save As makes the saved file current.) This exercise shows that you can edit template files just as you would regular drawing files.

**13.** Close the template file.

## Using a Template

Now let's see how a template is used. You'll use the template you just created as the basis for a new drawing you'll work on in this chapter:

**1.** Click the New tool from the Quick Access toolbar to open the Select Template dialog box. This is a typical file dialog box which should be familiar to you by now.

**2.** In the Select Template list box, click the filename Arch8x11h.dwt. Metric users should click the filename A4plan.dwt. Because this file is blank, you won't see anything in the preview window.

3. Click Open. It may not be obvious, but your new file is set up with the same architectural units and drawing limits as the bathroom drawing. It also contains the Door, Toilet, and Tub blocks.

4. You need to give your new file a name. Choose Save As from the Application menu to open the Save Drawing As dialog box. (Make sure you choose Save As, or you won't get the Save Drawing As dialog box.) Enter **Kitchen** for the filename, and select the folder in which to save your new kitchen file. For example, you can save your file in the My Documents folder by clicking the My Documents shortcut in the left column.

5. Click Save to create the Kitchen file, and close the dialog box.

You've created and used your own template file. Later, when you've established a comfortable working relationship with AutoCAD, you can create a set of templates that are custom-made to your particular needs.

However, if you're in a hurry you don't need to create a template every time you want to reuse settings from another file. You can use an existing file as the basis or prototype for a new file without creating a template. Open the prototype file, and choose Save As from the Application menu to create a new version of the file under a new name. You can then edit the new version without affecting the original prototype file.

## Copying an Object Multiple Times

CERT OBJECTIVE

Let's explore the tools that let you quickly duplicate objects. In the following sections, you'll begin to draw parts of a small kitchen. The first set of exercises introduces the Array command, which you can use to draw the gas burners of a range top.

As you'll see, an array can be either in a circular pattern, called a *polar array*, or a matrix of columns and rows, called a *rectangular array*. You can also create arrays that follow a curved or straight path, such as a spline curve, arc, or polyline.

### Making Circular Copies

To start the range top, first set the layer on which you want to draw, and then draw a circle representing the edge of one burner:

1. Set the current layer to Fixture by selecting Fixture from the layer drop-down list in the Home tab's Layers panel.

   Because you used the Bath file as a template, Running Osnap is already turned on for Endpoint, Midpoint, and Intersection.

2. Click the Center, Radius Circle tool on the Home tab's Draw panel, or type **C↵**.

3. At the Specify center point for circle or [3P/2P/Ttr (tan tan radius)]: prompt, pick a point at coordinate 4′,4′. Metric users should pick a point at coordinate 120,120.

4. At the Specify radius of circle or [Diameter]: prompt, enter **3↵**. Metric users should enter **7.6↵**. The circle appears.

Now you're ready to use the Array command to draw the burner grill. You'll first draw one line representing part of the grill and then use the Array command to create the copies:

1. Zoom into the circle you just drew, and then make sure Snap mode is off by unchecking the Snap Mode tool in the status bar.

2. Draw a 4″ line starting from the coordinate 4′-1″,4′-0″ and ending to the right of that point. Metric users should draw a 9 cm line starting at coordinate 122,120 and ending to the right of that point.

3. Adjust your view so it looks similar to Figure 6.2.

**FIGURE 6.2**
A close-up of the circle and line

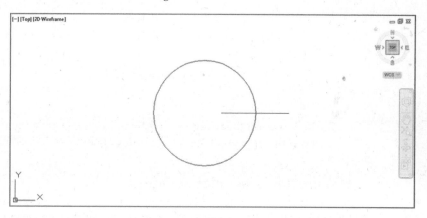

You've got the basic parts needed to create the burner grill. You're ready to make multiple copies of the line. For this part, you'll use the Array command:

1. Make sure Ortho mode is off and Polar Tracking is on.

2. Click the Polar Array tool from the Array flyout on the Modify panel as shown in Figure 6.3, or type **ARRAYPOLAR**↵.

**FIGURE 6.3**
The Array flyout

3. At the `Select Objects:` prompt, click the horizontal line and press ↵.

4. At the `Specify center point of array or [Base point/Axis of rotation]:` prompt, Shift+right-click and select Center. To select the center of the circle, hover over the circle perimeter until you see the Center osnap marker. When the marker appears, click. A circular array of the line appears.

5. At the Select grip to edit array or [Associative/Base point/Items/Angle between/Fill angle/ROWs/Levels/ROTate items/eXit]<eXit>: prompt, enter I⏎ or select Items from the command line.

6. At the Enter number of items in array or [Expression]: prompt, enter 8⏎. The lines appear evenly spaced in a circular array (Figure 6.4).

**FIGURE 6.4**
The lines evenly spaced in a polar array

7. Press ⏎ to exit the Arraypolar command, or if Dynamic Input is on, choose eXit from the menu that appears at the cursor. Your drawing should look like Figure 6.4.

## Making Row and Column Copies

Now you'll draw the other three burners of the gas range by creating a rectangular array from the burner you just drew. You'll first zoom back a bit to get a view of a larger area. Then you'll proceed with the Array command.

Follow these steps to zoom back:

Zoom Scale  1. Click Zoom Scale from the Navigation bar. You can also type Z⏎S⏎.

2. Enter 0.5x⏎. Your drawing will look like Figure 6.5.

**FIGURE 6.5**
The preceding view reduced by a factor of 0.5

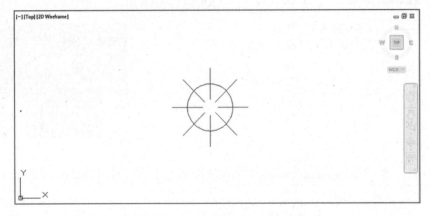

If you're not too fussy about the amount you want to zoom out, you can click Out from the Zoom flyout on the View tab's Navigate 2D panel to reduce your view quickly.

Entering 0.5x for the Zoom Scale factor tells AutoCAD you want a view that reduces the width of the current view to fill half the display area, enabling you to see more of the work area. If you specify a scale value greater than 1 (5, for example), you'll magnify your current view. If you leave off the *x*, your new view will be in relation to the drawing limits rather than the current view.

Next you'll finish the range top. You'll get a chance to use the Rectangular Array option to create three additional burners:

1. Click the Rectangular Array tool on the Array flyout on the Modify panel as shown in Figure 6.6, or type **ARRAYRECT**↵.

**FIGURE 6.6**
The Rectangular
Array tool on
the Array flyout

2. Select the entire burner, including the lines and the circle, and then press ↵ to confirm your selection.

3. At the `Select grip to edit array or [Associative/Base point/COUnt/Spacing/COLumns/Rows/Levels/eXit]<eXit>:` prompt, type **COU**↵ or select COUnt from the command line.

4. At the `Enter number of rows or [Expression] <4>:` prompt, enter **2**↵.

5. At the `Enter number of columns or [Expression] <4>:` prompt, enter **2**↵ again.

6. To set the array dimensions, type **S**↵ or select Spacing from the command line.

7. At the `Specify the distance between columns or [Unit cell] <1'-3">:` prompt, type **1'-4"**↵. Metric users enter **40.6**↵.

8. At the `Specify the distance between rows <1'-3">:` prompt, type **1'-2"**↵. Metric users enter **35.5**↵.

9. Press ↵, or right-click and select the eXit option in the context menu.

10. The array appears in the drawing, but a few of the array elements are off the top of the screen, as shown in Figure 6.7. In the next section, "Fine-Tuning Your View," you'll learn about the Pan tool, which will enable you to adjust the view so that the array is centered in the drawing area.

**FIGURE 6.7**
The burners arrayed

---

**QUICK ARRAY COPIES WITH GRIPS**

Sometimes the Array tool can be overkill if you need to make only a few evenly spaced copies. Fortunately, grip editing offers a feature that lets you quickly make evenly spaced copies. Here's how it's done:

1. Press the Esc key to make sure you aren't in the middle of a command; then select the objects you want to copy.

2. Click a grip point as your base point.

3. Right-click and select Move.

4. Ctrl+click a location at which to place a copy of the selected object. This first copy will determine the interval distance for additional copies.

5. Continue to hold down the Ctrl key, and select additional points to make copies at regularly spaced intervals.

The copies snap to the distance you indicate with the first Ctrl+click point (in step 4). You can use osnaps to select a distance based on the position of another object. Once you've made the first copy with the Ctrl+click, you can release the Ctrl key to make multiple copies at random intervals. Another option is to use PolarSnap while making grip edit copies. With PolarSnap, you can enter a specific distance for the intervals.

---

## Fine-Tuning Your View

Back in Figure 6.7, you may have noticed that parts of the burners don't appear on the display. To move the view over so that you can see all the burners, use the Pan command. Pan is similar to Zoom in that it changes your view of the drawing. However, Pan doesn't alter the magnification of the view the way Zoom does. Rather, Pan maintains the current magnification while moving your view across the drawing, just as you would pan a camera across a landscape.

To activate the Pan command, follow these steps:

1. Click the Pan tool on the Navigation bar, or type **P**↵. A small hand-shaped cursor appears in place of the AutoCAD cursor.

2. Place the hand cursor in the center of the drawing area, and then click and drag it down and to the left. The view follows the motion of your mouse.

3. Continue to drag the view until it looks similar to Figure 6.8; then release the mouse button.

**FIGURE 6.8**
The panned view of the range top

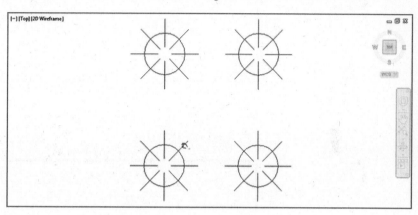

Zoom Realtime

4. To finish the kitchen, you want a view that shows more of the drawing area. Click the Zoom Realtime option in the Navigation bar's zoom flyout. The cursor changes to the Zoom Realtime cursor. The Zoom/Pan context menu also appears when you right-click during the Zoom Realtime command.

5. Place the cursor close to the top of the screen, and click and drag the cursor down to zoom out until your view looks like the top panel of Figure 6.9. You may need to click and drag the Zoom Realtime cursor a second time to achieve this view.

6. Right-click again, and choose Exit from the context menu. You're now ready to add more information to the kitchen drawing.

You can also exit the Pan or Zoom Realtime command without opening the context menu; just press the Esc key twice.

This exercise showed how you can fine-tune your view by easily switching between Pan and Zoom Realtime. After you get the hang of these two tools working together, you'll be able to access the best view for your needs quickly. The other options in the context menu—Zoom Window, Zoom Original, and Zoom Extents—perform the same functions as the options in the Zoom flyout on the View tab's Navigate 2D panel or in the Navigation bar.

The Zoom Window option in the Zoom/Pan context menu functions in a slightly different way from the standard Zoom Window option. Instead of clicking two points, you click and drag a window across your view.

**FIGURE 6.9**
The final view of the range top burners (top image) and the finished kitchen (bottom image). Metric dimensions are shown in brackets.

## Finishing the Kitchenette

Before you save and close the Kitchen file, you need to do one more thing. You'll be using this drawing as a symbol and inserting it into the overall plan of the studio apartment unit. To facilitate accurate placement of the kitchen, you'll change the location of the base point of this drawing to the upper-left corner of the kitchen. This will then be the drawing's *grip*:

1. Complete the kitchenette as indicated in the bottom panel of Figure 6.9, shown earlier in this chapter. As the figure indicates, make sure you put the kitchenette on the Fixture layer. This will help you control the visibility of the kitchenette in future edits of this file. Draw the sink roughly as shown in the figure.

2. Click the Set Base Point tool in the Insert tab's expanded Block Definition panel.

3. At the Enter base point: prompt, pick the upper-left corner of the kitchen, as indicated in the bottom image of Figure 6.9. The kitchen drawing is complete.

4. Select Save from the Quick Access toolbar, but keep the file open because you'll use it later.

> ### USING THE COPY COMMAND TO CREATE AN ARRAY
>
> In the previous section, you learned how you can quickly make an array of objects using the Array command. You can also create simple arrays using the Copy command. To see firsthand how this works, see "Copying and Editing Attribute Definitions" in Chapter 12, "Using Attributes."

## Array along a Path

Before you continue with the apartment drawings you're working on for the main part of the tutorial, we'd like to introduce you to one more Array feature. In AutoCAD 2015, you can create an array that follows a curved or straight path, such as an arc, spline curve, or complex polyline. Try the following exercise to see firsthand how it works:

1. Open the file called seating.dwg. You'll see a drawing of a chair in the lower-left corner along with an arc drawn across the width of the drawing area.

2. Click the Path Array tool in the Array flyout (see Figure 6.10), or type **ARRAYPATH**↵.

**FIGURE 6.10**
Select the Path Array tool from the Array flyout on the Home tab's Modify panel.

3. At the Select object: prompt, click the chair at the left end of the arc in the drawing and then press ↵ (see Figure 6.11).

**FIGURE 6.11**
Click the chair at the left end of the arc.

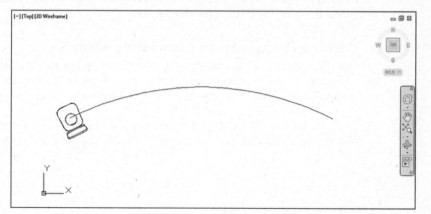

4. At the Select Path curve: prompt, select the arc toward the left end.

5. At the Select grip to edit array or [Associative/Method/Base point/Tangent direction/Items/Rows/Levels/Align items/Z direction/eXit] <eXit>: prompt, press ↵ to exit the command.

In this exercise, you made an array of a chair that follows the path of an arc. Note that the chair had been set up facing away from the center of the arc. In a later exercise, you'll see how you can easily rotate the chairs to face the center.

You could have used a spline curve or polyline (see Chapter 18, "Drawing Curves," for more on spline curves and polylines) instead of the arc and the results would have been similar.

Now suppose you want to adjust the curvature of your array. This is just a simple matter of adjusting the shape of the arc as in the following steps:

1. Click the arc to expose its grips.

2. Click the middle grip, drag it up until the arc dimension shows an Ortho value close to 30.0000 < 90 degrees, and then click. The array of chairs follows the arc (see Figure 6.12).

**FIGURE 6.12**
Change the radius of the arc and the array follows.

3. Press the Esc key twice to clear your selection of the arc.

Here you see how the associative feature of the Arraypath command enables you to control the array by adjusting the object you used for the path. Arrays can be edited through a variety of methods, as you'll see in the next section.

## Making Changes to an Associative Array

Now let's take a look at how you can make changes to an array. You may have noticed the Associative option in the Array command's prompt. By default, the Associative option is turned on, which enables you to edit array objects as a group. You'll see firsthand how this works in the following exercises.

You'll start by editing the array you created using the Path Array tool. Since you've changed the arc array path, the chairs no longer fill the arc. The last chair to the right is no longer at the end of the arc. This happened because when you changed the arc's radius, you made it a bit longer. By default, the chair array is set up to maintain the chairs' distance from each other. You can change that setting so that the chairs fill the arc. Here's how it's done:

1. Click the array of chairs. Notice that the Array contextual Ribbon tab appears (see Figure 6.13).

**FIGURE 6.13**
The Array tab displays a different set of panels and options when an array is selected.

2. Click the Measure flyout in the Array tab's Properties panel and then select the Divide Method option. The chairs are now evenly spaced along the arc.

The Divide and Measure options in the Array tab's Properties panel are similar to the Divide and Measure commands. Divide marks off an object into equal parts whereas Measure marks off an object based on a distance between the marks. You'll learn more about Divide and Measure in the section "Finding an Exact Distance along a Curve" later in this chapter.

You may have also noticed that the chairs are pointing away from the center of the arc. You can realign them so they face the center of the arc by making a simple change to the original chair. The following steps show you how this is done:

1. Click the Edit Source tool in the Array tab's Options panel.

2. Click the middle chair in the array. The Array Editing State message appears, informing you that you need to enter **ARRAYCLOSE** to exit the array editing state (see Figure 6.14).

**FIGURE 6.14**
The Array Editing State message

3. Click OK.

4. Press the Esc key to clear the selection of chairs.

5. Click the middle chair again, and then click the Rotate tool in the Home tab's Modify panel.

6. For the rotation base point, click the center of the circle in the chair seat.

7. Rotate the chair so that all of the chairs are facing the center of the arc, as shown in Figure 6.15.

**FIGURE 6.15**
Rotating the chairs

8. When the chairs are oriented so that they are pointing toward the center of the arc, click to fix their location.

9. Click the Save Changes tool in the Edit Array panel to save the changes and exit the array editing state. You can also type **ARRAYCLOSE**↵ and choose Yes in the dialog box that appears.

In this exercise, you saw how editing the source object of an array affects the other array copies. This is the Associative array feature at work. You could have made any number of other changes to the array.

Next, you'll make changes to the chair array spacing and add a few additional rows. Then you'll revisit the kitchenette to see how you can edit a nested array.

Try the following exercise to see how the Ribbon can be used to edit an array:

1. Click any chair in the array. Notice again that the Ribbon changes to show the Array tab with some new panels.

2. In the Rows panel, change the Row Count value in the top text box to **3**. Two more rows of chairs appear for a total of three rows.

3. Adjust your view so that you can see all of the rows.

4. In the Items panel, change the Item Count value at the top to **10**. If you are unable to change the item count value, open the Properties panel, click Measure, and select Divide.

5. Press the Esc key to clear your selection.

6. Exit the file without saving it so that you can come back and practice with it again.

---

**UNABLE TO CHANGE THE ITEM COUNT?**

If you can't change the Item Count value in the Items panel, select Divide Method from the Divide/Measure flyout in the Properties panel of the Array tab. The Measure option does not allow you to change the item count because Measure forces a fixed distance between objects in the array. Since the Divide option doesn't care about the distance between objects, it allows you to change the item count.

As you can see from these exercises, you can easily make changes to an array through the Ribbon panel options in the Array tab. Many of these options are also available through the multi-function grip menus when you have Dynamic Input turned on.

Several other tools become available on the Ribbon panel when you select an associative array. Table 6.1 gives you a rundown of the panels and tools and their function. The tools that appear in the Ribbon will be slightly different depending on whether the array is a polar, rectangular, or path array, but the features they offer are similar to those in the table.

**TABLE 6.1:** The panels and tools on the Array tab

| PANEL OR TOOL | PURPOSE |
| --- | --- |
| Items | Controls the number of items, their distance, and the overall width of the array. |
| Rows | Controls the number of rows, the distance between rows, and the overall distance between the first and last row. A fourth option, Incremental Elevation in the expanded Rows panel, enables you to control the z-axis height of rows for 3D models. |
| Levels | Controls the number of levels in the z-axis, their spacing, and the overall distance from the first to the last level. |
| Base Point | Enables you to adjust the base point of the array objects. |
| Measure/Divide | Controls how the arrayed objects behave when the path is modified. Measure Method maintains the distance between objects when the path object changes in length. Divide Method causes the distance between objects to adjust to changes in the path object's length. |
| Align Items | Controls whether the array objects are aligned with the path object. |
| Z Direction | Controls whether array objects are "banked" with a 3D path object. |
| Edit Source | Enables you to edit the source object in an array. |
| Replace Item | Enables you to replace the source object in the array. |
| Reset Array | Restores erased items and removes overrides. |

In the next exercise, you'll return to the kitchen drawing to see how you can use grips to modify an array:

1. If you have closed the kitchen drawing, open it again.

2. Click the array of burners that you created earlier. The grips appear for the array, and you see the Array tab in the Ribbon as you did earlier.

3. Hover over the grip in the upper-right burner. A menu appears.

4. Select the Row And Column Count option from the menu. Now, as you move the cursor up and to the right, additional burners appear. The farther to the upper right you move the cursor, the more rows and columns appear (see Figure 6.16).

**FIGURE 6.16**
The rows and columns increase as you move the cursor farther from the base point.

5. When you see one additional row and column, click and then press the Esc key to clear your selection. The additional burners are added to the drawing.

6. You don't want the changes to be permanent, so click the Undo tool to revert back to the four burners of the original drawing.

7. Close the kitchen drawing without saving it.

In step 4, you used the Row And Column Count multifunction grip option to add rows and columns to an array. This option combines the function of the Rows and Columns panels in the Array tab.

## Developing Your Drawing

As mentioned briefly in Chapter 3, when you're using AutoCAD you first create the basic geometric forms used in your drawing and then you refine them. In this section, you'll create two drawings—the studio apartment unit and the lobby—that demonstrate this process in more detail.

First, you'll construct a typical studio apartment unit by using the drawings you've created thus far. In the process, you'll explore the use of lines as reference objects.

You'll also further examine how to use existing files as blocks. In Chapter 4, "Organizing Objects with Blocks and Groups," you inserted a file into another file. The number of files you can insert is limitless, and you can insert files of any size. As you may already have guessed, you can also *nest* files and blocks; that is, you can insert blocks or files in other blocks or files. Nesting can help reduce your drawing time by enabling you to build one block out of smaller blocks. For example, you can insert your door drawing into the bathroom plan. In turn, you can insert the bathroom plan into the studio unit plan, which also contains doors. Finally, you can insert the unit plan into the overall floor plan for the studio apartment building.

### Importing Settings

In this exercise, you'll use the Bath file as a prototype for the studio unit plan. However, you must make a few changes to it first. After the changes are made, you'll import the bathroom and thereby import the layers and blocks contained in the bathroom file.

As you go through this exercise, observe how the drawings begin to evolve from simple forms to complex, assembled forms.

Use these steps to modify the Bath file:

1. Open the Bath file you worked on earlier. If you skipped drawing the Bath file in Chapter 5, "Keeping Track of Layers and Blocks," use the file 05c-bath.dwg (or 05c-bath-metric.dwg) from this book's companion web page.

 2. Click the Set Base Point tool in the Insert tab's expanded Block Definition panel, and select the upper-left corner of the bathroom as the new base point for this drawing so that you can position the Bath file more accurately.

3. Save the Bath file. If you use the sample from the book's web page, choose Save As from the Application menu and save it as **Bath**. You can save it to your Documents folder to keep the original in its unedited state.

4. Click the Close icon in the Drawing tab, or choose Close from the Application menu to close the bath drawing.

Next, you'll create a new file. Use the New option from the Quick Access toolbar to create a file from a template:

1. Click New from the Quick Access toolbar to open the Select Template dialog box.

2. Locate and select the acad.dwt template file. Metric users should locate the acadiso.dwt template file.

3. Click Open to open the new file.

4. If you're using Imperial measurements, choose Drawing Utilities ➢ Units from the Application menu; then, in the Drawing Units dialog box, select Architectural from the Length group's Type drop-down list and click OK. Metric users should use the default decimal length type and should select Centimeters in the Insertion Scale drop-down list.

5. Type **LIMITS**↵. At the Specify lower left corner or [ON/OFF] <0'-0",0'-0">: prompt, press ↵ to accept the default drawing origin for the lower-left corner.

6. If you're using Imperial measurements, enter **528,408**↵ at the next prompt. These are the appropriate dimensions for an 8-1/2" × 11" drawing at 1/4" = 1'-0" scale. Metric users should enter **1485,1050**. This is the work area for a 1:50 scale drawing on an A4 sheet.

7. Click Zoom All from the Navigation bar.

Let's continue by laying out a typical studio unit. You'll discover how importing a file also imports a variety of drawing items such as layers and linetypes. Follow these steps:

1. Begin the unit by drawing two rectangles, one 14' long by 24' wide and the other 14' long by 4' wide. Metric users should make the rectangles 426 cm wide by 731 cm long and 426 cm wide by 122 cm long. Place them as shown in Figure 6.17. The large rectangle represents the interior of the apartment unit, and the small rectangle represents the balcony. The size and location of the rectangles are indicated in the figure.

**FIGURE 6.17**

The apartment unit interior and balcony. Metric locations and dimensions are shown in brackets.

**2.** Click the Explode tool on the Home tab's Block panel, select the two rectangles, and then press ↵.

**3.** Click the Insert tool on the Home tab's Block panel to open the Insert dialog box.

**4.** Click the Browse button, and locate and select the bath drawing by using the Select Drawing File dialog box; then click Open. If you haven't saved a bathroom drawing from earlier exercises, you can use `05c-bath.dwg`.

**5.** If you're using the `05c-bath.dwg` file, do the following: After selecting `05c-bath.dwg` in step 4, change the name that appears in the Name text box to Bath instead of `05c-bath` before you click OK in step 6. This gives the inserted file a block name of Bath, even though its originating filename is `05c-bath`.

---

**IF YOU USED THE RECTANGLE TOOL TO DRAW THE INTERIOR AND BALCONY...**

...of the apartment unit, make sure you use the Explode tool on the Modify panel to explode the rectangles. The Rectangle tool draws a polyline rectangle instead of simple line segments, so you need to explode the rectangle to reduce it to its component lines. You'll learn more about polylines in Chapter 18.

---

**6.** Click OK in the Insert dialog box, and then click the upper-left corner of the unit's interior as the insertion point (see Figure 6.18). You can use the Endpoint osnap to place the bathroom accurately. If you are prompted for scale and rotation, use a scale factor of 1.0 and a rotation angle of 0°.

**FIGURE 6.18**
The unit after
the bathroom is
inserted

7. If running osnaps haven't been set up in this file, you need to use the Osnap context menu (Shift+right-click) to access the Endpoint osnap. You can set up running osnaps to take advantage of the AutoSnap functions by right-clicking the Object Snap button in the status bar and selecting Settings. Set the running osnaps as described in Chapter 3.

8. Assign the two rectangles that you drew earlier to the Wall layer. To do this, select the two rectangles so that they're highlighted, and then open the layer drop-down list in the Layers panel and select Wall. Press the Esc key to clear the selection.

By inserting the bathroom, you imported the layers and blocks contained in the Bath file. You were then able to move previously drawn objects to the imported layers. If you're in a hurry, this can be a quick way to duplicate layers that you know exist in another drawing. This method is similar to using an existing drawing as a template, but it lets you start work on a drawing before deciding which template to use.

## Using Osnap Tracking to Place Objects

You'll draw lines in the majority of your work, so it's important to know how to manipulate lines to your best advantage. In the following sections, you'll look at some common ways to use and edit these fundamental drawing objects. The following exercises show you the process of drawing lines rather than just how individual commands work. While you're building walls and adding doors, you'll get a chance to become more familiar with Polar Tracking and Osnap Tracking.

### ROUGHING IN THE LINE WORK

The bathroom you inserted in the preceding section has only one side of its interior walls drawn. (Walls are usually shown by double lines.) In this next exercise, you'll draw the other side. Rather than trying to draw the wall perfectly the first time, you'll sketch in the line work and then clean it up in the next section, in a way similar to manual drafting.

Use these steps to rough in the wall lines:

1. Zoom in to the bathroom so that the entire bathroom and part of the area around it are displayed, as shown in Figure 6.19.

**FIGURE 6.19**
The enlarged view
of the bathroom

2. Select Wall from the layer drop-down list in the Layers panel to make Wall the current layer.

3. Make sure that the Object Snap Tracking and Object Snap tools on the status bar are turned on.

Object Snap   Object Snap Tracking

4. Click Line from the Draw panel, or type L↵.

5. At the Specify first point: prompt, hover your cursor over the lower-right corner of the bathroom so that the Endpoint Osnap marker appears, but don't click it.

6. Now move the cursor downward and, as you do, the tracking vector appears. (If the tracking vector doesn't appear at first, hover your cursor over the corner again until it does appear.)

Remember that a little cross appears at the osnap location, telling you that Osnap Tracking has "locked on" to that location.

7. With the tracking vector visible, point the cursor directly downward from the corner and then type **5**↵. Metric users should type **13**↵. A line starts 5″ (or 13 cm) below the lower-right corner of the bathroom.

8. Continue the line horizontally to the left to cross the left wall of the apartment unit slightly, as illustrated in the top image in Figure 6.20. Press ↵.

**FIGURE 6.20**
The first wall line and the wall line by the door

Draw the line to the left past the vertical wall line.

End the line using the Perpendicular Osnap.

Add wall line from the endpoint of the jamb.

9. Draw another line upward from the endpoint of the top doorjamb to meet the top wall of the unit (see the bottom image in Figure 6.20). Use the Perpendicular osnap to pick the top wall of the unit. This causes the line to end precisely on the wall line in a perpendicular position, as seen in the bottom image in Figure 6.20.

You can also use the Perpendicular osnap override to draw a line perpendicular to a nonorthogonal line—one at a 45° angle, for instance.

10. Draw a line connecting the two doorjambs. Then assign that line to the Ceiling layer. (See the top panel in Figure 6.21.)

**11.** Draw a line 6″ down from the endpoint of the doorjamb nearest the corner. (See the top panel in Figure 6.21.) Metric users should draw a line 15 cm down.

**FIGURE 6.21**
The corner of the bathroom wall and the filleted wall around the bathroom

Add a door header and change it to the Ceiling layer.

Add a 6″ line. [15 cm line]

Fillet

---

### SMOOTHING THE ARC

You may notice that some of the arcs in your bathroom drawing aren't smooth. Don't be alarmed; this is how AutoCAD displays arcs and circles in enlarged views. The arcs will be smooth when they're plotted. If you want to see them now as they're stored in the file, you can regenerate the drawing by typing **RE**↵ at the Command prompt. Chapter 7, "Mastering Viewing Tools, Hatches, and External References," discusses regeneration in more detail.

In the previous exercise, Osnap Tracking mode enabled you to specify the starting point of a line at an exact distance from the corner of the bathroom. In step 7, you used the Direct Distance method for specifying distance and direction.

---

### SELECTING POINTS FROM A KNOWN LOCATION

Instead of using a tracking vector in step 6 of the previous exercise, you could choose From on the Osnap context menu and then open the context menu again and select Endpoint. Select the corner and enter a polar coordinate such as **@5<-90** to accomplish the same task as this exercise.

---

## CLEANING UP THE LINE WORK

You've drawn some of the wall lines, approximating their endpoint locations. Next, you'll use the Fillet command to join lines exactly end to end and then import the kitchen drawing.

---

### UNDERSTANDING THE OSNAP TRACKING VECTOR

The Osnap Tracking vector comes into play only after you've placed an osnap marker on a location—in this case, the corner of the bathroom. It won't appear at any other time. If you have both Running Osnaps and Osnap Tracking turned on, you'll get the tracking vector every time the cursor lands on an osnap location. This can be confusing to novice users, so you may want to use Osnap Tracking sparingly until you become more comfortable with it.

Because Polar Tracking also uses a tracking vector, you may get the two confused. Remember that Polar Tracking lets you point the cursor in a specific direction while selecting points. If you're an experienced AutoCAD user, you can think of it as a more intelligent Ortho mode. On the other hand, Osnap Tracking lets you align points to osnap locations. Experienced AutoCAD users can think of Osnap Tracking as a more intelligent XYZ filter option.

---

Follow these steps to join the lines:

1. Click the Fillet tool on the Modify panel or type **F↵**.

   The Fillet, Chamfer, and Blend Curves tools share the same location in the Modify toolbar, so the tool tip may say any of these. If it does, then click the flyout arrowhead next to the tool and select Fillet.

2. Type **R↵0↵** to make sure the fillet radius is set to 0.

3. Fillet the two lines by picking the vertical and horizontal lines, as indicated in the bottom panel in Figure 6.21 shown earlier in this chapter. Notice that these points lie on the portion of the line you want to keep. Your drawing will look like the bottom panel in Figure 6.21.

CERT OBJECTIVE

> ### CHAMFER VS. FILLET VS. BLEND CURVES
>
> The Chamfer command performs a similar function to the Fillet command, but unlike Fillet, it enables you to join two lines with an intermediate beveled line rather than with an arc. Chamfer can be set to join two lines at a corner in exactly the same manner as Fillet.
>
> The Blend Curves command will also join lines, but it does so by inserting a curved spline to intuitively bridge a gap between the ends of various types of objects.

4. Fillet the bottom wall of the bathroom with the left wall of the unit, as shown in Figure 6.22. Make sure the points you pick on the wall lines are on the side of the line you want to keep, not on the side you want trimmed.

5. Fillet the top wall of the unit with the right-side wall of the bathroom, as shown in Figure 6.22.

**FIGURE 6.22**
The cleaned-up wall intersections

You can select two lines at once for the fillet operation by using a crossing window; to do so, type **C⏎** at the Select first object or ...: prompt and then use a crossing window to select the two endpoints you want to join. The two endpoints closest to the fillet location are trimmed.

Where you select the lines affects the way the lines are joined. As you select objects to fillet, the side of the line where you click is the side that remains when the lines are joined. Figure 6.23 illustrates how the Fillet command works and shows what the Fillet options do.

**FIGURE 6.23**

Where you click the object to select it determines which part of an object will be filleted.

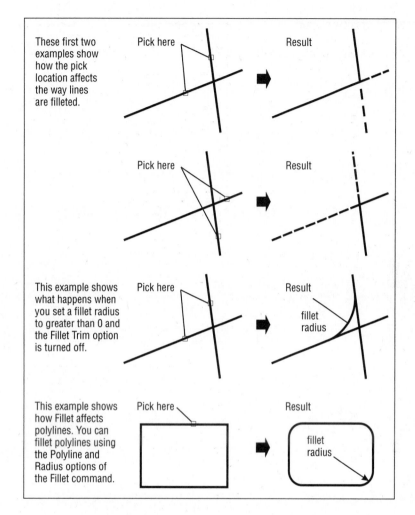

These first two examples show how the pick location affects the way lines are filleted.

Pick here     Result

Pick here     Result

This example shows what happens when you set a fillet radius to greater than 0 and the Fillet Trim option is turned off.

Pick here     Result

fillet radius

This example shows how Fillet affects polylines. You can fillet polylines using the Polyline and Radius options of the Fillet command.

Pick here     Result

fillet radius

If you select two parallel lines during the Fillet command, the two lines are joined with an arc. Now import the kitchen plan you drew earlier in this chapter:

1. Click Insert on the Block panel, and select More Options.

2. In the Insert dialog box, click the Browse button to locate the kitchen drawing you created earlier in this chapter. Make sure you leave the Specify On-Screen check box deselected under the Scale and Rotation groups of the Insert dialog box.

3. Place the kitchen drawing at the wall intersection below the bathtub. (See the top image in Figure 6.24.)

**FIGURE 6.24**
The view after using Pan and Zoom, with the door inserted and the jamb and header added

If you didn't complete the kitchen earlier in this chapter, you can insert the 06a-kitchen.dwg file. Metric users can insert 06-kitchen-metric.dwg.

**4.** Adjust your view with Pan and Zoom so that the upper portion of the apartment unit is centered in the drawing area, as illustrated in the top image in Figure 6.24.

## PLACING THE DOOR ACCURATELY

The next step is to add the entry door shown in the bottom image in Figure 6.24. In doing that, you'll use a number of new tools together to streamline the drawing process.

In this exercise, you'll practice using the Osnap Tracking feature and the From Osnap option to place the entry door at an exact distance from the upper corner of the floor plan:

1.  Right-click in the Command window, and choose Recent Commands ➤ Insert from the context menu to open the Insert dialog box.

2.  Select Door from the Name drop-down list.

3.  Make sure the Specify On-Screen option is checked in the Rotation group but not in the Scale group, and then click OK. You'll see the door follow the cursor in the drawing window.

4.  Shift+right-click to open the Osnap context menu, and then choose From.

5.  Make sure the Object Snap and Object Snap Tracking buttons on the status bar are on; then use the Endpoint Running Osnap to click the corner where the upper horizontal wall line meets the bathroom wall.

6.  Now move the cursor to the right, and you'll see the Osnap Tracking vector extend from the corner.

7.  Continue to move the cursor to the right so that the tracking vector readout shows roughly 6″, or 15 cm for metric users.

8.  With the cursor in this position, enter **5**↵. Metric users should enter **13**↵. The door is placed exactly 5 (or 13) units to the right of the corner.

9. At the Specify rotation angle <0>: prompt, enter **270.↵**. Or, if you prefer, turn on Polar Tracking to orient the door so that it's swinging *into the studio*. You've now accurately placed the entry door in the studio apartment.

10. Make sure the door is on the Door layer and the kitchen block is on the Fixture layer.

For a shortcut to setting an object's layer, you can select the object or objects and then select a layer from the layer drop-down list in the Layers panel.

Next, add the finishing touches to the entry door:

**CERT OBJECTIVE**

1. Add 5″ (13 cm for metric users) doorjambs as shown in the bottom image in Figure 6.24, and change their Layer property to the Jamb layer.

2. Choose the Break tool in the expanded Modify panel, and then select the header over the entry door. (See the bottom image in Figure 6.24.)

3. Type F↵ to use the first-point option; then select the endpoint of one of the doorjambs.

4. At the Specify second break point: prompt, select the endpoint of the other jamb, as shown in the bottom image in Figure 6.24. The line between the points disappears.

5. Draw the door header on the Ceiling layer, as shown in Figure 6.25.

**FIGURE 6.25**
The other side of the wall

6. Click Offset on the Modify panel, and offset the top wall lines of the unit and the door header up 5″ (13 cm for metric users) so they connect with the top end of the doorjamb, as shown in Figure 6.25. Don't forget to include the short wall line from the door to the bathroom wall.

7. Choose Save As from the Application menu to save your file as **Unit**.

## USING POLAR AND OSNAP TRACKING AS CONSTRUCTION LINE TOOLS

**CERT OBJECTIVE**

So far, you've been using existing geometry to place objects in the plan accurately. In this section, you'll use the Polar and Osnap Tracking tools to extend the upper wall line 5″ (13 cm for metric users) beyond the right interior wall of the unit. You'll also learn how to use the Construction Line tool to locate doorjambs accurately near the balcony.

**CERT OBJECTIVE**

### OTHER METHODS FOR USING THE BREAK COMMAND

In the exercise for finishing the unit plan, you used the Break command to place a gap in a line accurately over the entry door. In Chapter 5, you broke a line at a single point to create multiple, contiguous line segments.

In this chapter, you used the Break command's first-point (F) option, which allows you to specify the first point of a break. You can also break a line without the F option, but with a little less accuracy. When you don't use the F option, the point at which you select the object is used as the first breakpoint. If you're in a hurry, you can dispense with the F option and place a gap in an approximate location. You can later use other tools to adjust the gap.

In addition, you can use locations on other objects to select the first and second points of a break. For example, you might want to align an opening with another opening some distance away. After you've selected the line to break, you can then use the F option and select two points on the existing opening to define the first and second breakpoints. The breakpoints will align in an orthogonal direction to the selected points.

Start by changing the Polar Tracking setting to include a 45° angle:

1. Right-click the Polar Tracking button in the status bar at the bottom of the AutoCAD window, and choose Settings to open the Drafting Settings dialog box at the Polar Tracking tab (see Figure 6.26).

2. Select 45 from the Increment Angle drop-down list in the Polar Angle Settings group.

3. In the Object Snap Tracking Settings group, make sure the Track Using All Polar Angle Settings option is selected and click OK.

**FIGURE 6.26**

The Polar Tracking tab in the Drafting Settings dialog box

You're ready to extend the wall line. For this operation, you'll use grip editing:

1. Click the wall line at the top of the plan and to the right of the door to select the line and expose its grips.

2. Click the Ortho Mode button in the status bar to turn on Ortho mode. This keeps the wall line straight as you edit it.

3. Click the rightmost grip of the line to make it hot.

4. Place the cursor on the upper-right corner of the plan until you see the Endpoint osnap marker; then move the cursor away from the corner at a 45° angle. The Osnap Tracking vector appears at a 45° angle. Notice the small X that appears at the intersection of the Osnap Tracking vector and the line (see Figure 6.27).

   With the Osnap Tracking vector and the line intersecting, click the mouse button. The line changes to extend exactly 5 units beyond the vertical interior wall of the plan.

5. Press the Esc key twice to clear your selection. Then repeat steps 1 through 4 for the horizontal wall line to the left of the door to extend that line to the left corner (see Figure 6.28).

**FIGURE 6.27**

The Osnap
Tracking vector

**FIGURE 6.28**

Extend the wall line
using the Osnap
Tracking vector.

6. Click Zoom All from the Zoom flyout on the Navigation bar, or type **Z**↵**A**↵ to view the entire drawing. It looks like Figure 6.29.

**FIGURE 6.29**

The studio unit
so far

With Polar Tracking set to 45° and Osnap Tracking turned on in a crowded drawing, you may find that you're selecting points you don't really want to select. Just remember that if a drawing becomes too crowded, you can turn off these options temporarily by clicking the Object Snap Tracking or Polar Tracking button in the status bar.

In this exercise, you used Polar Tracking and Ortho mode to position the two lines used for the exterior walls of the studio unit accurately. This shows how you can take advantage of existing geometry with a combination of tools in the status bar.

Now you'll finish the balcony by adding a sliding-glass door and a rail. This time, you'll use lines for construction as well as for parts of the drawing. First, you'll add the doorjamb by drawing a construction line. A *construction line* is a line that has an infinite length, but unlike a ray, it extends in both directions. After drawing the construction line, you'll use it to position the doorjambs quickly.

Follow these steps:

1. Zoom in to the balcony area, which is the smaller rectangle at the bottom of the drawing.

   Click the Construction Line tool on the expanded Draw panel. You can also type **XL↵**. You'll see this prompt:

   ```
   Specify a point or [Hor/Ver/Ang/Bisect/Offset]:
   ```

2. Type **O↵** or select Offset from the command line.

3. At the `Specify offset distance or [Through] <0'-5">:` prompt, type **4'↵**. Metric users should type **122↵**.

4. At the `Select a line object:` prompt, click the wall line at the right of the unit.

5. At the `Specify side to offset:` prompt, click a point to the left of the wall to display the construction line. (See the top image of Figure 6.30.)

6. At the `Select a line object:` prompt, click the left wall line and then click to the right of the selected wall to create another construction line. Your drawing should look like the top image in Figure 6.30.

   Next, you'll edit the construction lines to form the jambs.

7. Press the Esc key to exit the Xline command.

8. Click Trim on the Modify panel or type **Tr↵**.

9. Select the construction lines and the two horizontal lines representing the wall between the unit and the balcony and press ↵. You can either use a crossing window or select each line individually. You've just selected the objects to trim.

   You can also use the Fence selection option to select the lines to be trimmed.

10. Click the horizontal lines at any point between the two construction lines. Then click the construction lines above and below the horizontal lines to trim them. Your drawing looks like the bottom image in Figure 6.30.

11. Assign the trimmed construction lines to the Jamb layer.

**12.** Add lines on the Ceiling layer to represent the door header.

**13.** Draw lines between the two jambs (on the Door layer) to indicate a sliding-glass door (see Figure 6.31).

**FIGURE 6.30**
Drawing the door opening

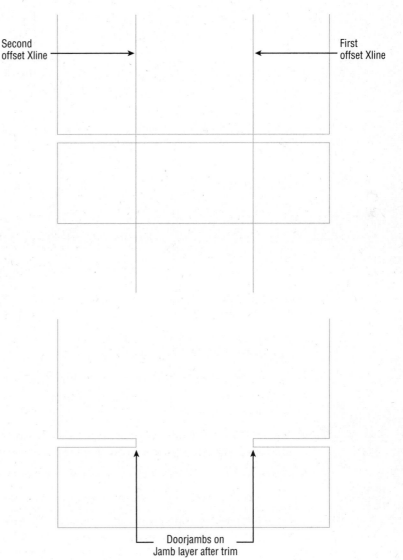

Second offset Xline

First offset Xline

Doorjambs on
Jamb layer after trim

**FIGURE 6.31**
Finishing the slid-
ing-glass door and
the railing

Sliding door on Door layer

Base point    Change to    Header on Ceiling layer
              F-rail layer

5" [13 cm] line on Wall layer

The wall facing the balcony is now complete. To finish the unit, you need to show a handrail and the corners of the balcony wall:

1. Offset the bottom line of the balcony 3" toward the top of the drawing. Metric users should offset the line 7.6 units.

2. Create a new layer called **F-rail**, and assign this offset line to it.

3. Add a 5" (13 cm for metric users) horizontal line to the lower corners of the balcony, as shown in Figure 6.31.

 4. Click the Set Base Point tool from the Insert tab's expanded Block Definition panel to set the base point at the lower-left corner of the balcony at the location shown in Figure 6.31.

5. Zoom back to the previous view. Your drawing should now look like Figure 6.32.

 6. Click Save from the Quick Access toolbar to save the drawing, and then close the file.

Your studio apartment unit plan is now complete. The exercises you've just completed demonstrate a typical set of operations you'll perform while building your drawings. In fact, nearly 80 percent of what you'll do in AutoCAD is represented here.

Now, to review the drawing process and to create a drawing you'll use later, you'll draw the apartment building's lobby. As you follow the steps, refer to Figure 6.33.

**FIGURE 6.32**
The completed studio apartment unit

**FIGURE 6.33**
Drawing the lobby plan. Metric dimensions are shown in brackets.

16'-4"
[498 cm]

Corner coordinate:
12'-6", 17'-7"
[381,537]

8'-6"
[258 cm]

Corner coordinate:
19'-11", 8'-2"
[607,250]

9'
[274 cm]

Corner coordinate:
12'-6", 8'-2"
[381,250]

7'
[213 cm]

8'-11"
[272 cm]

**1. Draw rectangles on Wall layer.**

Next, array steps 11" [28 cm]

First, copy wall line for stair steps 4' [122 cm]

Finally, draw line at midpoint of stairs

**2. Add stairs on Floor layer.**

Insert door at 28'-5", 17'-7" [866,537] on Door layer

Draw elevator 5'-4"× 7'-4" [223 cm x 162 cm] on Fixture layer

Erase line

**3. Add door and elevator.**

Copy interior wall line up 5" [13 cm]

Add door opening, jambs, and header on appropriate layers

Pick base point at corner

**4. Add door openings.**

**THE CONSTRUCTION LINE OPTIONS**

There is more to the Construction Line command than you've seen in the exercises in this chapter. Here is a list of the Construction Line options and their uses:

**Hor**   Draws horizontal construction lines as you click points

**Ver**   Draws vertical construction lines as you click points

**Ang**   Draws construction lines at a specified angle as you pick points

**Bisect**   Draws construction lines bisecting an angle or an area between two points

**Offset**   Draws construction lines offset at a specified distance from an existing line

As is usual in floor plans, the elevator shaft is indicated by the box with the large *X* through it, and the stair shaft is indicated by the box with the row of parallel lines through it. If you're in a hurry, use the finished version of this file, called Lobby.dwg (Lobby-metric.dwg for metric users). To draw the apartment building lobby, follow these steps:

1. Create a new file called Lobby.dwg, using the Unit.dwg file as a prototype. (Open the Unit.dwg file, choose Save As from the Application menu, and enter **Lobby** for the new filename.)

2. Erase the entire unit (select the Erase tool from the Modify panel, and then type **All↵↵**).

3. Draw the three main rectangles that represent the outlines of the stair shaft, the elevator shaft, and the lobby.

4. To draw the stairs, copy or offset the stair shaft's left wall to the right a distance of 4″ (122 cm). This creates the first line representing the steps.

5. Array this line in one row of 10 columns, using an 11″ (28 cm) column offset.

6. Draw the center line dividing the two flights of stairs.

7. Draw the elevator, insert the door, and assign the door to the Door layer. Practice using construction lines here.

8. Draw the doorjambs. Edit the door openings to add the doorjambs and headers and add the interior walls to the stairwell.

9. Use the Base command to set the base point of the drawing. Your plan should resemble the one in Figure 6.33, step 4.

10. Save the Lobby.dwg file and close it.

**USING RAYS**

If you like the Construction Line tool but you would like to have one endpoint, you can use a ray (click Ray in the expanded Draw panel). A *ray* is like a line that starts from a point you select and continues off to an infinite distance. You specify the start point and angle of the ray. You can place a ray at the corner at a 45° angle and then fillet the ray to the horizontal wall line to shorten or lengthen the line to the appropriate length.

# Finding an Exact Distance along a Curve

To find an exact distance along a curve or to mark off specific distance increments along a curve, do the following:

1. With a file open, click the Point Style tool in the Home tab's expanded Utilities panel, or enter **ddptype**↵ to open the Point Style dialog box (Figure 6.34).

**FIGURE 6.34**
The Point Style
dialog box

2. Click the X icon in the top row. Also be sure the Set Size Relative To Screen radio button is selected. Then click OK.

   You can also set the point style by setting the Pdmode system variable to 3.

3. Click Measure from the expanded Draw panel, or type **ME**↵ (see Figure 6.35).

**FIGURE 6.35**
The Measure tool
on the expanded
Draw panel

Measure tool

---

### THE DIFFERENCE BETWEEN DIVIDE AND MEASURE

The Divide tool (Divide from the expanded Draw panel) marks off a line, an arc, or a curve into equal divisions as opposed to divisions of a length you specify. You might use Divide to divide an object into 12 equal segments, for example. Aside from this difference in function, Divide works exactly the same as Measure.

4. At the `Select object to measure:` prompt, click the end of the curve that you want to use as the starting point for your distance measurement.

5. At the `Specify length of segment or [Block]:` prompt, enter the distance you want. A series of Xs appears on the curve, marking off the specified distance along the curve. You can select the exact location of the Xs by using the Node osnap override (see Figure 6.36).

**FIGURE 6.36**

Finding an exact distance along a spline curve by using points and the Measure command

Distance found by the Measure command

Point entity

---

**USING BLOCKS INSTEAD OF POINTS**

With the Block option of the Measure command you can specify a block to be inserted at the specified segment length in place of point objects on the arc. You can align the block with the arc as it's inserted. Or you can use the Arraypath command described earlier in this chapter.

---

The Measure command also works on most objects, including arcs and polylines. You'll get a more detailed look at the Measure command in Chapter 18.

As you work with AutoCAD, you'll find that constructing temporary geometry will help you solve problems in new ways. Don't hesitate to experiment! Remember, you always have the Save and Undo commands to help you recover from mistakes.

---

**DIVIDE AND MEASURE AS AUTOLISP CUSTOMIZATION TOOLS**

Divide and Measure are great tools for gathering information about objects in a drawing. A colleague of ours found it to be an excellent way to find the length of a complex object while working on an AutoLISP® macro. In AutoLISP, you have to write some elaborate code just to find the length of a complex polyline. After struggling with his program code, our colleague realized that he could use the Measure command to mark off known distances along a polyline and then count the points to find the overall length of the polyline.

## Changing the Length of Objects

Suppose that, after finding the length of an arc, you realize you need to lengthen the arc by a specific amount. The Lengthen tool in the expanded Modify panel lets you lengthen or shorten arcs, lines, polylines, splines, and elliptical arcs. Here's how to lengthen an arc:

1. Select Lengthen from the expanded Modify panel, or type **LEN**↵.

2. At the Select an object or [DElta/Percent/Total/DYnamic]: prompt, type **T**↵, or select Total from the command line.

3. At the Specify total length or [Angle] <1.0000)>: prompt, enter the length you want for the arc.

4. At the Select an object to change or [Undo]: prompt, click the arc you want to change. Be sure to click at a point nearest the end you want to lengthen. The arc increases in length to the size you specified.

The Lengthen command also shortens an object if it's currently longer than the value you enter. In this short example, you've learned how to change an object to a specific length. You can use other criteria to change an object's length using these options available for the Lengthen command:

**Delta** Lengthens or shortens an object by a specific length. To specify an angle rather than a length, use the Angle suboption.

**Percent** Increases or decreases the length of an object by a percentage of its current length.

**Total** Specifies the total length or angle of an object.

**Dynamic** Lets you graphically change the length of an object using your cursor.

## Creating a New Drawing by Using Parts from Another Drawing

Next, we'll explain how to use the Export command. Export can be used to turn parts of a drawing into a separate file in a way similar to the Wblock command described in Chapter 4. Here you'll use the Export command to create a separate staircase drawing by using the staircase you've already drawn for the lobby.

Follow these steps:

1. If you closed the lobby drawing, open it now. If you didn't create the drawing, open the 06-Lobby.dwg (or 06-Lobby-metric.dwg) file.

2. Chose Export ➤ Other Formats from the Application menu, or type **export**↵ to open the Export Data dialog box.

3. Enter **stair.dwg** in the File Name text box, and click Save. By including the .dwg filename extension, you let AutoCAD know that you want to export to a drawing file and not a file in some other file format, such as DXF or WMF.

4. At the Enter name of existing block or [= (block=output file)/* (whole drawing)] <define new drawing>: prompt, press ↵. When you export to a DWG format, AutoCAD assumes you want to export a block. Bypassing this prompt by pressing

↵ tells AutoCAD that you want to create a file from part of the drawing rather than from a block.

5. At the `Specify insertion base point:` prompt, pick the lower-right corner of the stair shaft. This tells AutoCAD the base point for the new drawing.

6. At the `Select objects:` prompt, use a standard window (not a crossing window) to select the stair shaft, as shown in Figure 6.37.

**FIGURE 6.37**
A selection window enclosing the stair shaft

← Selection window

← Base point

7. When the stair shaft, including the door, is highlighted, press ↵ to confirm your selection. The stairs disappear.

8. Because you want the stairs to remain in the lobby drawing, click the Undo button to bring them back. Undo doesn't affect any files you might export by choosing Export ➢ Other Formats from the Application menu, by using Wblock, or by using the Block tool.

## Eliminating Unused Blocks, Layers, Linetypes, Shapes, Styles, and More

A template can contain blocks and layers you don't need in your new file. For example, the lobby you just completed contains the bathroom block because you used the Unit file as a prototype. Even though you erased this block, it remains in the drawing file's database. It's considered unused because it doesn't appear as part of the drawing. Such extra blocks can slow you down by increasing the amount of time needed to open the file. They also increase the size of your file unnecessarily. You can eliminate unused elements from a drawing by using the Purge command.

### SELECTIVELY REMOVING UNUSED ELEMENTS

You use the Purge command to remove unused individual blocks, layers, linetypes, shapes, text styles, and other drawing elements from a drawing file. To help keep the file size small and to make layer maintenance easier, you should purge your drawing of unused elements. Bear in mind, however, that the Purge command doesn't delete certain primary drawing elements— namely, layer 0, the Continuous linetype, and the Standard text style.

Use these steps to practice using the Purge command:

**1.** In the lobby drawing, choose Drawing Utilities ➢ Purge from the Application menu to open the Purge dialog box (see Figure 6.38). You'll see a listing of drawing components that can be purged. If the drawing contains any of the types of components listed, a plus sign appears to the left of the component name.

**FIGURE 6.38**

The Purge dialog box

**2.** Click the plus sign of the component you want to purge. In this exercise, click the plus sign next to the Blocks listing. The list expands to show the names of the items under the component category.

**3.** Select the name BATH from the expanded list. If you want to select more than one item, you can Ctrl+click individual names or Shift+click to select a group of names.

**4.** After the components are selected, click the Purge button in the lower-left corner of the dialog box. You then see a message box asking you to confirm that you want to purge the block.

**5.** Click Purge This Item and then click Close to close the Purge dialog box.

### REMOVING ALL UNUSED ELEMENTS

In the previous exercise, you selected a single block for removal from the lobby drawing. If you want to clear all the unused elements from a file at once, you can click the Purge All button at the bottom of the Purge dialog box (see Figure 6.38).

Here are the steps:

1. Choose Drawing Utilities ➢ Purge from the Application menu to open the Purge dialog box again.

2. Click the Purge Nested Items check box to turn on this option.

3. Click Purge All to open the Confirm Purge dialog box, which asks whether you want to purge a block.

4. Click Purge This Item. The Confirm Purge dialog box displays the name of another block, asking you to confirm the purge. You can continue to click Purge This Item, and AutoCAD will display the Confirm Purge dialog box for each unused element still in the drawing.

5. Click the Purge All Items option to purge everything at once. The Confirm Purge dialog box closes.

6. In the Purge dialog box, click Close.

7. Close and save the Lobby file, and exit AutoCAD.

The Lobby file is now trimmed down to the essential data it needs and nothing else. You may have noticed that when you returned to the Purge dialog box in step 6, the items in the list box no longer showed plus signs. This indicates that there are no longer any unused items in the drawing.

In this last exercise, you used the Purge Nested Items option at the bottom of the dialog box. The Purge Nested Items option automatically purges unused blocks, including those nested within other blocks. If this option isn't checked, you might have to repeat the Purge operation to remove all unused elements in a drawing.

---

#### PURGING ZERO-LENGTH GEOMETRY AND BLANK TEXT

At the very bottom of the Purge dialog box, you'll see the option Purge Zero-Length Geometry And Empty Text Objects. This has long been on the wish list of AutoCAD users, and it does just what it says: It purges objects that have no length as well as text objects that do not contain any text. They are offered in the Purge dialog box because they cannot be selected and deleted like normal AutoCAD objects.

## The Bottom Line

**Create and use templates.**   If you find that you're using the same settings when you create a new drawing file, you can set up an existing file the way you like and save it as a template. You can then use your saved template for any new drawings you create.

**Master It**   Describe the method for saving a file as a template.

**Copy an object multiple times.**   Many tools in AutoCAD allow you to create multiple copies. The Array command offers a way to create circular copies, row and column copies, and copies that follow a path.

**Master It**   What names are given to the three types of arrays offered in the Modify panel?

**Develop your drawing.**   When laying down simple line work, you'll use a few tools frequently. The exercises in the early part of this book showed you some of these commonly used tools.

**Master It**   What tool can you use to join two lines end to end?

**Find an exact distance along a curve.**   AutoCAD offers some tools that allow you to find an exact distance along a curve.

**Master It**   Name the two tools you can use to mark off exact distances along a curve.

**Change the length of objects.**   You can accurately adjust the length of a line or arc in AutoCAD using a single command.

**Master It**   What is the keyboard alias for the command that changes the length of objects?

**Create a new drawing by using parts from another drawing.**   You can save a lot of time by reusing parts of drawings. The Export command can help.

**Master It**   True or false: The Export command saves only blocks as drawing files.

# Chapter 7

# Mastering Viewing Tools, Hatches, and External References

Now that you've created drawings of a typical apartment unit and the apartment building's lobby and stairs, you can assemble them to complete the first floor of the apartment building. In this chapter, you'll take full advantage of the features of the AutoCAD® 2015 software to enhance your drawing skills and to reduce the time to create accurate drawings.

As your drawing becomes larger, you'll find that you need to use the Zoom and Pan commands more often. Larger drawings also require some special editing techniques. You'll learn how to assemble and view drawings in ways that will save you time and effort as your design progresses. Along the way, you'll see how you can enhance the appearance of your drawings by adding hatch patterns.

In this chapter, you will learn to

♦ Assemble the parts

♦ Take control of the AutoCAD display

♦ Use hatch patterns in your drawings

♦ Understand the boundary hatch options

♦ Use external references

## Assembling the Parts

One of the best timesaving features of AutoCAD is its ability to duplicate repetitive elements quickly in a drawing. In this section, you'll assemble the drawings you've been working on into the complete floor plan of a fictitious apartment project. Doing so will demonstrate how you can quickly and accurately copy your existing drawings in a variety of ways.

---

**DON'T SEE THE NAVIGATION BAR?**

In this chapter, you'll be asked to use the Zoom and Pan tools on the Navigation bar frequently. If you don't see it in the AutoCAD window, then go to the View tab's Windows panel, click the User Interface tool, and turn on the Navigation Bar option. Or, if you prefer, you can also find the Zoom and Pan tools in the View tab's Navigate 2D panel.

---

Start by creating a new file for the first floor:

1. Create a new file named Plan to contain the drawing of the apartment building's first floor. This is the file you'll use to assemble the unit plans into an apartment building. If you want to use a template file, use acad.dwt. Metric users can use the acadiso.dwt template file. (These are AutoCAD template files that appear in the Select Template dialog box when you choose New from the Quick Access toolbar.)

2. In the Length group of the Drawing Units dialog box, set the unit Type to Architectural (choose Drawing Utilities ➢ Units from the Application menu). Metric users can leave the Type as Decimal but change the insertion scale to centimeters.

3. Set up the drawing for a 1/8" = 1'-0" scale on a 24" by 18" drawing area. (You can use the Limits command for this.) Such a drawing requires an area 2,304 units wide by 1,728 units deep. Metric users should set up a drawing at 1:100 scale on an A2 sheet size. Your drawing area should be 5940 cm by 4200 cm.

4. Create a layer called **Plan1**, and make it the current layer.

5. Right-click the Snap Mode tool in the status bar and select Settings.

6. Set Snap Spacing to **1**.

7. Choose Zoom All from the Navigation bar or type **Z↵A↵** to get an overall view of the drawing area.

Now you're ready to start building a floor plan of the first floor from the unit plan you created in the previous chapter. You'll begin by creating a mirrored copy of the apartment plan:

1. Make sure the Object Snap tool is turned off, and then insert the 07a-unit.dwg drawing at coordinate 31'-5",43'-8". Metric users should insert the 07a-unit-metric.dwg drawing at coordinate 957,1330. If you don't already have them, you can download these and other exercise files for this book at www.sybex.com/go/masteringautocad2015.

2. Accept the Insert defaults. 07a-unit and 07a-unit-metric are the same drawings as the Unit.dwg file you were asked to create in earlier chapters.

   If you prefer, you can specify the insertion point in the Insert dialog box by removing the check mark from the Specify On-Screen check box. The input options in the Insertion Point group then become available to receive your input.

If you happen to insert a block in the wrong coordinate location, you can use the Properties palette to change the insertion point for the block.

Continue the drawing by making mirrored copies of the inserted plan:

1. Zoom into the apartment unit plan.

2. Click Mirror on the Home tab's Modify panel, select the unit plan, and press ↵.

3. At the Specify first point of the mirror line: prompt, Shift+right-click, and choose From.

4. Shift+right-click again, and choose Endpoint.

**5.** Select the endpoint of the upper-right corner of the apartment unit, as shown in Figure 7.1.

**FIGURE 7.1**
The unit plan mirrored

Select this corner in step 5
for the Mirror command.

**6.** Enter **@2.5<0**↵. Metric users should enter **@6.5<0**↵. A rubber-banding line appears, indicating the mirror axis.

**7.** Turn on the Ortho mode tool, and select any point to point the mirror axis in a vertical orientation. You can also hold down the Shift key as you make your point selection to turn on Ortho mode temporarily.

**8.** At the `Erase Source Objects? [Yes/No] <N>:` prompt, press ↵. You'll get a 5″ wall thickness between two studio units. Your drawing should be similar to the one shown in Figure 7.1.

You now have a mirror-image copy of the original plan in the exact location required for the overall plan. Next, make some additional copies for the opposite side of the building:

**1.** Press ↵ to reissue the Mirror command and select both units.

**2.** Use the From osnap option again, and using the Endpoint osnap, select the same corner you selected in step 5 of the previous exercise.

**3.** Enter **@24<90** to start a mirror axis 24″ directly above the selected point. Metric users should enter **@61<90**.

**4.** With Ortho mode on, select a point so that the mirror axis is exactly horizontal.

**5.** At the `Erase source objects? [Yes/No] <N>:` prompt, press ↵ to keep the two unit plans you selected in step 1 and complete the mirror operation.

With the tools you've learned about so far, you've quickly and accurately set up a fairly good portion of the floor plan. Continue with the next few steps to "rough in" the main components of the floor:

> Zoom Extents

1. Click Zoom Extents on the Navigation bar's Zoom flyout to get a view of the four plans, or you can type Z↵E↵. The Extents option forces the entire drawing to fill the screen at the center of the display area. Your drawing will look like Figure 7.2.

**FIGURE 7.2**
The unit plan, dupli-cated four times

2. Copy the four units to the right at a distance of 28'-10" (878 cm for metric users), which is the width of two units from center line to center line of the walls.

3. Insert the Lobby.dwg file from Chapter 6, "Editing and Reusing Data to Work Efficiently," at coordinate 89'-1",76'-1"(2713,2318 for metric users).

4. Copy all the unit plans to the right 74'-5" (2267 cm for metric users), the width of 4 units plus the width of the lobby.

> Zoom All

5. Click Zoom All on the Navigation bar's Zoom flyout or type Z↵A↵ to view the entire drawing, which should look like Figure 7.3.

6. Click Save on the Quick Access toolbar to save this Plan.dwg file.

## Taking Control of the AutoCAD Display

By now, you should be familiar with the Pan and Zoom functions in AutoCAD. Many other tools can also help you get around in your drawing. In the following sections, you'll get a closer look at the ways you can view your drawing.

### Understanding Regeneration and Redrawing

AutoCAD uses two commands for refreshing your drawing display: Regen (drawing regeneration) and Redraw. Each command serves a particular purpose, although it may not be clear to a new user.

**FIGURE 7.3**
The Plan drawing

To understand the difference between Regen and Redraw, keep in mind that AutoCAD stores drawing data in two ways:

♦ In a database of highly accurate coordinate information that is part of the properties of objects in your drawing

♦ In a simplified database used just for the display of the objects in your drawing

As you draw, AutoCAD starts to build an accurate, core database of objects and their properties. At the same time, it creates a simpler database that it uses just to display the drawing quickly. AutoCAD uses this second database to allow quick manipulation of the display of your drawing. For the purposes of this discussion, we'll call this simplified database the *virtual display* because it's like a computer model of the overall display of your drawing. This virtual display is, in turn, used as the basis for what is shown in the drawing area. When you issue a Redraw command, you're telling AutoCAD to reread this virtual display data and display that information in the drawing area. A Regen command, on the other hand, tells AutoCAD to rebuild the virtual display based on information from the core drawing database.

You may notice that the Pan Realtime and Zoom Realtime commands don't work beyond a certain area in the display. When you reach a point where these commands seem to stop working, you've come to the limits of the virtual display data. To go beyond these limits, AutoCAD must rebuild the virtual display data from the core data; in other words, it must regenerate the drawing. You can usually do this by zooming out to the extents of the drawing.

Sometimes, when you zoom in to a drawing, arcs and circles may appear to be faceted instead of smooth curves. This faceting is the result of the virtual display simplifying curves to conserve memory. You can force AutoCAD to display smoother curves by typing **RE↵**, which is the shortcut for the Regen command.

## Saving Views

Another way to control your views is by saving them. You might think of saving views as a way of creating a bookmark or a placeholder in your drawing.

## CREATING MULTIPLE VIEWS

So far, you've looked at ways that will help you get around in your drawing while using a single view window. You can also set up multiple views of your drawing, called *viewports*. With viewports, you can display more than one view of your drawing at one time in the AutoCAD drawing area. For example, one viewport can display a close-up of the bathroom, another viewport can display the overall plan view, and yet another can display the unit plan.

When viewports are combined with the Paper Space feature, you can plot multiple views of your drawing. Paper Space is a display mode that lets you arrange multiple views of a drawing. To find out more about viewports and Paper Space, see Chapter 15, "Laying Out Your Printer Output," and Chapter 22, "Editing and Visualizing 3D Solids."

## CONTROLLING DISPLAY SMOOTHNESS

As you work in AutoCAD, you may notice that linetypes sometimes appear continuous even when they're supposed to be dotted or dashed. You may also notice that arcs and circles occasionally appear to be segmented lines although they're always plotted as smooth curves. A command called Viewres controls how smoothly linetypes, arcs, and circles are displayed in an enlarged view. The lower the Viewres value, the fewer the segments and the faster the redraw and regeneration. However, a low Viewres value causes noncontinuous linetypes, such as dashes or center lines, to appear as though they're continuous, especially in drawings that cover very large areas (for example, civil site plans).

Finding a Viewres value that best suits the type of work you do will take some experimentation. The default Viewres setting is 1000. You can try increasing the value to improve the smoothness of arcs and see if a higher value works for you. Enter **Viewres**↵↵ at the Command prompt to change the value. If you work with complex drawings, you may want to keep the value at 1000 and then, when you zoom in close to a view, use the Regen command to display smooth arcs and complete linetypes.

For example, a few walls in the Plan drawing aren't complete. To add the lines, you'll need to zoom into the areas that need work, but these areas are spread out over the drawing. AutoCAD lets you save views of the areas in which you want to work and then jump from one saved view to another saved view. This technique is especially helpful when you know you'll often want to return to a specific area of your drawing.

You'll see how to save and recall views in the following set of exercises. Here's the first one:

1. Click the View Manager tool in the View tab's Views panel. If you don't see the Views panel, right-click in the View tab and select Show Panel ➢ Views. You can also type **V**↵ to open the View Manager dialog box (see Figure 7.4).

## MANAGING SAVED VIEWS

In the View Manager dialog box, you can call up an existing view (Set Current), create a new view (New), or get detailed information about a view. You can also select from a set of predefined views that include orthographic and isometric views of 3D objects. You'll learn more about these options in Chapter 20, "Creating 3D Drawings."

**FIGURE 7.4**
The View Manager
dialog box

2. Make sure the Current option is selected in the list to the left, and then click the New button to open the New View / Shot Properties dialog box (see Figure 7.5). You'll notice some options related to the User Coordinate System (UCS) plus an option called View Category. You'll get a chance to look at the UCS in Chapter 20 and Chapter 21, "Using Advanced 3D Features." The View Category option relates to the Sheet Set feature described in the bonus chapter "Keeping a Project Organized with Sheet Sets," available at www.omura.com/chapters. Other options, including Visual Style, Background, and Boundary, give you control over the appearance of the background and layout of a saved view. For now, you'll concentrate on creating a new view.

**FIGURE 7.5**
The New View /
Shot Properties
dialog box

3. Click the Define Window radio button. The dialog boxes momentarily disappear, and the Dynamic Input display turns on.

4. At the `Specify first corner:` prompt, click two points to place a selection window around the area that surrounds the elevator lobby, as shown in Figure 7.6. Notice that the display changes so that the nonshaded area shows the area you selected. If you aren't satisfied with the selection area, you can place another window in the view.

**FIGURE 7.6**

Select this area for your saved view.

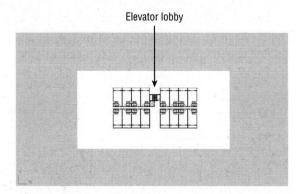

Elevator lobby

5. When you're satisfied with your selection, press ↵ or right-click. The dialog boxes reappear.

6. Click the View Name input box, and type **Elevator Lobby** for the name of the view you just defined.

7. Click the OK button. The New View / Shot Properties dialog box closes, and you see Elevator Lobby in the Views list.

8. Click OK to close the View Manager dialog box.

9. Let's see how to recall the view that you've saved. Type **V**↵ to open the View Manager, expand the Model Views option in the Views list, and select Elevator. Click Set Current and then click Apply and OK.

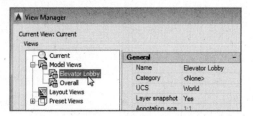

Your view changes to a close-up of the area you selected in step 4.

If you need to make adjustments to a view after you've created it, you can do so by following these steps: Right-click the view name in the View Manager dialog box, select Edit Boundaries, and then select a window as you did in steps 2 and 3.

---

**REPEAT THE LAST COMMAND**

Remember that when no command is active, you can right-click the Command window and then select Recent Commands to repeat a recently issued command. You can also right-click the drawing area when AutoCAD is idle and repeat the last command.

---

If you prefer, you can use the keyboard to invoke the View command and thus avoid all the dialog boxes:

1. Click Zoom Extents on the Navigation bar's Zoom flyout, or type Z↵E↵.

2. Enter **-View**↵**S**↵ at the Command prompt, or use the **-V**↵**S**↵ shortcut. (Remember to use the minus sign in front of *View* or *V*.)

3. At the Enter view name to save: prompt, enter **Overall**↵.

4. Save the Plan file.

As you can see, this is a quick way to save a view. With the name Overall assigned to this view, you can easily recall it at any time. (Choosing the Zoom All flyout option from the Navigation bar gives you an overall view too, but it may zoom out too far for some purposes, or it may not show what you consider an overall view.)

---

**OPENING A FILE TO A PARTICULAR VIEW**

The Select File dialog box contains a Select Initial View check box. If you open a drawing with this option selected, you're greeted with a Select Initial View dialog box just before the opened file appears on the screen. This dialog box lists any views saved in the file. You can then go directly to a view by double-clicking the view name. If you've saved views and you know the name of the view you want, using Select Initial View saves time when you're opening large files.

---

## Understanding the Frozen Layer Option

As mentioned earlier, you may want to turn off certain layers to plot a drawing containing only selected layers. But even when layers are turned off, AutoCAD still takes the time to redraw and regenerate them. The Layer Properties Manager offers the Freeze option; this acts like the Off option, except that Freeze causes AutoCAD to ignore frozen layers when redrawing and regenerating a drawing. By freezing layers that aren't needed for reference or editing, you can reduce the time AutoCAD takes to perform regens. You'll find this capability helpful when working with large files.

Be aware, however, that the Freeze option affects blocks in an unusual way. Try the following exercise to see firsthand how the Freeze option makes entire blocks disappear:

1. Close the Plan file, and open the 07b-plan.dwg file from the sample files. Metric users should open 07b-plan-metric.dwg. This file is similar to the Plan file you created but with a few walls and stairs added to finish off the exterior. Also note that the individual units are blocks named 07a-unit or 07a-unit-metric. This will be important in a later exercise.

2. Open the Layer Properties Manager dialog box, and then set the current layer to 0.

3. Click the yellow lightbulb icon in the Plan1 layer listing to turn off that layer. Nothing changes in your drawing. Even though you turned off the Plan1 layer, the layer on which the unit blocks were inserted, the unit blocks remain visible.

4. Right-click in the layer list, choose Select All from the context menu, and then click a lightbulb icon (not the one you clicked in step 3). You see a message warning you that the current layer will be turned off. Click Turn The Current Layer Off. Now everything is turned off, including objects contained in the unit blocks.

5. Right-click in the layer list, choose Select All from the context menu, and then click a lightbulb icon to turn all the layers back on.

6. Click the Plan1 layer to select it and then click its Freeze/Thaw icon. (You can't freeze the current layer.) The yellow sun icon changes to a gray snowflake, indicating that the layer is now frozen (see Figure 7.7). Only the unit blocks disappear.

**FIGURE 7.7**
Freezing the
Plan1 layer

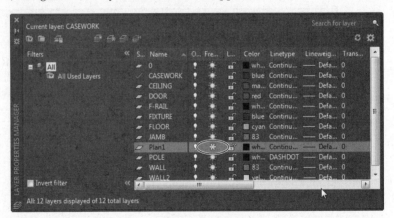

Even though none of the objects in the unit blocks were drawn on the Plan1 layer, the entire contents of the blocks assigned to the Plan1 layer are frozen when Plan1 is frozen. Another way to freeze and thaw individual layers is by clicking the Freeze/Thaw icon (which looks like a sun) in the layer drop-down list in the Home tab's Layers panel.

You don't really need the Plan1 layer frozen. You froze it to see the effects of Freeze on blocks. Do the following to turn Plan1 back on:

1. Thaw layer Plan1 by going back to the Layer Properties Manager and clicking the snowflake icon in the Plan1 layer listing.

2. Turn off the Ceiling layer. Exit the dialog box by clicking the X in the Layer Properties Manager's title bar.

The previous exercise showed the effect of freezing on blocks. When a block's layer is frozen, the entire block is made invisible regardless of the layer assignments of the objects contained in the block.

Keep in mind that when blocks are on layers that aren't frozen, the individual objects that are part of the block are still affected by the status of the layer to which they're assigned. This means that if some objects in a block are on a layer called Wall and the Wall layer is turned off or frozen, then those objects become invisible. Objects within the block that aren't on the layer that is off or frozen remain visible.

# Using Hatch Patterns in Your Drawings

To help communicate your ideas to others, you'll want to add graphic elements that represent types of materials, special regions, or textures. AutoCAD provides hatch patterns for quickly placing a texture over an area of your drawing. In the following sections, you'll add a hatch pattern to the floor of the studio apartment unit, thereby instantly enhancing the appearance of one drawing. In the process, you'll learn how to update all the units in the overall floor plan quickly to reflect the changes in the unit.

## Placing a Hatch Pattern in a Specific Area

It's always a good idea to provide a separate layer for hatch patterns. By doing so, you can turn them off if you need to. For example, the floor paving pattern might be displayed in one drawing but turned off in another so it won't distract from other information.

In the following exercises, you'll set up a layer for a hatch pattern representing floor tile and then add that pattern to your drawing. This will give you the opportunity to learn the different methods of creating and controlling hatch patterns.

Follow these steps to set up the layer:

1. Open the 07a-unit.dwg file. Metric users should open 07a-unit-metric.dwg. These files are similar to the Unit drawing you created in earlier chapters, and they are used to create the overall plan in the 07b-plan and 07b-plan-metric files. Remember that you also still have the 07b-plan or 07b-plan-metric file open.

2. Zoom into the bathroom and kitchen area.

3. Create a new layer called **FLR-PAT**.

4. Make FLR-PAT the current layer.

Now that you've set up the layer for the hatch pattern, you can place the pattern in the drawing:

1. Click the Hatch tool on the Home tab's Draw panel, or type **H↵**. The Hatch Creation Ribbon tab appears (see Figure 7.8).

**FIGURE 7.8**

The Hatch Creation
Ribbon tab

Select
Boundary Object —

Hatch Type —

Delete
Boundary Object —

Hatch Color —

Background Color —

Recreate
Boundary Object —

Transparency

Angle

Hatch Spacing/Hatch Pattern Scale

**2.** In the Pattern drop-down list box of the Properties panel, select User Defined. The User Defined option lets you define a simple crosshatch pattern by specifying the line spacing of the hatch and whether it's a single- or double-hatch pattern.

**3.** Click the Hatch Spacing text box in the lower-right corner of the Properties panel (see Figure 7.8), and enter **6** (metric users should enter **15**). This tells AutoCAD you want the hatch's line spacing to be 6″, or 15 cm. Leave the Hatch Angle value at 0 because you want the pattern to be aligned with the bathroom.

**4.** Expand the Properties panel, and click the Double button. This tells AutoCAD that you want the hatch pattern to run both vertically and horizontally.

**5.** Hover the cursor over different parts of the bathroom layout, but don't click anything. You will see a preview of your hatch pattern appear in each area over which you hover.

**6.** Click inside the area representing the bathroom floor. The hatch pattern is placed in the floor area. Notice that the area inside the door swing is not hatched. This is because the door swing area is not a contiguous part of the floor.

**7.** Click inside the door swing to place the hatch pattern.

**8.** Right-click and select Enter to exit the Hatch command, or press the Enter key.

---

### HATCHING AROUND TEXT

If you have text in the hatch boundary, AutoCAD will avoid hatching over it unless the Ignore option is selected in the Island Display Style options of the Advanced Hatch settings. See the section "Using Additional Hatch Features" later in this chapter for more on the Ignore setting.

---

As you saw from the exercise, AutoCAD gives you a preview of your hatch pattern before you place it in the drawing. In the previous steps, you set up the hatch pattern first by selecting the User Defined option, but you can reverse the order if you like. You can click in the areas you want to hatch first and then select a pattern, adjust the scale, and apply other hatch options.

**NOTE** Also note that in step 3, you are asked to change the Hatch Spacing setting. The name of this setting changes from Hatch Spacing to Hatch Pattern Scale when you use a predefined pattern instead of a user-defined one.

---

### MATCHING PATTERNS

Say you want to add a hatch pattern that you've previously inserted in another part of the drawing. With the Match Properties tool in the Options panel of the Hatch Creation tab, you can select a previously inserted hatch pattern as a prototype for the current hatch pattern. However, this feature doesn't work with exploded hatch patterns.

---

## Adding Predefined Hatch Patterns

In the previous exercise, you used the User Defined option to create a simple crosshatch pattern. You also have a number of other predefined hatch patterns from which to choose. You can find other hatch patterns on the Internet, and if you can't find the pattern you want, you can create your own (see Chapter 24, "Customizing Toolbars, Menus, Linetypes, and Hatch Patterns").

Try the following exercise to see how you can add one of the predefined patterns available in AutoCAD:

**1.** Pan your view so that you can see the area below the kitchenette. Using the Rectangle tool in the Draw panel, draw the 3′-0″ by 8′-0″ outline of the floor tile area, as shown in Figure 7.9. Metric users should create a rectangle that is 91 cm by 228 cm. You can also use a closed polyline.

**FIGURE 7.9**
The area below the kitchen, showing the outline of the floor tile area

Outline of floor tile area

2. Click the Hatch tool in the Draw panel.

3. In the Properties panel of the Hatch Creation Ribbon tab, select the Pattern option in the Hatch Type drop-down list.

4. Click the Hatch Pattern tool in the Pattern panel. (If you don't see the Hatch Pattern tool, skip to step 6.) A flyout appears that displays a selection of hatch patterns (see Figure 7.10). This list has a scroll bar to the right that lets you view additional patterns.

**FIGURE 7.10**
The Hatch Pattern flyout (left) and the Hatch Pattern panel in a full-screen AutoCAD window (right)

Hatch pattern tool

Scroll through the patterns using the arrows.

Click this arrow to open the panel to show more of the patterns.

5. Scroll down the flyout, and locate and select AR-PARQ1 (see Figure 7.10).

6. If you didn't see the Hatch Pattern tool in step 4, scroll through the patterns in the Pattern panel using the down arrow to the right of the panel to locate and select the AR-PARQ1 pattern. You can also expand the list by clicking the arrowhead below the scroll arrows (see Figure 7.10).

7. Click inside the rectangle you just drew.

8. Right-click and select Enter, or press the Enter key.

The predefined patterns with the *AR* prefix are architectural patterns that are drawn to full scale. In general, you should leave their Hatch Pattern Scale settings at 1. You can adjust the scale after you place the hatch pattern by using the Properties palette, as described later in this chapter.

CERT OBJECTIVE

### Adding Solid Fills

You can use the Solid option from the Hatch Type drop-down list in the Hatch Creation tab's Properties panel to create solid fills. The Hatch Color drop-down list lets you set the color of your solid fill. Remember that you can drag and drop solid fills and hatch patterns from the tool palettes you saw in Chapter 1, "Exploring the Interface."

## Positioning Hatch Patterns Accurately

If you've ever laid tile in a bathroom, you know that you have to select the starting point for your tiles carefully in order to get them to fit in an area with pleasing results. If you need to fine-tune the position of a hatch pattern within an enclosed area, you can do so by using the options in the Origin panel of the Hatch Creation tab.

The main tool in the panel, Set Origin, lets you select an origin point for your hatch pattern. You can also use the Hporigin system variable to accomplish this. Or you can expand the Origin panel for a set of predefined origin locations. These locations are Bottom Left, Bottom Right, Top Left, Top Right, Center, and Use Current Origin. The Use Current Origin option refers to the X,Y origin of the drawing.

If you are hatching an irregular shape, these origin locations are applied to the *boundary extents* of the shape. An imaginary rectangle represents the outermost boundary, or the boundary extents of the shape, as shown in Figure 7.11.

**FIGURE 7.11**
The origin options shown in relation to the boundary extents of an irregular shape

The boundary extents and a sample hatch pattern

The Store As Default Origin option lets you save your selected origin as the default origin for future hatch patterns in the current drawing.

Now that you've learned how to add a hatch pattern, let's continue with a look at how your newly edited plan can be used. In the next exercise, you'll use this updated 07a-unit file to update all the units in the Plan file.

## Updating a Block from an External File

As you progress through a design project, you make countless revisions. With traditional drafting methods, revising a drawing, such as the studio apartment floor plan, takes a good deal of time. If you changed the bathroom layout, for example, you would have to erase every occurrence of the bathroom and redraw it 16 times. With AutoCAD, revising this drawing can be a quick operation. You can update the studio unit you just modified throughout the overall Plan drawing by replacing the current Unit block with the updated Unit file. AutoCAD can update all occurrences of the Unit block. The following exercise shows how this is accomplished.

For this exercise, remember that the blocks representing the units in the 07b-plan and 07b-plan-metric files are named 07a-unit and 07a-unit-metric:

1. Make sure you've saved the 07a-unit (07a-unit-metric for metric users) file with the changes, and then return to the 07b-plan file that is still open. Click the Open Documents tool from the Application menu, and then select 07b-plan.dwg. Metric users should use 07b-plan-metric.dwg.

**YOU CAN'T UPDATE EXPLODED BLOCKS**

Exploded blocks won't be updated when you update blocks from an external file. If you plan to use this method to update parts of a drawing, don't explode the blocks you plan to update. See Chapter 4, "Organizing Objects with Blocks and Groups."

**2.** Click the Insert tool on the Home tab's Block panel and select More Options to open the Insert dialog box.

**3.** Click the Browse button. In the Select Drawing File dialog box, double-click the 07a-unit filename (07a-unit-metric for metric users).

**4.** Click OK in the Insert dialog box. A warning message tells you that a block already exists with the same name as the file. You can cancel the operation or redefine the block in the current drawing.

**5.** Click Redefine Block. The drawing regenerates.

**6.** At the Specify insertion point or [Basepoint/Scale/X/Y/Z/Rotate]: prompt, press the Esc key. You do this because you don't want to insert the 07a-unit file into your drawing; you're just using the Insert feature to update an existing block.

**7.** Zoom into one of the units. The floor tile appears in all the units as you drew it in the Unit file (see Figure 7.12).

**FIGURE 7.12**
The Plan drawing with the tile pattern

Nested blocks must be updated independently of the parent block. For example, if you modified the Toilet block while editing the 07a-unit file and then updated the 07a-unit drawing in the 07b-plan file, the old Toilet block wouldn't be updated. Even though the toilet is part of the 07a-unit file, it's still a unique, independent block in the Plan file, and AutoCAD won't modify it unless specifically instructed to do so. In this situation, you must edit the original Toilet block and then update it in both the Plan and Unit files.

**SUBSTITUTING BLOCKS**

In the exercise in "Updating a Block from an External File," you updated a block in your `Plan` file by using the Browse option in the Insert dialog box. In that exercise, the block name and the filename were the same. You can also replace a block with another block or a file of a different name. Here's how to do it:

1. Open the Insert dialog box.

2. Click the Browse button next to the Name input box, locate and select the file you want to use as a substitute, and then click Open to return to the Insert dialog box.

3. Change the name in the Name input box to the name of the block you want replaced.

4. Click OK. A warning message appears, telling you that a block with this name already exists. Click OK to proceed with the block substitution.

Another method is to **-Insert**↵. (Don't forget the minus sign in front of *Insert*.) At the `Enter Block name or [?]:` prompt, enter the block name followed by an equal sign (=), and then enter the name of the new block or the filename. Don't include spaces between the name and the equal sign.

You can use this method of replacing blocks if you want to see how changing one element of your project can change your design. You might, for example, draw three different apartment unit plans and give each plan a unique name. You could then generate and plot three apartment building designs in a fraction of the time it would take you to do so by hand.

Also, block references and layer settings of the current file take priority over those of the imported file. For example, if a file to be imported has layers of the same name as the layers in the current file but those layers have color and linetype assignments that are different from those in the current file, the current file's layer color and linetype assignments determine those of the imported file. This doesn't mean, however, that the imported file on disk is changed; only the insertion in the active drawing is affected.

## Changing the Hatch Area

You may have noticed the Associative option in the Hatch Creation tab's Options panel. When this option is turned on, AutoCAD creates an associative hatch pattern. *Associative* hatches adjust their shapes to any changes in their associated boundary, hence the name. The following exercise demonstrates how this works.

Suppose you want to enlarge the tiled area of the kitchen by one tile. Here's how it's done:

1. Click the 07a-unit Drawing tab to switch to that drawing.

2. Click the outline border of the hatch pattern you created earlier. Notice the grips that appear around the hatch-pattern area.

3. Shift+click the grip in the lower-left corner of the hatch area.

4. With the lower-left grip highlighted, Shift+click the lower-right grip.

5. Click the lower-right grip again, but don't Shift+click this time.

---

### SELECTING HATCH GRIPS

If the boundary of the hatch pattern consists of line segments, you can use a crossing window or polygon-crossing window to select the corner grips of the hatch pattern.

---

6. Enter @12<–90↵↵ (@30<–90 for metric users) to widen the hatch pattern by 1′, or 30 cm for metric users. The hatch pattern adjusts to the new size of the hatch boundary.

7. Press the Esc key twice to clear any grip selections.

8. Choose Save from the Quick Access toolbar to save the Unit file.

9. Return to the 07b-plan file using the drawing tab, and repeat the steps in the section "Updating a Block from an External File" earlier in this chapter to update the units again.

The Associative feature of hatch patterns can save time when you need to modify your drawing, but you need to be aware of its limitations. A hatch pattern can lose its associativity when you do any of the following:

◆ Erase or explode a hatch boundary

◆ Erase or explode a block that forms part of the boundary

◆ Move a hatch pattern away from its boundary

These situations frequently arise when you edit an unfamiliar drawing. Often, boundary objects are placed on a layer that is off or frozen, so the boundary objects aren't visible. Also, the hatch pattern might be on a layer that is turned off and you proceed to edit the file not knowing that a hatch pattern exists. When you encounter such a file, take a moment to check for hatch boundaries so you can deal with them properly.

## Modifying a Hatch Pattern

**CERT OBJECTIVE**

Like everything else in a project, a hatch pattern may eventually need to be changed in some way. Hatch patterns are like blocks in that they act like single objects. You can explode a hatch pattern to edit its individual lines. The Properties palette contains most of the settings you'll need to make changes to your hatch patterns. But the most direct way to edit a hatch pattern is to use the Hatch Editor Ribbon tab.

### EDITING HATCH PATTERNS FROM THE HATCH EDITOR TAB

Follow these steps to modify a hatch pattern by using the Hatch Editor Ribbon tab:

1. Return to the Unit drawing.

2. Press the Esc key to clear any grip selections that may be active from earlier exercises.

3. Click the hatch pattern in the kitchen to open the Hatch Editor Ribbon tab. It's the same as the Hatch Creation Ribbon tab.

**A Double-Click Opens the Properties Palette**

Clicking on a hatch pattern opens a Ribbon tab in which you can edit the pattern using the same tools you used to create it. If you prefer, you can right-click and select Properties to access the Properties palette.

4. In the Pattern panel, locate and click the pattern named AR-BRSTD. It's the pattern that looks like a brick wall.

5. Press the Esc key to clear your selection of the hatch pattern. The AR-BRSTD pattern appears in place of the original parquet pattern.

6. Save and exit your file.

In this exercise, you were able to change the hatch just by clicking it. Although you changed only the pattern type, other options are available. You can, for example, modify a predefined pattern to a user-defined one by selecting User Defined from the Hatch Type drop-down list in the Properties panel of the Hatch Editor tab.

You can then enter angle and scale values for your hatch pattern in the options provided in the Properties panel of the Hatch Editor tab.

The other items in the Hatch Editor Ribbon tab are duplicates of the options in the Hatch Creation tab. They let you modify the individual properties of the selected hatch pattern. The upcoming section, "Understanding the Boundary Hatch Options," describes these other properties in detail.

### Editing Hatch Patterns from the Properties Palette

If you prefer, you can use the older method to edit a hatch pattern. To open the Properties palette, select and right-click the hatch pattern you want to edit and then select Properties. The Properties palette displays a Pattern category, which offers a Pattern Name option (see Figure 7.13). The actual pattern name appears to the right of the option.

When you click this option, an ellipsis button appears, enabling you to open the Hatch Pattern Palette dialog box (see Figure 7.14). You can then select a new pattern from the dialog box. The Type option in the Properties palette lets you change the type of hatch pattern from Predefined to User Defined or Custom.

**FIGURE 7.13**
The Pattern
category in the
Properties palette

**FIGURE 7.14**
The Hatch Pattern
Palette dialog box

# Understanding the Boundary Hatch Options

The Hatch Creation and Hatch Editor Ribbon panels offer many other options that you didn't explore in the previous exercises. For example, instead of clicking in the area to be hatched, you can select the objects that bound the area you want to hatch by clicking the Select Boundary Objects tool in the Boundaries panel. You can use the Select Boundary Objects tool to add boundaries to existing hatch patterns as well.

## Controlling Boundaries with the Boundaries Panel

The previous exercises in this chapter have just touched on the tools in the Boundaries panel. Other options in the Boundaries panel are Pick Points, Select Boundary Objects, Remove Boundary Objects, and Recreate Boundary.

**Pick Points**   Lets you place a hatch pattern across several enclosed areas by clicking inside the areas. This is the default selection mode.

**Select Boundary Objects**   Lets you select objects to define a hatch boundary.

**Remove Boundary Objects**   Lets you remove a bounded area, or *island*, in the area to be hatched. An example is the toilet seat in the bathroom. This option is available only when you select a hatch area by using the Pick Points option and an island has been detected.

**Recreate Boundary**   Draws a region or polyline around the current hatch pattern. You're then prompted to choose between a region and a polyline and to specify whether to reassociate the pattern with the re-created boundary. (See the Associative Boundary option discussed in a moment.)

## Fine-Tuning the Boundary Behavior

The Boundary Hatch feature is view dependent; that is, it locates boundaries based on what is visible in the current view. If the current view contains a lot of graphic data, AutoCAD can have difficulty finding a boundary or can be slow in finding a boundary. If you run into this problem, or if you want to single out a specific object for a point selection boundary, you can further limit the area that AutoCAD uses to locate hatch boundaries by using the Boundary Set options found in the expanded Boundaries panel:

**Display Boundary Objects**   Highlights the objects that have been selected as the hatch boundary by AutoCAD.

**Don't Retain/Retain Boundary Objects**   Retains outlines used to create the hatch pattern, a capability that can be helpful if you want to duplicate the shape of the boundary for other purposes. Typically this option is set to Don't Retain Boundaries, but you can use two other settings: Retain Boundaries – Polyline and Retain Boundaries – Regions.

**Select New Boundary Set**   Lets you select the objects you want AutoCAD to use to determine the hatch boundary instead of searching the entire view. The screen clears and lets you select objects. This option discards previous boundary sets. It's useful for hatching areas in a drawing that contains many objects that you don't want to include in the hatch boundary.

**Use Current Viewport**   Uses the current viewport extents to define the boundary set.

The Boundary Set options give you more control over the way a point selection boundary is created. These options have no effect when you use the Select Boundary Objects button to select specific objects for the hatch boundary.

---

**BOUNDARY RETENTION**

The Hatch command can also create an outline of the hatch area by using one of two objects: 2D regions, which are like 2D planes, or polyline outlines. Hatch creates such a polyline boundary temporarily to establish the hatch area. These boundaries are automatically removed after the hatch pattern is inserted. If you want to retain the boundaries in the drawing, make sure the Retain Boundaries – Polyline option is selected. Retaining the boundary can be useful if you know you'll be hatching the area more than once or if you're hatching a fairly complex area.

Retaining a hatch boundary is useful if you want to know the hatched area's dimensions in square inches or feet because you can find the area of a closed polyline by using the List command. See Chapter 2, "Creating Your First Drawing," for more on the List command.

---

## Controlling Hatch Behavior with the Options Panel

The Options panel offers a set of tools that control some additional features of the Hatch command. These features affect the way a hatch pattern fills a boundary area as well as how it behaves when the drawing is edited. Note that the Gap Tolerance, Create Separate Hatches, Normal Island Detection, and Send Behind Boundary options are on the expanded Options panel. The following gives you a brief description of each of the Options panel's options:

**Associative Boundaries**   Allows the hatch pattern to adjust to changes in its boundary. With this option turned on, any changes to the associated boundary of a hatch pattern cause the hatch pattern to flow with the changes in the boundary.

**Annotative Scale**   Allows the hatch pattern to adjust to different scale views of your drawing. With this option turned on, a hatch pattern's size or spacing adjusts to the annotation scale of a viewport layout or Model Space view. See Chapter 4 for more on the annotation scale.

**Match Properties**   This group allows you to use an existing hatch pattern when inserting additional hatch patterns into a drawing. Select Use Current Origin when you want to use the current default hatch origin. Select Use Source Hatch Origin when you want to use the origin from the existing hatch pattern.

**Gap Tolerance**   Lets you hatch an area that isn't completely enclosed. The Gap Tolerance value sets the maximum gap size in the perimeter of an area you want to hatch. You can use a value from 0 to 5000.

**Create Separate Hatches**   Creates separate and distinct hatches if you select several enclosed areas while selecting hatch areas. With this option off, separate hatch areas behave as a single hatch pattern.

**Normal Island Detection (Island Detection Options)**   Controls how islands within a hatch area are treated. Islands are enclosed areas that are completely inside a hatch boundary. There are four options in this list:

> **Normal Island Detection**   This causes the hatch pattern to alternate between nested boundaries. The outer boundary is hatched; if there is a closed object within the boundary, it isn't hatched. If *another* closed object is inside the first closed object, *that* object is hatched. This is the default setting.

**Outer Island Detection**    This applies the hatch pattern to an area defined by the outermost boundary and a closed object within that boundary. Any boundaries nested in that closed object are ignored.

**Ignore Island Detection**    This supplies the hatch pattern to the entire area within the outermost boundary, ignoring any nested boundaries.

**No Island Detection**    This turns off island detection. This option is not available if you have already added a hatch pattern to your drawing.

**Send Behind Boundary (Draw Order)**    Allows you to specify whether the hatch pattern appears on top of or underneath its boundary. This is useful when the boundary is of a different color or shade and must read clearly or when the hatch pattern must cover the boundary. The options in this list are self-explanatory and are Do Not Assign/Do Not Change, Send To Back, Bring To Front, Send Behind Boundary, and Bring In Front Of Boundary. See "Overlapping Objects with Draw Order" later in this chapter.

## Controlling Hatch Default Layer, Layout Scale, and ISO Line Weight

The expanded Properties panel contains a few items that you'll want to be aware of as you become more familiar with AutoCAD. You've already seen how the Double option works when you are creating user-defined hatch patterns. The following list describes several other options that are available:

**Hatch Layer Override**    Allows you to select the default layer for hatch patterns. Select a layer name from the drop-down list. New hatch patterns you add to the drawing will be placed on the selected layer instead of the current one.

**Relative To Paper Space**    Allows you to change a hatch pattern's scale to one that is relevant to the current Paper Space view. This option is available only while you are in a layout tab and when you're using a pattern that is not user defined.

**ISO Pen Width**    Allows you to select an ISO pen width for the lines of a hatch pattern. This option is available only when you are using ISO patterns.

---

### ANNOTATIVE HATCH PATTERNS

In Chapter 4, you learned about a feature called the *annotation scale*. With this tool, you can assign several scales to certain types of objects and AutoCAD displays the object to the proper scale of the drawing. You can take advantage of this feature to allow hatch patterns to adjust their spacing or pattern size to the scale of your drawing. The Annotative option in the Options panel of the Hatch Creation Ribbon tab turns on the annotation scale feature for hatch patterns. Once this capability is turned on for a hatch pattern, you can set up the drawing scales that you want to apply to the hatch pattern using the same methods described for blocks in Chapter 4.

---

## Using Additional Hatch Features

The Hatch command has a fair amount of "intelligence." As you saw in an earlier exercise, it was able to detect not only the outline of the floor area but also the outline of the toilet seat that represents an island in the pattern area. If you prefer, you can control how AutoCAD treats these island conditions and other situations by selecting options available in the Hatch Creation and Hatch Editor Ribbon tab. You can also create and edit hatch patterns using the Hatch And Gradient dialog box (see Figure 7.15), which should be familiar to anyone who has used AutoCAD before.

**FIGURE 7.15**

The expanded Hatch And Gradient dialog box

To open the Hatch And Gradient dialog box, start the Hatch command by clicking the Hatch tool in the Home tab's Draw panel, and then click the Hatch Settings tool in the right side of the Options panel title bar. This opens the Hatch And Gradient dialog. Click the More Options button in the lower-right corner of this dialog box.

This button expands the dialog box to show additional hatch options (Figure 7.15).

Nearly all of the settings and tools in the Hatch And Gradient dialog box are repeated in the Hatch Creation and Hatch Editor Ribbon tabs. They are just presented in a different way.

---

### HATCH BOUNDARIES WITHOUT THE HATCH PATTERN

The Boundary command creates a polyline outline or region in a selected area. It works much like the Retain Boundary – Polyline option but doesn't add a hatch pattern.

## Using Gradient Shading

CERT
OBJECTIVE

You may have noticed Solid and Gradient options in the Pattern drop-down list. The solid hatch pattern lets you apply a solid color instead of a pattern to a bounded area. AutoCAD also offers a set of gradient patterns that let you apply a color gradient to an area.

You can apply a gradient to an area using the same method you used to apply a hatch pattern, but when you select the Gradient option, you'll see a slight change in the Hatch Creation tab panels. The Hatch Pattern Scale input box in the Properties panel changes to a Tint slider, and the Pattern panel changes to show a set of different gradient patterns. The Origin panel also changes to show Centered as the only option (see Figure 7.16). The Hatch Color and Background Color options in the Properties panel change to Gradient Color 1 and Gradient Color 2, enabling you to set the gradient colors.

**FIGURE 7.16**
The Gradient Shading feature

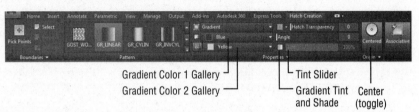

Instead of offering hatch patterns, the Pattern panel offers a variety of gradient patterns. If you don't see the gradient patterns, you can click the Hatch Pattern tool to open a flyout of the gradient patterns. The Properties panel lets you control the colors of the gradient. You can select the colors from the two-color drop-down lists in the Properties panel.

If you don't see a color you want, you can click the Select Colors option at the bottom of the list to open the Select Color dialog box. This dialog box lets you choose from Index, True Color, or Color Books colors (see Figure 7.17).

The Gradient Tint And Shade slider just to the right of the color drop-down lists lets you control the shade of the single-color gradient.

### CHOOSING BETWEEN A SINGLE COLOR OR TWO COLORS

You can choose a gradient that transitions between shades of a single color by clicking the Gradient Tint And Shade tool in the Properties panel just to the left of the Tint slider. This turns on the Gradient Tint And Shade slider and disables the Color 2 drop-down list. When you turn off the Gradient Tint And Shade button, the Gradient Tint slider is disabled and the Gradient Color 2 drop-down list is enabled.

**FIGURE 7.17**
The True Color options in the Select Color dialog box

### SELECTING GRADIENT PATTERNS

As mentioned earlier, you can choose from a set of gradient patterns in the Pattern panel. The Angle slider gives you further control over the gradient pattern by allowing you to rotate the angle of the pattern. The Centered option in the Origin panel places the center of the gradient at the center of the area selected for the pattern. This option is a toggle that is either on or off.

To place a gradient pattern, select a set of objects or a point in a bounded area, just as you would for a hatch pattern.

## Tips for Using Hatch

Here are a few tips for using the Hatch feature:

◆ Watch out for boundary areas that are part of a large block. AutoCAD examines the entire block when defining boundaries. This can take time if the block is large. Use the Specify Boundary Set option to focus on the set of objects you want AutoCAD to use for your hatch boundary.

◆ The Hatch feature is view dependent; that is, it locates boundaries based on what is visible in the current view. To ensure that AutoCAD finds every detail, zoom into the area to be hatched.

◆ If the area to be hatched is large yet requires fine detail, first outline the hatch area by using a polyline. (See Chapter 18, "Drawing Curves," for more on polylines.) Then use the Select Boundary Objects option in the Hatch Creation tab's Boundaries panel to select the polyline boundary manually instead of depending on Hatch to find the boundary for you.

◆ Consider turning off layers that might interfere with the ability of AutoCAD to find a boundary.

◆ Hatch works on nested blocks as long as the nested block entities are parallel to the current User Coordinate System. You'll learn more about the User Coordinate System in Chapter 20 and Chapter 21.

## Space Planning and Hatch Patterns

Suppose you're working on a plan in which you're constantly repositioning equipment and furniture, or you're in the process of designing the floor covering. You might be a little hesitant to place a hatch pattern on the floor because you don't want to have to rehatch the area each time you move a piece of equipment or change the flooring. You have two options in this situation: You can use the Hatch feature's associative capabilities to include the furnishings in the boundary set, or you can use the Display Order feature.

### USING ASSOCIATIVE HATCH

Associative Hatch is the most straightforward method. Make sure the Associative option is selected in the Hatch Creation tab's Options panel, and include your equipment or furniture in the boundary set. You can do this by using the Select option in the Boundaries panel.

After the pattern is in place, the hatch pattern automatically adjusts to its new location when you move the furnishings in your drawing. One drawback, however, is that AutoCAD attempts to hatch the interior of your furnishings if they cross the outer boundary of the hatch pattern. Also, if any boundary objects are erased or exploded, the hatch pattern no longer follows the location of your furnishings. To avoid these problems, you can use the method described in the next section, "Overlapping Objects with Draw Order."

### OVERLAPPING OBJECTS WITH DRAW ORDER

The Draw Order feature lets you determine how objects overlap. In the space-planning example, you can create furniture by using a solid hatch to indicate horizontal surfaces (see Figure 7.18).

**FIGURE 7.18**
Using Draw Order to create an overlapping effect over a hatch pattern

Draw an outline of the furniture or equipment; then use the Hatch tool to fill the outline with a Solid hatch pattern.

In the Hatch And Gradient dialog box, make sure that Send Behind Boundary is selected in the Draw Order drop-down list before you add the hatch pattern.

Place the drawing of the equipment on the floor pattern; then click the Send To Back tool from the Draworder flyout on the Home tab's Modify panel.

The equipment will appear to sit on top of the floor pattern.

## MATCHING A HATCH PATTERN AND OTHER PROPERTIES QUICKLY

Another tool to help you edit hatch patterns is Match Properties, which is similar to Format Painter in the Microsoft Office system. This tool lets you change an existing hatch pattern to match another existing hatch pattern. Here's how to use it:

**1.** Choose Match Properties from the Home tab's Clipboard panel or type **Matchprop**↵.

**2.** Click the source hatch pattern you want to copy.

**3.** Click the target hatch pattern you want to change. The target pattern changes to match the source pattern.

The Match Properties tool transfers other properties as well, such as layer, color, and linetype settings. You can select the properties that are transferred by opening the Property Settings dialog box.

To open this dialog box, type **S**↵ after selecting the object in step 2, or right-click and choose Settings from the context menu. You can then select the properties you want to transfer from the options shown. All the properties are selected by default. You can also transfer text and dimension style settings. You'll learn more about text and dimension styles in Chapter 9, "Adding Text to Drawings," and Chapter 11, "Using Dimensions."

You can then place the furniture on top of a floor-covering pattern and the pattern will be covered and hidden by the furniture. Here's how to do that. (These steps aren't part of the regular exercises of this chapter. They're shown here as general guidelines when you need to use the Draw Order feature.)

**1.** Draw the equipment outline, and make sure the outline is a closed polygon.

**2.** Start the Hatch tool described earlier in this chapter, and place a solid hatch pattern inside the equipment outline.

**3.** In the Hatch Creation tab's expanded Options panel, make sure Send To Back is selected in the Draw Order drop-down list.

**4.** Turn the outline and solid hatch into a block, or use the Group command to group them.

**5.** Move your equipment drawing into place over the floor pattern.

**6.** Click on the floor hatch pattern and then, in the Hatch Editor tab's expanded Options panel, select Send To Back from the Draw Order drop-down list.

After you take these steps, the equipment will appear to rest on top of the pattern. (See the bottom panel in Figure 7.18.) You can also change the display order of objects relative to other objects in the drawing using the Draworder flyout in the Home tab's Modify panel.

The Draworder options are all part of the Draworder command. As an alternative to using the Ribbon, you can type **Draworder.⏎** at the Command prompt, select an object, and then enter an option at the prompt:

```
Enter object ordering option
[Above objects/Under objects/Front/Back] <Back>:
```

For example, the equivalent of choosing the Send To Back tool from the Draworder flyout is entering **Draworder.⏎B.⏎**. You can also select the object you want to edit, right-click, and then choose Draw Order from the context menu.

You've now had a detailed look at hatch patterns and fills. Remember that you can also use the tool palettes to help organize and simplify access to your favorite hatch patterns, or you can use the patterns already available in the tool palettes. The patterns in the tool palettes can be edited and manipulated in the same way as described in this chapter. If you want to know how to make full use of the tool palettes, check out the discussion on the AutoCAD DesignCenter™ in Chapter 25, "Managing and Sharing Your Drawings."

---

**TAKE A BREAK**

If you're working through the tutorial in this chapter, this would be a good place to take a break or stop. You can pick up the next exercise in the section "Attaching a Drawing as an External Reference" at another time.

---

# Using External References

CERT OBJECTIVE

AutoCAD allows you to import drawings in a way that keeps the imported drawing independent from the current one. A drawing imported in this way is called an *external reference (Xref)*. Unlike drawings that have been imported as blocks, Xref files don't become part of the drawing's database. Instead, they're loaded along with the current file at startup time. It's as if AutoCAD were opening several drawings at once: the currently active file you specify when you start AutoCAD and any file inserted as an Xref.

If you keep Xref files independent from the current file, any changes you make to the Xref automatically appear in the current file. You don't have to update the Xref file manually as you do blocks. For example, if you use an Xref to insert the Unit file into the Plan file and you later make changes to the Unit file, you will see the new version of the Unit file in place of the old the next time you open the Plan file. If the Plan file was still open while edits were made, AutoCAD will notify you that a change has been made to an Xref.

---

### BLOCKS AND XREFS CAN'T HAVE THE SAME NAME

You can't use a file as an Xref if the file has the same name as a block in the current drawing. If this situation occurs but you still need to use the file as an Xref, you can rename the block of the same name by using the Rename command. You can also use Rename to change the name of various objects and named elements.

---

Another advantage of Xref files is that, because they don't become part of a drawing's database, drawing size is kept to a minimum. This results in more efficient use of your hard disk space.

Xref files, like blocks, can be edited only by using special tools. You can, however, use osnaps to snap to a location in an Xref file, or you can freeze or turn off the Xref file's insertion layer to make it invisible.

## Attaching a Drawing as an External Reference

The next exercise shows how to use an Xref in place of an inserted block to construct the studio apartment building. You'll first create a new unit file by copying the old one. Then you'll bring a new feature, the External References palette, to the screen. Follow these steps to create the new file:

1. Use the Drawing tab at the top of the drawing area to return to the 07a-unit file.

2. Choose Save As from the Application menu to save it under the name unitxref.dwg, and then close the unitxref.dwg file. This will make a copy of the 07a-unit.dwg file for the following steps. Or, if you prefer, you can use the unitxref.dwg file for the following steps.

3. Return to the 07b-plan file, choose Save As, and save the file under the name Planxref. The current file is now Planxref.dwg.

4. Erase all the unit plans (E↵All↵). In the next step, you'll purge the unit plans from the file. (By completing steps 2 through 4, you save yourself from having to set up a new file.)

5. Choose Drawing Utilities ➤ Purge from the Application menu to open the Purge dialog box, and then click the Purge All button to open the Confirm Purge dialog box. This purges blocks and layers that aren't in use in the drawing.

6. Click Purge All Items and close the Purge dialog box.

Now you're ready to use the External References palette:

1. Click the External References tool in the Insert tab's Reference panel title bar or type **XR**↵ to open the External References palette (see Figure 7.19).

**FIGURE 7.19**
The External References palette

2. Click the Attach DWG button in the upper-left corner of the palette to open the Select Reference File dialog box. This is a typical AutoCAD file dialog box complete with a preview window.

3. Locate and select the `unitxref.dwg` file, and then click Open to open the Attach External Reference dialog box (see Figure 7.20). Notice that this dialog box looks similar to the Insert dialog box. It offers the same options for insertion point, scale, and rotation.

4. You'll see a description of the options presented in this dialog box. For now, click OK.

**FIGURE 7.20**

The Attach External Reference dialog box

5. Enter **31'-5",43'-8"** (metric users enter **957,1330**) for the insertion point.

6. The inserted plan may appear faded. If it does, click the Xref Fading tool in the Insert tab's expanded Reference panel to turn off the Xref Fading feature. This will give the plan a more solid appearance.

7. After the `unitxref.dwg` file is inserted, re-create the same layout of the floor plan you created in the first section of this chapter by copying and mirroring the `unitxref.dwg` external reference.

8. Save the `Planxref` file.

You now have a drawing that looks like the `07b-plan.dwg` file you worked with earlier in this chapter, but instead of blocks that are detached from their source file, you have a drawing composed of Xrefs. These Xrefs are the actual `unitxref.dwg` file, and they're loaded into AutoCAD at the same time that you open the `Planxref.dwg` file. An icon in the lower-right corner of the AutoCAD window tells you that the current drawing contains Xrefs.

Not only does this icon alert you to Xrefs, but it also enables you to open the External References palette, as you'll see in the next exercise.

---

**FADING XREFS**

In step 6 of the previous exercise, you saw the Xref Fading tool. This tool is an aid to help you visualize which objects in your drawing are Xrefs. To the right of the Xref tool is the Xref Fading slider, which lets you control the amount of fading that is applied to the Xrefs in your drawing. You can either move the slider or enter a fading value in the input box to the far right. The Xref Fading tool affects only the appearance of the Xref in the drawing. It does not cause the Xref to fade in your printed or plotted output.

---

Next, you'll modify the `unitxref.dwg` file and see the results in the `Planxref.dwg` file:

1. To open the `unitxref.dwg` file, from the current `Planxref` file select and then right-click a unit and choose Open Xref from the context menu. You can also enter **Xopen**⏎ at the Command prompt and then select the unit plan Xref.

2. Erase the hatch patterns and kitchen outline for the floors, and save the `unitxref.dwg` file.

3. Use the drawing tab to return to the `Planxref.dwg` file. You see a message balloon pointing to the Manage Xrefs icon in the lower-right corner of the AutoCAD window. The balloon warns you that an Xref has changed. Right-click the Manage Xrefs icon in the lower-right corner of the AutoCAD window, and then choose External References from the pop-up menu to open the External References palette.

4. Right-click the unitxref name in the list box and then click Reload. Notice that the units in the Planxref drawing have been updated to include the changes you made to the `unitxref` file.

You may have noticed that there is a Reload DWG Xrefs option in the Manage Xrefs icon context menu. This option will reload all Xrefs in the current drawing without requiring you to select the individual file to reload in the External References palette.

Also, you may have noticed the Open option in step 4 when you used the right-click menu in the External References palette. This option performs the same function as the Xopen command, which opens the selected Xref for editing.

Be aware that when an Xref has been modified, the Manage Xrefs icon at the lower right in the AutoCAD window changes to show an exclamation point. This alerts you to changes in an Xref being used by the current drawing.

Click the Manage Xrefs icon to open the External References palette. The Xref that has been changed is indicated by a warning icon in the Status column of the list box along with the "Needs reloading" message.

You can then select the Xref that needs to be updated, right-click, and choose the Reload option from the context menu to reload the selected Xref. You can also select multiple Xrefs if more than one needs updating. Another option is to select Reload All References from the Refresh flyout at the top of the External References palette.

Here you saw how an Xref file is updated in a different way than a block. Because Xrefs are loaded along with the drawing file that contains them, the containing file, which in this case was the Planxref file, automatically displays any changes made to the Xref when it's opened. Also, you avoid having to update nested blocks because AutoCAD updates nested Xrefs as well as non-nested Xrefs. When an Xref is modified while you're editing a file, you're alerted to the change through the Xref icon located in the lower-right corner of the AutoCAD window. You can click the balloon message that appears from that icon to update any modified Xrefs.

## Other Differences between External References and Blocks

Here are a few other differences between Xrefs and inserted blocks that you'll want to keep in mind:

◆ Any new layers, text styles, or linetypes brought in with Xref files don't become part of the current file. If you want to import any of these items, you can use the Xbind command (described in Chapter 14, "Advanced Editing and Organizing").

◆ If you make changes to the layers of an Xref file, those changes aren't retained when the file is saved unless you checked the Retain Changes To Xref Layers option in the Open And Save tab of the Options dialog box. This option, found in the External References (Xrefs) group, instructs AutoCAD to remember any layer color or visibility settings from one editing session to the next. In the standard AutoCAD settings, this option is on by default.

◆ Another way to ensure that layer settings for Xrefs are retained is to enter **Visretain**↵ at the Command prompt. At the New value for VISRETAIN <0>: prompt, enter **1**.

◆ To segregate layers in Xref files from layers in the current drawing, AutoCAD prefixes the names of the Xref file's layers with their file's name. A vertical bar separates the filename prefix and the layer name when you view a list of layers in the layer drop-down list or the Layer Properties Manager dialog box (as in unitxref | wall).

◆ You can't explode Xrefs. You can, however, convert an Xref into a block and then explode it. To do this, select the Xref in the External References palette, then right-click and choose Bind to open another dialog box that offers two ways of converting an Xref into a block. See the section "Other External Reference Options" later in this chapter for more information.

◆ If an Xref is renamed or moved to another location on your hard disk, AutoCAD won't be able to find that file when it opens other files to which the Xref is attached. If this happens, you must select the path in the Found At field at the bottom of the External References palette and then click the Browse button (the ellipsis) to tell AutoCAD where to find the cross-referenced file.

◆ Take care when retargeting an Xref file with the Browse button. The Browse button can assign a file of a different name to an existing Xref as a substitution.

♦ Xref files are especially useful in workgroup environments in which several people are working on the same project. For example, one person might be updating several files that are inserted into a variety of other files. If blocks are used, everyone in the workgroup would have to be notified of the changes and would have to update all the affected blocks in all the drawings that contained them. With Xref files, however, the updating is automatic; you avoid confusion about which files need their blocks updated.

---

### IMPORTING BLOCKS, LAYERS, AND OTHER NAMED ELEMENTS FROM EXTERNAL FILES

You can use the Xbind command to import blocks and other named elements from another file. First, use the External References palette to cross-reference a file; type **Xbind** at the Command prompt. In the Xbind dialog box, click the plus sign next to the Xref filename, and then click the plus sign next to Block. Select the name of the block you want to import, click the Add button, and click OK. Finally, open the External References palette, select the Xref filename from the list, right-click, and select Detach to remove the Xref file. The imported block remains as part of the current file. (See Chapter 14 for details on importing named elements.) You can also use the AutoCAD Content Explorer™ to import named elements from external files. Content Explorer is described in Chapter 25.

The tool palettes give you access to frequently used blocks and hatch patterns that reside in other drawings. You can open the tool palettes by clicking the Tool Palettes tool in the View tab's Palettes panel.

In standard AutoCAD installations, the tool palette window is configured with sample 3D commands (not in the AutoCAD LT® software), blocks, and hatch patterns that you can drag and drop into your current drawing. Select a tab for the tool palette that contains the block or pattern you want, and then click and drag the item into your drawing. In the case of hatch patterns, click and drag the pattern into an area that is bounded on all sides by objects. When you're ready to customize the tool palette window, you do so by clicking and dragging objects or tools into a new or existing palette. See Chapter 24 for more on customizing tool palettes.

---

## Other External Reference Options

Many other features are unique to external reference files. Let's briefly look at some of the other options in the External References palette.

### OPTIONS IN THE EXTERNAL REFERENCES PALETTE

Several options are available when you right-click an external reference name listed in the External References palette, shown in Figure 7.20 earlier in this chapter. You saw the Reload option in an earlier exercise. The following other options are available:

**Attach**  Opens the Attach External Reference dialog box, in which you can select a file to attach and set the parameters for the attachment.

**Detach**    Detaches an Xref from the current file. The file is then completely disassociated from the current file.

**Reload**    Restores an unloaded Xref.

**Unload**    Similar to Detach, but maintains a link to the Xref file so that it can be quickly reattached. This has an effect similar to freezing a layer and can reduce redraw, regeneration, and file-loading times.

**Bind**    Converts an Xref into a block. Bind offers two options: Bind and Insert. The Bind option maintains the Xref's named elements (layers, linetypes, and text and dimension styles) by creating new layers in the current file with the Xref's filename prefix (discussed again in Chapter 14). The Insert option doesn't attempt to maintain the Xref's named elements but merges them with named elements of the same name in the current file. For example, if both the Xref and the current file have layers of the same name, the objects in the Xref are placed in the layers of the same name in the current file.

**Open**    Lets you open an Xref. Select the Xref from the list, and then click Open. The Xref opens in a new window when you close the External References palette.

**Path**    Enables you to remove the path to the Xref file (shown in the Found At option of the Details panel) or change it from a full path to a relative path.

**Details**    A panel at the bottom of the External References palette. It's similar to the Properties palette in that it displays the properties of a selected external reference and also allows you to modify some of those properties. For example, the Reference Name option in the Details panel lets you give the external reference a name that is different from the Xref filename. Table 7.1 gives you a rundown of the options in the Details panel.

**TABLE 7.1:**    The Details panel of the External References palette

| OPTION | FUNCTION |
| --- | --- |
| Reference Name | Lets you give the Xref a different name from the Xref's filename. This can be helpful if you want to use multiple external references of the same file. |
| Status | Tells you whether the Xref is loaded, unloaded, or not found (read only). |
| Size | Gives you the file size information (read only). |
| Type | Lets you choose between the Attach and Overlay attachment methods for the Xref file. Xrefs attached as overlays don't include nested Xrefs. |
| Date | Gives you the date and time the file was attached (read only). |
| Found At | Tells you where AutoCAD expects to find the Xref file (read only). |
| Saved Path | Lets you select the location of the Xref file. When you click the text box for this option, a Browse button appears to the right. You can click this button to locate a lost Xref or use a different file from the original attached Xref. |

### THE ATTACH EXTERNAL REFERENCE DIALOG BOX

The Attach External Reference dialog box, shown in Figure 7.20 earlier in this chapter, offers these options:

**Browse**  Opens the Select Reference File dialog box to enable you to change the file you're importing as an Xref.

**Attachment**  Tells AutoCAD to include other Xref attachments that are nested in the selected file.

**Overlay**  Tells AutoCAD to ignore other Xref attachments that are nested in the selected file. This avoids multiple attachments of other files and eliminates the possibility of circular references (referencing the current file into itself through another file).

**Path Type**  Offers options for locating Xrefs. Xref files can be located anywhere on your system, including network servers. For this reason, you can easily lose links to Xrefs either by moving them or by rearranging file locations. To help you manage Xrefs, the Path Type option offers three options: Full Path, Relative Path, and No Path.

> **Full Path**  Retains the current full path.
>
> **Relative Path**  Maintains paths in relation to the current drawing. The current drawing must be saved before using the Relative Path option.
>
> **No Path**  Used for drawings in which Xrefs are located in the same folder as the current drawing or in the path specified in Support File Search Path in the Files tab of the Options dialog box (choose Options from the Application menu).

**Specify On-Screen**  Appears in three places. It gives you the option to enter an insertion point, scale factors, and rotation angles in the dialog box or in the Command window, in a way similar to inserting blocks. If you clear this option for any of the corresponding parameters, the parameters change to allow input. If they're selected, you're prompted for those parameters after you click OK to close the dialog box. With all three Specify On-Screen check boxes cleared, the Xref is inserted in the drawing using the settings indicated in the dialog box.

**Show Details/Hide Details**  Displays or hides the path information for the selected Xref file.

**Block Unit**  Displays the insert scale setting for the external reference. Values are shown as the unit type and scale factor.

## Clipping Xref Views and Improving Performance

Xrefs are frequently used to import large drawings for reference or backgrounds. Multiple Xrefs, such as a floor plan, column grid layout, and site-plan drawing, might be combined into one file. One drawback to multiple Xrefs in earlier versions of AutoCAD was that the entire Xref was loaded into memory even if only a small portion of it was used for the final plotted output. For computers with limited resources, multiple Xrefs could slow the system to a crawl.

AutoCAD offers two tools that help make display and memory use more efficient when using Xrefs: the Clip command and the Demand Load option in the Options dialog box.

## CLIPPING VIEWS

The Clip command, found in the Insert tab's Reference panel, lets you clip the display of an Xref or a block to any shape you want, as shown in Figure 7.21. For example, you might want to display only an L-shaped portion of a floor plan to be part of your current drawing. Clip lets you define such a view. To access the command, choose Clip from the Insert tab's Reference panel.

**FIGURE 7.21**
The first panel shows a polyline outline of the area to be isolated with the Clip option. The second panel shows how the Xref appears after Clip is applied. The last panel shows a view of the plan with the polyline's layer turned off.

a.

Polyline

b.

c.

You can clip blocks and multiple Xrefs as well. You can also specify a front and back clipping distance so that the visibility of objects in 3D space can be controlled. You can define a clip area by using polylines or spline curves, although curve-fitted polylines revert to de-curved polylines. (See Chapter 18 for more on polylines and spline curves.)

## CONTROLLING XREF SETTINGS IN THE OPTIONS DIALOG BOX

The External References (Xrefs) group in the Open And Save tab of the Options dialog box offers some tools to help you manage memory use and other features related to Xrefs. If you're working on large projects with others in a workgroup, you should be aware of these settings and what they do.

The Demand Load Xrefs drop-down list offers three settings: Disabled, Enabled, and Enabled With Copy. Demand Load is set to Enabled With Copy by default in the standard AutoCAD setup. In addition to reducing the amount of memory an Xref consumes, Demand Load prevents other users from editing the Xref while it's being viewed as part of your current drawing. This helps aid drawing version control and drawing management. The Enabled With Copy option creates a copy of the source Xref file and then uses the copy, thereby enabling other AutoCAD users to edit the source Xref file.

Demand loading improves performance by loading only the parts of the referenced drawing that are needed to regenerate the current drawing. You can set the location for the Xref copy in the Files tab of the Options dialog box under Temporary External Reference File Location.

Two other options are also available in the Options dialog box:

**Retain Changes To Xref Layers**   Instructs AutoCAD to remember any layer color or visibility settings of Xrefs from one editing session to the next. In the standard AutoCAD settings, this option is on by default.

**Allow Other Users To Refedit Current Drawing**   Lets others edit the current drawing by choosing Edit Reference from the Insert tab's expanded Reference panel (Refedit). You'll learn about this command in the next section.

---

 **Real World Scenario**

### EXTERNAL REFERENCES IN THE SAN FRANCISCO MAIN LIBRARY PROJECT

Although the exercises in this chapter demonstrate how Xrefs work, you aren't limited to using them in the way shown here. Perhaps one of the most common ways of using Xrefs is to combine a single floor plan with different title block drawings, each with its own layer settings and title block information. In this way, single-drawing files can be reused in several drawing sheets of a final construction document set. This helps keep data consistent across drawings and reduces the number of overall files needed.

This is exactly how Xrefs were used in the San Francisco Main Library drawings. One floor plan file contained most of the main information for that floor. The floor plan was then used as an Xref in another file that contained the title block as well as additional information such as furnishings or floor finish reference symbols. Layer visibility was controlled in each title block drawing so that only the data related to that drawing appeared.

Multiple Xref files were also used by segregating the structural column grid layout drawings from the floor-plan files. In other cases, portions of plans from different floors were combined into a single drawing by using Xrefs, as shown here:

## Editing Xrefs in Place

You've seen different methods for editing blocks and Xrefs as external files. There is also a way to edit a block or an Xref directly in a file without having to edit an external file: You can use the Edit Reference option in the Insert tab's expanded Reference panel or the Edit Reference In-Place option in the External Reference tab's Edit panel. These options issue the Refedit command.

The following exercise demonstrates how Refedit works. If you are a metric user, note that for this exercise we're using a file set up with Imperial units. The unit type is not important to the exercise:

1. Open the 07-planxref.dwg file. This file is set up like the Planxref.dwg file you created in the previous exercises. 07-planxref uses a file called 07-unitxref.dwg instead of the unitxref.dwg file for the Xref units.

2. Zoom into the unit plan in the lower-left corner of the drawing so you see a view similar to Figure 7.22.

3. Click the corner unit to select it. Notice that the External Reference ribbon tab appears, offering several options that allow you to edit the Xref. You'll learn more about these options later.

**FIGURE 7.22**
The enlarged view
of the unitxref
in the Planxref
drawing

**4.** Double-click the wall of the corner unit. The Reference Edit dialog box appears (see Figure 7.23).

**FIGURE 7.23**
The Reference Edit
dialog box

The Reference Edit dialog box contains two main areas. The right side shows a thumbnail view of the item that you're editing. The left side shows a list of the specific item you selected in the Xref. Notice that the list box shows the hierarchical relationship of the kitchenette block in relation to the 07-unitxref Xref.

**5.** In the list, click the 07-unitxref|KITCHEN listing and then click OK. The Edit Reference panel appears in the current Ribbon tab. You may see a previous release warning message. Click OK at the warning.

**6.** Use a selection window to select the entire lower-left corner unit. Notice that only the grips in the kitchenette appear, indicating that the objects in the kitchenette are selected. Although the rest of the unit appears to be selected, it appears lighter in color. This shows you that only the kitchen is available for editing.

**7.** Press the Esc key to clear your selection.

**SPECIAL SAVE AS OPTIONS THAT AFFECT DEMAND LOADING**

AutoCAD offers a few additional settings that boost the performance of the Demand Load feature. When you choose Save As from the Application menu to save a file in the standard DWG format, you see the Tools button in the upper-right corner of the Save Drawing As dialog box. Choosing Tools ➤ Options opens the Save As Options dialog box. Using the options in the Index Type drop-down list on the DWG Options tab can help improve the speed of demand loading. The index options are as follows:

**None**   No index is created.

**Layer**   AutoCAD loads only layers that are both turned on and thawed.

**Spatial**   AutoCAD loads only portions of an Xref or raster image within a clipped boundary.

**Layer & Spatial**   This option turns on both the Layer and Spatial options.

In step 5 of the previous exercise, the Refedit command isolates the objects you select for editing. You can't edit anything else in the Xref until you exit the Refedit command and start over.

At this point, you can edit a block in an Xref. Now let's continue editing the kitchenette:

1. Zoom in on the kitchenette, and move the four burners to the right 8".

2. Erase the sink.

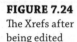

3. Click the Save Changes tool on the Edit Reference panel. If your screen resolution is fairly low, you may have to expand the Edit Reference panel to see the Save Changes tool.

4. A warning message appears, telling you that the changes you've made to the Xref will be saved. Click OK.

5. Zoom back to your previous view. Notice that the other units reflect the changes you made to the 07-unitxref Xref (see Figure 7.24).

**FIGURE 7.24**
The Xrefs after being edited

6. Open the 07-unitxref.dwg file, which can be found in the Chapter 7 sample file folder. The kitchen reflects the changes you made to the Xref of the unit in the 07-planxref file. This shows you that by choosing to save the reference edit in step 3, you saved the changes back to the Xref's source file.

As you saw from these two exercises, it's possible to edit a specific block in an Xref, but to do that you must select the block name in the Reference Edit dialog box.

In these exercises, you edited a block contained in an Xref, but you could have just as easily edited a block in the current drawing. You can also edit nested blocks by using the Refedit command. Changes in blocks in the current file don't affect other files because blocks aren't linked to external files. The changes to blocks remain in the current file until you explicitly export the changed block to a file, as you saw in earlier exercises.

## Using the External Reference Tab

Earlier, you saw that when you click an Xref, the External Reference tab appears. This tab offers several tools divided into three panels: Edit, Clipping, and Options. See Table 7.2 for a complete description of these tools.

**TABLE 7.2:**     The External Reference tab options

| TOOL NAME | FUNCTION |
| --- | --- |
| Edit Reference In-Place | Starts the Refedit command, which allows you to edit an Xref within the current drawing. |
| Open Reference | Opens the selected Xref. |
| Create Clipping Boundary | Starts the Xclip command, which allows you to hide portions of an Xref. This feature is similar to the image clipping command described in Chapter 13, "Copying Existing Drawings from Other Sources." |
| Removing Clipping | Removes a clipping boundary. |
| External References | Opens or closes the External References palette. |

## Adding and Removing Objects from Blocks and Xrefs

In the previous exercises, you removed objects from the Kitchen block by using the Erase command. You can also move objects from a block or an Xref into the current drawing without erasing them. To do this, choose Remove From Working Set from the Edit Reference panel while in the Refedit command. This removes the objects from the block or Xref without erasing them. Likewise, you can add new objects to the block or Xref by choosing Add To Working Set from the Edit Reference panel. Both menu options invoke the Refset command, with different options applied. Also note that the Edit Reference panel appears in all the Ribbon tabs when you are in the Refedit command.

To see how Refset works, try the following exercise:

1. Close the 07-unitxref.dwg file.

2. In the 07-planxref file, zoom in to the kitchenette to get a view similar to the top panel of Figure 7.25.

**FIGURE 7.25**
Moving the burners out of the Kitchen block and adding the rectangle

Move burners here.
Add rectangle.

Burners removed from working set remain in their moved position.

Rectangle appears in all copies of the Unit XRef.

3. Double-click the unit plan drawing. You can also choose Edit Reference from the Insert tab's expanded Reference panel and then click the unit plan.

4. Click the 07-unitxref|KITCHEN listing in the Reference Edit dialog box, and then click OK.

5. Use the Move tool to move the two burners on the right just to the right of the kitchenette, as shown in Figure 7.25.

6. Click the Remove From Working Set tool in the expanded Edit Reference panel.

7. Select the two burners you just moved, and then press ↵.

Notice that the burners become grayer to show that they're removed from the working set. They remain as part of the Planxref drawing, but they're no longer part of the Kitchen block. Now add a rectangle to the Kitchen block in place of the burners:

1. Draw a 7″ by 16″ rectangle in place of the moved burners, as shown in the top panel of Figure 7.26. Anything you add to the drawing automatically becomes part of the working set.

2. Click Save Changes in the Edit Reference panel. You'll see a warning message stating that all reference edits will be saved. Click OK.

3. Zoom out enough to see the other units in the drawing (see Figure 7.26).

**FIGURE 7.26**
The Planxref drawing with the changes made to the `07-unitxref` Xref

You can see that the burners have been replaced by the rectangle in all the other Xref units. The burners you moved are still there in the lower-left corner unit, but they have been removed from all the Xrefs. It's as if you extracted them from the block and placed them in the Plan drawing.

While you were using the Refedit command, any new objects you created were added to the working set automatically. When you drew the rectangle in step 1, for example, it was automatically included in the *working set*, which is the set of objects included in the block or Xref on which you're currently working. You didn't have to add it specifically to the working set.

If you want to include existing objects in the working set, choose the Add To Working Set tool from the Edit Reference panel.

You've completed the exercises in this chapter, so you can exit AutoCAD without saving these changes.

## Understanding the Reference Edit Dialog Box Options

The Reference Edit dialog box offers you the option to isolate specific blocks in the Xref by selecting them from the hierarchy list. You may have noticed the two radio button options: Automatically Select All Nested Objects and Prompt To Select Nested Objects. The default option, Automatically Select All Nested Objects, lets you select any object contained in the selected object in the hierarchy listing. If you select the Prompt To Select Nested Objects option, you're prompted to select objects on the screen before the Edit Reference panel appears.

In addition to the options you used in the exercises, the Reference Edit dialog box includes the Settings tab, which provides a few options (see Figure 7.27).

**FIGURE 7.27**

The Settings tab of the Reference Edit dialog box

## CREATE UNIQUE LAYER, STYLE, AND BLOCK NAMES

When you use the Refedit command with the Automatically Select All Nested Objects option turned on, you can import nested blocks into the current drawing. For example, if you selected the Bath block in the hierarchy list in the previous exercise, you would have access to the Tub and Toilet blocks in the Bath block. You could then copy either of those blocks into the current file.

When you make a copy of a block from an Xref, AutoCAD needs to assign that block a name. The Create Unique Layer, Style, And Block Names option tells AutoCAD to use the original block name and append a $#$ prefix to the name (# is a numeric value starting with 0). If you were to import the Bath block, for example, it would become $0$bath in the current drawing. This ensures that the block maintains a unique name when it's imported, even if there is a block with the same name in the current drawing. If you turn off the Create Unique Layer, Style, And Block Names option, the original name is maintained. If the current drawing contains a block of the same name, the imported block uses the current file's definition of that block.

## DISPLAY ATTRIBUTE DEFINITIONS FOR EDITING

If your drawing contains attributes (see Chapter 12, "Using Attributes," for more on attributes), this option is offered. If you turn on this option, you can then edit attribute definitions by using the Refedit command. If you select a block that contains an attribute definition while you're using the Refedit command, the attribute definition is exposed, enabling you to make changes. Changes to attribute definitions affect only new attribute insertions. Except for the attribute of the edited block, existing attributes aren't affected. If you want to update existing attributes to a newly edited definition, use the Sync option of the Block Attribute Manager (choose Manage Attributes from the Home tab's expanded Block panel).

## LOCK OBJECTS NOT IN WORKING SET

In the Refedit exercises, you saw that objects that aren't selected in the Reference Edit dialog box are grayed out and aren't selectable. The Lock Objects Not In Working Set option controls this feature and is turned on by default.

## The Bottom Line

**Assemble the parts.** Technical drawings are often made up of repetitive parts that are drawn over and over. AutoCAD makes quick work of repetitive elements in a drawing, as shown in the first part of this chapter.

**Master It** What is the object used as the basic building block for the unit plan drawing in the beginning of this chapter?

**Take control of the AutoCAD display.** Understanding the way the AutoCAD display works can save you time, especially in a complex drawing.

**Master It** Name the dialog box used to save views in AutoCAD. Describe how to recall a saved view.

**Use hatch patterns in your drawings.** Patterns can convey a lot of information at a glance. You can show the material of an object or you can indicate a type of view, like a cross section, by applying hatch patterns.

**Master It** How do you open the Hatch And Gradient dialog box?

**Understand the boundary hatch options.** The hatch options give you control over the way hatch patterns fill an enclosed area.

**Master It** Describe an island as it relates to boundary hatch patterns.

**Use external references.** External references are drawing files that you've attached to the current drawing to include as part of the drawing. Because external references aren't part of the current file, they can be worked on at the same time as the referencing file.

**Master It** Describe how drawing files are attached as external references.

# Chapter 8

# Introducing Printing, Plotting, and Layouts

Getting hard-copy output from the AutoCAD® 2015 software is something of an art. You'll need to be intimately familiar with both your output device and the settings available in AutoCAD. You'll probably spend a good deal of time experimenting with the plotter settings in AutoCAD and with your printer or plotter to get your equipment set up just the way you want.

With the huge array of output options available, this chapter can provide only a general discussion of plotting and printing. As a rule, the process for using a plotter isn't much different from that for a printer; you just have more media-sized options with plotters. Still, every output device is different. It's up to you to work out the details and fine-tune the way you and AutoCAD together work with your particular plotter or printer.

This chapter describes the features available in AutoCAD and discusses some general rules and guidelines to follow when setting up your plots. We'll start with an overview of the plotting features in AutoCAD and then delve into the finer details of setting up your drawing and controlling your plotter or printer.

In this chapter, you will learn to

♦ Understand the plotter settings

♦ Use layout views to control how your plots look

♦ Add an output device

♦ Store a page setup

## Plotting the Plan

To see firsthand how the Plot command works, you'll plot the plan drawing by using the default settings on your system. You'll start by getting a preview of your plot before you commit to printing your drawing. As an introduction, you'll plot from the model view of an AutoCAD drawing, but be aware that typically you should plot from a layout view. Layout views give you a greater degree of control over how your output will look. You'll be introduced to layout views later in this chapter. Now let's get started!

First, try plotting your drawing to no particular scale:

1. Be sure your printer or plotter is connected to your computer and is turned on.

2. Start AutoCAD, and open the plan.dwg file; open plan-metric.dwg if you are using the metric system. These files can be found in the Chapter 8 sample files download at www.sybex.com/go/masteringautocad2015.

**3.** Select Zoom All from the Zoom flyout in the navigation bar to display the entire drawing, or type **Z↵A↵**.

**4.** Click the Plot tool from the Quick Access toolbar to open the Plot dialog box (see Figure 8.1).

**FIGURE 8.1**
The Plot dialog box

**5.** If the Name option in the Printer/Plotter group shows None, click the drop-down arrow and select your current Windows system printer.

**6.** In the Plot Area group, select the Display option from the What To Plot drop-down list (see Figure 8.2). This tells AutoCAD to plot the drawing as it appears in the drawing window. You also have the option to plot the limits of the drawing or to select an area to plot with a window. In addition, you can choose to plot the extents of a drawing or a saved view.

**FIGURE 8.2**
Choose the Display option.

**7.** Select the Fit To Paper option in the Plot Scale group.

**8.** Click the Preview button in the lower-left corner of the dialog box. AutoCAD works for a moment and then displays a sample view of how your drawing will appear when printed. Notice that the view also shows the Zoom Realtime cursor. You can use the Zoom/Pan Realtime tools to get a close-up of your print preview.

**9.** Go ahead and plot the file: Right-click and choose Plot from the context menu. AutoCAD sends the drawing to your printer.

**10.** Your plotter or printer prints the plan to no particular scale.

You've just plotted your first drawing to see how it looks on paper. You used the minimal settings to ensure that the complete drawing appears on the paper.

You may notice that a message bubble appears in the lower-right corner of the AutoCAD window (see Figure 8.3). If you click the text that reads "Click to view plot and publish details," the Plot And Publish Details dialog box opens to display some detailed information about your plot.

**FIGURE 8.3**
Click the message text to open the Plot And Publish Details dialog box.

As you become more experienced with AutoCAD and your projects become more demanding, the information presented in the Plot And Publish Details dialog box may be useful to you. For now, make a mental note that this information is available should you need it.

---

**SET THE APPROPRIATE UNITS**

It's important to make sure you use the appropriate unit settings in this chapter. For example, if you've been using the metric measurements for previous exercises, make sure you use the metric settings in the exercises of this chapter; otherwise, your results won't coincide.

---

Next, try plotting your drawing to an exact scale. This time, you'll expand the Plot dialog box to show a few more options:

**1.** In the status bar, click the Annotation Scale tool and select 1/16" = 1'-0" from the flyout. Metric users should select 1:20.

**2.** Click Plot on the Quick Access toolbar again to open the Plot dialog box. If the Name option in the Printer/Plotter group shows None, click the drop-down arrow and select your current Windows system printer.

**3.** Click the More Options button. You'll see some additional options appear on the right side of the dialog box (see Figure 8.4).

**FIGURE 8.4**
Open the additional options on the right.

New options appear to the right.

4. If your last printout wasn't oriented correctly on the paper, select the Landscape option in the Drawing Orientation group.

---

**PRINT PREVIEW DEPENDENCIES**

The appearance of the print preview depends on the type of output device you chose when you installed AutoCAD or when you last selected a Plotter Device option (described in the section "WYSIWYG Plotting Using Layout Views" later in this chapter). The print preview is also affected by other settings in the Plot dialog box, such as those in the Drawing Orientation, Plot Offset, and Plot Area groups. This example shows a typical preview view using the Windows default system printer in Landscape mode.

---

5. In the Plot Scale group, clear the Fit To Paper check box. Then, select 1/16" = 1'-0" from the Scale drop-down list. Metric users should select 1:20. As you can see, you have several choices for the scale of your output.

6. In the Paper Size group, select Letter. Metric users should select A4. The options in this drop-down list depend on your Windows system printer or the output device you configured for AutoCAD.

7. In the Plot Area group, select Limits from the drop-down list. This tells AutoCAD to use the limits of your drawing to determine which part of your drawing to plot.

8. Click the Preview button again to get a preview of your plot.

9. Right-click and choose Plot from the context menu. This time, your plot is to scale.

Here, you were asked to specify a few more settings in the Plot dialog box. Several settings work together to produce a drawing that is to scale and that fits properly on your paper. Here is where it pays to understand the relationship between your drawing scale and your paper's size, discussed in Chapter 3, "Setting Up and Using the Drafting Tools." You also saw how you can expand the options in the Plot dialog box.

The following sections are lengthy but don't contain many exercises. If you prefer to continue with the exercises in this chapter, skip to the section "WYSIWYG Plotting Using Layout Views." Be sure to come back and read the following sections while the previous exercises are still fresh in your mind.

## Understanding the Plotter Settings

In the following sections, you'll explore all the settings in the Plot dialog box. These settings give you control over the size and orientation of your image on the paper. They also let you control which part of your drawing gets printed. All these settings work together to give you control over how your drawing fits on your printed output.

---

**AUTOCAD REMEMBERS PLOTTER SETTINGS**

AutoCAD 2015 relies mainly on the Windows system printer configuration instead of its own plotter drivers. However, it does remember printer settings that are specific to AutoCAD, so you don't have to adjust your printer settings each time you use AutoCAD. This gives you more flexibility and control over your output. Be aware that you'll need to understand the Windows system printer settings in addition to those offered by AutoCAD.

---

## Paper Size

You use the options in the Paper Size group to specify the paper size for your output. You can select a paper size from the Paper Size drop-down list. These sizes are derived from those available from your selected system printer. You'll find out how to select a different printer later in this chapter.

AutoCAD 2015 offers sheet sizes in both Imperial and metric measurements in the Paper Size group. AutoCAD assumes that if you pick a metric sheet size such as A4 or A5, you'll want the sheet dimensions specified in metric measurements, and it adjusts the dialog box settings accordingly.

## Drawing Orientation

When you used the Preview button in the first exercise in this chapter, you saw your drawing as it would be placed on the paper. In that example, it was positioned in a *landscape orientation*, which places the image on the paper so that the width of the paper is greater than its height. You can rotate the image on the paper 90° into what is called a *portrait orientation* by selecting the Portrait radio button in the Drawing Orientation group. A third option, Plot Upside-Down, lets you change the orientation further by turning the landscape or portrait orientation upside down. These three settings allow you to print the image in any one of four orientations on the sheet.

In AutoCAD, the preview displays the paper in the orientation it's in when it leaves the printer. For most small-format printers, if you're printing in the portrait orientation the image appears in the same orientation you see when you're editing the drawing. If you're using the landscape orientation, the preview image is turned sideways. For large-format plotters, the preview may be oriented in the opposite direction. The graphic in the Drawing Orientation group displays a capital *A* on a sheet showing the orientation of your drawing on the paper output.

Remember that you need to click the More Options button in the lower-right corner of the Plot dialog box to access the Drawing Orientation group. The More Options button looks like a circle with a greater-than sign. You can also press Alt+Shift+>.

## Plot Area

The What To Plot drop-down list in the Plot Area group lets you specify which part of your drawing you want to plot. You may notice some similarities between these settings and the Zoom command options. The Plot Area options are described next. Most of these options are used only in a model view. Typically, when plotting from a layout view, you'll use the Layout option.

**Display**   Display is the default option; it tells AutoCAD to plot what is currently displayed on the screen. If you let AutoCAD fit the drawing onto the sheet (that is, you select the Fit To Paper check box in the Plot Scale group), the plot is exactly the same as what you see on your screen, adjusted for the width and height proportions of your display.

**Extents**   The Extents option uses the extents of the drawing to determine the area to print. If you let AutoCAD fit the drawing onto the sheet (by selecting the Fit To Paper check box in the Plot Scale group), the plot displays exactly the same image that you would see on the screen if you chose the Zoom Extents tool from the Zoom flyout in the Navigation bar.

**Layout**   The Layout option (available in layout views only) replaces the Limits option when you plot from a layout view. (See the section "WYSIWYG Plotting Using Layout Views" later in this chapter.) This option plots everything displayed within the paper margins shown in the layout view. Typically, this is the only option you'll use when printing from a layout.

**Limits**   The Limits option (available in Model Space only) uses the limits of the drawing to determine the area to print. If you let AutoCAD fit the drawing onto the sheet (by selecting the Fit To Paper check box in the Plot Scale group), the plot displays exactly the same image that you would see on the screen if you selected Zoom All from the Zoom flyout on the Navigation bar.

---

### GETTING A BLANK PLOT?

Do you get a blank printout even though you selected Extents or Display? Chances are the Fit To Paper check box isn't selected, or the Inches = Units (mm = Units for metric users) setting is inappropriate for the sheet size and scale of your drawing. If you don't care about the scale of the drawing, make sure the Fit To Paper option is selected. Otherwise, make sure the Plot Scale settings are set correctly. If you select Display for the plot area, try Extents instead. The next section, "Plot Scale," describes how to set the scale for your plots.

---

**View**   The View option is available when you've saved a view in the drawing by using the View command. When you select View from the What To Plot drop-down list, another drop-down list appears offering a list of views available in the drawing. You can then select the view that you want to plot. If you let AutoCAD fit the drawing onto the sheet (by selecting Fit To Paper from the Plot Scale group), the plot displays exactly the same thing that you would see on the screen if you recalled the view you're plotting. Objects that don't appear in the view are clipped in the plotted view.

**Window**   The Window option enables you to use a window to indicate the area you want to plot. Nothing outside the window prints. When you select this option, the Plot dialog box temporarily closes to allow you to select a window. After you've done this the first time, a Window button appears next to the drop-down list. You can click the Window button and then indicate a window in the drawing area, or AutoCAD will use the last indicated window. If you use the Fit To Paper option in the Plot Scale group to let AutoCAD fit the drawing onto the sheet, the plot displays exactly what you enclose in the window.

## Plot Scale

In the previous section, you could select Fit To Paper for several of the Plot Area options. Bear in mind that when you instead apply a scale factor to your plot, the results of the Plot Area settings change, and some problems can arise. This is where most new users have difficulty.

For example, the apartment plan drawing fits nicely on the paper when you use Fit To Paper. But if you try to plot the drawing at a scale of 1" = 1', you'll probably get a blank piece of paper because, at that scale, hardly any of the drawing fits on your paper. AutoCAD will tell you that it's plotting and then tell you that the plot is finished. You won't have a clue as to why your sheet is blank.

If an image is too large to fit on a sheet of paper because of improper scaling, the plot image is placed on the paper differently, depending on whether the plotter uses the center of the image or the lower-left corner for its origin. Keep this in mind as you specify scale factors in this area of the dialog box.

### SCALE

You can select a drawing scale from a set of predefined scales in the Scale drop-down list. These options cover the most common scales you'll need to use.

You've already seen how the Fit To Paper option lets you avoid giving a scale and forces the drawing to fit on the sheet when you're plotting from the model view. This works fine if you're plotting illustrations that aren't to scale. If you select another option, such as ⅛"= 1'-0", the inches and units text boxes change to reflect this scale. The Inches = text box changes to 0.125, and the Units text box changes to 12.

If you're plotting from a layout, you'll use the 1:1 scale option or perhaps a 1:2 scale if you're plotting a half-size drawing. In a layout, the drawing scale is typically set up through the viewport. While you're plotting from a layout, AutoCAD automatically determines the area to plot based on the printer and sheet size you select. For more information, see "WYSIWYG Plotting Using Layout Views" later in this chapter.

### CUSTOM SCALE

In some cases, you may need to set up a nonstandard scale (not shown in the drop-down list) to plot your drawing. If you can't find the scale you want in the Scale drop-down list, you can select Custom and then enter custom values in the Inches or mm and Units text boxes.

Through these text boxes, you can indicate how the drawing units in your drawing relate to the final plotted distance in inches or millimeters. For example, if your drawing is of a scale factor of 96, you would follow these steps:

1. In the Plot Scale group of the Plot dialog box, double-click the text box just below the Scale drop-down list, and enter **1**.

2. Double-click the Units text box, enter **96**, and press the Tab key.

   Metric users who want to plot to a scale of 110 should enter **1** in the mm text box and **10** in the Units text box.

If you're more used to the Architectural unit style in the Imperial measurement system, you can enter a scale as a fraction. For example, for a ⅛″ scale drawing, do this:

1. Double-click the Inches = text box, enter **1/8**, and press the Tab key. The value in the text box changes to 0.125, which is the decimal equivalent of ⅛″.

2. Double-click the Units text box, enter **12**, and press the Tab key.

If you specify a different scale than the one you chose while setting up your drawing, AutoCAD plots your drawing to that scale. You aren't restricted in any way as to scale, but entering the correct scale is important: If it's too large, AutoCAD will think your drawing is too large to fit on the sheet, although it will attempt to plot your drawing anyway. See Chapter 3 for a discussion of unit styles and scale factors.

---

### DON'T FORGET YOUR ANNOTATION SCALE

You may see a message saying that the "annotation scale is not equal to the plot scale" when you attempt to plot your drawing. You can click Continue at the message and your drawing will still be plotted to the scale you specify. If you are using any text or blocks that use the annotation scale feature, those items will be plotted at the Annotation scale setting for the model view or layout you are trying to plot. See Chapter 4, "Organizing Objects with Blocks and Groups," for more on the annotation scale.

---

If you plot to a scale that is different from the scale you originally intended, objects and text appear smaller or larger than is appropriate for your plot. You'll need to edit your text size to match the new scale. You can do so by using the Properties palette. Select the text whose height you want to change, right-click and choose Properties from the context menu, and then change the Height setting in the Properties palette.

## ADDING A CUSTOM SCALE TO THE SCALE DROP-DOWN LIST

If you use a custom scale frequently, you may find it annoying to have to input the scale every time you plot. AutoCAD offers the ability to add your custom scale to the Scale drop-down list shown earlier. You can then easily select your custom scale from the list instead of entering it through the text box.

**CERT OBJECTIVE**

Here are the steps you use to add a custom scale to the Scale drop-down list:

1. Choose Options from the Application menu to open the Options dialog box.

2. Select the User Preferences tab, and then click the Default Scale List button at the bottom of the dialog box.

3. In the Default Scale List dialog box, click the Add button.

4. In the Add Scale dialog box, enter a name for your custom scale in the Name Appearing In Scale List text box, and then enter the appropriate values in the Scale Properties text boxes.

5. Click OK in each dialog box to close it.

There are several options besides Add in the Default Scale List dialog box. Clicking the Edit button lets you edit an existing scale in the list. Clicking the Move Up and Move Down buttons lets you change the location of an item in the list. Clicking Delete deletes an item or a set of items from the list. Clicking the Reset button restores the list to its default condition and removes any custom items you may have added.

---

**SHORTCUT TO THE EDIT SCALE LIST DIALOG BOX**

Instead of opening the Options dialog box and clicking Default Scale List on the User Preferences tab, you can enter **Scalelistedit**↵ at the Command prompt to open the Edit Drawing Scales dialog box directly.

### SCALE LINEWEIGHTS

AutoCAD offers the option to assign lineweights to objects either through their layer assignments or by directly assigning a lineweight to individual objects. The lineweight option, however, doesn't have any meaning until you specify a scale for your drawing. After you specify a scale, the Scale Lineweights option becomes available. Select this check box if you want the lineweight assigned to layers and objects to appear correctly in your plots. You'll get a closer look at lineweights and plotting later in this chapter.

## Shaded Viewport Options

Most of your plotting will probably involve 2D technical line drawings, but occasionally you may need to plot a shaded or rendered 3D view. You may need to include such 3D views combined with 2D or 3D Wireframe views. AutoCAD offers the Shaded Viewport Options group, which enables you to plot shaded or rendered 3D views of your AutoCAD drawing. These options give you control over the quality of your rendered output. (Users of the AutoCAD LT® software don't have the Shaded Viewport Options group.)

Remember that you need to click the More Options button in the lower-right corner of the Plot dialog box to get to the Shaded Viewport Options group. You also need to select a printer name in the Printer/Plotter group before these options are made available.

### SHADE PLOT

The Shade Plot drop-down list lets you control how a Model Space view or layout is plotted. You can choose from the following options:

**As Displayed**    Plots the Model Space view as it appears on your screen.

**Legacy Wireframe**    Plots the Model Space view of a 3D object as a Wireframe view.

**Legacy Hidden**    Plots your Model Space view with hidden lines removed.

**3D Hidden/3D Wireframe/Conceptual/Hidden/Realistic…**    Plots the Model Space using one of several visual styles. These selections override the current Model Space visual style. See Chapter 20, "Creating 3D Drawings," for more on visual styles.

**Rendered**    Renders your Model Space view before plotting (see the bonus chapter "Rendering 3D Drawings," available at http://www.omura.com/chapters).

**Draft/Low/Medium/High/Presentation**    Sets the quality of the plot.

The Shade Plot options aren't available if you're plotting from a layout view. You can control the way each layout viewport is plotted through the viewport's Properties settings. You'll learn more about layout viewport properties later in this chapter.

### QUALITY AND DPI

The Quality drop-down list determines the dots per inch (dpi) setting for your output. These options aren't available if you select Legacy Wireframe or Legacy Hidden from the Shade Plot drop-down list:

**Draft**    Plots 3D views as wireframes.

**Preview**    Offers 150 dpi resolution.

**Normal**    Offers 300 dpi resolution.

**Presentation**    Offers 600 dpi resolution.

**Maximum**    Defers dpi resolution to the current output device's settings.

**Custom**    Lets you set a custom dpi setting. When you select Custom, the DPI text box is made available for your input.

If some of the terms discussed for the Shaded Viewport Options group are unfamiliar, don't be alarmed. You'll learn about 3D shaded views in Part 4 of this book. When you start to explore 3D modeling in AutoCAD, come back and review the Shaded Viewport Options group.

## Plot Offset

Sometimes, your first plot of a drawing shows the drawing positioned incorrectly on the paper. You can fine-tune its location by using the Plot Offset settings. To adjust the position of your drawing on the paper, enter the location of the view origin in relation to the plotter origin in x- and y-coordinates (see Figure 8.5).

**FIGURE 8.5**
Adjusting the image location on a sheet

For example, suppose you plot a drawing and then realize that it needs to be moved 1″ to the right and 3″ up on the sheet. You can replot the drawing by making the following changes:

1. Double-click the X text box, type **1**, and press the Tab key.

2. Double-click the Y text box, type **3**, and press the Tab key.

Now proceed with the rest of the plot configuration. With these settings, the image is shifted on the paper exactly 1″ to the right and 3″ up when the plot is done.

You can also tell AutoCAD the location from which the offset is to occur. The Plot And Publish tab of the Options dialog box (choose Application ➤ Options) offers the Specify Plot Offset Relative To button group. This group offers two radio buttons: Printable Area and Edge Of Paper. You can select the option that makes the most sense for you.

## Plot Options

The options in the Plot Options group provide you with greater control over your output and require some detailed instruction. Here is a brief description of these options. You'll learn more about them later in this chapter.

**Plot In Background**   If you think your plot will take some time to complete, this option plots your drawing in the background so that, after you begin a plot, you can immediately return to your drawing work. You can also control this option through the Backgroundplot system variable.

**Plot Object Lineweights**   As mentioned earlier, AutoCAD lets you assign lineweights to objects either through their layer assignment or by assigning them directly. If you use this feature in your drawing, this option lets you turn lineweights on or off in your output.

**Plot With Transparency**   You can apply a transparency of objects and layers in your drawing. This option lets you control whether transparency is used when your drawing is plotted.

**Plot With Plot Styles**   Plot styles give you a high degree of control over your drawing output. You can control whether your output is in color or black and white, and you can control whether filled areas are drawn in a solid color or a pattern. You can even control the way lines are joined at corners. You can learn more about these options and how they affect your work in in the bonus chapter "Understanding Plot Styles," available at http://www.omura.com/chapters.

**Plot Paperspace Last**   When you're using a layout view, otherwise known as Paper Space, this option determines whether objects in Paper Space are plotted before or after objects in Model Space. You'll learn more about Model Space and Paper Space later in this chapter.

**Hide Paperspace Objects**   This option pertains to 3D models in AutoCAD. When you draw in 3D, you can view your drawing as a *Wireframe view*. In a Wireframe view, your drawing looks like it's transparent even though it's made up of solid surfaces. Using hidden-line removal, you can view and plot your 3D drawings so that solid surfaces are opaque. To view a 3D drawing in the drawing area with hidden lines removed, use the Hide command or use one of the visual styles other than Wireframe. To plot a 3D drawing with hidden lines removed, choose the Hidden option or a visual style from the Shade Plot drop-down list.

Hide Paperspace Objects doesn't work for views in the Layout viewport described later. Instead, you need to set the viewport's Shade Plot setting to Hidden. (Click the viewport border, right-click, and choose Shade Plot ➤ Hidden from the context menu.)

**Plot Stamp On**   The Plot Stamp feature lets you place pertinent data on the drawing in a location you choose. This includes the drawing name, date and time, scale, and other data. When you click the Plot Stamp On check box to turn on this option, the Plot Stamp Settings button appears.

Click this button to gain access to the Plot Stamp dialog box (see Figure 8.6). This dialog box offers many controls over the plot stamp. It is a fairly extensive tool, so rather than us filling this chapter with a description of all its features, see the bonus chapter "Hardware and Software Tips," available at http://www.omura.com/chapters for a complete rundown of the Plot Stamp options.

**FIGURE 8.6**
The Plot Stamp
dialog box

**Save Changes To Layout**   When this option is turned on, the changes you make to Plot dialog box settings are saved with the current layout. You'll learn more about layouts in the section "WYSIWYG Plotting Using Layout Views."

## Exit Options

The Plot dialog box has the usual OK, Cancel, and Help buttons at the bottom. You'll also see the Apply To Layout button. This button lets you save the plot settings you make without sending your drawing to the printer or plotter for output. It is convenient for those times when you decide halfway through your plot setup not to plot your drawing.

# WYSIWYG Plotting Using Layout Views

So far you've done all your work in the model view, also known as Model Space. There are other views to your drawing that are specifically geared toward printing and plotting. The *layout* views enable you to control drawing scale, add title blocks, and set up layer settings different from those in the model view. You can think of the layout views as page layout spaces that act like a desktop publishing program.

This part of the chapter introduces you to layout views as they relate to plotting. You'll also learn more about layout views in Chapter 15, "Laying Out Your Printer Output."

You can have as many layout views as you like, each set up for a different type of output. You can, for example, have two or three layout views, each set up for a different scale drawing or with different layer configurations for reflected ceiling plans, floor plans, or equipment plans. You can even set up multiple views of your drawing at different scales in a single layout view. In addition, you can draw and add text and dimensions in layout views just as you would in Model Space.

To get familiar with the layout views, try the following exercise:

1. Hover over the Plan file's Drawing tab at the top of the drawing area (see Figure 8.7) and then click the Layout1 preview panel.

**FIGURE 8.7**

Choose the Layout1 panel.

---

**OPTIONS IN THE PREVIEW PANEL**

When you hover over a Drawing tab, you see two printer icons along the top of the preview images. The icon in the upper-left corner lets you plot the layout. The icon in the upper-right corner lets you start the Publish feature. See Chapter 25, "Managing and Sharing Your Drawings," for more on the Publish feature.

---

**2.** A view of your drawing appears on a gray background, as shown in Figure 8.8. This is a view of your drawing as it will appear when plotted on your current default printer or plotter. The white area represents the printer or plotter paper.

**FIGURE 8.8**

A view of Layout1

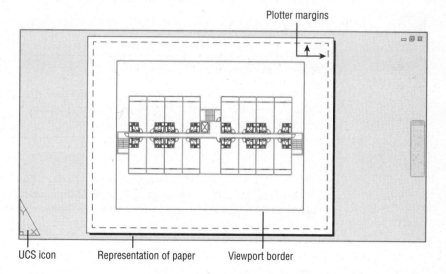

**3.** Try zooming in and out using the Zoom Realtime tool or the scroll wheel of your mouse. Notice that the entire image zooms in and out, including the area representing the paper.

Layout views give you full control over the appearance of your drawing printouts. You can print a layout view just as you did the view in Model Space.

Let's take a moment to look at the elements in the Layout1 view. As mentioned previously, the white area represents the paper on which your drawing will be printed. The dashed line immediately inside the edge of the white area represents the limits of your plotter's margins. Finally, the solid rectangle that surrounds your drawing is the outline of the viewport border. A *viewport* is an AutoCAD object that works like a window into your drawing from the layout view. Also notice the triangular symbol in the lower-left corner of the view; this is the UCS icon for the layout view. It tells you that you're currently in layout view space. You'll see the significance of this icon in the following exercise:

1. Try using a selection window to select the lobby area of your drawing. Nothing is selected.

2. Click the viewport border, which is the rectangle surrounding the drawing, as shown in Figure 8.8. This is the viewport into Model Space. Notice that you can select it.

3. Open the Properties palette by clicking the Properties arrow icon in the title bar of the Home tab's Properties panel. You can see from the Properties palette that the viewport is just like any other AutoCAD object with layer, linetype, and color assignments. You can even hide the viewport outline by turning off its layer.

4. Close the Properties palette.

5. With the viewport still selected, click the Erase tool in the Modify toolbar. The view of your drawing disappears when you erase the viewport. Remember that the viewport is like a window into the drawing you created in the model view. After the viewport is erased, the drawing view goes with it.

6. Type **U⏎** or click the Undo button in the Quick Access toolbar to restore the viewport.

---

**CREATING NEW VIEWPORTS**

You can create new viewports using the Vports command (the Rectangular/Polygon/From Object tool in the View tab's Viewports panel). See the section "Creating New Paper Space Viewports" in Chapter 15 for more information.

---

7. Double-click anywhere within the viewport's boundary. Notice that the UCS icon you're used to seeing appears in the lower-left corner of the viewport. The Layout UCS icon disappears. The Navigation bar and ViewCube® also appear inside the viewport.

8. Click the lobby in your drawing. You can now select parts of your drawing.

9. Try zooming and panning your view. Changes in your view take place only within the boundary of the viewport.

10. Click Zoom All from the Zoom flyout in the Navigation bar or type **Z⏎A⏎** to display the entire drawing in the viewport.

11. To return to Paper Space, double-click an area outside the viewport. You can also type **PS⏎** to return to Paper Space or **MS⏎** to access the space within the viewport.

This exercise shows you the unique characteristics of layout views. The objects in the viewport are inaccessible until you double-click the interior of the viewport. You can then move about and edit your drawing in the viewport, just as you would while in the model view.

Layout views can contain as many viewports as you like, and each viewport can hold a different view of your drawing. You can size and arrange each viewport any way you like, or you can create multiple viewports, giving you the freedom to lay out your drawing as you would a page in a page layout program. You can also draw in the layout view or import Xrefs and blocks for title blocks and borders.

## Setting Plot Scale in the Layout Viewports

In the first part of this chapter, you plotted your drawing from the model view. You learned that to get the plot to fit on your paper, you had to either use the Fit To Paper option in the Plot dialog box or indicate a specific drawing scale, plot area, and drawing orientation.

The layout view works in a different way: It's designed to enable you to plot your drawing at a 1-to-1 scale. Instead of specifying the drawing scale in the Plot dialog box, as you did when you plotted from the model view, you let the size of your view in the layout view viewport determine the drawing scale. You can set the viewport view to an exact scale by making changes to the properties of the viewport.

To set the scale of a viewport in a layout view, try the following exercise:

**1.** Press the Esc key to clear any selections. Then, click the viewport border to select it. You'll see the Viewport Scale tool appear in the status bar.

**2.** Click the Viewport Scale tool, and a list of common drawing scales appears (see Figure 8.9).

**FIGURE 8.9**
Choose a viewport scale.

3. Select 1/16" = 1' (metric users should select 1:20). The view in the drawing window changes to reflect the new scale for the viewport. Now most of the drawing fits into the viewport, and it's to scale. The scale of 1/16" = 1' is similar to the metric 1:200 scale, but because you used centimeters instead of millimeters as the base unit for the metric version of the plan drawing, you drop the second 0 in 200. The metric scale becomes 1:20.

4. Use the viewport grips to enlarge the viewport enough to display all of the drawing, as shown in Figure 8.10. As you move a corner grip, notice that the viewport maintains a rectangular shape.

**FIGURE 8.10**
The enlarged viewport

5. Click Plot from the Quick Access toolbar, and in the Plot dialog box, make sure the Scale option is set to 1:1 and your system printer is selected in the Printer/Plotter group; then click OK. Your drawing is plotted as it appears in the Layout tab, and it's plotted to scale.

In step 2, you used the Viewport Scale tool in the status bar to select a scale for a viewport. If you look just below the Standard Scale option, you see the Custom Scale option. Both options work like their counterparts, the options in the Plot Scale group in the Plot dialog box.

Layout views and viewports work in conjunction with your plotter settings to give you a better idea of how your plots will look. There are numerous plotter settings that can dramatically change the appearance of your layout view and your plots. Next, you'll learn how some of the plotter settings can enhance the appearance of your drawings. You'll also learn how layout views can display those settings, letting you see on your computer screen exactly what will appear on your paper output.

## Adding an Output Device

We mentioned earlier that you can set up AutoCAD for more than one output device. You can do this even if you have only one printer or plotter connected to your computer. You might want multiple printer configurations in AutoCAD for many reasons. You might want to set up your system so that you can print to a remote location over a network or the Internet. Some printer configurations are strictly file oriented, such as the AutoCAD DWF format for Internet web pages or raster file output. (See Chapter 25 for more on DWF files.)

AutoCAD works best with printers and plotters configured as Windows system devices. Although you can add devices through the AutoCAD Plot Manager, Autodesk recommends that you set up your plotters and printers as Windows devices and then use the System Printer option in AutoCAD to select your output device. (In Windows 7, choose Start ➢ Devices And Printers, and then select Add A Printer from the menu bar to configure a new printer.) You can use the Add-A-Plotter Wizard in AutoCAD to create predefined settings for your system printer so that you can quickly choose a printer or plotter setup.

You can also configure additional printers through the AutoCAD Plot Manager; this method also uses the Add-A-Plotter Wizard. Here's how it's done:

1. Click the Plotter Manager tool on the Output tab's Plot panel to open the Plotters window (see Figure 8.11). Your view of the Plotters window may look a little different, depending on your operating system, but the same basic information is there.

**FIGURE 8.11**
The Plotters window

You can also open this window by clicking the Add Or Configure Plotters button in the Plot And Publish tab of the Options dialog box. It's just an Explorer window showing you the contents of the `Plotters` folder that is buried in the `Users` folder for your Windows 8 or Windows 7 user profile (`C:\Users\`*User Name*`\AppData\Roaming\Autodesk\AutoCAD 2015\R20.0\enu\Plotters`, where *User Name* is your login name).

2. Double-click the Add-A-Plotter Wizard icon to open the Add Plotter dialog box. You see the Introduction screen, which describes the purpose of the wizard.

3. Click Next. The next screen lets you select the type of setup you want. You're offered three options: My Computer, Network Plotter Server, and System Printer. The first two options offer plotter options based on drivers specific to AutoCAD. They offer the same set of options, except the Network Plotter Server option asks you for a network server name. The System Printer option uses the existing Windows system printer as the basis for the setup.

4. Click the My Computer radio button and click Next, and you will see a listing of plotter models that are supported by AutoCAD directly through its own drivers. If you use a PostScript device, or if you want to convert drawings to raster formats, this is the place to select those options. You can select the plotter or printer manufacturer name from the Manufacturers list on the left and then select a specific model from the list on the right.

If you have a driver for a specific plotter or printer that isn't listed, you can click the Have Disk button to browse to your driver location.

5. After you've made a printer or plotter selection, click Next. You're then asked if you want to use an existing PCP or PC2 configuration file for the selected plotter. PCP and PC2 configuration files are plotter configuration files from earlier releases of AutoCAD.

6. Unless you plan to use one of those files, click Next on the Import PCP Or PC2 screen. If you selected My Computer in step 3, the Ports screen opens (see Figure 8.12). With the Plot To A Port option selected, you can use the list to select a port to which your printer or plotter is connected. The Configure Port button lets you set up the port if you have a specific requirement for it. If you intend to plot to a file instead of to a port, you can select the Plot To File radio button at the top as an alternative. An AutoSpool option is also offered if your printer requires this feature.

**FIGURE 8.12**

The Ports screen of the Add-A-Plotter Wizard

If you selected an option in step 4 that doesn't require a port setup, click the Next button to skip this option; the Plotter Name screen opens. You can enter a descriptive name in the Plotter Name text box. This name will appear in the Printer Name drop-down list of the Plot Or Page Setup dialog box.

7. Enter a name for this configuration in the space provided, and then click Next to open the Finish screen.

8. From this screen you can make adjustments to the configuration you've just created by clicking the Edit Plotter Configuration button. Click Finish to exit the Add-A-Plotter Wizard. Your new configuration appears in the Plotters window.

The Edit Plotter Configuration button lets you fine-tune your plotter settings. For example, you can calibrate your plotter for more accurate scaling of your plots, or if you're creating a raster file output configuration, you can create a custom page setting for extremely high-resolution raster images.

After you've set up a plotter, the plotter information is stored as a file with the .pc3 filename extension in the Plotters folder described earlier.

## Editing a Plotter Configuration

In step 8 of the previous exercise, you exited the Add-A-Plotter Wizard without editing the newly created plotter configuration. You can always go back and edit the configuration by opening the Plotters window (choose Plotter Manager on the Output tab's Plot panel) and double-clicking the configuration you want to edit. You can recognize a plotter configuration file by its .pc3 filename extension.

Most users use their Windows system printer or plotter for other applications besides AutoCAD, and frequently the AutoCAD settings for that printer are different from the settings used for other applications. You can set up AutoCAD to use its own settings automatically so you don't have to reconfigure your Windows system printer every time you switch applications. To do so, follow these steps:

1. Click the Page Setup Manager tool on the Output tab's Plot panel to open the Page Setup Manager dialog box. You can also right-click the Quick View Layouts tool in the status bar and choose Page Setup Manager.

2. Click the Modify button to open the Page Setup dialog box.

3. Select the printer that you want to configure in the Name drop-down list of the Printer/Plotter group.

---

### CONTROLLING THE APPEARANCE OF THE LAYOUT VIEWS

The Options dialog box offers a set of controls dedicated to the layout views. If you don't like some of the graphics in the layout views, you can turn them off. Open the Options dialog box and click the Display tab to see a set of options in the Layout Elements group in the lower-left side of the dialog box.

As you can see, you can control the display of the tabs themselves, the margins, the paper background, and the paper shadow. In addition, you can specify whether AutoCAD automatically creates a viewport or opens the Page Setup dialog box when you open a layout view for the first time.

4. Click the Properties button just to the right of the drop-down list to open the Plotter Configuration Editor dialog box. A list box displays all the properties of the printer or plotter. Not all these properties are editable, however. Each time you click a property in the list box, the lower half of the dialog box displays the options associated with that property.

5. Click the Custom Properties item in the list box. In the lower half of the dialog box you'll see the Custom Properties button (see Figure 8.13).

**FIGURE 8.13**
Click Custom Properties.

6. Click the Custom Properties button. You'll see the Windows system printer options. These are the same options you see when you edit the properties of your printer by choosing Start ➤ Printers And Faxes or Start ➤ Control Panel ➤ Printers And Other Hardware.

7. Adjust these settings the way you want them when you plot from AutoCAD and then click OK.

8. Back in the Plotter Configuration Editor dialog box, click the Save As button. A standard Save As dialog box appears.

9. Enter the name of the plot configuration you've set up or accept the default name (which is usually the name of the Windows printer or plotter), and click Save.

10. Click OK in the Plotter Configuration Editor dialog box; then click OK in the Page Setup dialog box and close the Page Setup Manager.

The Plotter Configuration Editor offers a wide variety of options that are fairly technical in nature. If you want to know more about the Plotter Configuration Editor, see the bonus chapter "Hardware and Software Tips," available at http://www.omura.com/chapters.

## Plotting Image Files and Converting 3D to 2D

If your work involves producing manuals, reports, or similar documents, you may want to add the Raster File Export option to your list of plotter configurations. The Raster File Export option lets you plot your drawings to a wide range of raster file formats, including CALS, JPEG, PCX, Targa, Tiff, and BMP. You can then import your drawings into documents that accept bitmap images. Images can be up to 8,000 × 8,000 pixels (set through the Plotter Configuration Editor) and can contain as many colors as the file format allows. If you need several raster formats, you can use multiple instances of this or any plotter configuration.

To convert your 3D wireframe models into 2D line drawings, use the Flatshot tool described in Chapter 20. You can then include your 2D line drawings with other 2D drawings for plotting and printing.

## Storing a Page Setup

Unlike most other programs, AutoCAD offers hundreds of page setup options. It can be quite a chore to keep track of and maintain all these options. But as you settle into using AutoCAD, you'll probably find that you'll set up a few plotter configurations and stick to them. AutoCAD 2015 lets you save a page setup under a name to help you store and manage the settings you use most.

You've already seen the Page Setup Manager dialog box on your way to preparing a page for printing. In this section, you'll take a closer look at this useful tool.

Follow these steps to create a page setup:

1. In AutoCAD, click the Page Setup Manager tool in the Output tab's Plot panel. The Page Setup Manager dialog box opens (see Figure 8.14). So far, you've used only the Modify option in this dialog box to modify an existing page setup. Now you'll try creating a new setup.

**FIGURE 8.14**
The Page Setup Manager

**2.** Click the New button to open the New Page Setup dialog box (see Figure 8.15).

**FIGURE 8.15**
Naming a new
page setup

**3.** To create a new page setup, first enter a name in the New Page Setup Name text box, and then select a setup from the Start With list box. AutoCAD will use the setup you select as the basis for the new setup. Notice that AutoCAD offers the name Setup1 as a default name for a new setup.

**4.** Click OK when you're finished. AutoCAD opens the Page Setup dialog box, where you can choose the settings for your new page setup.

**5.** Click OK to return to the Page Setup Manager and then close it. Your new page setup is listed in the Current Page Setup list box. From here, you can select a page setup from the list box and then click the Set Current button to make it the current page setup for the layout.

You can also import other user-defined page setups by clicking the Import button. Because page setups are stored in the drawing, the Import button opens a standard file dialog box that displays drawing files. You can then select a file from which you want to import a page setup.

The current page setup applies to the current Layout tab, but after you create a new page setup, it's offered as an option in the Page Setup Manager dialog box for all other Layout tabs in this file. You can also select a page setup directly from the Plot dialog box by using the Name drop-down list in the Page Setup group.

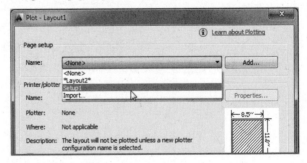

Page setups can be used with the Publish feature described in Chapter 25 to set up batch plots or in the Sheet Set feature described in the bonus chapter "Keeping a Project Organized with Sheet Sets," available at http://www.omura.com/chapters. You can also create an entirely new page setup on the fly while in the Plot dialog box. To do this, click the Plot tool in the Quick Access toolbar and then click the Add button in the Page Setup group of the Plot dialog box. This opens a simple dialog box where you can enter a name for your new setup. After you enter a new name and click OK, you can proceed to choose your page settings. Then click OK or Apply To Layout, and the setup will be saved under the new name.

# Plotter and Printer Hardware Considerations

Positioning an AutoCAD drawing on the printer output is something of an art. Before you face a deadline with hundreds of plots to produce, you may want to create some test plots and carefully refine your plotter settings so that you have AutoCAD set up properly for those rush jobs.

As part of the setup process, you'll need to understand how your particular printer or plotter works. Each device has its own special characteristics, so a detailed description of printer hardware setup is beyond the scope of this book. The following sections include a few guidelines.

## Understanding Your Plotter's Limits

If you're familiar with a word processing or page layout program, you know that you can set the margins of a page, thereby telling the program exactly how far from each edge of the paper you want the text to appear. With AutoCAD, you don't have that luxury. To place a plot on your paper accurately, you must know the plotter's actual printable area. These are the margins, beyond which the plotter won't plot. These limits vary from plotter to plotter (see Figure 8.16).

**FIGURE 8.16**
Visual representation of the printable area on a sheet

Printer margins, which vary with plotter

Plotter media

It's crucial that you know your printer's or plotter's margins in order to place your drawings accurately on the sheet. Take some time to study your plotter manual and find out exactly what these limits are. Then make a record of them and store it somewhere in case you or someone else needs to format a sheet in a special way.

Margins for printers often depend on the software that drives them. You may need to consult your printer manual or use the trial-and-error method of plotting several samples to see how they come out.

## UNDERSTANDING THE PLOT AND PUBLISH TAB IN THE OPTIONS DIALOG BOX

We mentioned the Plot And Publish tab in the Options dialog box earlier in this chapter. This tab contains several options related to plotting that can be useful. Here's a summary of those options and their purposes.

### DEFAULT PLOT SETTINGS FOR NEW DRAWINGS

The options in this group let you control the default plot settings for new drawings and for drawings from earlier versions of AutoCAD that are opened for the first time in AutoCAD 2015. The Use As Default Output Device radio button and drop-down list let you select the default plotter or printer to be used with new drawings. When the Use Last Successful Plot Settings radio button is selected, the last successful plotter settings for subsequent plots are used. This is how earlier versions of AutoCAD worked. The Add Or Configure Plotters button opens the Plotters window. This is the same as choosing the Plot Manager tool from the Output tab's Plot panel. From the Plotters window, you can launch the Add-A-Plotter Wizard to add new plotter configurations. You can also edit existing plotter configurations.

## GENERAL PLOT OPTIONS

These options control some of the general plotter parameters. The Keep The Layout Paper Size If Possible radio button causes AutoCAD to attempt to plot to the paper size specified in the Plot dialog box, regardless of the paper size in the plotter. If the specified size is larger than the capacity of the plotter, a warning message is displayed. The Use The Plot Device Paper Size option causes AutoCAD to use the paper size specified by the system printer or the PC3 plot configuration file currently in use. Both settings are also controlled by the Paperupdate system variable.

The System Printer Spool Alert drop-down list offers control over printer-spooling alert messages. The OLE Plot Quality drop-down list lets you control the quality of OLE objects embedded in or linked to a drawing. This setting can also be controlled through the Olequality system variable.

When the Use OLE Application When Plotting OLE Objects check box is selected, AutoCAD launches any application that is associated with an OLE object embedded or linked to the AutoCAD drawing that is currently being plotted. This helps improve the plot quality of OLE objects. You can also set this option through the Olestartup system variable. See Chapter 19, "Getting and Exchanging Data from Drawings," for more information about Object Linking and Embedding (OLE).

The Hide System Printers option affects the Printer/Plotter group's Name drop-down list in the Plot and Page Setup dialog boxes. With this option turned on, you see only printers that have a .pc3 filename extension associated with them. These include printers that have been set up using the Add-A-Plotter Wizard discussed earlier in this chapter.

## PLOT TO FILE

You have the option to plot to a file that can be downloaded to your printer or plotter at a later date. The Plot To File group lets you specify the default destination for the plot files.

## PLOT AND PUBLISH LOG FILE

You can maintain a plot log file that records information about each plot you make. This can be helpful when you must keep records of hard-copy output for billing purposes. You can specify the location of the plot and publishing log file in the Files tab of the Options dialog box under the Plot And Publishing Log File Location listing. The log file has a .csv filename extension.

## BACKGROUND PROCESSING OPTIONS

AutoCAD performs background plots so that after you begin a plot, you can immediately return to your drawing work instead of waiting for the plot to be completed. The options in this group let you turn on this feature either for standard plotting or for the Publish feature discussed in Chapter 25. You can also control this option through the Backgroundplot system variable.

## PLOT STAMP SETTINGS

This button opens the Plot Stamp dialog box, which you saw in the section "Plot Options" earlier in this chapter. The Plot Stamp dialog box lets you determine what information is displayed in a plot stamp, which is a label placed on the print of a drawing to provide information about the source file.

### PLOT STYLE TABLE SETTINGS

When you click this button, the Plot Style Table Settings dialog box opens. This dialog box controls the type of plot styles used in AutoCAD. In the case of named plot styles, you can also select a default plot style for layer 0 and a default plot style for objects. Note that the Use Color Dependent Plot Styles and Use Named Plot Styles radio buttons don't have an effect on the current drawing; they affect only new drawings and pre–AutoCAD 2000 drawings being opened for the first time in AutoCAD 2015. The Default Plot Style Table drop-down list lets you select a default plot style table for new and pre–AutoCAD 2000 drawings. These settings are also controlled by the Pstylepolicy system variable.

The Add Or Edit Plot Style Tables button in the Plot Style Table Settings dialog box opens the Plot Styles dialog box. From there, you can double-click an existing plot style table file or start the Add-A-Plot Style Table Wizard to create a new plot style.

### SPECIFY PLOT OFFSET RELATIVE TO

Here you can determine whether the plot offset is set in relation to the printable area of your printer or to the edge of the paper. The printable area is determined by the printer margin.

### AUTO PUBLISH

You can set up AutoCAD to automatically publish your file to a DWF, DWFx, or PDF file when you save or close a drawing. Place a check mark in the Automatic Publish check box to enable this feature. The Automatic Publish Settings button gives you control over the location of the published files as well as the file format, password protection, and other file features. Note that this feature will increase the time it takes to save or close a file.

---

After you've established the limits of your plotter or printer, you'll be better equipped to fit your drawing within those limits. You can then establish some standard drawing limits based on your plotter's limits, such as to define custom sheet sizes. Although AutoCAD offers standard sheet sizes in the Paper Size group of the Page Setup and Plot dialog boxes, these sizes don't always take into account the printable area.

## Knowing Your Plotter's Origins

Another important consideration is the location of your plotter's origin. For example, on some plotters the lower-left corner of the plot area is used as the origin. Other plotters use the center of the plot area as the origin. When you plot a drawing that is too large to fit the sheet on a plotter that uses a corner for the origin, the image is pushed toward the top and to the right of the sheet (see Figure 8.17). When you plot a drawing that is too large to fit on a plotter that uses the center of the paper as the origin, the image is pushed outward in all directions from the center of the sheet.

In each situation, the origin determines a point of reference from which you can relate your drawing in the computer to the physical output. After you understand this, you're better equipped to place your electronic drawing accurately on the physical medium.

**FIGURE 8.17**
Plotting an over-sized image on a plotter that uses the lower-left corner for its origin

Plot origin —

Clipped portion of drawing —

---

**USING BATCH AND ELECTRONIC PLOTS**

The focus of this chapter has been printer or plotter hard-copy output. But a major part of your work will involve the transmission of electronic versions of your documents. More than ever, architects and engineers are using the Internet to exchange documents of all types, so AutoCAD offers several tools to make the process easier.

We've mentioned that you can control some of your output settings through the Plot And Publish tab of the Options dialog box. The Publish feature includes items that enable you to "print" your drawings as a file that can be emailed to clients and consultants or posted on an FTP site or website. The Publish feature lets you create a single file that contains multiple pages so that you can combine several drawing sheets into one file.

The Publish feature also enables you to plot several drawings at once without having to load and print each one individually. This can be helpful when you've finished a set of drawings and want to plot them during a break or overnight. Chapter 25 gives you a detailed look at the Publish feature.

---

## The Bottom Line

**Understand the plotter settings.**   Unlike other types of documents, AutoCAD drawings can end up on nearly any size sheet of paper. To accommodate the range of paper sizes, the AutoCAD plotter settings are fairly extensive and give you a high level of control over your output.

**Master It**   Name a few of the settings available in the Plot dialog box.

**Use layout views to control how your plots look.**　The Layout tabs in AutoCAD offer a way to let you set up how a drawing will be plotted. You can think of the layout views as paste-up areas for your drawings.

**Master It**　Name some of the items that you see in a layout view.

**Add an output device.**　Typically, AutoCAD will use the Windows system printer as an output device, but often you will find that the printer you use is a dedicated plotter that is not connected to Windows in the usual way. AutoCAD lets you add custom plotters and printers through the Add-A-Plotter Wizard.

**Master It**　How do you start the Add-A-Plotter Wizard?

**Store a page setup.**　Most of the time, you will use the same plotter settings for your drawings. You can save plotter settings using the Page Setup feature.

**Master It**　Describe a way to create a page setup. Describe how to retrieve a setup.

# Chapter 9

# Adding Text to Drawings

One of the most tedious drafting tasks is applying notes to your drawing. The AutoCAD® 2015 software makes this job faster by enabling you to type your notes, insert text from other sources, and copy notes that repeat throughout a drawing, and it helps you create professional-looking notes using a variety of fonts, type sizes, and type styles.

In this chapter, you'll add notes to your apartment building plan. In the process, you'll explore some of the AutoCAD text-creation and text-editing features. You'll learn how to control the size, slant, type style, and orientation of text and how to import text files. You'll start by working through some exercises that show you the process of preparing a drawing for text. You'll then add a few lines of text to the drawing and learn how text size and drawing scale interrelate. The rest of the chapter shows you the tools available for formatting text to fit your application.

In this chapter, you will learn to

- ♦ Prepare a drawing for text
- ♦ Set the annotation scale and add text
- ♦ Explore text formatting in AutoCAD
- ♦ Add simple single-line text objects
- ♦ Use the Check Spelling feature
- ♦ Find and replace text

## Preparing a Drawing for Text

In these first sections, you'll go through the process of adding text to a drawing that currently has none. By doing so, you'll gain firsthand experience in using all the tools you'll need for adding text to a drawing. Start by setting up a drawing to prepare it for the addition of text:

1. Start AutoCAD, and open the Unit file. If you haven't created this file, you can use the file called 9a-unit.dwg (metric users should use 9a-unit-metric.dwg), which you'll find among this chapter's files at the book's web page, www.sybex.com/go/masteringautocad2015. After the file is open, choose Save As from the Application menu to save the Unit drawing to a file called Unit.dwg.

2. Create a layer called **Notes**, and make it the current layer. Notes is the layer on which you'll keep all your text information.

3. If the FLR-PAT layer is on, turn it off. Otherwise, the floor pattern you added previously will obscure the text you enter during the exercises in this chapter.

4. Set up your view so it looks similar to the top image in Figure 9.1.

**FIGURE 9.1**

The top image shows the points to pick to place the text boundary window. The bottom image shows the completed text.

Click here to start text boundary.

Text boundary window

Text flow direction indicated by arrow

Click here to finish.

---

### ORGANIZE TEXT WITH LAYERS

It's a good idea to keep your notes on a separate layer so you can plot drawings containing only the graphics information or freeze the Notes layer to save redraw/regeneration time.

---

## Organizing Text by Styles

**CERT OBJECTIVE**

Before you begin to add text to your drawing, you should set up a text style or two. You can think of text styles as a tool to store your most common text formatting. Styles store text height and font information so you don't have to set these options every time you enter text. Generally, you'll need only a few text styles.

Even if you started to add text without creating your own text style, you would still be using a text style. That's because every text object must have a style, so AutoCAD includes the Standard text style in every new drawing. The Standard style uses an AutoCAD font called Txt and includes numerous other settings that you'll learn about in this section. These other settings include width factor, oblique angle, and default height.

**SET UP DEFAULT FONTS IN TEMPLATES**

If you don't like the way the AutoCAD default style is set up, open the acad.dwt template file and change the Standard text style settings to your liking. You can also add other styles that you use frequently. Remember, AutoCAD files with the .dwt filename extension in their name are just AutoCAD DWG files with a slightly different extension to set them apart as templates.

In this next exercise, you'll create a text style called Note1, which you'll use to add notes to the unit plan on which you've been working:

1. Click the Text Style drop-down list from the Home tab's expanded Annotation panel and select Manage Text Styles, or type **St↵**. This opens the Text Style dialog box (see Figure 9.2).

**FIGURE 9.2**

The Text Style dialog box

2. Click the New button to the right in the dialog box to open the New Text Style dialog box.

3. Enter **Note1** for the name of your new style, and then click OK.

4. In the Text Style dialog box again, click the Font Name drop-down list in the Font group and select a font for your style.

5. Locate the Courier New TrueType font and select it. A quick way to locate the font is to click in the list and start typing the font name.

6. Select the Annotative option in the Size group (see Figure 9.3).

**FIGURE 9.3**

The Annotative option in the Text Style dialog box

**7.** In the Paper Text Height box, enter **0.1**. You'll see your input change to ⅛" if you are using the architectural unit style. Metric users should enter **0.15**.

**8.** Close the dialog box.

The Annotative option you turned on in step 6 is an important feature for keeping your text at the proper size for your drawing scale. You'll see how it works in the exercises later in the section "Setting the Annotation Scale and Adding Text."

---

**MAKING A STYLE THE DEFAULT**

Once you've created a style, you can make it the default current style by selecting it from the Text Style drop-down list in the Annotate tab's Text panel.

---

## Getting Familiar with the Text and Annotation Scale Control Panels

Before you get much further into the AutoCAD text features, take a moment to familiarize yourself with the Annotate tab's Text and Annotation Scaling panels (see Figure 9.4). You'll be using a few of these panel tools in this chapter. If you need to, you can refer to this figure as you work through the exercises.

**FIGURE 9.4**
The Text panel (left) and the Annotation Scaling panel (right)

If your Annotation panel doesn't look like the one in this figure, hover over it and the panel will expand to display the options.

## Setting the Annotation Scale and Adding Text

You've got a text style set up and ready to use. Now you'll add some text to your unit plan. Before you begin, you should determine a drawing scale. This is important because with the

Annotative feature turned on, AutoCAD needs to know the drawing scale in order to set the size of the text. Follow these steps:

1. In the right side of the status bar, click the drop-down arrow next to Annotation Scale.

2. Select ¼″ = 1′-0″. Metric users, select 1:100.

You've just set the drawing scale for the Model Space view. This isn't a permanent setting; you can change it at any time, as you'll see later. The settings you used for the annotation scale are somewhat arbitrary for the purposes of demonstrating the Annotative Scale feature.

## Inserting Text

Finally, you can begin to add text. To start, you'll add some text to label the entrance to the floor plan. The process is similar to the process in other graphics programs that offer a text feature. You draw a boundary in the area where you want the text to appear, and then you start typing:

1. Turn off the Object Snap tool in the status bar.

2. Click the Multiline Text tool in the Annotate tab's Text panel. You can also type **MT⏎**. You see a prompt that tells you the current text style and height:

```
Current text style: "Note1" Text height: 4 13/16"
Annotative: Yes
Specify first corner:
```

3. Click the first point indicated in the top image in Figure 9.1 to start the text boundary window. This boundary window indicates the area in which you'll place the text. Notice the arrow near the bottom of the window; it indicates the direction of the text flow. You don't have to be too precise about where you select the points for the boundary because you can adjust the location and size later.

4. At the `Specify opposite corner or [Height/Justify/Line spacing/Rotation/ Style/Width/Columns]:` prompt, click the second point indicated in the top image in Figure 9.1. The Text Editor tab appears with the text editor superimposed over the area you just selected (see Figure 9.5).

5. Click the text editor and type **Entry**. As you type, the word appears in the text editor just as it will appear in your drawing.

6. Press ⏎ to advance one line; then enter **6′ by 7′**.

7. Press ⏎ to advance another line, and enter **[182 cm by 213 cm]**.

8. Press ⏎ again to advance another line, and enter **carpet floor**.

9. Click Close Text Editor on the Close panel. The text appears in the drawing just as it did in the text editor. (See the bottom image in Figure 9.1.)

**FIGURE 9.5**

The text editor floats over the selected area.

After you've added text, if the text doesn't quite fit in the area you've indicated, you can make adjustments to the text boundary. Click the text to expose the text boundary, including the boundary grips. Then click and drag the grips to resize the boundary. The word-wrap feature automatically adjusts the text formatting to fit the text boundary.

You may have noticed that the Text Editor tab and text editor work like any text editor; if you make a typing error, you can highlight the error and retype the letter or word. You can perform other word processing functions too, such as using search and replace, importing text, and changing fonts.

You also saw that the text editor shows how your text will appear in the location you selected using the text boundary. If your view of the drawing is such that the text is too small to be legible, the text editor enlarges the text so that you can read it clearly. Likewise, if you're zoomed in too closely to see the entire text, the text editor adjusts the text to enable you to see all of it.

---

### MAKING TEXT READABLE OVER HATCH PATTERNS

If text is included in a selection where a hatch pattern is to be placed, AutoCAD automatically avoids hatching over the text. If you add text over a hatched area, you can use the Background Mask tool in the Text Editor tab to make the text more readable. Another option is to use the Select Boundary Objects tool in the Hatch Edit tab to add text to a hatch selection.

---

## Exploring Text and Scale

Even though your text height is 0.1′, or 0.15 cm, it appears at the appropriately enlarged size for the current scale. If the text were drawn to the size of 0.1′, it would be very small and barely visible. However, the Annotative Scale feature makes the adjustment to your text size based on the Annotation Scale setting.

You can see how the Annotation Scale setting affects your text:

1. First, make sure the Show Annotation Objects tool is turned on in the status bar, or type **Annoallvisible**↵**1**↵.

2. Click the Annotation Scale setting, and select 1/2″ = 1″-0″. Metric users should select 1:50. The new text changes to the appropriate size for the selected scale.

3. Click the Add/Delete Scales tool in the Annotate tab's Annotation Scaling panel, or enter **Objectscale**↵.

4. At the `Select annotative objects:` prompt, select the text and press ↵. You see the Annotation Object Scale dialog box (see Figure 9.6) listing the annotation scales you have used for this drawing.

**FIGURE 9.6**
The Annotation
Object Scale
dialog box

5. You can add additional scales to your text object. Click the Add button, which opens the Add Scales To Object dialog box (see Figure 9.7).

6. Select 1/2″ = 1′-0″ from the list (metric users should select 1:50) and click OK, and then click OK again in the Annotation Object Scale dialog box.

Now test your settings by changing the Annotation Scale value back to the previous setting:

1. In the status bar, click the Annotation Scale setting, and select 1/4″= 1′-0″. Metric users should select 1:100.

2. The text changes back to its original size.

**FIGURE 9.7**

The Add Scales To
Object dialog box

In steps 2 through 4 of the first exercise in this section, you added a new annotation scale to
the text. This is necessary for the text to be aware of the new annotation scale you want to use.
Each time you include a new scale for your drawing, you need to add an annotation scale to the
text in your drawing.

If you prefer, you can turn on the Automatically Add Scales To Annotative Objects tool
in the status bar, which does just what its name says. The keyboard command for this tool is
**Annoautoscale**⌐4⌐. Once a scale is added, you can quickly change between scales by selecting
a scale from the Annotation Scale list.

So far, you've used only a single multiline text object. However, if you have many notes distrib-
uted throughout a drawing, you'll need to add an annotation scale to all of them before they can
automatically adjust themselves to the different scales you'll use with your drawing. If you have
the Automatically Add Scales To Annotative Objects tool turned on in the status bar, this happens
automatically. Otherwise, you'll have to add the scales to each annotative object. This is easy to do
because you have the option to select as many objects as you need when adding annotation scales.

---

### Text and Scale in Legacy Drawings

AutoCAD 2015 offers the Annotative Scale feature to automate the scaling of text and other objects
to their proper size based on the drawing's annotation scale. But there is a good chance that you'll
encounter drawings that were created before the Annotative Scale feature was available. For that
reason, you should have a basic understanding of scale factors as they apply to text.

As you know by now, AutoCAD lets you draw at full scale—that is, you can represent distances
as values equivalent to the actual size of the object. When you later plot the drawing, you tell
AutoCAD the scale at which you want to plot, and the program reduces the drawing accordingly.
This gives you the freedom to enter measurements at full scale and not worry about converting
them to various scales every time you enter a distance. Unfortunately, in earlier versions of
AutoCAD this feature created problems when users entered text and dimensions. You had to
make the text height very large in order for it to be readable when scaled down.

To illustrate this point, imagine you're drawing the unit plan at full size on a very large sheet of
paper. When you're finished with this drawing, it will be reduced to a scale that enables it to fit
on an 8½″ × 11″ sheet of paper. So you have to make your text large to keep it legible after it's
reduced. If you want text to appear ⅛″ high when the drawing is plotted, you must convert it to
a considerably larger size when you draw it. To do so, you multiply the desired height of the final
plotted text by a scale conversion factor. (See Chapter 3, "Setting Up and Using the Drafting
Tools," for more on scale conversion factors.)

For example, if your drawing is at a ⅛" = 1'-0" scale, you multiply the desired text height, ⅛", by the scale conversion factor of 96 to get a height of 12". This is the height you must make your text to get ⅛" high text in the final plot.

With AutoCAD 2015, you don't have to work through the math to get the right text size for your drawing. But if you encounter a drawing that was created in an earlier version of AutoCAD and you notice that the text size is very large, you'll know why.

## Understanding the Text Style Dialog Box Options

You've just taken nearly all the steps you'll need to know to add text to any drawing. Now let's take a step back and look more closely at some of the finer points of adding text, starting with text styles. The following sections give you more detailed information about the text style settings you saw in the early part of this chapter. They explain those settings and their purposes. Some of them, such as Width Factor, can be quite useful. Others, such as the Backwards and Vertical options, are rarely used. Take a moment to study these settings to become familiar with what is available and make a mental note of these items for future reference.

### Styles

In the Styles list box, you'll see a list showing the current style. This list also contains other styles that may be present in the drawing. The drop-down list below the Styles list box lets you control whether all styles are listed or just those that are being used in the drawing. In addition, there are the Set Current, New, and Delete buttons and options in the Font and Effects groups. You have already seen the Size group.

### Set Current/New/Delete

Set Current makes the selected style the current one. New lets you create a new text style. Delete lets you delete the selected style.

The Delete option isn't available for the Standard style.

### Font

In the Font group, you have the following options:

**Font Name** Lets you select a font from a list of available fonts. The list is derived from the font resources available to Windows 8, Windows 7, Windows Vista, or Windows XP plus the standard AutoCAD fonts.

**Font Style** Offers variations of a font, such as italic or bold, when they're available.

**Use Big Font** Applicable to Asian fonts. This option is offered only with AutoCAD fonts.

### Size

The Size group offers settings relating to text size, scale, and orientation.

**Annotative** Causes the text size to adjust automatically to the current annotation scale setting.

**Match Text Orientation To Layout**   Causes the text orientation to match the orientation of a layout view. This option is available only when the Annotative option is on.

**Height/Paper Text Height**   Lets you enter a font size. With the Annotative option turned off, this option is named *Height* and will set the absolute height of the text. With the Annotative option turned on, it shows *Paper Text Height* and will set the height of the text when printed. A 0 height has special meaning when you use the Text command to enter single-line text as described later in this chapter.

## Effects

In the Effects group, you have the following options:

**Upside Down**   Displays text upside down.

**Backwards**   Displays text backward.

**Vertical**   Displays text in a vertical column.

**Width Factor**   Adjusts the width and spacing of the characters in the text. A value of 1 keeps the text at its normal width. Values greater than 1 expand the text, and values less than 1 compress the text.

This is the Simplex font expanded by 1.4

This is the Simplex font using a width factor of 1

This is the Simplex font compressed by .6

**Oblique Angle**   Skews the text at an angle. When this option is set to a value greater than 0, the text appears italicized. A value of less than 0 (–12, for example) causes the text to lean to the left.

*This is the Simplex font using a 12–degree oblique angle*

You can also set the width factor and oblique angle directly for text using the Width Factor and Oblique Angle tools in the expanded Formatting panel under the Text Editor Ribbon panel. This tab is available when you create new text or double-click existing text.

---

**RENAMING A TEXT STYLE OR OTHER NAMED OBJECT**

If you need to rename a text style or other named object in AutoCAD, you can do so using the Rename command. Enter **Ren⏎** at the Command prompt to open the Rename dialog box. In the Named Objects list box to the left, choose Text Styles. Click the name of the style you want to change from the Items list on the right; the name appears in the Old Name box below the list. In the box next to the Rename To button, enter the new name. Click the Rename To button, and click OK.

---

# Exploring Text Formatting in AutoCAD

CERT
OBJECTIVE

You've seen how you can set up a style and make scale adjustments. AutoCAD also offers a wide range of text-formatting options that are typical of the options in most word processing programs. You can control fonts, text height, justification, line spacing, and width. You can even include special characters such as degree symbols or stacked fractions. With these additional formatting tools, you can make adjustments to the text style with which you started.

## Adjusting the Text Height and Font

To get some experience using the text-formatting tools in AutoCAD, try the following exercise. You'll use the Multiline Text tool again, but this time you'll get to try out some of its other features.

In this exercise, you'll see how you can use the Ribbon tools to adjust the size and font of text:

1. Pan your view so the kitchen is just at the top of the drawing, as shown in the first image in Figure 9.8.

**FIGURE 9.8**
Placing the text-boundary window for the living-room label and the final label

carpet floor

Click here to start the text boundary.

Click here to finish.

Living Room
14'-0" by 16'-5"
[427 cm by 500 cm]

carpet floor

2. In the status bar, make sure Annotation Scale is set to 1/4" = 1'-0" (1:100 for metric users).

**3.** Click the Multiline Text tool on the Annotate tab's Text panel, and then select a text boundary window, as shown in the first image in Figure 9.8.

**4.** In the text editor, type the following:

```
Living Room
14'-0" by 16'-5" [427 cm by 500 cm]
```

Be sure you press ↵ after *Living Room*, but make the rest of the text a continuous string. As you type, the words wrap. AutoCAD uses word wrap to fit the text inside the text boundary area.

**5.** Highlight the text *14'-0" by 16'-5" [427 cm by 500 cm]* as you would in any word processor. For example, you can click the end of the line to place the cursor there and then Shift+click the beginning of the line to highlight the whole line.

**6.** In the Text Editor tab's Style panel, click in the Text Height text box and enter **1/16**↵. Metric users, enter **0.08**↵. The highlighted text changes to a smaller size.

**7.** Highlight the words *Living Room*.

**8.** In the Formatting panel, click the Font drop-down list to display a list of font options.

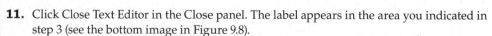

**9.** Scroll up the list until you find Arial. The text in the text editor changes to reflect the new font.

**10.** With the words *Living Room* still highlighted, click the Underline button in the Formatting panel.

**11.** Click Close Text Editor in the Close panel. The label appears in the area you indicated in step 3 (see the bottom image in Figure 9.8).

**12.** To see how you can go back to the Text Editor tab, double-click the text. The Text Editor tab and text editor appear, enabling you to change the text.

**13.** Click Close Text Editor in the Close panel.

While using the Multiline Text tool, you may have noticed the [Height/Justify/Line spacing/Rotation/Style/Width/Columns]: prompt immediately after you picked the first point of the text boundary. You can use any of these options to make on-the-fly modifications to the height, justification, line spacing, rotation style, or width of the multiline text.

For example, after clicking the first point for the text boundary, you can type **R**↵ and then specify a rotation angle for the text window, either graphically with a rubber-banding line or by entering an angle value. After you've entered a rotation angle, you can resume selecting the text boundary.

## Understanding the Text Editor Tab

CERT
OBJECTIVE

You've just experimented with a few of the Text Formatting features of the Text Editor tab. A variety of additional formatting tools are available. Figure 9.9 shows where these tools are, and Table 9.1 describes their uses. Note that Figure 9.9 shows the Ribbon with the AutoCAD window at a 1024-pixel width. The Style panel will display the text styles as a list in large displays. These Ribbon tools are fairly straightforward, and if you've used other word processing programs, you should find them easy to use. Most are common to the majority of word processors, although a few—such as Symbol, Oblique Angle, and Width Factor—are unique to AutoCAD. Look at Table 9.1 and see if there are any tools you think you'll find useful.

**FIGURE 9.9**
Additional features of the Text Editor tab

---

**TABLE 9.1:** Text formatting tools

| TOOL | USE |
| --- | --- |
| Text Style (appears when the AutoCAD window is 1024 pixels wide or smaller) | Select a text style. |
| Annotative Toggle | Turn the Annotative feature on or off. |
| Text Height | Set the paper text height of text currently being entered or edited. |

**TABLE 9.1:** Text formatting tools  *(continued)*

| TOOL | USE |
|---|---|
| Stack/Unstack Fraction | Change fractions to stacked or unstacked. |
| Bold/Italic/Underline/Overline/ Strikethrough | Select text, and then select one of these options to add bold, italic, underline, overline, or strikethrough to the text. |
| Match Text Formatting | Select text with desired formatting, click Match, and then select text to change format. |
| Color | Select text, and then choose a color from this drop-down list. |
| Font | Select a font different from the font for the current text style. |
| Background Mask | Control the background mask feature, which places a background behind text to make it more readable when placed over hatch patterns. |
| Change Case | Change the case of text. |
| Line Spacing | Set the line spacing in paragraphs. You can also set line spacing in the Properties palette for an Mtext object or by using the Paragraph dialog box. (See "Setting Indents and Tabs" later in this chapter.) |
| Bullets And Numbering | Select a text list, click this tool, and then select Lettered, Numbered, or Bulleted to add letters, numbers, or bullets to the list. |
| Default/Left/Center/Right/Justify/ Distribute | Click the appropriate tool to align the text to the left, center, or right side of the text boundary. Justify adds space between words to force left and right alignment. Distribute adds space between letters to force left and right alignment. |
| Paragraph Dialog Box | Open a dialog box that lets you set up paragraph formatting, including tabs, indents, and paragraph spacing. |
| Columns | Indicate the number of columns and how the columns are set up. |
| Symbol | Place the cursor at a location for the symbol, and then click the Symbol tool to find and add a symbol. (See Figure 9.10 later in this chapter for the available symbols.) |
| Field | Click to open the Field dialog box where you can add a text field. See "Adding Formulas to Cells" in Chapter 10, "Using Fields and Tables," for more about fields. |
| More | Use Character Set to insert foreign language characters, such as Cyrillic or Greek. Use Editor Settings to choose settings for the text editor. |
| Ruler | Click to turn the ruler at the top of the Text panel on or off. |

## Adding Symbols and Special Characters

The Text Editor tab also offers a tool called Symbol. This tool lets you add special symbols common to technical drawing and drafting. Figure 9.10 shows the symbols that are offered in the Symbol tool in the form of a drop-down list.

**FIGURE 9.10**
The AutoCAD symbols

| | | | |
|---|---|---|---|
| Degrees | $x°$ | Identity | $\equiv$ |
| Plus/Minus | $\pm$ | Initial Length | $\bigcirc$ |
| Diameter | $\phi$ | Monument Line | Ⴊ |
| Almost Equal | $\approx$ | Not Equal | $\neq$ |
| Angle | $\angle$ | Ohm | $\Omega$ |
| Boundary Line | Ɓ | Omega | $\Omega$ |
| Center Line | Ȼ | Property Line | Ʀ |
| Delta | $\Delta$ | Subscript 2 | $x_2$ |
| Electrical Phase | $\Phi$ | Squared | $x^2$ |
| Flow Line | Ƒ | Cubed | $x^3$ |

At the bottom of the Symbol drop-down list is an option called Other. By clicking the Other option, you open the Windows Character Map dialog box (see Figure 9.11). Characters such as the trademark (™) and copyright (©) symbols are often available in the fonts offered in the Character Map. The contents of the Character Map depend on the font currently selected.

**FIGURE 9.11**
The Character Map

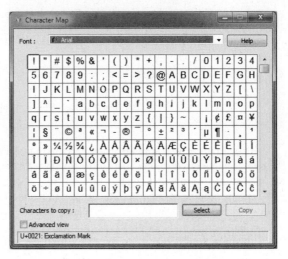

The Character Map is a Windows accessory. If it doesn't appear when you choose Other from the Symbol tool menu, you may need to install the Character Map from your Windows installation CD.

Finally, if your application requires music, math, astronomy, Greek, or other symbols, AutoCAD offers a set of fonts with special symbols. Figure 9.17, later in this chapter, shows these fonts and the symbols they contain. You can set up text styles with these fonts or call them up directly from the Formatting panel's Font option.

### TEXT JUSTIFICATION AND OSNAPS

You may have noticed that the object-justification list offers three center options: Top Center, Middle Center, and Bottom Center. All three of these options have the same effect on the text's appearance, but they each have a different effect on how osnaps act on the text. Figure 9.12 shows where the osnap point occurs on a text boundary depending on which justification option is selected. A multiline text object has only one insertion point on its boundary, which you can access with the Insert osnap.

**FIGURE 9.12**

The location of the Insert osnap point on a text boundary, based on its justification setting

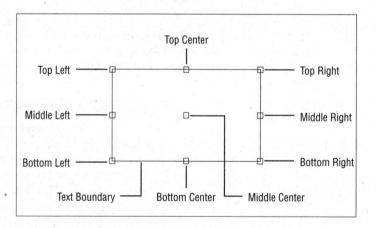

The osnap point also appears as an extra grip point on the text boundary when you click the text. If you were to center-justify the text you just entered, you would see that a grip point appears at the top center of the text boundary.

Knowing where the osnap points occur can be helpful when you want to align the text with other objects in your drawing. In most cases, you can use the grips to align your text boundary, but the Top Center and Middle Center justification options enable you to use the center and middle portions of your text to align the text with other objects.

## CHANGING JUSTIFICATION OF MULTIPLE TEXT OBJECTS

You've seen how you can change the justification of an individual text object, but you'll often find that you need to change the justification of several text objects at one time. AutoCAD offers the Justifytext command for this purpose. To use it, click the Justify tool in the Annotate tab's Text panel, or type **Justifytext**↵ at the Command prompt. At the Select objects: prompt, select the text you want to change and then press ↵ to confirm your selection. You'll see the following prompt in the command line (or at the cursor if Dynamic Input is on):

```
[Left/Align/Fit/Center/Middle/Right/TL/TC/TR/ML/MC/MR/BL/BC/BR] <Left>:
```

Enter the letters corresponding to the type of justification you want to use for the text. (See the section "Justifying Single-Line Text Objects" later in this chapter for a description of these options.) After you enter an option, the selected text changes to conform to the selected justification option.

## Setting Indents and Tabs

You should also know about the indent and tab features of the text editor. You may have noticed the ruler at the top of the text editor. Figure 9.13 shows that ruler, including tabs and indent markers.

**FIGURE 9.13**
The ruler at the top of the text editor lets you quickly set tabs and indents for text.

The indent markers let you control the indention of the first line and the rest of the paragraph. The tab markers give you control over tab spacing. For new text, the tab markers don't appear until you add them by clicking the ruler. The following exercises will demonstrate the use of these markers.

Start by practicing with the indent markers:

1. Save the Unit drawing, and then open the indent.dwg file. This file contains some text with which you'll experiment.

2. Double-click the text at the top of the drawing to open the Text Editor tab.

3. Press Ctrl+A to highlight all the text in the text editor. This is necessary to indicate the text group to be affected by your indent settings.

4. Click and drag the top indent marker two spaces to the right. The indent of the first line moves with the marker. A note appears above the ruler showing you how much indent you're applying. Also notice that the text at the first tab remains at its starting location.

**5.** Click and drag the bottom indent marker two spaces to the left. The rest of the paragraph moves with the marker. Again, you see a note by the ruler showing how much indent you're applying.

**6.** Click the Close Text Editor tool in the Text Editor tab to exit.

Here you see how you can control the indents of the selected text with the indent markers. You can set paragraphs of a single Mtext object differently, giving you a wide range of indent-formatting possibilities. Just select the text you want to set, and then adjust the indent markers.

Now try the tab markers. For this exercise, you'll try the text-import feature to import a tab-delimited text file:

**1.** Click the Multiline Text tool on the Annotate tab's Text panel.

**2.** For the first corner of the text boundary, click the upper-left corner of the large rectangle in the drawing, just below the paragraph.

**3.** For the opposite corner of the text boundary, click the lower-right corner of the rectangle.

**4.** Right-click in the text editor, and select Import Text.

**5.** In the Select File dialog box, locate and select the `tabtest.txt` file and then click Open. The contents of the `tabtest.txt` file are displayed in the text editor.

The file you just imported was generated from the Attribute Extraction Wizard in AutoCAD. You'll learn more about this feature in Chapter 12, "Using Attributes." This file contains tabs to align the columns of information. You can adjust those tabs in the Text Formatting toolbar, as you'll see in the next set of steps.

Now use the tab markers to adjust the tab spacing of the columns of text:

**1.** Press Ctrl+A to select all the text.

**2.** Click the ruler at a point that is at the 12th mark from the left (that's three of the taller tick marks in the ruler). An L-shaped marker appears, and the first tab column of text moves to this position.

**3.** Click the ruler again at the 20th mark. The second tab column aligns to this position.

**4.** Continue to click the ruler to add more tab markers so the text looks similar to Figure 9.14. Don't worry about being exact; this is just for practice. After you've placed a marker, you can click and drag it to make adjustments.

**FIGURE 9.14**
Add tab markers
so your text looks
similar to
this figure.

**5.** Click Close Text Editor in the Text Editor tab's Close panel. The text appears in the drawing as a door schedule.

Here you saw how you can create a table or a schedule from an imported text file. You can also create a schedule from scratch by composing it directly in the text editor of the Multiline Text command. AutoCAD also offers the Table feature, which is specifically designed for creating tables (see Chapter 10). Still, the previous example offers a way to demonstrate the tab feature in the Multiline Text tool, and you may encounter a file in which a table is formatted in the way described here.

In addition to using the indent and tab markers on the ruler, you can control indents and tabs through the Paragraph dialog box. Do the following to get a firsthand look:

**1.** Double-click the text at the top of the `indent.dwg` drawing (the one you edited in the first part of this section), and then press Ctrl+A to select all the text.

**2.** Right-click the ruler above the text editor, and select Paragraph to open the Paragraph dialog box (see Figure 9.15). The Paragraph dialog box also lets you set other paragraph settings, such as alignment, spacing between paragraphs, and line spacing in the paragraph.

**FIGURE 9.15**
The Paragraph
dialog box

3. Change the value in the First Line box to **1.5** and the Hanging box to **2.2**.

4. Double-click the tab position box in the upper-left corner, just below the row of tab symbols in the Tab group. Enter **2.2**, and click the Add button.

5. Click OK. The text now appears indented from the numbers.

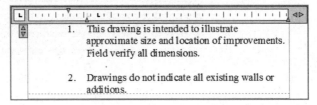

6. Click the Close Text Editor tool in the Close panel. The text in the drawing is now formatted as it appeared in the text editor.

7. Close but do not save the `indent.dwg` file.

In this exercise, you used the Paragraph dialog box to set the paragraph indent and the first tab marker to be the same value. This causes the text portion of the list to be aligned at a distance of 2.2 drawing units from the left text boundary, leaving the list number extended farther to the left. This gives the list a more professional appearance.

---

### SETTING EXACT MTEXT WIDTH AND HEIGHT

You may have noticed the options Set Mtext Width and Set Mtext Height in the right-click context menu in step 2 of the exercise using the Paragraph dialog box. The Set Mtext Width option opens a dialog box that enables you to enter a width for paragraph columns where there are multiple columns. The Set Mtext Height allows you to enter an exact height for columns.

---

The Paragraph dialog box gives you fine control over the formatting of your text. It lets you delete tabs by highlighting them in the list and clicking the Remove button. You can also add tabs at specific distances from the left margin of the text boundary by entering new tab locations in the Tab box and clicking the Add button.

You specify distances in drawing units. If your drawing is set up to use architectural units, for example, you can enter values in feet and inches or just inches. In the First Line and Hanging boxes, you enter a numeric value for paragraph indents. As you've just seen, you can use the First Line and Hanging boxes to create a numbered list by setting the Hanging box value to be the same as the first tab stop position.

## What Do the Fonts Look Like?

You've already seen a few of the fonts available in AutoCAD. Chances are that you're familiar with the TrueType fonts available in Windows. You have some additional AutoCAD fonts from which to choose. You may want to stick with the AutoCAD fonts for all but your presentation drawings because other fonts can consume more memory.

Figure 9.16 shows the basic AutoCAD text fonts. The Romans font is perhaps the most widely used because it offers a reasonable appearance while consuming little memory. Figure 9.17 lists some of the symbols and Greek fonts.

**FIGURE 9.16**
Some of the standard AutoCAD text fonts

| | |
|---|---|
| This is Txt | |
| This is Monotxt | |
| This is Simplex | (Old version of Roman Simplex) |
| This is Complex | (Old version of Roman Complex) |
| This is Italic | (Old version of Italic Complex) |
| This is Romans | (Roman Simplex) |
| This is Romand | (Roman double stroke) |
| This is Romanc | (Roman Complex) |
| This is Romant | (Roman triple stroke) |
| This is Scripts | (Script Simplex) |
| This is Scriptc | (Script Complex) |
| This is Italicc | (Italic Complex) |
| This is Italict | (Italic triple stroke) |
| Τηισ ισ Γρεεκσ | (This is Greeks - Greek Simplex) |
| Τηισ ισ Γρεεκχ | (This is Greekc - Greek Complex) |
| This is Gothice | (Gothic English) |
| Thif if Gothicg | (Gothic German) |
| This is Gothici | (Gothic Italian) |

**FIGURE 9.17**
Some of the Auto-CAD symbols and Greek fonts

### IMPORTING TEXT FILES

With multiline text objects, AutoCAD enables you to import ASCII text (TXT) or Rich Text Format (RTF) files. RTF files can be exported from Microsoft Word and most other word processing programs and retain most of their formatting in AutoCAD. Here's how you import text files:

1. With the multiline text editor open, right-click in the text area and choose Import Text.

2. In the Select File dialog box, locate a valid text file. It must be a file in either a raw text (ASCII) format, such as a Notepad file (with the filename extension.txt) or RTF (with the filename extension.rtf). RTF files can store formatting information such as boldface and varying point sizes.

3. After you've highlighted the file you want, double-click it or click Open. The text appears in the text editor window.

4. Click the Close Text Editor button, and the text appears in your drawing.

You can use the Windows Clipboard and the Cut and Paste functions to add text to a drawing. To do this, follow these steps:

1. Select some text and then choose Cut or Copy in any Windows program to place the text on the Windows Clipboard.

2. Open AutoCAD. Right-click in the drawing area, and choose Clipboard ➢ Paste from the Home tab's Clipboard panel; the pasted text appears in your drawing. However, it isn't editable in AutoCAD.

Additionally, you may drag and drop TXT and RTF files directly from Windows Explorer into AutoCAD, with the same results.

If the text is from a text editor like Windows Notepad, it is inserted as AutoCAD text. If the text contains formatting from a word processor, like Microsoft Word, the text is an OLE object.

Because AutoCAD is an OLE client, you can also attach other types of documents to an AutoCAD drawing file. See Chapter 19, "Getting and Exchanging Data from Drawings," for more on OLE support in AutoCAD.

In the following sections, you'll work with some of the AutoCAD fonts. You can see samples of all the fonts, including TrueType fonts, in the preview window of the Text Style dialog box. If you use a word processor, you're probably familiar with at least some of the TrueType fonts available in Windows and AutoCAD.

### THE *TEXTFILL* SYSTEM VARIABLE

Unlike the standard sticklike AutoCAD fonts, TrueType and PostScript fonts have filled areas. These filled areas take more time to generate, so if you use these fonts for a lot of text, your redraw and regen times will increase. To help reduce redraw and regen times, you can set AutoCAD to display and plot these fonts as outline fonts while still printing them as solid fonts.

To change this setting, type **Textfill**↵, and then type **0**↵. Doing so turns off text fill for PostScript and TrueType fonts.

# Adding Simple Single-Line Text Objects

You might find that you're entering a lot of single words or simple labels that don't require all the bells and whistles of the multiline text editor. AutoCAD offers the *single-line text object*, which is simpler to use and can speed text entry if you're adding only small pieces of text.

Continue the tutorial on the Unit.dwg or the 9b-unit.dwg sample file by trying the following exercise:

1. Adjust your view so that you see the part of the drawing shown in Figure 9.18.

**FIGURE 9.18**
Adding simple labels to the kitchen and bath by using the Text command

2. Make sure Note1 is the current text style, and then, from the Multiline Text flyout on the Annotate tab's Text panel, click the Single Line tool, or enter **Dt⏎**.

3. At the Specify start point of text or [Justify/Style]: prompt, pick the starting point for the text you're about to enter, just below the kitchen at coordinate 17'-2",22'-5" (490,664 for metric users). Note that the prompt offers the Justify and Style options.

**4.** At the Specify rotation angle of text <0>: prompt, press ↵ to accept the default, 0. You can specify any angle you like at this prompt (for example, if you want your text aligned with a rotated object). You see a text I-beam cursor at the point you picked in step 3.

**5.** Type **Kitchenette**. As you type, the word appears directly in the drawing.

---

### PASTING TEXT FROM OTHER SOURCES

You can paste text from the Clipboard into the cursor location by using the Ctrl+V keyboard shortcut or by right-clicking in the drawing area to access the context menu.

---

**6.** This time, you want to label the bathroom. Pick a point to the right of the door swing; you can approximate the location since you can always adjust the text location later. The text cursor moves to that point.

**7.** Type **Bathroom**↵. Figure 9.18 shows how your drawing should look now.

**8.** Press ↵ again to exit the Text command.

---

### CONTINUING WHERE YOU LEFT OFF

If for some reason you need to stop entering single-line text objects to do something else in AutoCAD, you can continue the text where you left off by starting the Text command and then pressing ↵ at the Specify start point of text or [Justify/Style]: prompt. The text continues immediately below the last line of text entered.

---

Here you were able to add two single lines of text in different parts of your drawing fairly quickly. Text uses the current default text style settings. If you want to create a column of single-line text, you can press ↵ to move the cursor down to start a new line below the one you just entered.

To edit single-line text, you can double-click the text. The text is highlighted, and you can begin typing to replace it all, or you can click a location in the text to make single word or character changes.

This is the end of the tutorial section of this chapter. The rest of this chapter offers additional information about text.

## Justifying Single-Line Text Objects

Justifying single-line text objects is slightly different than justifying multiline text. For example, if you change the justification setting to Center, the text moves so that the center is placed at the text-insertion point. In other words, the insertion point stays in place while the text location adjusts to the new justification setting. Figure 9.19 shows the relationship between single-line text and the insertion point based on different justification settings.

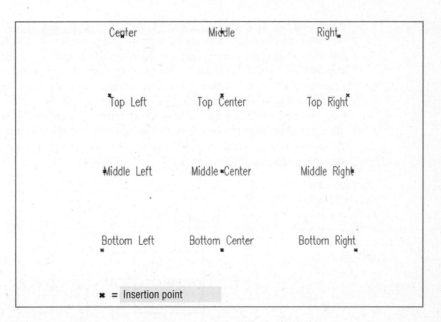

**FIGURE 9.19**
Text inserted using the various justification options

To set the justification of text as you enter it, you must enter **J**↵ at the Specify start point of text or [Justify/Style]: prompt after issuing the Text command. You can also change the current default style by entering **S**↵ and then the name of the style at the Specify start point of text or [Justify/Style]: prompt.

After you've issued Text's Justify option, you get the following prompt:

```
Enter an option
[Align/Fit/Center/Middle/Right/TL/TC/TR/ML/MC/MR/BL/BC/BR]:
```

Here are descriptions of each of these options. (We've left Fit and Align until last because they require more explanation.)

**Center**    Centers the text on the start point with the baseline on the start point.

**Middle**    Centers the text on the start point with the baseline slightly below the start point.

**Right**    Justifies the text to the right of the start point with the baseline on the start point.

**TL, TC, and TR**    TL, TC, and TR stand for Top Left, Top Center, and Top Right. When you use these justification styles, the text appears entirely below the start point, justified left, center, or right, depending on which option you choose.

**ML, MC, and MR**    ML, MC, and MR stand for Middle Left, Middle Center, and Middle Right. These styles are similar to TL, TC, and TR except that the start point determines a location midway between the baseline and the top of the lowercase letters of the text.

**BL, BC, and BR**    BL, BC, and BR stand for Bottom Left, Bottom Center, and Bottom Right. These styles too are similar to TL, TC, and TR, but here the start point determines the bottommost location of the letters of the text (the bottom of letters that have descenders, such as *p*, *q*, and *g*).

**Align and Fit**   With the Align and Fit justification options, you must specify a dimension in which the text is to fit. For example, suppose you want the word *Refrigerator* to fit in the 26"-wide box representing the refrigerator. You can use either the Fit or the Align option to accomplish this. With Fit, AutoCAD prompts you to select start and end points and then stretches or compresses the letters to fit within the two points you specify. You use this option when the text must be a consistent height throughout the drawing and you don't care about distorting the font. Align works like Fit, but instead of maintaining the current text style height, the Align option adjusts the text height to keep it proportional to the text width without distorting the font. Use this option when it's important to maintain the font's shape and proportion. Figure 9.20 demonstrates how Fit and Align work.

**FIGURE 9.20**
The word Refrigerator as it appears normally and with the Fit and Align options selected

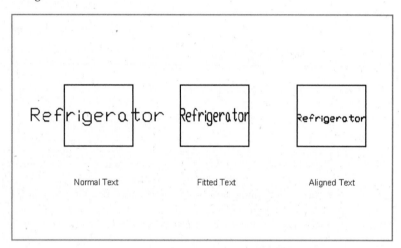

Normal Text                    Fitted Text                    Aligned Text

**A  Justify**

You can change the justification of single-line text by using the Properties palette, but the text moves from its original location while maintaining its insertion point. If you want to change the justification of text without moving the text, you can use the Justifytext command. Click the Justify tool in the Annotate tab's Text panel, or type **Justifytext** at the Command prompt, and then select the text you want to change. Justifytext works on both multiline and single-line text.

## Using Special Characters with Single-Line Text Objects

Just as with multiline text, you can add a limited set of special characters to single-line text objects. For example, you can place the degree symbol (°) after a number, or you can *underscore* (underline) text. To accomplish this, you use double percent signs (%%) in conjunction with a special code. For example, to underscore text, you enclose that text with %% followed by the letter *u*, which is the underscore code. So to create the text "This is underscored text," you enter the following at the prompt:

```
This is %%uunderscored%%u text.
```

*Overscoring* (putting a line above the text) operates in the same manner. To insert codes for symbols, you place the codes in the correct positions for the symbols they represent. For example, to enter 100.5, you type **100.5%%d**. Table 9.2 shows some other examples of special character codes.

### KEEPING TEXT FROM MIRRORING

At times, you'll want to mirror a group of objects that contain some text. This operation causes the mirrored text to appear backward. You can change a setting in AutoCAD to make the text read normally even when it's mirrored:

**1.** At the Command prompt, enter **Mirrtext**↵.

**2.** At the `Enter new value for MIRRTEXT <1>:` prompt, enter **0**↵.

Now any mirrored text that isn't in a block will read normally. The text's position, however, will still be mirrored, as shown in the following example. Mirrtext is set to 0 by default.

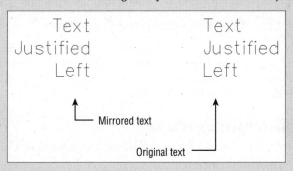

**TABLE 9.2:**     Special character codes

| CODE | WHAT IT DOES |
| --- | --- |
| %%o | Toggles overscore on and off. |
| %%u | Toggles underscore on and off. |
| %%c | Places a diameter symbol where the code occurs. |
| %%d | Places a degree sign (°) where the code occurs. |
| %%p | Places a plus/minus sign where the code occurs. |
| %%% | Forces a single percent sign. This is useful when you want a percent sign in conjunction with another code. |
| %%*nnn* | Allows the use of extended characters or Unicode characters when these characters are available for a given font. *nnn* is the three-digit value representing the ASCII extended character code. |

### Using the Character Map Dialog Box to Add Special Characters

You can add special characters to a single line of text in the same way you add special characters to multiline text. You may recall that to access special characters, you use the Character Map dialog box.

To open the Character Map dialog box, choose Start ➢ All Programs ➢ Accessories ➢ System Tools ➢ Character Map. You can then use the procedure discussed in the section "Adding Symbols and Special Characters" earlier in this chapter to cut and paste a character from the Character Map dialog box. If you use the Character Map dialog box often, create a shortcut for it and place the shortcut in your Start menu or on your Desktop.

## Using the Check Spelling Feature

Although AutoCAD is primarily a drawing program, you'll find that some of your drawings contain more text than graphics, and so AutoCAD does include a spell checking tool. If you've ever used the spelling checker in a typical word processor, such as Microsoft Word, the operation in AutoCAD will be familiar to you.

### How Check Spelling Works

The hardest part to using the Check Spelling tool is locating it in the Ribbon. Try the following to see how it works:

1. Click the Check Spelling tool in the Annotate tab's Text panel. You can also type **Sp↵**. The Check Spelling dialog box appears (see Figure 9.21).

**FIGURE 9.21**
The Check Spelling dialog box

2. You can click the Start button to check the spelling in the entire drawing. Or if you prefer, you can be more selective by choosing an option from the Where To Check drop-down list. You can select a mixture of multiline and single-line text as well as dimension text, attributes, and text in Xrefs.

When the spelling checker finds a word it doesn't recognize, the Check Spelling dialog box shows you the word along with a suggested spelling. If the spelling checker finds more than one spelling, a list of suggested alternate words appears below the box. You can then highlight the desired replacement and click the Change button to change the misspelled word, or you can click Change All to change all occurrences of the word in the selected text. If the suggested word is inappropriate, choose another word from the replacement list (if any) or enter your own spelling in the Suggestions box. Then click Change or Change All.

Here is a list of the options available in the Check Spelling dialog box:

**Add To Dictionary** Adds the word in question to the current dictionary.

**Ignore** Skips the word.

**Ignore All** Skips all occurrences of the word in the text being checked.

**Change** Changes the word in question to the word you've selected from (or entered into) the Suggestions box.

**Change All** Changes all occurrences of the current word when there are multiple instances of the misspelling.

**Dictionaries** Lets you use a different dictionary to check spelling. This option opens the Dictionaries dialog box, described in the upcoming section.

The Check Spelling feature includes types of notations that are more likely to be found in technical drawings. It also checks the spelling of text that is included in block definitions, externally referenced files, and dimensions.

## Choosing a Dictionary

Clicking the Dictionaries button in the Check Spelling dialog box opens the Dictionaries dialog box (see Figure 9.22), where you can select a main dictionary for foreign languages or create or choose a custom dictionary. The names of main dictionary files have the .dct extension. The main dictionary for the US version of AutoCAD is Enu.dct.

**FIGURE 9.22**
Choosing a
dictionary

In the Dictionaries dialog box, you can also add or delete words from a custom dictionary. Custom dictionary files are ASCII files with names that end with the .cus extension. Because they're ASCII files, you can edit them outside of AutoCAD. Click the Current Custom Dictionary drop-down list to view a list of existing custom dictionaries.

If you prefer, you can select a main or custom dictionary by using the Dctmain system variable. Click the Help button and then, in the Autodesk® Exchange window, select the Search tab. Enter **Dctmain** to learn more about the Dctmain system variable.

You can also select a dictionary from the Files tab of the Options dialog box (see Figure 9.23; choose Options from the Application menu). You can find the dictionary list under Text Editor, Dictionary, And Font File Names. Click the plus sign next to this item, and then click the plus sign next to the Main Dictionary item to display the dictionary options. From here, you can double-click the dictionary you prefer.

**FIGURE 9.23**
Choosing a dictionary via the Options dialog box

## Substituting Fonts

At times, you'll want to change all the fonts in a drawing quickly. For instance, you might need to convert the font of a drawing received from another office to a font that conforms to your own office standards. The Fontmap system variable works in conjunction with a font-mapping table, enabling you to substitute fonts in a drawing easily.

The font-mapping table is an ASCII file called Acad.fmp, which is located in the C:\ Users\*User Name*\AppData\Roaming\Autodesk\AutoCAD 2015\R20.0\enu\Support folder. You can also use a file you create yourself. You can give this file any name you choose, as long as it has the .fmp extension.

This font-mapping table contains one line for each font substitution you want AutoCAD to make. A typical line in this file reads as follows:

```
romant; C:\Program Files\Autodesk\AutoCAD 2015\Fonts\txt.shx
```

In this example, AutoCAD is directed to use the `txt.shx` font in place of the `romant.shx` font. To execute this substitution, you type **Fontmap⏎*Fontmap_filename*⏎**.

*Fontmap_filename* is the font-mapping table you created. This tells AutoCAD where to look for the font-mapping information. Then you issue the Regen command to view the font changes. To disable the font-mapping table, type **Fontmap⏎**.

You can also specify a font-mapping file in the Files tab of the Options dialog box. Look for the Text Editor, Dictionary, And Font File Names listing. Click the plus sign next to this listing, and then click the plus sign next to the Font Mapping File listing to display the name and location of the current default font-mapping file. If you hold the cursor over the name, AutoCAD displays the full location of the file (see Figure 9.24).

**FIGURE 9.24**
AutoCAD shows the full path to the font-mapping file.

You can double-click this filename to open the Select A File dialog box. From there, you can select a different font-mapping file.

# Finding and Replacing Text

One of the most time-consuming tasks in drafting is replacing text that appears repeatedly throughout a drawing. Fortunately, you have a Find And Replace tool to help simplify this task. Find And Replace in AutoCAD works like any other find-and-replace tool in a word processing program. A few options work specifically with AutoCAD. Here's how it works:

1. Enter the text you want to locate in the Find Text box located in the middle of the Annotate tab's Text panel (see Figure 9.25), and then click the magnifying glass to the right. The Find And Replace dialog box opens, and the drawing area displays the part where the text has been found.

**FIGURE 9.25**
Using Find And
Replace

2. Enter the replacement text in the Replace With box.

3. When you've made certain that this is the text you want to change, click Replace. If you want to replace all occurrences of the text in the drawing, click Replace All.

4. If you want to skip over the found text, click Find Next to locate the next instance of the text in your drawing. If the text is not found, AutoCAD returns to your original view.

You can also enter **Find**↵ at the Command prompt to open the Find And Replace dialog box and then enter the text you want in the Find What text box.

To limit your find-and-replace operation to a specific set of objects in your drawing, choose Selected Objects from the Find Where drop-down list. Once you've selected this option, click the Select Objects tool in the upper-right corner of the Find And Replace dialog box (see Figure 9.26).

**FIGURE 9.26**
The Select
Objects tool

Select Objects tool

---

**MAKING SUBSTITUTIONS FOR MISSING FONTS**

When text styles are created, the associated fonts don't become part of the drawing file. Instead, AutoCAD loads the needed font file at the same time the drawing is loaded. If a text style in a drawing requires a particular font, AutoCAD looks for the font in the AutoCAD search path; if the font is there, it's loaded. Usually this isn't a problem if the drawing file uses the standard fonts that come with AutoCAD or Windows. But occasionally, you'll encounter a file that uses a custom font.

In earlier versions of AutoCAD, you saw an error message when you attempted to open such a file. This missing-font message often sent new AutoCAD users into a panic.

Fortunately, now AutoCAD automatically substitutes an existing font for the missing font in a drawing. By default, AutoCAD substitutes the `simplex.shx` font, but you can specify another font by using the `Fontalt` system variable. Type **Fontalt.⏎** at the Command prompt, and then enter the name of the font you want to use as the substitute.

You can also select an alternate font through the Files tab of the Options dialog box. Locate the Text Editor, Dictionary, And Font File Names listing, and then click the plus sign at the left. Locate the Alternate Font File item, and click the plus sign at the left. The current alternate is listed. You can double-click the font name to select a different font through the Alternate Font dialog box.

Be aware that the text in your drawing will change in appearance, sometimes radically, when you use a substitute font. If the text in the drawing must retain its appearance, substitute a font that is as similar in appearance to the original font as possible.

When you click the Select Objects tool, the Find And Replace dialog box closes temporarily to enable you to select a set of objects or a region of your drawing. Find And Replace then limits its search to those objects or the region you select.

You can further control the types of objects that Find And Replace looks for by clicking the More Options tool in the lower-left corner of the Find And Replace dialog box. The dialog box expands to show more options (see Figure 9.27).

**FIGURE 9.27**

More extensive options for Find And Replace

With this dialog box, you can refine your search by limiting it to blocks, dimension text, standard text, or hyperlink text. You can also specify whether to match the case and find whole words only.

**SPEEDING UP AUTOCAD WITH QTEXT**

If you need to edit a large drawing that contains a lot of text but you don't need to edit the text, you can use the Qtext command to help accelerate redraws and regenerations when you're working on the drawing. Qtext turns lines of text into rectangular boxes, saving AutoCAD from having to form every letter. This enables you to see the note locations so that you don't accidentally draw over them. To use it, enter **qtext.⏎** at the Command prompt and enter **On** or select the On option from the Dynamic Input display.

**CREATE PARAGRAPH COLUMNS**

You can format Mtext into multiple columns. This can be useful for long lists or to create a newspaper column appearance for your text. Text formatted into columns will automatically flow between columns as you add or remove text.

To format text into columns, do the following:

1. Create the text using the Mtext tool as usual.

2. Click and drag the corner resizer at the bottom-right corner of the text upward. As you do this, a second column appears.

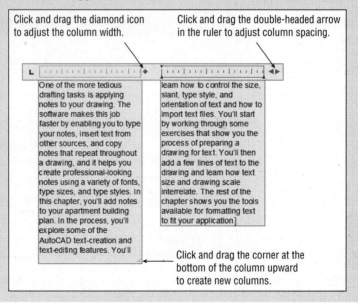

Click and drag the diamond icon to adjust the column width.

Click and drag the double-headed arrow in the ruler to adjust column spacing.

One of the more tedious drafting tasks is applying notes to your drawing. The software makes this job faster by enabling you to type your notes, insert text from other sources, and copy notes that repeat throughout a drawing, and it helps you create professional-looking notes using a variety of fonts, type sizes, and type styles. In this chapter, you'll add notes to your apartment building plan. In the process, you'll explore some of the AutoCAD text-creation and text-editing features. You'll

learn how to control the size, slant, type style, and orientation of text and how to import text files. You'll start by working through some exercises that show you the process of preparing a drawing for text. You'll then add a few lines of text to the drawing and learn how text size and drawing scale interrelate. The rest of the chapter shows you the tools available for formatting text to fit your application]

Click and drag the corner at the bottom of the column upward to create new columns.

**3.** If you want to create another column, click and drag the bottom edge of the right-most column upward.

**4.** To adjust the column width, click and drag the diamond icon that appears just to the right of the first column in the ruler. All the columns will adjust to the width of the first column.

Once you've set up your columns, click the Close Text Editor tool. You can adjust the column width and spacing by using grips that appear when you click on the text.

To adjust the column width of existing Mtext, click and drag the arrow grip at the top and to the right of the first column. To adjust the width between columns (the column spacing), click and drag the arrow grip at the top and to the right of the last column. The grips at the bottom of each column allow you to adjust the height of the columns.

You can manually set column features through the Column Settings dialog box. To open it, double-click on the Mtext and then choose Column Settings from the Columns flyout in the Text Editor tab's Insert panel.

The Dynamic Columns option is the default for the Column Type group, and it allows you to adjust the column size using grips.

# The Bottom Line

**Prepare a drawing for text.**   AutoCAD offers an extensive set of features for adding text to a drawing, but you need to do a little prep work before you dive in.

**Master It**   Name two things you need to do to prepare a drawing for text.

**Set the annotation scale and add text.**   Before you start to add text, you should set the annotation scale for your drawing. Once this is done, you can begin to add text.

**Master It**   In a sentence or two, briefly describe the purpose of the annotation scale feature. Name the tool you use to add text to a drawing.

**Explore text formatting in AutoCAD.**   Because text styles contain font and text-size settings, you can usually set up a text style and then begin to add text to your drawing. For those special cases where you need to vary text height and font or other text features, you can use the Formatting panel of the Text Editor tab.

**Master It**   What text formatting tool can you use to change text to boldface type?

**Add simple single-line text objects.**   In many situations, you need only a single word or a short string of text. AutoCAD offers the single-line text object for these instances.

**Master It**   Describe the methods for starting the single-line text command.

**Use the Check Spelling feature.**   It isn't uncommon for a drawing to contain the equivalent of several pages of text, and the likelihood of having misspelled words can be high. AutoCAD offers the Check Spelling feature to help you keep your spelling under control.

**Master It**   What option do you select in the Check Spelling dialog box when it finds a misspelled word and you want to accept the suggestion it offers?

**Find and replace text.**   A common activity when editing technical drawings is finding and replacing a word throughout a drawing.

**Master It**   True or false: The Find And Replace feature in AutoCAD works very differently from the find-and-replace feature in other programs.

# Chapter 10

# Using Fields and Tables

Adding text to a set of drawings can become a large part of your work. You'll find that you're editing notes and labels almost as frequently as you're editing the graphics in your drawings. To make some of those editing tasks easier, the AutoCAD® 2015 software provides a few special text objects.

In this chapter, we'll look at fields and tables, two features that can help automate some of the most common tasks in AutoCAD.

Fields are a special type of text object that can automatically update to reflect changes in the drawing. The Table feature is a tool that helps automate the process of creating and editing tables and schedules. Tables are a common part of technical drawings and are similar to spreadsheets. In fact, AutoCAD tables behave much like spreadsheets, giving you the ability to add formulas to cells.

We'll start this chapter with an introduction to fields and then go on to explore tables. Toward the end, we'll revisit fields to see how they can be used to add formulas to tables.

In this chapter, you will learn to

◆ Use fields to associate text with drawing properties

◆ Add tables to your drawing

◆ Edit the table line work

◆ Add formulas to cells

◆ Import and export tables

◆ Create table styles

## Using Fields to Associate Text with Drawing Properties

The text labels you worked with in Chapter 9, "Adding Text to Drawings," are static and don't change unless you edit them by using the tools described in that chapter. Another type of text object, called a *field*, behaves in a more dynamic way than the multiline text. A field can be linked to the properties of other objects so that it updates itself automatically as the associated properties change. For example, you can create a field that is associated with a block name. If the block name changes, the field text automatically changes as well.

Try the following exercise to see how this works:

1. Open the 10c-unit.dwg file. This file is similar to the drawing you worked on in Chapter 9.

2. Double-click the Kitchen text to highlight it and make it available for editing.

**3.** Right-click the highlighted Kitchen text, and then choose Insert Field to open the Field dialog box (see Figure 10.1). A list to the left shows the types of fields available.

**FIGURE 10.1**
Choose the field you want to insert.

**4.** In the Field Category drop-down list, select Objects. This limits the display of field types to object fields.

**5.** In the Field Names list, select NamedObject.

**6.** Make sure that Block is selected in the Named Object Type drop-down list in the top of the dialog box, and then select KITCHEN from the Name list. This associates the field with the KITCHEN block name.

**7.** In the Format list to the far right, select First Capital. This causes the field text to be lowercase with a capital first letter (also referred to as sentence case), regardless of how the block name is spelled.

**8.** Click OK to exit the Field dialog box, and then press ↵ to return to the Command prompt.

When you return to the drawing, the text appears in a gray background. This tells you that the text is a field rather than an Mtext or text object. The gray background is a device to help you keep track of field text; it doesn't plot.

You've converted existing text into a field that is linked to a block name. Now let's see how the field works:

**1.** Enter **Rename**↵ at the Command prompt to open the Rename dialog box.

**2.** Make sure Blocks is selected in the Named Objects list, and then select KITCHEN from the Items list. The word *KITCHEN* appears in the Old Name box near the bottom of the dialog box.

3. Enter **Kitchenette** in the box just below the Old Name box, and then click the Rename To button.

4. Click OK to close the Rename dialog box.

5. Type **Re**↵. The field you created changes to reflect the new block name.

Fields can be associated with a wide variety of properties. You've just seen how a block name can be associated with a field. In this exercise, you'll use a field to display the area of an object:

1. Click Zoom Extents from the Zoom flyout on the Navigation bar or type **Z**↵**E**↵ to view the entire plan.

2. Use the Rectangle command to place a rectangle in the living room area, as shown in Figure 10.2.

**FIGURE 10.2**
Place a rectangle that fills the living room.

Rectangle

3. Double-click the Living Room text to open the Text Editor tab and the text editor.

4. Highlight the text that reads *230 square feet*. Right-click the selected text, and choose Insert Field from the context menu.

5. In the Field dialog box, select Object from the Field Names list.

6. Click the Select Object button next to the Object Type box at the top of the Field dialog box (see Figure 10.3). The Field dialog box momentarily closes to enable you to select an object.

**FIGURE 10.3**
Click the Select Object button.

**7.** Select the rectangle you just added. The Field dialog box returns.

**8.** In the Property list just below the Object Type box, select Area.

**9.** Select Architectural from the Format list to the far right (see Figure 10.4).

**FIGURE 10.4**
The Architectural
option in the
Format list

**10.** Click OK. The field you just added appears in the drawing as the area of the rectangle.

**11.** Click Close Text Editor in the Text Editor tab's Close panel.

Next, you'll alter the rectangle to see how it affects the field:

**1.** Click the rectangle to expose its grips (see Figure 10.5). Then select the top-middle grip of the rectangle, and move it upward so that the top edge aligns with the bathroom wall.

**FIGURE 10.5**
Expose the grips.

Move this grip
upward.

**2.** Type **Re↵**. The field you just added updates to reflect the new area of the rectangle.

**3.** After reviewing the results, close `10c-unit.dwg` without saving it.

In previous exercises, you changed existing text into fields. You can create new fields in either the Text or the Mtext command by selecting Insert Field from the context menu whenever you're typing the text content.

In this exercise, you used a rectangle, but you can use any closed polyline to create an area field.

We've touched on just two of the many possible uses for fields. You can associate other types of properties, including the current layer, the drawing name, linetypes, and more. You can include Diesel macros as part of fields. (You'll learn about Diesel macros in Chapter 24, "Customizing Toolbars, Menus, Linetypes, and Hatch Patterns.") Fields can also be used in the Table feature (described in the next section), which enables you to create tables and schedules quickly. Fields are used to coordinate sheet labels with reference symbols in the AutoCAD Sheet Set feature described in the online bonus chapter "Keeping a Project Organized with Sheet Sets," available at www.omura.com/chapters.

For most of your projects, the standard text objects will work just fine, but you may find fields useful when you know a label has to be associated with specific types of data in your drawing. In later chapters, you'll have more opportunities to work with fields.

## Adding Tables to Your Drawing

One of the most common text-related tasks you'll do for your drawings is create schedules, such as door and window schedules or parts schedules. Such schedules are tables used to provide detailed information about the elements in your design.

In the past, AutoCAD users used Mtext or Text to create the content of schedules and then used line-drawing tools to create the cells of the schedule. Since AutoCAD 2006, you have been able to use tables to help you generate schedules more quickly. Tables allow you to format the columns and rows of text automatically, similar to formatting in spreadsheet programs.

### Creating a Table

The first step in creating a table is to determine the number of rows and columns you want. Don't worry if you aren't certain of the exact number of rows and columns; you can add or subtract them at any time. In this exercise, you'll create a table that contains 12 rows and 9 columns, as shown in Figure 10.6.

**FIGURE 10.6**

A sample table created with the Table tool

| Number | Room | \(Finish\) Floor | Base | Wall | Ceiling | Ceiling Ht. | Area | Remarks |
|--------|------|-------|------|------|---------|-------------|------|---------|
| \multicolumn{9}{c}{Room Finish Schedule} | | | | | | | | |
| 110 | Lobby | B | 1 | A | 1 | 10'-0" | 200sf | |
| 111 | Office | A | 1 | B | 2 | 8'-0" | 96sf | |
| 112 | Office | A | 1 | B | 2 | 8'-0" | 96sf | |
| 113 | Office | A | 1 | B | 2 | 8'-0" | 96sf | |
| 114 | Meeting | C | 1 | B | 2 | 8'-0" | 150sf | |
| 115 | Breakout | C | 1 | B | 2 | 8'-0" | 150sf | |
| 116 | Womens | D | 2 | C | 3 | 8'-0" | 50sf | |
| 117 | Mens | D | 2 | C | 3 | 8'-0" | 50sf | |
| | | | | | | | | |

Start by creating the basic table layout:

1. Click New on the Quick Access toolbar, and use the standard acad.dwt drawing template.

2. Click Table in the Home tab's Annotation panel to open the Insert Table dialog box (see Figure 10.7). You can also click the Table tool in the Annotate tab's Tables panel or type **Tb**↵.

**FIGURE 10.7**
The Insert Table dialog box

3. In the Column & Row Settings group, enter **9** for Columns and **12** for Data Rows.

4. Click OK. The dialog box closes and the outline of a table follows your cursor.

5. Position the table in the center of your drawing area, and click to place it. The table appears with a cursor in the top cell. You also see the Text Editor tab in the Ribbon.

6. Enter **Room Finish Schedule**, and press ↵. The cursor moves to the next cell.

7. Click Close Text Editor in the Text Editor tab's Close panel.

## Adding Cell Text

You've just created a table and added a title. Notice that the table actually contains 14 rows, including the title row at the top and an additional row for the headings of each column. You can delete these additional rows if you don't need them, but for now you'll start to add some text to the table:

1. Adjust your view so the table fills most of the drawing area.

2. Double-click in the first cell at the top left, just below the Room Finish Schedule label (see Figure 10.8). The cell turns gray, and the Text Editor tab appears in the Ribbon. You also see labels across the top and left side showing the row and column addresses.

**FIGURE 10.8**
Double-click
the first cell
shown here.

3. Enter **Number** for the room number column at the far left, and then press the Tab key to advance to the next cell to the right.

4. Enter **Room**, and press the Tab key again.

5. Enter **Finish**, and press the Tab key four times to advance four columns. You do this because the Finish heading shown in Figure 10.6, earlier, has four columns under it: Floor, Base, Wall, and Ceiling. In the next exercise, you'll learn how to format those four columns under the single heading.

6. Enter **Ceiling Ht.** and press the Tab key again.

7. Enter **Area**, press the Tab key, and enter **Remarks**.

8. Click Close Text Editor in the Text Editor tab's Close panel.

You have the column headings in place. Now you need to do a little extra formatting. In step 5, you left three cells blank because four of the columns will be combined under one heading: the Finish heading covers the Floor, Base, Wall, and Ceiling columns. Next, you'll combine the blank cells with the Finish heading:

1. Click in the center of the cell with the Finish label to select it.

2. Shift+click in the third cell to the right of the Finish cell to select all four cells (see Figure 10.9).

**FIGURE 10.9**
Select a group of
four cells.

| A | B | C | D | E | F | G | H | I |
|---|---|---|---|---|---|---|---|---|
| | | | | Room Finish Schedule | | | | |
| Number | Room | Finish | | | | Ceiling Ht. | Area | Remarks |
| | | | | | | | | |
| | | | | | | | | |
| | | | | | | | | |

3. Right-click in the selected cells, and choose Merge ➢ All. The four selected cells merge into a single cell with the word *Finish*.

Now you need to add the subheads under the Finish header:

1. Double-click in the leftmost cell below the Finish cell. The Text Editor tab appears in the Ribbon (see Figure 10.10).

2. Enter **Floor**, and press the Tab key.

**FIGURE 10.10**

Double-click this cell and the Text Editor tab appears.

3. Enter **Base**, **Wall**, and **Ceiling** in each of the following columns as you've been doing. Remember that the Tab key advances you to the next cell to the right. Your table should look like Figure 10.11.

**FIGURE 10.11**

The table so far

4. Click Close Text Editor in the Text Editor tab's Close panel.

## Adjusting Table Text Orientation and Location

You now have the basic layout of the table, with one difference: The Floor, Base, Wall, and Ceiling labels you just added are oriented horizontally, but you want them oriented vertically, as shown earlier in Figure 10.6. The following steps will show you how to rotate a set of labels in a table so they appear in the orientation you want:

1. Click in the cell labeled Floor to select it. The Table Cell tab appears in the Ribbon.

2. Shift+click in the cell labeled Ceiling to select all four of the cells below the Finish heading. The combined cells have four grips, one on each side of the group.

3. Click the grip at the bottom of the selected group, and move it down about four rows. Click to "fix" the row height in place. The entire row becomes taller. This provides room for the text when you rotate it.

4. Right-click in the selected cells, and choose Properties from the context menu to open the Properties palette.

**5.** In the Properties palette, click the Text Rotation box under the Content group.

**6.** Enter **90↵** for a 90 rotation of the text. The text rotates into a vertical orientation.

**7.** Close the Properties palette.

With the text in this orientation, the columns are too wide, so you'll change the cell width for the selected cells.

**8.** Move the right grip to the left to decrease the width of the cells.

**9.** For the final touch, you'll center the text in the cells. With the cells still selected, right-click in the selected cells, and choose Alignment ➤ Bottom Center. The text becomes centered in the cells and aligned at the bottom of the cells.

---

### SETTING MARGINS WITH THE PROPERTIES PALETTE

You can also control the margin between the text and the cell border by using the Cell Margin options in the Properties palette. Select a group of cells in the table, right-click, and choose Properties. In the Properties palette, click the Vertical Cell Margin option or the Horizontal Cell Margin option in the Cell group.

---

In the previous exercise, you learned how you could adjust the text orientation through the Properties palette. You can also adjust the width of cells through the Properties palette. Or if you prefer, you can adjust the width of multiple cells by adjusting the grip location of selected cells.

Now continue to add text to the cells and adjust their sizes:

1. Double-click in the cell in the Number column just below the row that contains the Floor, Base, Wall, and Ceiling cells. A text cursor appears in the cell, and the Text Editor tab appears in the Ribbon.

2. Enter **110**, and press ↵. Instead of advancing to the next cell to the right, you advance to the next cell below.

3. Enter **111**, and press ↵ again. Continue to enter each room number in this way until you reach room number 117. When you've finished entering the room numbers, click Close Text Editor in the Text Editor tab's Close panel.

   Next, you'll reduce the width of the column to fit the text a bit better.

4. Click in the cell with the Number text label. It's the first column heading in the table.

5. Shift+click in the bottom cell of the Number column to select the entire column.

6. Click the grip to the left of the column, and move the grip to the right so that the column width is approximately half the width of the Room column. You can zoom in on the column to allow more control over the positioning of the grip.

7. Press Esc to exit the selection and view your table so far (see Figure 10.12).

**FIGURE 10.12**

The table with the columns resized

Now, suppose you want to delete one of the extra rows of cells at the bottom of the table or add a new row. Here's how:

1. Click the bottom-left cell of the table to select it.

2. Right-click, and choose Rows ➢ Delete from the context menu. The row disappears.

3. To add a row, select a cell, right-click, and choose Rows ➢ Insert Above or Rows ➢ Insert Below, depending on where you want the new row. (You don't have to do this last step.)

You may notice the Delete Columns and Insert Columns options in the context menu that let you add or delete columns. These options function in a way that's similar to how the Delete Rows and Insert Rows options function. You can also use the tools in the Rows and Columns panels of the contextual Table Cell tab to insert and delete rows and columns.

# Editing the Table Line Work

So far, you've concentrated on how you can format text and cells in a table, but you'll also want some control over the lines in the table. Typically, heavier lines are used around the border of the table and between the title and the rest of the table.

Selecting a cell, right-clicking, and selecting Borders from the context menu option lets you modify the outline of the border. When you select this option, the Cell Border Properties dialog box opens (see Figure 10.13).

**FIGURE 10.13**

Setting border properties

You can use this dialog box to fine-tune the appearance of the line work of the table. Try the following exercise to see firsthand how this dialog box works:

1. Make sure you do not have a cell selected, and then turn on the display of lineweights by typing **LW↵**.

2. In the Lineweight Settings dialog box, turn on the Display Lineweight setting and then click OK.

3. Click in the title cell at the top of the table to select the cell, and then right-click and choose Borders to open the Cell Border Properties dialog box.

4. Click the Lineweight drop-down list, and select 0.30 mm.

5. Click the Outside Borders button that appears just above the preview panel to tell AutoCAD to change the borders of the cell to the selected lineweight (see Figure 10.14).

**FIGURE 10.14**
Click to display
outside borders.

6. Click OK. The title cell is now outlined in a heavier line. To see it clearly, press the Esc key.

You can also adjust the lineweights of the borders that encircle a group of cells, as demonstrated in the following exercise:

1. Click the cell in the upper-left corner with the Number label.

2. Shift+click the cell in the lower-right corner of the table so that all the cells from the second-from-the-top row down are selected.

3. Right-click and choose Borders.

4. Select 0.30 mm from the Lineweight drop-down list. Then click the Outside Borders button as you did in step 5 of the previous exercise.

5. Click OK. The outlines of the selected cells are given the new lineweight setting (see Figure 10.15).

**FIGURE 10.15**
The borders
updated

| Room Finish Schedule | | | | | | | | |
|---|---|---|---|---|---|---|---|---|
| Number | Room | Finish | | | | Ceiling Ht. | Area | Remarks |
| | | Floor | Base | Wall | Ceiling | | | |
| 110 | | | | | | | | |
| 111 | | | | | | | | |
| 112 | | | | | | | | |
| 113 | | | | | | | | |
| 114 | | | | | | | | |
| 115 | | | | | | | | |
| 116 | | | | | | | | |
| 117 | | | | | | | | |

6. Save this file for future reference.

---

**CHANGING THE BACKGROUND COLOR**

In addition to the table borders, you can change the background color for the cells of the table using the Table Cell Background Color drop-down list in the Cell Styles panel of the contextual Table Cell tab. You can also use the Background Fill option in the Properties palette to set cell background colors.

The Cell Border Properties dialog box also lets you set the line colors by selecting a color from the Color drop-down list before selecting an Apply To option. In addition, there are several other buttons around the preview panel (see Figure 10.16) that let you select the lines that are affected by the Cell Border Properties settings.

**FIGURE 10.16**
Setting which borders will be affected

You can also use the preview panel to select individual borders by clicking the sample border in the preview panel. The sample changes to show you which border lines are affected.

## Adding Formulas to Cells

In the beginning of this chapter, we mentioned that you can include formulas in cells of AutoCAD tables. This can be a great time-saver because you can set up a table with quantities that automatically adjust to changes in values in individual cells. You don't have to calculate the changes manually.

You may recall that formulas are a type of field and that a field can be linked with objects in a drawing so that the field displays the linked object's properties. The formula field can be linked to several numeric text values.

Although fields are the tools you use for formulas, you don't have to choose deliberately to add a field to a cell every time you want to add a formula. The exercise in the following section will demonstrate how you can add a formula by typing directly in a cell. AutoCAD takes care of converting your input into a field.

## Using Formulas Directly in Cells

The simplest way to add a formula to a cell is to double-click the cell and then, when the Text Editor tab appears in the Ribbon, enter the formula directly in the cell with the addition of an = (equal sign) at the beginning. Try the following exercise to see how it works:

1. Open the FieldSample.dwg file.

2. Double-click in the cell, as shown in Figure 10.17, to select the location for your formula.

**FIGURE 10.17**

Selecting the cell for your formula

| Sample Table | | | | |
|---|---|---|---|---|
| 100 | 200 | 300 | 400 | |
| 150 | 250 | 350 | 450 | |
| 250 | 350 | 450 | 550 | |
| | | | | |

← Double-click this cell.

3. Enter **=A2+D4** in the cell to add the values in cell A2 and cell D4.

4. Press ⏎ after you enter the formula. The value of A2 plus D4 appears in the cell (see Figure 10.18).

**FIGURE 10.18**

The cell with the sum of two other cells

| Sample Table | | | | |
|---|---|---|---|---|
| 100 | 200 | 300 | 400 | |
| 150 | 250 | 350 | 450 | |
| 250 | 350 | 450 | 550 | |
| | | | | 650 |

In step 3, the equal sign tells AutoCAD to convert the text into a formula field. You may have noticed that when you start to edit a cell in a table, the row and column labels appear along the top and left side of the table. You can use these labels to determine the cell addresses for your formula.

In typical spreadsheet fashion, you can change the formula in a cell at any time. Double-click the cell containing the formula, and then edit the formula values and operators.

You can also use the Formula drop-down list from the Table Cell tab's Insert panel to select from a set of predefined math operations (see Figure 10.19).

**FIGURE 10.19**

The Formula drop-down list in the Insert panel

Click in the cell where you want to place the formula; then, in the Table Cell tab, click the Formula drop-down list in the Insert panel and select the operation you want to use. Next, place a selection window around the cells you want to include in the formula. Click in the first cell that you want to include in the formula, and then click in the second cell. As you do this, a selection window appears. All the cells that are included in the selection window are included in the formula.

## Using Other Math Operations

In the previous exercise, you used the plus sign to add the value of two cells. You can string together several cells' addresses to add multiple cells, as follows:

```
=A2+A3+A4...
```

You can also subtract, multiply, or divide by using the – (subtract or minus), * (multiply or asterisk), or / (divide) signs. To perform multiple operations on several cells, you can group operations within parentheses in a way similar to how you would in a typical spreadsheet formula. For example, if you want to add two cells together and then multiply their sum by another cell, use the following format:

```
=(A2+A3)*A4
```

The Average, Sum, and Count buttons that appear in the Formula flyout on the Table Cell tab's Insert panel give you quick access to these frequently used functions. You can add to a cell the average value of a set of cells, the sum of a set of cells, or the count of the number of cells. When you click one of these options after selecting a cell, you're prompted to select several cells with a selection window. Once you've selected a set of cells, you see the appropriate formula in the currently selected cell. Clicking the Average button, for example, produces a formula similar to the following:

```
=Average(A1:B5)
```

Clicking the Sum button produces a formula like the following:

```
=Sum(A1:B5)
```

In both cases, a range of cells is indicated by a colon, as in A1:B5. You can use this format when entering formulas manually. You can also include a single cell with a range by using a comma:

```
=Sum(A1:B5,C6)
```

# Importing and Exporting Tables

Data of the kind found in tables is often shared with others who may not be AutoCAD users. For this reason, you'll want to be able to move table data to and from your drawing to other applications so that it can be viewed and edited by others. AutoCAD offers the following methods for importing and exporting tables.

## Importing a Table

Frequently, tables are created outside AutoCAD in a spreadsheet program such as Microsoft Excel. You can import an Excel worksheet as an AutoCAD table by using the AutoCAD Entities option in the Paste Special feature. The ability to import tables lets non-AutoCAD users create the table data while you concentrate on the drawing.

Try the following exercise to see how you can import a table from a worksheet:

1. Open a new drawing; then open the Excel worksheet called 10a-plan.xls, and highlight the door data, as shown in Figure 10.20. You may see a security message in Excel.

**FIGURE 10.20**

Selecting the door data in the 10a-plan.xls spreadsheet

| | A | B | C | D | E | F | G | H |
|---|---|---|---|---|---|---|---|---|
| | A1 | | ƒx | D-TYPE | | | | |
| 1 | D-TYPE | D-SIZE | D-NUMBER | D-THICK | D-RATE | D-MATRL | D-CONST | |
| 2 | B | 3'-0" | 116 | 1 3/4" | 20 min. | Wood | Solid Core | |
| 3 | B | 3'-0" | 114 | 1 3/4" | 20 min. | Wood | Solid Core | |
| 4 | B | 3'-0" | 112 | 1 3/4" | 20 min. | Wood | Solid Core | |
| 5 | B | 3'-0" | 110 | 1 3/4" | 20 min. | Wood | Solid Core | |
| 6 | B | 3'-0" | 106 | 1 3/4" | 20 min. | Wood | Solid Core | |
| 7 | B | 3'-0" | 108 | 1 3/4" | 20 min. | Wood | Solid Core | |
| 8 | B | 3'-0" | 102 | 1 3/4" | 20 min. | Wood | Solid Core | |
| 9 | B | 3'-0" | 104 | 1 3/4" | 20 min. | Wood | Solid Core | |
| 10 | B | 3'-0" | 115 | 1 3/4" | 20 min | Wood | Solid Core | |
| 11 | B | 3'-0" | 111 | 1 3/4" | 20 min. | Wood | Solid Core | |
| 12 | B | 3'-0" | 107 | 1 3/4" | 20 min. | Wood | Solid Core | |
| 13 | B | 3'-0" | 103 | 1 3/4" | 20 min. | Wood | Solid Core | |
| 14 | B | 3'-0" | 101 | 1 3/4" | 20 min. | Wood | Solid Core | |
| 15 | B | 3'-0" | 105 | 1 3/4" | 20 min. | Wood | Solid Core | |
| 16 | B | 3'-0" | 109 | 1 3/4" | 20 min. | Wood | Solid Core | |
| 17 | B | 3'-0" | 113 | 1 3/4" | 20 min. | Wood | Solid Core | |
| 18 | | 116 | | | | | | |
| 19 | | 108 | | | | | | |

2. Right-click and select Copy to place a copy of the selected data into the Windows Clipboard, and then switch back to AutoCAD.

3. Choose Paste Special from the Paste flyout on the Home tab's Clipboard panel (see Figure 10.21) to open the Paste Special dialog box. If you don't see the Clipboard panel, enter **PASTESPEC**↵.

**FIGURE 10.21**

The Paste flyout

— Flyout

Paste
Paste as Block
Paste as Hyperlink
Paste to Original Coordinates
Paste Special

4. With the Paste radio button selected, click AutoCAD Entities in the list and then click OK.

5. At the Specify insertion point or [paste as Text]: prompt, click a point in the lower-right area of the drawing. The worksheet data appears in the drawing as a table.

If the text is difficult to read because of a dark drawing area background, you can change the background color of the table to white.

1. Select all of the cells of the table by selecting cell 1A and then Shift+clicking on cell 17G. Note that the Table Cell tab appears automatically in the ribbon.

**2.** In the Table Cell tab's Cell Style panel, select white from the Table Cell Background Color drop-down list.

In this exercise, you imported the worksheet by using the default standard table style. This gives you a simple-looking table using the AutoCAD Txt font. You can set up a custom table style, as described later in this chapter, with the fonts and borders you want and then import the table for a more customized appearance. Make sure your custom table style is the current style before you import the worksheet.

## Exporting Tables

You might want to export your AutoCAD table to a spreadsheet program or database. You can do this using a somewhat hidden option in a context menu. Follow these steps:

**1.** Select the entire table. You can do so by clicking in a spot above and to the right of the table. With the crossing selection window, completely enclose the table and click.

**2.** Right-click anywhere in the table, and choose Export from the context menu to open the Export Data dialog box.

**3.** Specify a name and location for your exported table data, and click Save.

The file is saved with a `.csv` filename extension. This type of file is comma delimited and can be read by most spreadsheet programs, including Excel. Unfortunately, the CSV file doesn't retain the AutoCAD table formatting.

---

### ADDING GRAPHICS TO TABLE CELLS

One of the most interesting features of the Table tool is its ability to include blocks in a cell. This ability can be useful if you want to include graphic elements in your table. Adding a block to a cell is a simple process. Here are the steps:

**1.** Click in a cell to select it.

**2.** Right-click, and choose Insert ➤ Block from the context menu to open the Insert A Block In A Table Cell dialog box.

**3.** Select a block name from the Name drop-down list. You can also click the button to the right of the list to open the Select Drawing File dialog box, which lets you select a drawing file for import to the cell.

> **4.** After you've selected a block and specified the settings in the Properties group of the dialog box, click OK. The block appears in the cell you've selected.
>
> The dialog box enables you to specify the alignment (Overall Cell Alignment) and size (Scale) of the inserted block. By default, the AutoFit option is turned on. This option adjusts the size of the block to make it fit in the current cell size.

To open the exported file from Excel, choose File ➤ Open in the Excel menu bar; then, in the Open dialog box, select Text Files (*.prn, *.txt, *.csv) in the Files Of Type drop-down list. You can then locate the exported table and open it.

# Creating Table Styles

If you find that you're creating the same table layout over and over, you can set up predefined table styles. You can set up the properties of the title, column headings, and data in advance so that you don't have to set them up each time you create a table. For example, if you prefer to use Arial bold at 0.25" for the title and standard Arial at 0.125" for the column headings, you can create a table style with those settings. The next time you need to create a table, you can select your custom table style and specify the number of columns and rows; then you'll be ready to add the data without having to format the text.

## Adding or Modifying a Table Style

The method you use to create a table style in AutoCAD is similar to the method used to modify an existing one.

To create a table style, follow these steps:

**1.** Click Table Style in the Home tab's expanded Annotation panel to open the Table Style dialog box.

You can also select the Table Style tool from the Annotate tab's Tables panel title bar. The Table Style tool is the arrowhead at the right end of the Tables panel title bar. You see the Standard table style in the Styles list box (see Figure 10.22). This is the one you used in the previous exercises.

**FIGURE 10.22**
The Table Style
dialog box

**2.** Click the New button to open the Create New Table Style dialog box. This is where you give your new table style a name.

**3.** Enter **My Table Style**, and click Continue to open the New Table Style dialog box (see Figure 10.23).

**FIGURE 10.23**

The New Table Style dialog box

**4.** You'll learn more about the options in this dialog box next. For now, click OK to close the dialog box.

**5.** Your new table style now appears in the Styles list of the Table Style dialog box. If you want to edit an existing table style, you can select the style from the list and click the Modify button. The Modify Table Style dialog box will appear, enabling you to edit the existing style. The Modify Table Style dialog box is identical to the New Table Style dialog box shown in Figure 10.23.

**6.** Click Close to exit the dialog box.

After you've created a style, you can select it from the Table Style group of the Insert Table dialog box that you used to create the sample table (see Figure 10.24). To open the Insert Table dialog box, click Table in the Home tab's Annotation panel.

**FIGURE 10.24**

Select the table style in the Insert Table dialog box.

You can also open the New Table Style dialog box by clicking the Launch The Table Style Dialog button just to the right of the Table Style drop-down list in the Insert Table dialog box.

## The Table Style Options

Let's take a closer look at the New Table Style dialog box, shown earlier in Figure 10.23. It may seem a bit bewildering at first, but once you take the time to explore the parts of this dialog box, it's fairly straightforward. The following offers a description of the parts of the New Table Style dialog box by group:

**Starting Table**   Typically, you can set up a new table style using the settings in the other groups of this dialog box, but the Starting Table group gives you the ability to use an existing table in the drawing as the basis for your new table style. This can be helpful if you've already done some work formatting a table in your drawing. This group includes two buttons. The one on the left lets you select an existing table in the drawing for your new style. If you click this button, the dialog box closes temporarily to allow you to select a table in your drawing. The button on the right removes your in-drawing table selection and reverts to the settings in the dialog box.

**General**   The General group offers only one setting: the direction for the table. Typically, you'll use the Down option, which means the table reads from top to bottom. If for some reason you need a table with titles at the bottom, choose the Up option.

**Cell Styles**   You have a high degree of control over the appearance of individual cells through the cell styles. By default, your new table style will have three cell styles, called Data, Header, and Title. You can select these cell styles from the drop-down list at the top of the Cell Styles group. You can then edit the selected style using the three tabs below the drop-down list. Here are brief descriptions of the function of each tab:

◆ General gives you control over the fill color, alignment, format, and type of information presented in the cell. The Margins options control the margins in the cell. The Merge Cells On Row/Column Creation option at the bottom of the General tab causes the cells to merge into a single cell for the selected cell style.

◆ Text gives you control over the default text style, the height and color, and the angle of the text in the cell.

◆ Borders lets you control the lineweight for the borders of the cell.

You can also create your own cell style using the two buttons to the right of the Cell Styles drop-down list. The left button lets you create a new cell style. The button on the right lets you create, rename, or delete a cell style through the Manage Cell Styles dialog box.

**Cell Style Preview**   This window gives you a preview of what the cell style will look like with the settings you make in the tabs of the Cell Styles group. This preview changes in real time as you change the settings in the General, Text, or Borders tab.

## The Bottom Line

**Use fields to associate text with drawing properties.**    Fields are a special type of text object that can be linked to object properties. They can help to automate certain text-related tasks.

**Master It**    Name two uses for fields that you learned about in the first part of this chapter.

**Add tables to your drawing.**    The Tables feature can help you make quick work of schedules and other tabular data that you want to include in a drawing.

**Master It**    What is the name of the dialog box that appears when you click the Table tool in the Annotate tab's Tables panel?

**Edit the table line work.**    Because tables include line work to delineate their different cells, AutoCAD gives you control over table borders and lines.

**Master It**    How do you get to the Cell Border Properties dialog box?

**Add formulas to cells.**    Tables can also function like a spreadsheet by allowing you to add formulas to cells.

**Master It**    What type of text object lets you add formulas to cells?

**Import and export tables.**    The Table feature allows you to import Microsoft Excel spreadsheets into AutoCAD.

**Master It**    Describe how to import a spreadsheet from Excel into AutoCAD.

**Create table styles.**    Table styles can save time by enabling you to set up preformatted tables with a title, column headings, and other data.

**Master It**    Name the four groups in the New Table Style dialog box.

# Chapter 11

# Using Dimensions

Before you determine the dimensions of a project, your design is in flux and many questions may be unanswered. After you begin dimensioning, you'll start to see whether things fit or work together. Dimensioning can be crucial to how well a design works and how quickly it develops. The dimensions answer questions about code conformance if you're an architect; they answer questions about tolerances, fit, and interference if you're involved in mechanical applications. After you and your design team reach a design on a schematic level, communicating even tentative dimensions to others on the team can accelerate design development. Dimensions represent a point from which you can develop your ideas further.

With the AutoCAD® 2015 software, you can easily add tentative or final dimensions to any drawing. AutoCAD gives you an accurate dimension without your having to take measurements. You pick the two points to be dimensioned and the dimension line location, and AutoCAD does the rest. The *associative dimensioning* capability of AutoCAD automatically updates dimensions whenever the size or shape of the dimensioned object changes. These dimensioning features can save you valuable time and reduce the number of dimensional errors in your drawings.

In this chapter, you will learn to

◆ Understand the components of a dimension

◆ Create a dimension style

◆ Draw linear dimensions

◆ Edit dimensions

◆ Dimension nonorthogonal objects

◆ Add a note with a leader arrow

◆ Apply ordinate dimensions

◆ Add tolerance notation

## Understanding the Components of a Dimension

Before you start the exercises in this chapter, it will help to know the names of the parts of a dimension. Figure 11.1 shows a sample of a dimension with the parts labeled. The *dimension line* is the line that represents the distance being dimensioned. It's the horizontal line with the diagonal tick marks on either end. The *extension lines* are the lines that originate from the object being dimensioned. They show you the exact location from which the dimension is taken. The *dimension text* is the dimension value, usually shown inside or above the dimension line.

**FIGURE 11.1**
The components of
a dimension

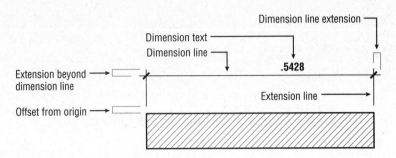

**FIGURE 11.1**
The components of
a dimension

Another component of a dimension line is the *dimension line extension*. This is the part of the dimension line that extends beyond the extension line. Dimension line extensions are usually used only on architectural dimensions. The extension lines typically extend beyond the dimension lines in all types of dimensions. The extension line *offset from origin* is the distance from the beginning of the extension line to the object being dimensioned. The *extension beyond dimension line* is the distance the dimension line extends past the extension line.

You can control each of these components by creating or editing dimension styles. *Dimension styles* are the settings that determine the look of your dimensions. You can store multiple styles in a single drawing. The first exercise in this chapter will show you how to create a dimension style.

---

**DIMENSIONING STANDARDS**

In addition to the components of a dimension, you should know about the standards that govern the placement and style of dimensions in a drawing. Each industry has a different set of standards for text size, text style, arrow style, dimension placement, and general dimensioning methods. These issues are beyond the scope of this book; however, we urge you to become familiar with the standards associated with your industry. Many resources are available to you if you want to find out more about dimension standards. Here are a few resources on the subject:

♦ For mechanical drafting in the United States, check the American Society of Mechanical Engineers (ASME) website: www.asme.org.

♦ For European standards, see the International Organization for Standardization (ISO) website: www.iso.org.

♦ For architectural standards in the United States, see the American Institute of Architects (AIA) website: www.aia.org.

---

## Creating a Dimension Style

**CERT OBJECTIVE**

Dimension styles are similar to text styles. They determine the look of your dimensions as well as the size of dimensioning features, such as the dimension text and arrows. You can set up a dimension style to have special types of arrows, for instance, or to position the dimension text above or in line with the dimension line. Dimension styles also make your work easier by enabling you to store and duplicate your most common dimension settings.

AutoCAD gives you one of two default dimension styles, *ISO-25* or *Standard,* depending on whether you use the metric or Imperial (also called English) measurement system. You'll probably add many other styles to suit the types of drawings you're creating. You can also create variations of a general style for those situations that call for only minor changes in the dimension's appearance.

In this section, you'll learn how to set up your own dimension style based on the Standard dimension style (see Figure 11.2). For metric users, the settings are different, but the overall methods are the same.

**FIGURE 11.2**

The AutoCAD Standard dimension style compared with an architectural-style dimension

A dimension using the Standard default settings

A dimension set up for architectural drawings

A sample of other arrows

Follow these steps to create a dimension style:

1. Open the 11a-unit.dwg file and rename it **Unit.dwg**. Metric users should open 11a-unit-metric.dwg and rename it **Unit.dwg**. These files are the same as the Unit.dwg file you used in the previous chapter before the exercises.

2. Choose Zoom All from the Zoom flyout in the Navigation bar or type **Z↵A↵** to display the entire floor plan.

3. Click the Dimension Style tool on the Annotate tab's Dimensions panel title bar. You can also choose the Dimension Style tool from the Home tab's expanded Annotation panel (it looks like a dimension with a paintbrush) or type **D↵** at the Command prompt to open the Dimension Style Manager.

4. Select Standard from the Styles list box. Metric users should select ISO-25 (see Figure 11.3).

5. Click New to open the Create New Dimension Style dialog box (see Figure 11.4).

6. With the Copy of Standard or ISO-25 name highlighted in the New Style Name box, enter **My Architectural**.

7. Click Continue to open the detailed New Dimension Style dialog box (see Figure 11.5).

**FIGURE 11.3**

The Dimension Style Manager

**FIGURE 11.4**

The Create New Dimension Style dialog box

**FIGURE 11.5**

The New Dimension Style dialog box

You've just created a dimension style called My Architectural, but at this point it's identical to the Standard style on which it's based. Nothing has happened to the Standard style; it's still available if you need to use it.

## Setting Up the Primary Unit Style

Now you need to set up your new dimension style so that it conforms to the US architectural style of dimensioning. Let's start by changing the unit style for the dimension text. Just as you changed the overall unit style of AutoCAD to a feet-and-inches style for your bath drawing in Chapter 3, "Setting Up and Using the Drafting Tools," you must change your dimension styles. Setting the overall unit style doesn't automatically set the dimension unit style. Follow these steps:

1. In the New Dimension Style dialog box, click the Primary Units tab (see Figure 11.6).

**FIGURE 11.6**
The Primary Units options

2. In the Linear Dimensions group, open the Unit Format drop-down list and choose Architectural. Notice that this drop-down list contains the same unit styles as the main Drawing Units dialog box (choose Drawing Utilities ➤ Units from the Application menu), with the addition of the Windows Desktop option. Metric users can skip this option.

---

### Using Commas or Periods for Decimals

The Decimal Separator option a few settings below the Unit Format option lets you choose between a period and a comma for decimal points. Metric users often use the comma for a decimal point, and US users use a period. This option doesn't have any meaning for measurements other than decimal, so it's dimmed when the Architectural unit format is selected.

3. Select 0'-0 1/4" from the Precision drop-down list, just below the Unit Format list. Metric users should select 0.00. The Precision option enables you to set the level of precision that is displayed in the dimension text. It doesn't limit the precision of the AutoCAD drawing database. This value is used to limit only the display of dimension text values.

4. Just below the Precision drop-down list, open the Fraction Format drop-down list and select Diagonal. Notice what happens to the graphic: The fractional dimensions change to show how your dimension text will look. Metric users can skip this step because it isn't available when the Decimal unit format is selected.

5. In the Zero Suppression group in the lower-left corner, click 0 Inches to deselect this check box. If you leave it turned on, indications of 0 inches will be omitted from the dimension text. (In architectural drawings, 0 inches are shown as in this dimension: 12'-0".) Metric users can ignore this option.

If you use the Imperial measurement system, you've set up My Architectural's dimension unit style to show dimensions in feet and inches, the standard method for US construction documents. Metric users have changed the Precision value and have kept the Decimal unit system.

## Setting the Height for Dimension Text

Along with the unit style, you should adjust the size of the dimension text. The Text tab of the New Dimension Style dialog box lets you set a variety of text options, including text location relative to the dimension line, style, and height.

Follow these steps to set the height of your dimension text:

1. Click the Text tab to display the text options (see Figure 11.7).

**FIGURE 11.7**
The Text options

2. Highlight the contents of the Text Height box.

3. The Text Height box can accept typed values, or you can use the up and down arrows on the right side of the input to increase or decrease the value. Press the down arrow to reach the 1/8" setting. Metric users should enter **0.3**↵ for the text height.

Unlike with the text you created in Chapter 9, "Adding Text to Drawings," you specify dimension text height by its final plot size. You then specify an overall dimension scale factor that affects the sizing of all dimensioning settings, such as text and arrows.

If you want to use a specific text style for your dimensions, select a text style in the Text Style drop-down list in the Text tab. If the style you select happens to have a height specification greater than 0, that height will override any text height settings you enter in the Text tab.

## Setting the Location and Orientation of Dimension Text

The default AutoCAD setting for the placement of dimension text puts the text in line with the dimension line, as shown in the example at the top of Figure 11.2 earlier in this chapter. Suppose you want the new My Architectural style to put the text above the dimension line instead, as shown in the second example in Figure 11.2. To do that, you'll use the Text Placement and Text Alignment group options in the Text tab of the New Dimension Style dialog box:

1. In the Text Alignment group in the lower-right corner of the dialog box, click the Aligned With Dimension Line radio button.

2. In the Text Placement group, open the Vertical drop-down list and select Above. The appearance of the sample image changes to show how your new settings will look.

3. Again in the Text Placement group, change the Offset From Dim Line value to 1/16". Metric users can leave this setting at 0.625. This setting controls the size of the gap between the dimension line and the dimension text.

Each time you change a setting, the graphic gives you immediate feedback about how your changes will affect your dimension style.

## Choosing an Arrow Style and Setting the Dimension Scale

Next you'll specify a different type of arrow for your new dimension style. For linear dimensions in architectural drawings, a diagonal line, or *tick* mark, is typically used instead of an arrow.

In addition, you want to set the scale for the graphical components of the dimension, such as the arrows and text. Recall from Chapter 9 that text must be scaled up in order to appear at the proper size in the final output of the drawing. Dimensions too must be scaled so that they look correct when the drawing is plotted. The arrows are controlled by settings in the Symbols And Arrows tab, and the overall scale of the dimension style is set in the Fit tab.

Here are the steps for specifying the arrow type and scale:

1. Click the Symbols And Arrows tab to display the options for controlling the arrow style and dimension line extensions (see Figure 11.8).

**FIGURE 11.8**
The Symbols And
Arrows options

2. In the Arrowheads group, open the First drop-down list and choose Architectural Tick. The graphic next to the arrowhead name shows you what the arrowhead looks like. Note that the Second drop-down list automatically changes to Architectural Tick to maintain symmetry on the dimension.

3. In the Arrowheads group, change the Arrow Size setting to 1/8". Metric users should enter **0.3**.

Next you need to set the behavior of the dimension line and extension lines:

1. Click the Lines tab to display the options for controlling the dimension and extension lines (see Figure 11.9).

2. In the Dimension Lines group, highlight the value in the Extend Beyond Ticks box and change the value to **1/16**. (Metric users should enter **0.15**.) This causes the dimension lines

to extend past the tick arrows. This is a standard graphic practice used for dimensioning linear dimensions in architectural plans.

Dimension line extension

**FIGURE 11.9**
The options for controlling the dimension and extension lines

**3.** In the Extension Lines group, change the Extend Beyond Dim Lines setting to ⅛". Metric users should change this to **0.3**. This setting determines the distance the extension line extends past the dimension line.

4. Again in the Extension Lines group, change the Offset From Origin setting to ⅛". Metric users should change this to **0.3**. This sets the distance from the point being dimensioned to the beginning of the dimension extension line.

5. Click the Fit tab of the New Dimension Style dialog box to display the options for overall dimension scale and miscellaneous settings (see Figure 11.10).

**FIGURE 11.10**

The Fit options

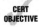
**CERT OBJECTIVE**

6. Turn on the Annotative option in the Scale For Dimension Features group. You may recall from Chapter 9 that the Annotative option allows AutoCAD to scale an object automatically to the drawing's annotation scale.

7. Click OK to close the New Dimension Style dialog box. The Dimension Style Manager appears again.

**CREATE CUSTOM ARROWHEADS**

See the online bonus chapter "System Variables and Dimension Styles," available at `www.omura.com/chapters`, for details on how you can create your own arrowheads. AutoCAD also lets you set up a separate arrow style for leaders.

**SCALE FOR DIMENSIONS IN LEGACY DRAWINGS**

Drawings created prior to AutoCAD 2008 relied on scale factors to determine the scaling of dimensions. Because it's likely that you'll run into legacy drawing files, here is some information about the settings used for those earlier dimensions.

Instead of the Annotative option, the Use Overall Scale Of option is used in the Scale For Dimension Features group. You select the Use Overall Scale Of radio button, and enter a drawing scale factor in the Use Overall Scale Of box.

All the values you enter for the options in the New Dimension Style dialog box are multiplied by this Use Overall Scale Of value to obtain the final size of the dimension components. For example, the text height you entered earlier, 1/8″, is multiplied by 48 for a dimension text height of 6″. For metric users, the text height of 0.3 is multiplied by 50 for a text height of 15 cm. For more on the scaling of text and other objects in AutoCAD, see Chapter 3.

**USING THE LAYOUT VIEWPORT SCALE FOR DIMENSIONS**

If you use the Scale Dimensions To Layout option in the Scale For Dimension Features group of the Fit tab, AutoCAD uses the layout viewport scale to size the dimension components. See Chapter 8, "Introducing Printing, Plotting, and Layouts," for more information about viewport scale settings. The Scale Dimension To Layout option can be useful if you have a drawing that you want to print at multiple scales.

## Setting Up Alternate Units

You can use the Alternate Units tab of the New Dimension Style dialog box to set up AutoCAD to display a second dimension in centimeters or millimeters. Likewise, if you're a metric user, you can set up a second dimension to display feet and inches. The following exercise shows you how to set up alternate dimensions. You don't have to do this exercise now; it's here for your information. If you like, come back later and try it to see how it affects your dimensions. You can pick up the tutorial in the next section, "Setting the Current Dimension Style."

If you decide later that you don't want the alternate units to be displayed, you can turn them off by returning to the Modify Dimension Style dialog box and removing the check mark from the Display Alternate Units check box.

Here are the steps for setting up alternate dimensions:

1. In the Dimension Style Manager, select a style and then click Modify. Or if you want to create a new style, click New.

2. In the Modify Dimension Style dialog box, click the Alternate Units tab (see Figure 11.11). This is virtually identical to the New Dimension Style dialog box with which you've been working.

**FIGURE 11.11**

The Alternate Units options

3. Click the Display Alternate Units check box. The options in the tab become available for your input.

4. Select the appropriate option from the Unit Format drop-down list. Imperial users should select Decimal to show metric alternate units. Metric users should select Architectural.

5. Select an appropriate precision value from the Precision drop-down list.

6. Enter a scale factor for your alternate dimension in the Multiplier For Alt Units box. For Imperial users, the default value is 25.4. This value converts feet-and-inch dimensions to millimeters. In our metric examples, you've been using centimeters, so change this setting to **2.54**. Metric users should enter **0.3937** to convert centimeters to feet and inches.

7. In the Placement group, select where you want the alternate dimension to appear in relation to the main dimension.

8. You don't want to display alternate units now, so turn off the Display Alternate Units setting.

9. Click OK to close the Modify Dimension Style dialog box. The Dimension Style Manager appears again.

## Setting the Current Dimension Style

Before you can begin to use your new dimension style, you must make it the current default:

1. Click My Architectural in the Styles list box in the Dimension Style Manager.

2. Click the Set Current button at the far right.

3. Click Close to exit the Dimension Style Manager.

You can also select a dimension style from the drop-down list in the Annotate tab's Dimensions panel or the Home tab's expanded Annotation panel. You're now ready to use your new dimension style.

---

**FITTING TEXT AND ARROWS IN TIGHT PLACES**

Every now and then, you'll need to dimension a small gap or a small part of an object in which dimension text won't fit. The Fit tab includes a few settings (other than the ones you've already worked with) that control how dimensions act when the extension lines are too close. The Text Placement group contains three options to place the text in tight situations:

**Beside The Dimension Line** Places text next to the extension line but close to the dimension line. You'll see how this affects your dimension later.

**Over Dimension Line, With Leader** Places the dimension text farther from the dimension line and includes an arrow or a leader from the dimension line to the text.

**Over Dimension Line, Without Leader** Does the same as the previous setting, but doesn't include the leader.

The options in the Fit Options group let you control how text and arrows are placed when there isn't enough room for both between the extension lines.

---

In the next set of exercises, you'll use the My Architectural style you just created. To switch to another style, open the Dimension Style Manager again, select the style you want from the Styles list, and click Set Current, as you did in the previous exercise.

## Modifying a Dimension Style

CERT OBJECTIVE

To modify an existing dimension style, open the Dimension Style Manager dialog box, highlight the style you want to edit, and then click Modify to open the Modify Dimension Style dialog box. You can then make changes to the various components of the selected dimension style. When you've finished making changes and closed both dialog boxes, all the dimensions associated with the edited style update automatically in your drawing. For example, if you're not using the Annotative Scale feature and you decide you need to change the dimension scale of a style, you can open the Modify Dimension Style dialog box and change the Use Overall Scale Of value in the Scale For Dimension Features group of the Fit tab.

So far, you've been introduced to the various settings that let you determine the appearance of a dimension style. We haven't discussed every option; to learn more about the other dimension style options, consult the online bonus chapter "System Variables and Dimension Styles," available at www.omura.com/chapters. There you'll find descriptions of all the items in the New Dimension Style and Modify Dimension Style dialog boxes, plus reference material covering the system variables associated with each option.

If your application is strictly architectural, you may want to make these same dimension-style changes to the acad.dwt template file or create a set of template files specifically for architectural drawings of different scales.

# Drawing Linear Dimensions

CERT
OBJECTIVE

The most common type of dimension you'll be using is the *linear dimension*. The linear dimension is an orthogonal dimension measuring the width and length of an object. AutoCAD provides three dimensioning tools for this purpose: Linear (Dimlinear), Continue (Dimcont), and Baseline (Dimbase). These options are readily accessible from the Annotate tab's Dimensions panel.

In the following set of exercises, you'll see figures displaying dimensions in both Imperial and metric units. We've included both measurements so that both Imperial and metric users can more easily follow the tutorial. But in your own drawing, you'll see only one dimension value displayed above the dimension line.

## Understanding the Dimensions Panel

Before you apply any dimension, you should study the Annotate tab's Dimensions panel (see Figure 11.12). This panel contains nearly all the tools necessary to draw and edit your dimensions.

**FIGURE 11.12**
The Annotate tab's
Dimensions panel

Many of the dimensioning tools discussed in this chapter can be found in the Home tab's Annotation panel. However, since the focus of this chapter is on dimensioning, unless otherwise noted, use the panels on the Annotate tab.

**SELECTING OPTIONS FROM THE DIMENSION FLYOUT**

In this chapter, you'll be selecting options from the large flyout on the left side of the Dimensions panel. This flyout starts out showing the Linear tool, but since the flyout name changes depending on the last tool selected, we'll refer to this flyout as the Dimension flyout.

## Placing Horizontal and Vertical Dimensions

Let's start by looking at the basic dimensioning tool, Linear. The Linear button (the Dimlinear command) on the Annotate tab's Dimensions panel accommodates both the horizontal and vertical dimensions.

In this exercise, you'll add a vertical dimension to the right side of the unit plan:

1. Before you start to dimension your drawing, you need to set its scale. Select 1/4"= 1'-0" from the Annotation Scale drop-down list. Metric users should select 1:50.

2. To start either a vertical or horizontal dimension, choose Linear from the Dimension flyout in the Annotate tab's Dimensions panel, or enter **DLI**↵ at the Command prompt.

3. The Specify first extension line origin or <select object>: prompt asks you for the first point of the distance to be dimensioned. An extension line connects the object being dimensioned to the dimension line. Use the Endpoint osnap override, and pick the upper-right corner of the entry, as shown in Figure 11.13.

**FIGURE 11.13**
The dimension line added to the Unit drawing

4. At the Specify second extension line origin: prompt, pick the lower-right corner of the living room, as shown in Figure 11.13.

---

**SELECTING OBJECTS TO BE DIMENSIONED**

The prompt in step 3 gives you the option of pressing ↵ to select an object. If you do this, you're prompted to pick the object you want to dimension rather than the distance to be dimensioned. This method is discussed later in this chapter.

---

5. At the next prompt, `Specify dimension line location or [Mtext/Text/Angle/ Horizontal/Vertical/Rotated]:`, the dimension line indicates the direction of the dimension and contains the arrows or tick marks. Move your cursor from left to right to display a temporary dimension. Doing so enables you to select a dimension-line location visually.

6. Enter **@4'<0**↵ to tell AutoCAD you want the dimension line to be 4' to the right of the last point you selected. Metric users should enter **@122<0**↵. (You could pick a point by using your cursor, but this doesn't let you place the dimension line as accurately.) After you've done this, the dimension is placed in the drawing as shown in Figure 11.13.

## Continuing a Dimension

You'll often want to enter a group of dimensions strung together in a line. For example, you may want to continue dimensioning the balcony and align the continued dimension with the dimension you just entered.

To do this, use the Continue option found in the Dimensions panel's Continue/Baseline flyout:

[⊢†⊣ Continue]  1. Click the Continue tool on the Dimensions panel, or enter **DCO**↵.

2. At the `Specify a second extension line origin or [Undo/Select] <Select>:` prompt, pick the upper-right corner of the balcony. (See the top image in Figure 11.14.)

3. Pick the right end of the rail on the balcony. See the bottom image in Figure 11.14 for the results.

4. Press ↵ twice to exit the command.

If you select the wrong location for a continued dimension, you can click the Undo tool or press **U**↵ to undo the last dimension.

The Continue option adds a dimension from where you left off. The last-drawn extension line is used as the first extension line for the continued dimension. AutoCAD keeps adding dimensions as you continue to pick points, until you press ↵.

You probably noticed that the 5" dimension is placed away from the dimension line with a leader line pointing to it. This is the result of the 5" dimension's text not having enough space to fit between the dimension extension lines. You'll learn about dimension style settings that can remedy this problem. For now, let's continue adding dimensions to the plan.

### CONTINUING A DIMENSION FROM A PREVIOUS DIMENSION

If you need to continue a string of dimensions from an older linear dimension instead of the most recently added one, press ↵ at the `Specify a second extension line origin or [Undo/ Select] <Select>:` prompt you saw in step 2 of the previous exercise. Then, at the `Select continued dimension:` prompt, click the extension line from which you want to continue.

**FIGURE 11.14**
The dimension string, continued and completed

Pick this corner to
continue the dimension string.

Pick this corner to
complete the dimension string.

## Drawing Dimensions from a Common Base Extension Line

Another way to dimension objects is to have several dimensions originate from the same extension line. To accommodate this, AutoCAD provides the Baseline option on the Dimensions control panel and the Dimension drop-down menu.

To see how this works, you'll start another dimension—this time a horizontal one—across the top of the plan:

1. Click the Linear tool in the Dimension flyout on the Dimensions panel. Or, as you did for the vertical dimension, type **DLI**↵ to start the horizontal dimension.

2. At the Specify first extension line origin or <select object>: prompt, use the Endpoint osnap to pick the upper-left corner of the bathroom, as shown in Figure 11.15.

**FIGURE 11.15**
The bathroom with horizontal dimensions

Start the dimension at this corner.

Select this corner for the second point.

3. At the Specify second extension line origin: prompt, pick the upper-right corner of the bathroom, as shown in Figure 11.15.

4. At the Specify dimension line location or [Mtext/Text/Angle/ Horizontal/ Vertical/Rotated]: prompt, pick a point above the unit plan, like the 7'-6" dimension in Figure 11.15. If you need to, pan your view downward to fit the dimension in.

---

**USE OSNAPS WHILE DIMENSIONING**

Because you usually pick exact locations on your drawing as you dimension, you may want to turn on the Object Snap tool in the status bar to avoid the extra step of selecting osnaps from the Osnap context menu.

---

5. You're set to draw another dimension continuing from the first extension line of the dimension you just drew. Click the Baseline tool on the Continue/Baseline flyout of the Dimensions panel. Or type **DBA**↵ at the Command prompt to start a baseline dimension.

**6.** At the `Specify a second extension line origin or [Undo/Select] <Select>:` prompt, click the upper-right corner of the entry as shown in Figure 11.16.

**FIGURE 11.16**
The overall width dimension

**7.** Press ↵ twice to exit the Baseline command.

**8.** Pan your view down so it looks similar to Figure 11.16.

In this example, you see that the Baseline option is similar to the Continue option except that the Baseline option enables you to use the first extension line of the previous dimension as the base for a second dimension. The distance between the two horizontal dimension lines is controlled by the Baseline Spacing setting in the Lines tab of the New Dimension Style and Modify Dimension Style dialog boxes.

### CONTINUING FROM AN OLDER DIMENSION

You may have noticed in step 7 that you had to press ↵ twice to exit the command. As with Continue, you can draw the baseline dimension from an older dimension by pressing ↵ at the `Specify a second extension line origin [Undo/Select] <Select>:` prompt. You then get the `Select base dimension:` prompt, at which you can either select another dimension or press ↵ again to exit the command.

---

#### CONTROL THE STYLE USED WITH CONTINUE OR BASELINE

A system variable called `DIMCONTINUEMODE` lets you control the style of a continue or baseline dimension. At the `Type a command` prompt, enter **dimcontinuemode**↵**1**↵ to have the baseline or continue dimension use the style of the selected dimension. Type **dimcontinuemode**↵**0**↵ to have the baseline or continue dimension use the current dimension style.

## Adjusting the Distance between Dimensions

As you work toward a deadline, you may find that you cut a few corners, or someone else does, when adding dimensions, and a set of parallel dimension lines isn't accurately placed.

You can quickly adjust the spacing between dimension lines using the Adjust Space tool in the Dimensions panel:

1. Click the Adjust Space tool in the Dimensions panel or type **Dimspace**↵.

2. At the Select base dimension: prompt, click the dimension closest to the feature being dimensioned.

3. At the Select dimensions to space: prompt, click the next dimension.

4. Continue to select the other parallel dimensions. When you're finished with your selections, press ↵.

5. You see this prompt:

   ```
   Select dimensions to space:
   Enter value or [Auto] <Auto>:
   ```

   Enter a value for the distance between the dimension lines. This value should be in full-scale distances. You can also press ↵ and AutoCAD will adjust the distance between dimensions for you.

# Editing Dimensions

CERT
OBJECTIVE

As you add more dimensions to your drawings, you'll find that AutoCAD occasionally places the dimension text or line in an inappropriate location or that you may need to modify the dimension text. In the following sections, you'll take an in-depth look at how you can modify dimensions to suit those special circumstances that always crop up.

## Appending Data to Dimension Text

So far in this chapter, you've been accepting the default dimension text. You can append information to the default dimension value or change it entirely if you need to. At the point when you see the temporary dimension dragging with your cursor, enter **T**↵. Then, using the less-than and greater-than (< and >) symbols, you can add text either before or after the default dimension or replace the symbols entirely to replace the default text. The Properties palette lets you modify the existing dimension text in a similar way (see Chapter 2, "Creating Your First Drawing," for more on the Properties palette). You can open the Properties palette for a dimension by selecting the dimension and then right-clicking to open the context menu. Select Properties from there.

Let's see how this works by changing an existing dimension's text in your drawing:

1. Type **ED**↵. This starts the Ddedit command.

2. Click the last horizontal dimension you added to the drawing at the top of the screen. The Text Editor tab appears in the Ribbon (see Figure 11.17).

**FIGURE 11.17**
The Text Editor tab

3. Press the End key to place the cursor at the end of the 14'-0" text, and then type **to face of stud** beginning with a space. The space is included to ensure that the dimension doesn't run into the text.

4. Click Close Text Editor in the Close panel of the Text Editor tab, and then press ↵ to exit the Ddedit command. The dimension changes to read 14'-0" to face of stud.

5. Because you don't need the new appended text for the tutorial, click the Undo button in the Quick Access toolbar to remove the appended text.

---

**EDITING MULTIPLE DIMENSIONS**

In the exercise where you changed an existing dimension's text, you were able to edit only a single dimension. To append text to several dimensions at once, you need to use the Dimension Edit tool. See the sidebar "Making Changes to Multiple Dimensions" later in this chapter for more on this command.

---

If you need to restore the original dimension text for a dimension whose value has been completely replaced, you can use the steps shown in the previous exercise. However, in step 3 replace the text with the <> bracket symbols.

You can also have AutoCAD automatically add a dimension suffix or prefix to all dimensions instead of just a chosen few by using the Suffix or Prefix option in the Primary Units tab of the New Dimension Style or Modify Dimension Style dialog box. See the online bonus chapter "System Variables and Dimension Styles," available at www.omura.com/chapters, for more on this feature.

AutoCAD provides the associative dimensioning capability to update dimension text automatically when a drawing is edited. Objects called *definition points* determine how edited dimensions are updated.

The definition points are located at the same points you pick when you determine the dimension location. For example, the definition points for linear dimensions are the extension line origins. The definition points for a circle diameter are the points used to pick the circle and the opposite side of the circle. The definition points for a radius are the points used to pick the circle plus the center of the circle.

Definition points are point objects. They're difficult to see because they're usually covered by the feature they define. You can, however, see them indirectly by using grips. The definition points of a dimension are the same as the dimension's grip points. You can see them by clicking a dimension. Try the following:

1. Make sure the Grips feature is turned on. (See Chapter 2 to refresh your memory on the Grips feature.)

2. Click the longest of the three vertical dimensions you drew in the earlier exercise. You'll see the grips of the dimension, which is shown in Figure 11.18.

**FIGURE 11.18**

The grip points are the same as the definition points on a dimension.

Click this grip.

## Using Grips to Make Minor Adjustments to Dimensions

The definition points, whose location you can see through their grips, are located on their own unique layer called *defpoints*. Definition points are displayed regardless of whether the Defpoints layer is on or off.

To give you an idea of how these definition points work, the following exercises show you how to manipulate the definition points directly.

In this exercise, you'll use coordinates to move a dimension line:

1. With the grips visible, click the grip near the dimension text.

2. Move the cursor around. When you move the cursor vertically, the text moves along the dimension line. When you move the cursor horizontally, the dimension line and text

move together, keeping their parallel orientation to the dimensioned floor plan. Here the entire dimension line, including the text, moves. In a later exercise, you'll see how you can move the dimension text independently of the dimension line.

3.  Enter **@9'<0.⏎**. Metric users should enter **@275<0.⏎**. The dimension line, text, and dimension extensions stretch to the new location to the right of the text (see Figure 11.19).

**FIGURE 11.19**

Moving the dimension line by using its grip

**MOVING SEVERAL DIMENSION LINES AT ONCE**

If you need to move several dimension lines, select them all, and then Shift+click one set of dimension-line grips from each dimension. After you've selected the grips, click one of the hot grips again. You can then move all the dimension lines at once.

In step 3 of the previous exercise, you saw that you could specify an exact distance for the dimension line's new location by entering a relative polar coordinate. Cartesian coordinates work just as well. You can even use object snaps to relocate dimension lines.

Next, try moving the dimension line back by using the Perpendicular osnap:

1.  Click the grip at the bottom of the dimension line you just edited.

2.  Shift+right-click and choose Perpendicular from the Osnap context menu.

3.  Place the cursor on the vertical dimension line that dimensions the balcony and click it.

4.  Choose Zoom All from the Zoom flyout on the Navigation bar and then click Save in the Quick Access toolbar to save this file in its current state.

### MAKING CHANGES TO MULTIPLE DIMENSIONS

You can use the Dimension Edit tool to edit existing dimensions quickly. This tool gives you the ability to edit more than one dimension's text at one time. One common use for the Dimension Edit tool is to change a string of dimensions to read *Equal* instead of showing the actual dimensioned distance. The following example shows an alternative to using the Properties palette for appending text to a dimension:

1. Type **DED↵**.

2. At the prompt

   ```
   Enter type of dimension editing [Home/New/Rotate/Oblique]<Home>:
   ```

   type **N↵** to use the New option. The Text Editor opens, showing 0 in the text box.

3. Use the arrow keys to move the cursor behind or in front of the 0, and then enter the text you want to append to the dimension. You can remove the 0 and replace the dimension with your text as an alternative.

4. Click Close Text Editor in the Close panel of the Text Editor tab.

5. At the `Select objects:` prompt, pick the dimensions you want to edit. The `Select objects:` prompt remains, enabling you to select several dimensions.

6. Press ↵ to finish your selection. The dimension changes to include your new text or to replace the existing dimension text.

The Dimension Edit tool is useful in editing dimension text, but you can also use this tool to make graphical changes to the text. Here is a list of the other Dimension Edit tool options:

**Home**  Moves the dimension text to its standard default position and angle.

**Rotate**  Rotates the dimension text to a new angle.

**Oblique**  Skews the dimension extension lines to a new angle. (See the section "Skewing Dimension Lines" later in this chapter.)

The selected dimension line moves to align with the other vertical dimension, back to its original location.

## Changing Style Settings of Individual Dimensions

In some cases, you have to change an individual dimension's style settings in order to edit it. For example, if you try to move the text of a typical linear dimension, you may find that the text and dimension lines are inseparable. You need to make a change to the dimension style setting that controls how AutoCAD locates dimension text in relation to the dimension line. The following section describes how you can change the style settings of individual dimensions to facilitate changes in the dimension.

### MOVING FIXED DIMENSION TEXT

You've seen how dimension text is attached to the dimension line so that when the text is moved, the dimension line follows. You may encounter situations in which you want to move the text independently of the dimension line. The following steps show how you can separate dimension text from its dimension line. These steps also show how you can change a single dimension's style settings:

1. Make sure Dynamic Input is turned on in the status bar.

2. Click the dimension you want to edit to expose its grips.

3. Hover over the grip nearest the dimension text. The multifunction grip menu appears (see Figure 11.20).

**FIGURE 11.20**
The multifunction grip menu for a dimension text

4. Select the option you want to use to move the text. For example, to move the 5" dimension text in Figure 11.20, select Move Text Only or Move With Leader.

5. Move the text, and when you are satisfied with the new location, press the Esc key to clear your selection.

As you saw in Figure 11.20, you have a number of options for moving dimension text. The multifunction grip options are self-explanatory, but you might want to experiment with them to see how each one behaves.

When you use some of the dimension text multifunction grip options, you are changing the property of that dimension. In fact, the old way of moving dimension text involved changing a setting in the Properties palette for a selected dimension. The Move Text, Add Leader option in the Text Movement listing of the Fit category of the Properties palette lets you move the dimension text independently of the dimension line. This option is similar to the Move With Leader option in the multifunction grip menu. It also draws a leader from the dimension line to the text. Another option—Move Text, No Leader—does the same thing but doesn't include a leader. This option has the same effect as the Move Text Only option in the multifunction grip menu. You can also set these options for a dimension style by using the Text Placement options in the Fit tab of the New Dimension Style or Modify Dimension Style dialog box.

The Properties palette gives you access to many of the settings you saw for setting up dimension styles. The main difference here is that the Properties palette affects only the dimensions you've selected.

In a previous exercise, you changed the format setting of a single dimension *after* it was placed. These settings can be made a standard part of your Architectural dimension style by using the Modify button in the Dimension Style Manager.

If you have multiple dimension styles and you want to change an existing dimension to the current dimension style, use the Update tool. Choose Update on the Dimensions panel or type **Dimstyle↵A↵**. Then select the dimensions you want to change and press ↵. The selected dimensions will be converted to the current style.

---

### ROTATING AND POSITIONING DIMENSION TEXT

Once in a while, dimension text works better if it's kept in a horizontal orientation, even if the dimension itself isn't horizontal. To rotate dimension text, click the Text Angle tool from the Annotate tab's expanded Dimensions panel, select the dimension text, and then enter an angle or select two points to indicate an angle graphically. You can also enter **0↵** to return the dimension text to its default angle.

If you need to move the dimension text to the left, center, or right of the dimension line, you can use the Left Justify, Center Justify, or Right Justify tool in the Annotate tab's expanded Dimensions panel.

---

## Editing Dimensions and Other Objects Together

It's helpful to be able to edit a dimension directly by using its grips. But the key feature of dimensions in AutoCAD is their ability to adjust themselves *automatically* to changes in the drawing.

To see how this works, try moving the living room closer to the bathroom wall. You can move a group of lines and vertices by using the Stretch command and the Crossing option:

1. Click the Stretch tool in the Home tab's Modify panel, or type **S↵C↵**. You'll see the following prompts:

   ```
   At the Select objects to stretch
   by crossing-window or crossing-polygon...
   Select objects: C
   Specify first corner:
   ```

2. Pick a crossing window, as illustrated in Figure 11.21, and then press ↵ to confirm your selection.

3. At the `Specify base point or [Displacement] <Displacement>:` prompt, pick any point on the screen.

4. At the `Specify second point or <use first point as displacement>:` prompt, enter **@2'<90↵** to move the wall 2' in a 90° direction. Metric users should enter **@61<90↵**. The wall moves, and the dimension text changes to reflect the new dimensions, as shown in Figure 11.22.

5. After viewing the result of using the Stretch tool, click the Undo tool in the Quick Access toolbar or type **U↵** to change the drawing back to its previous state.

You can also use the Mirror, Rotate, and Stretch commands with dimensions. The polar arrays also work, and you can use Extend and Trim with linear dimensions.

**FIGURE 11.21**
The Stretch crossing window

**FIGURE 11.22**
The moved wall, with the updated dimensions

When you're editing dimensioned objects, be sure to select the dimension associated with the object being edited. As you select objects, using the crossing window (C) or crossing polygon (CP) selection option helps you include the dimensions. For more on these selection options, see Chapter 2.

---

**PLACING DIMENSIONS OVER HATCH PATTERNS**

If a hatch pattern or solid fill completely covers a dimension, you can use the Draworder command to have AutoCAD draw the dimension over the hatch or solid fill. See Chapter 7, "Mastering Viewing Tools, Hatches, and External References," and Chapter 13, "Copying Existing Drawings from Other Sources," for more on various uses of the Draworder command.

---

---

**MODIFYING THE DIMENSION STYLE SETTINGS BY USING OVERRIDE**

In the section "Moving Fixed Dimension Text," you used the Properties palette to facilitate moving the dimension text. You can also choose the Override tool in the Annotate tab's expanded Dimensions panel (Dimoverride command) to accomplish the same thing. The Override option enables you to change an individual dimension's style settings. Here's an example that shows how you can use the Override option in place of the Properties palette in the exercise in "Moving Fixed Dimension Text":

1. Press the Esc key twice to make sure you aren't in the middle of a command. Then choose Override from the Annotate tab's expanded Dimensions panel.

2. At the following prompt, type **Dimfit**⏎:

   ```
   Enter dimension variable name to override or [Clear overrides]:
   ```

3. At the `Enter new value for dimension variable <3>:` prompt, enter **4**⏎. This has the same effect as selecting Move Text, Add Leader from the Fit category of the Properties palette.

4. The `Enter dimension variable name to override:` prompt appears again, enabling you to enter another dimension variable. Press ⏎ to move to the next step.

5. At the `Select objects:` prompt, select the dimension you want to change. You can select a group of dimensions if you want to change several dimensions at once. Press ⏎ when you've finished with your selection. The dimension settings change for the selected dimensions.

As you can see from this example, the Dimoverride command requires that you know exactly which dimension variable to edit in order to make the desired modification. In this case, setting the Dimfit variable to 4 lets you move the dimension text independently of the dimension line. If you find the Dimoverride command useful, consult the online bonus chapter "System Variables and Dimension Styles," available at www.omura.com/chapters, to determine which system variable corresponds to the Dimension Style dialog box settings.

---

## Associating Dimensions with Objects

You've seen how dimensions and the objects with which they're associated can move together so that the dimension remains connected to the object. When you're in the process of editing a drawing, dimensions may lose their association with objects, so you may need to re-create an association between a dimension and an object. The following steps show you how this is done:

1. Choose Reassociate from the Annotate tab's expanded Dimensions panel. You can also type **Dimreassociate.⏎** at the Command prompt.

2. At the following prompt, select the dimension that you want to reassociate with an object, and then press ⏎:

   ```
   Select dimensions to reassociate
   Select Objects or [Disassociated]:
   ```

3. At the `Specify first extension line origin or [Select object] <next>:` prompt, note that an X appears at one of the dimension's definition points.

4. Use the Endpoint osnap, and click the end of the object you want to have connected to the definition point indicated in step 3.

5. An X appears at the dimension's other definition point. Use the Endpoint osnap again, and click the other endpoint of the object you want associated with the dimension. You now have the dimension associated with the endpoints of the object. You may have to adjust the location of the dimension line at this point.

In step 3, you see an X at the location of a dimension definition point. If the definition point is already associated with an object, the X appears with a box around it. The box is a reminder that the definition point is already associated with an object and that you'll be changing its association. In this situation, you can press ⏎ to switch to the dimension's other definition point.

Also in step 3, you have the option to select an object. This option enables you to associate the dimension with an entire object instead of with just one endpoint. If you type **S.⏎** at that prompt in step 3, you can then select the object you want to associate with the dimension. The dimension changes so that its definition points coincide with the endpoints of the object. The dimension remains in its original orientation. For example, a vertical dimension remains vertical even if you associate the dimension with a horizontal line. In this situation, the dimension dutifully dimensions the endpoints of the line but shows a distance of 0.

---

**REMOVING DIMENSION ASSOCIATIONS**

You can remove a dimension's association with an object by using the Dimdisassociate command. Type **Dimdisassociate**↵ at the Command prompt, select the dimension(s), and then press ↵.

---

## Adding a String of Dimensions with a Single Operation

In AutoCAD you can create a string of dimensions using a single operation. The Qdim command lets you select a set of objects instead of having to select points. The following exercise demonstrates how the Qdim command works:

1. If you haven't done so already, zoom out so you have an overall view of the Unit floor plan.

2. Click Quick Dimension on the Dimensions panel.

3. At the Select geometry to dimension: prompt, place a selection window around the entire left-side wall of the unit.

4. Press ↵ to finish your selection. The following prompt appears:

   ```
   Specify dimension line position, or
   [Continuous/Staggered/Baseline/Ordinate/Radius/Diameter/
   datumPoint/Edit/seTtings] <Continuous>:
   ```

5. Click a point to the left of the wall to place the dimension. A string of dimensions appears, displaying all the dimensions for the wall (see Figure 11.23).

6. When you've finished reviewing the results of this exercise, exit the file without saving it.

**FIGURE 11.23**
The dimensions for
the wall

The prompt in step 4 indicates several types of dimensions from which you can choose. For example, if you want the dimensions to originate from a single baseline, you can enter **B↵** in step 4 to select the Baseline option.

The Qdim command can be a time-saver when you want to dimension a wall quickly. It may not work in all situations, but if the object you're dimensioning is fairly simple, it can be all you need.

In this exercise, you used a simple window to select the wall. For more complex shapes, try using a crossing polygon selection window. See Chapter 2 for more on crossing polygons.

### Adding or Removing the Alternate Dimensions

You may eventually encounter a drawing that contains alternate dimensions, as shown in some of the figures earlier in this chapter. You can remove those alternate dimensions by turning off the alternate dimension features. Here's how it's done:

1. Click the Dimension Style tool in the Annotate tab's Dimensions panel title bar or enter **D↵** to open the Dimension Style Manager.

2. Select the style that uses the alternate units. In the Styles list box, choose Modify.

3. Select the Alternate Units tab.

4. Click the Display Alternate Units check box to remove the check mark.

5. Click OK, and then click Close to close the Dimension Style Manager.

---

#### USING OBJECT SNAP WHILE DIMENSIONING

When you pick intersections and endpoints frequently, as you do during dimensioning, it can be inconvenient to use the Osnap context menu. If you know you'll be using certain osnaps frequently, you can use running osnaps. (See the sidebar "The Osnap Options" in Chapter 3 for more on setting up running osnaps.)

After you've designated your running osnaps, the next time you're prompted to select a point the selected osnap modes are automatically activated. You can still override the default settings by using the Osnap context menu (Shift+click the right mouse button).

There is a drawback to setting a running osnap mode: When your drawing gets crowded, you can end up picking the wrong point by accident. However, you can easily toggle the running osnap mode off by clicking Object Snap in the status bar or by pressing F3.

---

The dimensions that use the style you just edited change to remove the alternate dimensions. You can also perform the reverse operation and add alternate dimensions to an existing set of dimensions. Follow the steps shown here, but instead of removing the check mark in step 4 add the check mark and make the appropriate setting changes to the rest of the Alternate Units tab.

## Dimensioning Nonorthogonal Objects

So far, you've been reading about how to work with linear dimensions. You can also dimension nonorthogonal objects, such as circles, arcs, triangles, and trapezoids. In the following sections, you'll practice dimensioning a nonorthogonal object.

For the following exercises, you'll use a drawing of a hexagonal-shaped window. Open the 11a-wind.dwg file from the sample files; metric users should open the 11a-wind-metric.dwg file. You can use this file to follow along.

## Dimensioning Nonorthogonal Linear Distances

Now you'll dimension the window. The unusual shape of the window prevents you from using the horizontal or vertical dimensions you've used already. However, choosing Aligned from the Dimension flyout in the Dimensions panel enables you to dimension at an angle:

1. Click the Aligned tool in the Dimension flyout on the Dimensions panel. You can also enter **DAL**↵ to start the aligned dimension.

2. At the Specify first extension line origin or <select object>: prompt, press ↵. You could pick extension-line origins as you did in earlier examples, but pressing ↵ shows you how the Select Object option works.

3. At the Select object to dimension: prompt, pick the upper-right face of the hexagon near coordinate 29,22 (75,55 for metric users). As the prompt indicates, you can also pick an arc or a circle for this type of dimension.

4. At the Specify dimension line location or [Mtext/Text/Angle]: prompt, pick a point near coordinate 34,24 (90,60 for metric users). The dimension appears in the drawing, as shown in Figure 11.24.

**FIGURE 11.24**
The aligned dimension of a nonorthogonal line

Just as with linear dimensions, you can enter **T**↵ in step 4 to enter alternate text for the dimension.

Next, you'll dimension a face of the hexagon. Instead of its actual length, however, you'll dimension a distance at a specified angle—the distance from the center of the face:

1. Select the Linear tool from the Dimension flyout on the Dimensions panel or type **DLI**↵.

2. At the Specify first extension line origin or <select object>: prompt, press ↵.

3. At the Select object to dimension: prompt, pick the lower-right face of the hexagon near coordinate 29,14 (77,33 for metric users).

4. At the Specify dimension line location or [Mtext/Text/Angle/Horizontal/ Vertical/Rotated]: prompt, type **R**↵ to select the Rotated option.

5. At the Specify angle of dimension line <0>: prompt, enter **30**↵.

6. At the `Specify dimension line location or [Mtext/Text/Angle/Horizontal/Vertical/Rotated]:` prompt, pick a point near coordinate 33,7 (88,12 for metric users). Your drawing will look like Figure 11.25.

**FIGURE 11.25**
A linear dimension using the Rotated option

The Dimrotate command accomplishes the same thing with a slight change in the sequence of steps.

## Dimensioning Radii, Diameters, and Arcs

To dimension circular objects, you use another set of options from the Dimension menu:

1. Select the Angular tool from the Dimension flyout on the Dimensions panel, or enter **DAN↵** at the Command prompt.

2. At the `Select arc, circle, line, or <specify vertex>:` prompt, pick the upper-left face of the hexagon near coordinate 15,22 (44,57 for metric users).

3. At the `Select second line:` prompt, pick the top face at coordinate 22,26 (54,62 for metric users).

4. At the `Specify dimension arc line location or [Mtext/Text/Angle]:` prompt, notice that as you move the cursor around the upper-left corner of the hexagon, the dimension changes, as shown in the top images of Figure 11.26.

5. Pick a point near coordinate 21,20 (49,50 for metric users). The dimension is fixed in the drawing. (See the bottom image of Figure 11.26.)

If you need to make subtle adjustments to the dimension line or text location, you can do so using grips after you place the angular dimension.

Now try the Diameter option, which shows the diameter of a circle:

1. Click the Diameter tool in the Dimension flyout on the Dimensions panel, or enter **DDI↵** at the Command prompt.

2. At the `Select arc or circle:` prompt, pick the circle.

3. At the `Specify dimension line location or [Mtext/Text/Angle]:` prompt, you see the diameter dimension drag along the circle as you move the cursor. If you move the cursor outside the circle, the dimension line and text also move outside the circle. (See the top image in Figure 11.27.)

**FIGURE 11.26**
The angular dimension added to the window frame

**FIGURE 11.27**
Dimension showing the diameter of a circle

If the dimension text can't fit in the circle, AutoCAD gives you the option to place the dimension text outside the circle as you drag the temporary dimension to a horizontal position.

4. Place the cursor inside the circle so the dimension arrow points in a horizontal direction, as shown in the bottom image of Figure 11.27.

5. With the text centered, click the mouse.

The Radius tool in the Dimension flyout on the Dimensions panel gives you a radius dimension, just as the Diameter tool provides a circle's diameter. Figure 11.28 shows a radius dimension on the outside of the circle, but you can place it inside in a manner similar to how you place the diameter dimension. The Center Mark tool on the expanded Dimensions panel places a cross mark in the center of the selected arc or circle.

**FIGURE 11.28**
A radius dimension shown on the outside of the circle

If you need to dimension an arc or a circle whose center isn't in the drawing area, you can use the jogged dimension. Here are the steps:

1. Click the Jogged tool from the Dimension flyout on the Annotate tab's Dimensions panel, or enter **DJO**↵ at the Command prompt.

2. At the Select arc or circle: prompt, select the object you want to dimension.

3. At the Specify center location override: prompt, select a point that indicates the general direction to the center of the arc or circle. A dimension line appears and follows the movement of your cursor.

4. Position the dimension line where you want it, and then click.

5. Position the dimension line jog where you want it, and then click. The jogged dimension is placed in the drawing (see Figure 11.29).

Arc lengths can also be given a dimension using the Arc Length tool. Choose the Arc Length tool from the Dimension flyout on the Dimensions panel, or enter **DAR**↵ at the Command prompt. At the Select Arc or polyline arc segment: prompt, select the arc you want to dimension. It can be either a plain arc or a polyline arc. Once you've selected the arc, the arc dimension appears and moves with the cursor. You can then select the location for the dimension.

**FIGURE 11.29**
The jogged dimension in the drawing

## Skewing Dimension Lines

At times, you may need to force the extension lines to take on an angle other than 90° to the dimension line. This is a common requirement of isometric drawings, in which most lines are at 30° or 60° angles instead of 90°. To facilitate nonorthogonal dimensions like these, AutoCAD offers the Oblique option:

1. Choose Oblique from the expanded Dimensions panel, or type **DED⏎RO⏎**.

2. At the `Select objects:` prompt, pick the aligned dimension in the upper-right portion of the drawing and press ⏎ to confirm your selection.

3. At the `Enter obliquing angle (Press ENTER for none):` prompt, enter **60⏎** for 60°. The dimension will skew so that the extension lines are at 60° (see Figure 11.30).

4. Save the drawing.

**FIGURE 11.30**
The extension lines at 60°

# Adding a Note with a Leader Arrow

One type of dimension is something like a text-dimension hybrid. The AutoCAD Multileader tool lets you add a text note combined with an arrow that points to an object in your drawing. Multileaders are easy to use and offer the same text-formatting tools as the Mtext tool. Try the following exercise to get familiar with multileaders:

1. Click the Multileader tool in the Annotate tab's Leaders panel (see Figure 11.31), or enter **MLD**↵.

**FIGURE 11.31**

The Leaders panel

2. At the Specify leader arrowhead location or [leader Landing first/Content first/Options] <Options>: prompt, pick a point near the top-left edge of the hexagon at coordinate 16,24 (45,59 for metric users).

3. At the Specify leader landing location: prompt, enter **@6<110**↵. Metric users should enter **@15<110**↵. The Text Editor tab appears, along with the text cursor at the note location.

4. Enter **Window Frame** for the note, and then click Close Text Editor in the Text Editor tab's Close panel. Your note appears with the leader arrow similar to the one shown in Figure 11.32.

**FIGURE 11.32**

The leader with a note added

The text in the note is in the current text style unless you specify another style in the Text tab of the New Dimension Style or Modify Dimension Style dialog box. (See the section "The Text Tab" in the bonus chapter "System Variables and Dimension Styles," available at www.omura.com/chapters, for more information.)

**SETTING THE SCALE OF LEADERS**

Multileaders have an Annotative option that allows them to adjust automatically to the scale of the drawing. You can find the Annotative option setting in the properties for a specific multileader in the drawing or in the multileader style setting. See the Scale option in Table 11.2, later in this chapter, under the Leader Structure tab.

The Multileader tool offers a lot of options that aren't obvious when you're using it. In step 1 of the previous example, after choosing Multileader you can press ↵ to modify the behavior of the Multileader tool. You'll see the following prompt:

```
Enter an option [Leader type/leader lAnding/Content
  type/Maxpoints/First angle/Second angle/eXit options]
  <eXit options>:
```

Table 11.1 gives you a rundown of these options and their functions.

**TABLE 11.1:**    The Multileader options

| OPTION | FUNCTION |
|---|---|
| Leader type | Allows you to choose between straight-line leaders, curved leaders, or no leaders. |
| leader lAnding | Determines whether a leader landing is used. The *leader landing* is the short line that connects the arrow to the note. Also lets you set landing distance. |
| Content type | Lets you select between Mtext or a block for the leader note. You also have the option to choose None. |
| Maxpoints | Lets you set the number of points you select for the leader. The default is 2. |
| First angle | Lets you constrain the angle of the leader line to a fixed value. |
| Second angle | Lets you constrain the angle of the arrow's second line segment if you're using more than two points for the Maxpoints option. |
| eXit options | Lets you return to the main part of the Multileader command to draw the leader. |

## Creating Multileader Styles

Besides using the options shown in Table 11.1, you can create multileader styles to control the appearance of multileaders. Multileader styles are similar in concept to text and dimension styles. They allow you to set up the appearance of the leader under a name that you can call up at any time. For example, you may want to have one type of leader that uses a block instead of text for the note and another leader that uses a dot in place of an arrow. Alternatively, you may want to set up a style that uses curved lines instead of straight ones for the leader line. You can create a multileader style for each of these types of leader features and then switch between the leader styles, depending on the requirements of your leader note.

To set up or modify a multileader style, click the Multileader Style Manager tool in the Annotate tab's Leaders panel title bar. You can also enter **MLS**↵ at the Command prompt. Doing so opens the Multileader Style Manager, shown in Figure 11.33. From here, you can select an existing style from the list on the left and click Modify to edit it, or you can click New to create a new one. If you click New, you're asked to select an existing style as a basis for your new style.

**FIGURE 11.33**
The Multileader
Style Manager

When you click Modify or New, the Modify Multileader Style (see Figure 11.34) or New Multileader Style dialog box opens.

**FIGURE 11.34**
The Modify
Multileader Style
dialog box

Table 11.2 describes the options in each of the tabs of the Modify Multileader Style dialog box. Some of these options are the same as those for the Multileader command.

**TABLE 11.2:**     The Modify Multileader Style dialog box options

| TAB AND GROUP | FUNCTION |
| --- | --- |
| **Leader Format tab** | |
| General | Lets you set the leader line to straight or curved. You can also set the color, lineweight, and linetype for the leader line. |
| Arrowhead | Controls the size and shape of the arrowheads. |
| Leader Break | Controls the size of the gap in a leader line when the Leaderbreak command is applied. Leaderbreak places a break on a leader line where two leader lines cross. |
| **Leader Structure tab** | |
| Constraints | Determines the number of line segments in the leader line. You can also apply angle constraints to the leader-line segments. |
| Landing Settings | Controls the leader-line landing segment. This is the last line segment that points to the note. |
| Scale | Lets you control the scale of the leader components. You can either apply a fixed scale or use the Annotative option to have the drawing annotation scale apply to the leader. |
| **Content tab** | |
| Multileader Type | Lets you select the type of object that will be used for the leader note. The options are Mtext, Block, and None. |
| Text Options | Gives you control over the way the leader note appears. You can control color, text style, size, justification, and orientation. |
| Leader Connection | Determines the position between the leader line and the note. |

Once you've set up a multileader style, you can make it the default style by selecting it from the Multileader Style drop-down list on the Annotate tab's Leaders panel.

The selected style will be applied to any new multileader you add to your drawing. You can also change the style of an existing multileader. To do this, click the multileader to select it, and then select the multileader style you want from the Leaders panel drop-down list.

## Editing Multileader Notes

If you need to make changes to the note portion of a multileader, you can do so by double-clicking the note. Doing so brings up the Text Editor tab in the Ribbon, allowing you to make changes as you would in a word processor.

At other times, you may want to change the leader line, arrows, or other graphic features of the multileader. For example, you may want to have all the notes aligned vertically for a neater appearance. As another option, you may want to add more leader arrows so that the note points to several objects in the drawing instead of just one.

The Leaders panel offers several tools that let you make these types of changes to your leader notes (refer back to Figure 11.31). The Add Leader and Remove Leader tools let you add or remove leaders from a multileader. Add Leader is a handy tool if you want a single note to point to several objects. The Align tool lets you align the note portion of several multileaders. Finally, the Collect tool lets you collect several multileaders that use blocks for notes into a single note.

## Breaking a Dimension Line for a Leader

In a crowded drawing, your multileader arrow may have to cross over a dimension line. In many drafting conventions, when a leader line crosses over a dimension line, the dimension line must be shown with a gap.

You can apply a gap to a dimension line using the Dimbreak tool. Here's how it works:

1. Choose Break from the Dimensions panel.

2. At the `Select dimension to add/remove break or [Multiple]:` prompt, select a dimension line, or enter **M**↵ and select multiple dimension lines.

3. When you're finished with your selection, press ↵. Note that this ↵ is necessary only when using the Multiple option.

4. At the `Select object to break dimension or [Auto/Manual/Remove] <Auto>:` prompt, press ↵. A gap appears wherever a leader line or other dimension line crosses over the selected dimension line.

If you prefer to indicate a break manually, enter **M**↵ at the prompt in step 4. Doing so allows you to select two points on the dimension, indicating where the gap is to occur. The drawback to adding a break manually is that the break will not follow the leader line if the leader line is moved. The break will have to be removed and replaced.

If additional dimension or leader lines are added that cross over the dimension line, repeat your use of the Dimbreak tool. To remove an existing break, use the Remove option in step 4 by entering **R↵**.

## Applying Ordinate Dimensions

In mechanical drafting, *ordinate dimensions* are used to maintain the accuracy of machined parts by establishing an origin on the part. All major dimensions are described as x-coordinates or y-coordinates of that origin. The origin is usually an easy-to-locate feature of the part, such as a machined bore or two machined surfaces.

Figure 11.35 shows a typical application of ordinate dimensions. In the lower-right corner, note the two dimensions whose leaders are jogged. Also note the origin location in the center circle.

**FIGURE 11.35**
A drawing using ordinate dimensions

To use the Ordinate command, perform the following steps:

1. Select Origin from the View tab's Coordinates panel, or type **UCS↵Or↵**. If you don't see the Coordinates panel in the View tab, go to the View tab, right-click in the Ribbon, and select Show Panels ➤ Coordinates.

2. At the `Specify new origin point <0,0,0>:` prompt, click the exact location of the origin of your part.

3. Toggle Ortho mode on in the status bar.

4. Click the Ordinate tool in the Dimension flyout on the Annotate tab's Dimensions panel. You can also enter **DOR↵** to start the ordinate dimension.

5. At the `Specify feature location:` prompt, click the item you want to dimension. The direction of the leader determines whether the dimension will be of the Xdatum or the Ydatum.

6. At the `Specify leader endpoint or [Xdatum/Ydatum/Mtext/Text/Angle]:` prompt, indicate the length and direction of the leader. Do this by positioning the rubber-banding leader perpendicular to the coordinate direction you want to dimension and then clicking that point.

In steps 1 and 2, you used the UCS feature to establish a second origin in the drawing. The Ordinate Dimension tool then uses that origin to determine the ordinate dimensions. You'll get a chance to work with the UCS feature in Chapter 21, "Using Advanced 3D Features." You may have noticed options in the Command window for the Ordinate Dimension tool. The Xdatum and Ydatum options force the dimension to be of the x- or y-coordinate no matter what direction the leader takes. The Mtext option opens the Text Editor tab in the Ribbon, enabling you to append or replace the ordinate dimension text. The Text option lets you enter replacement text directly through the Command window.

If you turn off Ortho mode, the dimension leader is drawn with a jog to maintain the orthogonal line segment to the dimension text (look back at Figure 11.35).

## Adding Tolerance Notation

In mechanical drafting, *tolerances* are a key part of a drawing's notation. They specify the allowable variation in size and shape that a mechanical part can have. To help facilitate tolerance notation, AutoCAD provides the Tolerance command, which offers common ISO tolerance symbols together with a quick way to build a standard feature-control symbol. *Feature-control symbols* are industry-standard symbols used to specify tolerances. If you're a mechanical engineer or drafter, the AutoCAD tolerance notation options will be a valuable tool. However, a full discussion of tolerances requires a basic understanding of mechanical design and drafting, and it is beyond the scope of this book.

### Inserting Tolerance and Datum Values

To use the Tolerance command, choose Tolerance from the expanded Dimensions panel, or type TOL↵ at the Command prompt to open the Geometric Tolerance dialog box (see Figure 11.36).

**FIGURE 11.36**
The Geometric Tolerance dialog box

This is where you enter tolerance and datum values for the feature-control symbol. You can enter two tolerance values and three datum values. In addition, you can stack values in a two-tiered fashion.

Click a box in the Sym group to open the Symbol dialog box.

The top section of Figure 11.37 shows what each symbol in the Symbol dialog box represents. The bottom image shows a sample drawing with a feature symbol used on a cylindrical object. The symbols in the sample drawing show that the upper cylinder needs to be parallel within 0.003″ of the lower cylinder. Note that mechanical drawings often use measurements in thousandths, so 0.3 means 0.003.

**FIGURE 11.37**
The tolerance symbols

In the Geometric Tolerance dialog box, you can click a box in any of the Datum groups or a box in the right side of the Tolerance groups to open the Material Condition dialog box. This dialog box contains standard symbols relating to the maximum and minimum material conditions of a feature on the part being dimensioned.

### Adding Inspection Dimensions

Another type of dimension related to tolerances is the inspection dimension. This is a type of dimension notation that indicates how often the tolerances of a dimension should be checked.

To add an inspection dimension, first add a regular linear dimension as described in the early part of this chapter. Next, follow these steps:

1. Choose Inspect from the Dimensions panel or type **Diminspect**↵. The Inspection Dimension dialog box appears (see Figure 11.38).

**FIGURE 11.38**
The Inspection Dimension dialog box

2. Click the Select Dimensions tool. The dialog box temporarily closes to allow you to select a dimension.

3. Select a shape option from the Shape group.

4. Enter a value for the Label and Inspection Rate boxes, and then click OK.

The dimension appears with the additional changes from the dialog box (see Figure 11.39).

**FIGURE 11.39**
The dimension with the additional changes

## The Bottom Line

**Understand the components of a dimension.** Before you start to dimension with AutoCAD, become familiar with the different parts of a dimension. Doing so will help you set up your dimensions to fit the style you need.

**Master It**  Name a few of the dimension components.

**Create a dimension style.** As you become more familiar with technical drawing and drafting, you'll learn that there are standard formats for drawing dimensions. Arrows, text size, and even the way dimension lines are drawn are all subject to a standard format. Fortunately, AutoCAD offers dimension styles that let you set up your dimension format once and then call up that format whenever you need it.

**Master It** What is the name of the dialog box that lets you manage dimension styles, and how do you open it?

**Draw linear dimensions.** The most common dimension that you'll use is the linear dimension. Knowing how to place a linear dimension is a big first step in learning how to dimension in AutoCAD.

**Master It** Name the three locations you are asked for when placing a linear dimension.

**Edit dimensions.** Dimensions often change in the course of a project, so you should know how to make changes to dimension text or other parts of a dimension.

**Master It** How do you start the command to edit dimension text?

**Dimension nonorthogonal objects.** Not everything you dimension will use linear dimensions. AutoCAD offers a set of dimension tools for dimensioning objects that aren't made up of straight lines.

**Master It** Name some of the types of objects for which a linear dimension isn't appropriate.

**Add a note with a leader arrow.** In addition to dimensions, you'll probably add lots of notes with arrows pointing to features in a design. AutoCAD offers the multileader for this purpose.

**Master It** What two types of objects does the multileader combine?

**Apply ordinate dimensions.** When accuracy counts, ordinate dimensions are often used because they measure distances that are similar to coordinates from a single feature.

**Master It** What AutoCAD feature do you use for ordinate dimensions that isn't strictly associated with dimensions?

**Add tolerance notation.** Mechanical drafting often requires the use of special notation to describe tolerances. AutoCAD offers some predefined symbols that address the need to include tolerance notation in a drawing.

**Master It** How do you open the Geometric Tolerance dialog box?

# Part 3

# Mastering Advanced Skills

# Chapter 12

# Using Attributes

Earlier in this book, you learned how to create blocks, which are assemblies of objects in AutoCAD® 2015. Blocks enable you to form parts or symbols that can be easily reproduced. Furniture, bolts, doors, and windows are a few common items that you can create with blocks. Whole rooms and appliances can also be made into blocks. There is no limit to a block's size.

AutoCAD also offers a feature called *attributes* that allows you to store text information as a part of a block. For example, you can store the material specifications for a bolt or other mechanical part that you've converted into a block. If your application is architecture, you can store the material, hardware, and dimensional information for a door or window that has been converted into a block. You can then quickly gather information about that block that may not be obvious from the graphics.

Attribute text can be set up to be invisible, or it can be displayed as text in the drawing. If it's invisible, you can easily view the attribute information by double-clicking the block that contains the attribute. The attribute information is displayed in a dialog box. This information can also be extracted to a database or spreadsheet, letting you keep an inventory of the blocks in your drawing. You can even convert attribute information into tables in an AutoCAD drawing. Doing so can help you make quick work of parts lists or door and window schedules. By using attributes, you can keep track of virtually any object in a drawing or maintain textual information in the drawing that can be queried.

Keeping track of objects is just one way to use attributes. You can also use them in place of text objects when you must keep text and graphic items together. One common example is the reference symbol in an architectural drawing. Reference symbols are used to indicate the location of more detailed information in a drawing set, such as the elevation views of a room or a cross-section of a wall or other part of a building. In this chapter, you'll use attributes for one of their common functions: maintaining lists of parts. In this case, the parts are doors. This chapter also describes how to import these attributes into a database-management program. As you go through the exercises, think about the ways attributes can help you in your particular application.

In this chapter, you will learn to

♦ Create attributes

♦ Edit attributes

♦ Extract and export attribute information

# Creating Attributes

Attributes depend on blocks. You might think of an attribute as text information attached to a block. The information can be a description of the block or some other pertinent text. For example, you can include an attribute definition with the Door block you created in Chapter 4, "Organizing Objects with Blocks and Groups." Subsequently, every time you insert the Door block, you'll be prompted for a value associated with that door. The value can be a number, a height or width value, a name, or any type of text information you want. After you enter a value, it's stored as part of the Door block in the drawing database. This value can be displayed as text attached to the Door block or it can be invisible. You can change the value at any time. You can even specify the prompts for the attribute value.

However, suppose you don't have the attribute information when you design the Door block. As an alternative, you can add the attribute to a *symbol* that is later placed by the door when you know enough about the design to specify what type of door goes where. Figure 12.1 shows a sample door symbol and a table to which the symbol refers. The standard door-type symbol suits this purpose nicely because it's an object that you can set up and use as a block independent of the Door block.

**FIGURE 12.1**

A door symbol tells you what type of door goes in the location shown. Usually, the symbol contains a number or a letter that is keyed to a table that shows more information about the door.

A door symbol placed by a door in a floor plan refers to a specification in a table in another drawing.

## Adding Attributes to Blocks

In the following exercise, you'll create a door-type symbol, which is commonly used to describe the size, thickness, and other characteristics of any given door in an architectural drawing. The symbol is usually a circle, a hexagon, or a diamond with a number in it. The number is generally cross-referenced to a schedule that lists all the door types and their characteristics.

You'll create a new block containing attribute definitions in the file for which the block is intended: the Plan.dwg file. You will use the 12a-plan.dwg file from the sample drawings, which is similar to the Plan file on which you've been working in previous chapters. You'll create the block in the file so that you can easily insert it where it belongs in the plan.

First, open the Plan file and set up a view appropriate for creating the block with the attribute:

1. Open the 12a-plan.dwg file. Metric users can use the file 12a-plan-metric.dwg. These are similar to the Plan.dwg file you've created on your own with a few additions to facilitate the exercises in this chapter.

Zoom Window 2. Select the Zoom Window option on the Navigation bar.

3. At the Specify first corner: prompt, enter **0,0⏎**.

4. At the Specify opposite corner: prompt, enter **12,9** (**30.5,22.8** for metric users). This causes your view to zoom in to a location near the origin of the drawing in a 12″ × 9″ area (30.5 cm × 22.8 cm for metric users).

You zoom into this small area because you'll draw the block at its paper size of ¼″ (or 0.6 cm for metric users). Now you're ready to create the block and attribute. You'll start by drawing the graphics of the block, and then you'll add the attribute definition:

1. Draw a circle with its center at coordinate 7,5 (15,11 for metric users) and a diameter of 0.25 (0.6 for metric users). The circle is automatically placed on layer 0, which is the current layer. Remember that objects in a block that are on layer 0 take on the color and linetype assignment of the layer on which the block is inserted.

2. Zoom into the circle so that it's about the same size as that shown in Figure 12.2.

**FIGURE 12.2**
The attribute
definition inserted
in the circle

3. If the circle looks like an octagon, type **RE⏎** to regenerate your drawing.

 4. Click the Define Attributes tool in the Home tab's Block Definition panel or type **ATT⏎** to open the Attribute Definition dialog box (see Figure 12.3).

**FIGURE 12.3**
The Attribute Definition dialog box

**5.** In the Attribute group, click the Tag box and enter **D-TYPE**.

---

### UNDERSTANDING THE ATTRIBUTE TAG

The attribute tag is equivalent to a field name in a database. You can also think of the tag as the attribute's name or ID. It can help to identify the purpose of the attribute. The tag can be a maximum of 255 characters but can't contain spaces. If you plan to use the attribute data in a database program, check that program's documentation for other restrictions on field names.

---

**6.** Press the Tab key or click the Prompt box, and enter **Door type**. This is the text for the prompt that will appear when you insert the block containing this attribute. Often the prompt is the same as the tag, but it can be anything you like. Unlike the tag, the prompt can include spaces and other special characters.

---

### GIVE YOUR PROMPTS MEANINGFUL NAMES

Use a prompt that gives explicit instructions so that the user will know exactly what is expected. Consider including an example in the prompt. (Enclose the example in square brackets to imitate the way AutoCAD prompts often display defaults.)

---

**7.** Click the Default box, and enter a hyphen (-). This is the default value for the door-type prompt.

**MAKE YOUR DEFAULTS USEFUL**

If an attribute will contain a number that will be used later for sorting in a database, use a default attribute value such as 000 to indicate the number of digits required. The zeros can also remind the user that values less than 100 must be preceded by a leading zero, as in 099.

8. Click the Justification drop-down list, and select Middle Center. This enables you to center the attribute on the circle's center. The Text Settings group includes several other options. Because attributes appear as text, you can apply the same settings to them as you would to single-line text.

9. In the Text Height box, make sure the value is ⅛" or **0.125**. (Metric users should enter **0.3**.) This makes the attribute text 0.125" (0.3 cm) high.

10. Select the Annotative option. Doing so allows the attribute to adjust in size automatically according to the annotation scale of the drawing.

11. In the Insertion Point group, make sure the Specify On-Screen check box is selected.

12. Click OK to close the dialog box.

13. Using the Center osnap, pick the center of the circle. You need to place the cursor on the circle's circumference, not in the circle's center, to obtain the center by using the osnap. The attribute definition appears at the center of the circle (see Figure 12.2).

You've just created your first attribute definition. The attribute definition displays its tag in all uppercase letters to help you identify it. When you later insert this file into another drawing, the tag turns into the value you assign to it when it's inserted. If you want only one attribute, you can stop here and save the file. The next section shows how you can quickly add several more attributes to your drawing.

## Copying and Editing Attribute Definitions

Next, you'll add a few more attribute definitions, but instead of using the Attribute Definition dialog box, you'll make an arrayed copy of the first attribute and then edit the attribute definition copies. This method can save you time when you want to create several attribute definitions that have similar characteristics. By making copies and editing them, you'll also get a chance to see firsthand how to change an attribute definition.

Follow these steps to make copies of the attribute:

1. Click Copy in the Home tab's Modify panel or type **CO**↵ to start the Copy command.

2. At the Select objects: prompt, select the attribute definition you just created and press ↵ to confirm your selection.

3. At the Specify base point or [Displacement/mOde] <Displacement>: prompt, select the center of the circle.

**4.** At the `Specify second point or [Array] <user first point as displacement>:` prompt, type **A.**↵ to enter the Array option.

**5.** At the `Enter number of items to array:` prompt, type **7.**↵.

**6.** At the `Specify second point or [Fit]:` prompt, point the cursor directly downward and enter **0.18**↵ (**0.432** for metric users). You can use the Polar Tracking tool in the status bar to help align the cursor in a downward direction.

**7.** The `Specify second point:` prompt appears again, allowing you to create another set of copies. Press ↵ to exit the Copy command.

**8.** Pan your view upward to center the attribute definition copies in the view.

CERT
OBJECTIVE

Now you're ready to modify the copies of the attribute definitions:

**1.** Press Esc twice to clear any selections or commands, and click all of the attribute definitions just below the original.

**2.** Right-click and choose Properties from the context menu to open the Properties palette.

**3.** Scroll down the list of properties until you see the Invisible option in the Misc category.

**4.** Select Yes from the Invisible option's drop-down list.

**5.** Press the Esc key to clear your selection, and close the Properties palette.

You've just turned off Visibility mode for all but the first attribute definition. Now change the Tag, Prompt, and Default values for the attribute definitions:

**1.** Double-click on the attribute definition just below the original one in the center of the circle. The Edit Attribute Definition dialog box appears.

**2.** Highlight the Tag text box, and type **D-SIZE**↵.

3. Highlight the Prompt text box, and type **Door size**↵.

4. In the Default text box, type **3′-0″**↵. Metric users should type **90**↵.

You've just learned how to edit an attribute definition. Now you'll make changes to the other attribute definitions:

1. Continue to edit the rest of the attribute definition properties by using the attribute settings listed in Table 12.1. To do so, click on the next attribute definition and repeat steps 2 through 5 of the preceding exercise, replacing the Tag and Prompt values with those shown in Table 12.1. Use a hyphen for the Default values. Also, make sure all but the original attributes have the Invisible option set to Yes.

2. When you've finished editing the last attribute definition, click OK or press ↵ on your last entry.

When you later insert a file or a block containing attributes, the attribute prompts will appear in the order in which their associated definitions were created. If the order of the prompts at insertion time is important, you can control it by editing the attribute definitions so that their creation order corresponds to the desired prompt order. You can also control the order by using the Block Attribute Manager, which you'll look at later in this chapter.

**TABLE 12.1:**     Attributes for the door-type symbol

| TAG | PROMPT | DEFAULT VALUE |
| --- | --- | --- |
| D-NUMBER | Door number | - |
| D-THICK | Door thickness | - |
| D-RATE | Fire rating | - |
| D-MATRL | Door material | - |
| D-CONST | Door construction | - |

*Make sure the Invisible option is selected for the attributes in this table.*

CERT OBJECTIVE

### USING PROPERTIES TO EDIT ATTRIBUTE DEFINITIONS

If you prefer, you can use the Properties palette to change an attribute definition's Tag, Prompt, or Default value (shown as Value). These values can be found under the Text group of the palette after an attribute definition is selected.

## Turning the Attribute Definitions into a Block

You need to perform one more crucial step before these attribute definitions can be of any use. You must turn the attribute definitions into a block, along with the circle:

1. Click the Create Block tool in the Home tab's Block panel, or enter **B**↵.

2. In the Block Definition dialog box, enter **S-DOOR** for the name.

3. In the Base Point group, click the Pick Point tool and then use the Center osnap to select the center of the circle.

4. In the Objects group, click the Select Objects tool and select the circle and all the attributes. Press ↵ when you've completed your selection.

5. In the Behavior group, select the Annotative option. This ensures that the block is scaled to the appropriate size for the scale of the drawing into which it's inserted.

6. Click OK. When the Edit Attribute dialog box opens, click OK to close it.

7. The attributes and the circle are now a block called S-DOOR. You can delete the S-DOOR block on your screen.

---

**UNDERSTANDING ATTRIBUTE DEFINITION MODES**

The Attribute Definition dialog box includes several choices in the Mode group; you've used one of these modes to see what it does. You won't use any of the other modes in this exercise, but here is a list describing all the modes for your reference:

**Invisible**   Controls whether the attribute is shown as part of the drawing.

**Constant**   Creates an attribute that doesn't prompt you to enter a value. Instead, the attribute has a constant, or fixed, value you give it during creation. Constant mode is used when you know you'll assign a fixed value to an object. After constant values are set in a block, you can't change them by using the standard set of attribute-editing commands.

**Verify**   Causes AutoCAD to review the attribute values you enter at insertion time and to ask you whether they're correct. This option appears only when the Attribute dialog box is turned off (the Attdia system variable is set to 0).

**Preset**   Causes AutoCAD to assign the default value to an attribute automatically when its block is inserted. This saves time because a preset attribute won't prompt you for a value. Unlike attributes created in Constant mode, a preset attribute can be edited.

**Lock Position**   Prevents the attribute from being moved from its original location in the block when you're grip editing.

**Multiple Lines**   Allows the attribute to contain multiple lines of text, similar to Mtext objects. When this option is turned on, you can specify a text boundary width.

With the exception of Invisible mode, none of these modes can be altered after the attribute becomes part of a block. Later in this chapter, we'll show you how to make an invisible attribute visible.

---

Once you've created the block, you can place it anywhere in the drawing using the Insert command or the Insert tool in the Home tab's Block panel. You'll insert this block in another location in the drawing. If you want to use the block in other drawings, you can use the Wblock command to save the block as a drawing file, or you can use the DesignCenter™ palette to drag and drop blocks from a drawing file. (See Chapter 25, "Managing and Sharing Your Drawings," for more on DesignCenter.)

## Inserting Blocks Containing Attributes

In the preceding section, you created a door-type symbol at the desired size for the plotted symbol. This size is known as the *paper size*. Because you turned on the Annotative option for the attribute and block, you can use the Annotation Scale setting to have the block insert at the appropriate size for the scale of the drawing. The following steps demonstrate the process of inserting a block that contains attributes. First, set up your view and annotation scale in preparation to insert the blocks:

1. Turn on Attribute Dialog mode by entering **Attdia↵1↵** at the Command prompt. This enables you to enter attribute values through a dialog box in the next exercise. Otherwise, you'd be prompted for the attribute values in the command-line interface.

2. Select ⅛"=1'-0" (1:100 for metric users) from the Annotation Scale drop-down list in the lower-right corner of the AutoCAD window. This ensures that the block appears at the proper size for the drawing scale.

3. Type **View↵** to open the View Manager dialog box.

4. Click the plus sign (+) to the left of the Model Views option to expand the Model Views list; then select FIRST from the list, select Set Current, and click OK. This is a view that has been saved in this drawing. (See "Taking Control of the AutoCAD Display" in Chapter 7, "Mastering Viewing Tools, Hatches, and External References," for more on saving views.)

5. Be sure the CEILING and FLR-PAT layers are off. Normally, in a floor plan, the door headers aren't visible anyway and their appearance will interfere with the placement of the door-reference symbol.

6. Finally, you can begin to place the blocks in the drawing. Click the Insert tool in the Home tab's Block panel, then More Options, or type I↵ to open the Insert dialog box.

7. Select S-DOOR from the Name drop-down list.

8. In the Insertion Point group, make sure the Specify On-Screen option is turned on.

9. In the Scale group, make sure the Uniform Scale check box is selected.

10. In the Rotation group, make sure the Specify On-Screen option is turned off, and then click OK.

   Now you're ready to place the block in your drawing in the appropriate location and enter the attribute values. AutoCAD is waiting for you to select a location for the symbol.

11. Click in the doorway of the lower-left unit, near coordinate 41'-3",72'-4". Metric users should use coordinate 1256,2202. You may want to temporarily turn off Osnaps to avoid accidentally clicking on an object. When you click the location, the Edit Attributes dialog box opens (see Figure 12.4).

**FIGURE 12.4**
The Edit Attributes
dialog box

12. In the Door Construction box, enter **Solid core**↵. Note that this is the prompt you created. Note also that the default value is the hyphen you specified. Attribute data is case sensitive, so any text you enter in all capital letters is stored in all capital letters.

13. In the Door Material box, change the hyphen to **Wood**. Continue to change the values for each box as shown in Table 12.2.

14. When you've finished changing values, click OK and the symbol appears. The only attribute you can see is the one you selected to be visible: the door type.

**TABLE 12.2:**    Attribute values for the typical studio entry door

| PROMPT | VALUE |
| --- | --- |
| Door Construction | Solid core |
| Door Material | Wood |
| Fire Rating | 20 min. |
| Door Thickness | 1¾" (4 cm for metric) |
| Door Number | (Same as room number; see Figure 12.6, later in this chapter) |
| Door Size | 3'-0" (90 cm for metric) |
| Door Type | A |

**15.** Add the rest of the door-type symbols for the apartment entry doors by copying or array-ing the door symbol you just inserted. You can use the previously saved views found in the Views drop-down list in the View tab's Views panel to help you get around the draw-ing quickly. Don't worry that the attribute values aren't appropriate for each unit; you'll see how to edit the attributes in the next section.

In addition to the S-DOOR block, you'll need a block for the room number. To save some time, we've included a block called S-APART that contains a rectangle and a single attribute definition for the room number (see Figure 12.5).

**FIGURE 12.5**

The apartment number symbol

Attribute definitions:
Tag = R-Number
Prompt = Room number
Default = 000
Text height = 0.125 (0.30 metric)
Justification = Middle

0.5625 × 0.25 rectangle
(1.37 × 0.6 metric)

R—NUMBER

Do the following to insert the room-number block:

**1.** Choose Insert from the Home tab's Block panel, and select S-APART from the Name drop-down list.

**2.** Make sure the Specify On-Screen setting is turned on only for the Insertion point, and then click OK.

**3.** Insert the S-APART block into the lower-left unit. Give the attribute of this block the value **116**.

4. Copy or array the S-APART block so that there is one S-APART block in each unit. You'll learn how to modify the attributes to reflect their proper values in the following section. Figure 12.6 shows what the view should look like after you've entered the door symbols and the apartment numbers.

**FIGURE 12.6**
An overall view of the plan with door symbols and apartment numbers added

## Editing Attributes

Because drawings are usually in flux even after construction or manufacturing begins, you'll eventually have to edit previously entered attributes. In the example of the apartment building, many things can change before the final set of drawings is completed.

Attributes can be edited individually or *globally*—you can edit several occurrences of a particular attribute tag all at one time. In the following sections, you'll use both individual and global editing techniques to make changes to the attributes you've entered so far. You'll also practice editing invisible attributes.

### Editing Attribute Values One at a Time

AutoCAD offers an easy way to edit attributes one at a time through a dialog box. The following exercise demonstrates this feature:

1. Restore the First view by selecting First from the Views flyout in the View tab's Views panel.

2. Double-click the apartment number attribute in the unit just to the right of the first unit in the lower-left corner to open the Enhanced Attribute Editor (see Figure 12.7).

3. Change the value in the Value box to **112**, and click OK to make the change.

4. Do this for each room, using Figure 12.8 as a reference for assigning room numbers.

5. Go back and edit the door number attribute for the S-DOOR blocks. Give each door the same number as the room number with which it's associated. See Figure 12.8 for the room numbers.

**FIGURE 12.7**
The Enhanced
Attribute Editor

**FIGURE 12.8**
Apartment num-
bers for one floor
of the studio apart-
ment building

## Editing Attribute Text Formats and Properties

You may have noticed that the Enhanced Attribute Editor in the preceding exercise has three tabs: Attribute, Text Options, and Properties. When you double-click a block containing attributes, the Enhanced Attribute Editor dialog box opens at the Attribute tab. You can use the other two tabs to control the size, font, color, and other properties of the selected attribute.

The Text Options tab (see Figure 12.9) lets you alter the attribute text style, justification, height, rotation, width factor, and oblique angle. (See Chapter 9, "Adding Text to Drawings," for more on these text options.)

**FIGURE 12.9**
The Enhanced
Attribute Editor's
Text Options tab

The Properties tab (see Figure 12.10) lets you alter the attribute's layer, linetype, color, line-weight (effective only on AutoCAD fonts), and plot-style assignments.

**FIGURE 12.10**

The Enhanced Attri-bute Editor's Prop-erties tab

In the previous exercise, you edited a block containing a single attribute. Double-clicking a block that contains multiple attributes, such as the S-DOOR block, opens the Enhanced Attribute Editor dialog box at the Attribute tab. This tab displays all the attributes whether they're visible or not, as shown in Figure 12.11. You can then edit the value, formats, and properties of the individual attri-butes by highlighting the attribute in the Attribute tab and using the other tabs to make changes. The changes you make affect only the attribute you've highlighted in the Attribute tab.

**FIGURE 12.11**

The Enhanced Attri-bute Editor showing the contents of a block that contains several attributes

The Enhanced Attribute Editor lets you change attribute values, formats, and properties one block at a time, but as you'll see in the next section, you can also make changes to several attri-butes at once.

---

#### MOVING THE LOCATION OF ATTRIBUTES

If you want to change the location of individual attributes in a block, you can do so by using grips. Click the block to expose the grips, and then click the grip connected to the attribute. Or if you've selected several blocks, Shift+click the attribute grips, and then move the attributes to their new location. They are still attached to their associated blocks. If you don't see grips appear for the attributes, then the attribute definition has its Lock Position property turned on. This is a setting that is available when you create the attribute in the Attribute Definition dialog box.

## Making Global Changes to Attribute Values

At times, you'll want to change the value of several attributes in a file so that they're all the same value. You can use the Edit Attribute Globally option to make global changes to the attribute values.

Suppose you decide you want to change all the entry doors to a type designated as B rather than A. Perhaps door-type A was an input error or type B is better suited for an entry door. The following exercise demonstrates how this is done:

1. Type **View**↵ to open the View Manager dialog box and select the view named FOURTH from the Views list.

2. Click the Set Current option, and then click OK.

3. Pan your view down so you can see all of the "A" door-reference symbols for this view.

4. Click Multiple from the Edit Attribute flyout on the Home tab's Block panel or the Insert tab's Block panel. You can also type **-Attedit**↵ at the Command prompt. Make sure you include the hyphen at the beginning of the command.

5. At the `Edit Attributes one at a time? [Yes/No] <Y>:` prompt, enter **N**↵ for No. You see the message `Performing global editing of attribute values`. This tells you that you're in Global Edit mode.

6. At the `Edit only attributes visible on screen? [Yes/No] <Y>:` prompt, press ↵. As you can see from this prompt, you have the option to edit all attributes, including those out of the view area. You'll get a chance to work with this option later in this chapter.

7. At the `Enter block name specification <*>:` prompt, press ↵. Optionally, you can enter a block name to narrow the selection to specific blocks.

8. At the `Enter attribute tag specification <*>:` prompt, press ↵. Optionally, you can enter an attribute tag name to narrow your selection to specific tags.

9. At the `Enter attribute value specification <*>:` prompt, press ↵. Optionally, you can narrow your selection to attributes containing specific values.

10. At the `Select Attributes:` prompt, select the door-type symbol's attribute value for units 103 to 115. You can use a window to select the attributes if you prefer. Press ↵ when you've finished your selection.

11. At the `Enter string to change:` prompt, enter **A**↵.

12. At the `Enter new string:` prompt, enter **B**↵. The door-type symbols all change to the new value.

In step 8, you were asked to select the attributes to be edited. AutoCAD limits the changes to those attributes you select. If you know you need to change every attribute in your drawing, you can do so by answering the series of prompts in a slightly different way, as demonstrated in the following exercise:

1. Try the same procedure again, but this time enter **N** for the first prompt and again at the `Edit only attributes visible on screen? [Yes/No] <Y>:` prompt (step 4 in the previous exercise). The message `Drawing must be regenerated afterwards` appears. The AutoCAD Text Window appears.

2. Once again, you're prompted for the block name, the tag, and the value (steps 5, 6, and 7 in the previous exercise). Respond to these prompts as you did earlier.

3. You then get the message `128 attributes selected`. This tells you the number of attributes that fit the specifications you just entered.

4. At the `Enter string to change:` prompt, enter **A↵** to indicate you want to change the rest of the A attribute values.

5. At the `Enter new string:` prompt, enter **B↵**. A series of *Bs* appears, indicating the number of strings that were replaced.

In this exercise, AutoCAD skipped the `Select Attribute:` prompt and went directly to the `String to change:` prompt. AutoCAD assumes that you want it to edit every attribute in the drawing, so it doesn't bother asking you to select specific attributes.

## Making Invisible Attributes Visible

You can globally edit invisible attributes, such as those in the door-reference symbol, by using the tools just described. You may, however, want to be more selective about which invisible attribute you want to modify. Optionally, you may want to make invisible attributes temporarily visible for other editing purposes.

This exercise shows you how to make invisible attributes visible:

1. On the Insert tab's expanded Block panel, click the Retain Display flyout and select Display All Attributes. You can also enter **Attdisp↵On↵**. Your drawing looks like Figure 12.12.

**FIGURE 12.12**
The drawing with all the attributes visible. (Door-type symbols are so close together that they overlap.)

**2.** At this point, you could edit the invisible attributes individually as in the first attribute-editing exercise. For now, set the attribute display back to Normal. On the Insert tab's Expanded Block panel, click the Display All Attributes flyout and select Retain Attribute Display. You can also enter **Attdisp↵N↵**.

---

### USING SPACES IN ATTRIBUTE VALUES

At times, you may want the default value to begin with a blank space. This enables you to specify text strings more easily when you edit the attribute globally. For example, suppose you have an attribute value that reads 3334333. If you want to change the first 3 in this string of numbers, you have to specify 3334 when prompted for the string to change. Then, for the new string, you enter the same set of numbers again with the first 3 changed to the new number. If you specify only 3 for the string to change, AutoCAD will change all the 3s in the value. If you start with a space, as in _3334333 (I'm using an underscore here only to represent the space; it doesn't mean you type an underscore character), you can isolate the first 3 from the rest by specifying _3 as the string to change (again, enter a space instead of the underscore).

You must enter a backslash character (\) before the space in the default value to tell AutoCAD to interpret the space literally rather than as a press of the spacebar (which is equivalent to pressing ↵).

---

You've seen the results of the On and Normal options. The Off option makes all attributes invisible regardless of the mode used when they were created.

Because the attributes weren't intended to be visible, they appear to overlap and cover other parts of the drawing when they're made visible. Remember to turn them back off when you're done reviewing them.

## Making Global Format and Property Changes to Attributes

While we're on the subject of global editing, you should know how to make global changes to the format and properties of attributes. Earlier, you saw how to make format changes to individual attributes using the Enhanced Attribute Editor dialog box. You can also use the Edit Attribute dialog box to make global changes, as the following exercise demonstrates.

Follow these steps to make the global changes:

**1.** Click the Block Attribute Manager in the Home tab's expanded Block panel to open the Block Attribute Manager dialog box. You can also enter **battman↵**.

**2.** Select S-APART from the Block drop-down list at the top of the dialog box. This list displays all the blocks that contain attributes. The only attribute defined for the selected block is displayed in the list box below it.

**3.** Click the attribute value in the list, and click the Edit button to open the Edit Attribute dialog box. The Edit Attribute dialog box is nearly identical to the Enhanced Attribute Editor you saw earlier.

**4.** Click the Properties tab, select Red from the Color drop-down list, and click OK.

**5.** Click OK to exit the Block Attribute Manager dialog box.

The Edit Attribute dialog box you saw in this exercise offers a slightly different set of options from those in the Enhanced Attribute Editor dialog box. In the Attribute tab of the Edit Attribute dialog box, you can change some of the mode settings for the attribute, such as visibility and the Verify and Preset modes. You can also change the Tag, Prompt, and Default values. In contrast, the Attribute tab in the Enhanced Attribute Editor dialog box enables you to change the attribute value but none of the other attribute properties.

## Other Block Attribute Manager Options

The Block Attribute Manager dialog box includes a few other options that weren't covered in the exercises. Here's a rundown of the Settings, Move Up, Move Down, Remove, and Sync buttons:

**Settings** Click this button to open the Block Attribute Settings dialog box (see Figure 12.13), which lets you control which attribute properties are displayed in the list box of the Block Attribute Manager.

The Emphasize Duplicate Tags option highlights duplicate tag names by showing them in red. The Apply Changes To Existing References option forces any changes you make to the attribute properties to be applied to existing attributes. If this setting is turned off, you have to use the Sync button in the Block Attribute Manager dialog box to update existing attributes, and the changes you make to attribute properties are applied only to new attributes added after the change. You can also enter **Attsync↵** at the Command prompt to synchronize older attributes.

**FIGURE 12.13**
The Block Attribute
Settings dialog box

**Move Up and Move Down** Clicking these buttons moves a selected attribute up or down the list of attributes in the list box. If you move an item down the list, the item changes its position when viewed using the Ddatte command or when you're viewing the attribute's properties in the Enhanced Attribute Editor dialog box. Of course, this has an effect only on blocks containing multiple attributes.

**Remove** Clicking this button removes the selected attribute from the block, so make sure you mean it before you click.

**Sync** This option updates attribute properties such as order, text formatting, mode, and so on. It can also be used to update blocks globally that have had new attribute definitions added or deleted. It doesn't affect the individual attribute values.

## Redefining Blocks Containing Attributes

Attributes act differently from other objects when they're included in redefined blocks. Normally, blocks that have been redefined change their configuration to reflect the new block definition. But if a redefined block contains attributes, the attributes maintain their old properties, including their position in relation to other objects in the block. This means the old attribute position, style, and so on don't change even though you may have changed them in the new definition.

Fortunately, AutoCAD offers a tool that's specifically designed to let you update blocks with attributes. The following steps describe how to update attribute blocks:

1. Before you use the command to redefine an attribute block, you must create the objects and attribute definitions that will make up the replacement attribute block. The simplest way to do this is to explode a copy of the attribute block you want to update. This ensures that you have the same attribute definitions in the updated block.

2. Make your changes to the exploded attribute block.

> **EXPLODE ATTRIBUTE BLOCKS AT A 1-TO-1 SCALE**
>
> Before you explode the attribute block copy, be sure it's at a 1-to-1 scale. This is important because if you don't use the original size of the block, you could end up with all your new attribute blocks at the wrong size. Also be sure you use a marker device, such as a line, to locate the insertion point of the attribute block before you explode it. Doing so will help you locate and maintain the original insertion point for the redefined block.

**3.** Type **Attredef**↵.

**4.** At the `Enter name of block you wish to redefine:` prompt, enter the appropriate name.

**5.** At the `Select objects:` prompt, select all the objects, including the attribute definitions, that you want to include in the revised attribute block.

**6.** At the `Specify insertion base point of new Block:` prompt, pick the same location used for the original block.

After you pick the insertion point, AutoCAD takes a few seconds to update the blocks. The amount of time depends on the complexity of the block and the number of times the block occurs in the drawing. If you include a new attribute definition with your new block, it too is added to all the updated blocks, with its default value. Attribute definitions that are deleted from your new definition are removed from all the updated blocks.

You can also use the Refedit command to modify an attribute definition. Click the Edit Reference tool in the Insert tab's expanded Reference panel to modify attribute definitions. After editing, you must use the Sync option in the Block Attribute Manager to update all instances of the modified block.

## Extracting and Exporting Attribute Information

After you enter the attributes in your drawing, you can extract the information contained in the attributes and use it to generate reports or to analyze the attribute data in other programs. You might, for example, want to keep track of the number and type of doors in your drawing through a database manager. This is especially useful if you have a project such as a large hotel that contains thousands of doors.

When you extract attribute data, AutoCAD creates a text file. You can choose to export the file in either comma-delimited or tab-delimited format. If you have Microsoft Excel or Access installed, you can also export the attribute data in a format compatible with these programs.

### Performing the Extraction

In the past, extracting the attribute data from a drawing was an error-prone task requiring the creation of a template file. This template file had to contain a series of codes that described the data you wanted to extract. AutoCAD has a greatly improved system for attribute data extraction in the form of the Data Extraction Wizard. The following exercises will walk you through a sample extraction.

**EXTRACTING DATA IN AUTOCAD 2015 LT**

The AutoCAD LT® software doesn't offer the Data Extraction Wizard. Instead, you see the more simplified Attribute Extraction dialog box, which offers the file-format options (comma- or space-delimited or DXF output), the output filename, and template file options. For AutoCAD LT, the template file is used as an option to filter the attributes.

## USING THE DATA EXTRACTION WIZARD

In this first exercise, you'll explore the Data Extraction Wizard. You can use the `12c-plan.dwg` sample file if you haven't done the tutorials from the beginning of the chapter.

1. Go back to the `Plan.dwg` file, and click Extract Data from the Insert tab's Linking & Extraction panel. On the Begin page (Figure 12.14), you can choose to start an extraction from scratch or use an existing data-extraction setup that you've created from previous extractions.

**FIGURE 12.14**
Starting the Data
Extraction Wizard

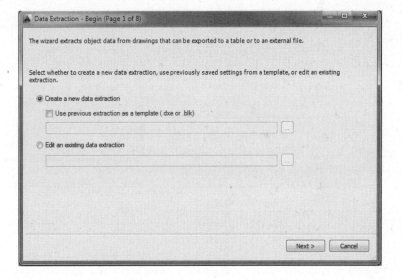

2. Click Next to open the Save Data Extraction As dialog box. This dialog box lets you save the data-extraction settings you're about to set up in a file with the `.dxe` filename extension. Enter a name, pick a location for your file, and then click Save. The Define Data Source page opens (see Figure 12.15).

3. Click Settings to view other options. These options (see Figure 12.16) let you further refine the content of your extraction.

4. Click Cancel to close the Additional Settings dialog box, and then click Next to open the Select Objects page (see Figure 12.17).

**FIGURE 12.15**
Defining a
data source

**FIGURE 12.16**
Additional settings

**FIGURE 12.17**
The Select
Objects page

Take a moment to study the Select Objects page. It's the heart of the extraction process. Here you select the blocks that contain attributes as well as the specific attributes you want to extract. The list shows all the object types in the drawing. You'll pare down this list to show only the blocks with attributes.

## SELECTING WHAT TO EXTRACT

Let's continue by selecting specific information for the extraction:

1. Click the Display All Object Types option in the Display Options group to turn it off, and make sure the Display Blocks Only radio button is selected.

2. Select the Display Blocks With Attributes Only option.

3. In the Object list, remove the check mark next to all but the S-DOOR item. If you have a lot of blocks listed, you can select groups of names from the list by clicking the item at the top of the list, then Shift+clicking the item at the bottom. (Click any check box in a selected item to remove the check marks.) You can also Ctrl+click in the list to select multiple, nonconsecutive items.

4. Click Next to open the Select Properties page (see Figure 12.18), which displays a list of the different types of data available for extraction.

**FIGURE 12.18**
The Select Properties page

5. In the Category Filter group list on the right, deselect all the options except Attribute. Now you see only the attribute data listed in the Properties panel.

6. Make sure that each item in the Properties panel is selected. A check mark should appear by each item.

7. Click Next. The Refine Data page appears (see Figure 12.19). Here you can continue to filter out data. For example, you can deselect the Show Count Column and Show Name Column options because they may be unnecessary for your purpose. You can also get a preview of your extracted data by clicking the Full Preview button.

**FIGURE 12.19**
The Refine
Data screen

**SORTING COLUMNS**

If you want to sort your data by column, you can do so by clicking the column title. To change the order of the columns, click and drag the column titles horizontally.

## SAVING THE ATTRIBUTE DATA TO A FILE

Now let's complete the extraction process:

1. Click Next. The Choose Output page appears (see Figure 12.20). This window lets you determine whether to convert the data into a table in the drawing, extract the data as an external data file, or do both.

2. Select the Output Data To External File option. The box just below the option becomes available for input (see Figure 12.21). You can type a location for the external file, or you can click the Browse button to browse to a location.

**FIGURE 12.20**
Decide how to
convert your
attribute data.

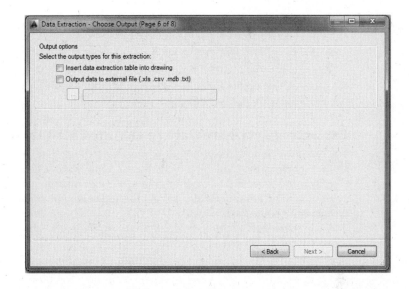

**FIGURE 12.21**
Enter the location
to which you'll
extract the data.

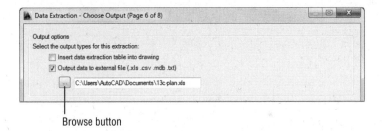

Browse button

3. You have the option to extract an XLS, CSV, MDB, or TXT file. You can select the type of file to use when you click the Browse button to show where you want the file to go. The Browse button opens a Save As dialog box, where you can select the type of file to save from the File Of Type drop-down list. The default filename is the current drawing filename with an .xls extension. Click Save to go to the next step.

4. Click Next to open the Finish screen (see Figure 12.22). It gives you a brief message explaining what to do next.

**FIGURE 12.22**
Completing
the wizard

5. Click Finish. A file with the current drawing name and the `.xls` filename extension is created. By default, the file is placed in the Documents folder unless you specify a different location in step 3.

You now have a file called `Plan.xls` (`12c-plan.xls` if you used the sample file) that contains the data you saw earlier in the Full Preview window of the Data Extraction Wizard. You can open this file with Microsoft Excel.

## Extracting Attribute Data to an AutoCAD Table

You may have noticed the option to extract the attribute data to an AutoCAD table in the Choose Output screen of the Data Extraction Wizard. This option lets you convert the attribute data directly into a table in the current drawing. Besides making it easy to create parts lists or other types of tables in your drawing, you get the added benefit of having tables update automatically whenever attribute data changes.

If you turn on this option and click Next, you'll see the Table Style screen (see Figure 12.23) instead of the Finish screen.

**FIGURE 12.23**
Styling your table

From here, you can follow these steps:

1. Select a table style for the extracted data, enter a title, and click Next. The Finish screen opens.

2. Click Finish. You're prompted to select a point. Click in the drawing to place the table.

The table may appear at a small size depending on the scale of your drawing. Zoom in to the location where you clicked and you'll see the table (see Figure 12.24). You'll also see the Data Link icon in the lower-right corner of the AutoCAD window.

**FIGURE 12.24**

The table and the Data Link icon

| Quantity | D-CONST | D-MATRL | D-NUMBER | D-RATE | D-SIZE | D-THICK | D-TYPE | Name |
|---|---|---|---|---|---|---|---|---|
| 1 | Solid Core | Wood | 103 | 20 min. | 3'-0" | 1 3/4' | B | S-DOOR |
| 1 | Solid Core | Wood | 111 | 20 min. | 3'-0" | 1 3/4' | B | S-DOOR |
| 1 | Solid Core | Wood | 108 | 20 min. | 3'-0" | 1 3/4' | B | S-DOOR |
| 1 | Solid Core | Wood | 107 | 20 min. | 3'-0" | 1 3/4' | B | S-DOOR |
| 1 | Solid Core | Wood | 115 | 20 min. | 3'-0" | 1 3/4' | B | S-DOOR |
| 1 | Solid Core | Wood | 102 | 20 min. | 3'-0" | 1 3/4' | B | S-DOOR |
| 1 | Solid Core | Wood | 101 | 20 min. | 3'-0" | 1 3/4' | B | S-DOOR |
| 1 | Solid Core | Wood | 105 | 20 min. | 3'-0" | 1 3/4' | B | S-DOOR |
| 1 | Solid Core | Wood | 113 | 20 min. | 3'-0" | 1 3/4' | B | S-DOOR |
| 1 | Solid Core | Wood | 109 | 20 min. | 3'-0" | 1 3/4' | B | S-DOOR |
| 1 | Solid Core | Wood | 112 | 20 min. | 3'-0" | 1 3/4' | B | S-DOOR |
| 1 | Solid Core | Wood | 116 | 20 min. | 3'-0" | 1 3/4' | B | S-DOOR |
| 1 | Solid Core | Wood | 106 | 20 min. | 3'-0" | 1 3/4' | B | S-DOOR |
| 1 | Solid Core | Wood | 104 | 20 min. | 3'-0" | 1 3/4' | B | S-DOOR |
| 1 | Solid Core | Wood | 110 | 20 min. | 3'-0" | 1 3/4' | B | S-DOOR |
| 1 | Solid Core | Wood | 114 | 20 min. | 3'-0" | 1 3/4' | B | S-DOOR |

With the table in place, you can make changes to the attribute data. When you're ready to update the table, right-click the Data Link icon in the lower-right corner of the AutoCAD window and select Update All Data Links. The table will be updated to reflect the latest attribute values.

## The Bottom Line

**Create attributes.**    Attributes are a great tool for storing data with drawn objects. You can include as little or as much data as you like in an AutoCAD block.

**Master It**    What is the name of the object you must include in a block to store data?

**Edit attributes.**    The data you include in a block is easily changed. You may have several copies of a block, each of which must contain its own unique set of data.

**Master It**    What is the simplest way to gain access to a block's attribute data?

**Extract and export attribute information.**    Attribute data can be extracted in a number of ways so that you can keep track of the data in a drawing.

**Master It**    How do you start the data-extraction process?

# Chapter 13

# Copying Existing Drawings from Other Sources

This chapter discusses ways to import existing drawings into the AutoCAD® 2015 software through tracing, scaling, and scanning. At times, you'll want to turn an existing drawing into an AutoCAD drawing file. The original drawing may be hand drawn, or it might be a PDF from another source. You may be modifying a design that someone else created or converting your library of older, hand-drafted drawings for AutoCAD use. Perhaps you want to convert a hand-drawn sketch into a formal drawing? In addition to importing drawings, you'll learn how to incorporate drawings in Portable Document Format (PDF) into your AutoCAD work.

In this chapter, you will learn to

♦ Convert paper drawings into AutoCAD files

♦ Import a raster image

♦ Work with a raster image

♦ Work with PDF files

♦ Use a geolocation map

## Methods for Converting Paper Drawings to AutoCAD Files

*Tracing* with a special piece of hardware known as a digitizing tablet used to be the only way to enter a hand-drafted drawing into AutoCAD. However, a traced drawing usually requires some cleanup and reorganization.

*Scaling* a drawing is the method of taking measurements directly from a paper drawing using an architect's or engineer's scale. It is the most flexible method because you don't need special peripherals to do it and, generally, you're faced with fewer cleanups afterward. Scaling also facilitates the most accurate input of orthogonal lines because you can read dimensions directly from the drawing and enter them into AutoCAD. The main drawback with scaling is that if the hand-drafted drawing does not contain written dimensions, it would be difficult to produce an accurate copy. In addition, you must constantly look at the hand-drafted drawing and measure distances with a scale, and irregular curves are difficult to scale accurately.

Programs are available that automatically convert an image file into an AutoCAD drawing file consisting of lines and arcs. These programs may offer some help, but they require some editing and checking for errors.

*Scanning*, much like tracing, is best used for drawings that are difficult to scale, such as complex topographical maps containing a large number of contours or nontechnical line art, such as letterhead and logos.

The simplest method for converting paper drawings, and the method we show you in this chapter, is to scan your drawings as image files to be used as a background in AutoCAD. You can import your image files into AutoCAD and then trace directly over them. This technique allows you to see the original drawing in the AutoCAD window, removing the need to constantly refer to documents in other programs.

## Importing a Raster Image

If you have a scanner and you'd like to use it to import drawings and other images into AutoCAD, you can take advantage of the program's ability to import raster images. There are many reasons you may want to import a scanned image. In architectural plans, a vicinity map is frequently used to show the location of a project. With the permission of its creator, you can scan a map into AutoCAD and incorporate it into a cover sheet. That cover sheet can also contain other images, such as photographs of the site, computer renderings and elevations of the project, and company logos. In architectural projects, scans of older drawings can be used as backgrounds for renovation work. This can be especially useful for historical buildings where the building's owner wishes to keep the original architectural detail.

Another reason for importing a scanned image is to use the image as a reference over which to trace. You can trace a drawing with a good deal of accuracy by using a scanned image. Now that the price of a scanner has fallen below $100, it has become a cost-effective tool for tracing a wide variety of graphic material. In this section, you'll learn how you can import an image as a background for tracing.

In an open drawing, click the External References tool on the Insert tab's Reference panel (see Figure 13.1) to open the External References palette, which lets you import a full range of raster image files.

**FIGURE 13.1**
The External References palette allows you to import raster images.

You can also type **XR**↵. This palette should look familiar from Chapter 7, "Mastering Viewing Tools, Hatches, and External References." It's the same palette you used to manage external references. Just like external references (Xrefs), raster images are loaded when the current file is open but they aren't stored as part of the current file when it is saved. This helps keep file sizes down, but it also means that you need to keep track of inserted raster files. You must make sure they're kept together with the AutoCAD files in which they're inserted. For example, you might want to keep image files in the same folder as the drawing file to which they're attached.

AutoCAD has a utility called eTransmit that collects AutoCAD files and their related support files, such as raster images, external references, and fonts, into any folder or drive you specify. See Chapter 25, "Managing and Sharing Your Drawings," for details.

Another similarity between Xrefs and imported raster images is that you can clip a raster image so that only a portion of the image is displayed in your drawing. Portions of a raster file that are clipped aren't stored in memory, so your system won't get bogged down even if the raster file is huge.

The following exercise gives you step-by-step instructions for importing a raster file. It also lets you see how scanned resolution translates into an image in AutoCAD. This is important if you're interested in scanning drawings for the purpose of tracing over them. Here are the steps:

1. Create a new file called `Rastertrace.dwg`.

2. Set up the file as an architectural drawing with a ¼" = 1' scale on an 8½" × 11" sheet (set the Limits settings to 0,0 for the lower-left corner and 528,408 for the upper-right corner). Make sure the drawing units type is set to Architectural. Metric users should set up their drawing at a 1:50 scale on an A4 size sheet. (The Limits settings for metric users should be 0,0 for the lower-left corner and 1480,1050 for the upper-right corner.)

Zoom All

3. Choose Zoom All from the Zoom flyout on the Navigation bar or type **Z**↵**A**↵ to make sure the entire area of the drawing limits is displayed on the screen.

4. Draw a line across the screen from coordinates 0,20' to 64',20'. Metric users should draw the line from 0,600 to 1820,600. You'll use this line in a later exercise.

5. Click the line you just drew, and then select Red from the Object Color drop-down list in the Home tab's Properties panel. This helps make the line more visible. If you have the Quick Properties feature turned on, you can select the color from the Quick Properties panel.

6. Click the External References tool in the title bar of the Insert tab's Reference panel.

7. On the External References palette's menu bar, click the arrowhead next to the Attach DWG tool and then choose Attach Image from the flyout.

   In the Select Reference File dialog box, locate and select the `raster1.jpg` project file. You can see a preview of the file on the right side of the dialog box.

8. Click Open to open the Attach Image dialog box (see Figure 13.2).

9. Uncheck the Specify On-Screen option in the Insertion Point group to accept the 0,0,0 coordinates.

**10.** Click OK, and then at the `Specify scale factor <1>:` prompt, use the cursor to scale the image so that it fills about half the screen, as shown in Figure 13.3. The `raster1.jpg` filename appears in the External References palette.

**FIGURE 13.2**
The Attach Image
dialog box

**FIGURE 13.3**
Manually scaling
the raster image

As the cursor moves, the outline of the raster image changes.

## Working with a Raster Image

Once you've imported a raster image, you can begin to work with it in a variety of ways. You can resize the image to suit your needs and even adjust its size to a particular scale. Raster images can be made to overlap AutoCAD objects, or you can have raster images appear in the background. There are also rudimentary controls for brightness, contrast, and transparency. In the following sections, you'll continue to use the image you attached to your drawing to explore some of these options.

## Real World Scenario

### TIPS FOR IMPORTING RASTER IMAGES

When you scan a document into your computer, you get a raster image file. Unlike AutoCAD files, *raster image files* are made up of a matrix of colored pixels that form a picture, which is why raster images are also sometimes called *bitmaps*. *Vector files*, like those produced by AutoCAD, are made up of instructions to draw lines, arcs, curves, and circles. The two formats, raster and vector, are so different that it's difficult to convert one format to the other accurately. It's easier to trace a raster file in AutoCAD than it is to try to use a computer program to make the conversion for you.

But even tracing a raster image file can be difficult if the image is of poor quality. Having worked with scanned images in AutoCAD for a variety of projects, we've discovered that you can make your work a lot easier by following a few simple rules:

♦ Scan in your drawing using a grayscale or color scanner, or convert your black-and-white scanned image to grayscale using your image-editing software. This will give you more control over the appearance of the image once it's in AutoCAD.

♦ Use an image-editing program, such as Adobe Photoshop or your scanner software, to clean up unwanted gray or spotted areas in the file before importing it into AutoCAD.

♦ If your scanner software or image-editing program has a "de-speckle" or "de-spot" feature, use it. It can help clean up your image and ultimately reduce the raster image's file size.

♦ Scan at a reasonable resolution. Scanning at 150 dpi to 200 dpi may be more than adequate.

♦ If you plan to make heavy use of raster imports, upgrade your computer to the fastest processor and install as much memory as you can afford.

The raster import commands can incorporate paper maps or plans into 3D AutoCAD drawings for presentations. We know of one architectural firm that produces impressive presentations with little effort by combining 2D scanned images with 3D massing models for urban design studies. (A *massing model* shows only the rough outline of buildings without giving too much detail, thus showing the general scale of a project without being too fussy.)

## Scaling a Raster Image

The `raster1.jpg` file was scanned as a grayscale image at 100 dpi. This shows that you can get a reasonable amount of detail at a fairly low scan resolution.

Now suppose you want to trace over this image to start an AutoCAD drawing. The first thing you should do is scale the image to the appropriate size. You can scale an image file to full size. Try the following steps to see how you can begin the process:

1. Choose Zoom Extents from the Zoom flyout on the Navigation bar, or type Z↵E↵.

2. Click Scale on the Home tab's Modify panel.

3. Click the edge of the raster image to select it.

4. Press ↵ to finish your selection.

5. At the Specify base point: prompt, click the X in the lower-left corner of the image.

6. At the Specify scale factor or [Copy/Reference]: prompt, enter **R**↵ to use the Reference option.

7. At the Specify reference length <0' -1">: prompt, type **@**↵. This tells AutoCAD that you want to use the last point selected as one end of the reference length. After you enter the @ symbol, you'll see a rubber-banding line emanating from the X.

8. At the Specify second point: prompt, click the X at the lower-right corner of the image.

9. At the Specify new length or [Points] <0' -1" >: prompt, enter **44'**↵. Metric users should enter **1341**↵. The image enlarges. Remember that this reference line is 44', or 1341 cm, in length.

The image is now scaled properly for the plan it portrays. You can proceed to trace over the image. You can also place the image on its own layer and turn it off from time to time to check your trace work. Even if you don't trace the scanned floor plan line for line, you can read the dimensions of the plan from your computer monitor instead of having to go back and forth between measuring the paper image and drawing the plan on the computer.

## Controlling Object Visibility and Overlap with Raster Images

With the introduction of raster image support, AutoCAD inherited a problem that's fairly common to programs that use such images: Raster images obscure other objects that were placed previously. The image you imported in the previous exercise, for example, obscures the line you drew when you first opened the file. In most cases, this overlap isn't a problem. However, in some situations, you'll want AutoCAD vector objects to overlap an imported raster image. An example is a civil-engineering drawing showing an AutoCAD drawing of a new road superimposed over an aerial view of the location for the road.

Paint and page-layout programs usually offer a "to front/to back" tool to control the overlap of objects and images. AutoCAD offers the Draworder command. Here's how it works:

1. Click Zoom Extents on the Navigation bar or type **Z**↵**E**↵ to get an overall view of the image.

2. Choose the Bring Above Objects tool from the Draworder flyout on the Home tab's expanded Modify panel.

**3.** At the `Select objects:` prompt, select the horizontal line you drew when you first opened the file.

**4.** If there are other objects in the drawing that you want to "bring above objects," you can select them as well. Press ↵ to finish your selection.

**5.** At the `Select reference objects:` prompt, click the edge of the raster image of the utility room and then press ↵.

The drawing regenerates, and the entire line appears, no longer obscured by the raster image.

---

### MASKING AN AREA OF AN IMAGE

You can mask out areas of an imported raster image by creating a solid hatch area and using the Draworder command to place the solid hatch on top of the raster image. Such masks can be helpful as backgrounds for text that must be placed over a raster image. You can also use the Wipeout command (select Wipeout on the Home tab's expanded Draw panel) to mask areas of a drawing.

---

The Draworder tool you just used has seven options in the Draworder flyout on the Home tab's Modify panel:

**Bring To Front**  Places an object or a set of objects at the top of the draw order for the entire drawing. The effect is that the objects are completely visible.

**Send To Back**  Places an object or a set of objects at the bottom of the draw order for the entire drawing. The effect is that other objects in the drawing may obscure those objects.

**Bring Above Objects**  Places an object or a set of objects above another object in the draw order. This has the effect of making the first set of objects appear above the second selected object.

**Send Under Objects**  Places an object or a set of objects below another object in the draw order. This has the effect of making the first set of objects appear underneath the second selected object.

**Bring Text To Front**  Automatically brings all text in a drawing in front of all objects.

**Bring Dimensions To Front**  Automatically brings all dimensions in a drawing in front of all objects.

**Bring Leaders To Front**  Automatically brings all dimension leaders in a drawing in front of all objects.

**Bring All Annotations To Front**  Automatically brings all annotation objects in a drawing, including dimensions, in front of all objects.

**Send Hatch To Back**  Automatically sends all hatch patterns in a drawing behind other objects.

You can also use the **DR** keyboard shortcut to issue the Draworder command. If you do this, you see these prompts:

```
Select objects:
Enter object ordering option [Above objects/Under objects/Front/Back]<Back>:
```

You must then select the option by typing the capitalized letter of the option.

Although this section discussed the Draworder tools in relation to raster images, they can also be invaluable in controlling visibility of line work in conjunction with hatch patterns and solid fills. See Chapter 7 for a detailed discussion of the Draworder tools and hatch patterns.

## Clipping a Raster Image

In Chapter 7, you saw how you could clip an external reference object so that only a portion of it appears in the drawing. You can clip imported raster images in the same way. Just as with Xrefs, you can create a closed outline of the area you want to clip, or you can specify a simple rectangular area.

---

### IMAGES AND THE EXTERNAL REFERENCES PALETTE

The External References palette you saw in Chapter 7 helps you manage your imported image files. It's especially helpful when you have a large number of images in your drawing. You can control imported images in a way similar to how you control Xrefs; you can temporarily unload images (to help speed up the editing of AutoCAD objects) and reload, detach, and relocate raster image files. See Chapter 7 for a detailed description of these options.

---

In the following exercise, you'll try the Clip command to control the display of the raster image.

**NOTE**   If you have difficulty viewing the cursor while hovering over the raster image, read the upcoming section "Adjusting Brightness, Contrast, and Fade" to learn how you can adjust the brightness of the raster image so you can see the cursor more clearly.

**1.** Select the Clip tool from the Insert tab's Reference panel, or type **Clip**↵.

**2.** At the Select object to clip: prompt, click the edge of the raster image.

**3.** At the Enter image clipping option [ON/OFF/Delete/New boundary]<New>: prompt, press ↵ to create a new boundary.

**4.** At the [Select polyline/Polygonal/Rectangular/Invert clip] <Rectangular>: prompt, enter **P**↵ or click Polygonal in the command-line interface to draw a polygonal boundary.

**5.** Select the points shown in the top image in Figure 13.4 and then press ↵. The raster image is clipped to the boundary you created, as shown in the second image in Figure 13.4.

As the prompt in step 3 indicates, you can turn the clipping off or on, or you can delete an existing clipping boundary through the Clip Image option.

**FIGURE 13.4**

Adjusting the boundary of a clipped image

After you clip a raster image, you can adjust the clipping boundary by using its grips:

1. Click the boundary edge of the raster image to expose its grips.

2. Click a grip in the upper-right corner, as shown in the final image in Figure 13.4.

3. Drag the grip up and to the right, and then click a point. The image adjusts to the new boundary.

In addition to hiding portions of a raster image that are unimportant to you, clipping an image file reduces the amount of RAM the raster image uses during your editing session. AutoCAD loads only the visible portion of the image into RAM and ignores the rest.

## Adjusting Brightness, Contrast, and Fade

AutoCAD offers a tool that enables you to adjust the brightness, contrast, and fade of a raster image. Try making some adjustments to the raster image of the utility room in the following exercise:

**1.** Click the edge of the raster image. The Image tab appears in the Ribbon (see Figure 13.5).

**FIGURE 13.5**
The Image tab appears when you select a raster image.

**2.** In the Adjust panel of the Image tab, click and drag the Fade slider to the right so that it's near the middle of the slider scale, or enter **50** in the Fade box to the right of the slider. The sample image fades to the AutoCAD background color as you move the slider.

**3.** Press the Esc key to unselect the raster image. The Image tab closes.

**4.** Save the file as **Rasterimport.dwg**.

You can adjust the brightness and contrast by using the other two sliders in the Adjust panel of the Image tab.

By using the Image tab in conjunction with image clipping, you can create special effects. Figure 13.6 shows an aerial view of downtown San Francisco with labels. This view consists of two copies of the same raster image. One copy serves as a background, which was lightened using the method demonstrated in the previous exercise. The second copy is the darker area of the image with a roughly triangular clip boundary applied. You might use this technique to bring focus to a particular area of a drawing you're preparing for a presentation.

**FIGURE 13.6**
Two copies of the same image can be combined to emphasize a portion of the drawing.

If the draw order of objects is incorrect after you open a file or perform a Pan or Zoom, issue a Regen to recover the correct draw-order view.

In addition to the tools in the Adjust panel, there are several tools in the Image tab that can be used to modify raster images. Table 13.1 gives you a rundown of their function.

**TABLE 13.1:**     The tools on the Image tab

| TOOL | FUNCTION |
|---|---|
| Brightness | Adjusts the brightness of an image. |
| Contrast | Adjusts the contrast of an image. |
| Fade | Adjusts the fade value of an image. |
| Create Clipping Boundary | Allows you to create a clipping boundary. This tools works just like the Clip tool. |
| Remove Clipping | Removes a clipping boundary. |
| Show Image | Toggles an image on and off. |
| Background Transparency | Toggles the transparency of an image on and off. |
| External References | Opens the External References palette. |

## Turning Off the Frame, Adjusting Overall Quality, and Controlling Transparency

You can make three other adjustments to your raster image: frame visibility, image quality, and image transparency.

By default, a raster image displays an outline, or a *frame*. In many instances, this frame can detract from your drawing. You can turn off image frames globally by typing **Imageframe┘0┘**. This sets the Imageframe setting to 0, which turns off the frame visibility. If it's set to 1, the frame is made visible. You can also set it to 2, which leaves the frame visible but doesn't plot it (see Figure 13.7).

Frames can also be controlled through the Frame flyout on the Insert tab's Reference panel. If you turn off a raster image's frame, you can't click the image to select it for editing, though you can still select an image using the All, Previous, or Last selection option (see Chapter 2, "Creating Your First Drawing," for more on selection options). To make a raster image selectable with your mouse, turn on the image frame using the Display And Plot Frames or the Display But Don't Plot Frames option.

If your drawing doesn't require the highest-quality image, you can set the image quality to Draft mode. You may use Draft mode when you're tracing an image or when the image is already of a high quality. To set the image quality, enter **Imagequality┘** and then enter **H** for High mode (high quality) or **D** for Draft mode. In Draft mode, your drawing will regenerate faster.

**FIGURE 13.7**

A raster image with the frame on (top) and off (bottom)

High mode softens the pixels of the raster image, giving the image a smoother appearance. Draft mode displays the image in a raw, pixelated state. If you look carefully at the regions between the motorcycle and the background in the second image in Figure 13.8, you'll see that the edges of the motorcycle appear a bit jagged. The top image in Figure 13.8 uses the High setting to soften the edges of the motorcycle. You may need to look closely to see the difference.

Finally, you can control the transparency of raster image files that allow transparent pixels. Some file formats, such as GIF (Global Interchange Format), allow you to set a color in the image to be transparent (usually the background color). Most image-editing programs support this format because it's a popular one used on web pages.

When you turn on the Transparency setting, objects normally obscured by the background of a raster image may show through. Select the raster image and then, in the Image tab's Options panel, select Background Transparency. You can also right-click and select Image ➢ Transparency, then select On or Off from the Dynamic Input menu. In addition, you can enter **Transparency**↵ and then select the raster image you want to make transparent. Press ↵, and then enter **On** or **Off**, depending on whether you want the image to be transparent. Unlike the Frame and Quality options, Transparency works on individual objects rather than operating globally.

The Properties palette offers many of the same adjustments described in this section. You can use it for quick access to the Transparency setting and other raster image settings.

**FIGURE 13.8**
A close-up of a raster image with quality set to High (top) and Draft (bottom)

### CAN'T GET TRANSPARENCY TO WORK?

The Transparency command does not work on all types of images. As mentioned, it works with GIF files that have the background removed. You can also use a bitonal image, meaning the image must have only two colors, typically black and white. A bitonal image is also referred to as a *bitmap* image in Photoshop. It cannot be grayscale or multicolor. PDF files that have been exported from AutoCAD may also work with the Transparency command.

You can put images that do not work with the Transparency command on a layer with transparency set to a value greater than 0. Transparency can also be set using the Transparency slider in the Home tab's Properties panel. To use the Transparency slider, select the object, such as an image or hatch pattern, and then adjust the slider to achieve the level of transparency you want. You can start at 50 and adjust downward or upward.

Note that if you want your image to print or plot with the transparency in effect, you must select the Plot Transparency option in the Plot or Page Setup dialog box.

# Working with PDF Files

If you're using a computer as part of your daily work activity, you will encounter a PDF document. PDFs have become a part of everyday life, so it's no surprise that AutoCAD offers a fair amount of support for PDFs.

In the following sections, you'll learn how to import a PDF document into AutoCAD and how you can control various properties of the document, such as fading and the ability to snap to objects in the PDF.

## Importing a PDF

To import a PDF, you use a method similar to the one you used earlier to import an image file. In fact, you could perform all of the steps in the exercise in the section "Importing a Raster Image" earlier in this chapter using a PDF file instead of the raster1.jpg file. You just need to know how to set up the Select Reference File dialog box to allow you to locate PDFs.

Try the following to see how to import a PDF:

1. Open a new file using the acad.dwt file as a template.

2. Use the Save As option in the Application menu, and save the drawing as **PDFimport.dwg**.

3. Click the Attach tool in the Insert tab's Reference panel, or type **attach↵**, to open the Select Reference File dialog box.

4. In the Files Of Type drop-down list at the bottom of the dialog box, select PDF Files (*.pdf).

5. Locate and select the SampleImport.pdf file.

6. Click Open to open the Attach PDF Underlay dialog box (see Figure 13.9). Notice that you have an option to select a specific page of the PDF document if you are opening a multipage PDF.

7. Click page 2 of the page preview on the left side of the dialog box.

8. Click OK and then, at the Specify insertion point: prompt, place the outline of the drawing so that it is roughly centered in the drawing area and click.

9. At the Specify scale factor or [Unit] <1.0000>: prompt, use the cursor to scale the image so that it fills the screen (Figure 13.10). Page 2 of the SampleImport.pdf file appears in the drawing.

**FIGURE 13.9**
The Attach PDF
Underlay dialog box

**FIGURE 13.10**
Manually scaling
the PDF image

## Scaling and Osnaps with PDFs

In an earlier exercise, you were able to scale an image file, though you had to use a reference line that was already in the image file to scale the drawing roughly to its proper size in AutoCAD. If you have a PDF that was created from an AutoCAD file or from another vector-based program, you can use osnaps to select exact locations in the PDF.

Try the following exercise to see how you can use osnaps to select geometry in the PDF. You'll scale the drawing so that the width of the stairs conforms to the known distance for that area.

First make sure the Snap To Underlays feature is turned on:

**1.** In the Insert tab's Reference panel, click the Snap To Underlays tool.

**2.** Select the Snap To Underlays ON option.

Now you are ready to scale the PDF drawing:

**1.** Click the Scale tool in the Home tab's Modify panel or type **SC**↵.

**2.** Select the attached PDF file and press ↵.

**3.** At the `Specify base point:` prompt, turn on the osnaps and select the left endpoint of the horizontal line at the top of the drawing, as shown in Figure 13.11.

**FIGURE 13.11**
Selecting the first endpoint of the line for the Scale command

**4.** At the `Specify scale factor or [Copy/Reference]:` prompt, type **R**↵ to use the Reference option.

**5.** At the `Specify Reference length <1.0000>:` prompt, click the same endpoint again or type **@**↵.

**6.** At the `Specify second point:` prompt, click the endpoint of the line shown in Figure 13.12.

**7.** At the `Specify new length or [Points] <1.0000>:` prompt, enter **196**, which is the inch equivalent of 16'-4". Metric users should enter **498** to match the dimension of the metric version of the lobby drawing.

**8.** In the Navigation bar, choose the Zoom Extents option from the Zoom flyout to center the drawing in the drawing area.

**FIGURE 13.12**
Selecting the second
endpoint of the
line for the Scale
command

Click this endpoint.

PDF (approximate): Endpoint

In this exercise, you were able to use object snaps directly on the imported PDF drawing. You may have noticed that a tooltip appeared with the message "PDF (approximate): Endpoint." The PDF drawing is not an exact representation of the original drawing, so the tooltip reminds you that, even though you are using an osnap to select a location in the drawing, it is not an exact location as it would be in an AutoCAD file.

## Controlling the PDF Display

You can take advantage of a number of other features of a PDF file. Just as with a typical Xref or image file, you can fade the PDF so it appears as a background image. You can also use the Clip feature you saw earlier in this chapter to clip the PDF to a specific area.

You can gain access to these and other PDF display features through the PDF Underlay Ribbon tab. This tab appears automatically whenever you select an attached PDF drawing. Click the PDF drawing of the lobby and you'll see the PDF Underlay tab appear in the Ribbon (see Figure 13.13).

**FIGURE 13.13**
The panels on
the PDF Underlay
Ribbon tab

Table 13.2 describes the tools in the PDF Underlay Ribbon tab. The tools are fairly self-explanatory. For example, the tools in the Adjust panel let you control the fade and contrast of the PDF drawing. The Display In Monochrome option displays a color PDF in monochrome.

One option you'll want to take a closer look at is the Edit Layers tool in the PDF Layers panel. If the source PDF is a drawing that contains layers, you can control the visibility of those layers using this tool. With an imported PDF selected, click the Edit Layers tool to open the Underlay Layers dialog box (see Figure 13.14).

**FIGURE 13.14**
The Underlay Layers
dialog box

**TABLE 13.2:** The PDF Underlay tab tools

| OPTION | USE |
| --- | --- |
| Contrast | Adjusts the contrast setting for the PDF |
| Fade | Adjusts the amount of fade applied to the PDF |
| Display In Monochrome | Displays the PDF in monochrome |
| Create Clipping Boundary | Adds a clipping boundary to the PDF |
| Remove Clipping | Removes a clipping boundary |
| Show Underlay | Shows or hides the PDF |
| Enable Snap | Enables or disables the PDF snap feature |
| External References | Opens the External References palette |
| Edit Layers | Opens the Underlay Layers dialog box, allowing you to control layer visibility |

You can turn the visibility of a layer on or off by clicking the light bulb icon to the left of it in the list. For example, if you turn off the WALL layer in the Underlay Layers dialog box for the SampleImport example, the PDF drawing will change so that the walls will not be shown (see Figure 13.15).

**FIGURE 13.15**
The imported PDF
with the WALL
layer turned off

---

**ADDING LAYERS TO YOUR PDF**

If you want to create a PDF with layers, you can do so by printing a drawing to a PDF file using the AutoCAD DWG To PDF.pc3 Printer/Plotter option. You can find this option in the Name drop-down list in the Page Setup or Plot dialog box. (See Chapter 8, "Introducing Printing, Plotting, and Layouts," for more on the Name drop-down list.) You don't have to do anything special. If your drawing contains layers, the DWG to PDF.pc3 plotter will include them in the PDF. Adobe Acrobat 6.0 and later will also include layers when used from AutoCAD.

---

# Coordinating Geographic Locations

Architects and engineers use geolocation and mapping tools to help place their projects on their chosen sites. Usually a program like Google Earth or another mapping program is used to get an idea of the site conditions. Street views from Google Maps can help designers get a better idea of how their buildings will appear from a street level.

Geolocation tools can help the designer coordinate information between the different disciplines involved in a project. Designers can place their projects over an aerial view of a site and coordinate the orientation and location of key features of their design.

The Geographic Location feature in AutoCAD allows you place an accurately scaled map or aerial view in your drawing. You can then draw your designs directly on the map or import an existing AutoCAD design. Unlike an imported image, the Geographic Location map will always remain in the background so you don't have to be concerned about an overlapping image. You can also easily switch between a map view and an aerial view as the need arises.

---

### START AN AUTODESK 360 ACCOUNT TO USE GEOGRAPHIC LOCATION

Before you start to work with the Geographic Location feature, you will need to create an Autodesk® 360 account and be signed in. Click the Sign In drop down list in the InfoCenter and select Sign In to Autodesk 360. A browser appears that takes you to the Autodesk 360 website where you can sign up for a free account. If you already have an account, just sign in.

---

Let's take a look at how the Geographic Location feature works:

1. In a new file, select the Insert Ribbon tab and in the Location panel, click Set Location and select From Map.

2. You will see a message asking "Do you want to use Live Map Data?". Click Yes.

3. The Geographic Location dialog box appears (see Figure 13.16). Here, you can enter an address, a location name, or the latitude and longitude of a site.

**FIGURE 13.16**
The Geographic
Location dialog box

4. Enter a location name or address in the input box at the top of the dialog box and click the magnifying glass icon. For this exercise, enter **Fort Mason, San Francisco**. The dialog box changes to show an aerial view map of Fort Mason. In the left side, you see a list keyed to numbered locations on the map (see Figure 13.17).

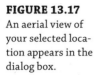

**FIGURE 13.17**
An aerial view of your selected location appears in the dialog box.

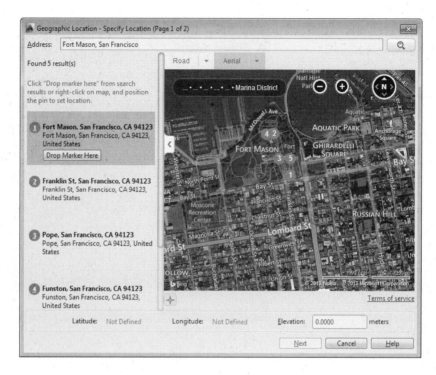

5. Click the Drop Marker Here button just under the first item in the list: Fort Mason, San Francisco, CA 94123. A red marker appears in the map.

6. Click the Next button at the bottom of the dialog box.

7. At the next dialog box, you are asked to select a coordinate system. Select CAHP-IIF, which is second from the top, and then select Next. The dialog box closes and you see the prompt:

   ```
   Select a point for the location <0.0000,0.0000.0.0000>:
   ```

8. Click a point at the center of the drawing area. The point you select corresponds to the red marker that appeared in the Geographic Location dialog box. You see the next prompt:

   ```
   Specify the north direction or [Angle]<angle>:
   ```

9. Click a point directly above the first point you selected to indicate a north direction pointing up. An aerial view of the northern tip of San Francisco appears (see Figure 13.18).

10. Once the aerial view appears in the drawing, you can zoom in and out using the standard AutoCAD view tools. Use the wheel of your mouse to zoom in to get a closer look at Fort Mason.

You may notice that the Geolocation Ribbon tab appears with a set of options (see Figure 13.19). These options allow you to modify your geolocation view. For example, the Map Aerial flyout lets you switch to a map view and back again.

**FIGURE 13.18**
The drawing area with the Geographic Location aerial view

**FIGURE 13.19**
The Geolocation Ribbon tab panels

Try it in the following exercise:

1. In the Online Map panel of the Geolocation tab, click the Map Aerial flyout and select Map Road. The view changes to show a graphic representation of the roads.

2. In the Online Map panel of the Geolocation tab, click the Map Road flyout and select Map Aerial. The view changes back to the aerial view.

## Making Adjustments to the Map

As you can see from the previous steps, you can easily switch between an aerial view and a map view. You also have the option to show a combined aerial and map view using the Map Hybrid option, or turn the geolocation background off entirely using the Map Off option.

### OPTIONS ON THE LOCATION PANEL

Besides controlling the geolocation background image, the Geolocation Ribbon tab lets you make other adjustments to your background. Here is a rundown of the tools and features you'll find in the Location panel:

**Edit Location**   Offers two options: From Map and From File. If you select From Map, the Geographic Location dialog box opens, enabling you to enter new location data. The From File option lets you find a location using a KML or KMZ file. KML files are used with Google Earth to enable location, tagging, and placement of 3D models on a Google Earth map. KMZ files are archive files similar to ZIP files and they contain KML files and any support files needed for the KML file.

**Reorient Marker**   Lets you reposition the original marker location and reset the north orientation. You are asked to select a point for the location of the address or latitude-longitude position, and then you are asked for the north orientation.

**Remove Location**   Lets you remove the geolocation map from the drawing. When you click this tool, you are asked if you want to remove the location data and the assigned coordinate system from the current drawing.

### OPTIONS ON THE TOOLS PANEL

The Map Tools palette in the Geolocation Ribbon panel offers tools that let you mark locations in the geolocation background. You've already seen what the Map Aerial and Map Road options do. The following list describes the other tools in this panel:

**Locate Me**   Lets you find your location on the aerial view or map. This feature is available only if your computer is equipped with a GPS or other feature that is able to provide your location data.

**Mark Position**   Lets you place a marker in the aerial or map view. The following options are available in the flyout: The Lat-Long option lets you specify the latitude and longitude for the marker location. The My Location option is similar to the Locate Me tool and places a marker at your current location. The Point option enables you to point to a location to place a marker. Once you click on a location, you are prompted to enter a text description for the location. AutoCAD opens the Text Editor Ribbon tab, giving you the ability to format your text description.

### OPTIONS ON THE ONLINE MAP PANEL

The Online Map panel in the Geolocation Ribbon panel gives you control over the map's appearance. It also lets you capture a portion of the map:

**Map Aerial**   Lets you select from a number of display options. You can choose to display a map (see Figure 13.20 later in this chapter) or a combined map and aerial view. You can also turn the map off completely.

**Capture Area**    Lets you place a selection rectangle over a portion of the displayed map. You can then to copy the selected area to the Clipboard. You can also capture the entire map that is in the display. Once you place a selection rectangle, the Map Image Ribbon tab appears, enabling you to adjust brightness, contrast, and fade of the selected area. You can also control the quality of the image. The captured map area is stored with the drawing and is not dependent upon an Internet connection. It can also be moved, rotated or resized in a manner similar to an imported raster image.

## Finding Measurements and Distances

In the first Geolocation exercise, you may have noticed the Drawing Unit option in the Geographic Location dialog box. By default, this option is set to inches, but you can set it to feet, meters, miles, or some other unit of measure. By accepting the default inches for the Drawing Unit option, any measurements you take on the map will return distances using inches as the drawing unit. If the unit style of your drawing is set to Architectural, distances will be displayed in feet and inches— inches are the base drawing unit. Try the following exercise to see how distances are displayed:

1. Type **Units**⏎ to open the Drawing Units dialog box.

2. Select Architectural from the Type drop-down list, and then click OK.

3. Choose Map Road from the Map Aerial flyout in the Map Tools Ribbon panel.

4. Zoom into the map view so it looks similar to Figure 13.20.

**FIGURE 13.20**
The Map Road view

5. Choose Measure from the Home tab's Utilities panel.

6. Measure the distance from Laguna Street to Van Ness Avenue. The Measure tool reports a distance of 2446', give or take a few feet.

In this exercise, the distance reported by the Measure tool is in feet. Had you not changed drawing unit in steps 1 and 2, the distance reported by the Measure tool would have been 29,043 units, which is the distance in inches.

You can use other methods to find measurements in your map. For example, you could get a rough estimate of the size of an existing building by drawing a closed polyline around the building outline (see Figure 13.21). Select the polyline and hover over a grip to view the dimensions of the outline closest to the grip.

**FIGURE 13.21**
Dimensions from a building outline

# The Bottom Line

**Convert paper drawings into AutoCAD files.**   AutoCAD gives you some great tools that let you convert your paper drawings into AutoCAD files. Several options are available. Depending on your needs, you'll find at least one solution that will allow you to convert your drawings quickly.

**Master It**   Describe the different methods available in AutoCAD for converting paper drawings into CAD files.

**Import a raster image.**   You can use bitmap raster images as backgrounds for your CAD drawings or as underlay drawings that you can trace over.

**Master It**   Import a raster image of your choice, and use the AutoCAD drawing tools to trace over your image.

**Work with a raster image.**   Once imported, raster images can be adjusted for size, brightness, contrast, and transparency.

**Master It**   Import a raster image of your choice, and fade the image so that it appears to blend into the background with less contrast.

**Work with PDF files.**   AutoCAD allows you to import and control the display of PDF files. This is significant since the PDF file format is so prevalent in the business world.

**Master It**   In a PDF that includes layers, how do you gain access to the layer settings?

**Use a geolocation map.**   You can include a correctly scaled background aerial view or road map of a site in your drawing to help you better coordinate your design with site conditions.

**Master It**   Name three types of information you can use to find a site in the Geographic Location dialog box.

# Chapter 14

# Advanced Editing and Organizing

Because you may not know all of a project's requirements when it begins, you usually base the first draft of a design on anticipated needs. As the plan goes forward, you adjust for new requirements as they arise. As more people enter the project, additional design restrictions come into play, and the design is further modified. This process continues throughout the project, from the first draft to the end product.

In this chapter, you'll gain experience with some tools that will help you edit your drawings more efficiently. You'll take a closer look at Xrefs and how they may be used to help streamline changes in a drawing project. You'll also be introduced to tools and techniques you can use to minimize duplication of work, such as the Quick Select tool and the QuickCalc feature. The AutoCAD® 2015 software can be a powerful timesaving tool if used properly. This chapter examines ways to harness that power.

In this chapter, you will learn to

♦ Use external references (Xrefs)

♦ Manage layers

♦ Use advanced tools: Filter and Quick Select

♦ Use the QuickCalc calculator

## Using External References

Chapter 7, "Mastering Viewing Tools, Hatches, and External References," mentioned that careful use of blocks, external references (Xrefs), and layers can help improve your productivity. In the following sections, you'll see firsthand how to use these features to help reduce design errors and speed up delivery of an accurate set of drawings. You do so by controlling layers in conjunction with blocks and Xrefs to create a common drawing database for several drawings. You can also use AutoCAD DWF and Acrobat PDF files as Xrefs. See Chapter 13, "Copying Existing Drawings from Other Sources," for more on PDF files and Chapter 25, "Managing and Sharing Your Drawings," for more on DWF files.

Later, you'll start to use Xrefs to create different floor plans for the building you worked on earlier in this book. To save you some time, we've created a second one-bedroom unit plan called Unit2 that you'll use in these exercises (see Figure 14.1). You can find this new unit plan in the Chapter 14 folder of sample files at this book's web page, www.sybex.com/go/masteringautocad2015.

**FIGURE 14.1**

The one-
bedroom unit

## Preparing Existing Drawings for External Referencing

Chapter 7 discussed how you can use Xrefs to assemble one floor of the apartment. In this section, you'll explore the creation and use of Xrefs to build multiple floors, each containing slightly differ-ent sets of drawing information. By doing so, you'll learn how Xrefs enable you to use a single file in multiple drawings to save time and reduce redundancy. You'll see that by sharing common data in multiple files, you can reduce your work and keep the drawing information consistent.

You'll start by creating the files that you'll use later as Xrefs:

1. Open the `Plan.dwg` file. If you didn't create the `Plan.dwg` file, you can use the `14a-plan .dwg` or `14a-plan-metric` file (see Figure 14.2). Select Zoom All from the Navigation bar to center the drawing.

**FIGURE 14.2**

The overall plan

2. Turn off the Ceiling and Flr-pat layers to get a clear, uncluttered view of the individual unit plans.

3. Use the Wblock command (enter **W**↵ at the Command prompt), and write the eight units in the corners of your plan to a file called Floor1.dwg in your My Documents folder (see Figure 14.3). When you select objects for the Wblock, be sure to include the S-DOOR door reference symbols and apartment number symbols for those units. Use 0,0 for the Wblock insertion base point. Also make sure the Delete From Drawing check box is selected in the Write Block dialog box before you click OK.

**FIGURE 14.3**

Units to be exported to the Floor1.dwg file

Select these units for the Wblock command.

4. Using Figure 14.4 as a guide, insert the Unit2.dwg file into the corners where the other eight units were previously. Metric users should use Unit2-metric.dwg. These files can be found in the Chapter 14 folder of sample files. If you didn't create the Unit2 file earlier in this chapter, use the 14a-unit2.dwg file.

**FIGURE 14.4**

Insertion information for Unit2. Metric coordinates are shown in brackets.

Insert Unit2 at coordinate 31'-5",104'-6" [957,3184]; x-scale factor = 1; y-scale factor = -1 (minus one).

Insert Unit2 at coordinate 31'-5", 43'-8" [957,1330]; x and y scale factor=1.

Mirror inserted Unit2 blocks to this side.

5. After you've accurately placed the corner units, use the Wblock command to write these corner units to a file called `Floor2.dwg`. Again, use the 0,0 coordinate as the insertion base point for the Wblock, and make sure the Delete From Drawing check box is selected.

6. Choose Save As from the Application menu to turn the remaining set of unit plans into a file called `Common.dwg`.

You've just created three files: `Floor1.dwg`, `Floor2.dwg`, and `Common.dwg`. Each file contains unique information about the building. Next, you'll use the Xref command to recombine these files for the different floor plans in your building.

## Assembling Xrefs to Build a Drawing

You'll now create composite files for each floor using Xrefs of only the files needed for the individual floors. You'll use the Attach option of the Xref command to insert all the files you exported from the `Plan.dwg` file.

Follow these steps to create a file representing the first floor:

1. Close the `Common.dwg` file, open a new file, and call it **Xref-1.dwg**.

2. For Imperial measurement users, use the Drawing Units dialog box (**Units↵**) to set the drawing units type to Architectural and the Insertion scale to Inches. Use the Limits command to set the lower-left corner at 0,0 and the upper-right corner at 2112,1632. Metric users should set the drawing units type to Decimal and the insertion scale to Centimeters. Set the lower-left corner limits to 0,0 and the upper-right corner limits to 5940 cm × 4200 cm. For both measurement systems, select All from the Zoom flyout on the View tab's Navigate panel or type **Z↵A↵** so that your drawing area is adjusted to the window.

3. Set the Ltscale value to 192. Metric users should set it to 200.

4. Click Attach in the Insert tab's Reference panel or type **XA↵** to open the Select Reference File dialog box.

5. Locate and select the `Common.dwg` file.

6. In the Attach External Reference dialog box, make sure the Specify On-Screen check box in the Insertion Point group isn't selected. Then make sure the X, Y, and Z values in the Insertion Point group are all 0 (see Figure 14.5). Because the insertion points of all the files are the same (0,0), they will fit together perfectly when they're inserted into the new files.

7. Click OK. The `Common.dwg` file appears in the drawing.

The drawing may appear faded. This is because AutoCAD has a feature that allows you to fade an Xref so that it is easily distinguished from other objects in your current drawing. You can quickly change the reference fade setting by doing the following:

1. In the Insert tab's expanded Reference panel, locate the Xref Fading slider.

2. Click and drag the Xref Fading slider all the way to the left, or you can click in the Xref Fading slider value box to the right and enter **0↵**.

Your Xref should now appear solid. Remember the Xref Fading slider; you may find that you'll need it frequently when working with Xrefs.

**FIGURE 14.5**

The Attach External Reference dialog box

Now continue to add some reference files:

1. Click Attach from the Reference panel, and then locate, select, and insert the Floor1.dwg or Floor1-metric.dwg file.

2. Repeat step 1 to insert the Col-grid.dwg or Col-grid-metric.dwg file as an Xref. You now have the plan for the first floor.

3. Save this file.

Next, use the current file to create another file representing a different floor:

1. Choose Save As from the Application menu and save this file as **Xref-2.dwg**.

2. Click the External References tool in the Insert tab's Reference panel title bar, or type **XR↵**.

3. In the External References palette, select Floor1 in the list of Xrefs. Notice that as you hover over the Floor1 name, a description of the file appears with a thumbnail view (see Figure 14.6). This can help you quickly identify Xref files in the list.

4. Right-click and select Detach from the context menu.

5. Right-click in the blank portion of the list in the External References palette and select Attach DWG from the context menu.

6. Locate and select Floor2.dwg.

**FIGURE 14.6**
Highlight Floor1 in
the list of Xrefs.

7. In the Attach External Reference dialog box, make sure the X, Y, and Z values in the Insertion Point group are all set to 0.

8. Click OK. The Floor2 drawing appears in place of Floor1. Turn off the Notes layer to see the plan clearly.

Now when you need to make changes to Xref-1.dwg or Xref-2.dwg, you can edit their individual Xref files. The next time you open Xref-1.dwg or Xref-2.dwg, the updated Xrefs will automatically appear in their most recent forms.

Xrefs don't need to be permanent. As you saw in the previous exercise, you can attach and detach them easily at any time. This means that if you need to get information from another file—to see how well an elevator core aligns, for example—you can temporarily attach the other file as an Xref to check alignments quickly and then detach it when you're finished.

Think of these composite files as final plot files that are used only for plotting and reviewing. You can then edit the smaller, more manageable Xref files. Figure 14.7 illustrates the relationship of these files.

The combinations of Xrefs are limited only by your imagination.

---

### KEEPING TRACK OF XREF LOCATIONS

Because Xref files don't become part of the file into which they're referenced, you must take care to keep them in a location where AutoCAD can find them when the referencing file is opened. This can be a minor annoyance when you need to send files to others outside your office. To help keep track of Xrefs, choose Publish ▸ eTransmit from the Application menu. See Chapter 25 for details.

**LOCATING XREF FILES**

If you move an Xref file after you insert it into a drawing, AutoCAD may not be able to find it later when you attempt to open the drawing. If this happens, you can click the Browse button of the Saved Path option at the bottom of the External References palette to tell AutoCAD the new location of the Xref file. The Browse button appears at the far right of the Saved Path text box when you click in the text box.

If you know that you'll be keeping your project files in one place, you can use the Projectname system variable in conjunction with the Options dialog box to direct AutoCAD to look in a specific location for Xref files. Here's what to do:

1. Choose Options from the Application menu or type **OP**↵.

2. Click the Files tab and then locate and select the Project Files Search Path option.

3. Click Add and either enter a name for your project or accept the default name of Project1.

4. Click Browse and locate and select the folder where you plan to keep your Xref files.

5. Close the Options dialog box, and then enter *Projectname*↵ at the command-line interface. Enter the project name you used in step 3.

6. Save your file so it remembers this setting.

**FIGURE 14.7**
A diagram of Xref file relationships

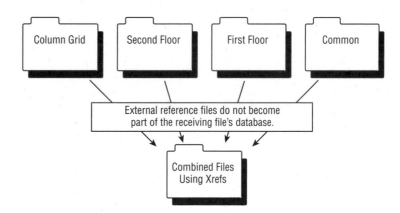

## Updating Blocks in Xrefs

Several advantages are associated with using Xref files. Because the Xrefs don't become part of the drawing file's database, the referencing files remain small. Also, because Xref files are easily updated, work can be split up among several people in a workgroup environment or on a network. For example, for your hypothetical apartment building project, one person can be editing the Common.dwg file while another works on Floor1.dwg, and so on. The next time the composite Xref-1.dwg or Xref-2.dwg file is opened, it automatically reflects any new changes made in the Xref files. If the Xref is updated while you still have the receiving file open, you see a balloon message telling you that an Xref requires a reload.

Let's see how to set this up:

1. Save and close the Xref-2.dwg file, and then open the Common.dwg file.

2. Update the unit plan you edited earlier in this chapter. Click Insert in the Home or Insert tab's Block panel, and then click More Options. You can also type **Insert⏎**.

3. In the Insert dialog box, click the Browse button and then locate and select your Unit.dwg file. If you can't find your Unit.dwg file, you can use 14b-unit.dwg (or 14b-dwg-metric .dwg for metric users) from the Chapter 14 sample files, but make sure you rename the file you use to **Unit.dwg** before you insert it. You may also use the method described in the "Substituting Blocks" sidebar in Chapter 7 to insert 14b-unit.dwg or 14b-dwg-metric .dwg without renaming the file.

4. At the warning message, click Redefine Block.

5. At the Insertion point: prompt, press the Esc key. You see the new unit plan in place of the old one (see Figure 14.8).

**FIGURE 14.8**
The Common.dwg file with the revised unit plan

6. If the Notes layer is on, use the layer drop-down list to turn it off.

7. Click the Insert tool in the Block panel again, and replace the empty room across the hall from the lobby with the utility room (utility.dwg or utility-metric.dwg) (see Figure 14.9).

8. Save the Common.dwg file.

9. Open the Xref-1.dwg file, right-click Common in the External References palette, and select Reload from the context menu. You can also right-click the Manage Xrefs icon in the lower-right corner of the AutoCAD window and select Reload DWG Xrefs. You see the utility room and the typical units in their new form. Your drawing should look like the top image in Figure 14.10.

**FIGURE 14.9**
The utility room
inserted

Add the Utility file.

10. Open Xref-2.dwg. You see that the utility room and typical units are updated in this file as well. (See the bottom image in Figure 14.10.)

**FIGURE 14.10**
The Xref-1.dwg
and Xref-2.dwg
files with the units
updated

## Importing Named Elements from Xrefs

Chapter 5, "Keeping Track of Layers and Blocks," discussed how layers, blocks, linetypes, and text styles—called *named elements*—are imported along with a file that is inserted into another file. Xref files don't import named elements. You can, however, review their names and use a special command to import the ones you want to use in the current file.

---

### SAVING XREF LAYER SETTINGS

You can set the Visretain system variable to 1 to force AutoCAD to remember layer settings of Xref files. Another choice is to turn on the Retain Changes To Xref Layers option in the Open And Save tab of the Options dialog box. You can also use the Layer States Manager in the Layer Properties Manager dialog box to save layer settings for later recall. The Layer States Manager is described in detail in the section "Saving and Recalling Layer Settings" later in this chapter.

---

AutoCAD renames named elements from Xref files by giving them the prefix of the filename from which they come. For example, the Wall layer in the Floor1.dwg file is called Floor1|WALL in the Xref-1.dwg file; the Toilet block is called Floor1|TOILET. You can't draw on the layer Floor1|WALL, nor can you insert Floor1|TOILET, but you can view Xref layers in the Layer Properties Manager dialog box, and you can view Xref blocks by using the Insert dialog box.

Next, you'll look at how AutoCAD identifies layers and blocks in Xref files, and you'll get a chance to import a layer from an Xref:

1. With the Xref-1.dwg file open, open the Layer Properties Manager palette. Notice that the names of the layers from the Xref files are all prefixed with the filename and the vertical bar (|) character. Exit the Layer Properties Manager palette. You can also open the Layer drop-down list to view the layer names.

2. Enter **XB**↵ to open the Xbind dialog box. You see a listing of the current Xrefs. Each item shows a plus sign to the left. This list box follows the Microsoft Windows format for expandable lists, much like the tree view in Windows Explorer (see Figure 14.11).

**FIGURE 14.11**
The Xbind
dialog box

3. Click the plus sign next to the Floor1 Xref item. The list expands to show the types of elements available to bind (see Figure 14.12).

**FIGURE 14.12**
The expanded
Floor1 list

**4.** Click the plus sign next to the Layer item. The list expands further to show the layers available for binding (see Figure 14.13).

**FIGURE 14.13**
The expanded
Layer list

**5.** Locate Floor1|WALL in the list, click it, and then click the Add button. Floor1|WALL is added to the list to the right, Definitions To Bind.

**6.** Click OK to bind the Floor1|WALL layer.

**7.** Open the Layer Properties Manager dialog box.

**8.** Scroll down the list and look for the Floor1|WALL layer. You won't find it. In its place is a layer called Floor1$0$WALL.

---

### IMPORT DRAWING COMPONENTS WITH DESIGNCENTER

The AutoCAD DesignCenter™ lets you import settings and other drawing components from any drawing, not just Xref drawings. You'll learn more about the DesignCenter in Chapter 25.

---

As you can see, when you use Xbind to import a named item, such as the Floor1|WALL layer, the vertical bar (|) is replaced by two dollar signs surrounding a number, which is usually 0. (If for some reason the imported layer name Floor1$0$WALL already exists, the 0 in that name is changed to 1, as in Floor1$1$WALL.) Other named items are renamed in the same way, using the $0$ replacement for the vertical bar.

You can also use the Xbind dialog box to bind multiple layers as well as other items from Xrefs attached to the current drawing. You can bind an entire Xref to a drawing, converting it to a simple block. By doing so, you have the opportunity to maintain unique layer names of the Xref being bound or to merge the Xref's similarly named layers with those of the current file. See Chapter 7 for details.

---

### NESTING XREFS AND USING OVERLAYS

Xrefs can be nested. For example, if the Common.dwg file created in this chapter used the Unit.dwg file as an Xref rather than as an inserted block, you would still get the same result in the Xref-1.dwg file. That is, you would see the entire floor plan, including the unit plans, when you opened Xref-1.dwg. In this situation, Unit.dwg would be nested in the Common.dwg file, which is in turn externally referenced in the Xref-1.dwg file.

Although nested Xrefs can be helpful, take care in using Xrefs this way. For example, you might create an Xref by using the Common.dwg file in the Floor1.dwg file as a means of referencing walls and other features of the Common.dwg file. You might also reference the Common.dwg file into the Floor2.dwg file for the same reason. After you did this, however, you'd have three versions of the Common plan in the Xref-1.dwg file because each Xref would have Common.dwg attached to it. And because AutoCAD would dutifully load Common.dwg three times, Xref-1.dwg would occupy substantial computer memory, slowing your computer when you edited the Xref-1.dwg file.

To avoid this problem, use the Overlay option in the Attach External Reference dialog box. An overlaid Xref can't be nested. For example, if you use the Overlay option when inserting the Common.dwg file into the Floor1.dwg and Floor2.dwg files, the nested Common.dwg files are ignored when you open the Xref-1.dwg file, thereby eliminating the redundant occurrence of Common.dwg. In another example, if you use the Overlay option to import the Unit.dwg file into the Common.dwg file and then attach the Common.dwg into Xref-1.dwg as an Xref, you don't see the Unit.dwg file in Xref-1.dwg. The nested Unit.dwg drawing is ignored.

If you have used the Attach option to insert an Xref and want to change it to Overlay, you can do so in the External References palette. Click the External References icon in the Insert tab's Reference panel's title bar, and then in the External References palette, right-click the name of the Xref you want to change and select Xref Type ▸ Overlay. Use the same steps to convert an Overlay Xref into an Attached Xref, but use Xref Type ▸ Attach after you right-click on the Xref name.

---

## Controlling the Xref Search Path

One problem AutoCAD users encountered in the past was lost or broken links to an Xref. This occurs when an Xref file is moved from its original location or when you receive a set of drawings that includes Xrefs. The Xref links are broken because AutoCAD doesn't know where to look.

When you insert an Xref, the Attach External Reference dialog box opens, offering you options for insertion point, scale, and rotation. This dialog box also provides the Path Type option, which enables you to select a method for locating Xrefs. You can choose from three path type options:

**Absolute Path**    Lets you specify the exact filename and path for an Xref, including the disk drive or network location. Use this option when you want AutoCAD to look in a specific location for the Xref.

**Relative Path**    Lets you specify a file location relative to the location of the current or host drawing. For example, if the host drawing is in a folder called C:\mycadfiles and the Xrefs are in a folder called C:\mycadfiles\xrefs, you can specify .\xrefs for the location of the Xref file. This option is useful when you know you'll maintain the folder structure of the host and Xref files when moving or exchanging these files. Note that because this is a relative path, this option is valid only for files that reside on the same local hard disk.

**No Path**    Perhaps the most flexible option, No Path tells AutoCAD to use its own search criteria to find Xrefs. When this option is selected, AutoCAD first looks in the same folder of the host drawing; then it looks in the project search path defined in the Files tab of the Options dialog box. (See Appendix B, "Installing and Setting Up AutoCAD," for more on the Options dialog box.) Finally, AutoCAD looks in the Support File Search Path option, also defined in the Files tab of the Options dialog box. If you plan to send your files to a client or a consultant, you may want to use this option.

You can change the path type using two features in the External References palette. First, select the Xref or Xrefs you want to change, then right-click and select Path in the context menu. You will see three options: Make Absolute, Make Relative, and Remove Path. Select the option you desire for the selected Xrefs. You can also click the Change Path tool in the External References palette toolbar.

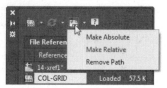

# Managing Layers

In a survey of AutoCAD users, Autodesk discovered that one of the most frequently used features in AutoCAD is the Layer command. You'll find that you turn layers on and off to display and edit the many levels of information contained in your AutoCAD files. As your files become more complex, controlling layer visibility becomes more difficult. Fortunately, AutoCAD offers the Layer States Manager to make your work a little easier.

## Saving and Recalling Layer Settings

The Layer States Manager lets you save layer settings. This can be crucial when you're editing a file that serves multiple uses, such as a floor plan and reflected ceiling plan. You can, for example, turn layers on and off to set up the drawing for a reflected ceiling plan view and then save the layer settings. Later, when you need to modify the ceiling information, you can recall the layer settings to view the ceiling data.

The following steps show you how the Layer States Manager works:

Layer
Properties

**1.** In AutoCAD, open the 14b-unit.dwg file. Click the Layer Properties tool in the Home tab's Layers panel to open the Layer Properties Manager, and turn on all the layers except Notes and Flr-pat. Your drawing should look similar to the top image in Figure 14.14.

**FIGURE 14.14**

The view of the 14b-unit.dwg file before and after changing layer settings

**2.** Click the Unsaved Layer State drop-down list in the Home tab's expanded Layers panel.

**3.** Click Manage Layer States to open the Layer States Manager dialog box. Take a moment to look at the options in this dialog box. This is where you can specify which layer settings you want saved with this layer state (see Figure 14.15).

**FIGURE 14.15**
The Layer States
Manager dialog box

**4.** You're ready to save the current layer state. Click the New button in the Layer States Manager dialog box. The New Layer State To Save dialog box opens (see Figure 14.16).

**FIGURE 14.16**
The New Layer State
To Save dialog box

**5.** Enter **blank floor plan** in the New Layer State Name box. Note that you can also enter a brief description of your layer state. Click OK to return to the Layer States Manager dialog box.

**6.** Click the More Restore Options button (see Figure 14.17) in the lower-right corner of the Layer States Manager dialog box to expand the list of options.

**FIGURE 14.17**
The More Restore
Options button

7. Make sure the On/Off check box is selected, and then click Close. Several other options are available, but you can leave them as they are.

8. Back in the Layer Properties Manager dialog box, turn on the Flr-pat and Notes layers and turn off the Ceiling layer.

   Your drawing looks like the bottom image in Figure 14.14.

You've just saved a layer state and then changed the layer settings to something different from the saved state. The following steps demonstrate how you can restore the saved layer state:

1. In the Home tab's expanded Layers panel, click the Unsaved Layer State drop-down list and select Blank Floor Plan. Your drawing reverts to the previous view with the Notes and Flr-pat layers turned off and the Ceiling layer turned on.

2. This brings you to the end of the Layer States Manager exercise. Save the file and close it.

The layer states are saved with the file so that you can retrieve them at a later date. As you can see in the Layer States Manager dialog box, you have a few other options, as shown in Table 14.1.

**TABLE 14.1:**     Layer States Manager dialog box options

| OPTION | PURPOSE |
| --- | --- |
| New | Creates a new layer state. |
| Save | Saves the selected layer state after edits. |
| Edit | Lets you edit the layer settings for the selected layer state. |
| Rename | Renames a selected layer state. |
| Delete | Deletes a layer state from the list. |
| Import | Imports a set of layer states that have been exported using the Export option of this dialog box. |
| Export | Saves a set of layer states as a file. By default, the file is given the name of the current layer state with the `.las` filename extension. You can import the layer-state file into other files. |
| Layer Properties To Restore (in the expanded dialog box) | Lets you select the layer properties to be controlled by the Layer States Manager. |

In addition to saving layer states by name, you can quickly revert to a previous layer setting by clicking the Previous tool on the Home tab's expanded Layers panel. This tool enables you to revert to the previous layer settings without affecting other settings in AutoCAD. Note that Previous mode doesn't restore renamed or deleted layers, nor does it remove new layers.

After you become familiar with these layer-state tools, you'll find yourself using them frequently in your editing sessions.

## Other Tools for Managing Layers

There are quite a number of tools that help you quickly set up layers as you work. In the following sections, you'll learn about some of those other tools you've seen in the Layers panel. All the tools discussed in these sections have keyboard command equivalents. Check the tool tip for the keyboard command name when you select one of these tools from the Layers panel.

### USING LAYER WALK TO EXPLORE LAYERS

When you work with a file that was produced by someone else, you usually have to spend some time becoming familiar with the way layers are set up in it. This process can be tedious, but the Layer Walk tool can help.

As the name implies, the Layer Walk tool lets you "walk through" the layers of a file, visually isolating each layer as you select its name from a list. You can use Layer Walk to select the layers that you want visible, or you can turn layers on and off to explore a drawing without affecting the current layer settings. To open the LayerWalk dialog box, do the following:

1. Click the Layer Walk tool on the expanded Layers panel, or enter **Laywalk**↵.

2. The LayerWalk dialog box appears (see Figure 14.18).

**FIGURE 14.18**
The LayerWalk
dialog box

You can click and drag the bottom edge of the dialog box to expand the list so that you can see all the layers in the drawing. When you first open the LayerWalk dialog box, you see the current visible layers selected. Layers that are off aren't selected. Click a single layer and AutoCAD displays just that layer. With a single layer selected, you can "walk" through the layers by pressing the down and up arrow keys.

You can use this dialog box to set up layer settings visually by Ctrl+clicking layer names to make them visible. Turn off Restore On Exit to maintain the layer settings you set up in the LayerWalk dialog box, or turn it on if you want the drawing to revert to the layer settings that were in place before you opened the LayerWalk dialog box. Right-click the list of layers to display a set of other options that let you save the layer state and invert the selection.

### CHANGING THE LAYER ASSIGNMENT OF OBJECTS

In addition to the Layer Walk tool, the Layers panel includes two tools that change the layer assignments of objects: the Match Layer tool and the Change To Current Layer tool on the expanded Layers panel.

The Match Layer tool is similar to the Match Properties tool, but it's streamlined to operate only on layer assignments. After clicking this tool in the Layers panel, select the object or objects you want to change, press ↵, and then select an object whose layer you want to match.

The Change To Current Layer tool on the expanded Layers panel changes an object's layer assignment to the current layer.

## CONTROLLING LAYER SETTINGS THROUGH OBJECTS

The remaining Layer tools let you make layer settings by selecting objects in the drawing. These tools are easy to use: click a tool, and then select an object.

The following list describes each tool:

**Layer Isolate/Layer Unisolate**   Layer Isolate turns off all the layers except for the layer of the selected object. Layer Unisolate restores the layer settings to the way the drawing was set before you used Layer Isolate.

**Freeze**   Freezes the layer of the selected object.

**Off**   Turns off the layer of the selected object.

**Lock/Unlock**   Locks the layer of the selected object. A locked layer is visible but can't be edited.

**Layer Walk**   Lets you dynamically change layer visibility.

**Copy Objects To New Layer**   Copies an object or a set of objects to a different layer.

**Make Object's Layer Current**   Enables you to set the current layer by selecting an object that is on the desired layer.

**Turn All Layers On**   Turns all layers on.

**Thaw All Layers**   Thaws all layers.

**Isolate To Current Viewport**   Enables you to freeze layers in all but the current viewport by selecting objects that are on the layers to be frozen.

**Merge**   Combines several layers into one layer. First select objects whose layers you want to merge, press ↵, and then select an object whose layer you want to merge with.

**Delete**   Deletes all objects on a layer and then deletes the layer.

## MERGING MULTIPLE LAYERS INTO ONE LAYER

If you find that you have several layers that you want to merge into one layer, you can use the Merge option in the Layer Manager. You can merge a single layer or a set of layers into an existing layer, other than one that has been selected. If the layer you want to use for the merge does not exist, create it first. Then in the Layer Manager, select the layer or layers you want to merge, right-click, and select the Merge Selected Layer(s) To option. The Merge To Layer dialog box appears (see Figure 14.19). You can select the layer name from the list. The merged layers are automatically purged from the drawing.

**FIGURE 14.19**

The Merge To Layer
dialog box

# Using Advanced Tools: Filter and Quick Select

Two other tools are extremely useful in your day-to-day work with AutoCAD: selection filters and Quick Select. We've saved the discussion of these tools until this part of the chapter because you don't need them until you've become accustomed to the way AutoCAD works. Chances are that you've already experimented with some of the AutoCAD menu options not yet discussed in the exercise. Many of the drop-down menu options and their functions are self-explanatory. Selection filters and QuickCalc (the latter is discussed later in this chapter) don't appear in any of the menus and require further explanation.

Let's start with selection filters. AutoCAD includes two selection-filtering tools: The *Quick Select tool* offers a quick way to locate objects based on their properties. The *Filter tool* lets you select objects based on a more complex set of criteria.

## Filtering Selections

Suppose you need to isolate just the walls of your drawing in a separate file. One way to do this is to turn off all the layers except the Wall layer. You can then use the Wblock command and select the remaining walls, using a window to write the wall information to a file. Filters can simplify this operation by enabling you to select groups of objects based on their properties.

Follow these steps to select objects based on their layer assignment:

1. Open the Unit.dwg file.

2. Type **W**⏎ to start the Wblock command. Then, in the Write Block dialog box, enter **Unitwall** in the File Name And Path text box.

3. Make sure the Objects and Retain radio buttons are selected in the dialog box, and then click the Select Objects button in the Objects group. The dialog box closes so that you can select objects.

4. At the Select Objects: prompt, type **'Filter**⏎ to open the Object Selection Filters dialog box (see Figure 14.20).

## GETTING NOTIFICATION OF NEW LAYERS

AutoCAD can notify you when new layers are added to Xrefs in a drawing or to the current drawing itself. Such new layers are called *unreconciled* layers. This feature can be helpful when you are working with others and need to stay informed about the condition of a drawing. By default, the notification comes in two forms. When new layers are added, a warning icon appears in the right side of the status bar. If you attempt to plot a drawing that contains new layers, the following message appears: Unreconciled new layers exist in the drawing. The warning will not prevent you from doing anything. It is just intended as a way to notify you of changes. In addition, the unreconciled layers are grouped into a layer property filter called Unreconciled New Layers, which can be viewed in the Layer Properties Manager.

To "reconcile" unreconciled layers, open the Layer Properties Manager, select the unreconciled layers, and right-click and select Reconcile Layers from the context menu.

New layer notification is turned on by default and is controlled by the Layerevalctl system variable. Type **Layerevalctl↵1↵** to turn it on and **Layerevalctl↵0↵** to turn it off.

You can also set how you are notified of new layers through the Layereval and Layernotify system variables. Layereval controls when the Unreconciled New Layer filter displays new layers and can be set to 0, 1, or 2. The setting 0 turns Layereval off, 1 sets it to detect new layers in Xrefs, and 2 sets it to detect new layers in Xrefs and the current drawing. Layernotify determines how you are notified of new layers. The setting 0 means no notification; 1 means notify when you start a plot; 2 when the drawing is open; 4 when Xrefs are loaded, reloaded, or attached; 8 when you are restoring a layer state; 16 when you are saving a file; and 32 when you are inserting a drawing.

**FIGURE 14.20**

The Object Selection Filters dialog box

5. Open the drop-down list in the Select Filter group.

6. Scroll down the list, and find and highlight the Layer option.

7. Click the Select button next to the drop-down list to display a list of layers. Highlight Wall, and click OK.

8. Click the Add To List button toward the bottom of the Select Filter group to add Layer = Wall to the list box.

9. Click Apply to close the Object Selection Filters dialog box.

10. Type **ALL**↵ to select everything in the drawing. Only the objects assigned to the Wall layer are selected. You see a message in the Command window indicating how many objects were found.

11. Press ↵. You see the message Exiting Filtered selection Resuming WBLOCK command - Select objects: 20 found.

12. Press ↵ again to complete the selection, and then click OK to complete the Wblock command. All the walls are written out to a file called Unitwall.

In this exercise, you filtered out a layer by using the Filter command. After you designate a filter, you then select the group of objects through which you want AutoCAD to filter. AutoCAD finds the objects that match the filter requirements and passes those objects to the current command.

As you've seen from the previous exercise, you can choose from many options in this utility. Let's take a closer look.

### WORKING WITH THE OBJECT SELECTION FILTERS DIALOG BOX

To use the Object Selection Filters dialog box, first select the criterion for filtering from the drop-down list. If the criterion you select is a named item (layer, linetype, color, or block), you can then click the Select button to choose specific items from a list. If there is only one choice, the Select button is dimmed.

After you've determined what to filter, you must add it to the list by clicking the Add To List button. The filter criterion then appears in the list box at the top of the Object Selection Filters dialog box, and you can apply that criterion to your current command or to a later command. AutoCAD remembers your filter settings, so if you need to reselect a filtered selection set, you don't have to redefine your filter criteria.

### SAVING FILTER CRITERIA

If you prefer, you can preselect filter criteria. Then, at any Select objects: prompt, you can type **Filter**↵, highlight the appropriate filter criteria in the list box, and click Apply. The specifications in the Object Selection Filters dialog box remain in place for the duration of the current editing session.

You can also save a set of criteria by entering a name in the text box next to the Save As button and then clicking the button. The criteria list data is saved in a file called Filter.nfl in the C:\Users\*User Name*\AppData\Roaming\Autodesk\AutoCAD 2015\R20.0\enu\Support folder. You can access the criteria list at any time by opening the Current drop-down list and choosing its name.

### FILTERING OBJECTS BY LOCATION

Notice the X, Y, and Z drop-down lists just below the main Select Filter drop-down list in the Object Selection Filters dialog box. These lists become accessible when you select a criterion that describes a geometric property or a coordinate (such as an arc's radius or center point). You can use these lists to define filter selections even more specifically, using greater than (>), less than (<), equal to or greater than (>=), equal to or less than (<=), equal to (=), or not equal to (!=) (called *relational operators*).

For example, suppose you want to grab all the circles whose radii are greater than 4.0 units. To do this, choose Circle Radius from the Select Filter drop-down list. Then, in the X list, select >. Enter **4.0** in the text box to the right of the X list, and click Add To List. The items

```
Circle Radius > 4.0000
Object = Circle
```

are added to the list box at the top of the dialog box. You used the > operator to indicate a circle radius greater than 4.0 units.

## CREATING COMPLEX SELECTION SETS

At times, you'll want to create a specific filter list. For instance, say you need to filter out all the Door blocks on the layer Floor2 *and* all arcs with a radius equal to 1. To do this, you use the *grouping operators* found at the bottom of the Select Filter drop-down list. You'll need to build a list as follows:

```
** Begin OR
** Begin AND
Block Name = Door
Layer = Floor2
** End AND
** Begin AND
Entity = Arc
Arc Radius = 1.0000
** End AND
** End OR
```

Notice that the Begin and End operators are balanced; that is, for every Begin OR or Begin AND, there is an End OR or End AND.

This list may look simple, but it can get confusing. If criteria are bounded by the AND grouping operators, objects must fulfill *both* criterion before they're selected. If criteria are bounded by the OR grouping operators, objects fulfilling *either* criterion will be selected. If you add the wrong option accidentally, select it from the list and click the Delete button. If you need to insert an option in the middle of the list, select the item that comes after the item you want to insert, and then select and add the item.

Here are the steps to build the previous list:

1. In the Select Filter drop-down list, choose **Begin OR, and then click Add To List. Do the same for **Begin AND.

2. Click Block Name in the Select Filter drop-down list, click the Select button, and select Door from the list that appears. Click Add To List.

3. For the layer, click Layer in the Select Filter drop-down list. Click Select, choose the layer name, and click Add To List.

4. In the Select Filter drop-down list, choose **End AND, and then click Add To List. Do the same for **Begin AND.

**5.** Select Arc from the Select Filter drop-down list, and click Add To List.

**6.** Select Arc Radius from the Select Filter list, and enter **1.0** in the text box next to the X drop-down list. Be sure the equal sign (=) shows in the X drop-down list, and then click Add To List.

**7.** Choose **End AND, and click Add To List. Do the same for **End OR.

If you make an error in any step, highlight the item, select an item to replace it, and click the Substitute button instead of the Add To List button. If you need only to change a value, click the Edit Item button near the center of the dialog box.

---

### QUICK ACCESS TO YOUR FAVORITE COMMANDS

As IT managers, we've discovered that AutoCAD users are possessive of their keyboard and tool shortcuts, and they are usually the first custom item that a new employee will install. You can collect your favorite commands into a single toolbar or Ribbon panel by using the AutoCAD customization feature. This way, you can have ready access to your most frequently used commands. Chapter 24, "Customizing Toolbars, Menus, Linetypes, and Hatch Patterns," gives you all the information you need to create your own custom toolbars and Ribbon panels.

---

## Using Quick Select

The Filter command offers a lot of power in isolating specific types of objects, but in many situations you may not need such an elaborate tool. The Quick Select dialog box can filter your selection based on the object properties, which are the more common filter criteria. To access the Quick Select dialog box, click Quick Select in the Home tab's Utilities panel, or right-click the drawing area when no command is active and choose Quick Select from the context menu.

Quick Select is also offered as an option in a few other dialog boxes. Try using the Wblock command again, this time using the Quick Select option offered in its dialog box:

**1.** With the Unit.dwg file open, type **W**↵ to start the Wblock command. Then, in the Write Block dialog box, enter **Unitwall2** in the File Name And Path text box.

**2.** Make sure the Objects radio button is selected at the top of the dialog box and the Delete From Drawing option is selected from the Objects group.

**3.** Click the Quick Select tool to the right of the Select Objects button in the Objects group to open the Quick Select dialog box (see Figure 14.21).

**4.** Select Layer from the Properties list.

**5.** Select Wall from the Value drop-down list near the bottom of the dialog box.

**6.** Click the Select Objects button in the upper-right corner of the dialog box. The dialog boxes close so that you can select objects.

**7.** Select the entire drawing by using a window; press ↵ to finish your selection. Both dialog boxes return.

**FIGURE 14.21**
The Quick Select
dialog box

8. Click OK, and then click OK in the Write Block dialog box. The walls disappear, indicating that they have been written to a file.

9. Click the Undo button to undo the deletion.

The Qselect command selects objects based on their properties, as shown in the Properties list box. You can apply the selection criteria based on the entire drawing, or you can use the Select Objects button in the upper-right corner of the dialog box to isolate a set of objects to which you want to apply the selection criteria.

In the previous exercise, you used Quick Select from within another dialog box. As mentioned earlier, you can also use Quick Select by clicking Quick Select in the Home tab's Utilities panel or by right-clicking the drawing area when no command is active and choosing Quick Select from the context menu. Quick Select then uses the Noun/Verb selection method: You select objects using Quick Select first, and then you apply editing commands to the selected objects.

If you want to use Quick Select with a command that doesn't allow the Noun/Verb selection method, you can select objects by using Quick Select, start the command you want to use, and then use the Previous Selection option.

Here is a description of the Quick Select dialog box options:

**Apply To** Lets you determine the set of objects to which you want to apply the Quick Select filters. The default is the entire drawing, but you can use the Select Objects button to select a set of objects. If you select a set of objects before issuing the Quick Select command, you also see the Current Selection option in the Apply To drop-down list.

**Object Type** Lets you limit the filter to specific types of objects such as lines, arcs, circles, and so on. The Multiple option lets you filter your selection from all the objects in the drawing regardless of type.

**Properties** Lets you select the property of the object type you want to filter, after you select an object type. The Properties list changes to reflect the properties that are available to be filtered.

**Operator** Offers a set of criteria to apply to the property you select in the Properties list to make your selection. You can select objects that are equal to or not equal to the criteria you select in the Object Type and Properties lists. Depending on the property you select, you also may have the option to select objects that are greater than or less than a given property value. For example, you can select all lines whose x-coordinate is less than 5 by choosing Line from the Object Type drop-down list and Start X from the Properties list. You then select < Less Than from the Operator drop-down list and enter **5** in the Value box.

**Value** Displays the values of the property you select in the Properties list. For example, if you select Layer from the Properties list, the Value option lists all the layers available.

**How To Apply** Lets you specify whether to include or exclude the filtered objects in a new selection set.

**Append To Current Selection Set** Lets you append the filtered objects to an existing selection set or create an entirely new selection set.

---

**SELECT SIMILAR OBJECTS OR ISOLATE OBJECT FOR EASIER EDITING**

There are a few features in the context menu that can help speed up object selection. If you select an object and right-click, you'll see the Select Similar option:

Just as the name implies, it will select all objects in the drawing that are similar to the one currently selected. For example, if you select a hatch pattern, right-click, and then click Select Similar, all the hatch patterns in the drawing will be selected. Click on a line, right-click, and then click Select Similar and all the lines that are on the selected line's layer will be selected. You can also use the Selectsimilar command to do the same thing.

You can control how the Select Similar feature behaves by entering **Selectsimilar⏎SE⏎**. This opens the Select Similar Settings dialog box, which lets you set the basis for the similar selection such as layer, color, or linetype, to name a few.

Another handy right-click option is Isolate. If you have a set of objects and you right-click and select Isolate ➤ Isolate Objects, all but the selected objects will be made invisible. Or you can right-click and select Isolate ➤ Hide Objects to hide the selected objects. To bring back the objects that were made invisible, right-click and select Isolate ➤ End Object Isolation.

# Using the QuickCalc Calculator

You may have noticed a calculator icon in some of the options in the Properties palette or in the context menu. This is the QuickCalc tool. If you click it, you'll see the QuickCalc calculator, shown in Figure 14.22. At first glance, it looks like a typical calculator. It has the standard math as well as the scientific functions that are available when you click the More button. If your view of QuickCalc doesn't look like Figure 14.22, click the More/Less button and then expand the Number Pad or Scientific section by clicking the arrow in the title bar. You'll also see a section for converting units, which comes in handy when you want to find the metric equivalent of an Imperial measurement.

**FIGURE 14.22**

QuickCalc and its parts

At the bottom is a section for variables. This area lets you store custom formulas and values to which you want to refer frequently.

Near the top is the display area. This is where QuickCalc keeps a running record of your calculation results. It also allows you to recall both the results and formulas you've used. Just below the display area is the text box. As you type, or as you click the keys of QuickCalc, your input appears in this box. Pressing Enter displays the resulting value both in the text box and in the display area.

Above the display area is a set of tools. These tools let you obtain other types of data from the drawing, such as the coordinate of a point or the intersection of two lines (see Figure 14.23).

**FIGURE 14.23**

The QuickCalc tools

The function of these tools will become clearer as you become familiar with QuickCalc. Table 14.2 describes each tool. Next, you'll get a chance to try out QuickCalc on some typical AutoCAD tasks.

**TABLE 14.2:**     QuickCalc tools

| TOOL | PURPOSE |
| --- | --- |
| Clear | Clears the value from the text box. |
| Clear History | Clears the display area. |
| Paste Value To Command Line | Pastes data from the text box to the command line. |
| Get Coordinates | Temporarily closes QuickCalc and prompts you to pick a point or points. Coordinates of the point or the angle value are placed in the input area. |
| Distance Between Two Points | Temporarily closes QuickCalc and prompts you to enter a point. Select two points; the distance between the points is placed in the input area of QuickCalc. |
| Angle Of Line Defined By Two Points | Returns the angle of two points. |
| Intersection Of Two Lines Defined By Four Points | Returns the coordinate of the intersection of four points. |

## Adding Foot and Inch Lengths and Finding the Sum of Angles

Although QuickCalc may look simple, it provides a powerful aid in your work in AutoCAD. Besides offering the typical calculator functions, QuickCalc also lets you quickly add and subtract angle values, feet-and-inches lengths, and much more. You can paste the results from calculations into the command line so that you can easily include results as part of command-line responses.

To get a full appreciation of what QuickCalc can do for you, try the following exercises.

Imagine that you have a renovation project for which someone has taken dimensions in the field. You may be asked to draw a section of wall for which the overall dimension isn't given but portions of the wall are dimensioned in a sketch, as shown in Figure 14.24.

**FIGURE 14.24**
A sketch of measurements taken from an existing building

You can use QuickCalc to add a series of feet-and-inches dimensions:

1. Open the `QuickCalc.dwg` sample file, which contains some lines with which you can work. It's set up to use architectural units.

2. Right-click, and select the QuickCalc tool from the context menu.

3. Double-click in the QuickCalc text box, and then enter **4'+36+5'6**. As you type, your entry appears in the text box (see Figure 14.25).

**FIGURE 14.25**

The QuickCalc text box

4. Press ↵. The sum of the lengths, 12'-6", appears in the text box and in the display area.

Notice that you only had to enter the foot (') sign. QuickCalc assumes that a value is in inches unless you specify otherwise. You can also enter distances in the more traditional way using dashes and zeros, as in 4'-0" or 5'-6". QuickCalc ignores the dashes.

Now, suppose you want to use your newfound length to draw a line. You can quickly add the results from the text box to the command line, as shown in the following exercise:

1. Click the Line tool, and then click a point in the left portion of the drawing area.

2. In the QuickCalc toolbar, click the Paste Value To Command Line tool. Notice that the value in the text box appears in the command line.

3. Make sure the Polar Tracking mode is turned on in the status bar.

4. While pointing the rubber-banding line directly to the right, press ↵. A horizontal line is drawn to the length of 12'-6".

5. Press ↵ to end the Line command.

In this example, you used the Paste Value To Command Line tool in the QuickCalc toolbar. If you want to use a value that has scrolled up in the display area, you can select that value, right-click, and choose Paste To Command Line (see Figure 14.26).

This approach is especially useful when you've used QuickCalc to add several strings of dimensions and you need to recall them individually from the display area. In addition to adding feet and inches, you can perform other math functions, such as dividing a length by 2 or multiplying a length. If the input value is in feet and inches, the resulting value is returned in feet and inches. For example, if you divide 25' by 6, the result is 4'-2".

**FIGURE 14.26**

The Paste To Command Line option in the context menu

Another useful QuickCalc tool is Angle Of Line Defined By Two Points, which allows you to obtain the angle defined by two points:

1. In QuickCalc, click the Angle Of Line Defined By Two Points tool. QuickCalc temporarily closes to allow you to select points.

2. With osnaps turned on, select the endpoints of the lower line, starting with the bottom endpoint, as shown in Figure 14.27.

**FIGURE 14.27**

Select these endpoints using the Angle Of Line Defined By Two Points option.

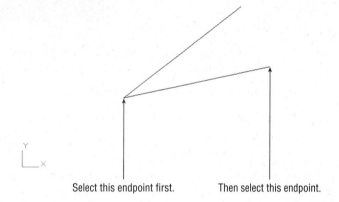

Select this endpoint first.  Then select this endpoint.

3. Back in QuickCalc, click the plus button in the number pad or enter **+**. Then click the Angle Of Line Defined By Two Points tool again.

4. Select the endpoints of the upper line, starting with the bottom end of the line.

5. Back in QuickCalc, you see the angle value of the second line added to the text box. Click the equal button in the QuickCalc number pad to get the total angle value.

Here you added the angle of two lines, but you could just as easily have subtracted one angle from another or multiplied the value of a single angle. This can be useful if you need to find a fraction or a multiple of an angle. For example, you might need to find one-quarter of the angle described by a line, or you might want to find the angle that bisects two lines. You can do so by adding the value of two angles, as described in the exercise, and then dividing by 2 using the number pad or by including **/2** in the text box. Once you've obtained a value, you can paste it into the command line while specifying angles for drawing input.

## Converting Units with QuickCalc

In addition to performing math functions on distances and angles, you can do some basic unit conversions. QuickCalc performs length, area, volume, and angle conversions in its Units Conversion group. Try the following exercise to learn how to convert a length from centimeters to feet and inches. In the process, you'll also learn how you can move a value from the Units Conversion area to the QuickCalc text box.

Suppose you have a paper drawing that was done in metric and you need to turn it into an AutoCAD drawing in feet and inches. Here's an example of how you can convert centimeters to feet and inches:

1. In QuickCalc, expand the Units Conversion section by clicking the arrow to the right of the Units Conversion title bar (see Figure 14.28).

**FIGURE 14.28**

The expanded Units Conversion section

2. Make sure Length appears for the Units Type option. If not, click in the box to the right of the Units Type option and select Length from the drop-down list that appears.

3. Select Centimeters from the Convert From drop-down list.

4. Select Feet from the Convert To drop-down list.

5. In the Value To Convert box, enter **450**↵ for 450 cm. The equivalent value in feet appears in the Converted Value box.

6. Click the Converted Value option, and you also see the QuickCalc icon to the far right. Click this icon to display the value in the text box at the top of QuickCalc.

The value is in feet and decimal feet. You can convert the value to feet and inches by doing the following:

1. Edit the value in the text box to read as follows: **14′ +(.7637795*12)**.

2. Press ↵. The value converts to a feet-and-inches value of 14′-9 3⁄16″.

One limitation to the unit-conversion feature is that it won't take feet-and-inches input when converting from feet. For example, if you want to convert 12′-4″ to centimeters, you have to enter **12.334**. In other words, you have to convert the inches to decimal feet. Because the Unit Conversion area is part of QuickCalc, this just means an extra step. You can quickly calculate the decimal feet equivalent of feet and inch values and then transfer them to the Units Conversion area.

Try the following to see how this works:

1. Click the Clear button in the QuickCalc toolbar (it looks like a calculator with a small red X next to it), and then double-click in the QuickCalc text box.

2. Enter **12 + (4 / 12)**↵ in QuickCalc's text box. The first 12 is the 12 feet. The 4 / 12 is for the 4 inches converted to decimal feet. Once you press ↵, the value of 12.3333333 appears.

3. Right-click in the QuickCalc text box, and then click in the Value To Convert box in the Units Conversion panel. The 12.3333333 value is pasted into the text box.

4. Select Feet from the Convert From drop-down list, and select Centimeters from the Convert To drop-down list. The centimeter equivalent of 12.3333333 feet appears in the Converted Value box.

Here you saw how values from the text box automatically transfer to the Units Conversion area. You can also cut and paste values from other sources into either the main calculator text box or the Units Conversion box.

## Using QuickCalc to Find Points

You've seen how QuickCalc will let you add values of distances and angles and how it can perform unit conversions. You can also use it to calculate coordinate locations. To work with coordinates, you need to use a few special functions built into QuickCalc that let you select points and manipulate their value.

AutoCAD offers the Midpoint Between Two Points osnap, which enables you to select a point midway between two other points without drawing a temporary line. The AutoCAD Cal command offers another way to accomplish this. In the following example, you'll use QuickCalc to perform the same function as an example of how you can acquire point data and manipulate it to derive other coordinate locations:

1. Click the Clear button on the QuickCalc toolbar; then double-click in the QuickCalc text box.

2. In the QuickCalc text box, enter **(end + end)/2**↵. QuickCalc closes temporarily to allow you to select points.

3. Select the endpoints of the two lines, as shown in Figure 14.29.

**FIGURE 14.29**
The endpoints of
the two lines

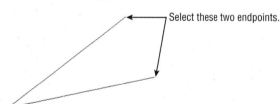

Select these two endpoints.

4. QuickCalc returns and displays the coordinates of a point exactly between the two endpoints you selected in step 3.

In step 2, you used the *end* function that is built into QuickCalc. As you saw, the end function lets you select the endpoint of an object (as you did in step 3). The end + end in the formula tells

QuickCalc to add the two coordinates you selected in step 3. The /2 in the formula divides the sum of the coordinates to find their average, which happens to be the midpoint between the two points.

If you were to perform this calculation using pencil and paper, you would add the x-, y-, and z-coordinate values of each point separately and then divide each coordinate by 2. Finally, you would combine the resulting x-, y-, and z-coordinates back into a single point location.

### USING OSNAP MODES IN QUICKCALC EXPRESSIONS

In the previous exercise, you used osnap modes as part of arithmetic formulas (or *expressions*, as they're called in AutoCAD). QuickCalc treats osnap modes as temporary placeholders for point coordinates until you pick the points.

The expression

```
(end + end)/2
```

finds the average of two values. In this case, the values are coordinates, so the average is the midpoint between the two coordinates. You can take this one step further and find the centroid of a triangle by using this expression:

```
(end + end + end)/3
```

Note that you enter only the first three letters of the osnap mode in calculator expressions. Table 14.3 shows what to enter in an expression for osnap modes. The table includes two items that aren't really osnap modes, although they work similarly when they're used in an expression. The first is Rad. When you include Rad in an expression, you get the following prompt:

```
Select circle, arc or polyline segment for RAD function:
```

You can then select an arc, a polyline arc segment, or a circle to obtain a radius for the expression.

**TABLE 14.3:** The geometry calculator's osnap modes

| CALCULATOR OSNAP | MEANING |
| --- | --- |
| End | Endpoint |
| Ins | Insert |
| Int | Intersection |
| Mid | Midpoint |
| Cen | Center |
| Nea | Nearest |
| Nod | Node |
| Qua | Quadrant |

| CALCULATOR OSNAP | MEANING |
|---|---|
| Per | Perpendicular |
| Tan | Tangent |
| Rad | Radius of object |
| Cur | Cursor pick |

The other item, Cur, prompts you for a point. Instead of looking for specific geometry on an object, it just locates a point. You could have used Cur in the previous exercise in place of the End and Cen modes to create a more general-purpose midpoint locator, as in the following formula:

```
(cur + cur)/2
```

### PASTING TO THE COMMAND LINE

Now that you have the coordinate for the midpoint, try the next exercise to apply that coordinate to a command. In this example, you'll use the coordinate found in step 3 as the starting point for a line:

1. Click the Line tool on the Draw panel.

2. In QuickCalc, right-click the (end + end)/2 listing in the display area, and then select Paste To Command Line (see Figure 14.30).

**FIGURE 14.30**
Select Paste To Command Line.

3. The coordinate value from the display area is pasted into the command line at the Line command's Specify first point: prompt. Press ↵ to accept the input from QuickCalc. You see a rubber-banding line beginning at a point midway between the two endpoints of the lines you selected in the previous exercise (see Figure 14.31).

4. Click another point to place the line in the drawing, and then press ↵ to exit the Line command.

**FIGURE 14.31**

Starting a line between two endpoints

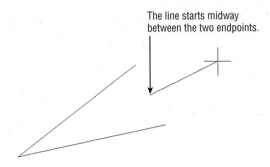

The line starts midway between the two endpoints.

## Finding Fractional Distances between Two Points

Another ability AutoCAD users commonly need is to find a location that is a fractional distance along a line. For example, users frequently need to find a point that is one-third the distance from the endpoint of a line. Here's how that can be accomplished using QuickCalc:

1. If the QuickCalc text box is not clear, click the Clear tool in the QuickCalc toolbar.

2. Enter **plt (end, end, 0.333).⏎** in the QuickCalc text box. QuickCalc closes temporarily to allow you to select points.

3. Click the endpoints of the line shown in Figure 14.32, starting with the lower-left endpoint. QuickCalc returns with the coordinates of a point that is 33.33 percent of the length of the line from the first endpoint you selected.

**FIGURE 14.32**

Select these points to find a point that is one-third the distance from an endpoint.

Click the endpoints of this line.

4. Click the Line tool.

5. Click in the QuickCalc display area on the last entry, right-click, and choose Paste To Command Line.

6. Press ⏎ and you see a line start at a point that is one-third the distance from the endpoint (see Figure 14.33).

7. Press Esc to exit the Line command. You don't need to draw the line because this exercise is intended to show you only how the formula in step 1 works.

**FIGURE 14.33**
A line starting at a
point that is one-
third the distance
from the endpoint

In step 1, you used a formula that contained the plt function. This function finds a point that is a particular percentage between two points. You specify the two points first, using the now-familiar end function, and then you specify the percentage between the two endpoints as a decimal value. The (end, end, 0.333) indicates the two endpoints you selected in step 2 and the percentage as a decimal value of 0.333.

In the formulas you've seen so far, you've used the end function to select endpoints. If you prefer to select your own osnaps during the point-selection process, you can use the cur function. Cur lets you use any osnap you want when selecting points. In the first example, you could use (cur + cur)/2 instead of (end + end)/2.

The plt function is just one of several special functions you can use with QuickCalc. Table 14.4 lists other functions you can use to find points in your drawing and gather other data. In the table, 2D points are represented as pt1, pt2, and so on. Three-dimensional points, or points describing a plane, are indicated by ptp1, ptp3, and so on. The center of an arc or a circle is indicated with *apex* for a 2D location and *apex1* and *apex2* for a 3D axis.

**TABLE 14.4:**   Functions in QuickCalc and the formats for their use

| FUNCTION AND FORMAT | DESCRIPTION |
| --- | --- |
| Getvar(*system variable name*) | Gets the value of a system variable |
| Vec(*pt1,pt2*) | Returns the vector described by the distance between the two points |
| Vec1(*pt1,pt2*) | Returns the vector described by 1 unit length |
| Abs(*vector*) | Returns the absolute value of the length of a vector |
| Cur(no arguments required) | Gets a point |
| @(no arguments required) | Returns the last point |
| w2u(*point*) and u2w(*point*) | Converts world coordinates to current user coordinates (w2u) or user coordinates to world |
| Pld(*pt1,pt2,distance*) | Returns the point on a line at a specified distance |
| Plt(*pt1,pt2,percent*) | Returns the point on a line at a percentage (decimal) of the line length |
| Rot(*pt1,apex,angle*) or Rot(*pt1,apex1,apex2,angle*) | Returns the rotation angle of a point (pt1) about an apex |

**TABLE 14.4:** Functions in QuickCalc and the formats for their use *(continued)*

| FUNCTION AND FORMAT | DESCRIPTION |
|---|---|
| Ill(*pt1,pt2,pt3,pt4*) | Returns the intersection between two lines |
| Ilp(*pt1,pt2,ptp1,ptp2,ptp3*) | Returns the intersection between a line and a plane; five points required |
| Dist(*pt1,pt2*) | Returns the distance between two points |
| Dpl(*point,pt1,pt2*) | Returns the shortest distance between a point and a line |
| Dpp(*point,ptp1,ptp2,ptp3*) | Returns the shortest distance between a point and a plane |
| Rad (no arguments required) | Returns a radius |
| Ang(*vector* or *pt1,pt2* or *apex,pt1,pt2* or *apex1,pt1,pt2,apex2*) | Returns an angle; can use up to four parameters when working in 3D |
| Nor(*vector* or *pt1,pt2* or *ptp1,ptp2,ptp3*) | Finds the normal of a vector or plane |

## Using QuickCalc While in the Middle of a Command

In all the previous examples, you've used QuickCalc as a stand-alone calculator. You've also seen how you can insert a calculation into the command line while a command is in progress. A third way to work with QuickCalc is to open it while in the middle of a command.

In a previous exercise, you used the (end + end)/2 formula to find the midpoint between two points, and then you inserted the resulting value into the Line command. Suppose you start the Line command before you open QuickCalc. Try the following to see how you can use QuickCalc once a command has been initiated:

1. Close QuickCalc.

2. Start the Line command.

3. Enter **'qc↵** to open QuickCalc.

4. In the QuickCalc text box, type **(end + end)/2** but don't press ↵. Instead, click the Apply button at the bottom of the QuickCalc window.

5. Select the endpoints of two lines. A line starts at the midpoint between the two points.

6. Click another point to draw the line, and then press ↵ to end the Line command.

In this exercise, you saw that an Apply option appears at the bottom of the QuickCalc window along with Close and Help buttons. These buttons aren't present when you open QuickCalc with no command active. The Apply button executes the formula and then immediately returns the resulting value to the command. Using QuickCalc in this way eliminates a few steps.

You may have also noticed that QuickCalc appeared with a light background instead of a dark one. This can serve as a reminder that you are using QuickCalc in the middle of another command.

### FINDING A POINT RELATIVE TO ANOTHER POINT

Now, suppose you want to start a line at a relative distance from another line. The following steps describe how to use the calculator to start a line from a point that is 2.5" in the x-axis and 5.0" in the y-axis from the endpoint of another line:

1. Make sure QuickCalc is closed, start the Line command, and select a point.

2. Right-click, select the QuickCalc tool, and type **end + [2.5,5.0]** in the text box.

3. Click the Apply button at the bottom of the QuickCalc window.

4. Click the endpoint of the line you just drew. The new line connects to a point that is at a distance of 2.5 in the x-axis and 5.0 in the y-axis from the endpoint you selected.

In this example, you used the Endpoint osnap mode to indicate a point of reference. This is added to Cartesian coordinates in square brackets, describing the distance and direction from the reference point. You could enter any coordinate value within the square brackets. You also could enter a polar coordinate in place of the Cartesian coordinate, as in the following: **end + [5.59<63]**.

You can replace the *end* in the expression with the at sign (@) to continue from the last point you selected. Also, it's not necessary to include every coordinate in the square brackets. For example, to indicate a displacement in only one axis, you can leave out a value for the other two coordinates while leaving in the commas, as in the following examples:

```
[4,5] = [4,5,0]
[,1] = [0,1,0]
[,,2] = [0,0,2]
```

### COMBINING COORDINATES AND EXPRESSIONS

In the previous two examples, you saw that you can use an expression or enter coordinates. But what if you want to combine an expression within a coordinate? For example, in the beginning of this section, you added feet and inches and then transferred the result to the command line. In that example, you had to switch back and forth between QuickCalc and the command line to create the response for the Command prompt. If you prefer, you can create an expression that supplies the entire command input. Here are the steps to do this:

1. Close QuickCalc, and then start the Line command.

2. Enter **'qc↵** to open QuickCalc.

3. Enter the following in the text box:

   ```
   End + [(4'+36+5'6)<45]
   ```

4. Click Apply.

5. In the drawing area, click the endpoint of a line. AutoCAD draws a line that begins at 12'-6" and at a 45 angle to the endpoint you select.

In this exercise, you used the expression (4′+36+5′6) right in the middle of a coordinate value. As described earlier, the coordinate is within square brackets. By using this method, you can calculate measurements and apply them to commands more easily. The trick is to become familiar with the syntax QuickCalc requires so you can write these expressions without errors.

## Storing Expressions and Values

The ability to create expressions to manipulate coordinates can be useful, but you may find it difficult to remember an expression once you've created it. Fortunately, QuickCalc offers the Variables section, which allows you to store frequently used expressions and values.

At the bottom of the QuickCalc window is the Variables section, which has its set of tools in its title bar (see Figure 14.34).

**FIGURE 14.34**

The Variables group

These tools let you add items to the list, edit items, or delete items from the list. A fourth option lets you send a variable to the main calculator text box. You can also right-click in the Variables section list box and select the same options from a context menu. In addition, the context menu lets you create a new category and rename an existing one.

The Variables section also contains a list of currently stored variables. Some sample variables are shown in the list. If you select a variable, you see a description of that variable's function at the bottom of the group. You may need to click the bottom edge of the QuickCalc window and drag downward to see the description.

To use an existing variable, select it from the list and click the Return Variable To Input Area button; it looks like a calculator. To add a variable to the list, click the New Variable button, which opens the Variable Definition dialog box (see Figure 14.35).

This dialog box lets you enter the properties of the variable and choose the type. In the Variable Properties group, you enter the name of the variable in the Name text box. In the Group With drop-down list, you select a category under which your formula will appear in the Variables list. You can also create a new category. The Value Or Expression box is where you put your formula; it can also be a single value, such as a number or a coordinate. At the bottom is a space to enter a description for the variable. This description will appear in the Variables group's detail box at the bottom of QuickCalc.

At the top, in the Variable Type group, you see two options: Constant and Function. If you choose Function, your variable will behave as it normally does when you enter it in the text box.

If you choose Constant and your variable is a formula, your variable will be executed when you close the Variable Definition dialog box. The resulting value will become the value for the variable.

**FIGURE 14.35**
The Variable Defini-
tion dialog box

To edit an existing variable, highlight it in the Variables group list, and then click the Edit Variable button to open the Variable Definition dialog box.

## Guidelines for Working with QuickCalc

You may notice some patterns in the way expressions are formatted for the calculator. Here are some guidelines to remember:

♦ Coordinates are enclosed in square brackets.

♦ Nested or grouped expressions are enclosed in parentheses.

♦ Operators are placed between values, as in simple math equations.

♦ Object snaps can be used in place of coordinate values.

Table 14.5 lists all the operators and functions available in QuickCalc. You may want to experiment with these functions on your own. You can enter many of these operators using the keys on the number pad or in the scientific group.

**TABLE 14.5:**   The QuickCalc functions

| OPERATOR/FUNCTION | WHAT IT DOES | EXAMPLE |
| --- | --- | --- |
| + or – | Adds or subtracts numbers or vectors | $2 – 1 = 1$[a,b,c] + [x,y,z] = [a+x, b+y, c+z] |
| * or / | Multiplies or divides numbers or vectors | $2 * 4.2 = 8.4$a*[x,y,z] = [a*x, a*y, a*z] |

**TABLE 14.5:** The QuickCalc functions *(continued)*

| OPERATOR/FUNCTION | WHAT IT DOES | EXAMPLE |
|---|---|---|
| ^ | Returns the exponent of a number | 3^2 = 9 |
| Sin | Returns the sine of an angle | sin (45) = 0.707107 |
| Cos | Returns the cosine of an angle | cos (30) = 0.866025 |
| Tang | Returns the tangent of an angle | tang (30) = 0.57735 |
| Asin | Returns the arcsine of a real number | asin (0.707107) = 45.0 |
| Acos | Returns the arccosine of a real number | acos (0.866025) = 30.0 |
| Atan | Returns the arctangent of a real number | atan (0.57735) = 30.0 |
| Ln | Returns the natural log | ln (2) = 0.693147 |
| Log | Returns the base-10 log | log (2) = 0.30103 |
| Exp | Returns the natural exponent | exp (2) = 7.38906 |
| exp10 | Returns the base-10 exponent | exp10 (2) = 100 |
| Sqr | Squares a number | sqr (9) = 81.0 |
| Abs | Returns the absolute value | abs (–3.4) = 3.4 |
| Rnd | Rounds to the nearest integer | round (3.6) = 4 |
| trunk | Drops the decimal portion of a real number | trunc (3.6) = 3 |
| r2d | Converts radians to degrees | r2d (1.5708) = 90.0002 |
| d2r | Converts degrees to radians | d2r (90) = 1.5708 |
| Pi | Provides the constant pi | 3.14159 |

QuickCalc is capable of much more than the typical uses you've seen here. A description of its full capabilities extends beyond the scope of this book. However, the processes described in these sections will be helpful as you use AutoCAD. If you want to know more about QuickCalc, consult the AutoCAD Help User Documentation (enter **QuickCalc** in the InfoCenter text box).

### SINGLING OUT PROXIMATE OBJECTS

You'll sometimes need to select an object that overlaps or is very close to another object. Often in this situation, you end up selecting the wrong object. To select the exact object you want, you can use the Selection Cycling tool and the Draworder command.

*Selection Cycling* lets you cycle through objects that overlap until you select the one you want. To use this feature, hover over the overlapping objects so that one of them is highlighted; then hold down the Shift key and press the spacebar. With each press of the spacebar, a different overlapping object will be highlighted. When the object you want to select is highlighted, click it.

Another way to gain access to an overlapped object is to use the Draworder command. You can select the overlapping object and then choose Send To Back from the Draworder flyout in the Home tab's expanded Modify panel.

One reason you would want to select an overlapping object is simply to delete a redundant line. AutoCAD offers the Delete Duplicate Object tool, which can be found in the Home tab's expanded Modify panel.

This tool is designed to help you easily remove overlapping objects that are not easily seen. To use it, click the Delete Duplicate Object tool or type **Overkill**↵. At the Select objects: prompt, select the objects that are overlapping. A selection window can be used to select an area. Press ↵ and the Delete Duplicate Objects dialog box appears.

This dialog box gives you control over the criteria AutoCAD uses to determine whether an object should be deleted. Make any changes necessary to the dialog box, and then click OK to remove duplicate overlapping objects.

# The Bottom Line

**Use external references (Xrefs).** You've seen how you can use Xrefs to quickly build variations of a floor plan that contain repetitive elements. This isn't necessarily the only way to use Xrefs, but the basic idea of how to use Xrefs is presented in the early exercises.

**Master It** Try putting together another floor plan that contains nothing but the Unit2 plan.

**Manage layers.** Once you start to edit complex drawings, you'll find that you'll want to save the On/Off or Freeze/Thaw layer states so you can access parts of a drawing more easily. The Layer States Manager lets you save as many layer conditions as you may need in the course of a project.

**Master It** What part of the Layer States Manager dialog box lets you control the layer properties that are affected by a saved layer state?

**Use advanced tools: Filter and Quick Select.** The Filter and Quick Select tools are great for isolating objects in a crowded drawing. You can select objects by their color or layer assignment. You can select all instances of a specific block.

**Master It** True or false: The Quick Select tool lets you select a set of objects to limit your selections.

**Use the QuickCalc calculator.** The QuickCalc calculator offers many standard calculator tools plus a few that you may not see in other calculators.

**Master It** Name a few of the more unusual features offered by the QuickCalc calculator.

# Chapter 15

# Laying Out Your Printer Output

Your set of drawings for the studio apartment building would probably include a larger-scale, more detailed drawing of the typical unit plan. You already have the beginnings of this drawing in the form of the Unit.dwg file.

As you've seen, the notes and dimensions you entered into the Unit.dwg file can be turned off or frozen in the Plan.dwg file so that they don't interfere with the graphics of the drawing. The Unit.dwg file can be part of another drawing file that contains more detailed information about the typical unit plan at a larger scale. To this new drawing, you can add notes, symbols, and dimensions. Whenever the Unit.dwg file is altered, you update its occurrence in the large-scale drawing of the typical unit as well as in the Plan.dwg file. The units are thus quickly updated, and good coordination is ensured among all the drawings for your project.

Now, suppose you want to combine drawings that have different scales in the same drawing file—for example, the overall plan of one floor plus an enlarged view of one typical unit. You can do so using the layout views and a feature called paper space.

In this chapter, you will learn to

♦ Understand model space and paper space

♦ Work with paper space viewports

♦ Create odd-shaped viewports

♦ Understand lineweights, linetypes, and dimensions in paper space

## Understanding Model Space and Paper Space

So far, you've explored ways to get around in your drawing while using a single view. This single-view representation of your AutoCAD® drawing is called *Model Space* display mode. You can also set up multiple views of your drawing by using what are called *floating viewports*. You create floating viewports in layout views in what is called *Paper Space* mode.

To get a clear understanding of the Model Space and Paper Space modes, imagine that your drawing is a full-sized replica or model of the object you're drawing. Your computer screen is your window into a "room" where this model is being constructed, and the keyboard and mouse are your means of access to this room. You can control your window's position in relation to the object through the use of Pan, Zoom, View, and other display-related commands. You can also construct or modify the model by using drawing and editing commands. Think of this room as your model space.

You've been working on your drawings by looking through a single window into model space. Now, suppose you can step back and add windows with different views looking into your model space; the effect is like having several video cameras in your model space room, each connected to a different monitor. You can view all your windows at once on your computer screen or enlarge a single window to fill the entire screen. Further, you can control the shape of your windows and easily switch from one window to another. This is what paper space is like.

Paper space lets you create and display multiple views of model space. Each view window, called a *viewport*, acts like an individual virtual screen. One viewport can have an overall view of your drawing while another can be a close-up. You can also control layer visibility individually for each viewport and display different versions of the same area of your drawing. You can move, copy, and stretch viewports and even overlap them. You can set up another type of viewport, called the *tiled viewport*, in model space. Chapter 21, "Using Advanced 3D Features," discusses this type of viewport.

One of the more powerful features of paper space is the ability to plot several views of the same drawing on one sheet of paper. You can also include graphic objects such as borders and notes that appear only in paper space. In this function, paper space acts much like a page-layout program such as QuarkXPress or Adobe InDesign. You can paste up different views of your drawing and then add borders, title blocks, general notes, and other types of graphic and textual data. Figure 15.1 shows the Plan drawing set up in Paper Space mode to display several views.

**FIGURE 15.1**
Different views of the same drawing in paper space

## Switching from Model Space to Paper Space

You can get to paper space by clicking any of the Layout tabs below the drawing area. You can also use the layout previews in the drawing tab.

**DON'T SEE THE LAYOUT TABS?**

If your version of AutoCAD does not show the Layout and Model tabs, you can turn them on by doing the following: Right-click on the Layout1 tool in the status bar and select Display Layout And Model Tabs. To turn the tabs off, right-click on any tab and select Hide Layout And Model Tabs. If you still do not see the tabs, you may need to maximize the drawing area window.

Let's start with the basics of switching between model and paper space:

1. Open the Xref-1 file you saved from the previous chapter, and make sure that your display shows the entire drawing. You can also use 15-xref1.dwg or 15-xref1-metric.dwg.

2. Click the Layout1 tab in the lower-left corner of the drawing area. You see your drawing appear in a kind of page preview view (see Figure 15.2).

**FIGURE 15.2**
Your drawing in a page preview view

3. Click the Model tab in the lower-left corner of the drawing area to return to model space.

This brief exercise shows you how quickly you can shift between model space and paper apace by using the Model and Layout1 tabs.

1. Hover over the drawing tab and you'll see preview images of the model and paper space layouts (see Figure 15.3). The current layout is highlighted with a blue border.

**FIGURE 15.3**
The Drawing tab's model and paper space preview

**2.** Point to Layout1 preview image; the drawing area will temporarily display a full view of the layout.

**3.** Click in the Layout1 image to confirm your selection of the layout view.

**4.** Hover over the drawing tab again, but this time click the preview panel to the left labeled Model.

**5.** Click the Model image to go back to the model space view.

Note that when you hover over a preview image, the Plot and Publish icons appear in the top corners of the image (see Figure 15.4).

**FIGURE 15.4**
The Plot and
Publish icons

If you prefer, you can use keyboard shortcuts to switch between model and paper space. Press Ctrl+PgDn to go from model space to paper space. Press Ctrl+PgUp to go from paper space to model space. If there are several paper space layout tabs, Ctrl+PgDn opens the next layout tab to the right and Ctrl+PgUp opens the next layout tab to the left.

## Setting the Size of a Paper Space Layout

We mentioned that paper space is like a page-layout program, and you saw how a paper space layout looks like a print preview. You can set up your layout for a specific set of printer settings, including the paper size and printer.

Let's continue with our look at paper space by seeing how you can set up a paper space layout for your printer:

**1.** Click the Layout1 tab.

**2.** Right-click the Layout1 tab and choose Page Setup Manager to open the Page Setup Manager. Notice that the name of the current layout is shown in the list of current page setups (see Figure 15.5).

**3.** Click the Modify button to open the Page Setup dialog box.

**4.** Select the Letter paper-size option from the Paper Size drop-down list. Metric users should select A4 (210 mm × 297 mm). The paper size you select here determines the shape and margin of the paper space layout area.

**5.** Select a printer from the Printer/Plotter Name drop-down list.

**6.** Click OK to close the Page Setup dialog box, and then click Close to close the Page Setup Manager.

**FIGURE 15.5**

The Page Setup
Manager

AutoCAD bases the paper space layout on the paper size and printer you specify in steps 4 and 5. The area shown in paper space reflects the area of the paper size you selected in step 4, and the paper margin shown by a dashed line is determined by the printer. If for some reason you need to change the paper size, repeat steps 2 through 5. You can also store the way you've set up your paper space layout using the Page Setup Manager you saw in step 2. See Chapter 8, "Introducing Printing, Plotting, and Layouts," for more on this feature.

## Creating New Paper Space Viewports

As you saw in Chapter 8, the different look of the layout view tells you that you're in paper space. You also learned that a viewport is automatically created when you first open a layout view. The layout viewport displays an overall view of your drawing to no particular scale.

In this section, you'll work with multiple viewports in paper space instead of just the default single viewport you get when you open the layout view.

This first exercise shows you how to create three new viewports at once:

1. Click the viewport's outline to select it. The viewport is the solid rectangle surrounding your drawing, just inside the dashed rectangle.

2. Click the Erase tool in the Home tab's Modify panel to erase the viewport. Your drawing disappears. Don't panic; remember that the viewport is like a window to model space. The objects in model space are still there.

3. Click the Named tool in the Layout tab's Layout Viewports panel to open the Viewports dialog box. You can also type **Vports⏎**.

4. Click the New Viewports tab. This tab contains a set of predefined viewport layouts (see Figure 15.6). You'll learn more about the Viewports dialog box and its options in Chapter 21.

**FIGURE 15.6**
The Viewports
dialog box

5. Click the Three: Above option in the Standard Viewports list box. The box to the right shows a sample view of the Three: Above layout you selected.

6. Click OK. The `Specify first corner or [Fit] <Fit>:` prompt appears.

7. Press ↵ to accept the default Fit option. The Fit option fits the viewport layout to the maximum area allowed in your paper space view. Three rectangles appear in the formation, as shown in Figure 15.7. Each of these is a viewport to your model space. The viewport at the top fills the whole width of the drawing area; the bottom half of the screen is divided into two viewports.

**FIGURE 15.7**
The newly created
viewports

When you create new viewports, AutoCAD automatically fills them with the extents of your model space drawing. You can specify an exact scale for each viewport, as you'll see later.

Notice that the dashed line representing your paper margin has disappeared. That's because the viewports are pushed to the margin limits, thereby covering the dashed line.

You could have kept the original viewport that appeared when you first opened the Layout1 view and then added two new viewports. Completely replacing the single viewport is a bit simpler because the Viewports dialog box fits the viewports in the allowed space for you.

After you've set up a paper space layout, it remains part of the drawing. You may prefer to use model space for doing most of your drawing and then use paper space layouts for setting up views for printing. Changes that you make to your drawing in model space will automatically appear in your paper space layout viewports.

## Reaching Inside Viewports

Now, suppose you need access to the objects in the viewports in order to adjust their display and edit your drawing. Try these steps:

1. Double-click inside a viewport. This gives you control over model space even though you're in paper space. (You can also enter **MS**↵ as a keyboard shortcut to enter Model Space mode.)

   The first thing you notice is that the UCS icon changes back to its L-shaped form. It also appears in each viewport as if you had three AutoCAD windows instead of just one.

2. Move your cursor over each viewport. In one of the viewports, the cursor appears as the AutoCAD crosshair cursor, whereas in the other viewports it appears as an arrow pointer. The viewport that shows the AutoCAD cursor is the active one; you can pan, zoom, and edit objects in the active viewport.

3. Click in the lower-left viewport to activate it.

4. Click Window from the Zoom flyout on the View tab's Navigate 2D panel, and place a window selection around the elevator area.

5. Click the lower-right viewport, and choose Zoom Window from the Zoom flyout on the Navigation bar to enlarge your view of a typical unit. You can also use the Pan and Zoom Realtime tools. If you don't see the UCS icon, it has been turned off. Type **UCSicon**↵**On**↵ to turn it on. See Chapter 21 for more on the UCS icon.

You can move from viewport to viewport even while you're in the middle of most commands. For example, you can issue the Line command, pick the start point in one viewport, go to a different viewport to pick the next point, and so on. To activate a different viewport, you click inside the viewport (see Figure 15.8).

**FIGURE 15.8**
The three viewports, each with a different view of the plan

Model Space UCS icon

---

### SWITCHING BETWEEN VIEWPORTS

We've found that users will have a need to overlap viewports from time to time. When they do this, they are often at a loss over how to switch between the overlapping viewports, especially when one is completely surrounded by another or when they are exactly the same size and in the same position. In this situation, you can move between viewports by pressing Ctrl+R repeatedly until you get to the viewport you want.

---

You've seen how you can zoom into a viewport view, but what happens when you use the Zoom command while in paper space? Try the following exercise to find out:

1. Double-click an area outside the viewports to get out of Floating model space.

2. Click Zoom Realtime from the Zoom flyout in the Navigation bar and then zoom into the paper space view. The entire view enlarges, including the views in the viewports.

> Zoom Realtime

3. Right-click, and select Close Preview Window. Click All from the Zoom flyout or enter Z↵A↵ to return to the overall view of paper space.

This brief exercise showed that you can use the Zoom tool in paper space just as you would in model space. All the display-related commands are available, including the Pan Realtime command.

## Working with Paper Space Viewports

Paper space is intended as a page-layout or composition tool. You can manipulate viewports' sizes, scale their views independently of one another, and even set layering and linetype scales independently.

Let's try manipulating the shape and location of viewports by using the Home tab's Modify panel options:

1. Make sure Object Snap is turned off in the status bar.

2. Make sure you're in a layout view. Then click the bottom edge of the lower-left viewport to expose its grips (see the top image in Figure 15.9).

3. Click the upper-right grip, and drag it to the location shown in the top image in Figure 15.9.

4. Press the Esc key, and erase the lower-right viewport by selecting it and clicking Erase in the Home tab's Modify panel or by pressing the Delete key.

5. Move the lower-left viewport so that it's centered in the bottom half of the window as shown in the bottom image in Figure 15.9.

In this exercise, you clicked the viewport edge to select it for editing. If while in paper space you attempt to click the image in the viewport, you won't select anything. Later, you'll see that you can use the osnap modes to snap to parts of the drawing image in a viewport.

Because viewports are recognized as AutoCAD objects, you can manipulate them by using all the editing commands just as you would manipulate any other object. In the previous exercise, you moved, stretched, and erased viewports. Next, you'll see how layers affect viewports:

1. Create a new layer called **Vport**.

2. Using the Properties palette, assign the viewports to the Vport layer.

3. Turn off the Vport layer. The viewport outlines disappear.

4. After reviewing the results of step 3, turn the Vport layer back on.

You can assign a layer, a color, a linetype, and even a lineweight to a viewport's outline. If you put the viewport on a layer that has been turned off or frozen, that outline becomes invisible, just like any other object on such a layer. Or you can put the viewport on a nonprinting layer so that the outline will be visible while you're editing. Making a viewport's outlines invisible or putting them on a nonprinting layer is helpful when you want to compose a final sheet for printing. Even when turned off, the active viewport has a heavy outline around it when you switch to Floating model space, and all the viewports still display their views.

**FIGURE 15.9**
Stretching, erasing, and moving viewports

Stretch the viewport grip to this location.

Move the viewport here.

## Scaling Views in Paper Space

Paper space has its own unit of measure. You've already seen how you're required to specify a paper size when opening a layout view to a paper space view. When you first enter paper space, regardless of the area your drawing occupies in model space, you're given limits that are set by the paper size you specify in the Page Setup dialog box. If you keep in mind that paper space is like a paste-up area that is dependent on the printer you configured for AutoCAD, this difference of scale becomes easier to comprehend. Just as you might paste up photographs and maps representing several square miles onto an 11″ × 17″ board, so too can you use paper space to paste up views of scale drawings representing city blocks or houses on an 8½″ × 11″ sheet of paper. But in AutoCAD, you have the freedom to change the scale and size of the objects you're pasting up.

While in paper space, you can edit objects in a model space viewport, but to do so you must use Floating model space. To get to Floating model space, double-click inside a viewport. You can then click inside any viewport and edit in that viewport. In this mode, objects that were created in paper space can't be edited. Double-click outside a viewport to go back to the paper space environment.

If you want to be able to print your drawing at a specific scale, you must indicate a scale for each viewport. Viewport scales are set in a way similar to the annotation scale in the Model tab. Let's see how to put together a sheet in paper space and still maintain accuracy of scale:

1. Make sure you're in paper space. You can tell by the shape and location of the UCS icon. If it looks like a triangle in the lower-left corner of the layout view, then you are in paper space.

2. Click the topmost viewport's outline to select it.

3. In the lower-right portion of the AutoCAD window, click the Viewport Scale drop-down list, and select 1/32″ = 1'-0″. Metric users should click Custom and add a custom scale of 1:400. Then select the 1:400 scale from the Viewport Scale drop-down list. Notice how the view in the upper viewport changes.

4. Press the Esc key twice to clear the selection of the viewport.

5. Click the lower viewport border.

6. Click the Viewport Scale drop-down list again, and select 3/16″ = 1'-0″ from the list. Metric users should select 1:50. The view in the viewport changes to reflect the new scale (see Figure 15.10).

**FIGURE 15.10**
Paper space view-
port views scaled
to 1/32″ = 1'-0″ and
3/16″ = 1'-0″ (1:400
and 1:100 for
metric users)

It's easy to adjust the width, height, and location of the viewports so that they display only the parts of the unit you want to see. While in paper space, use the Stretch, Move, Scale, or Rotate command to edit any viewport border, or use the viewport's grips to edit its size and shape. The view in the viewport remains at the same scale and location while the viewport changes in size. You can move and stretch viewports with no effect on the size and location of the objects in the view. When you rotate the viewport, the view inside the viewport will also rotate.

If you need to overlay one drawing on top of another, you can overlap viewports. Use the osnap overrides to select geometry in each viewport, even while in paper space. This lets you align one viewport on top of another at exact locations.

You can also add a title block in paper space at a 1:1 scale to frame your viewports and then plot this drawing from paper space at a scale of 1:1. Your plot appears just as it does in paper space at the appropriate scale. Paper space displays a dashed line to show you where the non-printable areas occur near the edge of the paper.

While you're working in paper space, pay close attention to whether you're in paper space or Floating model space. It's easy to pan or zoom in a Floating model space viewport accidentally when you intend to pan or zoom your paper space view. This can cause you to lose your viewport scaling or alignment with other parts of the drawing.

It's a good idea to save viewport views in case you happen to change a viewport view accidentally. You can do this by using the following procedure: Double-click inside a viewport whose view you want to save. Select View Manager from the View tab's Views panel, and then, in the View Manager, click the New button (see "Saving Views" in Chapter 7, "Mastering Viewing Tools, Hatches, and External References," for a description of the View Manager dialog box).

Another way to prevent your viewport view from being accidentally altered is to turn on View Lock. To do this, while in paper space click a viewport's outline. Right-click to open the context menu, and then choose Display Locked ➤ Yes. After the view is locked, you can't pan or zoom within a viewport. This setting is also available in the viewport's Properties palette and in the status bar to the left of the Viewport Scale tool when a viewport is selected or when you are in Floating model space.

## Setting Layers in Individual Viewports

Another unique feature of paper space viewports is their ability to freeze layers independently. You can, for example, display the usual plan information in the overall view of a floor but show only the walls in the enlarged view of one unit.

You control viewport layer visibility through the Layer Properties Manager. You may have noticed that there are three sun icons for each layer listing.

To see all of the layer options, you may need to widen the Layer Properties Manager to view all the columns. To do so, click and drag the right border of the dialog box to the right.

You're already familiar with the sun icon farthest to the left. This is the Freeze/Thaw icon that controls the freezing and thawing of layers globally. Several columns to the right of that icon are two sun icons with transparent rectangles. These icons control the freezing and thawing of layers in individual viewports. Of this pair, the one on the left controls existing viewports and the one on the right controls settings for newly created viewports.

This exercise shows you firsthand how the sun icon for existing viewports works:

1. Double-click inside a viewport to go to Floating model space.

2. Activate the lower viewport.

3. Open the Layer Properties Manager.

4. Locate the COMMON|WALL layer, and then click its name to help you see the layer clearly.

5. Click the column labeled VP Freeze for the selected layer (see Figure 15.11). You may need to widen the Layer Properties Manager to do this; the column title may show only V until you widen the column. The VP Freeze column is the seventh column from the right side of the dialog box. Click the icon, which looks like a transparent rectangle behind a sun. The sun changes to a snowflake, telling you that the layer is now frozen for the current viewport.

**FIGURE 15.11**
Select the VP Freeze option for the COMMON|WALL layer.

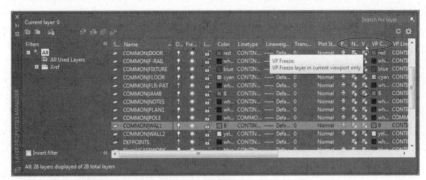

The Wall layer of the Common Xref becomes invisible in the current viewport. However, the walls remain visible in the other viewport (see Figure 15.12).

**FIGURE 15.12**
The drawing with the COMMON|WALL layer turned off in the active viewport

6. After reviewing the effects of the VP Freeze setting, go back to the Layer Properties Manager and thaw the COMMON|WALL layer by clicking its VP Freeze icon again so it turns back into a sun.

7. Take a moment to study the drawing, and then save the Xref-1.dwg file.

You may have noticed another, identical sun icon next to the one you used in the previous exercise. This icon controls layer visibility in any new viewports you create next rather than in existing viewports.

If you prefer, you can use the layer drop-down list in the Layers panel to freeze layers in individual viewports. Double-click in the viewport you want to modify, select the layer from the list, and then click the same sun icon with the small rectangle behind it.

In addition to setting the visibility of layers, you can set the other layer properties—such as color, linetype, and lineweight—for each viewport. First, make sure you're in Floating model space for the viewport whose layers you want to set up, and then open the Layer Properties Manager. You can set the properties for the current viewport using the VP Freeze, VP Color, VP Linetype, VP Lineweight, VP Transparency, and VP Plot Style settings for each layer (see Figure 15.13).

**FIGURE 15.13**

The VP Freeze, VP Color, VP Linetype, VP Lineweight, VP Transparency, and VP Plot Style columns in the Layer Properties Manager

This section concludes the apartment building tutorial. Although you haven't drawn the complete building, you've learned all the commands and techniques you need to do so. Figure 15.14 shows you a completed plan of the first floor. To complete your floor plans and get some practice using AutoCAD, you may want to add the symbols shown in this figure to your Plan.dwg file.

**FIGURE 15.14**

A completed floor of the apartment building

Because buildings like this one often have the same plans for several floors, the plan for the second floor can also represent the third floor. Combined with the first floor, this gives you a three-level apartment building. This project might also have a ground-level garage, which would be a separate file. You can use the `Col-grid.dwg` or `Col-grid-metric.dwg` file in the garage file as a reference for dimensions. The other symbols can be blocks stored as files that you can retrieve in other files.

---

### MASKING OUT PARTS OF A DRAWING

Chapter 7 described a method for using the AutoCAD Draworder feature to hide floor patterns under equipment or furniture in a floor layout. You can use a similar method to hide irregularly shaped areas in a paper space viewport. This is desirable for plotting site plans, civil plans, or floor plans that require portions of the drawing to be masked out. You may also want to mask part of a plan that is overlapped by another to expose dimension or text data.

---

## Creating and Using Multiple Paper Space Layouts

You're not limited to just one or two paper space layouts. You can have as many as you want, with each layout set up for a different sheet size containing different views of your drawing. You can use this feature to set up multiple drawing sheets based on a single AutoCAD drawing file. For example, suppose a client requires full sets of plans in both $\frac{1}{8}$" = 1' scale and $\frac{1}{16}$" = 1' scale. You can set up two Layout tabs, each with a different sheet size and viewport scale.

You can also set up different paper space layouts for the various types of drawings. A single drawing can contain the data for mechanical layout, equipment and furnishings, floor plans, and reflected ceiling plans. Although a project can require a file for each floor plan, a single file with multiple layout views can serve the same purpose in AutoCAD 2015.

To create new layout views, do the following:

**1.** Click the New Layout tab from the layout tabs in the lower-left corner of the drawing area (see Figure 15.15). A new preview panel appears, labeled Layout2.

**FIGURE 15.15**
The New Layout tab

**2.** Click the new Layout2 tab. The new layout appears with a single default viewport.

You've just seen how you can create a new layout using the New Layout tab. You can also right-click any layout tab to open a context menu that offers a New Layout option (see Figure 15.16). The New Layout option also appears when you right-click the Drawing tab at the top of the drawing area.

**FIGURE 15.16**
The New Layout
context menu
option

The Layout tab context menu also includes the From Template option. The From Template option lets you create a paper space layout based on an AutoCAD template file. AutoCAD provides several standard layouts that include title blocks based on common sheet sizes.

Finally, if you want to delete or rename a layout, right-click the layout tab you want to edit. You can then select Delete or Rename from the context menu that appears. If you select Delete, you'll see a warning message telling you that AutoCAD will permanently delete the layout you have chosen to delete. Click OK to confirm your deletion.

## Creating Odd-Shaped Viewports

In many situations, a rectangular viewport doesn't provide a view appropriate for what you want to accomplish. For example, you might want to isolate part of a floor plan that is L shaped or circular. You can create viewports for virtually any shape you need. You can grip-edit a typical rectangular viewport to change its shape into a trapezoid or other irregular four-sided polygon. You can also use the Clip tool to create more complex viewport shapes, as the following exercise demonstrates.

Follow these steps to set up a layout view that shows only the lower apartment units and the elevators and stairs:

1. Click the Clip tool in the Layout tab's Layout Viewports panel. You can also type **Vpclip**↵.

2. At the Select viewport to clip: prompt, click the viewport border.

3. At the Select clipping object or [Polygonal] <Polygonal>: prompt, press ↵.

4. Turn off Object Snap, and draw the outline shown in the top portion of Figure 15.17.

**FIGURE 15.17**

Drawing a polygon outline for a viewport

Draw this polygon outline.

5. After you finish selecting points, press ↵. The viewport changes to conform to the new shape.

6. Click the viewport border to expose its grips.

7. Click a grip, and move it to a new location. The viewport view conforms to the new shape.

The new viewport shape gives you more flexibility in isolating portions of a drawing. This can be especially useful if you have a large project that is divided into smaller sheets. You can set up several layout views, each displaying a different portion of the plan.

What if you want a viewport that isn't rectilinear? This exercise shows you how to create a circular viewport:

1. Erase the viewport you just modified.

2. Draw a circle that roughly fills the paper space area.

3. In the Layout tab's Layout Viewports panel, choose Object from the Viewport flyout. You can also type **-VPORTS↵O↵**.

4. Click the circle. The plan appears inside the circle, as shown in Figure 15.18.

**FIGURE 15.18**
A circular viewpoint

To simplify this exercise, you were asked to draw a circle as the basis for a new viewport. However, you aren't limited to circles; you can use a closed polyline or spline of any shape. (See Chapter 18, "Drawing Curves," for a detailed discussion of polylines and splines.) You can also use the Polygon tool on the Home tab's Draw panel to create a shape and then turn it into a viewport.

If you look carefully at the series of prompts for the previous exercise, you'll notice that the Layout Viewports Object tool invokes a command-line version of the Vports command (-vports), which offers some options that the standard Vports command doesn't. The following options are available with the command-line version of Vports:

```
_-VPORTS
Specify corner of viewport or
[ON/OFF/Fit/Shadeplot/Lock/Object/Polygonal/Restore/LAyer/2/3/4] <Fit>:
```

You used two of the options—Polygonal and Object—in the two previous exercises.

# Understanding Lineweights, Linetypes, and Dimensions in Paper Space

The behavior of several AutoCAD features depends on whether you're in paper space or model space. The most visible of these features are lineweights, linetypes, and dimensions. In the following sections, you'll take a closer look at these features and see how to use them in conjunction with paper space.

## Controlling and Viewing Lineweights in Paper Space

Lineweights can greatly improve the readability of technical drawings. You can make important features stand out with bold lineweights while keeping the noise of smaller details from overpowering a drawing. In architectural floor plans, walls are traditionally drawn with heavier lines so that the outline of a plan can be easily read. Other features exist in a drawing for reference only, so they're drawn in a lighter weight than normal.

If you look at the bonus chapter "Understanding Plot Styles," available at www.omura.com/chapters, you will see how to control lineweights in AutoCAD by using plot style tables. You can apply either a named plot style table or a color plot style table to a drawing. If you already have a library of AutoCAD drawings, you may want to use color plot style tables for backward compatibility. AutoCAD also enables you to assign lineweights directly to layers or objects and to view the results of your lineweight settings in paper space.

Here's an exercise that demonstrates how to set lineweights directly:

1. Open the Layer Properties Manager.

2. Right-click the Layer list, and choose Select All.

3. Click the Lineweight column (not the column header) to open the Lineweight dialog box (see Figure 15.19).

4. Select 0.13 mm from the list, and click OK. You've just assigned the 0.13 mm lineweight to all layers.

5. Right-click the Layer list again, and choose Clear All.

6. Click the COMMON|WALL layer, and Ctrl+click the Floor1|WALL layer to select these two layers.

**FIGURE 15.19**
The Lineweight
dialog box

7. Click the Lineweight column for either of the two selected layers to open the Lineweight dialog box again.

8. Select 0.40 mm from the dialog box, and click OK. You've just assigned the 0.40 mm lineweight to the two selected layers.

9. Click Close in the Layer Properties Manager.

Although you set the lineweights for the layers in the drawing, you need to make a few more changes to the file settings before they're visible in paper space:

1. Type **LW⏎** to open the Lineweight Settings dialog box (see Figure 15.20).

**FIGURE 15.20**
The Lineweight Settings dialog box

2. Select the Display Lineweight check box, and then click OK.

3. Make sure you're in paper space, and then zoom into the drawing.

4. Type **REA⏎**. The lines representing the walls are now thicker, as shown in Figure 15.21.

5. After reviewing the results of this exercise, close the file. You may save it for future reference.

**FIGURE 15.21**
An enlarged view of the plan with lineweights displayed

With the ability to display lineweights in paper space, you have better control over your output. Instead of using a trial-and-error method to print your drawing and then checking your printout to see whether the lineweights are correct, you can see the lineweights on your screen.

This exercise showed you how to set lineweights so that they appear in paper space as they will when you plot your drawing. If you normally plot your drawings in black, you can go one step further and set all your layer colors to black to see how your plots will look. But you'll need to save your layer settings so you can restore the layers to their original colors. Another way to view your drawing in black and white without affecting your layer settings is to use the color plot style table described in the bonus chapter "Understanding Plot Styles," available at www.omura.com/chapters.

---

### LINEWEIGHT DISPLAY SHORTCUT

When lineweight display is turned on, you see lineweights in model space as well as in paper space. Lineweights can be distracting while you work on your drawing in model space, but you can quickly turn them off by entering **Lwdisplay.↵Off.↵** at the command line. Entering **Lwdisplay.↵On.↵** turns the lineweight display back on.

---

## The Lineweight Settings Dialog Box

The Lineweight Settings dialog box includes a few other settings that you didn't use in the previous exercise. Here is a description of those settings for your reference:

**Units For Listing**   You can choose between millimeters and inches for the unit of measure for lineweights. The default is millimeters.

**Adjust Display Scale**   This setting lets you control just how thick lineweights appear in the drawing. Move the slider to the right for thicker lines and to the left for thinner lines. This setting affects only the display on your monitor. As you move the slider, you can see a sample of the results in the Lineweights list box just to the left of the slider. You may have to scroll down the list box to view the effects.

**Default Drop-Down List**   This drop-down list lets you select the default lineweight you see in the Layer Properties Manager. You may want to lower the default lineweight to 0.005″ (0.13 mm) as a matter of course because most printers these days can print lines that size and even smaller.

## Linetype Scales and Paper Space

As you've seen in previous exercises, you must carefully control drawing scales when creating viewports. Fortunately, this is easily done through the Properties palette. Although paper space offers the flexibility of combining images of different scale in one display, it also adds to the complexity of your task in controlling that display. Your drawing's linetype scale in particular needs careful attention.

In Chapter 5, "Keeping Track of Layers and Blocks," you saw that you had to set the linetype scale to the scale factor of the drawing in order to make the linetype visible. If you intend to plot that same drawing from paper space, you have to set the linetype scale back to 1 to get the linetypes to appear correctly. This is because AutoCAD faithfully scales linetypes to the current unit system. Remember that paper space units are different from model space units. When you scale a model space image down to fit in the smaller paper space area, the linetypes remain scaled to the increased linetype scale settings. In the Chapter 5 example, linetypes are scaled up by a factor of 24. This causes noncontinuous lines to appear as continuous in paper space because you see only a small portion of a greatly enlarged noncontinuous linetype.

The Psltscale system variable enables you to determine how linetype scales are applied to paper space views. You can set Psltscale so that the linetypes appear the same regardless of whether you view them directly in model space or through a viewport in paper space. By default, this system variable is set to 1. This causes AutoCAD to scale all the linetypes uniformly across all the viewports in paper space. You can set Psltscale to 0 to force the viewports to display linetypes exactly as they appear in model space. Psltscale is not a global setting. You must set it for each layout view that you create; otherwise, the default value of 1 will be used.

You can also control this setting in the Linetype Manager dialog box (type **LT**⏎). When you click the Show Details button, you see a setting called Use Paper Space Units For Scaling in the lower-left corner. When this check box is selected, Psltscale is set to 1. When it isn't selected, Psltscale is set to 0.

## Dimensioning in Paper Space Layouts

At times, you may find it more convenient to add dimensions to your drawing in paper space rather than directly on your objects in model space. This can be useful if you have a small project with several viewports in a layout and you want to keep dimensions aligned between viewports. You have two basic options when dimensioning model space objects in paper space. The Associative Dimensioning feature can make quick work of dimensions for layout views containing drawings of differing scales. Alternatively, if you prefer not to use Associative Dimensioning, you can adjust settings for individual dimension styles.

### USING ASSOCIATIVE DIMENSIONING IN PAPER SPACE

Perhaps the simplest way to dimension in paper space is to use the Associative Dimensioning feature. With this feature turned on, you can dimension model space objects while in a paper space layout. Furthermore, paper space dimensions of model space objects are automatically updated if the model space object is edited.

Try the following exercise to see how Associative Dimensioning works:

1. Click New from the Quick Access toolbar, and use the acad.dwt template to create a new blank file. Metric users should use the acadiso.dwt template.

2. Draw a rectangle 12 units wide by 4 units high. If you're using a metric file, make the rectangle 480 units wide by 160 units high.

3. Select the Layout1 tab.

4. Right-click the Layout1 tab and select Page Setup Manager.

5. In the Page Setup Manager, click Modify. Then, in the Page Setup dialog box, select a printer from the Printer/Plotter group's Name drop-down list.

6. Choose the Letter paper size in the Paper Size section. Metric users can pick ISO A4 (297.00 × 210.00 mm).

7. Click OK, and then close the Page Setup Manager.

8. Right-click in the drawing area, and choose Options from the context menu.

9. In the Options dialog box, click the User Preferences tab and make sure the Make New Dimensions Associative option in the Associative Dimensioning group is turned on (shows a check mark). Click OK to exit the dialog box.

Next, you'll use the rectangle you drew in model space to test the Associative Dimensioning feature in the Layout1 view:

1. Click Linear from the Annotate tab's Dimensions panel. Using the Endpoint osnap, dimension the bottom edge of the rectangle you drew in model space. The dimension shows 12.0000 (480 for metric drawings), the actual size of the rectangle.

**2.** Double-click inside the viewport, and use the Zoom Realtime tool to zoom out a bit so that the rectangle appears smaller in the viewport. Do not use the scroll wheel of your mouse to do this (see the next section, "Updating Associative Dimensions"). After you exit the Zoom Realtime tool, the dimension follows the new view of the rectangle.

**3.** While you're in Floating model space, click the rectangle and then click the grip in the lower-left corner and drag it upward and to the right.

**4.** Click again to place the corner of the rectangle in a new location. The dimension changes to conform to the new shape.

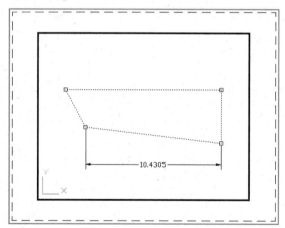

**5.** Close the rectangle file without saving it. You won't need it in the future.

You've just seen how you can dimension an object in model space while in paper space. You can dimension model space Xrefs in paper space in much the same way. The only difference is that changes to the Xref file don't automatically update dimensions made in paper space. You need to employ the Dimregen command to refresh paper space dimensions of Xref objects.

### Updating Associative Dimensions

If you use a wheel mouse to pan and zoom in a Floating model space viewport, you may need to use the Dimregen command to refresh an associative dimension. To do so, type **Dimregen**⏎ at the command line. You can also use Dimregen to refresh dimensions from drawings that have been edited in earlier versions of AutoCAD or, as mentioned already, to refresh dimensions of objects contained in external references.

### Paper Space Dimensioning without Associative Dimensioning

In some situations, you may not want to use Associative Dimensioning although you still want to dimension model space objects in paper space. For example, you might be in an office that has different versions of AutoCAD, or you might be sharing your drawings with other offices that aren't using AutoCAD 2015 and the use of Associative Dimensioning creates confusion.

To dimension model space objects in paper space without Associative Dimensioning, you need to have AutoCAD adjust the dimension text to the scale of the viewport from which you're dimensioning. You can have AutoCAD scale dimension values in paper space so that they correspond to a viewport zoom-scale factor. The following steps show you how this setting is made:

1. Open the Dimension Style Manager by clicking the Dimension Style tool in the Home tab's expanded Annotation panel.

2. Select the dimension style you want to edit and click Modify.

3. Click the Primary Units tab.

4. In the Measurement Scale group, enter the scale factor of the viewport you intend to dimension in the Scale Factor text box. For example, if the viewport is scaled to a ½" = 1'-0" scale, enter **24**.

5. Click the Apply To Layout Dimensions Only check box.

6. Click OK, and then click Close in the Dimension Style Manager. You're ready to dimension in paper space without associative dimensions.

Remember that you can snap to objects in a floating viewport so you can add dimensions as you normally would in model space. If you're dimensioning objects in viewports of different scales, you need to set up multiple dimension styles, one for each viewport scale.

## Other Uses for Paper Space

The exercises in the preceding sections should give you a sense of how you work in paper space and layout views. We've given examples that reflect common uses of paper space. Remember that paper space is like a page-layout portion of AutoCAD—separate yet connected to model space through viewports.

You needn't limit your applications to floor plans. You can take advantage of paper space with interior and exterior elevations, 3D models, and detail sheets. When used in conjunction with the raster-import capabilities in AutoCAD, paper space can be a powerful tool for creating large-format presentations.

---

**EXPORTING LAYOUT VIEWS TO MODEL SPACE**

You may encounter a situation where you want to export a layout view as a model space drawing. You can do so by following these steps:

**1.** At the bottom of the drawing area, click the Layout tab of the layout you want to export.

**2.** Right-click the tab and select Export Layout To Model from the context menu. The Export Layout To model space Drawing dialog box appears. This is a typical Save dialog box that allows you to select the location and name for your exported layout.

**3.** Select a folder location, enter a name for your exported layout, and then click Save.

Your layout view will be saved as a separate drawing file with the layout appearing in the model space of that file. It will also be in the same scale as the original layout view instead of in full scale. Other drawing elements such as layers, blocks, linetypes, and styles will also be exported, although they may be scaled down to fit the drawing.

---

## The Bottom Line

**Understand model space and paper space.** AutoCAD offers two viewing modes for viewing and printing your drawings. Model space is where you do most of your work; it's the view you see when you create a new file. Layouts, also called paper space, are views that let you arrange the layout of your drawing, similar to the way you would in a page-layout program.

**Master It** What are three ways of moving from model space to paper space?

**Work with paper space viewports.** While in paper space, you can create views in your drawing using viewports. You can have several viewports, each showing a different part of your drawing.

**Master It** Name some of the ways you can enlarge a view in a viewport.

**Create odd-shaped viewports.** Most of the time, you'll probably use rectangular viewports, but you have the option to create a viewport of any shape.

**Master It** Describe the process for creating a circular viewport.

**Understand lineweights, linetypes, and dimensions in paper space.** You can get an accurate view of how your drawing will look on paper by making a few adjustments to AutoCAD. Your layout view will reflect how your drawing will look when plotted.

**Master It** Name the two dialog boxes you must use to display lineweights in a layout view.

# Chapter 16

# Making "Smart" Drawings with Parametric Tools

Don't let the term *parametric drawing* scare you. *Parametric* is a word from mathematics, and in the context of AutoCAD® drawings, it means that you can define relationships between different objects in a drawing. For example, you can set up a pair of individual lines to stay parallel or set up two concentric circles to maintain an exact distance between the circles no matter how they may be edited.

Parametric drawing is also called *constraint-based modeling*, and you'll see the word *constraint* used in the AutoCAD Ribbon to describe sets of tools. The term *constraint* is a bit more descriptive of the tools you'll use to create parametric drawings because when you use them, you are applying a constraint upon the objects in your drawing.

In this chapter, you'll see firsthand how the parametric drawing tools work and how you might apply them to your needs.

In this chapter, you will learn to

♦ Use parametric drawing tools

♦ Connect objects with geometric constraints

♦ Control sizes with dimensional constraints

♦ Use formulas to control dimensions

♦ Put constraints to use

## Why Use Parametric Drawing Tools?

If you're not familiar with parametric drawing, you may be wondering what purpose it serves. With careful application of the parametric tools, you can create a drawing that you can quickly modify with just a change of a dimension or two instead of actually editing the lines that make up the drawing. Figure 16.1 shows a drawing that was set up so that the arcs and circles increase in size to an exact proportion when the overall length dimension is increased. This approach can save a lot of time if you're designing several parts that are similar with only a few dimensional changes.

**FIGURE 16.1**
The d1 dimension in the top image was edited to change the drawing to look like the one in the lower half.

You can also mimic the behavior of a mechanical assembly to test your ideas. The parametric drawing tools let you create linkages between objects so that if one moves, the others maintain their connection like a link in a chain. For example, you can create 3D AutoCAD models of a crankshaft and piston assembly of a car motor (see Figure 16.2) or the parallel arms of a Luxo lamp. If you move one part of the model, the other parts move in a way consistent with a real motor or lamp.

**FIGURE 16.2**
Move one part of the drawing and the other parts follow.

# Connecting Objects with Geometric Constraints

You'll start your exploration of parametric drawing by adding geometric constraints to an existing drawing and testing the behavior of the drawing with the constraints in place. Geometric constraints let you assign constrained behaviors to objects to limit their range of motion. Limiting motion to improve editing efficiency may seem counterintuitive, but once you've seen these tools in action, you'll see their benefits.

## Using AutoConstrain to Add Constraints Automatically

Start by opening a sample drawing and adding a few geometric constraints. The sample drawing is composed of two parallel lines connected by two arcs, as shown in Figure 16.3. These are just lines and arcs and are not polylines.

**FIGURE 16.3**
The Paramet-
ric01.dwg file
containing simple
lines and arcs

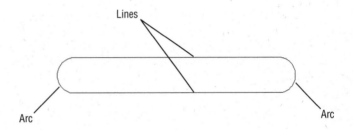

Here are the steps:

1. Open the Parametric01.dwg file from the sample files for this chapter (see Figure 16.3).

2. Select the Parametric tab, and click the AutoConstrain tool in the Geometric panel of the Parametric Ribbon Tab, or type **Autoconstrain**↵.

3. Select all of the objects in the drawing, and press ↵.

You've just used the AutoConstrain command to add geometric constraints to all of the objects in the drawing. You can see a set of icons that indicate the constraints that have been applied to the objects (see Figure 16.4). The AutoConstrain command makes a "best guess" at applying constraints.

**FIGURE 16.4**
The drawing with
geometric con-
straints added

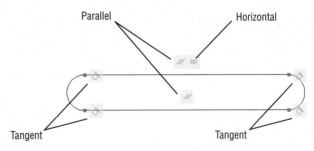

Notice that the constraint icons in the drawing match those you see in the Geometric panel. If you hover your mouse pointer over an icon, you'll see a tool tip that shows the name of the constraint.

The Tangent constraints that you see at the ends of the lines keep the arcs and the lines tangent to each other whenever the arcs are edited. The Parallel constraint keeps the two lines parallel, and the Horizontal constraint keeps the lines horizontal.

There is one constraint that doesn't show an icon, but you see a clue to its existence by the small blue squares where the arcs join the lines:

1. Place your cursor on one of the blue squares. A new icon appears below the tangent icon along with a description of the arc. The arc description may hide the new icon, so look carefully or move the cursor away and try again. The new icon appears immediately whereas the arc description takes a second to appear.

2. Hover your cursor over the icon that has just appeared. You see the icon appear for the Coincident constraint.

The Coincident constraint makes sure that the endpoints of the lines and arcs stay connected, as you'll see in the next few exercises.

## Editing a Drawing Containing Constraints

Now try editing the drawing to see how these constraints work:

1. Click the arc on the left side of the drawing (see the top of Figure 16.5).

2. Click the grip at the bottom of the arc and move it downward to increase the radius of the arc. The objects move in unison to maintain their geometric constraints (see the bottom of Figure 16.5).

3. Click again to accept the change in the arc radius.

4. Click the Undo tool in the Quick Access toolbar to undo your change.

**FIGURE 16.5**

Moving the end-point of one arc causes the other parts of the drawing to follow because of their geometric constraints.

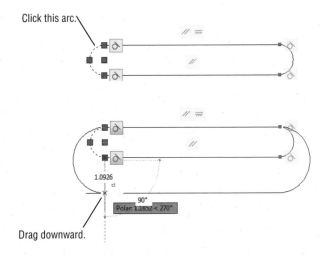

In this exercise, you saw how the Tangent, Parallel, Horizontal, and Coincident constraints worked to keep the objects together while you changed the size of one object. Next, you'll see what happens if you remove a constraint.

## Removing a Constraint

The AutoConstrain tool applied quite a few geometric constraints to the drawing. Suppose you want to remove a constraint to allow for more flexibility in the drawing. In the next exercise, you'll remove the Parallel constraint and then try editing the drawing to see the results:

1. Click the Parallel constraint icon that is just above the lower line.

2. Right-click and select Delete. Notice that the Parallel icon disappears from both the top and bottom line.

3. Click the line at the bottom of the drawing.

4. Click the grip at the left end of the line, drag it downward, and then click. This time, the left end of the line moves downward. The lines are no longer parallel, but they remain tangent to both arcs and their endpoints remain connected (see Figure 16.6).

**FIGURE 16.6**
Editing the arc with
the Parallel con-
straint removed

Notice that the top line remains horizontal as you edit the arc. The top line still has the Horizontal constraint. Next try removing the Horizontal constraint:

1. Click the Undo tool in the Quick Access toolbar to return to the previous shape.

2. Right-click the Horizontal constraint icon above the top line and select Delete.

3. Select the arc on the left side again as you did earlier.

4. Hover over the bottom grip of the arc, and select Stretch from the multifunction grip menu.

5. Move the grip downward. This time both the lines change their orientation, as shown in Figure 16.7.

**FIGURE 16.7**
Without the Hori-
zontal constraint,
both lines change as
the arc is edited.

Notice that lines and arcs remain connected and tangent to each other. This is because the Coincident and Tangent constraints are still in effect.

## ADDING A CONSTRAINT

You've seen how the AutoConstrain tool applies a set of constraints to a set of objects. You can also add constraints "manually" to fine-tune the way objects behave. In the next exercise, you'll add a circle to the drawing and then add a few specific constraints that you'll select from the Geometric panel:

1. Click the Undo tool in the Quick Access toolbar to change the drawing back to its original shape.

2. From the Home tab, click the Circle tool in the Draw panel.

3. Click a location roughly above and to the left of the drawing, as shown in Figure 16.8. You don't need to be exact because you will use a geometric constraint to move the circle into an exact location.

**FIGURE 16.8**
Place the circle roughly in the location shown here.

Place the circle here and give it a 0.25 radius.

4. Type **0.25.↵** for the radius of the circle.

5. Select the Parametric tab, and click the Concentric tool in the Geometric panel.

6. Click the arc at the left side of the drawing, and then click the circle you just added. The circle moves to a location that is concentric to the arc, as shown in Figure 16.9.

**FIGURE 16.9**
The circle is concentric to the arc on the left side.

In this exercise, you used the geometric constraint as an editing tool to move an object into an exact location. The Concentric constraint will also keep the circle inside the arc no matter where the arc moves.

---

### THE ORDER MAKES A DIFFERENCE

When you add constraints, sometimes the order in which you add them makes an important difference. In the Concentric constraint example, you selected the arc first and then the circle. Had you selected the circle first, the arcs and lines would have moved to the circle. Instead, as you saw in the exercise, the circle moved to the inside of the arc.

---

## Using Other Geometric Constraints

You've seen how several of the geometric constraints work. For the most part, each constraint is fairly easy to understand. The Tangent constraint keeps objects tangent to each other. The Coincident constraint keeps the location of objects together, such as endpoints or midpoints of lines and arcs. The Parallel constraint keeps objects parallel.

You have many more geometric constraints at your disposal. Table 16.1 gives you a concise listing of the constraints and their purposes. Note that, with the exception of Fix and Symmetric, all of the constraints affect pairs of objects.

**TABLE 16.1:** The geometric constraints

| NAME | USE |
| --- | --- |
| Coincident | Keeps point locations of two objects together, such as the endpoints or midpoints of lines. Allowable points vary between objects, and they are indicated by a red circle marked with an X while points are being selected. |
| Collinear | Keeps lines collinear. The lines need not be connected. |
| Concentric | Keeps circles and arcs concentric. |
| Fix | Fixes a point on an object to a location in the drawing. |
| Parallel | Keeps lines parallel. |
| Perpendicular | Keeps lines or polyline segments perpendicular. |
| Horizontal | Keeps lines horizontal. |
| Vertical | Keeps lines vertical. |
| Tangent | Keeps curves, or a line and curve, tangent to each other. |
| Smooth | Maintains a smooth transition between splines and other objects. The first object selected must be a spline. You can think of this constraint as a tangent constraint for splines. |
| Symmetric | Maintains symmetry between two curves about an axis that is determined by a line. Before using this constraint, draw a line that you will use for the axis of symmetry. You can also use the Fix, Horizontal, or Vertical constraint to fix the axis to a location or orientation. |
| Equal | Keeps the length of lines or polylines equal, or the radius of arcs and circles equal. |

The behavior of the geometric constraints might sound simple, but you may find that they can act in unexpected ways. With the limited space of this book, we can't give exercise examples for every geometric constraint, so we encourage you to experiment with them on your own. And have some fun with them!

### Using Constraints in the Drawing Process

Earlier you saw how the Concentric constraint allowed you to move a circle into a concentric location to an arc. You can use other geometric constraints in a similar way. For example, you can move a line into a collinear position with another line using the Collinear constraint. Or you can move a line into an orientation that's tangent to a pair of arcs or circles, as shown in Figure 16.10. The top image shows the separate line and circles, and the bottom image shows the objects after applying the Tangent constraint. Note that although the line is tangent to the two circles, its length and orientation does not change.

**FIGURE 16.10**

You can connect two circles so that they are tangent to a line by using the Tangent constraint.

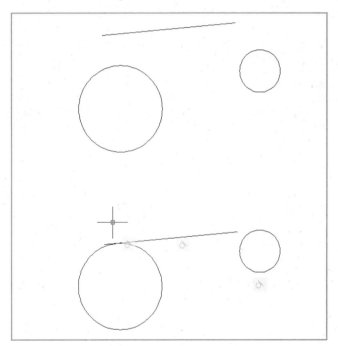

## Controlling Sizes with Dimensional Constraints

At the heart of the AutoCAD parametric tools are the dimensional constraints. These constraints allow you to set and adjust the dimension of an assembly of parts, thereby giving you an easy way to adjust the size and even the shape of a set of objects.

For example, suppose you have a set of parts that you are drafting, each of which is just slightly different in one dimension or another. You can add geometric constraints and then add dimensional constraints, which will let you easily modify your part just by changing the value of a dimension. To see how this works, try the following exercises.

## Adding a Dimensional Constraint

In this first dimensional constraint exercise, you'll add a horizontal dimension to the drawing you've been working on already. The drawing already has some geometric constraints with which you are familiar, so you can see how the dimensional constraints interact with the geometric constraints.

Start by adding a dimensional constraint between the two arcs:

1. In the Parametric tab, click the Aligned tool in the Dimensional panel.

2. Shift+right-click, and select the Center osnap option from the context menu.

3. Place the cursor on the arc on the left side of the drawing so that the Center osnap marker appears for the arc (see Figure 16.11). Notice that the arc is highlighted as you select the center.

**FIGURE 16.11**
Use the Center osnap to select the center of the arc.

4. Shift+right-click, and select the Center osnap option as you did in step 2.

5. Click the arc on the right side of the drawing (see Figure 16.12).

**FIGURE 16.12**
Adding the dimensional constraint

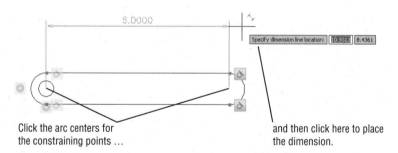

6. Click a location above the drawing, as shown in Figure 16.12.

7. At the `Dimension text =` prompt, press ↵ to accept the current value.

The dimensional constraint appears above the drawing and shows a value of d1=6.0000. The d1 is the name for that particular dimensional constraint. Each dimensional constraint is assigned a unique name, which is useful later when you want to make changes.

Now let's see how you can use the dimensional constraint you just added.

## Editing a Dimensional Constraint

A dimensional constraint is linked to objects in your drawing so that when you modify a dimension value, the objects to which the constraint is linked change. To see how this works, try editing the part by changing the dimension:

**1.** Double-click the dimension value of the dimensional constraint (see Figure 16.13).

**FIGURE 16.13**
Double-click the dimension value.

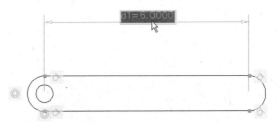

**2.** Type **4.5**↵. The part shortens to the dimension you entered.

---

### OSNAPS ARE FORCED OFF

In an earlier exercise, you had to select the Center osnap from the Osnap menu. When placing dimensional constraints, you'll need to use the Osnap menu to select Center osnaps. Running osnaps are automatically turned off when you use the dimensional constraint tools. This is because the dimensional constraint tools use their own method of finding locations on objects.

---

Next, add a dimension to the arc on the left side:

**1.** Click the Aligned tool from the Dimensional panel.

**2.** Select the top endpoint of the arc on the left side (top of Figure 16.14). Do this by first hovering over the arc near the endpoint. When you see the endpoint marker, click the mouse. If the constraint icons are in the way, you can zoom in to the drawing to see the marker.

**3.** Select the bottom endpoint of the arc in the same way.

**4.** Click a point to the left of the arc to place the dimension (bottom of Figure 16.14).

**5.** At the `Dimension text =` prompt, press ↵ to accept the current value.

**FIGURE 16.14**
Adding a dimensional constraint to the arc

Select the arc at this location so that the red circle appears.

Specify first constraint point or ⊞

d1=4.5000 🔒

Click here to place the dimension.

1.0000

Specify dimension line location: 2.7553 5.8174

Notice that the new dimensional constraint has been given the name d2. Now try changing the size of the arc using the dimensional constraint:

**1.** Double-click the dimension value of the d2 dimensional constraint (see Figure 16.15).

**FIGURE 16.15**
Adjusting the arc dimension

d1=4.5000 🔒

d2=2.000 🔒

**2.** Enter 2↵. The part adjusts to the new dimension.

As you can see from this example, you can control the dimensions of your drawing by changing the dimensional constraint's value. This is a much faster way of making accurate changes to your drawing. Imagine what you would have to do to make these same changes if you didn't have the geometric and dimensional constraints available.

# Using Formulas to Control and Link Dimensions

In the previous exercise, you saw how the dimensional constraint attached to the arc affected the drawing. But in that example, the circle on the left end of the drawing remained unaffected by the change in the arc size. Now suppose that you want that circle to adjust its size in relation to the size of the arc. To do this, you can employ the Parameters Manager and include a formula that manages the size of the circle.

In the following exercise, you'll add a dimensional constraint to the circle and then apply a formula to that constraint so that the circle will always be one half the diameter of the arc, no matter how the arc is modified.

Start by adding a Diameter constraint to the circle:

1. Click the Undo tool in the Quick Access toolbar to change the drawing back to its previous shape.

2. Click the Diameter tool in the Dimensional panel.

3. Click the circle to select it.

4. Click a location inside the drawing to place the constraint, as shown in Figure 16.16.

**FIGURE 16.16**
Adding a Diameter
constraint to
the circle

5. Press ↵ to accept the constraint value.

The Diameter constraint you just added is given the name dia1. It controls only the diameter of the circle; you could change the value of that constraint, but it would affect only the circle.

## Adding a Formula Parameter

Now let's add a formula that will "connect" the value of the circle diameter to the diameter of the arc:

1. Click the Parameters Manager tool in the Manage panel. The Parameters Manager appears (see Figure 16.17). Notice that the Parameters Manager gives a list of all of the dimensional constraints that exist in the drawing.

**FIGURE 16.17**
The Parameters
Manager

2. Click the Creates A New User Parameter tool at the top of the Parameters Manager. A new category appears in the list called User Parameters, and you see a user1 parameter appear.

3. Double-click in the Expression column for the user1 parameter (see Figure 16.18).

4. With the user1 expression value highlighted, type **d2 * 0.5**↲. You will see your entry replace the expression value (see Figure 16.18). This expression is saying, "Give the user1 variable the value of half the d2 constraint." Remember that the d2 constraint is the one given to the arc.

**FIGURE 16.18**
Adding an expres-
sion to the user1
parameter

Change this
expression to
d2 * 0.5.

5. Now double-click the Expression column for the dia1 parameter (see Figure 16.19). This is the parameter for the circle's diameter.

**FIGURE 16.19**

Applying the user1 parameter to the dia1 parameter

Change the expression for the dia1 parameter to user1.

6. Type **user1↵** to change the dia1 expression from 0.5 to user1. This tells AutoCAD to use the expression in the user1 parameter in place of the fixed 0.5 diameter value.

You've set up your circle to follow any changes to the width of the part. Now any changes to the d2 dimensional constraint will affect the circle.

## Testing the Formula

Try the following to see the parameters in action:

1. In the Parameters Manager, double-click the Expression column for the d2 parameter.

2. Change the value from 1 to 2 and observe the effect on the part (see Figure 16.20).

**FIGURE 16.20**

Change the d2 parameter and the part changes in size, including the circle.

The part changes in width and the circle also enlarges to maintain its proportion to the width of the part. Here you see that you can apply a formula to a constraint so that it is "linked" to another constraint's value. In this case, you set the circle's diameter to follow the width constraint of the part.

In addition, you can adjust the constraint value from the Parameters Manager. You could also have changed the width of the part as before by double-clicking the dimensional constraint for the arc.

## Using Other Formulas

In the previous exercise, you used a simple formula that multiplied a parameter, d2, by a fixed value. You used the asterisk to indicate multiplication. You could have used the minus sign in the formula if, for example, you wanted the circle to be an exact distance from the arc. Instead of d2 * 0.5, you could use d2 – 0.125, which would keep the circle 0.125 from the overall width of the part.

You can also choose from a fairly large list of formulas. If you double-click an expression in the Parameters Manager and then right-click, you can select Expressions from the context menu that appears. You can then select from a list of expressions for your parameter (see Figure 16.21).

**FIGURE 16.21**

The expressions offered from the Parameters Manager

As you can see from the list, you have quite a few expressions from which to choose. We won't try to describe each expression, but you should recognize most of them from your high school math class.

---

**ORGANIZING PARAMETERS**

If you find that you have a lot of parameters in the Parameters Manager, you can organize them using groups and filters. In the Parameters Manager, click the double arrowhead in the bar to the left of the parameter list.

The bar expands to display the Filters list. Click the funnel-shaped tool in the upper-left corner of the Parameters Manager to create a new group filter. Click and drag parameters from the parameters list to the group filter name to add parameters to your group filter.

---

# Editing the Constraint Options

AutoCAD offers a number of controls that you can apply to the constraints feature. Like most other controls, these are accessible through a settings dialog box that is opened from the Ribbon panel title bar. If you click the Constraint Settings tool on the Geometric panel title bar, the Constraint Settings dialog box opens (see Figure 16.22).

You can see that the Constraint Settings dialog box offers three tabs across the top: Geometric, Dimensional, and AutoConstrain. The settings in the Geometric tab let you control the display of the constraint bars, which are the constraint icons you see in the drawing when you add constraints. You can also control the transparency of the constraint bars using the slider near the bottom of the dialog box.

Like the Geometric tab, the Dimensional tab (see Figure 16.23) gives you control over the display of dimensional constraints. You can control the format of the text shown in the dimension and whether dynamic constraints are displayed.

**FIGURE 16.22**
The Constraint
Settings dialog
box showing the
Geometric tab

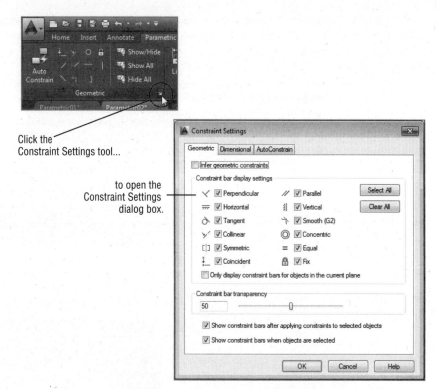

Click the
Constraint Settings tool...

to open the
Constraint Settings
dialog box.

**FIGURE 16.23**
The Dimensional
tab of the Con-
straint Settings
dialog box

Finally, the AutoConstrain tab (see Figure 16.24) gives you control over the behavior of the AutoConstrain command. You can control the priority of the constraints applied to a set of objects as well as which geometric constraints are allowed.

**FIGURE 16.24**
The AutoConstrain
tab of the Con-
straint Settings
dialog box

## Putting Constraints to Use

So far, you've seen some simple applications of the parametric tools available in AutoCAD. Although the parametric tools may seem simple, you can build some fairly elaborate parametric models using the geometric and dimensional constraints you've learned about here.

Besides having a drawing of a part that adjusts itself to changes in dimensional constraints, you can create assemblies that will allow you to study linkages and motion. For example, you can create a model of a piston and crankshaft from a gas engine and have the piston and crankshaft move together.

In the next exercise, you'll look at a drawing that has been established to show just how constraints can be set up to mimic the way a mechanical part behaves:

1. Open the `piston.dwg` file from the sample drawings.

2. Click the arc in the right side of the drawing (see Figure 16.25).

**FIGURE 16.25**
The piston drawing
in motion

Click the arc
to select it.

Click the center grip, right-click,
and select Rotate.

Rotate the arc and watch
how the drawing changes.

**3.** Click the center grip of the arc, and then right-click and select Rotate.

**4.** Move the cursor to rotate the arc. Notice that the "piston" that is connected to the arc with a fixed-length line follows the motion of the arc just as a piston would follow the motion of a crankshaft in a gas engine.

As you can see from this example, you can model a mechanical behavior using constraints. The piston in this drawing is a simple rectangle that has been constrained in both its height and width. A Horizontal constraint has also been applied so that it can move only in a horizontal direction. The line connecting the piston to the arc is constrained in its length. The Coincident constraint connects it to the piston at one end and the arc at the other end. The arc itself, representing the crankshaft, uses a Diameter constraint, and a Fix constraint is used at its center to keep its center fixed in one location. The net result is that when you rotate the arc, each part moves in unison.

## The Bottom Line

**Use parametric drawing tools.**   Parametric drawing tools enable you to create an assembly of objects that are linked to each other based on geometric or dimensional properties. With the parametric drawing tools, you can create a drawing that automatically adjusts the size of all of its components when you change a single dimension.

**Master It**   Name two examples given in the beginning of the chapter of a mechanical assembly that can be shown using parametric drawing tools.

**Connect objects with geometric constraints.**   You can link objects together so that they maintain a particular orientation to each other.

**Master It**   Name at least six of the geometric constraints available in AutoCAD.

**Control sizes with dimensional constraints.**   Dimensional constraints, in conjunction with geometric constraints, let you apply dimensions to an assembly of objects to control the size of the assembly.

**Master It**   Name at least four dimensional constraints.

**Use formulas to control dimensions.**   Dimensional constraints allow you to link dimensions of objects so that if one dimension changes, another dimension follows.

**Master It**   What example was used to show how formulas could be used with dimensional constraints?

**Put constraints to use.**   Constraints can be used in a variety of ways to simulate the behavior of real objects.

**Master It**   Name at least three geometric or dimensional constraints used in the piston.dwg sample file to help simulate the motion of a piston and crankshaft.

# Chapter 17

# Using Dynamic Blocks

Blocks are a great way to create and store ready-made symbols. They can be a real time-saver, especially when you have assemblies that you use often. Earlier in this book you learned how to create a basic, no-frills block. When you understand the basics of block creation, you can begin to work with *dynamic blocks*.

Dynamic blocks have properties that you can modify using grips. For example, you can create a dynamic block of a door and then easily grip-edit its size and orientation. Or you can use a single block to represent several versions of a similar object. You can have a single block of a bed that can be modified to show a double, queen-sized, or king-sized shape.

In this chapter, you'll explore the use of dynamic blocks through a series of tutorials. Each tutorial will show you a different way to use dynamic blocks. This will help you become familiar with the methods involved in creating dynamic blocks. You'll start by looking at the Block Editor, which in itself makes editing blocks much easier. Then you'll be introduced to the tools used to create dynamic blocks.

In this chapter, you will learn to

♦   Work with the Block Editor

♦   Create a dynamic block

♦   Add Scale and Stretch actions to a parameter

♦   Add more than one parameter for multiple grip functions

♦   Create multiple shapes in one block

♦   Rotate objects in unison

♦   Fill in a space automatically with objects

## Exploring the Block Editor

CERT
OBJECTIVE

Before you start to add dynamic block features to blocks, you'll want to get familiar with the Block Editor. The Block Editor offers an easy way to make changes to existing blocks, and as you'll see a bit later, it's also the tool you'll use to give your blocks some additional capabilities.

## Opening the Block Editor

As an introduction to the Block Editor, you'll make changes to the now familiar unit plan from earlier tutorials. Start by editing the Kitchen block in the unit:

1. Open the Unit.dwg file you saved from earlier exercises and freeze the Notes layer. You can also use the 17-unit.dwg file.

2. Double-click the kitchenette in the plan to open the Edit Block Definition dialog box (see Figure 17.1). Notice that all the blocks in the drawing are listed in the dialog box and that the Kitchen block is highlighted. You also see a preview of the block in the preview group.

**FIGURE 17.1**

The Edit Block Definition dialog box

3. With the KITCHEN block name selected, click OK. You see an enlarged view of the kitchenette in the drawing area with a light gray background (see Figure 17.2).

**FIGURE 17.2**

The Block Editor and its components

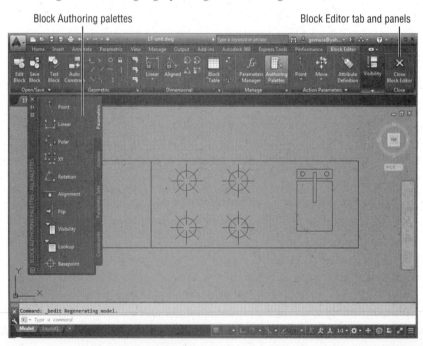

The gray background tells you that you're in the Block Editor. You'll also see the Block Editor tab along the top of the drawing area and the Block Authoring palettes, as shown in Figure 17.2.

Take a moment to look over the panels and tools on the Block Editor tab. This tab offers several housekeeping tools that let you open and save blocks and exit the Block Editor. You can point to each tool in the tab's panels to see its description. Figure 17.3 shows the Block Editor tab and tools.

**FIGURE 17.3**
The Block Editor tab

Both the Block Editor tab and the Block Authoring palettes offer tools for adding dynamic block features that you'll explore later in this chapter. You may notice that the Block Editor tab contains the geometric and dimensional constraint panels that you learned about in Chapter 16, "Making 'Smart' Drawings with Parametric Tools." Let's continue our look at the basic features of the Block Editor.

## Editing a Block and Creating New Blocks

The Block Editor lets you edit a block using all the standard AutoCAD® editing tools. In the following exercise, you'll modify the kitchen sink and save your changes to the drawing:

1. Delete the rectangle that represents the sink in the Kitchen block.

2. Click Close Block Editor on the Block Editor tab's Close panel (see the right side of Figure 17.3).

3. A message appears asking if you want to save your changes to the Kitchen block. Click Save The Changes To KITCHEN. Your view returns to the standard AutoCAD drawing area, and you can see the changes you made to the kitchen, as shown in Figure 17.4.

**FIGURE 17.4**
The unit plan with the edited Kitchen block

As you can see, editing blocks with the Block Editor is straightforward. In this example, you deleted part of the block, but you can perform any type of drawing or editing to modify the block.

The Block Editor tab also offers other block-saving options in its panels. You can save the block as you work by clicking the Save Block Definition button. If you need to create a variation on the block you're currently editing, you can click the Save Block As tool on the Block Editor's expanded Open/ Save panel to create a new block or overwrite an existing one with the drawing that is currently in the Block Editor.

If you want to edit a different block after editing the current one, you can click the Save Block tool on the Block Editor's Open/Save panel to save your current block and then click the Edit Block tool.

This tool opens the Edit Block Definition dialog box that you saw earlier. You can then select another block to edit or create a new block by entering a name for your block in the Block To Create Or Edit box.

## Creating a Dynamic Block

Now that you've seen how the Block Editor works, you can begin to explore the creation of dynamic blocks. As an introduction, you'll create a rectangle that you'll use to replace the sink in the kitchen. You'll add a dynamic block feature that will allow you to adjust the width of the sink using grips. In addition, you'll add a control that limits the size to one-unit increments.

Start by creating a block from scratch using the Block Editor:

**1.** Click the Block Editor tool in the Home tab's Block panel.

**2.** In the Edit Block Definition dialog box, enter **Sink** in the Block To Create Or Edit box and then click OK.

**3.** Use the Rectangle tool on the Home tab's Draw panel to draw a rectangle that is 12 units in the x-axis and 15 units in the y-axis.

**4.** Zoom into the rectangle so your view looks similar to Figure 17.5.

You could save this block now and you'd have a simple, static block. Next, you'll add a couple of features called *parameters* and *actions*. As their names imply, parameters define the parameters, or limits, of what the dynamic block will do, and actions describe the particular action taken when the grips of the dynamic block are edited. For example, in the next section you'll add a Linear parameter that tells AutoCAD that you want to restrain the grip editing to a linear direction. You'll also add a Stretch action that tells AutoCAD that you want the grip edit to behave like a Stretch command that pulls a set of vertices in one direction or another.

**FIGURE 17.5**
The rectangle for
the Sink block

## Adding a Parameter

The first parameter you'll add establishes the base point for the block. This will let you determine the point used when inserting the block in your drawing:

1. In the Block Authoring palettes, select the Parameters tab.

2. Click the Basepoint tool, Shift+right-click, select the Endpoint osnap, and then click the lower-left corner of the rectangle. This is how you determine the base point, or insertion point, of a block while using the Block Editor.

Next, you'll add a parameter that will determine the type of editing you want to add to the block. In this case, you want to be able to grip-edit the width of the block. For that you'll use the Linear Parameter tool:

1. Click the Linear tool on the Parameters tab of the Block Authoring palettes, or expand the Parameter tool (Point) on the Block Editor tab's Action Parameters panel and click Linear.

2. At the prompt

   ```
   Specify start point or [Name/Label
   /Chain/Description/Base/Palette/Value set]:
   ```

   Shift+right-click and select the Midpoint osnap; then select the left side of the rectangle.

3. Shift+right-click again, select Midpoint from the Osnap menu, and select the right side of the rectangle.

4. At the `Specify label location:` prompt, the parameter name appears with the parameter label at the cursor. Click below the rectangle to place the label as shown in Figure 17.6.

**FIGURE 17.6**

Placing the Linear
parameter

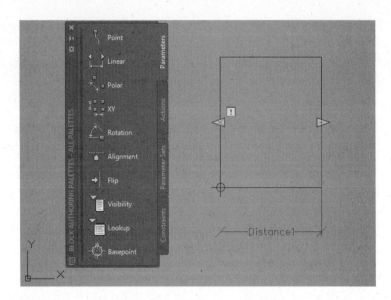

The parameter you just added lets you modify the block in a linear fashion. In this case, it will allow you to change the width of the rectangle. As you'll see, the locations of the parameter's arrows later become the grip locations for the dynamic block.

But just adding the parameter doesn't make the block dynamic. You need to include an action before a parameter can be used. You may have noticed the warning symbol in the parameter you just added. It tells you that you need to take some further steps to make the parameter useful.

## Adding an Action

Next, you'll add a Stretch action that will enable you to use the Linear parameter you just added. The Stretch action will let you stretch the block horizontally using grips. As you add the action, notice that it's similar to the Stretch command. The only difference is that you don't stretch the object; you only specify the vertices to stretch and the object you want to stretch.

Follow these steps:

1. Turn off osnaps and then click the Actions tab in the Block Authoring palettes and select Stretch.

2. At the Select parameter: prompt, click the parameter you just created.

3. At the Specify parameter point to associate with action or enter [sTart point/Second point] <Start>: prompt, point to the left-pointing arrow. You see a

circle with an X through it showing the location of a parameter point plus an osnap marker on one of the corners.

4. Click the circle with the arrow.

5. At the `Specify first corner of stretch frame or [CPolygon]:` prompt, place a selection window around the entire left side of the rectangle. This selects the portion of the rectangle that is to be stretched when you grip-edit the block.

6. At the `Specify objects to stretch Select Object:` prompt, select the rectangle and the base point you added earlier and then press ↵ to complete your selection.

You've just added an action to the Linear parameter you added earlier. You'll see an action icon appear below and to the right of the Distance1 linear parameter. The icon looks like the Stretch tool in the Actions tab to help you identify the action. If you hover over the icon, the parts affected by the action are highlighted.

Notice that the warning symbol is still showing. You need to add another action to the right side of the parameter because the parameter expects that you'll want to be able to grip-edit both sides:

1. Repeat the previous set of steps, but instead of clicking the left circle with the arrow of the Linear parameter as you did in step 4 of the preceding exercise, click the right arrow.

2. Place a window selection around the right side of the rectangle (as you did around the left side in step 5 in the preceding exercise).

3. At the `Specify objects to stretch:` prompt, select the rectangle again.

A second action icon appears next to the first one to the lower right of the Distance1 linear parameter. This time the warning symbol disappears, telling you that you've completed the steps you need for the parameter. You're ready to save the block and try it out:

1. Click Close Block Editor on the Block Editor tab's Close panel.

2. At the message asking if you want to save changes to the Sink block, click Save The Changes To Sink.

Next insert the sink to see how it works:

1. Click the Insert tool in the Home tab's Block panel.

2. Select Sink from the Insert flyout. The sink appears at the cursor.

3. Place the block at the location shown in Figure 17.7.

4. Click the newly inserted sink. You see two arrows at the vertical midpoints of the block.

5. Turn on Ortho mode, and click and drag the arrow on the right side of the block. The width of the block follows the arrow as you drag it. You also see the dimension of the sink as you drag the arrow.

6. Enter 15↵. The width of the block changes to 15 inches from the original 12.

**FIGURE 17.7**
The Sink block
in place

Place the block in this location.

Although you entered a value in step 6 to change the width of the sink, you could have clicked the mouse to change the width visually. The rectangle is still a block. You didn't have to explode it to change its width. If you hover the cursor over the dynamic block grip, you see the block's width dimension.

## Adding an Increment Value

You can grip-edit your dynamic Sink block to modify its width, and as you saw in the previous exercise, you can enter a specific value for the width as well. But suppose you'd like to limit grip movement so that the sink changes in only 1" steps. You can set parameters to have an increment value so that grip edits are limited to a specific distance.

The following steps show how you can set up the Linear parameter of the Sink block so that the sink width can be grip-edited to 1" increments:

1. Double-click the Sink block. Then, in the Edit Block Definition dialog box, make sure Sink is selected and click OK.

2. Click the Linear parameter's Distance1 label, right-click, and choose Properties.

**3.** In the Properties palette, scroll down to the Value Set group and click the Dist Type listing. The Dist Type option changes to a drop-down list.

**4.** Expand the list and select Increment.

**5.** Click in the Dist Increment text box just below the Dist Type options, and enter **1** for an increment distance of 1 inch.

**6.** Close the Properties palette, and then click Close Block Editor on the Block Editor tab's Close panel.

**7.** Save the changes.

**8.** Click the Sink block to expose its grips.

**9.** Click and drag the right arrow grip to the right. As soon as you click the grip, you see a set of increment marks appear indicating the increment steps for the grip. As you move the grip, the sink width jumps to the increment marks, which are 1″ apart, as shown in Figure 17.8.

**10.** Set the width of the sink back to 12″.

**FIGURE 17.8**
Grip-editing the
Sink block with the
Linear parameter's
increment value
set to 1

The width changes in 1″ increments.

In addition to an increment distance, you can set a range of movement for the Linear parameter. You may have noticed the minimum and maximum text boxes in the Properties palette in steps 3 through 5. You can enter values for these settings that define the range of movement allowed for the grip edits.

---

**UNDERSTANDING THE CYCLING OPTION**

You can turn on the Cycling option in the Misc group of the Properties palette of any parameter grip. Cycling allows you to use the parameter grip as an insertion point. With this option turned on, you can press the Ctrl key to cycle between the standard insertion point and the cycle-enabled grip of a parameter while inserting the block.

---

The sink exercise is a simple demonstration of how you can create and use dynamic blocks. But as you can see from the Block Authoring palettes, you can add many other parameters and actions to a block.

## Editing Parameters and Actions

In the previous exercises, you inserted parameters and actions using the default settings. These settings give you default names and labels for the parameters and actions, but you can always change them later. To change the label that appears for a parameter, double-click the label. The label will then appear in a rectangular box showing you that you can change its text.

If you want to include additional objects for an action, click the action icon to select it and then right-click and select Action Selection Set ➢ Modify Selection Set. You can also choose Action Selection Set ➢ New Selection Set if you want to change the object of the action.

## Keeping an Object Centered

Now suppose you want to add a drain to the sink, but to make things a little more complicated, you want to make sure the drain remains centered if the sink is widened or made narrower. You can alter the way the Linear parameter behaves so that both sides of the sink move symmetrically. Here's how it works:

1. Double-click the Sink block to open the Edit Block Definition dialog box. Make sure Sink is selected, and click OK.

2. Add a 3″ diameter circle in the center of the rectangle. This circle will represent the drain (see Figure 17.9).

3. Select the Distance1 linear parameter, and then right-click and select Properties.

4. In the Properties palette, scroll down to the bottom and look for the Base Location setting under the Misc section.

**FIGURE 17.9**
Adding the
sink drain

**5.** Click the Base Location option, and then select Midpoint from the drop-down list that appears to the right.

**6.** Close the Properties palette.

**7.** Click Close Block Editor in the Close panel, and save the Sink block changes.

Now try grip-editing the block to see how the Stretch action affects the sink drain:

**1.** Click the sink to select it.

**2.** Click and drag the right arrow grip to the right. The drain stays centered in the sink while the two sides expand outward.

In this exercise, you changed the Base Location option for the Linear parameter, which causes the block to behave differently when you edit its grips. You can also employ a completely different method to achieve similar results. The Geometric and Dimensional panels of the Block Editor tab offer a set of tools that work in a way that's similar to how the parameters and actions you've already worked with function. You will learn how these tools work next.

## Using Constraints in Dynamic Blocks

In the sink example, you added two Stretch actions to a Linear parameter. This enabled the block to be stretched in both the left and right directions. The actions and parameters offer one way of creating dynamic blocks, but you can also use the geometric and dimensional constraints to which you were introduced in the previous chapter.

In this section, you'll turn a simple door block into a dynamic block that will allow you to resize the door to any opening. In the process, you'll learn how to apply geometric and dimensional constraints to create a dynamic block.

At first, you may think that all you need to do to resize a door is change the scale. But when you scale the door, all its features, including the door width, are scaled proportionally. To be very accurate, you only want to stretch the door width and scale the door swing, leaving the door thickness at the same dimension. This can be accomplished by adding two aligned dimensional constraints and a few geometric constraints to the door.

Start by opening the Door block in the Block Editor and adding the geometric constraints to the door:

1. Click the Block Editor tool in the Home tab's Block panel.

2. In the Edit Block Definition dialog box, select DOOR and then click OK.

3. Click the AutoConstrain tool in the Block Editor tab's Geometric panel, and then select the rectangle representing the door, as shown in Figure 17.10. To select the door using a window, click above and to the left of the door, and then click below and to the right.

**FIGURE 17.10**
Select the rectangle representing the door.

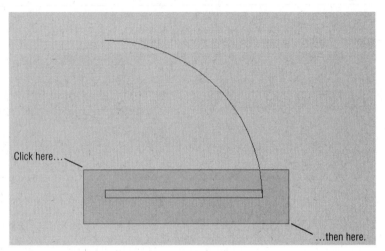

4. Press ⏎ when the door has been selected. You'll see the geometric constraint icons appear around the door.

The geometric constraints will make sure that the door maintains its rectangular shape when you apply changes to the door through the dynamic block feature. The constraints used are parallel, perpendicular, coincident, and horizontal. Note that the coincident constraint will not show an icon unless you hover over one of the corners of the rectangle.

You'll need to add a constraint to keep the arc connected to the rectangle:

1. Click the Coincident tool in the Geometric panel.

2. Place the cursor near the right end of the bottom horizontal line of the rectangle.

3. When you see the red circle and X marker, click.

4. Place the cursor near the lower end of the arc where it meets the rectangle. When you select this end, make sure the arc is highlighted, indicating that the arc will be selected.

You may need to zoom in to the location to ensure that you are selecting the correct point.

**5.** When you see the red circle and X marker, click the mouse.

The coincident constraint you just added will keep the arc and rectangle connected at the bottom-right corner of the rectangle.

Next, add a dimensional constraint. Most likely, you'll need to scale the door based only on the door opening, so place a dimensional constraint between the door hinge and the end of the door swing arc:

**1.** Click the Aligned tool in the Block Editor tab's Dimensional panel.

**2.** At the `Specify first constraint point or [Object/Point & line/2Lines] <Object>:` prompt, point to the line at the bottom of the drawing near the left endpoint, as shown in Figure 17.11.

**FIGURE 17.11**
Select the locations for the door opening dimensional constraint.

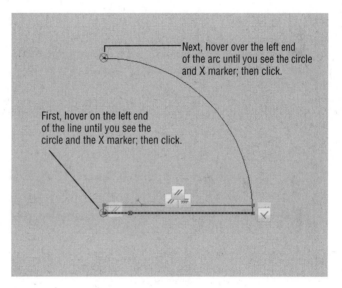

Next, hover over the left end of the arc until you see the circle and X marker; then click.

First, hover on the left end of the line until you see the circle and the X marker; then click.

**3.** When you see the red circle with the X appear at the left endpoint of the line, click.

**4.** At the `Specify second constraint point:` prompt, place the cursor on the top end of the arc so that you see the circle and X marker again at the left end of the arc, as indicated in Figure 17.11.

**5.** At the `Specify dimension line location:` prompt, place the dimension to the left of the arc (see Figure 17.12).

**6.** With the dimension highlighted, press ↵. Your drawing will look similar to Figure 17.12.

Notice that the constraint you just added is named d1. This will be an important feature in the next two constraints that you add.

**FIGURE 17.12**
The aligned dimensional constraint applied to the door opening

Next add another dimensional constraint to the width of the door rectangle. This time, you want the constraint to follow the door opening constraint, so instead of accepting the default value for the dimension, you'll enter the name of the first dimensional constraint:

1. Click the Aligned tool again from the Dimensional panel.

2. Select the left end of the bottom horizontal line again, as you did in the previous exercise (see Figure 17.13).

3. Select the right end of the bottom horizontal line, as shown in Figure 17.13.

4. Place the dimension line below the door roughly the same distance away from the door as the first dimensional constraint.

5. With the newly placed dimension highlighted, enter **d1.**↲. This will cause the door rectangle to follow the dimension of the d1 door opening dimensional constraint.

**FIGURE 17.13**
The door with the opening and door constraints added

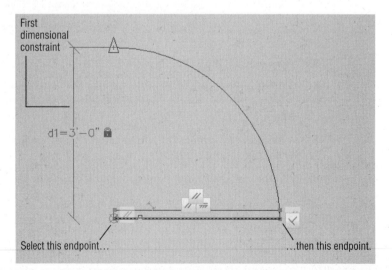

First dimensional constraint

d1=3'-0"

Select this endpoint… …then this endpoint.

Finally, add the dimensional constraint for the arc:

**1.** Click the Radius tool in the Block Editor tab's Dimensional panel.

**2.** Click anywhere on the arc.

**3.** Position the radius dimensional constraint anywhere toward the outside of the arc.

**4.** With the radius dimension highlighted, enter **d1**↵. This will cause the arc to follow the dimension of the door opening dimensional constraint.

**5.** You now have all of the constraints in place and are ready to try out your dynamic block (see Figure 17.14). Click Close Block Editor in the Close panel to save the block and return to the drawing.

**FIGURE 17.14**
The door
with all the
constraints added

Now try out your new dynamic block by adjusting the door size:

**1.** Pan your view so you can see the entry door clearly, as shown in Figure 17.15.

**2.** Click the door to select it. The added aligned constraint arrow appears as a grip on the right end of the Door block.

**FIGURE 17.15**
The Door block with
its grips exposed

**3.** Click the arrow grip. The length dimension becomes available for your input, and as you move the mouse, the door changes in size. Note that the thickness of the door doesn't change as you alter its width.

**4.** Enter 24↵ to change the door width to 24".

Notice that, although you were able to enter a door dimension directly to the block, you didn't change the door thickness when the door size changed. Only the door swing and width changed to accommodate the new door size. This is most apparent if you scale the door to a small size such as 6" or 12".

## Adding a List of Predefined Options

Earlier, you saw how you can add an increment value set to make a dynamic block stay in a set range of sizes. You can also set up a dynamic block to offer a range of sizes in a pop-up list. To do so, you need to employ the Block Table feature.

In the following exercise, you'll add a selectable list to the Door block to allow the door size to be selected from a list. Start by adding the block table that will allow you to define a set of predefined door dimensions:

**1.** Double-click the door to open the Edit Block Definition dialog box and then click OK.

**2.** In the Block Editor tab's Dimensional panel, click the Block Table tool.

**3.** At the Specify parameter location or [Palette]: prompt, place the block table in the location shown in Figure 17.16.

**FIGURE 17.16**
Placing the
block table

**4.** At the Enter number of grips [0/1] <1>: prompt, press ↵. The Block Properties Table dialog box appears (see Figure 17.17).

**5.** Click the Add Properties tool in the upper-left corner of the Block Properties Table dialog box. The Add Parameter Properties dialog box appears (see Figure 17.18).

**FIGURE 17.17**
The Block
Properties Table
dialog box

**FIGURE 17.18**
The Add Parameter
Properties
dialog box

6. Click the d1 listing at the top of the Add Parameter Properties dialog box and click OK. The Block Properties Table returns with a d1 heading in the list box.

7. Click just below the d1 listing, then type **12↵**. You see 1'-0" added to the list.

8. Type **18↵**; 1'-6" is added to the list.

9. Type **24↵30↵36↵**. The values you enter are added to the list in feet and inches format (see Figure 17.19).

10. Click OK to exit the Block Properties Table dialog box.

11. Click Close Block Editor in the Close panel and save the changes to return to your drawing.

**FIGURE 17.19**
The Block Properties Table dialog box with the values added

Now you can select from the door sizes in a pop-up list:

**1.** Click the door to select it.

**2.** Click the down-pointing grip below the door, as shown at the left side of Figure 17.20.

**FIGURE 17.20**
Selecting a door size from a list

**3.** Select the 3′-0″ door from the list that appears. (See the view to the right in Figure 17.20.) The door changes to a 36″-wide door.

If at a later time you need to make changes to the list or add more dimensions, you can open the block in the Block Editor and then click the Block Table tool. The Block Properties Table dialog box will appear with the data you entered earlier. You can then make changes to the table.

In this example, you saw that you can easily add predefined sizes to the dimensional constraint that appear in a selectable list. You can also give the list a more meaningful name. Right now, when you click on the grip that opens the list, you see d1 as the name. Try the following to change the name from d1 to Width:

1. Double-click the door, and in the Edit Block Definition dialog box, click OK.

2. Select the d1 dimensional constraint, and then right-click and select Properties.

3. In the Properties palette, select the Name option under the Constraint group and then type **Width**↵. Notice that all of the dimensional constraints that reference the dimension will change to show the name Width instead of d1.

4. Close the Properties palette, and then click the Close Block Editor tool in the Close panel.

5. To see the change, click the down-pointing grip below the door as you did in the previous exercise. Now you see the word *Width* as the heading in the list of door widths (see Figure 17.21).

**FIGURE 17.21**
The list with the word Width appearing as the column title

6. Save and close the file.

As you can see, you have a lot of control over the behavior of various components of the dynamic block. In the next section, you'll learn how you can control the visibility of different parts of your block.

## Creating Multiple Shapes in One Block

Depending on circumstances, you may need a block to display a completely different form. For example, you might want a single generic bath that can morph into a standard bath, a corner bath, or a large spa-style bath with jets.

Using dynamic blocks, you can hide or display elements of a block by selecting a *visibility state* from a list. For example, you can draw the three different bath sizes and then set up a visibility state for each size. Each visibility state displays only one bath size. You can then select a visibility state depending on the bath size you want.

Try the following exercise to see how this works firsthand:

1. Open the `visibilitysample.dwg` file, and then click the Block Editor tool on the Home tab's Block panel.

2. In the Edit Block Definition dialog box, select Bathtub from the list and click OK.

You see the contents of the Bathtub block (see Figure 17.22). It's just the three existing blocks—Standard, Jetted, and Corner—inserted at the same origin.

**FIGURE 17.22**
The Bathtub block

If you were to insert this block in a drawing, it would appear just as you currently see it, with each bathtub type overlaid on another. Next you'll see how you can add control over the visibility of each bathtub type so that only one is displayed at a time.

The first thing you need to do is add a Visibility parameter:

1. On the Parameters tab of the Block Authoring palettes, click Visibility.

2. Click below the blocks to place the Visibility parameter as shown in Figure 17.23.

**FIGURE 17.23**
Adding the Visibility parameter

**3.** Double-click the Visibility parameter you just added to open the Visibility States dialog box (see Figure 17.24). One visibility state, VisibilityState0, is already provided.

**FIGURE 17.24**
The Visibility States
dialog box

You'll need three visibility states: one for each type of bathtub whose visibility you want to control. You've already got one, but you want a name that is more appropriate to the application:

**1.** Click the Rename button. The existing visibility state in the list to the left becomes editable.

**2.** Enter **Standard**↵. This is the visibility state for your standard bathtub.

**3.** Click the New button to open the New Visibility State dialog box (see Figure 17.25).

**FIGURE 17.25**
Adding a
visibility state

**4.** Enter **Jetted** in the Visibility State Name box.

**5.** Make sure the Leave Visibility Of Existing Objects Unchanged In New State radio button is selected, and then click OK.

**6.** Click the New button again.

**7.** In the New Visibility State dialog box, enter **Corner** in the Visibility State Name box.

**8.** Make sure Leave Visibility Of Existing Objects Unchanged In New State is selected, and click OK.

You've just created all the visibility states you need.

9. Select Standard from the list in the Visibility States dialog box, and click the Set Current button. (You can also double-click the Standard item.) A check mark appears to the left of Standard, showing you that it's now the current state.

10. Click OK to exit the Visibility States dialog box.

You have the visibility states you need, and you have the objects whose visibility you want to control. Now you need to determine which block is visible for each state.

Remember that in step 9 of the previous exercise, you made Standard the current visibility state. You'll want only the standard Bathtub block visible for this state. Do the following to turn off the other two Bathtub blocks for the current state:

1. Select the Jetted and Corner blocks (see Figure 17.26).

**FIGURE 17.26**
Locating the blocks

Jetted

Standard

Corner

2. Right-click, and choose Object Visibility ➤ Hide For Current State. You can also click the Make Invisible tool on the right side of the Block Editor tab's Visibility panel.

The selected blocks disappear. They didn't go anywhere; they are just made invisible.

3. Click the drop-down list on the Block Editor tab's Visibility panel, and select Jetted. The hidden blocks appear.

The current visibility state is now Jetted, so you want only the Jetted block to be visible. Select the Standard and Corner blocks, and then right-click and choose Object Visibility ➢ Hide For Current State. You can also click the Make Invisible tool from the Visibility panel. Now only the Jetted block is visible.

**4.** On the Block Editor tab's Visibility panel, click the drop-down list again and select Corner. All the blocks appear.

**5.** Select the Standard and Jetted blocks, and click the Make Invisible tool. Now only the Corner block is visible.

You've created visibility states and set up the blocks so that they appear only when the appropriate visibility state is current. Next you'll test the blocks:

**1.** Click Close Block Editor, and save the changes you've made.

**2.** Click the Insert tool on the Home tab's Block panel, then More Options, and then select Bathtub from the Name drop-down list in the Insert dialog box.

**3.** Make sure Specify On-Screen is checked for the Insertion Point group and unchecked for the Scale and Rotation groups.

**4.** Click OK, and then place the block to the right of the other three blocks.

**5.** Click the Bathtub block you just inserted, and then click the Visibility grip (see the left image in Figure 17.27).

**6.** Select Jetted from the list. The jetted bathtub appears (see the right image in Figure 17.27).

**7.** Click the Bathtub block again, click the Visibility grip, and select Corner. The Corner tub appears.

**8.** Save and close the drawing.

**FIGURE 17.27**
Using the Visibility grip to change the bathtub

---

### CONTROLLING THE VISIBILITY OF INVISIBLE OBJECTS

While you're editing in the Block Editor, you can set up AutoCAD to display objects whose visibility has been turned off. If you set the bvmode system variable to 1, objects appear gray when their visibility has been turned off. You can also click the Visibility Mode tool in the Block Editor tab's Visibility panel.

---

In this example, you used a set of bathtubs but you can use the Visibility parameter for anything that requires a different appearance. As mentioned at the beginning of this chapter, another use might be a block that contains a double, a queen-sized, and a king-sized bed. Going back to the door example, you can create a left- and right-hand door in the same block and then use the Visibility parameter to display a left- or right-hand door in the drawing. Figure 17.28 shows such a door block. The Visibility parameter has been renamed Hand in the block. When the door is inserted in the drawing, you see a list that allows you to select Left or Right.

**FIGURE 17.28**
The Door dynamic block showing a left- and right-hand door (left), and the Door block as it appears in the drawing (right)

The Visibility parameter renamed Hand

## Rotating Objects in Unison

You've seen how actions and parameters can control the behavior of a single object in a block. You can also apply actions to multiple objects so that they move or change in unison. The following example shows how you can apply more than one Angular Constraint parameter to control two objects:

1. Open the gatesample.dwg file. In this sample file, the part that will move consists of the two non-red objects. The red lines have been added to help facilitate the rotation feature of the block.

2. Double-click the object in the drawing to open the Edit Block Definition dialog box, and then click OK. The Gate block opens for editing.

3. Click the Show All Geometric Constraints tool in the Block Editor tab's Geometric panel to reveal some of the existing constraints.

You can see how this drawing has been prepared for this exercise. The non-red parts of the drawing, which we'll call gates, are blocks that are constrained to the red lines with coincident constraints. The endpoints of the lines are constrained to the center of the arcs. The horizontal red lines are constrained to the vertical ones, also with coincident constraints, and the vertical lines are constrained at both ends with a fixed constraint (see Figure 17.29).

**FIGURE 17.29**

How the parts of the block are constrained

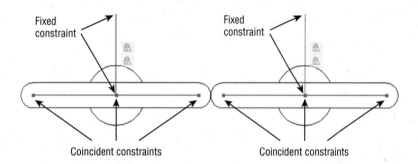

You'll use the red lines to define the rotation angle of the parts. The vertical line is fixed in place whereas the rest of the parts are constrained in such a way as to allow a rotational motion. Now add some angular constraints to define the rotation:

1. In the Dimensional panel, click the Angular tool.

2. Click the left vertical line toward the top, as shown in Figure 17.30.

3. Next, click the left horizontal line toward the right end of the line, as shown in Figure 17.30.

**FIGURE 17.30**

Adding the angular constraint to the gatesample.dwg drawing

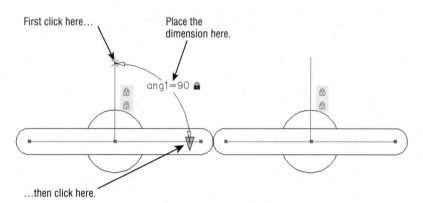

4. Place the dimension as shown in Figure 17.30.

5. The dimension text is highlighted. You want to keep the current value, so press ↵ to accept the default.

You have the first angular dimensional constraint in place. Next add a second one to the gate on the right, but this time, you'll use the name of the first angular constraint as the dimension for the second one:

1. In the Dimensional panel, click the Angular tool.

2. Click the right vertical line near its top, as shown in Figure 17.31.

3. Click the right horizontal line near its right end (see Figure 17.31).

4. Place the dimension as shown in Figure 17.31.

**FIGURE 17.31**
Adding the angular constraint to the second gate

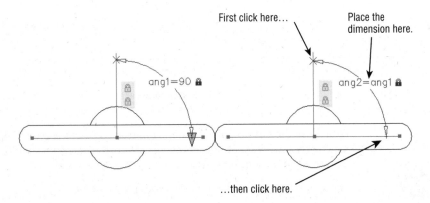

First click here…

Place the dimension here.

ang1=90

ang2=ang1

…then click here.

5. At the highlighted text, type **ang1**↵. This will cause this constraint to follow the first one you added.

Now you're ready to save the block and try it out:

1. Click Close Block Editor on the Block Editor tab's Close panel, and save the block.

2. Click the block to expose its grips.

3. Click the arrow grip on the horizontal line.

4. Type **45**↵. Both sides of the block rotate about their own centers to a 45-degree angle (see Figure 17.32).

5. Click the arrow grip again, and type **90**↵ to set the gate back to its original position.

**FIGURE 17.32**
The two parts rotate in unison.

You've got the basic function of the gate working, but you don't want the red lines to appear in the drawing since they are there to facilitate the action of the gate and are not really part of the drawing. Do the following to hide the red lines:

**1.** Double-click the Gate block to open the Edit Block Definition dialog box, and then click OK. The Gate block opens for editing.

**2.** Click the Construction Geometry tool in the Manage panel.

**3.** Select the four red lines and press ⊠. Notice that the lines change from solid to dashed, indicating that they are now construction geometry.

**4.** Click the Close Block Editor tool, and save the block. The block now appears without the red lines. If you click on the block, the rotation grip still appears, and you can alter the block as before.

Now suppose you want to have the gates rotate in opposite directions instead of in the same direction. You can add a user-defined formula to modify the behavior of the angular constraints:

**1.** Double-click the Gate block to open the Edit Block Definition dialog box, and then click OK. The Gate block opens for editing.

**2.** Click the Parameters Manager tool to open the Parameters Manager palette. You may recall that in Chapter 16, you used this palette to control the size of a concentric circle.

**3.** Double-click in the Expression column of the ang2 option, and type **ang1 * -1**↵.

**4.** Close the Parameters Manager palette, and then save and close the block.

**5.** Click the gate to select it, and then click the arrow grip.

**6.** Type **22**↵. Now the two parts rotate in opposite directions (see Figure 17.33).

**FIGURE 17.33**
The gates moving in opposite directions

**7.** Save and close the file.

You can go on to add a block table using the Block Table tool to create a predefined set of angles, just as you did for the Door block earlier in this chapter. You can also add incremental values by using the Properties palette to change the angle constraint in a way similar to how you changed constraints in the sink exercise in the first part of this chapter.

Next take a look at a way to array objects automatically with dynamic blocks.

## Filling in a Space Automatically with Objects

Perhaps one of the more tedious tasks you'll face is drawing the vertical bars of a hand railing for an elevation view. You can draw a single bar and then use the Array command to repeat the bar as many times as needed, but when you have to edit the railing, you may find that you're spending more time adding and erasing bars.

In the next example, you'll see how you can create a block that automatically fills in vertical bars as the width of the railing changes. You'll start with an existing drawing of a single vertical bar and an outline of the railing opening around the bar:

1. Open the `railsample.dwg` file.

2. Double-click the object in the drawing to open the Edit Block Definition dialog box, and then click OK. This opens the Railvertical block for editing.

   When the Block Editor opens, notice that the block already has a Linear parameter and a Stretch action added. Recall from the sink example at the beginning of this chapter that the Linear parameter and Stretch action let you vary the width of an object. In this case, the outermost rectangle is being stretched.

3. On the Actions tab of the Block Authoring palettes, click the Array action.

4. At the `Select parameter:` prompt, click the blue Linear parameter (labeled as Distance), as shown in Figure 17.34.

**FIGURE 17.34**
Adding the Array action to the Rail-vertical block

Select the inner rectangle.

Click the Distance parameter.

5. At the `Select objects:` prompt, select the dark vertical rectangle representing the vertical bar of the railing, as shown in Figure 17.34, and then press ↵.

6. At the `Enter the distance between columns (|||):` prompt, enter **4**↵.

7. Click Close Block Editor on the Block Editor tab's Close panel and save the changes.

8. Click the block to expose its grips.

9. Click and drag the blue arrow grip to the right. As the rail expands, additional vertical bars are added at 4" intervals (see Figure 17.35).

**FIGURE 17.35**

The Railvertical block adds vertical bars as its width expands.

10. Exit and save the file.

You can now use this block wherever you need to draw a simple railing with vertical bars. Another example of how the Array action might be used is in a side view of a bolt. You could show the threads of the bolt and use the Array action to increase the number of threads as the bolt is lengthened.

---

**USING PARAMETER SETS**

You probably noticed the Parameter Sets tab in the Block Authoring palettes. The options in this tab are predefined combinations of parameters and actions that are commonly used together. For example, the Polar Array set inserts a Polar parameter with an Array action. You only need to supply the object. The Polar Array set causes the associated object to rotate about a center point with a grip. You can also array the object by stretching the grip away from the rotation center.

To associate an object with a parameter set, right-click the action icon associated with a parameter (usually appearing below the parameter), and then select Action Selection Set ➤ New Selection Set. At the `Select objects:` prompt, select an object. If a stretch is employed, select a stretch frame and an object to stretch.

# Including Block Information with Data Extraction

In Chapter 12, "Using Attributes," you learned how you could attach data to blocks through attributes and then extract that data to spreadsheets or AutoCAD tables. You can also include dynamic block information that has been included in a property lookup table. This can be extremely useful for generating data for a bill of materials or in other situations if you need to track the numbers and types of items in your drawing.

To see how this works, you'll return to a version of the Door block that has some additions. This enhanced version of the Door block includes a left- and right-hand version of the door that is controlled with the Visibility parameter. Figure 17.36 shows the door inserted into a drawing using different door sizes and left and right variations.

**FIGURE 17.36**
The door block inserted several times into a drawing with various widths and handedness

You'll use the Attribute Extraction command to see how the dynamic block data appears as an exported table or a spreadsheet:

1. Open the `17-extractsample.dwg` file. This file contains a dynamic door block that is similar to the one you created earlier with the addition of a left and a right Visibility parameter.

 2. From the Annotate tab's Tables panel, click the Extract Data tool to start the Data Extraction Wizard.

3. On the Begin screen, click Next.

4. In the Save Data Extraction As dialog box, enter **Test** for the name and click Save.

5. On the Define Data Source screen, click Next.

6. On the Select Objects screen, remove the check mark from the Display All Object Types option so that only the Door block appears in the list and then click Next.

7. On the Select Properties screen, remove the check mark from all but the Dynamic Block option in the right column, and make sure the Hand and Width options in the left column are the only ones selected (see Figure 17.37).

**FIGURE 17.37**
Set up the Select
Properties screen to
look like this.

**8.** Click Next. On the Refine Data page, you see the data that will be exported to a spread-sheet file or a table (see Figure 17.38).

**FIGURE 17.38**
The resulting table
to be extracted,
as shown on the
Refine Data screen
of the Data Extrac-
tion Wizard

**9.** You don't really want to extract this data, so once you've taken a good look at this screen, click Cancel and then Yes in the Quit Wizard dialog box.

This is the end of the door example, so you can exit this file. Save it for future reference if you like.

As you can see in Figure 17.38, a list is generated that shows each door in the drawing with its size and handedness. You could use this data as part of a door schedule.

---

**TAKE CARE USING THE MIRROR TOOL**

If you use the Mirror command to mirror a block that contains a Visibility parameter to control left- and right-hand doors, the Attribute Extraction command will report erroneous results. Therefore, be sure that if you set up a block with a visibility parameter to control mirrored states, you use those actions to edit the door and don't rely on standard editing tools. That way, you'll ensure the accuracy of your extracted data.

---

## The Bottom Line

**Work with the Block Editor.**   To create dynamic blocks, you need to become familiar with the Block Editor. You can use the Block Editor to modify existing blocks in your drawing.

> **Master It**   What does the Edit Block Definition dialog box allow you to do?

**Create a dynamic block.**   A dynamic block is a block you add grips to so you can modify the block in a number of ways.

> **Master It**   Name some of the features of the Block Editor that let you add additional grip editing functions to a block.

**Add Scale and Stretch actions to a parameter.**   You can set up a dynamic block to perform multiple operations with a single grip.

> **Master It**   What do you need to do to have one grip perform two functions?

**Add more than one parameter for multiple grip functions.**   In addition to having one grip perform multiple operations, you can add as many grips as you need to make your block even more customizable.

> **Master It**   What feature do you use to set up a list of options for a block?

**Create multiple shapes in one block.**   Many of the dynamic block functions let you adjust the shape of the original block. Another feature lets you choose completely different shapes for the block.

> **Master It**   When a block uses the Visibility parameter to set up different shapes, how do you select a different block shape in the drawing?

**Rotate objects in unison.**   Blocks can be set up so that the action of one set of objects affects another set. This chapter gives the example of rotating objects in unison.

> **Master It**   Name the dimensional constraint that was used in the object rotation example in this chapter.

**Fill in a space automatically with objects.**   A dynamic block can help you automate the addition of repetitive elements to your drawing.

> **Master It**   What is the name of the action used to produce an array of an object in a block when the block is stretched?

# Chapter 18

# Drawing Curves

So far in this book, you've been using basic lines, arcs, and circles to create your drawings in the Autodesk® AutoCAD® software. Now it's time to add polylines and spline curves to your repertoire. Polylines offer many options for creating forms, including solid fills and free-form curved lines. Spline curves are perfect for drawing accurate and smooth nonlinear objects.

In this chapter, you will learn to

♦ Create and edit polylines

♦ Create a polyline spline curve

♦ Create and edit true spline curves

♦ Mark divisions on curves

## Introducing Polylines

*Polylines* are like composite line segments and arcs. A polyline may look like a series of line segments, but it acts like a single object. This characteristic makes polylines useful for a variety of applications, as you'll see in the upcoming exercises.

### Drawing a Polyline

First, to learn about the polyline, you'll begin a drawing of the top view of the joint shown in Figure 18.1.

**FIGURE 18.1**
A sketch of a
metal joint

Follow these steps to draw the joint:

1. Open a new file using the acad.dwt template, and save it as Joint2d.dwg. Don't bother to make special setting changes because you'll create this drawing with the default settings.

2. From the Navigation bar, choose Zoom All from the flyout or type **Z.⏎A.⏎**.

3. Click the Polyline tool on the Draw panel, or type **PL⏎**.

4. At the Specify start point: prompt, enter a point at coordinate 3,3 to start your polyline.

5. At the Specify next point or [Arc/Halfwidth/Length/Undo/Width]: prompt, enter **@3<0⏎** to draw a horizontal line of the joint.

6. At the Specify next point or [Arc/Close/Halfwidth/Length/Undo/Width]: prompt, click the Arc option in the prompt or enter **A⏎** to continue your polyline with an arc.

---

### USING THE ARC OPTION IN THE POLYLINE TOOL

The Arc option lets you draw an arc that starts from the last polyline point you selected. While in the Polyline tool, select the Arc option; as you move your cursor, an arc follows it in a tangential direction from the previous line segment of the polyline. You can return to drawing straight line segments by entering **L⏎**. If you want the arc to be drawn in the opposite direction from the last point instead of a tangent direction, hold down the Ctrl key.

---

7. At the prompt

```
Specify endpoint of arc or
[Angle/CEnter/CLose/Direction/Halfwidth/Line/Radius/Second pt/Undo/Width]:
```

enter **@4<90⏎** to draw a 180 arc from the last point you entered. Your drawing should now look similar to Figure 18.2.

8. To continue the polyline with another line segment, click the Line option in the prompt or enter **L⏎**.

**FIGURE 18.2**
A polyline consisting of a line segment and an arc

Polyline

9. At the `Specify next point or [Arc/Close/Halfwidth/Length/Undo/Width]:` prompt, enter @3<180↵. Another line segment continues from the end of the arc.

10. Press ↵ to exit the Polyline tool.

You now have a sideways, U-shaped polyline that you'll use in the next exercise to complete the top view of your joint.

## Setting Polyline Options

Let's take a break from the tutorial to look at some of the options that you didn't use in the Polyline prompt:

**Close**  Draws a line segment from the last endpoint of a sequence of line segments to the first point picked in that sequence. This works exactly like the Close option for the Line command.

**Length**  Enables you to specify the length of a line that will be drawn at the same angle as the last line entered.

**Halfwidth**  Creates a tapered line segment or an arc by specifying half its beginning and ending widths (see Figure 18.3).

**Width**  Creates a tapered line segment or an arc by specifying the full width of the segment's beginning and ending points.

**Undo**  Deletes the last polyline segment drawn.

**Radius/Second Pt**  The Radius and Second Pt options appear when you use the arc option to draw polyline segments. Radius lets you specify a radius for the arc and Second Pt lets you specify a second point in a three-point arc.

**FIGURE 18.3**
A tapered line segment and an arc created with Halfwidth

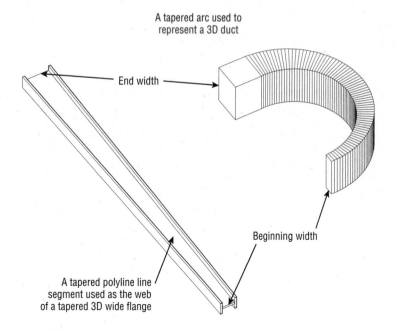

A tapered arc used to represent a 3D duct

End width

Beginning width

A tapered polyline line segment used as the web of a tapered 3D wide flange

If you want to break a polyline into simple lines and arcs, you can use the Explode option on the Modify panel, just as you would with blocks. After a polyline is exploded, it becomes a set of individual lines or arcs.

To turn off the filling of solid polylines, open the Options dialog box and click the Display tab. Clear the Apply Solid Fill check box in the Display Performance group.

> ### FILLETING A POLYLINE
>
> You can use the Fillet tool on the Modify panel to fillet all the vertices of a polyline at once. Click the Fillet tool, set your fillet radius by typing **R**⏎ and entering a radius value, type **P**⏎ to select the Polyline option, and then pick the polyline you want to fillet. If you want to fillet only two line segments of a polyline, use the fillet tool as you normally would to fillet simple lines.
>
> You can also close a polyline with a radius by using the fillet command on the polyline's endpoints.

## Editing Polylines

You can edit polylines with many of the standard editing commands. To change the properties of a polyline, click the polyline to select it, right-click, and select Properties to open the Properties palette. You can use the Stretch command on the Modify panel to move vertices of a polyline. The Trim, Extend, and Break commands on the Modify panel also work with polylines.

In addition, many editing capabilities are offered only for polylines. For instance, later you'll see how to smooth out a polyline using the Fit option in the Pedit command.

In this exercise, you'll use the Offset command on the Modify panel to add the inside portion of the joint:

1. Click the Offset tool in the Home tab's Modify panel, or type **O**⏎.

2. At the `Specify offset distance or [Through/Erase/Layer] <Through>:` prompt, enter **1**.

3. At the `Select object to offset or [Exit/Undo]<Exit>:` prompt, pick the U-shaped polyline you just drew.

4. At the `Specify point on side to offset or [Exit/Multiple/Undo] <Exit>:` prompt, pick a point on the inside of the U shape. You'll see a concentric copy of the polyline appear (see Figure 18.4).

5. Press ⏎ to exit the Offset command.

The concentric copy of a polyline made by choosing the Offset tool can be useful when you need to draw complex parallel curves like the ones shown in Figure 18.5.

**FIGURE 18.4**
The offset polyline

**FIGURE 18.5**
Sample complex curves drawn by using offset polylines

The outside profile was drawn first; then the Offset command was used to draw the inside profile.

120°

2.7500

1.1250

1.6250

4.7500

Next, complete the top view of the joint. To do this, you'll use the Edit Polyline tool, otherwise known as the Pedit command:

1. Connect the ends of the polylines with two short line segments (see Figure 18.6).

2. Choose Edit Polyline from the expanded Modify panel or type **PE↵**.

3. At the Select polyline or [Multiple]: prompt, pick the outermost polyline.

4. At the prompt

   ```
   Enter an option
   [Close/Join/Width/Edit vertex/Fit/Spline/Decurve/Ltype gen/Reverse/Undo]:
   ```

   click the Join option in the prompt or enter **J↵**.

**FIGURE 18.6**
The polyline so far

5. At the `Select objects:` prompt, select all the objects you've drawn so far.

6. Press ↵ to join all the objects into one polyline. It appears that nothing has happened.

7. Press ↵ again to exit the Pedit command.

8. Click the drawing to expose its grips. The entire object is highlighted, indicating that all the lines have been joined into a single polyline.

---

#### WHAT TO DO IF THE JOIN OPTION DOESN'T WORK

If the objects to be joined don't touch, you can use the *fuzz* join feature. Type **PE↵M↵** to start the Pedit command with the Multiple option, then select all the objects you want to join and press ↵. If you see a convert message, enter **Y↵**. At the `Enter an option [Close/Open/Join/Width/Fit/Spline/Decurve/Ltype gen/Reverse/Undo]:` prompt, click the Join option in the prompt or enter **J↵**. At the `Enter fuzz distance or [Jointype]:` prompt, enter a distance that approximates the size of the gap between objects. By default, AutoCAD extends the lines so they join end to end. You can use the Jointype option if you want Pedit to join segments with an additional segment.

---

By using the Width option under Edit Polyline, you can change the width of a polyline. Let's change the width of your polyline to give some width to the outline of the joint. To do this, you'll use the Edit Polyline tool again, but this time you'll use a shortcut:

1. Double-click the polyline.

2. At the `Enter an option [Open/Join/Width/Edit vertex/Fit/Spline/Decurve/Ltype gen/Reverse/Undo]:` prompt, enter **W↵** for the Width option.

3. At the `Specify new width for all segments:` prompt, enter **.03↵** for the new width of the polyline. The line changes to the new width (see Figure 18.7), and you now have a top view of your joint.

**FIGURE 18.7**
The polyline with a new thickness

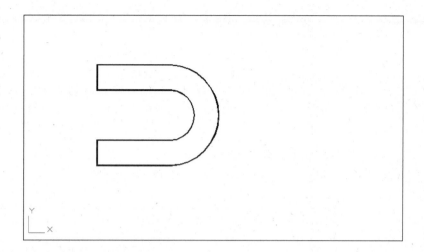

4. Press ↵ to exit the Pedit command.

5. Save this file.

In most cases, you can simply double-click on a polyline to start the Pedit command. But if you want to edit multiple polylines, or if you want to convert an object or set of objects into a polyline, use the Edit Polyline tool from the expanded Modify panel to start Pedit.

In addition, you can select the Edit Polyline options from a menu that appears at the cursor (see Figure 18.8) if dynamic input is on, or by selecting the polyline and then right-clicking anywhere in the drawing to access the Polyline options from the context menu.

**FIGURE 18.8**
The Edit Polyline options that appear at the cursor

## Setting Pedit Options

Here's a brief look at a few of the Pedit options you didn't try firsthand:

**Close**    Connects the two endpoints of a polyline with a line segment. If the polyline you selected to be edited is already closed, this option changes to Open.

**Open**    Removes the last segment added to a closed polyline.

**Spline/Decurve**    The Spline option smooths a polyline into a spline curve (discussed in detail later in this chapter). The Decurve option changes a spline or fit curve polyline back into its original shape before the Spline or Fit option was applied.

**Edit Vertex**   Lets you edit each vertex of a polyline individually (discussed in detail later in this chapter).

**Fit**   Turns polyline segments into a series of arcs.

**Ltype Gen**   Controls the way noncontinuous linetypes pass through the vertices of a polyline. If you have a fitted or spline curve with a noncontinuous linetype, turn on this option.

**Reverse**   Reverses the orientation of a polyline. The orientation is based on the order in which points are selected to create the polyline. The first point picked is the beginning (or point 1), the next point is point 2, and so on. In some cases, you may want to reverse this order using the Reverse option.

**Undo**   Removes the last polyline line segment.

---

**USING POLYLINES TO SET LINEWEIGHTS**

Typically, you would use the Lineweight feature of AutoCAD to set lineweights in your drawing. In cases where the Lineweight feature will not work, you can change the thickness of regular lines and arcs using Pedit to change them into polylines and then use the Width option to change their width.

---

## Smoothing Polylines

You can create a curve in AutoCAD in many ways. If you don't need the representation of a curve to be accurate, you can use a polyline curve. In the following exercise, you'll draw a polyline curve to represent a contour on a topographical map:

1. Open the topo.dwg file. The top image in Figure 18.9 contains the drawing of survey data. Some of the contours have already been drawn in between the data points.

2. Zoom in to the upper-right corner of the drawing so that your screen displays the area shown in the bottom image in Figure 18.9.

3. Click the Polyline tool on the Draw panel. Using the Center osnap, draw a polyline that connects the points labeled 254.00. Your drawing should look like the bottom image in Figure 18.9.

4. Press ↵.

5. Next you'll convert the polyline you just drew into a smooth contour line. Double-click the contour polyline line you just drew.

6. At the prompt

```
Enter an option
[Close/Join/Width/Edit vertex/Fit/Spline/Decurve/Ltype gen/Reverse/Undo]:
```

click the Fit option in the prompt or type F↵. The polyline smooths out into a series of connected arcs that pass through the data points.

7. Press ↵ to end the command.

**FIGURE 18.9**
The topo.dwg file shows survey data portrayed in an AutoCAD drawing. Notice the dots indicating where elevations were taken. The actual elevation value is shown with a diagonal line from the point.

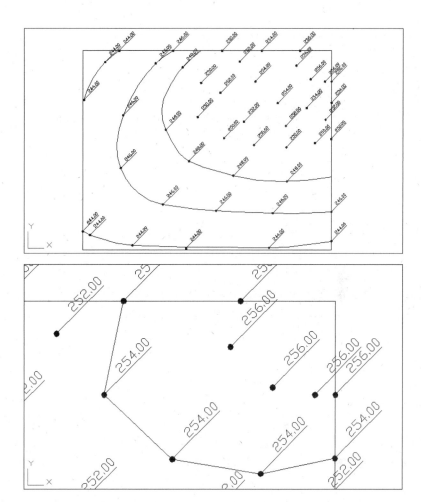

Your contour is now complete. The Fit option under the Pedit command causes AutoCAD to convert the straight-line segments of the polyline into arcs. The endpoints of the arcs pass through the endpoints of the line segments, and the curve of each arc depends on the direction of the adjacent arc. This gives the effect of a smooth curve. Next you'll use this polyline curve to experiment with some of the editing options unique to the Pedit command.

## Editing Vertices

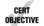

**CERT
OBJECTIVE**

One of the Pedit options that we haven't yet discussed, Edit Vertex, is like a command within a command. Edit Vertex has numerous suboptions that enable you to fine-tune your polyline by giving you control over individual vertices.

To access the Edit Vertex options, follow these steps:

1.  Turn off the DATA and BORDER layers to hide the data points and border.

2.  Double-click the polyline you just drew.

3.  Type E↵ to enter Edit Vertex mode. An X appears at the beginning of the polyline indicating the vertex that will be affected by the Edit Vertex options.

When using Edit Vertex, you must be careful about selecting the correct vertex to be edited. Edit Vertex has 10 options. You often have to exit the Edit Vertex operation and use Pedit's Fit option to see the effect of several Edit Vertex options on a curved polyline.

After you enter the Edit Vertex mode of the Pedit command, you can perform the following functions:

♦ Break the polyline between two vertices.

♦ Insert a new vertex.

♦ Move an existing vertex.

♦ Regenerate (type **RE**↵) the drawing to view the current shape of the polyline.

♦ Straighten a polyline between two vertices.

♦ Change the tangential direction of a vertex.

♦ Change the width of the polyline at a vertex.

These functions are presented in the form of the following prompt:

```
[Next/Previous/Break/Insert/Move/Regen/Straighten/Tangent/Width/eXit] <N>:
```

The following sections examine each of the options in this prompt, starting with Next and Previous.

### THE NEXT AND PREVIOUS OPTIONS

The Next and Previous options let you select a vertex for editing. When you start the Edit Vertex option, an X appears on the selected polyline to designate its beginning. As you select Next or Previous, the X moves from vertex to vertex to show which one is being edited. Let's try it:

**1.** Press ↵ a few times to move the X along the polyline. (Because Next is the default option, you only need to press ↵ to move the X.)

**2.** Type **P**↵ for Previous. The X moves in the opposite direction. The default option becomes P.

---

#### WHY REVERSE A POLYLINE

One of the more frequently asked questions we receive from readers is "How can I reverse the direction of a polyline?" It may seem like an odd question to someone new to AutoCAD, but reversing a polyline has quite a few uses. Perhaps the most common use is to turn a polyline that uses a complex linetype, one that includes text, right side up so that the text can be read more easily. (See Chapter 24, "Customizing Toolbars, Menus, Linetypes, and Hatch Patterns," for an example of a linetype that includes text.) If for some reason you need to reverse the direction of a polyline or spline, you can do so by using the Reverse option in the Pedit command.

**CERT OBJECTIVE**

## TURNING OBJECTS INTO POLYLINES AND POLYLINES INTO SPLINES

At times, you'll want to convert regular lines, arcs, or even circles into polylines. You might want to change the width of lines or join lines to form a single object such as a boundary. Here are the steps to convert lines, arcs, and circles into polylines:

1. Click the Edit Polyline tool from the Home tab's expanded Modify panel, or type **PE**↵ at the Command prompt.

2. At the `Select polyline or [Multiple]:` prompt, pick the object you want to convert. If you want to convert a circle to a polyline, first break the circle (using the Break tool on the expanded Modify panel) so that it becomes an arc of approximately 359.

3. At the prompt

   ```
   Object selected is not a polyline. Do you want to turn it into one? <Y>:
   ```

   press ↵. The object is converted into a polyline.

If you want to convert several objects to polylines, type **M**↵ at the `Select polyline or [Multiple]:` prompt, then select the objects you want to convert. You will see the `Convert Lines, Arcs and Splines to polylines [Yes/No]? <Y>:` prompt. Type **Y**↵, and all the selected objects are converted to polylines. You can then go on to use other Pedit options on the selected objects.

To turn a polyline into a true spline curve, do the following:

1. Click the Edit Polyline tool from the Home tab's expanded Modify panel, or type **PE**↵. Select the polyline you want to convert.

2. Type **S**↵ to turn it into a polyline spline, and then press ↵ to exit the Pedit command.

3. Click the Spline Fit tool on the Home tab's expanded Draw panel or type **SPL**↵.

4. At the `Specify first point or [Method/Knots/Object]:` prompt, click the Object option in the prompt or type **O**↵.

5. At the `Select spline-fit polyline:` prompt, click the polyline spline. Although it may not be apparent at first, the polyline is converted into a true spline.

You can also use the Edit Spline tool on the Home tab's expanded Modify panel (or enter **SPE**↵) to edit a polyline spline. If you do, the polyline spline is automatically converted into a true spline.

If you know you'll always want to convert an object into a polyline when using Pedit, you can turn on the `Peditaccept` system variable. Enter **peditaccept**↵ at the Command prompt, and then enter **1**↵.

## THE BREAK OPTION

The Break option breaks the polyline between two vertices:

1. Position the X on one end of the segment you want to break.

2. Enter **B**↵ at the Command prompt.

3. At the `Enter an option [Next/Previous/Go/eXit] <N>:` prompt, use Next or Previous to move the X to the other end of the segment to be broken.

4. When the X is in the proper position, enter **G↵** to break the polyline (see Figure 18.10).

**FIGURE 18.10**
How the Break
option works

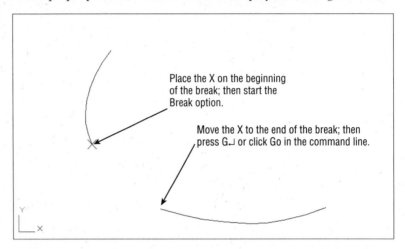

Place the X on the beginning of the break; then start the Break option.

Move the X to the end of the break; then press G↵ or click Go in the command line.

You can also use the Trim options on the Modify panel or the Break option on the expanded Modify panel to break a polyline anywhere, as you did when you drew the toilet seat in Chapter 3, "Setting Up and Using the Drafting Tools."

### THE INSERT OPTION

Next try the Insert option, which inserts a new vertex:

1. Type **X↵** to exit the Edit Vertex option temporarily. Then type **U↵** to undo the break.

2. Type **E↵** to return to the Edit Vertex option.

3. Press ↵ to advance the X marker to the next point.

4. Enter **I↵** to select the Insert option.

5. When the prompt `Specify location for new vertex:` appears, along with a rubber-banding line originating from the current X position (see Figure 18.11), pick a point indicating the new vertex location. The polyline is redrawn with the new vertex.

Notice that the inserted vertex appears between the currently marked vertex and the *next* vertex; this demonstrates that the Insert option is sensitive to the direction of the polyline. If the polyline is curved, the new vertex won't immediately be shown as curved. (See the first image in Figure 18.12.) You must smooth it out by exiting the Edit Vertex option and then using the Fit option, as you did to edit the site plan. (See the second image in Figure 18.12.) You can also use the Stretch command (on the Modify panel) to move a polyline vertex.

**FIGURE 18.11**
The new vertex location

**FIGURE 18.12**
The polyline before and after the curve is fitted

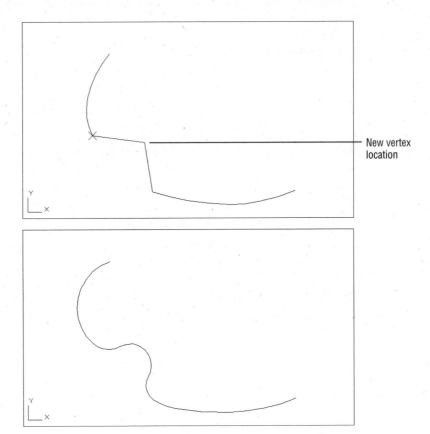

## THE MOVE OPTION

In this brief exercise, you'll use the Move option to move a vertex:

1. Undo the inserted vertex by exiting the Edit Vertex option (enter **X↵**) and typing **U↵**.

2. Restart the Edit Vertex option, and use the Next or Previous option to place the X on the vertex you want to move.

3. Enter **M↵** for the Move option.

4. When the Specify new location for marked vertex: prompt appears, along with a rubber-banding line originating from the X (see the first image in Figure 18.13), pick the new vertex. The polyline is redrawn (see the second image in Figure 18.13). Again, if the line is curved, the new vertex appears as a sharp angle until you use the Fit option (see the final image in Figure 18.13).

You can also move a polyline vertex by using its grip.

## THE REGEN OPTION

In some cases, the effect of an option does not appear in the drawing immediately. You can use the Regen option to update the display of the polyline and see any changes you've made up to that point.

## THE STRAIGHTEN OPTION

The Straighten option straightens a segment of a polyline by removing all the vertices between two selected vertices, replacing them with a straight-line segment. Using the Straighten option is a quick way to delete vertices from a polyline, as shown in the following exercise:

1. Undo the moved vertex (from the previous exercise).

2. Start the Edit Vertex option again, and select the starting vertex for the straight-line segment.

3. Enter **S↵** for the Straighten option.

4. At the Enter an option [Next/Previous/Go/eXit] <N>: prompt, move the X to the location for the other end of the straight-line segment.

5. After the X is in the proper position, enter **G↵** for the Go option. The polyline straightens between the two selected vertices (see Figure 18.14).

## THE TANGENT OPTION

The Tangent option alters the direction of a curve on a curve-fitted polyline:

1. Undo the straightened segment from the previous exercise.

2. Restart the Edit Vertex option, and position the X on the vertex you want to alter.

3. Enter **T↵** for the Tangent option. A rubber-banding line appears. (See the top image in Figure 18.15.)

**4.** Point the rubber-banding line in the direction of the new tangent, and click. An arrow appears, indicating the new tangent direction. (See the second image in Figure 18.15.)

**FIGURE 18.13**

Picking a new location for a vertex with the polyline before and after the curve is fitted

**FIGURE 18.14**

A polyline after straightening

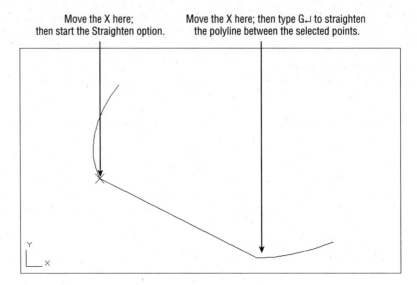

Move the X here; then start the Straighten option.

Move the X here; then type G↵ to straighten the polyline between the selected points.

Don't worry if the polyline shape doesn't change. You must use Fit to see the effect of the Tangent. (See the final image in Figure 18.15.)

### THE WIDTH OPTION

Finally, you'll try the Width option. Unlike the Pedit command's Width option, the Edit Vertex/Width option lets you alter the width of the polyline at any vertex. Thus you can taper or otherwise vary polyline thicknesses. Try these steps:

1. Undo the tangent arc from the previous exercise.

2. Return to the Edit Vertex option, and place the X at the beginning vertex of a polyline segment you want to change.

3. Type **W↵** to issue the Width option.

4. At the Specify starting width for next segment <0.0000>: prompt, enter a value—**12↵**, for example—indicating the polyline width desired at this vertex.

5. At the Specify ending width for next segment <12.0000>: prompt, enter the width—**24↵**, for example—for the next vertex.

The width of the polyline changes to your specifications (see Figure 18.16).

The Width option is useful when you want to create an irregular or curved area in your drawing that is to be filled in solid. This is another option that is sensitive to the polyline direction.

As you've seen throughout these exercises, you can use the Undo option to reverse the last Edit Vertex option used. You can also use the Exit option to leave Edit Vertex at any time. Enter **X**↵ to display the Pedit prompt:

```
Enter an option
[Close/Join/Width/Edit vertex/Fit/Spline/Decurve/Ltype gen/Reverse/Undo]:
```

**FIGURE 18.15**
Picking a new tangent direction

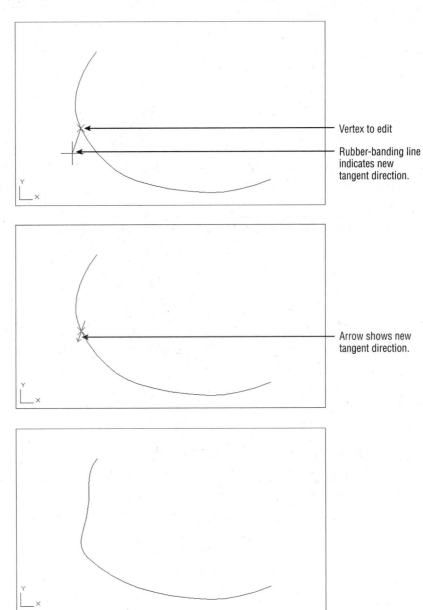

Vertex to edit

Rubber-banding line indicates new tangent direction.

Arrow shows new tangent direction.

**FIGURE 18.16**
A polyline with the width of one segment increased

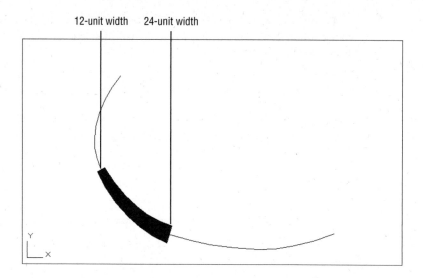

FILLING IN SOLID AREAS

You've learned how to create a solid area by increasing the width of a polyline segment. But suppose you want to create a solid shape or a thick line. AutoCAD provides the Solid, Trace, and Donut commands to help you draw simple filled areas. The Trace command acts just like the Line command (with the added feature of allowing you to draw wide line segments). Solid lets you create solid filled areas with straight sides, and Donut draws circles with a solid width.

You can create free-form, solid-filled areas by using the Solid hatch pattern. Create an enclosed area by using any set of objects, and then use the Hatch tool to apply a solid hatch pattern to the area. See Chapter 7, "Mastering Viewing Tools, Hatches, and External References," for details on using the Hatch tool.

# Creating a Polyline Spline Curve

The Pedit command's Spline option offers you a way to draw smoother and more controllable curves than those produced by the Fit option. A polyline spline doesn't pass through the vertex points as does a fitted curve. Instead, the vertex points act as weights pulling the curve in their direction. These "weighted" vertex points are called *control vertices*. The polyline spline touches only its beginning and end vertices. Figure 18.17 illustrates this concept.

**FIGURE 18.17**
The polyline spline
curve pulled toward
its control vertices

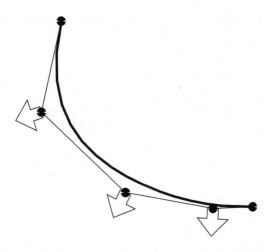

A polyline spline curve doesn't represent a mathematically true curve. See the next section, "Using True Spline Curves," to learn how to draw a more accurate spline curve.

Let's see how using a polyline spline curve may influence the way you edit a curve:

1. Undo the width changes you made in the previous exercise.

2. To change the contour into a polyline spline curve, double-click the polyline to be curved.

3. At the `Enter an option [Close/Join/Width/Edit vertex/Fit/Spline/Decurve/ Ltype gen/Reverse/Undo]:` prompt, type **S**↵. Your curve changes to look like Figure 18.18.

4. Press ↵ to exit Edit Polyline.

**FIGURE 18.18**
A spline curve

The curve takes on a smoother, more graceful appearance. It no longer passes through the points you used to define it. To see where the points went and to find out how spline curves act, do the following:

1. Click the curve. The original vertices appear as grips. (See the first image in Figure 18.19.)

2. Click the grip that is second from the top of the curve, as shown in the first image in Figure 18.19, and move the grip around. The curve follows your moves, giving you immediate feedback on how it will look.

3. Pick a point as shown in the second image in Figure 18.19. The curve is now fixed in its new position, as shown in the bottom image of Figure 18.19.

**FIGURE 18.19**
The fitted curve changed to a spline curve, with the location of the second vertex and the new curve

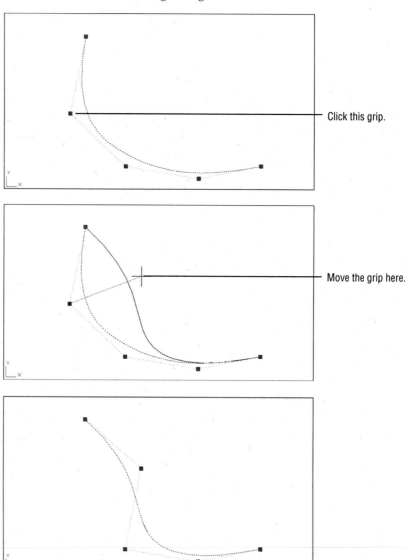

Click this grip.

Move the grip here.

---

**DISPLAYING THE CURVE FRAME**

You can set up AutoCAD to display both the curved and the straight segments defining the curve by turning on the Splframe system variable. Enter **splframe⏎1⏎**, and then issue a Regen command. You'll see a frame that connects the grips of the curve. To turn off the display of the straight segments, enter **splframe⏎0⏎**.

---

# Using True Spline Curves

So far, you've been working with polylines to generate spline curves. The advantage of using polylines for curves is that they can be enhanced in many ways. You can modify their width, for instance, or join several curves. But at times, you'll need a more exact representation of a curve.

The spline object, created by choosing the Spline Fit or Spline CV tool in the Home tab's expanded Draw panel, produces a more accurate model of a spline curve in addition to giving you more control over its shape.

The spline objects are true *Non-Uniform Rational B-Spline (NURBS)* curves. A full description of NURBS is beyond the scope of this book, but basically NURBS are standard mathematical forms used to represent shapes.

## Drawing a True Spline

The following steps describe the process used to create a spline curve. You don't have to create them now. Make a note of this section, and refer to it when you need to draw and edit a spline. Here are the steps:

1. Open the topo2.dwg file.

2. Choose the Spline Fit tool from the expanded Draw panel, or type **SPL⏎**.

3. At the Specify first point or [Method/Knots/Object]: prompt, select a point to start the curve. (See Figure 18.20.) The prompt changes to Enter next point or [start Tangency/toLerance]:.

4. Continue to select points until you've entered all the points you need. As you pick points, a curve appears and it bends and flows as you move your cursor. In Figure 18.20, the Center object snap was used to select the donuts that appear as dots in the survey plan.

5. After you've selected the last point, press ⏎ to exit the Spline command.

If you prefer, you can also control the tangency of the spline at its first and last points. The following steps describe how the start Tangency option can be used:

1. Start the spline just as before, and select the start point. At the Enter next point or [start Tangency/toLerance]: prompt, type **T⏎**. A rubber-banding line appears from the first point of the curve.

2. The prompt changes to Specify start tangent:. Select a point indicating the tangency of the first point.

3. Continue to select the other points of your spline. After you've selected the last point, type **T**↵.

4. Use the cursor to indicate the tangency of the spline at the last point.

**FIGURE 18.20**
Start the spline curve at the first data point and then continue to select points.

Click a point to start the spline.

You now have a smooth curve that passes through the points you selected. These points are called the *fit points.* If you click the curve, you'll see the grips appear at the location of these fit points and you can adjust the curve by clicking the grip points and moving them. You'll also see an arrowhead grip that appears at the beginning of the spline. If you click this arrowhead grip, you see two options: Fit and Control Vertices (see Figure 18.21).

**FIGURE 18.21**
The Fit and Control Vertices options

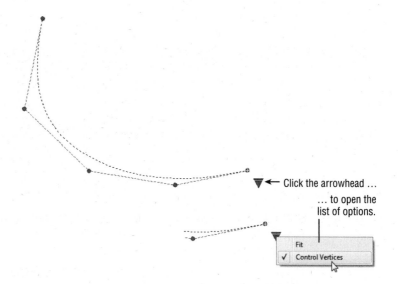

Click the arrowhead ...

... to open the list of options.

The Show Fit Points option will display the grips at the fit points, which are the points you used to draw the spline in the previous example. By default, these fit points lie on the spline, though you can adjust how closely the spline follows the fit points. You can also view the control vertices (CVs), which are points that control the curvature of the spline and do not lie on the spline itself (see Figure 18.17 earlier). Along with the CVs, you see a set of vectors called the control polyline. The control polyline helps you visualize the relationship between the CVs and the spline.

## Understanding the Spline Options

You may have noticed a few other options in the first Spline command prompt. When you start the Spline command, you see the Method, Knots, Degree, and Object options:

**Method**   Method lets you choose between Fit and CV. The Fit option causes the spline to be drawn through the lines you select. The CV, or Control Vertices, option causes the spline to use your selected points as control vertices (see Figure 18.17 earlier). After you've drawn a spline, you can switch between fit and CV views of your polyline (see Figure 18.21 earlier).

**Knots**   This option is available only if Fit is chosen in the Method option discussed previously. This option offers three additional options: Chord, Square Root, and Uniform. These options affect the shape of the spline as it passes through the fit point.

**Chord**   The Chord option numbers the knots with decimal values.

**Square Root**   The Square Root option numbers the knots based on the square root of the chord length between consecutive knots.

**Uniform**   The Uniform option numbers the knots in consecutive integers.

**Degree**   This option is available only if CV is chosen in the Method option discussed previously. The Degree option gives you control over the number of control vectors required to create a bend in the spline. You can use the values 1 through 10. The 1 value will cause the spline to produce straight lines, 2 will generate sharp curves, 3 will generate less sharp curves, and so on. In simple terms, the Degree value controls how closely the spline follows its control polyline.

**Object**   Object lets you convert a polyline into a spline. If the Fit option is selected under the Method option, you can convert only a spline-fitted polyline. If the CV option is selected under the Method option, you can select any polyline. With the CV Method option, the polyline will change shape so that the polyline vectors become control vectors.

After you start to select points for the spline, you see the end Tangency, toLerance, Undo, and Close options. Table 18.1 describes these options.

**TABLE 18.1:**   The Spline command options for selecting points

| OPTION | FUNCTION |
| --- | --- |
| end Tangency | Gives you control over the tangency at the beginning and end points of the spline. |
| toLerance | Lets you control how the curve passes through the fit points. The default value of 0 causes the curve to pass through the fit points. Any value greater than 0 causes the curve to pass close to, but not through, the points. |

**TABLE 18.1:** The Spline command options for selecting points *(continued)*

| OPTION | FUNCTION |
| --- | --- |
| Undo | Lets you undo a point selection in case you select the wrong point. |
| Close | Lets you close the curve into a loop. If you choose this option, you're prompted to indicate a tangent direction for the closing point. |

### JOINING SPLINES TO OTHER OBJECTS

While editing drawings, you may encounter a situation where a spline has been broken into two splines and you need the broken spline to behave as a single spline. The Join command will "mend" a broken spline, or any set of splines for that matter, as long as the splines are contiguous (touching end to end). To use the Join command, click the Join tool from the Home tab's expanded Modify panel or type **Join↵**. Select the splines you want to join.

Join can be used with other objects as well. You can join lines, polylines, 3D polylines, arcs, elliptical arcs, and helixes with the following restrictions:

♦ Any of these objects can be joined to a spline, polyline, 3D polyline, or helix.

♦ Lines cannot be joined to arcs or elliptical arcs.

♦ Arcs cannot be joined to elliptical arcs.

♦ Arcs must have the same center point and radius but can have a gap between the segments you wish to join. The same is true for elliptical arcs.

♦ Lines must be collinear, but there can be gaps between the lines to be joined.

♦ Unless you are joining to a polyline or 3D polyline, objects must be on the same plane.

## Fine-Tuning Spline Curves

Spline curves are different from other types of objects, and many of the standard editing commands won't work on splines. For making changes to splines, AutoCAD offers the Edit Spline tool, otherwise known as the Splinedit command, in the Home tab's expanded Modify panel.

### CONTROLLING THE FIT DATA OF A SPLINE

The Fit Data option of the Splinedit command lets you adjust the tangency of the beginning and endpoints, add new control points, and adjust spline tolerance settings. To get to these options, follow these steps:

1. Choose Edit Spline from the expanded Modify panel, or type **SPE↵** at the Command prompt.

2. At the Select spline: prompt, select the last spline you drew in the previous exercise.

3. At the `Enter an option [Close/Join/Fit data/Edit vertex/convert to Polyline/Reverse/Undo/eXit]:` prompt, type **F**⏎ to select the Fit Data option.

4. At the `[Add/Close/Delete/Kink/Move/Purge/Tangents/toLerance/eXit] <eXit>:` prompt, enter the option you want to use. For example, to change the tangency of the first and last points of your spline, type **T**⏎. You're prompted to select the tangent point of the first and last points. Table 18.2 lists the Splinedit Fit Data options and their purposes.

If you prefer, you can double-click on a spline to start the Splinedit command instead of selecting the Edit Spline tool in the Modify panel. If you have the Dynamic Input feature turned on, you can select Splinedit options from a menu that appears at the cursor (see Figure 18.22) instead of typing in the option keyboard shortcuts. If you double-click the polyline to select it and then right-click anywhere in the drawing, a context menu will appear that also shows the options.

**FIGURE 18.22**
The Splinedit options

**TABLE 18.2:**    The Fit Data options of the Splinedit command

| OPTION | FUNCTION |
| --- | --- |
| Add | Lets you add more control points |
| Close | Lets you close the spline into a loop |
| Delete | Removes a control point from the spline |
| Kink | Lets you add a control point, which does not maintain curvature |
| Move | Lets you move a control point |
| Purge | Deletes the fit data of the spline, thereby eliminating the Fit Data option for the purged spline |
| Tangents | Lets you change the tangency of the first and last points |
| toLerance | Controls the distance between the spline and a control point |
| eXit | Exits the Splinedit command |

## USING GRIP OPTIONS

The Splinedit command gives you a lot of control when you want to edit a spline. But if you want to make some minor changes, you can use the pop-up menu that appears when you hover over a grip on the spline. First, click on the spline to expose its grips, and then hover over a fit point or CV. The list of options appears.

The options are slightly different depending on whether you have the fit points or CVs displayed. The options enable you to add or remove a fit point or CV quickly, and in the case of CVs, you also have the Refine Vertices option. The Refine option lets you control the pull exerted on a spline by a CV.

## WHEN CAN'T YOU USE FIT DATA?

The Fit Data option of the Splinedit command offers many ways to edit a spline. However, this option isn't available to all spline curves. When you invoke certain other Splinedit options, a spline curve loses its fit data, thereby disabling the Fit Data option. These operations are as follows:

♦ Fitting a spline to a tolerance (Spline toLerance) and moving its control vertices.

♦ Fitting a spline to a tolerance and opening or closing it.

♦ Refining the spline.

♦ Purging the spline of its fit data by using the Purge option of the Splinedit command. (Choose Edit Spline from the expanded Modify panel, or enter **SPE↵**, and then select the spline and enter **F↵P↵**.)

Also note that the Fit Data option isn't available when you edit spline curves that were created from polyline splines. See the sidebar "Turning Objects into Polylines and Polylines into Splines" earlier in this chapter.

If you'd like to learn more about the Splinedit options, check the AutoCAD Exchange website. It offers a detailed description of how these options work.

# Marking Divisions on Curves

Perhaps one of the most difficult things to do in manual drafting is to mark regular intervals on a curve. AutoCAD offers the Divide and Measure commands to help you perform this task with speed and accuracy.

You can find the Divide and Measure tools on the expanded Draw Ribbon panel as shown in Figure 18.23. Click the title bar of the Draw panel to find the Divide and Measure tools.

---

**CONVERTING A SPLINE INTO A POLYLINE**

AutoCAD allows you to convert a spline object into a polyline. This can be very useful when you want to edit a spline using the polyline edit tools instead of the spline editing tools. You will lose some precision in the conversion, but more often than not this is not an issue.

To convert a spline to a polyline, double-click the spline and then, at the Enter an option prompt, type **P**↵. At the Specify a precision <10>: prompt, enter a value from 0 to 99. Note that a higher precision value may reduce the performance of AutoCAD, so use a reasonable value. You may want to experiment with different values and pick the lowest value that will still give you the results you want.

---

**FIGURE 18.23**
The Divide and Measure tools are in the expanded Draw Ribbon panel.

The Divide and Measure commands are discussed here in conjunction with polylines, but you can use these commands on any object except blocks and text.

## Dividing Objects into Segments of Equal Length

Use the Divide command to divide an object into a specific number of equal segments. For example, suppose you need to mark off the contour you've been working on in this chapter into nine equal segments. One way to do this is to first find the length of the contour by using the List command and then sit down with a pencil and paper to figure out the exact distances between the marks—but there is another, easier way.

The Divide command places a set of point objects on a line, an arc, a circle, or a polyline, marking off exact divisions. The following exercise shows how it works:

1. Open the 18a-divd.dwg file. This file is similar to the one with which you've been working in the previous exercises.

2. Click the Divide tool in the expanded Draw panel, or type **DIV**↵.

3. At the Select object to divide: prompt, pick the spline contour line that shows Xs in Figure 18.24.

4. The Enter the number of segments or [Block]: prompt that appears next is asking for the number of divisions you want on the selected object. Enter **9**↵.

   The Command prompt returns, and it appears that nothing has happened. But AutoCAD has placed several point objects on the contour that indicate the locations of the nine divisions you requested. To see these points more clearly, continue with the exercise.

5. Choose Point Style from the Home tab's Utilities panel or type **DDPTYPE**↵ to open the Point Style dialog box (see Figure 18.25).

**FIGURE 18.24**
Using the Divide
command on a
polyline

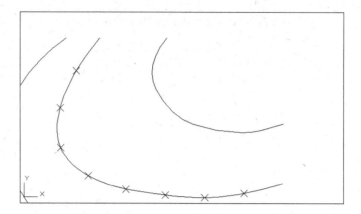

**FIGURE 18.25**
The Point Style
dialog box

**6.** Click the X point style in the top row of the dialog box, click the Set Size Relative To Screen radio button, and then click OK.

**7.** If the Xs don't appear, enter **RE↵**. A set of Xs appears showing the nine divisions (shown earlier in Figure 18.24).

You can also change the point style by changing the Pdmode system variable. When Pdmode is set to 3, the point appears as an X.

The Divide command uses *point* objects to indicate the division points. You create point objects by using the Point command. They usually appear as dots. Unfortunately, such points are nearly invisible when placed on top of other objects. But, as you've seen, you can alter their shape by using the Point Style dialog box. You can use these X points to place objects or references to break the object being divided. (The Divide command doesn't cut the object into smaller divisions.)

---

### SKETCHING WITH AUTOCAD

AutoCAD offers the Sketch command, which lets you do freehand drawing. The Sketch command can be set to draw polylines. If you'd like to know more about Sketch, the AutoCAD Help window offers several excellent descriptions of how it works. Click the Help tool (question mark icon) in the InfoCenter, and then at the AutoCAD 2015 Help website, enter **Sketch** in the search box.

---

**FINDING HIDDEN NODE POINTS**

If you're in a hurry and you don't want to bother changing the shape of the point objects, you can do the following: Set Running Osnaps to Node. Then, when you're in Point Selection mode, move the cursor over the divided curve. When the cursor gets close to a point object, the Node osnap marker appears.

---

## Dividing Objects into Specified Lengths

The Measure command acts just like Divide. However, instead of dividing an object into segments of equal length, the Measure command marks intervals of a specified distance along an object. For example, suppose you need to mark some segments exactly 60″ apart along the contour. Try the following exercise to see how the Measure command is used to accomplish this task:

1. Erase the X-shaped point objects.

2. Click Measure from the expanded Draw panel, or type **ME**↵.

3. At the `Select object to measure:` prompt, pick the contour at a point closest to its lower endpoint. We'll explain shortly why this is important.

4. At the `Specify length of segment or [Block]:` prompt, enter **60**↵. The X points appear at the specified distance.

5. Exit without saving this file.

Bear in mind that the point you pick on the object to be measured determines where the Measure command begins measuring. In the previous exercise, for example, you picked the contour near its bottom endpoint. If you picked the top of the contour, the results would be different because the measurement would start at the top, not the bottom. If the object's length is not equally divisible by the measured segment length, the last segment will be shorter than 60 units.

---

**MARKING OFF INTERVALS BY USING BLOCKS INSTEAD OF POINTS**

You can also use the Block option under the Divide and Measure commands to place blocks at regular intervals along a line, a polyline, or an arc. Here's how to use blocks as markers:

1. Be sure the block you want to use is part of the current drawing file.

2. Start either the Divide or Measure command and then select an object.

3. At the `Specify length of segment or [Block]:` prompt, enter **B**↵.

4. At the `Enter name of block to insert:` prompt, enter the name of a block.

5. At the `Align Block with Object? [Yes/No] <Y>:` prompt, press ↵ if you want the blocks to follow the alignment of the selected object. (Entering **N**↵ inserts each block at a 0 degree angle.)

6. At the `Enter the number of segments:` prompt, or the `Specify length of segment:` prompt, enter the number or length of the segments. The blocks appear at regular intervals on the selected object.

One example of using the Block option of Divide or Measure is to place a row of sinks equally spaced along a wall. Alternatively, you might use this technique to make multiple copies of an object along an irregular path defined by a polyline. In civil engineering projects, you can indicate a fence line by using Divide or Measure to place Xs along a polyline. You can also use the Array command to have blocks appear at regular intervals along a spline or polyline. See Chapter 6, "Editing and Reusing Data to Work Efficiently," for more on the Array command.

## The Bottom Line

**Create and edit polylines.**   Polylines are extremely versatile. You can use them in just about any situation where you need to draw line work that is continuous. For this reason, you'll want to master polylines early in your AutoCAD training.

**Master It**   Draw the part shown here.

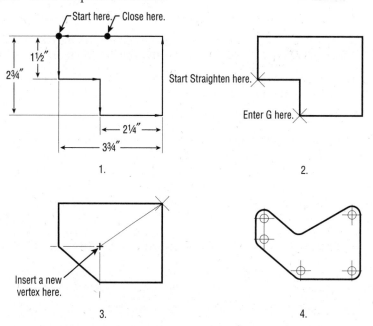

**Create a polyline spline curve.**   Polylines can be used to draw fairly accurate renditions of spline curves. This feature of polylines makes them very useful AutoCAD objects.

**Master It**   Try drawing the outline of an object that contains no or few straight lines as shown in the file lowerfairing.jpg, which is included in the Chapter 18 sample files. You can use the methods described in Chapter 13, "Copying Existing Drawings from Other Sources," to import a raster image of your object and then trace over the image using polyline splines.

**Create and edit true spline curves.** If you need an accurate spline curve, you'll want to use the Spline tool. Spline objects offer many more fine-tuning options that you won't find with polylines.

**Master It** Try tracing over the same image from the previous Master It section, but this time use the Spline tool.

**Mark divisions on curves.** The Divide and Measure tools offer a quick way to mark off distances on a curved object. This can be a powerful resource in AutoCAD that you may find yourself using often.

**Master It** Mark off 12 equal divisions of the spline curve you drew in the previous Master It exercise.

# Chapter 19

# Getting and Exchanging Data from Drawings

Autodesk® AutoCAD® drawings contain a wealth of data—graphic information such as distances and angles between objects as well as precise areas and the properties of objects. However, as you become more experienced with AutoCAD, you'll also need data of a different nature. For example, as you begin to work in groups, the various settings in a drawing become important. You'll need statistics on the amount of time you spend on a drawing when you're billing computer time. As your projects become more complex, file maintenance requires a greater degree of attention. To take full advantage of AutoCAD, you'll want to exchange information about your drawing with other people and other programs.

In this chapter, you'll explore the ways in which all types of data can be extracted from AutoCAD and made available to you, to your coworkers, and to other programs. First you'll learn how to obtain specific data about your drawings. Then you'll look at ways to exchange data with other programs—such as word processors, desktop publishing software, and even other CAD programs.

In this chapter, you will learn to:

♦ Find the area of closed boundaries

♦ Get general information

♦ Use the DXF file format to exchange CAD data with other programs

♦ Use AutoCAD drawings in page layout programs

♦ Use OLE to import data

## Finding the Area of Closed Boundaries

One of the most frequently sought pieces of data you can extract from an AutoCAD drawing is the area of a closed boundary. In architecture, you often need to find the area of a room or the footprint of a building. In civil engineering, you may want to determine the area covered by the boundary of a property line or the area of cut for a roadway. In the following sections, you'll learn how to use AutoCAD to obtain exact area information from your drawings.

### Finding the Area of an Object

Architects, engineers, and facilities planners often need to know the square footage of a room or a section of a building. A structural engineer might want to find the cross-sectional area of a beam. In this section, you'll practice determining the areas of regular objects.

First you'll determine the square-footage area of the living room and entry of your studio unit plan:

1. Start AutoCAD. Open the Unit.dwg file you created earlier, or use the 19a-unit.dwg file.

2. Zoom into the living room and entry area so you have a view similar to Figure 19.1.

**FIGURE 19.1**
Selecting the points to determine the area of the living room and entry

First point · Second point · Third point · Fourth point · Fifth point · Sixth point · Seventh point · Eighth point

3. On the Home tab's Utilities panel, click the Area tool on the Measure flyout, or type **MEA↵AR↵** at the Command prompt. This starts the Measuregeom command with the Area option.

4. Using the Endpoint osnap, start with the lower-left corner of the living room and select the points shown in Figure 19.1. You're indicating the boundary. Notice that as you click points, the area being calculated is indicated in green.

**5.** When you've come to the eighth point shown in Figure 19.1, press ↵. You'll see the following message:

```
Area = 39570.00 square in. (274.7917 square ft), Perimeter = 76'-0"
```

**6.** Type **X**↵ to exit the Measuregeom command.

The number of points you can pick to define an area is limitless, which means you can obtain the areas of complex shapes.

---

**FIND THE COORDINATE OF A POINT OR A DISTANCE IN A DRAWING**

To find absolute coordinates in a drawing, use the ID command. Click the ID Point tool on the Home tab's expanded Utilities panel, or type **ID**↵. At the Specify point: prompt, use the osnap overrides to pick a point; its x-, y-, and z-coordinates are displayed on the command line.

To find the distance between two points, choose Distance from the Measure flyout on the Home tab's Utilities panel, or type **Dist.**↵ and then click two points. AutoCAD will display the distance in the drawing as Delta X, Delta Y, and Delta Z coordinates and as a direct distance between the selected points. Angle information is also provided. The distance is also displayed in the command line.

---

## Using Hatch Patterns to Find Areas

Hatch patterns are used primarily to add graphics to your drawing, but they can also serve as a means for finding areas. You can use any hatch pattern you want because you're interested only in the area it reports back to you. You can also set up a special layer devoted to area calculations and then add to this layer the hatch patterns you use to find areas. That way, you can turn off the hatch patterns so that they don't plot, or you can turn off the Plot setting for that layer to ensure that it doesn't appear in your final output.

To practice using hatch patterns to find an area, do the following:

**1.** Set the current layer to FLOOR.

**2.** Turn off the DOOR and FIXTURE layers. Also make sure the CEILING layer is turned on. You want the hatch pattern to follow the interior wall outline, so you will need to turn off any objects that will affect the outline, such as the door and kitchen.

**3.** Click Hatch on the Home tab's Draw panel or type **H**↵ to open the Hatch Creation tab.

---

**MEASURING BOUNDARIES THAT HAVE GAPS**

If the area you're trying to measure has gaps, set the Gap Tolerance setting in the Hatch Creation tab's expanded Options panel to a value higher than the size of the gaps.

---

4.  At the `Pick internal point or [Select objects/seTtings]:` prompt, click in the interior of the unit plan. The outline of the interior is highlighted and the pattern is placed in the plan (see Figure 19.2). You might also notice that before you click in the unit plan, you get a preview of the hatch.

**FIGURE 19.2**

After you click a point on the interior of the plan to place a hatch pattern, an outline of the area is highlighted by a dotted line and the hatch appears.

5.  Press ↵ to complete the hatch.

6.  On the Home tab's Utilities panel, click the Area tool on the Measure flyout and then type **O↵**, or type **MEA↵AR↵O↵** at the Command prompt.

7.  Click the hatch pattern you just created. Again, you get the following message:

    ```
    Area = 39570.00 square in. (274.7917 square ft), Perimeter = 76'-0"
    ```

8.  Press **X↵** to exit the command.

If you need to recall the last area calculation value you received, enter **'Setvar↵Area↵**. The area is displayed in the prompt. Enter **'Perimeter↵** to get the last perimeter calculated.

The Hatch command creates a hatch pattern that conforms to the boundary of an area. This feature, combined with the ability of the Measuregeom command to find the area of a hatch pattern, makes short work of area calculations. Another advantage of using hatch patterns is that, by default, hatch patterns avoid islands within the boundary of the area you're trying to find.

The area of a hatch pattern is also reported by the Properties palette. Select the hatch pattern whose area you want to find, and then right-click and select Properties. Scroll down to the bottom of the Geometry group and you'll see the Area listing for the hatch pattern you selected. You can select more than one hatch pattern and find the cumulative area of the selected hatch patterns in the Properties palette.

## Adding and Subtracting Areas with the Area Command

CERT
OBJECTIVE

Hatch patterns work extremely well for finding areas, but if you find that you can't use hatch patterns for some reason, you have an alternative. You can still use a command called Boundary to generate a polyline outline of an enclosed boundary and then obtain the area of the outline using the Measuregeom command (Measure on the Home tab's Utilities panel). If islands are present within the boundary, you have to use the Subtract feature of the Measuregeom command to remove their area from the overall boundary area. In this section, you'll use the example of the flange part, which contains two islands, in the form of the two circles, at the lower end (see Figure 19.3).

**FIGURE 19.3**

A flange to a
mechanical device

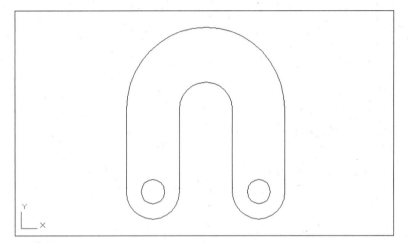

By using the Add and Subtract options of the Measuregeom command, you can maintain a running total of several separate areas being calculated, a capability that gives you flexibility in finding areas of complex shapes. This section guides you through the use of these options.

For the following exercise, you'll use a flange shape that contains circles. This shape is composed of simple arcs, lines, and circles. Use these steps to see how you can keep a running tally of areas:

1. Exit the Unit.dwg file, and open the file Flange.dwg (see Figure 19.3). Don't bother to save changes in the Unit.dwg file.

2. Click Boundary from the Hatch flyout on the Home tab's Draw panel or type **BO**↵ to open the Boundary Creation dialog box (see Figure 19.4).

**FIGURE 19.4**

The Boundary
Creation dialog box

3. Click the Pick Points icon.

4. Click in the interior of the flange shape. The entire shape is highlighted, including the circle islands.

5. Press ↵. You now have a polyline outline of the shape and the circles, although it won't be obvious that polylines have been created because they're drawn over the boundary objects.

6. Continue by using the Measuregeom command's Add and Subtract options. Select Area from the Measure flyout on the Home tab's Utilities panel.

7. Type **A**↵ to enter Add Area mode, and then type **O**↵ to select an object.

8. Click a vertical edge of the flange outline. You see the selected area highlighted in green, and the following message appears in the Command window:

```
Area = 27.7080, Perimeter = 30.8496
Total area = 27.7080
```

9. Press ↵ to exit Add Area mode.

10. Type **S**↵ to enter Subtract Area mode, and then type **O**↵ to select an object.

11. Click one of the circles. You see the following message:

```
Total area = 0.6070, Circumference = 2.7618
Total area = 27.1010
```

This shows you the area and perimeter of the selected object and a running count of the total area of the flange outline minus the circle. You also see the area of the subtracted circle change to a different color so you can distinguish between the calculated area and the subtracted area.

12. Click the other circle. You see the following message:

```
Total area = 0.6070, Circumference = 2.7618
Total area = 26.4940
```

Again, you see a listing of the area and circumference of the selected object along with a running count of the total area, which now shows a value of 26.4940. This last value is the true area of the flange.

13. Press ↵ and type **X**↵**X**↵ to exit the Measuregeom command. You can also press the Esc key to exit the command.

In this exercise, you first selected the main object outline and then subtracted the island objects. You don't have to follow this order; you can start by subtracting areas to get negative area values and then add other areas to come up with a total. You can also alternate between Add and Subtract modes, in case you forget to add or subtract areas.

You may have noticed that the Measuregeom Command prompt offered Specify first corner point or [Object/Add area/Subtract area/eXit]: as the default option for both the Add Area and Subtract Area modes. Instead of using the Object option to pick the circles, you can start selecting points to indicate a rectangular area as you did in the first exercise in this chapter.

Whenever you press ⏎ while selecting points for an area calculation, AutoCAD automatically connects the first and last points and returns the calculated area. If you're in Add or Subtract mode, you can then continue to select points, but the additional areas are calculated from the *next* point you pick.

As you can see from these exercises, it's simpler to outline an area first with a polyline wherever possible and then use the Object option to add and subtract area values of polylines.

In this example, you obtained the area of a mechanical object. However, the same process works for any type of area you want to calculate. It can be the area of a piece of property on a topographical map or the area of a floor plan. For example, you can use the Object option to find the area of an irregular shape such as the one shown in Figure 19.5, as long as it's a closed polyline.

**FIGURE 19.5**

The site plan with an area to be calculated

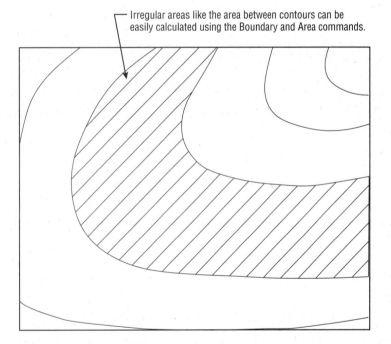

Irregular areas like the area between contours can be easily calculated using the Boundary and Area commands.

When issued through the keyboard as **MEA**⏎, the Measuregeom command offers a number of other options for measuring your drawing. The options appear in the Command window as [Distance/Radius/Angle/ARea/Volume]<Distance> or at the cursor as a Dynamic Input option. These options are automatically selected when you click the related tool from the Measure flyout on the Utilities panel. Remember that to use an option, you must type the capitalized letter or letters of the option shown in the list. Table 19.1 gives you descriptions of the options and how they are used.

**RECORDING AREA DATA IN A DRAWING FILE**

In just about every project we've worked on, area calculations were an important part of the drawing process. As an aid in recording area calculations, we created a block that contains attributes for the room number, the room area, and the date when the room area was last measured. The area and date attributes were made invisible so only the room number appears. The block with the attribute is then inserted into every room. Once the area of the room is discovered, it can be added to the block attribute with the Ddatte command. Such a block can be used with any drawing in which area data needs to be gathered and stored. See Chapter 12, "Using Attributes," for more on attributes. You can also use the Field object type to display the area of a polyline automatically as a text object. See Chapter 10, "Using Fields and Tables," for more on fields.

**TABLE 19.1:** The Measuregeom command options

| OPTION | USE |
| --- | --- |
| Distance | Returns the distance between two points. Type **D**↵ and select two points. You can also measure cumulative distances by typing **M**↵ after selecting the first point. |
| Radius | Returns the radius of an arc or circle. Type **R**↵ and select an arc or circle. |
| Angle | Returns the angle of an arc or the angle between two lines. Type **A**↵ and select the arc or two nonparallel lines. |
| ARea | Returns the area of a set of points or boundary. Type **AR**↵ to use this option. See previous exercises for instruction on the use of this option. |
| Volume | Returns the 3D volume based on an area times height. |
| eXit | Exits the current option. You can also press the Esc key. |

# Getting General Information

So far in this book, you've seen how to get data about the geometry of your drawings. AutoCAD also includes a set of tools that you can use to access the general state of your drawings. You can gather information about the status of current settings in a file or the time at which a drawing was created and last edited.

In the following sections, you'll practice extracting this type of information from your drawing, using the tools found in the Tools tab's Inquiry panel.

## Determining the Drawing's Status

When you work with a group of people on a large project, keeping track of a drawing's setup becomes crucial. You can use the Status command to obtain general information about the drawing on which you're working, such as the base point, current mode settings, and work-space or computer memory use. The Status command is especially helpful when you're editing a drawing on which someone else has worked because you may want to identify and change settings for your own style of working. Select Application ➤ Drawing Utilities ➤ Status to dis-play a list like the one shown in Figure 19.6.

**FIGURE 19.6**

The Status screen of the AutoCAD command-line interface

```
Command: STATUS
425 objects in C:\Users\AutoCAD\Documents\Mastering AutoCAD 2013\Projects
\Chapter 20\20a-unit.dwg
Undo file size:     3160 bytes
Model space limits are X:     0'-0"   Y:     0'-0"  (Off)
                       X:    44'-0"   Y:    34'-0"
Model space uses       X:    14'-7"   Y: 2'-3 1/2"
                       X:    33'-9"   Y: 35'-2 3/4" **Over
Display shows          X: 31'-0 7/16"  Y: -30'-9 1/4"
                       X: 37'-3 1/8"   Y: -27'-6 1/8"
Insertion base is      X:    15'-0"   Y:     2'-5"   Z:     0'-0"
Snap resolution is     X:     0'-1"   Y:     0'-1"
Grid spacing is        X:     4'-0"   Y:     4'-0"
Current space:        Model space
Current layout:       Model
Current layer:        "0"
Current color:        BYLAYER -- 7 (white)
Current linetype:     BYLAYER -- "CONTINUOUS"
Current material:     BYLAYER -- "Global"
Current lineweight:   BYLAYER
Current elevation:     0'-0"  thickness:     0'-0"
Fill on  Grid off  Ortho off  Qtext off  Snap off  Tablet off
Press ENTER to continue:
Object snap modes:    Center, Endpoint, Intersection, Extension
Free dwg disk (C:) space: 106091.7 MBytes
Free temp disk (C:) space: 106091.7 MBytes
Free physical memory: 5204.0 Mbytes (out of 7862.7M).
Free swap file space: 13125.5 Mbytes (out of 15723.6M).
```

---

**USE THE STATUS COMMAND TO GET YOUR BEARINGS**

If you have problems editing a file created by someone else, the difficulty can often be attributed to a setting that you aren't used to. If AutoCAD is acting in an unusual way, use the Status command to get a quick glimpse of the file settings before you start calling for help.

---

Here is a brief description of each item on the Status command's display in the expanded command line. Note that some of the items you see on the screen will vary somewhat from what we've shown here, but the information applies to virtually all situations except where noted:

**Number Objects In Drive:\Folder\Subfolder\Name.dwg**  The number of entities or objects in the drawing.

**Undo File Size**  The size of the Undo file located in the user temp folder.

**Model Space Limits Are**  The coordinates of the Model Space limits. Also indicates whether limits are turned off or on. (See Chapter 3, "Setting Up and Using the Drafting Tools," for more details on limits.)

**Model Space Uses**  The area the drawing occupies; equivalent to the extents of the drawing.

**\*\*Over**  If present, means that part of the drawing is outside the limit boundary.

**Display Shows**   The area covered by the current view.

**Insertion Base Is, Snap Resolution Is, and Grid Spacing Is**   The current default values for these mode settings.

**Current Space**   Model space or paper space.

**Current Layout**   The current tab.

**Current Layer**   The current layer.

**Current Color**   The color assigned to new objects.

**Current Linetype**   The linetype assigned to new objects.

**Current Material**   The material assigned to new objects.

**Current Lineweight**   The current default lineweight setting.

**Current Elevation/Thickness**   The current default z-coordinate for new objects, plus the default thickness of objects. These are both 3D-related settings. (See Chapter 20, "Creating 3D Drawings," for details.)

**Fill, Grid, Ortho, Qtext, Snap, and Tablet**   The status of these options.

**Object Snap Modes**   The current active osnap setting.

**Free Dwg Disk (Drive:) Space**   The amount of space available to store drawing-specific temporary files.

**Free Temp Disk (Drive:) Space**   The amount of space left on your hard drive for the AutoCAD resource temporary files.

**Free Physical Memory**   The amount of free RAM available.

**Free Swap File Space**   The amount of Windows swap-file space available.

When you're in paper space, the Status command displays information regarding the paper space limits. See Chapter 15, "Laying Out Your Printer Output," for more on model space and paper space.

In addition to being useful in understanding a drawing file, the Status command is an invaluable tool for troubleshooting. Frequently, a technical support person can isolate problems by using the information provided by the Status command.

## Keeping Track of Time

The Time command enables you to keep track of the time spent on a drawing for billing or analysis purposes. You can also use the Time command to check the current time and find out when the drawing was created and most recently edited. Because the AutoCAD timer uses your computer's time, be sure the time is set correctly in Windows.

To access the Time command, enter **Time** at the Command prompt. You get a message like the one shown in Figure 19.7.

**FIGURE 19.7**
The Time screen in the AutoCAD command-line interface

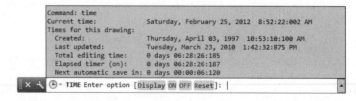

The first four lines of this message tell you the current date and time, the date and time the drawing was created, and the last time the drawing was saved.

The fifth line shows the total time spent on the drawing from the point at which the file was opened. This elapsed timer lets you time a particular activity, such as changing the width of all the walls in a floor plan or redesigning a piece of machinery. The last line tells you the timing of the next automatic save.

You can turn the elapsed timer on or off or reset it by entering **ON**, **OFF**, or **Reset** at the prompt shown at the bottom of the message, or you can press ↵ to exit the Time command.

## Getting Information from System Variables

If you've been working through this book's ongoing studio apartment building tutorial, you'll have noticed that we've occasionally mentioned a *system variable* in conjunction with a command. You can check the status or change the setting of any system variable while you're in the middle of another command. To do this, you type an apostrophe (') followed by the name of the system variable at the Command prompt.

For example, if you start to draw a line and suddenly decide you need to restrict your cursor movement to 45°, you can do the following:

1. At the `Specify next point or [Undo]:` prompt, enter '**snapang**.

2. At the `>>Enter new value for SNAPANG <0>:` prompt, enter a new cursor angle. You're returned to the Line command with the cursor in its new orientation.

You can also recall information such as the last area or distance calculated by AutoCAD. Type **Setvar**↵**Area**↵ to read the last area calculation. The Setvar command also lets you list all the system variables and their status as well as access each system variable individually by entering '**Setvar**↵**?**↵. You can then indicate which variables to list using wildcard characters such as the asterisk or question mark. For example, you can enter **g***↵ to list all the system variables that start with the letter *G*.

Many system variables give you direct access to detailed information about your drawing. They also let you fine-tune your drawing and editing activities. In the online bonus chapter "System Variables and Dimension Styles," available at `www.omura.com/chapters`, you'll find all the information you need to familiarize yourself with the system variables. Don't feel that you have to memorize them all at once; just be aware that they're available.

## Keeping a Log of Your Activity

At times, you may find it helpful to keep a log of your activity in an AutoCAD session. A *log* is a text file containing a record of your activities. It can also contain notes to yourself or others about how a drawing is set up. Such a log can help you determine how frequently you use a particular command, or it can help you construct a macro for a commonly used sequence of commands.

The following exercise demonstrates how to save and view a detailed record of an AutoCAD session by using the Log feature:

1. Press the Esc key to cancel any current commands and then choose Options from the Application menu to open the Options dialog box. Click the Open And Save tab. A new set of options appears.

2. In the File Safety Precautions group, click the Maintain A Log File check box and then click OK.

3. Type **Status↵** at the Command prompt.

4. Return to the Open And Save tab of the Options dialog box, and turn off the Maintain A Log File option.

5. Click OK to exit the dialog box.

6. Switch to Windows, and start the Notepad application or any text editor.

7. With the text editor, open the log file whose name starts with Flange in the folder listed here:

   `C:\Users\`*User Name*`\AppData\Local\Autodesk\AutoCAD 2015\R20.1\enu\`

   This file stores the text data from the command line whenever the Log File option is turned on. You must turn off the Log File option before you can view this file. When you're attempting to view the log file using Windows Notepad, make sure that you set Files Of Type in the Notepad Open dialog box to All Files. Note that this location is usually a hidden one. See the section "Finding Folders that Contain AutoCAD Files" in Appendix B, "Installing and Setting Up AutoCAD," for more information.

You can quickly turn the Maintain A Log File feature on and off by typing **Logfileon↵** and **Logfileoff↵**, respectively, at the Command prompt. As you can see in step 7, the log file is given the name of the drawing file from which the log is derived, with some additional numeric values. Because the Flange.dwg log file is a standard text file, you can easily send it to other members of your workgroup or print it for a permanent record.

---

#### FINDING THE LOG FILE

If you can't find the log file for the current drawing, you can enter **logfilename↵** at the Command prompt and AutoCAD will display the filename, including the full path. If you want to change the default location for the log file, open the Options dialog box and click the Files tab. Click the plus sign to the left of the Log File Location option in the list box. A listing appears showing you where the drawing log file is stored. You can then modify this setting to indicate a new location. Users of the AutoCAD LT® software should enter **Modemacro↵** and then **$(getvar, logfilepath)**.

---

## Capturing and Saving Text Data from the AutoCAD Text Window

If you're working in groups, it's often helpful to have a record of the status, editing time, and system variables for particular files readily available to other group members. It's also convenient to keep records of block and layer information so you can see whether a specific block is included in a drawing or what layers are normally on or off.

You can use the Windows Clipboard to capture and save such data from the AutoCAD Text Window. The following steps show you how it's done:

1. Move the arrow cursor to the Command prompt at the bottom of the AutoCAD Text Window. If the Text Window isn't open, enter **TEXTSCR↵**.

2. Right-click and choose Copy History from the context menu to copy the contents of the AutoCAD Text Window to the Clipboard.

3. Open Notepad or another text-editing application and paste the information.

---

### ENABLING THE FUNCTION KEYS

On some keyboards, the function keys, F1 through F12, serve a dual function. For example, on most laptops, you can use the Fn key to select an alternate function for the function keys, like toggling Wi-Fi on or off or switching to an external monitor. If you find that the F2 key on your PC is not expanding the AutoCAD command-line interface, make sure that you have disabled the special features of the function keys. There may be an F Lock or F Mode key near the row of function keys that performs this function.

---

If you want to copy only a portion of the command-line data to the Clipboard, perform the following steps:

1. Press the F2 function key to expand the command-line interface.

2. Using the I-beam text cursor, highlight the text you want to copy to the Clipboard.

3. Right-click and choose Copy from the context menu, or you can press Ctrl+C. The highlighted text is copied to the Clipboard.

4. Open Notepad or another text-editing application and paste the information.

You may notice other options on the context menu: Recent Commands, AutoComplete, Paste, Paste To Command Line, Transparency, and Options. Choosing Recent Commands displays a list of the most recent commands. For most activities, you'll use a handful of commands repeatedly; the Recent Commands option can save you time by giving you a shortcut to those commands that you use the most.

The AutoComplete feature automatically completes a command name as you type it. For example, if you start to type **cha** for the Change command, the AutoComplete feature will display a list of commands and system variables that begin with *cha* in a drop-down menu. As you continue to type, the list will also change to narrow down the options based on what you type. See Chapter 24, "Customizing Toolbars, Menus, Linetypes, and Hatch Patterns," for more on the AutoComplete options.

The Paste options paste the first line of the contents of the Clipboard into the command line or text box of a dialog box. This can be useful for entering repetitive text or for storing and retrieving a frequently used command. Choosing Options opens the Options dialog box.

Items copied to the Clipboard from the command-line interface or the AutoCAD Text Window can be pasted into dialog box text boxes. This can be a quick way to transfer layers, linetypes, or other named items into dialog boxes. You can even paste text into the drawing area.

## Storing Searchable Information in AutoCAD Files

As you start to build a library of AutoCAD files, you'll have to decide how to manage them. Keeping track of AutoCAD files can be a daunting task. Most AutoCAD users start to name files by their job number to keep things organized. But even the best organization schemes don't help if you need to find that one special file among thousands of files in your library. In this section, you'll learn how to include information in an AutoCAD file that you can use later to locate the file with the Windows Search utility.

AutoCAD includes DesignCenter™ and Content Explorer™, which are tools that can help you locate a file more easily based on a keyword or description. Chapter 25, "Managing and Sharing Your Drawings," provides a complete discussion of DesignCenter and Content Explorer.

To add general, searchable information about your drawing file, use the drawing's Properties dialog box (see Figure 19.8). Choose Drawing Utilities ➢ Drawing Properties from the Application menu.

**FIGURE 19.8**

A drawing's properties

Here are descriptions of the four tabs in this dialog box:

**General**    The General tab gives you general information about the file. This information is similar to what you see if you use the Properties options in Windows Explorer to view the properties of a file.

**Summary**    In the Summary tab, enter any text in the Title, Subject, Author, and Keywords fields that is appropriate to the drawing. The information you enter here is stored with the drawing and can be used to locate the file through the AutoCAD DesignCenter or the Windows Search utility.

In addition, you can enter a base location for hyperlinks that are applied to objects in your drawing. This base location can be a folder on your computer or network or an Internet web address. See Chapter 25 for more information on hyperlinks.

**Statistics**    The Statistics tab contains the Windows username of the person who last saved the drawing as well as the time spent on the file. The username is the name used to log in at the beginning of the Windows session.

**Custom**   The Custom tab contains two columns of text boxes. This tab lets you store additional custom data with the drawing that is also searchable. For example, you might enter Job Number in the Name column and then enter 9901 in the Value column. You might also include information such as project manager names, consultants, or revision numbers. You can then locate the file by using the AutoCAD DesignCenter or the Windows Search utility to search for those keywords from the Name and Value columns.

## Searching for AutoCAD Files

After you've included information in a file's Properties palette, you can use the AutoCAD DesignCenter, Content Explorer, the File dialog box, or the Windows Search function to locate your file.

A Find option is also located in the Tools menu in the upper-right corner of the AutoCAD Select File dialog box. To access it, click the Open tool from the Quick Access toolbar; then, in the Select File dialog box, choose Tools ➢ Find.

This option opens a Find dialog box that works just like the Windows Search Results window.

## Recovering Corrupted Files

No system is perfect. Eventually, you'll encounter a file that is corrupted in some way. Two AutoCAD tools can frequently salvage a corrupted file:

**Audit**   Enables you to check a file that you can open but suspect has a problem. Audit checks the currently opened file for errors and displays the results in the command-line interface.

**Recover/Recover With Xrefs**   Enables you to open a file that is so badly corrupted that AutoCAD is unable to open it in a normal way. A Select File dialog box appears in which you select a file for recovery. After you select a file, it's opened and checked for errors. The Recover With Xrefs option will attempt to recover the file and any attached Xrefs.

You can access these tools from the Drawing Utilities option on the Application menu. More often than not, these tools will do the job, although they aren't a panacea for all file corruption problems. In the event that you can't recover a file even with these tools, make sure your computer is running smoothly and that other systems aren't faulty.

If for some reason your computer shuts down while you're in the middle of editing a file, you'll see the Drawing Recovery Manager the next time you start AutoCAD. The Drawing Recovery Manager lets you recover the file on which you were working when AutoCAD unexpectedly shut down. This feature works just like the file recovery feature in Microsoft Office: A panel appears to the left of the AutoCAD Text Window showing you a list of recoverable files. You can then select the filename from the panel to open the file. You can open the Drawing Recovery Manager by choosing Application ➢ Drawing Utilities ➢ Open The Drawing Recovery Manager.

# Using the DXF File Format to Exchange CAD Data with Other Programs

AutoCAD offers many ways to share data with other programs. Perhaps the most common type of data exchange is to share drawing data with other CAD programs. In the following sections, you'll see how to export and import CAD drawings using the DXF file format.

A *Drawing Interchange Format (DXF) file* is a plain-text file that contains all the information needed to reconstruct a drawing. It's often used to exchange drawings created with other programs. Many CAD and technical drawing programs, including some 3D programs, can generate or read files in DXF format. You might want to use a 3D program to view your drawing in a perspective view, or you might have a consultant who uses a different CAD program that accepts DXF files.

Be aware that not all programs that read DXF files accept all the data stored therein. Many programs that claim to read DXF files throw away much of the DXF files' information. Attributes are perhaps the most commonly ignored objects, followed by many of the 3D objects, such as meshes and 3D faces.

## Exporting DXF Files

To export your current drawing as a DXF file, follow these steps:

1. Choose Save As from the Application menu or from the Quick Access toolbar to open the Save Drawing As dialog box.

2. Click the Files Of Type drop-down list. You can export your drawing under a number of formats, including six DXF formats.

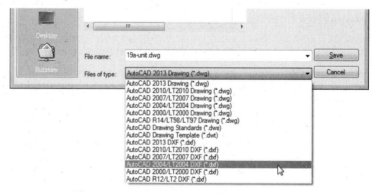

3. Select the appropriate DXF format, and then enter a name for your file. You don't have to include the .dxf filename extension.

4. Select a folder for the file and click Save.

In step 3, you can select from the following DXF file formats:

♦ AutoCAD 2013 DXF

♦ AutoCAD 2010 DXF (AutoCAD 2010, 2011, and 2012 share file formats)

♦ AutoCAD 2007/LT 2007 DXF (AutoCAD 2007, 2008, and 2009 share file formats)

♦ AutoCAD 2004/LT 2004 DXF

♦ AutoCAD 2000/LT 2000 DXF

♦ AutoCAD R12/LT2 DXF

Choose the appropriate format for the program to which you're exporting. In most cases, the safest choice is AutoCAD R12/LT2 DXF if you're exporting to another CAD program, although AutoCAD won't maintain the complete functionality of AutoCAD 2015 for such files.

After you've selected a DXF format from the Files Of Type drop-down list, you can set more detailed specifications by choosing Tools ➢ Options in the upper-right corner of the Save Drawing As dialog box. Doing so opens the Saveas Options dialog box. For DXF files, select the DXF Options tab (see Figure 19.9).

**FIGURE 19.9**
The Saveas Options dialog box open to the DXF Options tab

The DXF Options tab contains the following options:

**Format**   Lets you choose between ASCII (plain-text) and binary file formats. Most other programs accept ASCII, so it's the safest choice. Some programs accept binary DXF files, which have the advantage of being more compact than the ASCII format files.

**Select Objects**   Lets you select specific objects in the drawing for export. You can select objects after you close the Saveas Options dialog box and choose Save from the Save Drawing As dialog box.

**Decimal Places Of Accuracy (0 To 16)**   Enables you to determine the accuracy of the exported file. Keeping this value low helps reduce the size of the exported file, particularly if it's to be in ASCII format. Some CAD programs don't support the high accuracy of AutoCAD, so using a high value here may have no significance.

In addition to using the Save Drawing As tool, you can type **Dxfout**↵ at the Command prompt to open the Save Drawing As dialog box. This is a standard Windows file dialog box that includes the Options button described in the next section.

## Opening or Importing DXF Files

Some offices have made the DXF file format their standard for CAD drawings. This is most commonly seen in offices that use a variety of CAD software besides AutoCAD.

AutoCAD can be set up to read and write DXF files instead of the standard DWG file format by default. Here's how it's done:

1. Choose Options from the Application menu to open the Options dialog box.

2. Select the Open And Save tab.

3. In the File Save group, select any of the DXF formats from the Save As drop-down list.

4. Click OK.

After you do this, all your drawings are automatically saved in the DXF format of your choice. You can also set the default AutoCAD file type by clicking the Tools button in the Save Drawing As dialog box and clicking Options. As you saw in the preceding section, the Saveas Options dialog box includes the DWG Options tab (see Figure 19.10). You can select a default file type from the Save All Drawings As drop-down list.

**FIGURE 19.10**

The Saveas Options
dialog box open
to the DWG
Options tab

If you need to open a DXF file only once in a while, you can do so by selecting DXF from the Files Of Type drop-down list in the Select File dialog box. This is the dialog box you see when you click Open from the Quick Access toolbar. You can also use the Dxfin command:

1. Type **Dxfin**↵ at the Command prompt to open the Select File dialog box.

2. Locate and select the DXF file you want to import.

3. Double-click the filename. If the drawing is large, the imported file may take several minutes to open.

If you want to import a DXF file into the current drawing, you can use the Insert dialog box. (Click Insert on the Home tab's Block panel.) Click the Browse button to locate and select a file. Make sure the Files Of Type option is set to DXF.

## Using AutoCAD Drawings in Page Layout Programs

As you probably know, AutoCAD is a natural for creating line art, and because of its popularity, most page layout programs are designed to import AutoCAD drawings in one form or another.

Those of you who employ page layout software to generate user manuals or other technical documents will probably want to use AutoCAD drawings in your work. In this section, you'll examine ways to output AutoCAD drawings to formats that most page layout programs can accept.

You can export AutoCAD files to page layout software formats in two ways: by using raster export and by using vector file export.

## Exporting Raster Files

In some cases, you may need only a rough image of your AutoCAD drawing. You can export your drawing as a raster file that can be read in virtually any page layout or word processing program. To do this, you need to use the PublishToWebJPG.pc3 or PublishToWebPNG.pc3 printer option that comes with AutoCAD, as shown in these steps:

1. Click the Plot tool in the Quick Access toolbar.

2. In the Printer/Plotter group of the Plot dialog box, select PublishToWebJPG.pc3 or PublishToWebPNG.pc3 from the Name drop-down list.

3. The first time you use this printer option, you'll see the Plot – Paper Size Not Found dialog box. Select from the options presented in the dialog box.

4. Back in the Plot dialog box, you can select a size in pixels for your image file from the Paper Size drop-down list.

5. Click OK to create the image file.

6. In the Browse For Plot File dialog box, select a location for your file and click Save.

If you don't see a "paper size" you want to use, you can create a custom size using the Properties button in the Plot dialog box:

1. Follow the steps in the previous exercise, but at step 5, instead of clicking OK, click the Properties button to the right of the Printer/Plotter group's Name drop-down list. The Plotter Configuration Editor dialog box appears (see Figure 19.11).

2. Click Custom Paper Sizes in the large list box at the top of the dialog box. The options change in the lower half of the dialog box.

3. Click the Add button to start the Custom Paper Size Wizard.

4. Click the Start From Scratch radio button, and then click Next to open the Media Bounds screen.

5. Enter a height and width in pixels for your image file, and then click Next to open the Paper Size Name screen. Enter a name that best describes the size of the image file, and click Next to open the File Name screen.

6. On the Finish screen, click Finish. The Plotter Configuration Editor dialog box reappears. Click OK.

**FIGURE 19.11**
Editing the plotter
configuration

You can edit these settings at any time by opening the PC3 file in the `AppData\Roaming\`
`Autodesk\AutoCAD 2015\R20.0\enu\Plotters` subfolder of your profile folder. You can access
this file through Windows Explorer or from AutoCAD by clicking Plotter Manager in the Output
tab's Plot panel.

---

### FINDING THE *AppData* OR *APPLICATION DATA* FOLDER

The `AppData` or `Application Data` folder is typically a hidden folder. To get to it, you have to
turn off the "hide hidden folders" feature of Windows Explorer. See "Finding Folders That Contain
AutoCAD Files" in Appendix B for more information.

---

To create a raster file version of your drawing, click Plot on the Quick Access toolbar. Then,
in the Plot dialog box select your raster file plotter configuration from the Name drop-down list
of the Printer/Plotter group. You can then proceed to plot your drawing, but instead of paper
output, you'll get a raster file. You can specify the filename and location when you click the OK
button to plot the file.

If you need to make changes to your raster file configuration, click Plotter Manager in the
Output tab's Plot panel. Then, in the Plotters window double-click your raster file configuration file. You'll see the same Plotter Configuration Editor you used to set up the raster plotter
configuration.

You can set up a different plotter configuration for each type of raster file you use. You can
also set up plotter configurations for different resolutions if you choose. To learn more about
plotting in general, see Chapter 8, "Introducing Printing, Plotting, and Layouts." The online
bonus chapter "Hardware and Software Tips," available at www.omura.com/chapters, provides
detailed information on the Plotter Configuration Editor.

## Exchanging Files with Earlier Releases

One persistent dilemma that has plagued AutoCAD users is how to exchange files between earlier versions of the program. In the early days of CAD, if you upgraded AutoCAD, you were locked out from exchanging your drawings with people using earlier versions.

With Release 13, the file structure was changed radically from the file structure used in earlier versions of AutoCAD. Then, AutoCAD 14 made it possible to exchange files freely between Releases 13 and 14.

With a change in release numbering, starting with AutoCAD 2000, file formats have typically been used for three releases in a row. AutoCAD 2000 through 2002 files are compatible, as are 2004 through 2006. If you open the Save Drawing As dialog box and check the Files Of Type drop-down list, you'll see that R14, 2000, 2004, 2007, 2010, and 2013 are listed as options (AutoCAD 2015 uses the AutoCAD 2013 file format). Release numbers that are skipped in the list are compatible with only the next higher release. For example, if you want to save a file in a format that your colleague using AutoCAD 2005 can open, you would choose AutoCAD 2004 from the Files Of Type drop-down list. AutoCAD 2004 is a format compatible with AutoCAD releases 2004, 2005, and 2006. If compatibility with earlier releases is important, you can set the default behavior to save as AutoCAD 2010 format or earlier. Or, if you're willing to work with DXF files, you can set up AutoCAD 2015 to save drawings automatically as AutoCAD 2013 DXF files.

To set up AutoCAD to save drawings in the format used by an earlier version automatically, use the Options dialog box to set the default file type as described earlier in the section "Opening or Importing DXF Files." However, rather than selecting a DXF file type, select the DWG file type you want to use.

If you want to batch-convert multiple files to an earlier version, AutoCAD offers the DWG Convert dialog box. You can open this dialog box by typing **DWGCONVERT.** at the Command prompt. The DWG Convert dialog box enables you to create and save a list of files to convert in case you have a set of files that you need to down-convert often.

Select the Conversion Setups option in the dialog box to open the Conversion Setups dialog box. This dialog box lets you create or modify conversion setup presets to customize your most frequently used conversion methods.

Click New to create a new conversion preset option or to modify an existing one. You will see the New Conversion Setup or Modify Conversion Setup dialog box, either of which lets you set the parameters for your conversion setup.

Another option is to use a separate program to "downgrade" drawings to earlier versions. Autodesk offers its DWG TrueView™ software as a free download. DWG TrueView will batch-convert 2015 files to earlier versions, and it works in a way that is similar to the DWG Convert dialog box. The advantage to DWG TrueView is that it is a stand-alone application, so you don't need to have AutoCAD open to use it.

## Exporting Vector Files

If you need to preserve the accuracy of your drawing, or if you want to take advantage of TrueType or PostScript fonts, you can use the DXF, Windows Metafile (WMF), or PostScript vector format. You can also export to DGN and SAT file formats. Intergraph's DGN format is popular in civil engineering, mapping, and other CAD applications. SAT is a 3D modeling format associated with ACIS.

For vector format files, DXF is the easiest to work with, and with TrueType support, DXF can preserve font information between AutoCAD and page layout programs that support the DXF format. The WMF format is also a commonly accepted file format for vector information, and it preserves TrueType fonts and lineweights used in your drawings.

PostScript is a raster/vector hybrid file format that AutoCAD supports. Unfortunately, AutoCAD dropped direct PostScript font support with Release 14. However, you can still use substitute fonts to stand in for PostScript fonts. These substitute fonts are converted to true PostScript fonts when AutoCAD exports the drawing. You don't see the true results of your PostScript output until you print your drawing on a PostScript printer.

The DXF file export was covered in a previous section of this chapter, so the following sections will concentrate on the WMF and PostScript file formats.

---

### EXCHANGING 3D DATA WITH FBX

AutoCAD can export to the FBX file format, which is a platform-independent 3D authoring/interchange format. FBX can be exported through the Application Menu's Export option. To import FBX files, choose Import from the Insert tab's Import panel or type **Import**↵. Select FBX (*.fbx) from the Files Of Type drop-down menu.

---

### WMF OUTPUT

The WMF file type is one of the most popular vector file formats in Windows. It can be opened and edited by most illustration programs, including CorelDRAW and Adobe Illustrator. Most word processing, database, and worksheet programs can also import WMF files. It's a great option for AutoCAD file export because it preserves TrueType fonts and lineweight settings. You can export WMF files that preserve lineweights as well.

To export WMF files, do the following:

**1.** Select Export ➤ Other Formats from the Application menu to open the Export Data dialog box.

**2.** Enter a name and location for your WMF file, select Metafile (*.wmf) from the Files Of Type drop-down list, and then click Save. The dialog box closes, and you're prompted to select objects.

**3.** Select the objects you want to export to the WMF file and press ↵. The objects are saved to your WMF file.

## POSTSCRIPT OUTPUT

AutoCAD can export to the Encapsulated PostScript (EPS) file format. If you're using AutoCAD 2015, you can obtain PostScript output in two ways: You can choose Export ➤ Other Formats from the Application menu, or you can enter **Psout.┘** at the Command prompt. If you choose Export ➤ Other Formats, you can use the Files Of Type drop-down list in the Export Data dialog box to select Encapsulated PS. Another method is to install a PostScript printer driver and plot your drawing to an EPS file. If you're an AutoCAD LT user, you can't export to EPS by clicking Export; you must set up a PostScript plotter and use it to plot to a file.

To set up AutoCAD to plot your drawing to an EPS file, follow these steps:

1. Click Plotter Manager in the Output tab's Plot panel, and then, in the Plotters dialog box, double-click the Add-A-Plotter Wizard.

2. Choose Next on the Introduction Page screen.

3. On the Begin screen of the Add-A-Plotter Wizard, choose My Computer.

4. On the Plotter Model screen, select Adobe from the Manufacturers list and then select the appropriate PostScript level from the Models list.

5. Skip the Import PCP Or PC2 screen and the Ports screen.

6. Enter a name for your EPS output settings on the Plotter Name screen.

7. On the Finish screen, click the Finish button.

AutoCAD doesn't preserve font information when creating EPS files from the printer option. It also produces larger files, especially if your drawing contains a lot of area fills and filled fonts. As an alternative to EPS, you can "plot" to an Adobe PDF file. EPS files can often be replaced by PDF files. When you get to the Plotter Model screen, select the Autodesk ePlot (PDF) option from the Manufacturers list. You can also use the full version of Adobe Acrobat or Acrobat Professional to produce PDF files from AutoCAD.

The HPGL plot-file format is another vector format you can use to export your AutoCAD drawings. Use the method described earlier in the section "Exporting Raster Files" to add the HPGL plotter driver to your printer/plotter configuration.

---

### USING AUTOCAD DWF FILES

The Autodesk DWF file format is another format you can use to exchange drawing data with others. It offers features that are geared toward AutoCAD users. You can import DWF files as external references, and using a free DWF viewer, you can gather information about a drawing such as block information, attribute data, and distance measurements. See Chapter 25 for more on DWF.

---

# Using OLE to Import Data

To import data from other applications, you use the Cut and Paste features found in virtually all Windows programs. You cut the data from the source document and then paste it into AutoCAD.

Typically, you'll want to paste data into AutoCAD in its native object format, but if you prefer, you can use a Windows feature called Object Linking and Embedding (OLE) to import files.

---

### FINDING THE COPY AND PASTE TOOLS

There are several variations of the Copy and Paste tools in AutoCAD, so they have been combined into tools and flyouts on the Home tab's Clipboard panel. The Paste flyout is in the large icon to the left, and the Copy Clip tool is to the right of the Paste flyout.

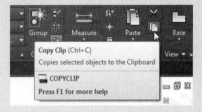

---

When you paste data into your AutoCAD file using OLE, you can link it to the source file or you can embed it. If you *link* it to the source file, the pasted data is updated whenever the source file is modified. This is similar to an AutoCAD Xref file. (See Chapter 14, "Advanced Editing and Organizing," for more on Xref files.) If you *embed* data, you're pasting it into AutoCAD without linking it. You can still open the application associated with the data by double-clicking it, but the data is no longer associated with the source file. Importing files using OLE is similar to other cut-and-paste operations. First, cut the data from the source application. This could be Microsoft Excel or Word. In AutoCAD, click Paste Special from the Paste flyout on the Home tab's Clipboard panel to open the Paste Special dialog box (see Figure 19.12).

Click the Paste Link radio button to tell AutoCAD that you want this paste to be a link. Notice that the list of source types changes to show only one option. This option will depend on the source document. Click OK. You're prompted to select an insertion point. Place the cursor in the location for the paste, and click. The imported data appears within the drawing. Depending on the type of data, it may appear in a bounding box. You can adjust the size of the bounding box to fit the scale of the drawing.

In addition to using the Paste Special tool, you can import an OLE object by clicking OLE Object in the Insert tab's Data panel to open the Insert Object dialog box (see Figure 19.13).

You can then select the type of object you want to import from the Object Type list box. Two radio buttons to the left of the list box let you import an existing object or create a new object of the type listed in the list box. If you choose the Create New radio button, the application associated with the object type will start and open a new file. If you choose the Create From File radio button (see Figure 19.14), the dialog box changes to show a filename and a Browse button.

You can then browse for an existing file to import. The Link check box lets you specify whether the imported file is to be linked and needs to be selected in order to use the Olelinks command described in the next section.

**FIGURE 19.12**
Use Paste Special to
link your data.

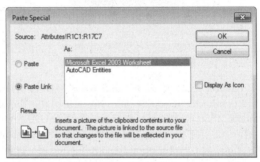

**FIGURE 19.13**
Inserting a
new object

**FIGURE 19.14**
Inserting an exist-
ing object

## Editing OLE Links

After you've pasted an object with links, you can control the links by typing **Olelinks.⏎** at the Command prompt. If there are no linked objects in the drawing, the Olelinks command does nothing; otherwise it opens the Links dialog box (see Figure 19.15).

**FIGURE 19.15**
Editing links

The options available in the Links dialog box are as follows:

**Cancel**   Cancels the link between a pasted object and its source file. After you use this option, changes in the source file have no effect on the pasted object. This is similar to using the Bind option in the Xref command.

**Update Now**   Updates an object's link when the Manual option is selected.

**Open Source**   Opens the linked file in the application associated with the object and lets you edit it.

**Change Source**   Lets you change the object's link to a different file. When you select this option, AutoCAD opens the Change Link dialog box, where you can select another file of the same type. For example, if you're editing the link to a sound file, the Change Link dialog box displays files with the .wav filename extension.

**Break Link**   Disconnects the link between the inserted data and the source document. The inserted data then becomes embedded rather than linked.

**Automatic and Manual**   Radio buttons that control whether linked objects are updated automatically or manually.

## Importing Worksheets as AutoCAD Tables

Although it can be beneficial to import worksheets as linked OLE objects, you may prefer to import worksheets as AutoCAD entities. You may not need the direct link to the source material that OLE linking offers. The ability to edit the imported worksheet directly in AutoCAD may have a higher priority for you.

In Chapter 10, you saw how you can create tables in AutoCAD by using the Table tool. You can import an Excel worksheet as an AutoCAD table by using the AutoCAD Entities option in the Paste Special dialog box. By importing worksheets as tables, you have more control over the layout and appearance of the worksheet data.

Try the following exercise to see how you can create a table from a worksheet:

1. Open the Excel worksheet called `19a-plan.xls`, and highlight the door data as shown in Figure 19.16.

**FIGURE 19.16**

The Excel worksheet

| | A | B | C | D | E | F | G | H | I | J |
|---|---|---|---|---|---|---|---|---|---|---|
| 1 | D-TYPE | D-SIZE | D-NUMBER | D-THICK | D-RATE | D-MATRL | D-CONST | | | |
| 2 | B | 3'-0" | 116 | 1 3/4" | 20 min. | Wood | Solid Core | | | |
| 3 | B | 3'-0" | 114 | 1 3/4" | 20 min. | Wood | Solid Core | | | |
| 4 | B | 3'-0" | 112 | 1 3/4" | 20 min. | Wood | Solid Core | | | |
| 5 | B | 3'-0" | 110 | 1 3/4" | 20 min. | Wood | Solid Core | | | |
| 6 | B | 3'-0" | 106 | 1 3/4" | 20 min. | Wood | Solid Core | | | |
| 7 | B | 3'-0" | 108 | 1 3/4" | 20 min. | Wood | Solid Core | | | |
| 8 | B | 3'-0" | 102 | 1 3/4" | 20 min. | Wood | Solid Core | | | |
| 9 | B | 3'-0" | 104 | 1 3/4" | 20 min. | Wood | Solid Core | | | |
| 10 | B | 3'-0" | 115 | 1 3/4" | 20 min. | Wood | Solid Core | | | |
| 11 | B | 3'-0" | 111 | 1 3/4" | 20 min. | Wood | Solid Core | | | |
| 12 | B | 3'-0" | 107 | 1 3/4" | 20 min. | Wood | Solid Core | | | |
| 13 | B | 3'-0" | 103 | 1 3/4" | 20 min. | Wood | Solid Core | | | |
| 14 | B | 3'-0" | 101 | 1 3/4" | 20 min. | Wood | Solid Core | | | |
| 15 | B | 3'-0" | 105 | 1 3/4" | 20 min. | Wood | Solid Core | | | |
| 16 | B | 3'-0" | 109 | 1 3/4" | 20 min. | Wood | Solid Core | | | |
| 17 | B | 3'-0" | 113 | 1 3/4" | 20 min. | Wood | Solid Core | | | |
| 18 | | 116 | | | | | | | | |
| 19 | | 114 | | | | | | | | |
| 20 | | 112 | | | | | | | | |
| 21 | | 110 | | | | | | | | |

2. Press Ctrl+C to place a copy of the selected data into the Windows Clipboard, and then switch back to AutoCAD.

3. Click Paste Special from the Paste flyout on the Home tab's Clipboard panel (see Figure 19.17) to open the Paste Special dialog box.

**FIGURE 19.17**

The Paste
Special tool

4. With the Paste radio button selected, select AutoCAD Entities from the list and click OK.

5. At the `Specify insertion point or [paste as Text]:` prompt, click a point in the lower-right area of the drawing. The worksheet data appears in the drawing as a table object (see Chapter 10 for more on tables).

6. Use the Scale tool to enlarge the table to a readable size (see Figure 19.18), and use the corner grips to adjust the width.

7. Close the Excel file.

**FIGURE 19.18**
Scale and size
the table.

| D-TYPE | D-SIZE | D-NUMBER | D-THICK | D-RATE | D-MATRL | D-CONST |
|--------|--------|----------|---------|--------|---------|---------|
| B | 3'-0" | 116 | 1 3/4" | no rating | Wood | Solid Core |
| B | 3'-0" | 114 | 1 3/4" | 20 min. | Wood | Solid Core |
| B | 3'-0" | 112 | 1 3/4" | 20 min. | Wood | Solid Core |
| B | 3'-0" | 110 | 1 3/4" | 20 min. | Wood | Solid Core |
| B | 3'-0" | 106 | 1 3/4" | 20 min. | Wood | Solid Core |
| B | 3'-0" | 108 | 1 3/4" | 20 min. | Wood | Solid Core |
| B | 3'-0" | 102 | 1 3/4" | 20 min. | Wood | Solid Core |
| B | 3'-0" | 104 | 1 3/4" | 20 min. | Wood | Solid Core |
| B | 3'-0" | 115 | 1 3/4" | 20 min | Wood | Solid Core |
| B | 3'-0" | 111 | 1 3/4" | 20 min | Wood | Solid Core |
| B | 3'-0" | 107 | 1 3/4" | 20 min. | Wood | Solid Core |
| B | 3'-0" | 103 | 1 3/4" | 20 min. | Wood | Solid Core |
| B | 3'-0" | 101 | 1 3/4" | 20 min. | Wood | Solid Core |
| B | 3'-0" | 105 | 1 3/4" | 20 min. | Wood | Solid Core |
| B | 3'-0" | 109 | 1 3/4" | 20 min. | Wood | Solid Core |
| B | 3'-0" | 113 | 1 3/4" | 20 min. | Wood | Solid Core |

You can edit this imported worksheet using the editing methods for AutoCAD tables described in Chapter 10. In that chapter, you learned that you could edit the text format, the border lineweight and color, and the background of cells. You can add rows and columns and rotate text so that it fits more uniformly in a vertical column.

In this exercise, the worksheet was imported using the default standard table style. This gives you a simple-looking table using the AutoCAD TXT font. You can set up a custom table style with the fonts and borders you want and then import the table for a more custom appearance. Make sure your custom table style is the current style before you import the worksheet.

## Understanding Options for Embedding Data

The Paste Special dialog box offers several other options that may better suit your needs. Here is a brief description of each format that is available:

**Microsoft Document**   Imports data from Microsoft Office documents. This option may show Word or Excel in the title, depending on the source. The pasted object will inherit the appearance of the source document. When using this option, you may receive a security warning message. Always make sure that your files are from a trusted source.

**Picture (Metafile)**   Imports the data as a vector or bitmap image, whichever is appropriate. If applicable, text is also maintained as text, although you can't edit it in AutoCAD.

**Bitmap**   Imports the data as a bitmap image, closely reflecting the appearance of the data as it appears on your computer screen in the source application.

**Picture (Enhanced Metafile)**   Similar to the Picture (Metafile) option, with support for more features.

**AutoCAD Entities**   Converts the data into AutoCAD objects such as lines, arcs, and circles. Text is converted into AutoCAD single-line text objects. Worksheets are converted into AutoCAD tables.

**Image Entity**   Converts the data into an AutoCAD raster image. You can then edit it by using the raster image–related tools such as Adobe Photoshop or the Microsoft Windows Paint program. See Chapter 13, "Copying Existing Drawings from Other Sources," for more on how to use raster images.

**Unicode Text**   Imports text data in the Unicode format. Unicode is an international standard for encoding text. If the Text option doesn't work, try Unicode Text.

**Text**   Converts the data into AutoCAD multiline text objects. Formatting isn't imported with text.

The options you see in the Paste Special dialog box depend on the type of data being imported. You saw how the Microsoft Excel Worksheet option maintains the imported data as an Excel worksheet. If the contents of the Clipboard come from another program, you're offered that program as a choice in place of Excel.

### Using the Clipboard to Export AutoCAD Drawings

Just as you can cut and paste data into AutoCAD from applications that support OLE, you can cut entities from AutoCAD and paste them as images to other applications. This can be useful as a way of including AutoCAD illustrations in word processing documents, worksheets, or page layout program documents. It can also be useful in creating background images for visualization programs such as Autodesk® 3ds Max® and 3ds Max® Design and for paint programs such as Corel Painter.

If you cut and paste an AutoCAD drawing to another file by using OLE and then send the file to someone using another computer, they must also have AutoCAD installed before they can edit the pasted AutoCAD drawing.

The receiving application doesn't need to support OLE, but if it does, the exported drawing can be edited with AutoCAD and will maintain its accuracy as a CAD drawing. Otherwise, the AutoCAD image will be converted to a bitmap graphic.

To use the Clipboard to export an object or a set of objects from an AutoCAD drawing, click Copy Clip from the Home tab's Clipboard panel. You're then prompted to select the objects you want to export. If you want to export and erase objects simultaneously from AutoCAD, click Cut from the Home tab's Clipboard panel.

In the receiving application, choose Edit ➢ Paste Special. You'll see a dialog box similar to the Paste Special dialog box in AutoCAD. Select the method for pasting your AutoCAD image, and then click OK. If the receiving application doesn't have a Paste Special option, choose Edit ➢ Paste. The receiving application converts the image into a format it can accept.

## The Bottom Line

**Find the area of closed boundaries.**   There are a number of ways to find the area of a closed boundary. The easiest way is also perhaps the least obvious.

**Master It**   Which AutoCAD feature would you use to find the area of an irregular shape quickly, such as a pond or lake?

**Get general information.**   A lot of information that is stored in AutoCAD drawings can tell you about the files. You can find out how much memory a file uses as well as the amount of time that has been spent editing the file.

**Master It**   What feature lets you store your own searchable information about a drawing file, and how do you get to this feature?

**Use the DXF file format to exchange CAD data with other programs.**   Autodesk created the DXF file format as a means of sharing vector drawings with other programs.

**Master It**   Name some of the versions of AutoCAD you can export to using the Save As option.

**Use AutoCAD drawings in page layout programs.**    AutoCAD drawings find their way into all types of documents, including brochures and technical manuals. Users are often asked to convert their CAD drawings into formats that can be read by page layout software.

**Master It**    Name some file formats, by filename extension or type, that page layout programs can accept.

**Use OLE to import data.**    You can import data into AutoCAD from a variety of sources. Most sources, such as bitmap images and text, can be imported as native AutoCAD objects. Other sources may need to be imported as OLE objects.

**Master It**    To link imported data to a source program through OLE, what dialog box would you use?

# Part 4

# 3D Modeling and Imaging

# Chapter 20

# Creating 3D Drawings

Viewing an object in three dimensions gives you a sense of its true shape and form. It also helps you conceptualize your design, which results in better design decisions. In addition, using three-dimensional objects helps you communicate your ideas to those who may not be familiar with the plans, sections, and side views of your design.

A further advantage to drawing in three dimensions is that you can derive 2D drawings from your 3D models, which may take considerably less time than creating them with standard 2D drawing methods. For example, you can model a mechanical part in 3D and then quickly derive its 2D top, front, and right-side views by using the techniques discussed in this chapter.

The AutoCAD LT® software does not support any of the 3D-related features described in this chapter.

In this chapter, you will learn to

♦ Know the 3D Modeling workspace

♦ Draw in 3D using solids

♦ Create 3D forms from 2D shapes

♦ Isolate coordinates with point filters

♦ Move around your model

♦ Get a visual effect

♦ Turn a 3D view into a 2D AutoCAD drawing

## Getting to Know the 3D Modeling Workspace

Most of this book is devoted to showing you how to work in the Drafting & Annotation workspace. This workspace is basically a 2D drawing environment, although you can certainly work in 3D as well.

The AutoCAD® 2015 program offers the *3D Modeling* and *3D Basics* workspaces, which give you a set of tools to help ease your way into 3D modeling. The 3D Modeling workspace gives AutoCAD a different set of Ribbon panels, but don't worry. AutoCAD behaves in the same basic way, and the AutoCAD files produced are the same regardless of whether they're 2D or 3D drawings. The 3D Basics workspace contains the minimum 3D tools needed to perform 3D functions.

To get to the 3D Modeling workspace, you first click the Workspace Switching tool in the status bar. Then select 3D Modeling (see Figure 20.1).

**FIGURE 20.1**

The Workspace Switching tool

If you're starting a new 3D model, you'll also want to create a new file using a 3D template. Try the following exercise to get started with 3D modeling:

1. Start AutoCAD. To create a new 3D modeling file, click New in the Quick Access toolbar to open the Select Template dialog box. Select acad3D.dwt and click Open. Your screen will look similar to Figure 20.2.

2. Click the Workspace Switching tool in the status bar at the bottom of the screen and select 3D Modeling. You'll see a new set of panels appear.

**FIGURE 20.2**

The AutoCAD 3D Modeling workspace

The drawing area displays the workspace as a perspective view with a dark gray background and a grid. This is just a typical AutoCAD drawing file with a couple of setting changes. The view has been set up to be a perspective view by default, and a feature called *Visual Styles* has been set to Realistic, which will show 3D objects as solid objects. You'll learn more about the tools you can use to adjust the appearance of your workspace later in this chapter. For now, let's look at the tool palette and Ribbon that appear in the AutoCAD window.

To the far right is the AutoCAD Materials Browser palette. It shows a graphical list of surface materials that you can easily assign to 3D objects in your model. If the Materials Browser does not open by default, you'll see how to open it and learn more about materials in Chapter 22, "Editing and Visualizing 3D Solids."

The Ribbon along the top of the AutoCAD window offers all the tools you'll need to create 3D models. The 3D Modeling workspace Ribbon offers a few of the tabs and panels with which you're already familiar, but many of the tabs will be new to you (see Figure 20.3). You see the familiar Draw and Modify panels in the Home tab, as well as several other panels devoted to 3D modeling: Modeling, Mesh, Solid Editing, Section, Coordinates, View, and Selection.

**FIGURE 20.3**
The Home Ribbon tab and panels of the 3D Modeling workspace

In addition, other Ribbon tabs offer more sets of tools designed for 3D modeling. For example, the Visualize tab contains tools that control the way the model looks. You can set up lighting and shadows and apply materials to objects such as brick or glass. You can also control the way AutoCAD illuminates the model through the Lights, Sun & Location, and Materials panels. In the next section, you'll gain firsthand experience creating and editing some 3D shapes using the Home tab's Modeling and View panels and the View tab's Visual Styles panel. This way, you'll get a feel for how things work in the 3D Modeling workspace.

## Drawing in 3D Using Solids

You can work with three types of 3D objects in AutoCAD: solids, surfaces, and mesh objects. You can treat solid objects as if they're solid material. For example, you can create a box and then remove shapes from the box as if you're carving it, as shown in Figure 20.4.

**FIGURE 20.4**
Solid modeling lets you remove or add shapes.

With surfaces, you create complex surface shapes by building on lines, arcs, or polylines. For example, you can quickly turn a series of curved polylines, arcs, or lines into a warped surface, as shown in Figure 20.5.

A mesh object is made up of edges, faces, and vertices. These basic parts create a series of square or triangular areas to define a three-dimensional form. You can create mesh objects with primitives in the same way as you create solid primitives. Their behavior is different, though. Mesh objects do not have mass properties like solids, but they can be altered through free-form modeling techniques. You can add creases as well as splits to the forms. You can alter the level of smoothness, which means you can add more edges, faces, and vertices for a more rounded and organic-looking object.

Next, you'll learn how to create a solid box and then make simple changes to it as an introduction to 3D modeling.

**FIGURE 20.5**
Using the Loft tool, you can use a set of 2D objects (left) to define a complex surface (right).

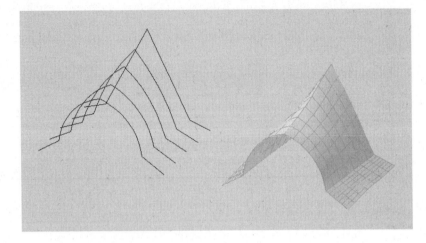

---

**CONVERTING OLD-STYLE SURFACE OBJECTS**

If you have some experience with AutoCAD 3D prior to AutoCAD® 2011, note that the current surface-modeling features aren't the same as the surface objects you may have created in the older version of AutoCAD. The current surface objects can interact with solid primitive objects and can be converted into 3D solids. You can convert the old-style surfaces into the new 3D surfaces using the Convtosurface command described in the sidebar "Converting Objects with Thickness into 3D Solids" later in this chapter.

---

## Adjusting Appearances

Before you start to work on the exercises, you'll want to change to a visual style that will make your work a little easier to visualize in the creation phase. Visual styles let you see your model in different modes, from sketch-like to realistic. You'll learn more about visual styles in the section "Getting a Visual Effect" later in this chapter. For now, you'll get a brief introduction by changing the style for the exercises that follow:

1. In the upper-left corner of the drawing area, click the Visual Style Control drop-down list to view the options.

2. Select the Shades Of Gray option. This will give the solid objects in your model a uniform gray color and will also "highlight" the edges of the solids with a dark line so you can see them clearly.

## Creating a 3D Box

Start by creating a box using the Box tool in the Home tab's Modeling panel:

1.  Close the Materials Browser by clicking the X on the title bar. You won't need it for this chapter. If you need it later, you can go to the Materials panel in the Visualize tab and click the Materials Browser tool.

2.  Select the Box tool from the Solids flyout on the Home tab's Modeling panel.

3.  Click a point near the origin of the drawing shown in Figure 20.6. You can use the coordinate readout to select a point near 0,0. After you click, you see a rectangle follow the cursor.

**FIGURE 20.6**

Drawing a 3D solid box

Your first selection should be a location near the drawing's origin at coordinate 0,0.

Select a location near the coordinate 20,15 for the other corner.

4.  Click another point near coordinate 20,15, as shown in Figure 20.6. As you move the cursor, the rectangle is fixed and the height of the 3D box appears.

5.  Enter 4↵ for a height of 4 units for the box. You can also click to fix the height of the box.

You used three basic steps in creating the box. First, you clicked one corner to establish a location for the box. Then, you clicked another corner to establish the base size. Finally, you selected a height. You use a similar set of steps to create any of the other 3D solid primitives found in the Solids flyout of the Home tab's Modeling panel. For example, for a cylinder you select the center, then the radius, and finally the height. For a wedge, you select two corners as you did with the box, and then you select the height.

---

**WHY THE SCREEN LOOKS DIFFERENT**

The display shown in this book is set up with a lighter background than the default background in AutoCAD so that you can see the various parts of the display more easily on the printed page.

In addition, when you start a 3D model using the acad3D.dwt template, the default layer 0 is set to a color that is a light blue instead of the white or black that is used in the standard acad.dwt template. The blue color is used so that you can see the 3D shapes clearly when the model is displayed using a shaded visual style. If you happen to start a 3D model using the acad.dwt template, you may want to change the default layer color to something other than white or black.

---

## Editing 3D Solids with Grips

After you've created a solid, you can fine-tune its shape by using grips:

1. Adjust your view so that it looks similar to Figure 20.7, and then click the solid to select it. Grips appear on the 3D solid as shown in the figure.

   You can adjust the location of the square grips at the base of the solid in a way that is similar to adjusting the grips on 2D objects. The arrow grips let you adjust the length of the site to which the arrows are attached. If you click an arrow grip and you have Dynamic Input turned on, a dimension appears at the cursor, as shown in Figure 20.7. You can enter a new dimension for the length associated with the selected grip, or you can drag and click the arrow to adjust the length. Remember that you can press the Tab key to shift between dimensions shown in the Dynamic Input display.

2. Click the arrow grip toward the front of the box, as shown at the upper left in Figure 20.7. Now, as you move the cursor, the box changes in length.

3. Press Esc twice to clear the grip selection and the box selection.

## Constraining Motion with the Gizmo

You can move individual edges by using a Ctrl+click. This will activate the gizmo. The gizmo is an icon that looks like the UCS icon and appears whenever you select a 3D solid or any part of a 3D solid. Try the next exercise to see how it works:

1. Hold down the Ctrl key and move the cursor over different surfaces and edges of the box. They will be highlighted as you do this. Ctrl+click the top-front edge of the box to expose the edge's grip. The gizmo will appear.

**FIGURE 20.7**
Grips appear on the
3D solid.

Click this arrow grip
to adjust the length of
the box.

Ctrl-click the top edge
to display the gizmo.

Click the base
of the gizmo.

**2.** The gizmo has three legs pointing in the x-, y-, and z-axes. It also has a grip at the base of
the three legs. If your Ctrl+click doesn't work as described, you may need to change the
setting for the Legacyctrlpick system variable. At the Type A Command prompt, enter
**legacyctrlpick↵**, and then enter **0↵**. Place the cursor on the blue z-axis of the gizmo, but
don't click. A blue line appears that extends across the drawing area, and the z-axis of the
gizmo changes color, as shown in Figure 20.8.

**FIGURE 20.8**
Using the gizmo to
constrain motion

Hover over the z-axis
of the gizmo and a
blue line appears.

The gizmo

**3.** Click the z-axis. Now as you move the cursor, the grip motion is constrained in the z-axis.

**4.** Click again to fix the location of the grip.

**5.** Press the Esc key to clear your grip selection.

**6.** Click the Undo tool to undo the grip edit.

Here you used the gizmo to change the Z location of a grip easily. You can use the gizmo to modify the location of a single grip or the entire object.

## Rotating Objects in 3D Using Dynamic UCS

Typically, you work in what is known as the *World Coordinate System (WCS)*. This is the default coordinate system that AutoCAD uses in new drawings, but you can also create your own coordinate systems that are subsets of the WCS. A coordinate system that you create is known as a *User Coordinate System (UCS)*.

UCSs are significant in 3D modeling because they can help you orient your work in 3D space. For example, you could set up a UCS on a vertical face of the 3D box you created earlier. You could then draw on that vertical face just as you would on the drawing's WCS. Figure 20.9 shows a cylinder drawn on the side of a box. If you click the Cylinder tool, for example, and place the cursor on the side of the box, the side will be highlighted to indicate the surface to which the cylinder will be applied. In addition, if you could see the cursor in color, you would see that the blue z-axis is pointing sideways to the left and is perpendicular to the side of the box.

**FIGURE 20.9**

Drawing on the side of a box

The face is highlighted.

The cursor's z-axis is perpendicular to the side of the box.

The UCS has always been an important tool for 3D modeling in AutoCAD. The example just described demonstrates the Dynamic UCS, which automatically changes the orientation of the x-, y-, and z-axes to conform to the flat surface of a 3D object.

You may have noticed that when you created the new 3D file using the `acad3D.dwt` template, the cursor looked different. Instead of the usual cross, you saw three intersecting lines. If you look carefully, you'll see that each line of the cursor is a different color. In its default configuration, AutoCAD shows a red line for the x-axis, a green line for the y-axis, and a blue line for the z-axis. This mimics the color scheme of the UCS icon, as shown in Figure 20.10.

**FIGURE 20.10**
The UCS icon at the left and the cursor in 3D to the right are color matched.

As you work with the Dynamic UCS, you'll see that the orientation of these lines changes when you point at a surface on a 3D object. The following exercise shows you how to use the Dynamic UCS to help you rotate the box about the x-axis:

1. Be sure the Object Snap and Allow/Disallow Dynamic UCS features are turned on.

2. Click Rotate in the Home tab's Modify panel or enter **RO**↵.

3. At the `Select objects:` prompt, click the box and then press ↵ to finish your selection.

4. At the `Specify base point:` prompt, don't click anything, but move the cursor from one surface of the box to a side of the box. As you do this, notice that the surface you point to becomes highlighted. The orientation of the cursor also changes depending on which surface you're pointing to.

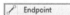

5. Place the cursor on the left side as shown in the top image of Figure 20.11; then Shift+right-click and select Endpoint from the Osnap context menu.

6. While keeping the side highlighted, place the osnap marker on the lower-front corner of the box, as shown in the top image in Figure 20.11. Click this corner. As you move the cursor, the box rotates about the y-axis.

7. Enter **-30** for the rotation angle. Your box should look like the image at the bottom in Figure 20.11.

Here you saw that you could hover over a surface to indicate the plane about which the rotation is to occur. Now suppose you want to add an object to one of the sides of the rotated box. The next section will show you another essential tool—one you can use to do just that.

**FIGURE 20.11**
Selecting a base point, and the resulting box orientation

The cursor on the left side of the box

The osnap marker

---

### USING OBJECT SNAPS AND OSNAP TRACKING IN 3D SPACE

If you need to place objects in precise locations in 3D, such as at endpoints or midpoints of other objects, you can do so using object snaps, just as you would in 2D. But you must take care when using osnaps where the Dynamic UCS is concerned.

In the exercise in the section "Rotating Objects in 3D Using Dynamic UCS," you were asked to make sure you placed the cursor on the side of the box that coincided with the rotational plane *before* you selected the Endpoint osnap. This ensures that the Dynamic UCS feature has selected the proper rotational plane; otherwise, the box may rotate in the wrong direction.

## Drawing on a 3D Object's Surface

In the rotation exercise, you saw that you could hover over a surface to indicate the plane of rotation. You can use the same method to indicate the plane on which you want to place an object. Try the following exercise to see how it's done:

1. Select Center, Radius from the Circle flyout on the Home tab's Draw panel or enter **C**↵.

2. Place the cursor on the top surface of the box, as indicated in the top image of Figure 20.12, and hold it there for a moment. The surface is highlighted and the cursor aligns with the angle of the top surface.

**FIGURE 20.12**
Drawing circles on the surface of a 3D solid

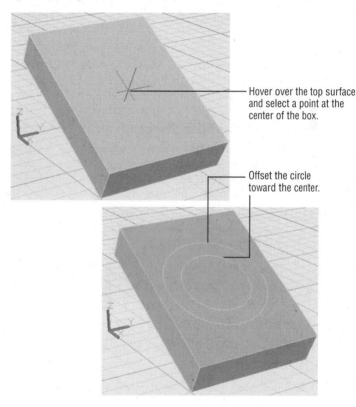

Hover over the top surface and select a point at the center of the box.

Offset the circle toward the center.

3. Click a point roughly at the center of the box. The circle appears on the surface, and as you move the cursor, the circle's radius follows.

4. Adjust the circle so that it's roughly the same 6-unit radius as the one shown on the lower image in Figure 20.12, and then click to set the radius. You can also enter **6**↵.

5. Select Offset from the Home tab's Modify panel, and offset the circle 2 units inward, as shown in the lower image of Figure 20.12. You can use the Center osnap to indicate a direction toward the center of the circle.

---

**USING A FIXED UCS**

If you're working in a crowded area of a drawing, or if you know you need to do a lot of work on one particular surface of an object, you can create a UCS that remains in a fixed orientation until you change it instead of relying on the Dynamic UCS feature. Select Face from the View flyout on the View tab's Coordinates panel, and then click the surface that defines the plane on which you want to work. The UCS aligns with the selected surface. Press ↵ to accept the face that the Face option has found, or you can use one of the options [Next/Xflip/Yflip] to move to another surface or flip the UCS. Once you've set the UCS, you won't have to worry about accidentally drawing in the wrong orientation. To return to the WCS, click UCS, World in the View tab's Coordinates panel. You'll learn more about the UCS in Chapter 21, "Using Advanced 3D Features."

---

This demonstrates that you can use Dynamic UCS to align objects with the surface of an object. Note that Dynamic UCS works only on flat surfaces. For example, you can't use it to place an object on the curved side of a cylinder.

## Pushing and Pulling Shapes from a Solid

You've just added two 2D circles to the top surface of the 3D box. AutoCAD offers a tool that lets you use those 2D circles or any closed 2D shapes to modify the shape of your 3D object. The Presspull tool in the Home tab's Modeling panel lets you "press" or "pull" a 3D shape to or from the surface of a 3D object. The following exercise shows how this works:

1. Make sure the Polar Tracking tool in the status bar is turned on, and then click the Presspull tool in the Home tab's Modeling panel. You can also enter **Presspull**↵ at the Type A Command prompt.

2. Move the cursor to the top surface of the box between both circles. (See the lower-right panel of Figure 20.13.)

3. With the cursor between the two circles, click. As you move the mouse, the circular area defined by the two circles moves.

4. Adjust the cursor location so that the cursor is positioned below the center of the circle, as shown in the top-left panel of Figure 20.13. Enter **3**↵ to create a 3-unit indentation, as shown in Figure 20.14.

You've created a circular indentation in the box by pressing the circular area defined by the two circles. You could have pulled the area upward to form a circular ridge on the box. Pressing the circle into the solid is essentially the same as subtracting one solid from another. When you press the shape into the solid, AutoCAD assumes you want to subtract the shape.

Presspull works with any closed 2D shape, such as a circle, closed polyline, or other completely enclosed area. An existing 3D solid isn't needed. For example, you can draw two concentric circles without the 3D box and then use Presspull to convert the circles into a 3D solid ring. In the previous exercise, the solid box showed that you can use Presspull to subtract a shape from an existing solid.

**FIGURE 20.13**

Move the cursor over different areas of the box and notice how the areas are highlighted.

Point inside the circle, and the center circle is highlighted.

Point between the circles, and the ring formed by the two circles is highlighted.

**FIGURE 20.14**

Creating an indentation in the box using Presspull

Enter 3 and a 3-unit indentation appears in the box.

As you saw in this exercise, the Presspull tool can help you quickly subtract a shape from an existing 3D solid. Figure 20.15 shows some other examples of how you can use Presspull. For example, you can draw a line from one edge to another and then use Presspull to extrude the resulting triangular shape. You can also draw concentric shapes and extrude them; you can even use offset spline curves to add a trough to a solid.

**FIGURE 20.15**
Creating complex shapes using the Presspull tool

---

**DRAWING OUTSIDE THE SURFACE**

If you use an open 2D object such as a curved spline or line on a 3D surface, the endpoints must touch exactly on the edge of the surface before Presspull will work.

---

## Making Changes to Your Solid

When you're creating a 3D model, you'll hardly ever get the shape right the first time. Suppose you decide that you need to modify the shape you've created so far by moving the hole from the center of the box to a corner. The next exercise will show you how to access the individual components of a 3D solid to make changes.

Your working model is composed of two objects: a box and a cylinder formed from two circles. These two components of the solid are referred to as *subobjects* of the main solid object. Faces and edges of 3D solids are also considered subobjects. When you use the Union, Subtract, and Intersect tools later in this book, you'll see that objects merge into a single solid—or at least that is how it seems at first. You can use Ctrl+click to access and modify the shapes of the subobjects. Try the following:

1. Press Esc to cancel the previous command. Place the cursor on the components of the solid you've made so far. They are highlighted as if they were one object. If you were to click it (don't do it yet), the entire object would be selected.

2. Hold down the Ctrl key, and move the cursor over the circular indentation. As you do this, the indentation is highlighted (see the top-left image in Figure 20.16).

3. While still holding down the Ctrl key, click both of the indentation sides. The grip for the indentation appears, as shown in the lower-right image in Figure 20.16. As you may guess, you can use these grips to change the shape and location of a feature of the selected solid.

4. Click the center square grip of the indentation, and move your cursor around. If you find it a bit uncontrollable, turn off Polar Tracking mode. As you move the cursor, the indentation moves with it.

5. Place the indentation in the location shown in Figure 20.17 and click. You've just moved the indentation from the center to the edge of the cylinder.

6. Press the Esc key to clear the selection. Exit the file and save it.

**FIGURE 20.16**
You can select subobjects of a 3D solid when you hold down the Ctrl key.

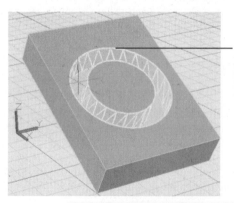

Hold down the Ctrl key and hover over the circular indentation. Click when the indentation is highlighted.

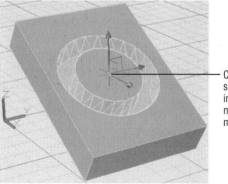

Click the center square grip. The indentation will move with the mouse.

**FIGURE 20.17**

You can move the indentation to a new location using its grip.

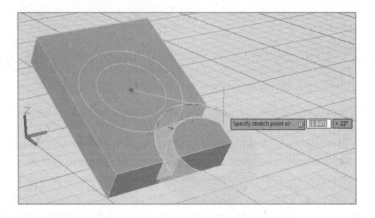

---

## THINGS TO WATCH OUT FOR WHEN EDITING 3D OBJECTS

You can use the Move and Stretch commands on 3D objects to modify their z-coordinate values—but you have to be careful with these commands when editing in 3D. Here are a few tips that we've picked up while working on various 3D projects:

♦ If you want to move a 3D solid using grips, you need to select the square grip at the bottom center of the solid. The other grips move only the feature associated with the grip, like a corner or an edge. When that bottom grip is selected, you can switch to another grip as the base point for the move by doing the following: After selecting the base grip, right-click, select Base Point from the context menu, and click the grip you want to use.

♦ The Scale command will scale an object's z-coordinate value as well as the standard x-coordinate and y-coordinate. Suppose you have an object with an elevation of 2 units. If you use the Scale command to enlarge that object by a factor of 4, the object will have a new elevation of 2 units times 4, or 8 units. If on the other hand that object has an elevation of 0, its elevation won't change because 0 times 4 is still 0. You can use the 3dscale command to restrict the scaling of an object to a single plane.

♦ You can also use Mirror and Rotate (on the Modify panel) on 3D solid objects, but these commands don't affect their z-coordinate values. You can specify z-coordinates for base and insertion points, so take care when using these commands with 3D models.

♦ Using the Move, Stretch, and Copy commands (on the Modify panel) with osnaps can produce unpredictable and unwanted results. As a rule, it's best to use coordinate filters when selecting points with osnap overrides. For example, to move an object from the endpoint of one object to the endpoint of another on the same z-coordinate, invoke the .XY point filter at the Specify base point: and Specify second point: prompts before you issue the Endpoint override. Proceed to pick the endpoint of the object you want, and then enter the z-coordinate or pick any point to use the current default z-coordinate.

♦ When you create a block, it uses the currently active UCS to determine its own local coordinate system. When that block is later inserted, it orients its own coordinate system with the current UCS. (The UCS is discussed in more detail in Chapter 21.)

This example showed that the Ctrl key can be an extremely useful tool when you have to edit a solid; it allows you to select the subobjects that form your model. Once the subobjects are selected, you can move them, or you can use the arrow grips to change their size.

## Creating 3D Forms from 2D Shapes

You've seen that 3D solid primitives are great for creating basic shapes, but in many situations you'll want to create a 3D form from a more complex shape. Fortunately, you can extrude 2D objects into a variety of shapes using additional tools found in the Home tab's Modeling panel. For example, you can draw a shape like a star and then extrude it along the z-axis, as shown in Figure 20.18. Alternatively, you can use several strategically placed 2D objects to form a flowing surface like the wing of an airplane.

**FIGURE 20.18**
The closed polyline on the left can be used to construct the 3D shape on the right.

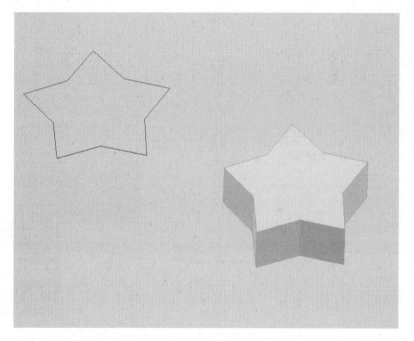

You can create a 3D solid by extruding a 2D closed polyline. This is a flexible way to create shapes because you can create a polyline of any shape and extrude it to a fairly complex form.

In the following set of exercises, you'll turn the apartment room from previous chapters into a 3D model. We've created a version of the apartment floor plan that has a few additions to make things a little easier for you. Figure 20.19 shows the file you'll use in the exercise. It's the same floor plan from earlier chapters but with the addition of closed polylines outlining the walls.

The plan isn't shaded as in the previous examples in this chapter. You can work in 3D in this display mode just as easily as in a shaded mode:

1. Open the 20-unit.dwg file. Metric users should open 20-unit-metric.dwg.

2. Choose SW Isometric from the 3D Navigation drop-down list in the Home tab's View panel (see Figure 20.20). You can also type **-View.⏎Swiso.⏎**.

**FIGURE 20.19**

The unit plan with closed polylines outlining the walls

Polyline outlines of the walls

**FIGURE 20.20**

Selecting a view from the 3D Navigation drop-down list

Your view now looks as if you're standing above and to the left of your drawing rather than directly above it (see Figure 20.21). The UCS icon helps you get a sense of your new orientation.

**3.** Click the Extrude tool in the Home tab's Modeling panel (see Figure 20.22).

You can also enter **Extrude.↵** at the command-line interface. You see the message `Current wire frame density: ISOLINES=4, Closed profiles creation mode = Solid` in the Command window followed by the `Select objects to extrude or [MOde]:` prompt.

**4.** Select the wall outlines shown in Figure 20.21, and then press ↵.

**FIGURE 20.21**
A 3D view of the
unit plan

Select these polylines for
the Extrude command.

**FIGURE 20.22**
Selecting the
Extrude tool from
the Modeling panel

**5.** At the Specify height of extrusion or [Direction/Path/Taper angle/
Expression] <-0'-3">: prompt, place the cursor near the top of the drawing area
and enter **8'**↵. Metric users should enter **224**↵. The walls extrude to the height you
entered, as shown in Figure 20.23.

**FIGURE 20.23**
The extruded walls

Unlike in the earlier exercise with the box, you can see through the walls because this is a Wireframe view. A *Wireframe view* shows the volume of a 3D object by displaying the lines representing the edges of surfaces. Later in this chapter, we'll discuss how to make an object's surfaces appear opaque as they do on the box earlier in this chapter.

Next you'll add door headers to define the wall openings:

1. Adjust your view so that you get a close look at the doorway shown in Figure 20.24. You can use the Pan and Zoom tools in this 3D view as you would in a 2D view.

**FIGURE 20.24**
Adding the door header to the opening at the balcony of the unit plan

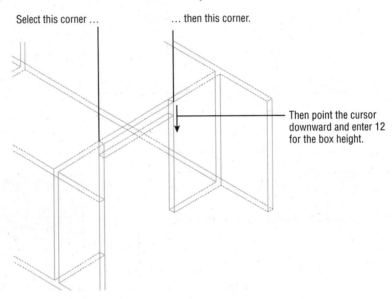

Select this corner … … then this corner.

Then point the cursor downward and enter 12 for the box height.

2. Turn off Dynamic UCS mode by clicking the Allow/Disallow Dynamic UCS tool in the status bar so that it's grayed out. This helps you avoid accidentally orienting your cursor to the wall behind the door header.

3. Click the Box tool in the Solids flyout of the Modeling panel.

4. Use the Endpoint osnaps, and click the two points shown in Figure 20.24.

5. At the `Specify height or [2Point] <8'-0">:` prompt, point the cursor downward from the points you just selected and enter **12**↵. Metric users should enter **30**↵. The door header appears.

6. Zoom and pan so that your view resembles Figure 20.25 and then repeat steps 4 and 5 to draw the other door headers.

The walls and door headers give you a better sense of the space in the unit plan. To enhance the appearance of the 3D model further, you can join the walls and door headers so that they appear as seamless walls and openings:

1. Zoom out so that you can see the entire unit. Click the Union tool in the Solid tab and Boolean panel (see Figure 20.26). You can also enter **UNI**↵.

**FIGURE 20.25**
Adding the remaining door headers

Add these three
door headers.

**FIGURE 20.26**
Select the
Union tool.

**2.** At the Select objects: prompt, select all the walls and headers, and then press ⏎.

Now the walls and headers appear as one seamless surface without any distracting joint lines. You can get a sense of the space of the unit plan. You'll want to explore ways of viewing the unit in 3D, but before you do that, you need to know about one more 3D modeling feature: *point filters*.

## Isolating Coordinates with Point Filters

AutoCAD offers a method for 3D point selection that can help you isolate the x-, y-, or z-coordinate of a location in 3D. Using *point filters* (described in the help files as "coordinate filters"), you can enter an X, Y, or Z value by picking a point on the screen and telling AutoCAD to use only the X, Y, or Z value of that point or any combination of those values. For example, suppose you want to start the corner of a 3D box at the x- and y-coordinates of the corner of the unit plan, but you want the Z location at 3′ instead of at ground level. You can use point or coordinate filters to select only the x- and y-coordinates of a point and then specify the z-coordinate as a separate value. The following exercise demonstrates how this works:

**1.** Zoom into the balcony door, and turn on the F-RAIL layer.

**2.** Choose the Box tool from the Solids flyout on the Modeling panel.

**3.** At the Specify first corner or [Center]: prompt, Shift+right-click to display the Object Snap menu and then choose Point Filters ➤ .XY. As an alternative, you can enter **.xy**⏎. By doing this, you are telling AutoCAD that first you're going to specify the x- and y-coordinates for this beginning point and then later indicate the z-coordinate.

You may have noticed the .X, .Y, and .Z options on the Object Snap menu (Shift+right-click) in step 3. These are the 3D point filters. By choosing one of these options as you select points in a 3D command, you can filter an X, Y, or Z value, or any combination of values, from that selected point. You can also enter filters through the keyboard.

**4.** At the Specify first corner or [Center]: .XY of: prompt, pick the corner of the unit plan, as shown in Figure 20.27.

**FIGURE 20.27**
Constructing
the rail using
point filters

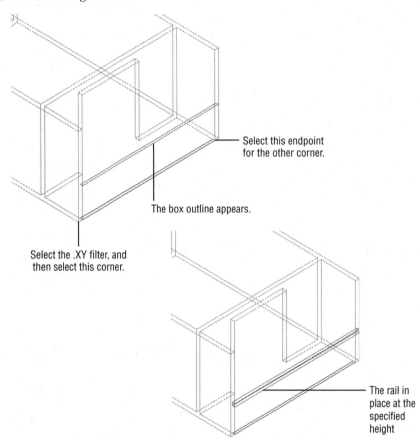

Select this endpoint
for the other corner.

The box outline appears.

Select the .XY filter, and
then select this corner.

The rail in
place at the
specified
height

**5.** At the (need Z): prompt, enter **36**↵ (the z-coordinate). Metric users enter **92**↵. The outline of the box appears at the 36" (or 92 cm) elevation and at the corner you selected in step 4.

**6.** At the Specify other corner or [Cube/Length]: prompt, Shift+right-click to display the Osnap menu again and choose Point Filters ➤ XY. Select the other endpoint indicated in Figure 20.27.

**7.** At the (need Z): prompt, a temporary outline of the box appears at the 36" height. Click at the endpoint indicated in Figure 20.27 to fix the base outline of the box.

**8.** Enter **4**↵ (**10**↵ for metric users) for the height of the box. The box appears as the balcony rail, as shown in the bottom image in Figure 20.27.

## CONVERTING OBJECTS WITH THICKNESS INTO 3D SOLIDS

If you've worked with 3D in AutoCAD before, you probably know that you can give an object a thickness property greater than 0 to make it a 3D object. For example, a line with a thickness property greater than 0 looks like a vertical surface.

In the unit plan exercise, you can do the same for the polylines used to draw the walls. Click the wall polylines, and then right-click and choose Properties. In the Properties palette, change the Thickness value to 8′ or 224 cm.

The walls appear in three dimensions. But be aware that these walls aren't 3D solids. If you zoom in to a detail of the walls, they appear hollow.

Fortunately, AutoCAD supplies a tool that converts a closed polyline with thickness into a solid. Expand the Home tab's Solid Editing panel, and then click the Convert To Solid tool. You can also enter **convtosolid**↵.

Select the polyline walls; press ↵ when you've finished your selection. After you do this, the walls become 3D solids. This operation works with any closed polyline, providing an alternate way of creating a 3D solid. If you have existing 3D models that have been produced using the Thickness property, you can use the Convert To Solid tool to bring your 3D models up-to-date. The Convert To Solid tool can also convert open polylines that have a width and thickness greater than 0. (See Chapter 18, "Drawing Curves," for more on polylines.)

Another tool, called Convert To Surface, converts objects with thickness into 3D surface objects. You can use 3D surfaces to slice or thicken 3D solids into full 3D solids. You'll learn more about 3D surfaces in Chapter 23, "Exploring 3D Mesh and Surface Modeling."

In step 4, you selected the corner of the unit, but the box didn't appear right away. You had to enter a Z value in step 5 before the outline of the box appeared. Then, in step 6, you saw the box begin at the 36″ elevation. Using point filters allowed you to place the box accurately in the drawing even though there were no features that you could snap to directly.

Now that you've gotten most of the unit modeled in 3D, you'll want to be able to look at it from different angles. Next you'll see some of the tools available to control your views in 3D.

**GET TO KNOW COORDINATE FILTERS**

In our own work in 3D, coordinate filters are a real lifesaver. They can help you locate a position in 3D when the drawing becomes crowded with objects. And because a lot of architectural models start from floor plans, you can easily "project" locations into 3D using coordinate filters. Understanding this tool will greatly improve your ability to work in 3D.

# Moving around Your Model

AutoCAD offers a number of tools to help you view your 3D model. You've already used one to get the current 3D view. Choosing Southwest Isometric from the View panel's drop-down list displays an isometric view from a southwest direction. You may have noticed several other isometric view options in that list. The following sections introduce you to some of the ways you can move around in your 3D model.

## Finding Isometric and Orthogonal Views

Figure 20.28 illustrates the isometric view options you saw earlier in the Home tab's View panel drop-down list: Southeast Isometric, Southwest Isometric, Northeast Isometric, and Northwest Isometric. The cameras represent the different viewpoint locations. You can get an idea of their location in reference to the grid and UCS icon.

**FIGURE 20.28**
The isometric viewpoints for the four isometric views available from the Home tab's View panel drop-down list

The Home tab's View panel's 3D Navigation drop-down list also offers another set of options: Top, Bottom, Left, Right, Front, and Back. These are orthogonal views that show the sides, top, and bottom of the model, as illustrated in Figure 20.29. In this figure, the cameras once again show the points of view.

When you use any of the view options described here, AutoCAD attempts to display the extents of the drawing. You can then use the Pan and Zoom tools to adjust your view.

**FIGURE 20.29**
This diagram shows the six viewpoints of the orthogonal view options on the View panel's 3D Navigation drop-down list.

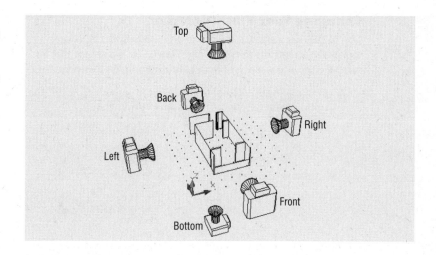

## Rotating Freely around Your Model

You may find the isometric and orthogonal views a bit restrictive. The Orbit tool lets you move around your model in real time. You can fine-tune your view by clicking and dragging the mouse using this tool. Try the following to see how it works:

1. Zoom out so you see an overall view of your model.

2. Click the Orbit tool in the Orbit flyout on the View tab's Navigate panel.

You can also enter **3dorbit**↵ and then right-click and select Other Navigation Modes ➤ Constrained Orbit.

3. Click and drag in the drawing area. As you drag the mouse, the view revolves around your model. The cursor changes to an orbit icon to let you know you're in the middle of using the Constrained Orbit tool.

If you have several objects in your model, you can select an object that you want to revolve around and then click the Orbit tool. It also helps to pan your view so that the object you select is in the center of the view.

When you've reached the view you want, right-click and choose Exit. You're then ready to make more changes or use another tool.

## Changing Your View Direction

One of the first tasks you'll want to do with a model is to look at it from all angles. The ViewCube® tool is perfect for this purpose. The ViewCube is a device that lets you select a view by using a sample cube. If it is not visible in your drawing, do the following:

1. First make sure Visual Styles is set to something other than 2D Wireframe by selecting an option from the Visual Styles drop-down list.

2. If you don't already see the ViewCube in the upper-right corner of the drawing area, go to the View tab's Viewport Tools panel and turn on the ViewCube option by clicking the View Cube button.

---

**CONSTRAINED ORBIT SHORTCUT**

If you have a mouse with a scroll wheel, you can hold down the Shift key while clicking and dragging the wheel to get the same effect as using the Constrained Orbit tool. If this doesn't work for you, try installing the manufacturer's software and drivers.

---

The following list explains what you can do with the ViewCube (see Figure 20.30):

♦ Click the Home icon to bring your view to the "home" position. This is helpful if you lose sight of your model.

♦ You can get a top, front, right-side, or other orthogonal view just by clicking the word *Top*, *Front*, or *Right* on the ViewCube.

♦ Click a corner of the cube to get an isometric-style view, or click an edge to get an "edge-on" view.

- Click and drag the N, S, E, or W label to rotate the model in the XY plane.

- To rotate your view of the object in 3D freely, click and drag the cube.

- From the icon at the bottom, select an existing UCS or create a new one from the UCS list.

**FIGURE 20.30**

The ViewCube and its options

Click the Home icon to bring your view to the "home" position. This is helpful if you lose sight of your model.

Click a corner to get an isometric-style view.

Click an edge to get an "edge-on" view.

Click the face of the cube to get an orthogonal view such as a top, front, or right-side view.

Click and drag the compass ring to rotate your view.

Click and drag a corner or edge to rotate your view freely in all directions.

Select an existing UCS or create a new one from the UCS list.

You can also change from a perspective view to a parallel projection view by right-clicking the cube and selecting Parallel Projection. To go from parallel projection to perspective, right-click and select Perspective or Perspective With Ortho Faces. The Perspective With Ortho Faces option works like the Perspective option except it will force a parallel projection view when you use the ViewCube to select a top, bottom, or side orthographic view.

When you are in a plan or top view, the ViewCube will look like a square, and when you hover your cursor over the cube, you'll see two curved arrows to the upper right of the cube (see Figure 20.31).

**FIGURE 20.31**

The ViewCube top view

You can click on any of the visible corners to go to an isometric view or click the double-curved arrows to rotate the view 90 degrees. The four arrowheads that you see pointing toward the cube allow you to change to an orthographic view of any of the four sides.

---

**SETTING THE HOME VIEW**

In a new file, the ViewCube's home view is similar to the SW Isometric view. To set your own home view, right-click the ViewCube and select Set Current View As Home.

---

## Using SteeringWheels

The ViewCube is great for looking at your model from different angles. But if your application requires you to be inside your model, you'll want to know how to use the *SteeringWheels*® feature. The SteeringWheels feature collects a number of viewing tools in one interface. You can open SteeringWheels by clicking the SteeringWheels tool in the View tab's Navigate panel (see Figure 20.32) or from the Navigation bar.

**FIGURE 20.32**

The SteeringWheels
tool

You can also type **Navswheel⏎**. When you do this, the SteeringWheels tool appears in the drawing area and moves with the cursor.

The SteeringWheels options are fairly self-explanatory. Just be aware that you need to use a click-and-drag motion to use them:

**Pan**   To pan your view, click and drag the Pan option.

**Zoom**   To zoom, click and drag the Zoom option.

**Orbit**   The Orbit option lets you revolve your view about your model.

**Look**   The Look option swivels your point of view around your model as if you were standing still and moving your "camera" around.

**Center**   The Center option is a bit less obvious, but it is an important tool for the SteeringWheels feature. Click and hold the Center option and then drag the circular cursor that appears onto a 3D object. In any visual style other than 2D Wireframe, you will see a green sphere that indicates the center of your view for the Orbit option. Place this green sphere on the object at the desired center of your orbit. For example, if you want to use the Orbit option to look at all sides of a cube, click and drag the Center option so that the green sphere is at the center of the cube. Release the mouse button when you've placed the sphere where you want it (see Figure 20.33).

**FIGURE 20.33**

Placing the green
sphere of the
Center option

If you are in a 2D Wireframe view, you will have to place the cursor on the edge of the object before you'll see the green sphere.

**Walk**   The Walk option is similar to the Walk tool in the Render tab's Animations panel. (See "Changing Where You Are Looking" later in this chapter for more on the Walk tool.) Click and drag the Walk option, and you'll see a blue circle and a cursor arrow that points in a direction away from the circle (see Figure 20.34). Your view moves smoothly in the direction of the arrow as if to follow it.

**FIGURE 20.34**
Using the
Walk option

**Rewind**   The Rewind option rewinds the views you've seen while using the SteeringWheels feature. Click and drag the Rewind option, and you see a series of panels like movie frames in a video-editing program (see Figure 20.35).

**FIGURE 20.35**
The frames of the
Rewind tool

As you move the mouse from right to left, the views in the AutoCAD drawing area are played back smoothly in reverse order. Move left to right to move forward in time through the views. This is especially helpful if your model has accidentally shifted out of view. You can roll back your views to one before the model flew out of view.

**Up/Down**   The Up/Down option will move your view up or down respectively along the z-axis using a slider control.

You can right-click on SteeringWheels for a number of options in the context menu. You can also open this menu by clicking the arrowhead in the lower-right corner of the wheel. Most of these context menu options are self-explanatory, but a few of them are worth a brief description.

If you click the Basic Wheels option in the SteeringWheels context menu, you'll see Tour Building and View Object. Select the Tour Building Wheel option. Figure 20.36 shows these variations on the basic SteeringWheels wheel, and they offer a pared-down set of options for the two types of viewing options indicated by the name of the wheels.

**FIGURE 20.36**
Variations of the
SteeringWheels
wheel

You'll also see mini versions available for the wheels from the SteeringWheels menu. The mini versions are much smaller, and they do not have labels indicating the options. Instead you see segmented circles, like a pie. Each segment of the circle is an option. Tool tips appear when you point at a segment, telling you what option that segment represents. Other than that, the mini versions work the same as the full-sized wheels.

The SteeringWheels feature takes a little practice, but when you've become familiar with it, you may find that you use it frequently when studying a 3D model. Just remember that a click-and-drag motion is required to use the tools effectively.

## Changing Where You Are Looking

AutoCAD uses a camera analogy to help you set up views in your 3D model. With a camera, you have a camera location and a target, and you can fine-tune both in AutoCAD. AutoCAD also offers the Swivel tool to let you adjust your view orientation. Using the Swivel tool is like keeping the camera stationary while pointing in a different direction. While viewing your drawing in perspective mode, click Pan on the View tab's Navigation bar, right-click in the drawing area, and select Other Navigation Modes ➢ Swivel. (Remember that you need to right-click on the ViewCube and select Perspective for the perspective mode.)

At first the Swivel tool might seem just like the Pan tool. But in the 3D world, Pan actually moves both the camera and the target in unison. Using Pan is a bit like pointing a camera out the side of a moving car. If you don't keep the view in the camera fixed on an object, you are panning across the scenery. Using the Swivel tool is like standing on the side of the road and turning the camera to take in a panoramic view.

To use the Swivel tool, do the following:

1.  While in a perspective view, click Pan on the View tab's Navigate panel or on the Navigation bar.

2.  Right-click in the drawing area, and choose Other Navigation Modes ➢ Swivel. You can also type **3dswivel**↵ at the Type A Command prompt.

3.  Click and drag in the drawing to swivel your point of view.

4.  When you have the view you want, right-click and select Exit.

If you happen to lose your view entirely, you can use the Undo tool in the Quick Access toolbar to return to your previous view and start over.

## Flying through Your View

Another way to get around in your model is to use the Walk or Fly view options. If you're familiar with computer games, this tool is for you. To get to these options, start the Pan tool as you did in the last exercise, and then right-click and select Other Navigation Modes ➢ Fly. If you don't see the Other Navigation Modes menu option, make sure that you are in a perspective view.

> ### WHERE TO FIND WALK
>
> The Walk tool is part of a flyout on the Animations panel. Typically, the Animations panel is not displayed. To display it, select the Visualize tab, right-click in a Ribbon panel, and select Show Panels ➢ Animations. The Walk tool is in the upper-right corner of the panel. The Fly tool is in the flyout of the Walk tool.

If you right-click while in this mode and click Display Instruction Window, a window will appear on the Communications Center. The message in the window tells you all you need to know about the Walk and Fly tools. You can use the arrow keys to move through your model. Click and drag the mouse to change the direction where you're looking.

If you press the F key, Walk changes to Fly mode. The main difference between Walk and Fly is that in Walk, both your position in the model and the point where you're looking move with the Up and Down arrow keys. Walk is a bit like Pan. When you're in Fly mode, the arrow keys move you toward the center of your view, which is indicated by a crosshair.

In addition to the crosshair, you'll see a palette that shows your position in the model from a top-down view (see Figure 20.37).

**FIGURE 20.37**
The Position Locator palette uses a top-down view.

You can use the palette to control your view by clicking and dragging the camera or the view target graphic. If you prefer, you can close the palette and continue to "walk" through your model. When you're finished using Walk, right-click and choose Exit.

## Changing from Perspective to Parallel Projection

When you create a new drawing using the acad3D.dwt template, you're automatically given a perspective view of the file. If you need a more schematic parallel projection style of view, you can get one from the ViewCube's right-click menu (see Figure 20.38). You can return to a perspective view by using the same context menu shown in the figure.

**FIGURE 20.38**
The Perspective pro-
jection and Parallel
projection tools

**FIGURE 20.38**
The Perspective pro-
jection and Parallel
projection tools

# Getting a Visual Effect

Although 3D models are extremely useful in communicating your ideas to others, sometimes you find that the default appearance of your model isn't exactly what you want. If you're only in a schematic design stage, you may want your model to look more like a sketch instead of a finished product. Conversely, if you're trying to sell someone on a concept, you may want a realistic look that includes materials and even special lighting.

AutoCAD provides a variety of tools to help you get a visual style, from a simple wireframe to a fully rendered image complete with chrome and wood. In the following sections, you'll get a preview of what is available to control the appearance of your model. Later, in Chapter 22, you'll get an in-depth look at rendering and camera tools that allow you to produce views from hand-sketched "napkin" designs to finished renderings.

## Using Visual Styles

In the earlier tutorials in this chapter, you drew a box that appeared to be solid. When you then opened an existing file to extrude the unit plan into the third dimension, you worked in a Wireframe view. These views are known as *visual styles* in AutoCAD. You used the Shades Of Gray visual style when you drew the box. The unit plan used the default 2D Wireframe view that is used in the AutoCAD Classic style of drawing.

Sometimes, it helps to use a different visual style, depending on your task. For example, the 2D Wireframe view in your unit plan model can help you visualize and select things that are behind a solid. AutoCAD includes several shaded view options that can bring out various features of your model. Try the following exercises to explore some of the other visual styles:

1. Click the Visual Styles drop-down list in the Home tab's View panel. You can also find the list in the View tab's Visual Styles panel, which will display the Visual Styles Manager palette. A set of graphic images appear that give you an idea of what each visual style shows you (see Figure 20.39). You can also access the visual styles from the Visual Styles drop-down list located at the upper-left side of the drawing screen, but you will not get the graphical images.

2. Select Wireframe. You can also enter **Vscurrent↵wireframe↵**. Your model appears as a transparent wireframe object with a gray background.

3. To get to the shaded view of your model, choose Realistic from the Visual Styles drop-down list or enter **Vscurrent↵Realistic↵**.

**FIGURE 20.39**
The Visual Styles
drop-down

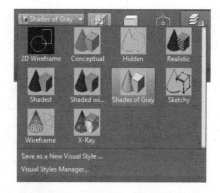

You may have noticed a few other visual styles options. Figure 20.40 shows a few of those options as they're applied to a sphere. 2D Wireframe and Wireframe may appear the same, but Wireframe uses a perspective view and a background color, whereas 2D Wireframe uses a parallel projection view and no background color.

**FIGURE 20.40**
Visual styles
applied to a sphere

| 2D Wireframe | Hidden | Wireframe | Conceptual | Realistic |

## Creating a Sketched Look with Visual Styles

You may notice blanks in the visual styles options in the View tab's Visual Styles drop-down list. These spaces allow you to create custom visual styles. For practice, you'll create a visual style similar to the existing Sketchy style so that you can learn how the rough look of that style was created. The following exercise will step you through the process:

1. Click the Visual Styles Manager from the Visual Styles drop-down. The Visual Styles Manager appears (see Figure 20.41). You can also enter **Visualstyles** ↵. This palette looks similar to the Properties palette with the addition of thumbnail examples of the visual styles at the top of the palette.

2. Click the Create New Visual Style tool in the Visual Styles Manager toolbar. The Create New Visual Style dialog box opens (see Figure 20.42).

3. Enter **Sketch** in the Name box.

4. Enter **Hand Drawn Appearance** in the Description box, and then click OK. You see a new thumbnail in the bottom-left corner of the samples at the top of the palette.

You've just created a new visual style. This new style uses the default settings that are similar to the Realistic visual style but without the Material Display option turned on. The material setting causes objects in your drawing to display any material assignments that have been given to objects. You'll learn more about materials in Chapter 22.

**FIGURE 20.41**
The Visual Styles
Manager

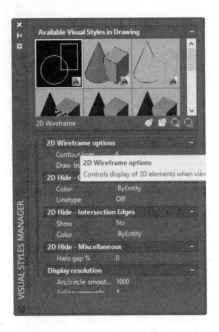

**FIGURE 20.42**
The Create New
Visual Style
dialog box

Now that you have a new visual style, you can begin to customize it. But before you start your customization, make your new visual style the current one so that you can see the effects of your changes as you make them:

1. Click the Apply Selected Visual Style To Current Viewport tool in the Visual Styles Manager toolbar.

   The display changes slightly, and you see the name Sketch appear in the Visual Styles drop-down list as well as the upper-left corner of the drawing area.

   Next you'll turn on the two features that will give your new visual style a sketch like appearance.

2. Use the scroll bar to the left of the Visual Styles Manager to scroll down to the bottom of the list of options.

3. Locate the Edge Modifiers option group, and click the Line Extensions Edges tool in the Edge Modifiers title bar.

   Edges of your model now appear to be drawn with lines extending beyond the corners.

**4.** Click the Jitter Edges tool in the Edge Modifiers title bar. The edges take on a sketched look, as shown in Figure 20.43.

**FIGURE 20.43**
The 3D unit plan
with the Sketch
visual style

**5.** Save the unit plan file.

The 3D view has taken on a hand-drawn appearance. Notice that the lines overhang the corners in a typical architectural sketch style. This is the effect of the Line Extensions Edges option you used in step 3. The lines are made rough and broken by the Jitter Edges setting. You can control the amount of overhang and jitter in the Edge Modifiers group of the Visual Styles Manager to exaggerate or soften these effects.

With your newly created Sketch visual style, the model looks like it's transparent. You can make it appear opaque by turning off the Show option under the Occluded Edges group in the Visual Styles Manager (see Figure 20.44).

**FIGURE 20.44**
The Show option in
the Occluded Edges
group in the Visual
Styles Manager

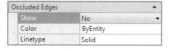

Finally, you can control some of the commonly used visual style properties using options in the Visualize tab's Visual Styles panel. This panel offers control over isolines, color, face style, shadows, and textures for the current visual style (see Figure 20.45).

**FIGURE 20.45**
Options in the
Visual Styles panel

## In-Canvas Viewport Controls

Beginning in AutoCAD® 2012, controls are built into each viewport that allow you to quickly change between visual styles and model views without starting either command. These controls are found in the upper-left portion of the viewport. Clicking the view name will bring up a list of the available views to choose from. Likewise, clicking on the visual style will bring up a list of available visual styles. Clicking on either of them will instantly make the selected style or view current in that viewport.

## Turning a 3D View into a 2D AutoCAD Drawing

Many architectural firms use AutoCAD 3D models to study their designs. After a specific part of a design is modeled and approved, they convert the model into 2D elevations, ready to plug into their elevation drawing.

If you need to convert your 3D models into 2D line drawings, you can use the Flatshot tool in the Home tab's expanded Section panel.

Set up your drawing view, and then click the Flatshot tool or enter **Flatshot**⏎ at the command-line interface to open the Flatshot dialog box (see Figure 20.46).

**FIGURE 20.46**
The Flatshot
dialog box

> ### PRINTING YOUR MODEL USING VISUAL STYLES
>
> You can print a drawing that uses visual styles either from the Model tab or from a Layout tab. If you're printing from the model view, click Plot from the Quick Access toolbar. Then, in the Plot dialog box, select the visual style from the Shade Plot drop-down list in the Shaded Viewport Options group. If you're plotting from a Layout tab, select the layout viewport border, right-click, and choose Shade Plot from the context menu. You can select from a list of visual styles on a cascading menu. Once you've done this, plot your layout as you normally would.

Select the options you want to use for the 2D line drawing, and then click Create. Depending on the options you select, you'll be prompted to select an insertion point or indicate a location for an exported drawing file. The 2D line drawing will be placed on the plane of the current UCS, so if you are viewing your model in a 3D view but you are in the World UCS, the 2D line drawing will appear to be projected onto the XY plane.

Flatshot lets you place the 2D version of your model in the current drawing as a block, to replace an existing block in the current drawing, or to save the 2D version as a DWG file. Table 20.1 describes the Flatshot options in more detail.

**TABLE 20.1:**    Flatshot options

| OPTION | WHAT IT DOES |
| --- | --- |
| **Destination** | |
| Inserts the 2D view in the current drawing as a block. You're prompted for an insertion point, a scale, and a rotation. | Insert As New Block |
| Replaces an existing block with a block of the 2D view. You're prompted to select an existing block. | Replace Existing Block |
| If Replace Existing Block is selected, lets you select a block to be replaced. A warning is shown if no block is selected. | Select Block |
| Exports the 2D view as a drawing file. | Export To A File |
| Displays the location for the export file. Click the Browse button to specify a location. | Filename And Path |
| **Foreground Lines** | |
| Color | Sets the overall color for the 2D view. |
| Linetype | Sets the overall linetype for the 2D view. |
| **Obscured Lines** | |
| Displays hidden lines. | Show |
| If Show is turned on, sets the color for hidden lines. | Color |

**TABLE 20.1:**    Flatshot options  *(continued)*

| OPTION | WHAT IT DOES |
|---|---|
| If Show is turned on, sets the linetype for hidden lines. The Current Linetype Scale setting is used for linetypes other than continuous. | Linetype |
| Displays edges for curved surfaces. | Include Tangential Edges |

One useful feature of Flatshot is that it can create a 2D drawing that displays the hidden lines of a 3D mechanical drawing. Turn on the Show option, and then select a linetype such as Hidden for obscured lines to produce a 2D drawing like the one shown in Figure 20.47.

**FIGURE 20.47**
A sample of a 2D drawing generated from a 3D model using Flatshot. Note the dashed lines showing the hidden lines of the view.

## Using the Point Cloud Feature

As you might guess from the name, a *point cloud* is a set of data points in a 3D coordinate system. They are often the product of 3D scanners, which are devices that can analyze and record the shape of real-world objects or environments. With point cloud data, you can reproduce an object or environment as a digital model that can then be used for a video game, movie production, 3D model, or even as-built drawings.

AutoCAD lets you import raw point cloud data through a set of tools that can be found in the Insert tab's Point Cloud panel (see Figure 20.48).

AutoCAD can import point cloud data in the form of RCP (Recap Project) or RCS (RecapScan) files. These file types can be produced with the Autodesk® ReCap™ program, a separate application that comes with AutoCAD (see the sidebar "Autodesk ReCap").

**FIGURE 20.48**
The Point Cloud
panel in the
Insert tab

---

**AUTODESK ReCAP**

Autodesk ReCap is an application that runs outside AutoCAD. This additional program lets you take raw data from 3D scans and package it in a way AutoCAD can use. ReCap can handle the massive amounts of data collected from 3D scanners so that you can aggregate the scans. It features tools that enable you to clean up the data, sort it, compress it, and visualize it. Once this is accomplished, ReCap will put the data into a file format that AutoCAD can easily digest and use. ReCap requires users to have and log into their Autodesk® 360 account.

---

After you import the point cloud data, AutoCAD displays it in your file. To import the data, use the Attach tool in the Point Cloud panel on the Insert tab. If you have raw point cloud data that hasn't been processed yet, click the Autodesk ReCap button to launch ReCap. Use the resulting dialog box to load the raw data and prepare it to use in AutoCAD.

Selecting an attached point cloud displays a bounding box around the data and activates the contextual Cloud Edit Ribbon tab. This tab provides a set of tools that you can use to manipulate your point cloud by clipping it (similar to the Clip tool), changing the point density, adjusting the color display of the point cloud, or running analysis tools.

Because point clouds can consume a great deal of memory, you can use the Level Of Detail slider in the Display panel to control the density of the point. The lower the density, the less impact the point cloud will have on performance. When you have the point cloud attached to a drawing, you can use the points to help guide you in building a 3D model. You can use the Node osnap to snap to the individual points in the point cloud. The referenced point cloud is selectable. When you do select it, a contextual Ribbon tab has several tools that will help you display your point cloud. It includes slider bars to increase or decrease the density of the points (how many are currently being displayed). You can change the color of the points or use any color data your scanning device may have gathered. Cropping tools are also available to help speed up the performance of your computer by reducing the number of points to process. This cropping feature can also help you control what is being displayed in your file.

## The Bottom Line

**Know the 3D Modeling workspace.**   When you work in 3D, you need a different set of tools from those for 2D drafting. AutoCAD offers the 3D Modeling workspace, which provides the tools you need to create 3D models.

**Master It**   Name some of the Ribbon panels that are unique to the 3D Modeling workspace.

**Draw in 3D using solids.** AutoCAD offers a type of object called a 3D solid that lets you quickly create and edit shapes.

**Master It** What does the Presspull command do?

**Create 3D forms from 2D shapes.** The Modeling panel offers a set of basic 3D shapes, but other tools enable you to create virtually any shape you want from 2D drawings.

**Master It** Name the command that lets you change a closed 2D polyline into a 3D solid.

**Isolate coordinates with point filters.** When you're working in 3D, selecting points can be a complicated task. AutoCAD offers point filters or coordinates to let you specify the individual x-, y-, and z-coordinates of a location in space.

**Master It** What does the .XY point filter do?

**Move around your model.** Getting the view you want in a 3D model can be tricky.

**Master It** Where is the drop-down list that lets you select a view from a list of pre-defined 3D views?

**Get a visual effect.** At certain points in your model making, you'll want to view your 3D model with surface colors and even material assignments. AutoCAD offers several ways to do this.

**Master It** What are the steps to take to change the view from Wireframe to Conceptual?

**Turn a 3D view into a 2D AutoCAD drawing.** Sometimes, it's helpful to convert a 3D model view into a 2D AutoCAD drawing. AutoCAD offers the Flatshot tool, which quickly converts a 3D view into a 2D line drawing.

**Master It** What type of object does Flatshot create?

# Chapter 21

# Using Advanced 3D Features

The Autodesk® AutoCAD® 2015 software has an extended set of tools for working with 3D drawings that lets you create 3D objects with few limitations on shape and orientation. This chapter focuses on the use of these tools, which help you easily generate 3D forms and view them in both perspective and orthogonal modes.

 The AutoCAD LT® software doesn't support any of the features described in this chapter. In this chapter, you will learn to

- ◆ Master the User Coordinate System
- ◆ Understand the UCS options
- ◆ Use viewports to aid in 3D drawing
- ◆ Use the array tools
- ◆ Create complex 3D surfaces
- ◆ Create spiral forms
- ◆ Create surface models
- ◆ Move objects in 3D space

## Setting Up AutoCAD for This Chapter

Before you start, we'd like you to set up AutoCAD in a way that will make your work a little easier. You'll use the 3D Modeling workspace to which you were introduced in Chapter 20, "Creating 3D Drawings." To do so, start AutoCAD. In Chapter 20, you started a new 3D model using a template set up for 3D modeling. Here you'll start to work with the default 2D drawing, acad.dwt.

Now click the Workspace Switching button in the status bar and select 3D Modeling, as shown in Figure 21.1. You'll see a new set of panels appear, as shown in Figure 21.2. The Home panel is different in that it now contains many of the 3D tools that we will be using. Additional panels include Solid, Surface, Mesh, and Visualize, which contain the 3D modeling and editing tools available in AutoCAD.

**FIGURE 21.1**
Select 3D Modeling
from the Workspace
drop-down.

**FIGURE 21.2**
The AutoCAD
window set up for
this chapter

## Mastering the User Coordinate System

The User Coordinate System (UCS) enables you to define a custom coordinate system in 2D and 3D space. You've been using the default coordinate system called the *World Coordinate System (WCS)* all along. By now, you're familiar with the L-shaped icon in the lower-left corner of the AutoCAD screen, containing a small square and the letters *X* and *Y*. The square indicates that you're currently in the WCS; the *X* and *Y* indicate the positive directions of the x- and y-axes. The WCS is a global system of reference from which you can define other UCSs.

It may help to think of these AutoCAD UCSs as different drawing surfaces or two-dimensional planes. You can have several UCSs at any given time. By setting up these different UCSs, you can draw as you would in the WCS in 2D and still create a 3D image.

Suppose you want to draw a house in 3D with doors and windows on each of its sides. You can set up a UCS for each of the sides, and then you can move from UCS to UCS to add your doors and windows (see Figure 21.3). In each UCS, you draw your doors and windows as you would in a typical 2D drawing. You can even insert elevation views of doors and windows that you created in other drawings.

**FIGURE 21.3**
Different UCSs in
a 3D drawing

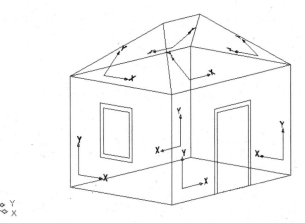

In this chapter, you'll experiment with several views and UCSs. All the commands you'll use are available both at the command line and via the Visualize tab's Coordinates panel.

## Defining a UCS

In the first set of exercises, you'll draw a chair that you can later add to your 3D unit drawing. In drawing this chair, you'll be exposed to the UCS as well as to some of the other 3D capabilities available in AutoCAD:

1. Open the barcelona1.dwg file. Metric users should open barcelona1_metric.dwg. This file contains two rectangles that you'll use to create a chair.

2. Select SW Isometric from the 3D Navigation drop-down list on the Home tab's View panel. You can also type **-V⏎SWISO⏎**. This gives you a 3D view from the lower-left corner of the rectangles, as shown in Figure 21.4. Zoom out a bit to give yourself some room to work.

**FIGURE 21.4**
The chair seat and
back in the Plan
(top) and Isometric
(bottom) views

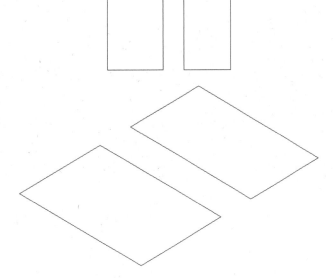

**3.** Select the two rectangles, and then right-click and select Properties.

**4.** In the Properties palette, enter **3** in the Thickness setting and press ↵. This gives the seat and back a thickness of 3″. Metric users should make the thickness 7.6 cm.

**5.** Press the Esc key, and close the Properties palette. Click the Convert To Solid tool in the Home tab's expanded Solid Editing panel.

**6.** Select the two rectangles, and then press ↵.

Notice that the UCS icon appears in the same plane as the current coordinate system. The icon will help you keep track of which coordinate system you're in. Now you can see the chair components as 3D objects.

Next you'll define a UCS that is aligned with one side of the seat:

**1.** Click UCS ➤ Named UCS in the Visualize tab's Coordinates panel or type **Ucsman↵** to open the UCS dialog box.

**2.** Select the Orthographic UCSs tab to view a set of predefined UCSs.

**3.** Select Front in the list box, as shown in Figure 21.5. Figure 21.6 shows the orientation of the Front UCS.

**FIGURE 21.5**

The UCS dialog box

**4.** Click the Set Current button to make the Front UCS current.

**5.** Click OK to close the dialog box.

The Orthographic UCSs tab offers a set of predefined UCSs for each of the six standard orthographic projection planes. Figure 21.6 shows these UCSs in relation to the WCS.

Because a good part of 3D work involves drawing in these orthographic planes, AutoCAD supplies the ready-made UCS orientations for quick access. But you aren't limited to these six orientations. If you're familiar with mechanical drafting, you'll see that the orthographic UCSs correspond to the typical orthographic projections used in mechanical drafting. If you're an architect, the Front, Left, Back, and Right UCSs correspond to the south, west, north, and east elevations of a building.

**FIGURE 21.6**

The six predefined
UCS orientations

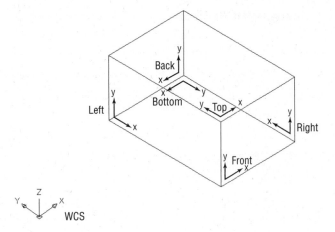

Before you continue building the chair model, you'll move the UCS to the surface on which you'll be working. Right now, the UCS has its origin located in the same place as the WCS origin. You can move a UCS so that its origin is anywhere in the drawing:

1. Click the Origin tool in the Visualize tab's Coordinates panel, or type **UCS⏎O⏎**.

2. Use the Endpoint osnap and click the bottom-front corner of the chair seat, as shown in Figure 21.7. The UCS icon moves to indicate its new origin's location. If you typed in the command, press Enter to accept the other default values.

**FIGURE 21.7**

Setting up a UCS

Click this corner for the new UCS origin.

You just created a new UCS based on the Front UCS you selected from the UCS dialog box. Now, as you move your cursor, the origin of the UCS icon corresponds to a 0,0 coordinate. Although you have a new UCS, the WCS still exists; you can always return to it when you need to.

## Saving a UCS

After you've gone through the work of creating a UCS, you may want to save it—especially if you think you'll come back to it later. Here's how to save a UCS:

1. Choose Named from the Coordinates panel or type **Ucsman.**↵ to open the UCS dialog box.

2. Make sure the Named UCSs tab is selected, and then highlight the Unnamed option in the Current UCS list box.

3. Click on the word *Unnamed*. The item changes to allow editing.

4. Type **3DSW.**↵ for the name of your new UCS.

5. Click OK to exit the dialog box.

Your UCS is now saved with the name 3DSW. You can recall it from the UCS dialog box or by using other methods that you'll learn about later in this chapter.

## Working in a UCS

Next, you'll arrange the seat and back and draw the legs of the chair. Your UCS is oriented so that you can easily adjust the orientation of the chair components. As you work through the next exercise, notice that, although you're manipulating 3D objects, you're really using the same tools you've used to edit 2D objects.

Follow these steps to adjust the seat and back and to draw legs:

1. Click the seat back to expose its grips. The seat back is the box to the right.

2. Click the bottom grip, as shown in the first image in Figure 21.8.

3. Right-click to open the Grip Edit context menu.

4. Choose Rotate from the menu. The seat back now rotates with the movement of the cursor. It rotates in the plane of the new UCS you created earlier.

5. Type **80.**↵ to rotate the seat back 80. Your view looks like the second image in Figure 21.8.

6. Click the bottom grip, as shown in the second image in Figure 21.8.

7. Right-click again and choose Move.

8. Using the Endpoint osnap, click the bottom-rear corner of the chair seat to join the chair back to the seat, as shown in the second image in Figure 21.8.

9. Click the chair seat, making sure that the chair back is also selected; then click the bottom-corner grip of the seat, as shown in the third image in Figure 21.8.

10. Right-click and choose Rotate from the Grip Edit context menu.

11. Enter **-10.**↵ to rotate both the seat and back negative 10. Press the Esc key to clear the grips. Your chair looks like Figure 21.9.

The new UCS orientation enabled you to use the grips to adjust the chair seat and back. All the grip rotation in the previous exercise was confined to the plane of the new UCS. Mirroring and scaling will also occur in relation to the current UCS.

**FIGURE 21.8**
Moving the components of the chair into place

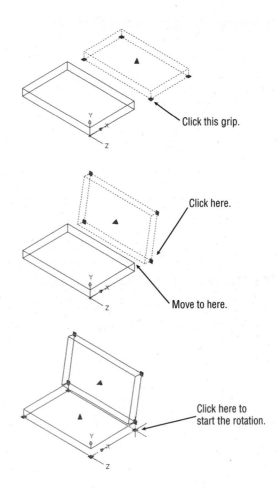

**FIGURE 21.9**
The chair after rotating and moving the components

## Building 3D Parts in Separate Files

As you work in 3D, your models will become fairly complex. When your model becomes too crowded for you to see things clearly, it helps to build parts of the model and then import them instead of building everything in one file. In the next set of exercises, you'll draw the legs of the chair and then import them to the main chair file to give you some practice in the procedure.

We've prepared a drawing called legs.dwg, which consists of two polylines that describe the shape of the legs. We did this to save you some tedious work that isn't related to 3D modeling. You'll use this file as a starting point for the legs, and then you'll import the legs into the barcelona1.dwg file:

1. Open the legs.dwg file. Metric users should open the legs_metric.dwg file. The file consists of two polyline splines that are in the shape of one set of legs. You'll turn these simple lines into 3D solids.

2. Click the Edit Polyline tool in the Home tab's expanded Modify panel.

3. At the Select polyline or [Multiple]: prompt, enter **M**⏎ to select multiple polylines. Then select the two polylines and press ⏎.

4. At the Enter an option [Close/Open/Join/Width/Fit/Spline/Decurve/Ltype gen/Reverse/Undo]: prompt, enter **W**⏎.

5. At the Specify new width for all segments: prompt, enter **0.5**⏎ to give the polylines a width of 0.5". Metric users should enter **1.27**⏎.

6. Press ⏎ to exit the Pedit command.

Next you need to change the Thickness property of the two polylines to make them 2", or 5 cm, wide:

1. With the two polylines selected, open the Properties palette and set their thickness to **2**. Metric users should set their thickness to **5**.

2. Close the Properties palette, or you can leave it open for the next exercise.

3. Click the Convert To Solid tool in the Home tab's expanded Solid Editing panel, or enter **convtosolid**⏎ at the Command prompt.

4. Select the two polylines if they're not already selected, and then press ⏎. The lines become 3D solids.

5. Click the Solid, Union tool in the Home tab's Solid Editing panel, select the two legs, and press ⏎. The two legs are now a single 3D solid, as shown in Figure 21.10.

As you've just seen, you can convert polylines that have both a width and a thickness into 3D solids. Now you're ready to add the legs to the rest of the chair:

1. Click the Tile Vertically tool in the View tab's User Interface panel. You see the legs drawing on the left and the rest of the chair on the right.

2. Adjust the views so that your screen looks similar to Figure 21.11. If you see a third Drawing1.dwg panel, close it and click the Tile Vertically tool again.

**FIGURE 21.10**
The polylines con-
verted to 3D solids

**FIGURE 21.11**
Click and drag the
leg from the left
window to the right
window, and align
the leg with the
chair seat and back.

 **Extents**

3. Click in the barcelona1 drawing, and select Extents from the Zoom flyout Navigation bar to get an overall view of the chair so far.

4. Click in the legs drawing, and then click the legs 3D solid to select it.

5. Click and hold the cursor on the legs until you see the arrow cursor with a small rectangle (see Figure 21.11, left).

6. When you see the rectangle, drag the mouse into the barcelona1 drawing. The legs appear in the proper orientation.

7. Release the mouse button to place the legs in the barcelona1 drawing. You don't need to be precise about placing the legs; you can move them into position next.

8. Use the Move tool to move the legs so that the endpoint of the horizontal leg joins the chair seat, as shown in the image in the right panel of Figure 21.11.

9. Save and close the legs.dwg file, and expand the barcelona1.dwg file to fill the AutoCAD window.

---

### USE COPY AND PASTE

You can also use Copy and Paste to copy the legs to the barcelona1 drawing. In step 4, right-click and select Copy from the context menu. Skip steps 5 through 7 and instead click in the barcelona1 drawing, right-click, and select Paste.

In these last few exercises, you worked on the legs of the chair in a separate file and then imported them into the main chair file with a click-and-drag motion. By working on parts in separate files, you can keep your model organized and more manageable. You may have also noticed that although the legs were drawn in the WCS, they were inserted in the 3DSW UCS that you created earlier. This shows you that imported objects are placed in the current UCS. The same would have happened if you inserted an Xref or another file.

## Understanding the UCS Options

You've seen how to select a UCS from a set of predefined UCSs. You can frequently use these preset UCSs and make minor adjustments to them to get the exact UCS you want.

You can define a UCS in other ways. You can, for example, use the surface of your chair seat to define the orientation of a UCS. In the following sections, you'll be shown the various ways you can set up a UCS. Learning how to move effortlessly between UCSs is crucial to mastering the creation of 3D models, so you'll want to pay special attention to the command options shown in these examples.

Note that these examples are for your reference. You can try them out on your own model. These options are accessible from the Visualize tab's Coordinates panel.

### UCS Based on Object Orientation

You can define a UCS based on the orientation of an object. This is helpful when you want to work on a predefined object to fill in details on its surface plane. The following steps are for information only and aren't part of the tutorial. You can try this at another time when you aren't working through an exercise.

Follow these steps to define a UCS this way:

1. Type **UCS↵OB↵**.

2. At the Select object to align UCS: prompt, pick the object that you want to use to define the UCS. For example, you could click a 3D solid that you want to edit. The UCS icon shifts to reflect the new coordinate system's orientation. Figure 21.12 shows an example of using the OB option to select the edge of the chair back.

**FIGURE 21.12**
Using the Object option of the UCS command to locate a UCS

Click this edge. ⸺

When you use the Object option, the UCS will align to the selected object.

## CONTROLLING THE UCS ICON

If the UCS icon isn't behaving as described in this chapter's exercises, chances are that its settings have been altered. You can control the behavior of the UCS icon through the UCS dialog box. To open the UCS dialog box, click Named in the Visualize tab's Coordinates panel or type **Ucsman↵**; then click the Settings tab.

The settings in the UCS Icon Settings group affect the way the UCS icon behaves. Normally, the On and Display At UCS Origin Point check boxes are selected. If On isn't selected, you won't see the UCS icon. If the Display At UCS Origin Point check box isn't selected, the UCS icon remains in the lower-left corner of the drawing window no matter where its origin is placed in the drawing.

If you have multiple viewports set up in a drawing, you can set these two options independently for each viewport. The third option, Apply To All Active Viewports, forces the first two settings to apply in all viewports.

Two more options appear in the UCS Settings group. If you have multiple viewports open, the Save UCS With Viewport option enables AutoCAD to maintain a separate UCS for each viewport. The Update View To Plan When UCS Is Changed option forces the display to show a plan view of the current UCS. This means that if you change a UCS orientation, AutoCAD automatically shows a plan view of the new UCS orientation. This option also forces viewport views to show the extents of plan views. If you find that your views are automatically zooming to extents when you don't want them to, turn off this setting.

Another tool for controlling the UCS icon is the UCS Icon dialog box. To open it, right-click the UCS Icon, click UCS Icon Settings, then Properties, and in the resulting dialog box, select the Visualize tab (or enter **Ucsicon↵P↵**).

Using this dialog box, you can fine-tune the appearance of the UCS icon, including its size and color. The 2D radio button in the UCS Icon Style group changes the UCS icon to the old-style UCS icon used in earlier versions of AutoCAD.

---

When you create a UCS using the Object option, the location of the UCS origin and its orientation depend on how the selected object was created. Table 21.1 describes how an object can determine the orientation of a UCS.

**TABLE 21.1:** Effects of objects on the orientation of a UCS

| OBJECT TYPE | UCS ORIENTATION |
|---|---|
| Arc | The center of the arc establishes the UCS origin. The x-axis of the UCS passes through the pick point on the arc. |
| Circle | The center of the circle establishes the UCS origin. The x-axis of the UCS passes through the pick point on the circle. |
| Dimension | The midpoint of the dimension text establishes the UCS origin. The x-axis of the UCS is parallel to the x-axis that was active when the dimension was drawn. |
| Face (of a 3D solid) | The origin of the UCS is placed on a quadrant of a circular surface or on the corner of a polygonal surface. |
| Line | The endpoint nearest the pick point establishes the origin of the UCS, and the XZ plane of the UCS contains the line. |
| Point | The point location establishes the UCS origin. The UCS orientation is arbitrary. |
| 2D polyline | The starting point of the polyline establishes the UCS origin. The x-axis is determined by the direction from the first point to the next vertex. |
| 3D polyline | Returns the message `This object does not define a coordinate system.` |
| Spline | The UCS is created with its XY plane parallel to the XY plane of the UCS that was current when the spline was created. |
| Solid | The first point of the solid establishes the origin of the UCS. The second point of the solid establishes the x-axis. |
| Trace | The direction of the trace establishes the x-axis of the UCS, and the beginning point sets the origin. |
| 3D Face | The first point of the 3D face establishes the origin. The first and second points establish the x-axis. The plane defined by the 3D face determines the orientation of the UCS. |
| Shapes, text, blocks, attributes, and attribute definitions | The insertion point establishes the origin of the UCS. The object's rotation angle establishes the x-axis. |

## UCS Based on Offset Orientation

At times, you may want to work in a UCS that has the same orientation as the current UCS but is offset. For example, you might be drawing a building that has several parallel walls offset with a sawtooth effect (see Figure 21.13).

You can easily hop from one UCS to a new, parallel UCS by using the Origin option. Click the Origin tool in the Coordinates panel, or type **UCS⏎O⏎**. At the Specify new origin point <0,0,0>: prompt, pick the new origin for your UCS.

Another UCS option, called Move, will move an existing, named UCS to a new location and keep its original orientation. You won't find the UCS Move option on any panel or toolbar, but you can use it by entering **UCS⏎M⏎** at the Command prompt.

The steps in the following section are for information only and aren't part of the tutorial. Again, you can try this at another time when you aren't working through an exercise.

**FIGURE 21.13**
Using the Origin option to shift the UCS

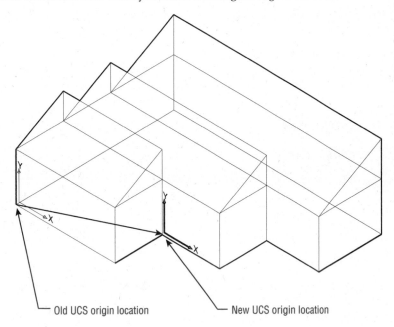

Old UCS origin location          New UCS origin location

## UCS Rotated around an Axis

Suppose you want to change the orientation of the x-, y-, or z-axis of a UCS. You can do so by using the X, Y, or Z flyout on the Visualize tab's Coordinates panel. These are perhaps among the most frequently used UCS options:

1. Click the X tool flyout arrowhead in the Visualize tab's Coordinates panel, and select Z from the flyout. You can also type **UCS⏎Z⏎**. This enables you to rotate the current UCS around the z-axis.

2. At the Specify rotation angle about Z axis <90>: prompt, press ⏎ to accept the default of 90. The UCS icon rotates about the z-axis to reflect the new orientation of the current UCS (see Figure 21.14).

Similarly, the X and Y options let you rotate the UCS about the current x- and y-axis, respectively, just as you did for the z-axis earlier. The X and Y tools are helpful in orienting a UCS to an inclined plane. For example, if you want to work on the plane of a sloped roof of a building, you can first use the Origin UCS tool to align the UCS to the edge of a roof and then use the X tool to rotate the UCS to the angle of the roof slope, as shown in Figure 21.15. Note that the default is 90°, so you only have to press ↵ to rotate the UCS 90°, but you can also enter a rotation angle.

Finally, you align the z-axis between two points using the Z-Axis Vector option. This is useful when you have objects in the drawing that you can use to align the z-axis. Here are the steps:

1. Click the Z-Axis Vector tool in the Coordinates panel, or type **UCS↵ZA↵**.

2. At the `Specify new origin point or [Object]<0,0,0>:` prompt, press ↵ to accept the default, which is the current UCS origin, or you can select a new origin.

3. At the prompt

   ```
   Specify point on positive portion of Z-axis
   <0'-0", 0'-0", 0'-1">:
   ```

   select another point to indicate the z-axis orientation. Figure 21.16 shows the resulting UCS if you use the bottom of the barcelona1 chair leg to define the z-axis.

**FIGURE 21.14**
Rotating the UCS about the z-axis

Click this edge.

When you use the Object option, the UCS will align to the selected object.

**FIGURE 21.15**
Moving a UCS to the plane of a sloping roof

Slope of roof

Because your cursor location is in the plane of the current UCS, it's best to pick a point on an object by using either the Osnap overrides or the coordinate filters.

**FIGURE 21.16**
Picking points
for the Z-Axis
Vector tool

Origin

Endpoint of chair leg for the
positive portion of the z-axis

## Orienting a UCS in the View Plane

Finally, you can define a UCS in the current view plane. This points the z-axis toward the user. This approach is useful if you want to switch quickly to the current view plane for editing or for adding text to a 3D view.

Click the View tool in the Coordinates panel, or type **UCS↵V↵**. Note that the View tool also has a flyout arrowhead that contains the Object and Face tools. If you accidentally click the flyout arrowhead, make sure to click the View tool in the flyout. The UCS icon changes to show that the UCS is aligned with the current view.

AutoCAD uses the current UCS origin point for the origin of the new UCS. By defining a view as a UCS, you can enter text to label your drawing, just as you would in a technical illustration. Text entered in a plane created this way appears normal.

You've finished your tour of the UCS command. Set the UCS back to the WCS by clicking the UCS, World tool in the Visualize tab's Coordinates panel, and save the barcelona1.dwg file.

You've explored nearly every option in creating a UCS except one. Later in this chapter, you'll learn about the 3-Point option for creating a UCS. This is the most versatile method for creating a UCS, but it's more involved than some of the other UCS options.

## Manipulating the UCS Icon

The UCS icon displays the direction of the axes in your drawing file. You can also directly manipulate it by selecting and right-clicking it or by using its multifunction grips. If your UCS icon is not selectable, or to turn off this selectable feature, open the UCS dialog box (click Named in the Visualize tab's Coordinates panel), click the Settings tab, and see if the Allow Selecting UCS Icon option is checked (see Figure 21.17).

There are essentially two selection options on the icon: the origin and the end of an axis. In either case, select the UCS icon, and then place your cursor over the appropriate grip and click the origin or endpoint (see Figure 21.18). Select how you want to change the UCS (move and align) and move the cursor. The UCS icon will relocate, showing you where your new coordinate system will be. You can move the origin to a new location or align it to another object or surface using this method. This makes working in a 3D environment a bit easier. Selecting the origin also lets you return the current UCS to the World Coordinate System (it resets the UCS). The x-, y-, and z-axes all work the same way. Pick the endpoint of the axis (the grip) to rotate the selected axis about the other axis (for example, if the x-axis is selected, it can rotate about either the y- or z-axis).

**FIGURE 21.17**
Making the UCS
icon selectable

**FIGURE 21.18**
Selecting and mov-
ing the UCS Icon
will alter your UCS.

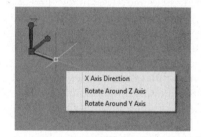

When you right-click the UCS icon, you will see a context menu containing a list of the UCS commands you can choose without having to leave the drawing area. Pick the UCS command you want to access.

## Saving a UCS with a View

In AutoCAD you can save a UCS with a view. Either click the View Manager option in the in-canvas View Controls (top-left corner of the drawing area) or click the View Manager option, found at the bottom of the 3D Navigation drop-down list in the Home tab's View panel (see Figure 21.19). In the View Manager dialog box, click the New button. This opens the New View/Shot Properties dialog box. Enter a name for your new view in the View Name box, and then choose a UCS to save with a new view by using the UCS drop-down list in the Settings group of the dialog box. Click OK to complete.

**FIGURE 21.19**
Select the View
Manager option in
either the in-canvas
View Controls or
the 3D Navigation
drop-down list.

# Using Viewports to Aid in 3D Drawing

In Chapter 15, "Laying Out Your Printer Output," you worked extensively with floating viewports in Paper Space. In this section, you'll use *tiled* viewports to see your 3D model from several sides at the same time. This is helpful in both creating and editing 3D drawings because it enables you to refer to different portions of the drawing without having to change views.

Tiled viewports are created directly in model space, as you'll see in the following exercise:

**1.** Click the Named tool in the Visualize tab's Model Viewports panel to open the Viewports dialog box (see Figure 21.20).

**FIGURE 21.20**
The Viewports
dialog box

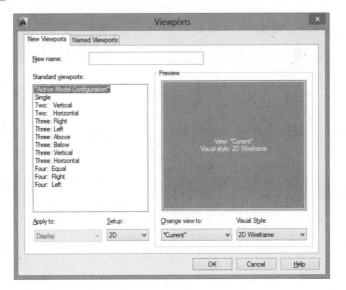

2. Make sure the New Viewports tab is selected, and then select Three: Right from the Standard Viewports list on the left.

   The window on the right changes to display a sample of the viewport configuration. It shows three rectangles, which represent the viewports, arranged with two on the left and one larger one to the right. Each rectangle is labeled as Current; this tells you that the current view will be placed in each viewport.

3. Open the Setup drop-down list at the bottom of the dialog box and select 3D.

   The labels in the viewport sample change to indicate Top, Front, and SE Isometric. This is close to the arrangement you want, but you need to make one more adjustment. The viewport to the right, SE Isometric, will show the back side of the chair. You want an SW Isometric view in this window.

4. Click the SE Isometric viewport sample. The sample viewport border changes to a double border to indicate that it's selected.

5. Open the Change View To drop-down list just below the sample viewports, and select SW Isometric. The label in the selected viewport changes to let you know that the view will now contain the SW Isometric view.

   The Change View To list contains the standard four isometric views and the six orthogonal views. By clicking a sample viewport and selecting an option from the Change View To drop-down list, you can arrange your viewport views nearly any way you want.

6. To name this viewport arrangement, enter **My Viewport Setup** in the New Name box.

7. Click OK. Your display changes to show three viewports arranged as they were indicated in the Viewports dialog box (see Figure 21.21).

**FIGURE 21.21**
Three viewports, each displaying a different view

You've set up your viewports. Let's check to see that your viewport arrangement was saved:

1. Click the Named tool in the Visualize tab's Model Viewports panel to open the Viewports dialog box again.

2. Click the Named Viewports tab. My Viewport Setup is listed in the Named Viewports list box. If you click it, a sample view of your viewport arrangement appears on the right.

3. After you've reviewed the addition to the Named Viewports list, close the dialog box.

Now, take a close look at your viewport setup. The UCS icon in the orthogonal views in the two left viewports is oriented to the plane of the view. AutoCAD lets you set up a different UCS for each viewport. The top view uses the WCS because it's in the same plane as the WCS. The side view has its own UCS, which is parallel to its view. The isometric view to the right retains the current UCS.

A Viewports dialog box option you haven't tried yet is the Apply To drop-down list in the New Viewports tab (see Figure 21.22).

**FIGURE 21.22**

The Apply To drop-down list

This list shows two options: Display and Current Viewport. When Display is selected, the option you choose from the Standard Viewports list applies to the overall display. When Current Viewport is selected, the option you select applies to the selected viewport in the sample view in the right side of the dialog box. You can use the Current Viewport option to build multiple viewports in custom arrangements.

You have the legs for one side. The next step is to mirror those legs for the other side:

1. Click the top view of the chair in the upper-left viewport.

2. Turn on Polar Tracking in the status bar, and then click the Mirror tool in the Home tab's expanded Modify panel.

3. In the upper-left viewport, click the 3D solid representing the chair legs and then press ↵.

4. At the Specify first point of mirror line: prompt, use the Midpoint osnap and select the midpoint of the chair seat, as shown in Figure 21.23.

**FIGURE 21.23**

Mirroring the legs from one side to another

Click the midpoint of this edge.

5. At the Specify second point of mirror line: prompt, pick any location to the right of the point you selected so that the rubber-banding line is exactly horizontal.

6. Press ↵ at the Erase source objects? [Yes/No] <N>: prompt. The legs are mirrored to the opposite side of the chair. Your screen should look similar to Figure 21.23.

Your chair is complete. Let's finish by getting a better look at it:

**1.** Click the viewport to the right showing the isometric view.

**2.** Click Single from the Viewport Configurations List drop-down list in the Visualize tab's Model Viewports panel (see Figure 21.24), or enter **-Vports⏎Si⏎**.

**FIGURE 21.24**
Click Single in the Viewport Configurations List drop-down list.

**3.** Use the Zoom tool to adjust your view so that it looks similar to Figure 21.25.

**FIGURE 21.25**
The chair in 3D with hidden lines removed

4. Click the Visual Styles drop-down list, and select Shades Of Gray. Note that your background may appear much darker.

5. Exit the file. You can save if you like or close without saving in case you want to do the exercise again.

## Using the Array Tools

In Chapter 6, "Editing and Reusing Data to Work Efficiently," you were introduced to the Array command. Let's take a look at how this works in the 3D world. In AutoCAD 2015, you can create a 3D array from any type of array, whether it is rectangular, polar, or path. Let's do an example using the path array:

1. Open the file `3Dseating.dwg`.

2. Click the Path Array tool in the Array flyout on the Modify panel of the Home tab, or type **ARRAYPATH**⏎.

3. At the `Select object :` prompt, click the chair at the left end of the arc in the drawing and then press ⏎.

4. At the `Select path curve :` prompt, select the magenta arc toward the left end.

5. At the `Select grip to edit array or [ASsociative / Method / Base point / Tangent direction / Items / Rows / Levels / Align items / Z direction / eXit] <eXit> :` prompt, enter **I**⏎.

6. At the `Specify the distance between items along the path or [Expression] <35.7596> :` prompt, press ⏎.

7. At the `Specify number of items or [Fill entire path / Expression] <6> :` prompt, enter **5**⏎.

8. At the `Select grip to edit array or [ASsociative / Method / Base point / Tangent direction / Items / Rows / Levels / Align items / Z direction / eXit] <eXit> :` prompt, enter **R**⏎.

9. At the `Enter the number of rows or [Expression] <1> :` prompt, enter **3**⏎.

10. At the `Specify the distance between rows or [Total / Expression] <40.7253> :` prompt, enter **48**⏎.

11. At the `Specify the incrementing elevation between rows or [Expression] <0.0000> :` prompt, enter **12**⏎.

12. Press ⏎ to exit the command.

In this exercise, you made an array of a chair that follows the path of an arc. The distance between chairs is 48" (1219.2 mm), and the vertical riser between each section is 12" (304.8 mm).

**CERT OBJECTIVE**

Now suppose you want to adjust the curvature of your array. This is a simple matter of adjusting the shape of the arc, as described here:

1. Click the arc to expose its grips.

2. Click the middle grip, and then drag it upward. Notice that all of the chairs adjust as you drag the arc.

Here you see how the associative feature of the Arraypath command lets you control the array by adjusting the object you used for the path. Arrays can be edited through a variety of methods, as you'll see in the next section.

### Making Changes to an Associative Array

Now let's take a look at how you can make changes to an array. You may have noticed the Associative option in the Array command's prompt. By default, the Associative option is turned on, which enables you to edit array objects as a group. You'll see how this works in the following exercises.

You'll start by editing the array you created using the Path Array tool. You'll see that the chairs are now skewed and are no longer pointing to the center of the arc. You can realign them by making a simple change to the original chair.

The following steps show you how this is done:

1. Click the array of chairs. Notice that the contextual Array tab appears (see Figure 21.26).

**FIGURE 21.26**
The Array tab appears and a new set of panels and options is displayed.

We'll change the number of chairs to allow for more seating.

2. In the contextual Array tab in the Properties panel, change from Measure Method to Divide Method by clicking the flyout arrow below the Measure button. Select the Divide Method button. In the Items panel, change the item count from 5 to **10** and press the Tab key.

The number of chairs dynamically changes to the new value.

3. Save the file.

Experiment with other values in the Array tab to see what effects they have.

As you can see from these exercises, you can easily make changes to an array through the Array tab options in the Ribbon. Many of these options are also available through the multi-function grip menus when you have Dynamic Input turned on.

## Creating Complex 3D Surfaces

In one of the previous exercises, you drew a chair composed of objects that were mostly straight lines or curves with a thickness. All the forms in that chair were defined in planes perpendicular to one another. For a 3D model such as this, you can get by using the orthographic UCSs. At times, however, you'll want to draw objects that don't fit so easily into perpendicular or parallel planes. In the following sections, you'll create more complex forms by using some of the other 3D commands in AutoCAD.

## Laying Out a 3D Form

In this next group of exercises, you'll draw a butterfly chair. This chair has no perpendicular or parallel planes with which to work, so you'll start by setting up some points that you'll use for reference only. This is similar in concept to laying out a 2D drawing. As you progress through the drawing construction, notice how the reference points are established to help create the chair. You'll also construct some temporary 3D lines to use for reference. These temporary lines will be your layout. These points will define the major UCSs needed to construct the drawing. The main point is to show you some of the options for creating and saving UCSs.

To save time, we've created the 2D drawing that you'll use to build your 3D layout. This drawing consists of two rectangles that are offset by 4″ (10 cm). To make it more interesting, they're also off-center from each other (see Figure 21.27).

**FIGURE 21.27**
Setting up a layout
for a butterfly chair

The first thing you'll need to do is set up the drawing for the layout:

1. Open the butterfly1.dwg file.

 2. Click SW Isometric in the 3D Navigation drop-down list, or type **–V↵SWISO↵**. This gives you a view from the lower-left side of the rectangles.

3. Zoom out so that the rectangles occupy about a third of the drawing area window.

Now you need to move the outer rectangle in the z-axis so its elevation is 30″ (76 cm):

1. Click the outer rectangle, and then click one of its grips.

2. Right-click to open the Grip Edit context menu.

3. Choose Move, and then enter **@0,0,30↵**; metric users should enter **@0,0,76↵**. This tells AutoCAD to move the rectangle a 0 distance in both the x- and y-axes and 30″ (or 76 cm) in the z-axis.

4. Pan your view downward so that it looks similar to Figure 21.28.

5. Use the Line tool to draw lines from the corners of the outer square to the corners of the inner square. Use the Endpoint osnap to select the exact corners of the squares. This is the layout for your chair—not the finished product.

**FIGURE 21.28**

The finished
chair layout

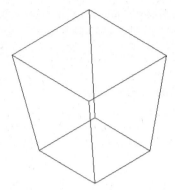

As an alternate method in step 3, after choosing Move from the Grip Edit context menu, you can turn on Ortho mode and point the cursor vertically so that it shows –Z in the coordinate readout. Then enter **30.⏎** (**76.⏎** for metric users).

## Spherical and Cylindrical Coordinate Formats

In the previous exercise, you used relative Cartesian coordinates to locate the second point for the Move command. For commands that accept 3D input, you can also specify displacements by using the Spherical and Cylindrical Coordinate formats.

The *Spherical Coordinate format* lets you specify a distance in 3D space while specifying the angle in terms of degrees from the x-axis of the current UCS and degrees from the XY plane of the current UCS (see the top image in Figure 21.29). For example, to specify a distance of 4.5″ (11.43 cm) at a 30° angle from the x-axis and 45° from the XY plane, enter **@4.5<30<45** (or **@11.43<30<45** for metric users). This refers to the direct distance followed by a < symbol, then the angle from the x-axis of the current UCS followed by another < symbol, and then the angle from the XY plane of the current UCS. To use the Spherical Coordinate format to move the rectangle in the exercise, enter **@30<0<90** (or **@76<0<90** for metric users) at the Second point: prompt.

The *Cylindrical Coordinate format,* on the other hand, lets you specify a location in terms of a distance in the plane of the current UCS and a distance in the z-axis. You also specify an angle from the x-axis of the current UCS (see the bottom image in Figure 21.29). For example, to locate a point that is a distance of 4.5″ (11.43 cm) in the plane of the current UCS at an angle of 30° from the x-axis and a distance of 3.3″ (8.38 cm) in the z-axis, enter **@4.5<30,3.3** (or **@11.43<30,8.38** for metric users). This refers to the distance of the displacement from the plane of the current UCS followed by the < symbol, then the angle from the x-axis followed by a comma, and then the distance in the z-axis. Using the Cylindrical Coordinate format to move the rectangle, you enter **@0<0,30** (or **@0<0,76** for metric users) at the Second point: prompt.

## Using a 3D Polyline

Now you'll draw the legs for the butterfly chair by using a 3D polyline. This is a polyline that can be drawn in 3D space. Here are the steps:

**1.** Click 3D Polyline in the Home tab's Draw panel, or type **3P.⏎**.

**2.** At the `Specify start point of polyline:` prompt, pick a series of points as shown in Figure 21.30 (top), by using the Endpoint and Midpoint osnaps. Use the Close option to close the series of lines.

**FIGURE 21.29**
The Spherical and Cylindrical Coordinate formats

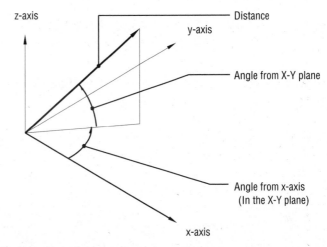

[Distance] < [Angle from x-axis] < [Angle from X-Y plane]

The Spherical Coordinate Format

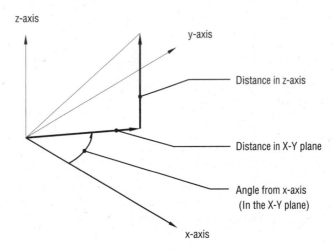

[Distance in X-Y plane] < [Angle from x-axis] , [Distance in z-axis]

The Cylindrical Coordinate Format

**FIGURE 21.30**
Using 3D polylines to draw the legs of the butterfly chair

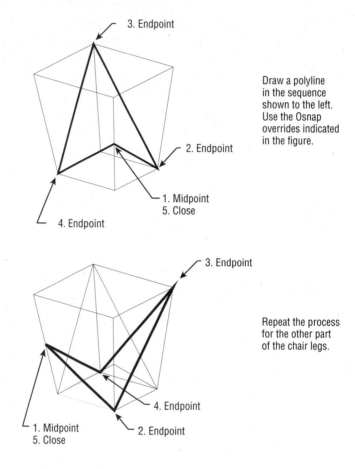

3. Endpoint

Draw a polyline in the sequence shown to the left. Use the Osnap overrides indicated in the figure.

2. Endpoint

1. Midpoint
5. Close

4. Endpoint

3. Endpoint

Repeat the process for the other part of the chair legs.

4. Endpoint

1. Midpoint
5. Close

2. Endpoint

**3.** Draw another 3D polyline in the mirror image of the first (see the lower image in Figure 21.30).

**4.** Erase the connecting vertical lines that make up the frame, but keep the rectangles. You'll use them later.

All objects, with the exception of lines and 3D polylines, are restricted to the plane of your current UCS. Two other legacy 3D objects, 3D faces and 3D meshes, are also restricted. You can use the Pline command to draw polylines in only one plane, but you can use the 3DPoly command to create a polyline in three dimensions. 3DPoly objects cannot, however, be given thickness or width.

## Creating a Curved 3D Surface

Next, you'll draw the seat of the chair. The seat of a butterfly chair is usually made of canvas, and it drapes from the four corners of the chair legs. You'll first define the perimeter of the seat by using arcs, and then you'll use the Edge Surface tool in the Home tab's Modeling panel to form the shape of the draped canvas. The Edge Surface tool creates a surface based on four objects defining the edges of that surface. In this example, you'll use arcs to define the edges of the seat.

To draw the arcs defining the seat edges, you must first establish the UCSs in the planes of those edges. In the previous example, you created a UCS for the side of the chair before you could draw the legs. In the same way, you must create a UCS defining the planes that contain the edges of the seat.

Because the UCS you want to define isn't orthogonal, you'll need to use the 3-point method. This lets you define the plane of the UCS based on three points:

1. Click the 3-Point tool on the Visualize tab's Coordinates panel, or type **UCS↵3↵**. With this option you can define a UCS based on three points that you select. Remember, it helps to think of a UCS as a drawing surface situated on the surface of the object you want to draw or edit.

2. At the `Specify new origin point <0,0,0>:` prompt, use the Endpoint osnap to pick the bottom of the chair leg to the far left, as shown in the left image of Figure 21.31. This is the origin point of your new UCS.

**FIGURE 21.31**
Defining and saving three UCSs

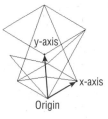

Set up the Front UCS.   Set up the Side UCS.   Set up the Back UCS.

3. At the `Specify point on positive portion of X-axis:` prompt, use the Endpoint osnap to pick the bottom of the next leg to the right of the first one, as shown in the left image in Figure 21.31.

4. At the `Specify point on positive-Y portion of the UCS XY plane:` prompt, pick the top corner of the butterfly chair seat, as shown in the left image in Figure 21.31. The UCS icon changes to indicate your new UCS.

5. Now that you've defined a UCS, you need to save it so that you can return to it later. Click UCS ➤ Named UCS in the Visualize tab's Coordinates panel, or type **UC↵** to open the UCS dialog box.

6. With the Named UCSs tab selected, right-click the Unnamed item in the list box, and choose Rename from the context menu.

7. Enter **Front↵**.

8. Click OK to exit the UCS dialog box.

You've defined and saved a UCS for the front side of the chair. As you can see from the UCS icon, this UCS is at a nonorthogonal angle to the WCS. Continue by creating UCSs for two more sides of the butterfly chair:

1. Define a UCS for the side of the chair, as shown in the middle image in Figure 21.31. Use the UCS dialog box to rename this UCS **Side**, just as you did for Front in steps 5 through 8 in the previous exercise. Remember that you renamed the unnamed UCS.

2. Repeat these steps for a UCS for the back of the chair, named **Back**. Use the right image in Figure 21.31 for reference.

3. Open the UCS dialog box again. In the Named UCSs tab, highlight Front.

4. Click the Set Current button, and then click OK. This activates Front as the current UCS.

5. Click the Start, End, Direction tool from the Arc flyout in the Home tab's Draw panel.

6. Draw the arc defining the front edge of the chair (see Figure 21.32). Use the Endpoint osnap override to pick the top endpoints of the chair legs as the endpoints of the arc.

**FIGURE 21.32**
Drawing the front and back seat edge using arcs and a polyline spline

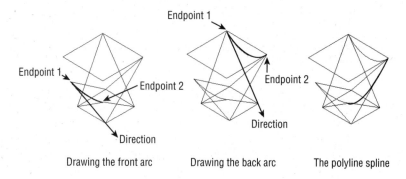

7. Repeat steps 3 through 6 for the UCS named Back, each time using the top endpoints of the legs for the endpoints of the arc.

8. Restore the UCS for the side, but instead of drawing an arc, use the Polyline tool and draw a polyline spline similar to the one in Figure 21.32. If you need help with polyline splines, see Chapter 18, "Drawing Curves."

Next you'll mirror the side-edge spline to the opposite side. This will save you from having to define a UCS for that side:

1. Click the World UCS tool on the Visualize tab's Coordinates panel to restore the WCS. You do this because you want to mirror the arc along an axis that is parallel to the plane of the WCS. Remember that you must use the coordinate system that defines the plane in which you want to work.

2. Click the polyline you drew for the side of the chair (the one drawn on the Side UCS).

3. Start the 3DMirror command on the Home tab's Modify panel. At the `Specify first point of mirror plane (3 points) or:` prompt, use the Midpoint override to pick the midpoints of the rectangle at the bottom of the model. Refer to Figure 21.33 for help. The polyline should mirror to the opposite side, and your chair should look like Figure 21.34.

4. Press the Esc key twice to clear the grips.

**FIGURE 21.33**
Set your UCS to World, and then mirror the arc that defines the side of the chair seat.

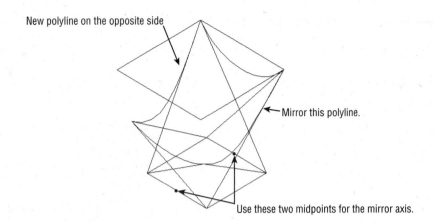

New polyline on the opposite side

Mirror this polyline.

Use these two midpoints for the mirror axis.

**FIGURE 21.34**
Your butterfly chair so far

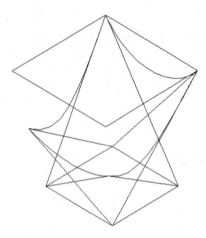

Finally, let's finish this chair by adding the mesh representing the chair seat:

1. Click the Loft tool from the Extrude flyout in the Home tab's Modeling panel, or enter **Loft.⏎** at the command line.

2. At the `Select cross-sections in lofting order or [POint/Join multiple edges/MOde]:` prompt, click the arc at the front of the layout.

3. At the `Select cross-sections in lofting order or [POint/Join multiple edges/MOde]:` prompt, click the arc at the back of the layout, and then press ⏎ to finish your selection of cross sections.

4. At the `Enter an option [Guides/Path/Cross sections only/settings] <Cross sections only>:` prompt, enter **G.⏎** for the Guides option. You'll use the two polylines as guides.

---

### QUICK HOPS TO YOUR UCSS

If you find you're jumping from one saved UCS to another, you'll want to know about the Named UCS Combo Control drop-down list. This list is located in the Visualize tab's Coordinates panel, and it contains the World and other standard UCS options as well as all the saved UCSs in a drawing. You can use this list as a quick way to move between UCSs that you've set up or between the predefined orthogonal UCSs.

Another great way to jump quickly between UCSs is to use the UCS Face option. The Face option requires a 3D solid, but once you have one in place, you can choose Face from the View flyout on the Visualize tab's Coordinates panel and then click on the face of the solid to which you want to align your UCS. For example, you can use the Loft command (see the section "Shaping the Solid" later in this chapter) to create a solid similar to the solid shown later in Figure 21.37 that connects the top and bottom rectangles of the butterfly chair. You can then use the UCS Face option to align to the sides of that solid to draw the arcs and polylines for the seat outline. This way, you're using the 3D solid as a layout tool.

---

5. At the Select guide profiles or [Join multiple edges]: prompt, select the two polylines on the sides of the layout, and then press ↵ to complete your selection. Your chair begins to take form, as shown in Figure 21.35.

6. Select Save from the Quick Access toolbar to save the chair so far.

You've got the beginnings of a butterfly chair with the legs drawn in schematically and the seat as a 3D surface. You can add some detail by using a few other tools, as you'll see in the next set of exercises.

## Converting the Surface into a Solid

In the previous example, you used the Loft tool to create a 3D surface. After you have a surface, you can convert it to a solid to perform other modifications.

You'll want to round the corners of the seat surface to simulate the way a butterfly chair hangs off its frame. You'll also round the corners of the frame and turn the frame into a tubular form. Start by rounding the seat surface. This will involve turning the surface into a solid so that you can use solid-editing tools to get the shape you want:

1. Click the Thicken tool in the Home tab's Solid Editing panel.

You can also enter **Thicken**↵ at the Command prompt.

**2.** Select the seat surface, and press ↵ to finish your selection.

**3.** At the `Specify thickness <0'-0">:` prompt, enter **0.01**↵ (**0.025**↵ for metric users).

**FIGURE 21.35**
The butterfly chair
with a mesh seat

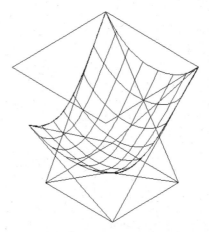

The seat surface appears to lose its webbing, but it has just been converted to a very thin 3D solid.

## Shaping the Solid

The butterfly chair is in a fairly schematic state. The corners of the chair are sharply pointed, whereas a real butterfly chair would have rounded corners. In this section, you'll round the corners of the seat with a little help from the original rectangles you used to form the layout frame.

First you'll use the Fillet command to round the corners of the rectangles. Then you'll use the rounded rectangles to create a solid from which you'll form a new seat:

**1.** Choose the Fillet tool from the Home tab's Modify panel, or enter **F**↵ at the command line.

**2.** At the `Select first object or [Undo/Polyline/Radius/Trim/Multiple]:` prompt, enter **R**↵.

**3.** At the `Specify fillet radius <0'-0">:` prompt, enter **3**↵. Metric users enter **7.5**↵.

**4.** At the `Select first object or [Undo/Polyline/Radius/Trim/Multiple]:` prompt, enter **P**↵ for the Polyline option.

**5.** At the `Select 2D polyline or [Radius]:` prompt, select the top rectangle, as shown at the top of Figure 21.36. The polyline corners become rounded.

**6.** Press ↵ to repeat the Fillet command.

**7.** Enter **P**↵ to use the Polyline option, and then click the bottom rectangle, as shown at the bottom of Figure 21.36. Now both polylines have rounded corners.

**FIGURE 21.36**
Round the corners
of the rectangles
with the Fillet
command.

Start the Fillet command —
and select the top
rectangle to round
its corners.

Repeat the Fillet command ——
to round the corners of
the bottom rectangle.

Next create a 3D solid from the two rectangles using the Loft tool:

1. Click the Loft tool in the Home tab's Modeling panel, or enter **Loft**↵.

2. At the `Select cross-sections in lofting order or [POint/Join multiple edges/MOde]:` prompt, select the two rectangles and press ↵ to finish your selection.

3. At the `Enter an option [Guides/Path/Cross sections only/Settings] <Cross sections only>:` prompt, press ↵. The rectangles join to form a 3D solid (see Figure 21.37).

**FIGURE 21.37**
The lofted rect-
angles form a
3D solid.

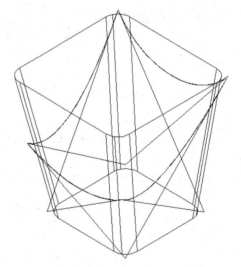

## Finding the Interference between Two Solids

In the next exercise, you'll use a tool that is intended to find the interference between two solids. This is useful if you're working with crowded 3D models and you need to check whether objects may be interfering with each other. For example, a mechanical designer might want to check that duct locations aren't passing through a structural beam.

You'll use Interfere as a modeling tool to obtain a shape that is a combination of two solids: the seat and the rectangular solid you just created. Here are the steps:

1. Click the Interfere tool in the Home tab's Solid Editing panel.

   You can also enter **Interfere**⏎ at the Command prompt.

2. At the `Select first set of objects or [Nested selection/Settings]:` prompt, select the chair seat solid and then press ⏎.

3. At the `Select second set of objects or [Nested selection/checK first set] <checK>:` prompt, click the rectangular solid you created in the previous exercise and press ⏎. The Interference Checking dialog box appears (see Figure 21.38), and the drawing temporarily changes to a view similar to the Realistic visual style.

**FIGURE 21.38**
Checking for interference

The view shows the interference of the two solids in red. Notice that the corners are rounded on the red interference.

4. In the Interference Checking dialog box, turn off the Delete Interference Objects Created On Close check box and click Close. The display returns to the Wireframe view. If you look carefully at the seat corners, you see a new solid overlaid on the seat (see Figure 21.39).

5. Delete the rectangular solid and the original seat, as shown in Figure 21.39.

As mentioned earlier, the Interference Checking tool is intended to help you find out whether objects are colliding in a 3D model; as you've just seen, though, it can be an excellent modeling tool for deriving a form that you could not otherwise create.

A number of other options are available when you're using the Interference Checking tool. Table 21.2 lists the options in the Interference Checking dialog box.

**FIGURE 21.39**
The interference
solid appears on top
of the original seat.

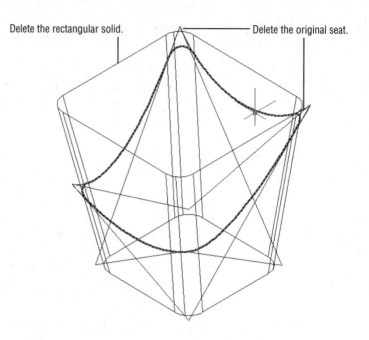

Delete the rectangular solid.

Delete the original seat.

---

**TABLE 21.2:**      Interference Checking dialog box options

| OPTION | WHAT IT DOES |
| --- | --- |
| First Set | Specifies the number of objects in the first set of selected objects |
| Second Set | Specifies the number of objects in the second set of selected objects |
| Interfering Pairs Found | Indicates the number of interferences found |
| Previous | Highlights the previous interference object |
| Next | Highlights the next interference object if multiple objects are present |
| Zoom To Pair | Zooms to the interference object while you're using the Previous and Next options |
| Zoom Realtime | Closes the dialog box to allow you to use Zoom Realtime |
| Pan Realtime | Closes the dialog box to allow you to use Pan |
| 3D Orbit | Closes the dialog box to allow you to use 3D Orbit |
| Delete Interference Objects Created On Close | Deletes the interference object after the dialog box is closed |

The prompt for the Interference Checking command also showed some options. The prompt in step 2 shows Nested selection/Settings. The Nested selection option lets you select objects that are nested in a block or an Xref. The Settings option opens the Interference Settings dialog box (see Figure 21.40).

**FIGURE 21.40**

Settings for
interference

This dialog box offers settings for the temporary display of interference objects while you're using the Interference command. Table 21.3 lists the options for this dialog box.

**TABLE 21.3:**     Interference Settings dialog box options

| OPTION | WHAT IT DOES |
| --- | --- |
| Visual Style | Controls the visual style for interference objects |
| Color | Controls the color for interference objects |
| Highlight Interfering Pair | Highlights the interfering objects |
| Highlight Interference | Highlights the resulting interference objects |
| Visual Style | Controls the visual style for the drawing while displaying the interference objects |

## Creating Tubes with the Sweep Tool

You need to take care of one more element before your chair is complete. The legs are currently simple lines with sharp corners. In this section, you'll learn how to convert lines into 3D tubes. To make it more interesting, you'll add rounded corners to the legs.

Start by rounding the corners on the lines you've created for the legs:

1. Use the Explode tool to explode the 3D polyline legs into simple lines.

2. Choose the Fillet tool from the Home tab's Modify panel, or enter F↵ at the command line.

**3.** At the `Select first object or [Undo/Polyline/Radius/Trim/Multiple]:` prompt, enter **R**↵.

**4.** At the `Specify fillet radius <0'-0">:` prompt, enter **2**↵. Metric users should enter **5**↵.

**5.** At the `Select first object or [Undo/Polyline/Radius/Trim/Multiple]:` prompt, enter **M**↵ and then select pairs of lines to fillet their corners.

**6.** When all the corners are rounded, press ↵ to exit the Fillet command.

**7.** Delete the two polyline splines you used to form the sides of the seat. Your drawing should look like Figure 21.41.

**FIGURE 21.41**
Drawing the circles
for the tubes

Draw a circle here and
make 15 copies for
a total of 16 circles.

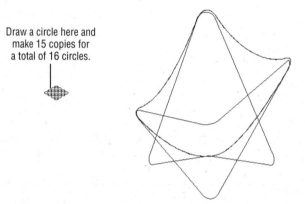

The chair is almost complete, but the legs are just wireframes. Next you'll give them some thickness by turning them into tubes. Start by creating a set of circles. You'll use the circles to define the diameter of the tubes:

**1.** Draw a ⅜" (0.95 cm) radius circle in the location shown in Figure 21.41. Don't worry if your location is a little off; the placement of the circle isn't important.

**2.** Use the Rectangular Array command to make 15 copies of the circle. In Figure 21.41, a 4 × 4 array is used with the default 1" spacing. Metric users should use a spacing of about 30 cm. Use the Explode command in the Home Tab's Modify panel to convert the circles from an associative array to regular circles. Start the explode command, and select the circles ↵.

Now you're ready to form the tubes:

**1.** Click the Sweep tool from the Extrude flyout in the Home tab's Modeling panel. You can also enter **sweep**↵ at the command line.

**2.** At the `Select objects to sweep or [MOde]:` prompt, click one of the circles you just created. It doesn't matter which circle you use because they're identical. Press ↵ when you're finished.

**3.** At the `Select sweep path or [Alignment/Base point/Scale/Twist]:` prompt, select one of the lines or fillet arcs that make up the legs.

4. Press ↵ to repeat the Sweep command, and then repeat steps 2 and 3 for each part of the leg segments, including the fillet arcs.

5. Continue with step 4 until all the lines in the legs have been converted into tubes.

6. Change the color of the solid representing the seat to cyan, and then select the Realistic visual style from the Visual Style viewport control. Your drawing will look similar to the image on the left of Figure 21.42, which shows a perspective view. The image on the right is the chair with some materials assigned to its parts and a slight adjustment to the seat location.

**FIGURE 21.42**
A perspective view of the butterfly chair with tubes for legs

7. Close the file. You can save it or, if you intend to repeat the exercise, close and do not save.

## Using Sweep to Create Complex Forms

Although you used circles with the Sweep command to create tubes, you can use any closed polyline shape. Figure 21.43 gives some examples of other shapes you can use with the Sweep command.

In step 3 of the previous exercise, you may have noticed some command-line options. These options offer additional control over the way Sweep works. Here is a rundown on how they work:

**Alignment** This option lets you determine whether the object to sweep is automatically set perpendicular to the sweep path. By default, this option is set to Yes. If set to No, Sweep assumes the current angle of the object, as shown in Figure 21.44.

**Base Point** By default, Sweep uses the center of the object to sweep as the location to align with the path, as shown in Figure 21.45. Base Point lets you set a specific location on the object.

**Scale** You can have Sweep scale the sweep object from one end of the path to the other to create a tapered shape, as shown in Figure 21.46. This option requires a numeric scale value.

**FIGURE 21.43**
You can use any closed shape with the Sweep command.

**FIGURE 21.44**
Alignment lets you set the angle between the object to sweep and the sweep path.

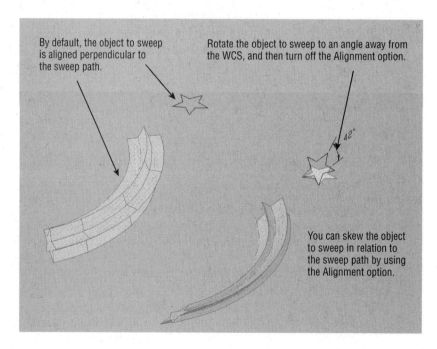

By default, the object to sweep is aligned perpendicular to the sweep path.

Rotate the object to sweep to an angle away from the WCS, and then turn off the Alignment option.

You can skew the object to sweep in relation to the sweep path by using the Alignment option.

**Twist**    You can have the object sweep twist along the path to form a spiral shape, as shown in Figure 21.47. This option requires a numeric value in the form of degrees of rotation.

**FIGURE 21.45**
Using the Base Point option

By default, the center of the object to sweep is aligned with the sweep path.

Base point

Center

Sweep path

With the Base Point option, you can select a location on the object to sweep that will align with the sweep path.

Sweep path

**FIGURE 21.46**
Scale lets you scale the object to sweep as it's swept along the path.

**FIGURE 21.47**
You can have the object sweep twist along the path to create a spiral effect.

These options are available as soon as you select the sweep object and before you select the path object. You can use any combination of options you need. For example, you can apply the Twist and Scale options together, as shown in Figure 21.48.

**FIGURE 21.48**
The Scale and Twist options applied together

## Creating Spiral Forms

You can use the Sweep tool in conjunction with the Helix tool to create a spiral form, such as a spring or the threads of a screw. You've already seen how the Sweep tool works. Try the following exercise to learn how the Helix tool works firsthand.

In this exercise, you'll draw a helicoil thread insert. This is a device used to repair stripped threads; it's basically a coiled steel strip that forms internal and external threads. Here are the steps:

1. Open the `Helicoil.dwg` file. This is a standard AutoCAD drawing containing a closed polyline in a stretched octagon shape. This is the cross section of the helicoil thread, and you'll use it as an object to sweep after you've created a helix.

2. Click the Helix tool in the Home tab's expanded Draw panel, or type **Helix**↵.

   You see the following prompt:

   ```
   Number of turns = 3.0000  Twist=CCW
   Specify center point of base:
   ```

3. Pick a point roughly in the center of the view. A rubber-banding line appears along with a circle.

4. At the `Specify base radius or [Diameter] <1.0000>:` prompt, enter **0.375**↵.

5. At the `Specify top radius or [Diameter] <0.3750>:` prompt, press ↵ to accept the default, which is the same as the value you entered in step 4.

6. At the `Specify helix height or [Axis endpoint/Turns/turn Height/tWist] <1.0000>:` prompt, enter **T**↵ to use the Turns option.

**7.** At the `Enter number of turns <3.0000>:` prompt, enter **15**↵ to create a helix with 15 turns total.

**8.** At the `Specify helix height or [Axis endpoint/Turns/turn Height/tWist] <1.0000>:` prompt, press ↵ to accept the default height of 1. The helix appears as a spiral drawn to the dimensions you've just specified for diameter, turns, and height (see Figure 21.49).

**FIGURE 21.49**
The helix and the helicoil after using Sweep

In step 6, you used the Turns option to specify the total number of turns in the helix. You also have other options that give you control over the shape of the helix. Figure 21.50 shows you the effects of the Helix command options. You may want to experiment with them on your own to become familiar with Helix.

**FIGURE 21.50**
The Helix command options

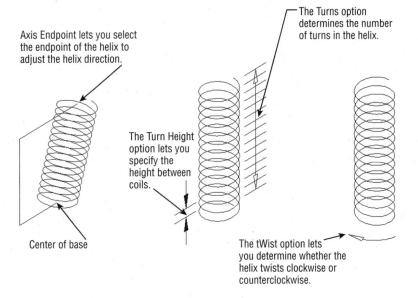

Axis Endpoint lets you select the endpoint of the helix to adjust the helix direction.

The Turns option determines the number of turns in the helix.

The Turn Height option lets you specify the height between coils.

Center of base

The tWist option lets you determine whether the helix twists clockwise or counterclockwise.

---

**EDIT A HELIX WITH THE PROPERTIES PALETTE**

If you find that you've created a helix with the wrong settings, you don't have to erase and re-create it. You can use the Properties palette to make adjustments to any of the helix options presented in Figure 21.50, even after a helix has been created. Select the helix, right-click, and choose Properties. Look in the Geometry section of the Properties palette for the helix settings.

---

Now use the Sweep tool to complete the helicoil:

1. Click the Sweep tool from the Extrude flyout in the Home tab's Modeling panel, or enter **Sweep** at the command line.

2. At the `Select objects to sweep or [MOde]:` prompt, select the thread cross section in the lower-left corner of the drawing and then press ↵.

3. At the `Select sweep path or [Alignment/Base point/Scale/Twist]:` prompt, select the helix. After a moment, the helicoil appears.

4. To see the helicoil more clearly, choose the Realistic option from the Visual Styles drop-down list, and then change the helicoil to the Helicoil layer.

5. Close and save the file. If you intend to repeat this exercise, close but don't save.

If the space between the coils is too small for the cross section, you may get an error message. If you get an error message at step 3, make sure you created the helix exactly as specified in the previous exercise. You may also try increasing the helix height.

In step 3, instead of selecting the sweep path, you can select an option to apply to the object to sweep. For example, by default, Sweep aligns the object to sweep at an angle that is perpendicular to the path and centers it. See "Using Sweep to Create Complex Forms" earlier in this chapter.

## Creating Surface Models

In an earlier exercise, you used the Loft command to create the seat of a butterfly chair. In this section, you'll return to the Loft command to explore some of its other uses. This time, you'll use it to create a 3D model of a hillside based on a set of site-contour lines. You'll also see how you can use a surface created from the Loft command to slice a solid into two pieces, imprinting the solid with the surface shape.

---

 **Real World Scenario**

**ARCHITECTURAL APPLICATIONS FOR THE HELIX TOOL**

In the exercises for the Helix tool, we used a device often used to repair spark plug threads that have been stripped, but the helix can be used in other applications besides mechanical modeling. For example, we've used a helix to draw a circular ramp for a parking garage. To do this, instead of multiple turns, you would use a single rotation or a half rotation. The radius of the helix would need to be much larger to accommodate the width of a car.

---

## 🌐 Real World Scenario

### OLD VS. NEW SURFACES

If you've used earlier (pre-2007) versions of AutoCAD to create 3D models, you've probably used surface modeling to create some of your 3D objects. If you open an old drawing file that contains those 3D surfaces, you'll see that they are called polygon meshes. You can convert those older mesh objects into new surface objects using the Convert To Surface tool, which is next to the Convert To Solid tool in the Home tab's expanded Solid Editing panel. If you prefer to use the older 3D surface modeling tools like Revsurf and Rulesurf, they are still available, though they now create mesh surfaces. You will learn more about mesh modeling in Chapter 23, "Exploring 3D Mesh and Surface Modeling."

Start by creating a 3D surface using the Loft command:

1. Open the contour.dwg file.

2. Select the Loft tool from the Extrude flyout on the Home tab's Modeling panel.

3. Select each brown contour in consecutive order from right to left or left to right. It doesn't matter whether you start at the left end or the right end, but you must select the contours in order.

4. When you're finished selecting all the contours, press ↵. You see the surface applied over the contour lines (see Figure 21.51).

**FIGURE 21.51**
Creating a 3D surface from contour lines

5. At the Enter an option [Guides/Path/Cross sections only/Settings] <Cross sections only>: prompt, press ↵ to exit the Loft command.

Once the loft surface has been placed, you can make adjustments to the way the loft is generated by using the arrow grip that appears when you select the surface:

1. Click the surface to select it.

2. Click the arrowhead that appears by the surface. This is known as a multifunction grip.

3. Select the Ruled option from the menu. The surface changes slightly to conform to the new Ruled surface option (see Figure 21.52). Press Esc to make sure you don't have any objects selected.

**FIGURE 21.52**
The surface showing the multifunction grip menu with the Ruled option selected

In the butterfly chair exercise, you used the Guides option in the Loft Command prompt. This allowed you to use the polyline curves to guide the loft shape from the front arc to the back arc. In this exercise, you didn't use the command options and went straight to the multifunction grip menu. The Ruled setting from step 3 generates a surface that connects the cross sections in a straight line.

## Slicing a Solid with a Surface

In the barcelona1.dwg chair example, you converted a surface into a solid using the Thicken command. Next, you'll use a surface to create a solid in a slightly different way. This time, you'll use the surface to slice a solid into two pieces. This will give you a form that is more easily read and understood as a terrain model:

1. Select the Extrude tool from the Extrude flyout in the Home tab's Modeling panel.

2. At the `Select objects to extrude or [MOde]:` prompt, select the large rectangle below the contours and press ⏎. The rectangle turns into a box whose height follows your cursor.

3. At the `Specify height of extrusion or [Direction/Path/Taper angle/ Expression]:` prompt, move the cursor upward so that the box looks similar to the one shown in Figure 21.53. Then click the mouse to fix the box's height.

**FIGURE 21.53**
The box extruded through the contours

You may have noticed that, as you raised the box height, you could see how it intersected the contour surface. Next you'll slice the box into two pieces:

1. Click the Slice tool in the Home tab's Solid Editing panel.

2. At the Select objects to slice: prompt, select the box and press ↵.

3. At the Specify start point of slicing plane or [planar Object/Surface/Zaxis/ View/XY/YZ/ZX/3points] <3points>: prompt, enter **S**↵ to use the Surface option.

4. At the Select a surface: prompt, select the contour surface.

5. At the Select solid to keep or [keep Both sides] <Both>: prompt, click the part of the box that is below the surface. The top part of the box disappears, and you see the surface once again.

6. Delete the contour surface and the contour lines. The box remains with an imprint of the surface, as shown in Figure 21.54.

**FIGURE 21.54**
The box with the contour surface imprinted

In step 3, you saw a prompt that offered a variety of methods for slicing the box. The Surface option allowed you to slice the box using an irregular shape, but most of the other options let you slice a solid by defining a plane or a series of planar objects.

## Finding the Volume of a Cut

Civil engineers frequently ask us how they can find the volume of earth from an excavated area. This is often referred to as a *cut* from a *cut and fill* operation. To do this, you first have to create the cut shape. Next you use the Interfere command to find the intersection between the cut shape and the contour surface. You can then find the volume of the cut shape using one of the inquiry commands in AutoCAD. The following exercise demonstrates how this is done.

Suppose that the contour model you've just created represents a site where you'll excavate a rectangular area for a structure. You want to find the amount of earth involved in the excavation. A rectangle has been placed in the contour drawing representing such an area:

1. Select Wireframe from the Visual Styles flyout on the Home tab's View panel (see Figure 21.55). This allows you to see the excavation rectangle more clearly.

2. Turn on the Selection Cycling tool in the status bar. This will help you select the rectangle in step 4.

**FIGURE 21.55**
Select Wireframe from the Visual Styles flyout.

**3.** Click the Extrude tool in the Home tab's Modeling panel.

**4.** Select the rectangle shown in Figure 21.56.

**FIGURE 21.56**
Selecting the rectangle representing the excavation area

**5.** In the Selection dialog box, select Polyline and then press ↵.

**6.** Extrude the rectangle to the height of 10′ (3 meters).

Here you used the Selection Cycling tool to help you select the rectangle, which is overlapped by the contour solid. The Selection Cycling tool presents the Selection dialog box, which lets you determine the type of object you want to select, thereby filtering out other objects nearby that might be selected accidentally.

With the excavation rectangle in place, you can use the Interfere command to find the volume of the excavation:

**1.** Click the Interfere tool in the Home tab's Solid Editing panel.

**2.** At the Select first set of objects or [Nested selection/Settings]: prompt, click the contour and press ↵.

**3.** At the Select second set of objects or [Nested selection/checK first set] <checK>: prompt, select the box and press ↵. The Interference Checking dialog box appears.

4. In the Interference Checking dialog box, deselect the Delete Interference Objects Created On Close check box and click Close.

5. Delete the box you used to represent the excavation area. The remaining shape contains the volume of the excavation.

6. Start the Region/Mass Properties tool by typing **Massprop**↵.

7. At the `Select objects:` prompt, select the excavation solid as shown in Figure 21.57 and then press ↵. The properties of the excavation area display in the command-line interface. At the top, you see the volume of the selected solid (see Figure 21.58).

8. Press ↵↵, and then at the `Write analysis to a file? [Yes/No] <N>:` prompt, press ↵ to exit the command or enter **Y**↵ to save the information to a text file.

**FIGURE 21.57**
The 3D solid representing the excavation

**FIGURE 21.58**
The mass and volume information from the Region/ Mass Properties tool

```
-------------- SOLIDS ---------------
Mass:                150725.8023 lb
Volume:              150725.8023 cu in
Bounding box:     X: 239.4168 -- 460.6312 in
                  Y: 79.8651 -- 232.3356 in
                  Z: 49.9963 -- 92.0158 in
Centroid:         X: 363.3381 in
                  Y: 180.4286 in
                  Z: 61.7502 in
Moments of inertia:  X: 5611072595.8413 lb sq in
                     Y: 20831685960.4080 lb sq in
                     Z: 25270149618.4929 lb sq in
Products of inertia: XY: 9719381763.3079 lb sq in
                     YZ: 1693061487.0124 lb sq in
                     ZX: 3374093264.1127 lb sq in
Radii of gyration:   X: 192.9431 in
                     Y: 371.7649 in
                     Z: 409.4587 in
Principal moments (lb sq in) and X-Y-Z directions about centroid:
```

## Understanding the Loft Command

As you've seen from the exercises in this chapter, the Loft command lets you create just about any shape you can imagine, from a simple sling to the complex curves of a contour map. If your loft cross sections are a set of closed objects like circles or closed polygons, the resulting object is a 3D solid instead of a surface.

The order in which you select the cross sections is important because Loft will follow your selection order to create the surface or solid. For example, Figure 21.59 shows a series of circles used for a lofted solid. The circles on each side are identical in size and placement, but the order of selection is different. The solid on the left was created by selecting the circles in consecutive order from bottom to top, creating an hourglass shape. The solid on the right was created by selecting the two larger circles first from bottom to top; the smaller, intermediate circle was selected last. This selection order created a hollowed-out shape with more vertical sides.

In addition to the selection order, several other settings affect the shape of a solid created by the Loft command. In the contour-map example, you selected the Ruled setting from a multifunction grip after you had completed the Loft command. You can also set Loft command options through the Loft Settings dialog box (see Figure 21.60). This dialog box appears during the Loft command when you select the Settings option after you've selected a set of cross sections.

**FIGURE 21.59**
The order in which you select the cross sections affects the result of the Loft command.

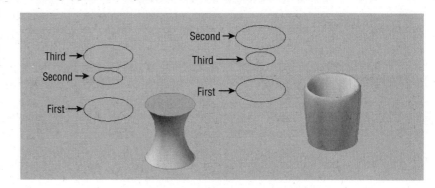

**FIGURE 21.60**
Loft Settings Smooth Fit

You can radically affect the way the Loft command forms a surface or a solid through the options in this dialog box, so it pays to understand what those settings do. Take a moment to study the following sections that describe the Loft Settings dialog box options.

## RULED AND SMOOTH FIT

The Ruled option connects the cross sections with straight surfaces, as shown in the sample to the left in Figure 21.61.

**FIGURE 21.61**
Samples of a Ruled loft at left and a Smooth Fit loft on the right

The Smooth Fit option connects the cross sections with a smooth surface. It attempts to make the best smooth transitions between the cross sections, as shown in the right image in Figure 21.61.

## NORMAL TO

Normal To is a set of four options presented in a drop-down list. To understand what this setting does, you need to know that *normal* is a mathematical term referring to a direction that is perpendicular to a plane, as shown in Figure 21.62. In these options, *normal* refers to the direction the surface takes as it emerges from a cross section.

**FIGURE 21.62**
A normal is a direction perpendicular to a plane.

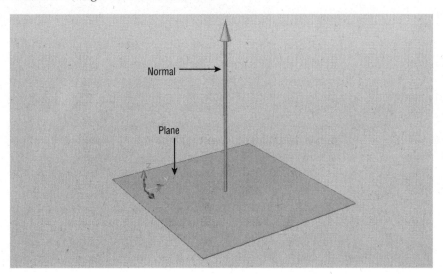

If you use the All Cross Sections option, the surfaces emerge in a perpendicular direction from all the cross sections, as shown in the first image in Figure 21.63. If you use the End Cross Section option, the surface emerges in a direction that is perpendicular to just the end cross section, as shown in the second image in Figure 21.63. The Start Cross Section option causes the surface to emerge in a direction perpendicular to the start cross section. The Start And End Cross Sections option combines the effect of the Start Cross Section and End Cross Section options.

**FIGURE 21.63**
Samples of the Normal To options applied to the same set of cross sections

## DRAFT ANGLES

The Draft Angles option affects only the first and last cross sections. This option generates a smooth surface with added control over the start and end angles. Unlike the Normal To option, which forces a perpendicular direction to the cross sections, Draft Angles allows you to set an angle for the surface direction. For example, if you set Start Angle to a value of 0, the surface will bulge outward from the start cross section, as shown in the first image of Figure 21.64.

**FIGURE 21.64**
The Draft Angles options

Likewise, an End Angle setting of 0 will cause the surface to bulge at the end cross section (see the second image in Figure 21.64).

The Start and End Magnitude settings let you determine a relative strength of the bulge. The right image in Figure 21.64 shows a draft angle of 0 and magnitude of 50 for the last cross section.

## CLOSE SURFACE OR SOLID

The Close Surface Or Solid option is available only when the Smooth Fit option is selected. It causes the first and last cross section objects to be connected, so the surface or solid loops back from the last to the first cross section. Figure 21.65 shows the cross sections at the left, a smooth version in the middle, and a smooth version with the Close Surface Or Solid option turned on. The Close Surface Or Solid option causes the solid to become a tube.

**FIGURE 21.65**
The Close Surface Or Solid option connects the end and the beginning cross sections.

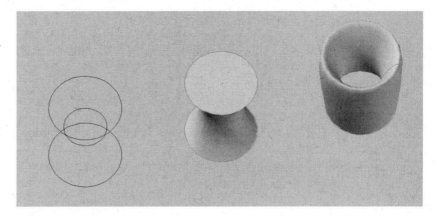

## Moving Objects in 3D Space

AutoCAD provides three tools specifically designed for moving objects in 3D space: 3D Align, 3D Move, and 3D Rotate. You can find all three commands in the Home tab's Modify panel. These tools help you perform common moves associated with 3D editing.

### Aligning Objects in 3D Space

In mechanical drawing, you often create the parts in 3D and then show an assembly of the parts. The 3D Align command can greatly simplify the assembly process. The following steps show how to use 3D Align to line up two objects at specific points:

1. Open the `align.dwg` file.

2. Click the 3D Align tool on the Home tab's Modify panel, or type **3dalign**↵.

3. At the `Select objects:` prompt, select the 3D wedge-shaped object and press ↵. (The *source object* is the object you want to move.)

4. At the `Specify base point or [Copy]:` prompt, pick a point on the source object that is the first point of an alignment axis, such as the center of a hole or the corner of a surface. For the align drawing, use the upper-left corner of the wedge.

5. At the `Specify second point or [Continue] <C>:` prompt, pick a point on the source object that is the second point of an alignment axis, such as another center point or other corner of a surface. For this example, select the other top corner of the wedge.

6. At the `Specify third source point or [Continue] <C>:` prompt, press ↵ if two points are adequate to describe the alignment. Otherwise, pick a third point on the source object that, along with the first two points, best describes the surface plane you want aligned with the destination object. Pick the lower-right corner of the wedge shown in Figure 21.66.

**FIGURE 21.66**
Aligning two 3D objects

Result

7. At the Specify first destination point: prompt, pick a point on the destination object to which you want the first source point to move. (The *destination object* is the object with which you want the source object to align.) This is the top corner of the rectangular shape. (See the first destination point in Figure 21.66.)

8. At the Specify second destination point or [eXit] <X>: prompt, pick a point on the destination object indicating how the first and second source points are to align in relation to the destination object. (See the second destination point in Figure 21.66.)

9. You're prompted for a third destination point. Pick a point on the destination object that, along with the previous two destination points, describes the plane with which you want the source object to be aligned. (See the third destination point in Figure 21.66.) The source object will move into alignment with the destination object.

## Moving an Object in 3D

CERT
OBJECTIVE

In Chapter 20, you saw how you can use the move gizmo tool to help restrain the motion of an object in the x-, y-, or z-axis. AutoCAD offers a Move command specifically designed for 3D editing that includes a move gizmo tool to restrain motion.

You don't need to perform these steps as an exercise. You can try the command on your own when you need to use it.

Here's how it works:

1. Click the 3D Move tool in the Home tab's Modify panel. You can also enter **3dmove**↵.

2. Select the object or set of objects you want to move and press ↵. The Move gizmo appears on the object (see Figure 21.67).

**FIGURE 21.67**
The Move gizmo

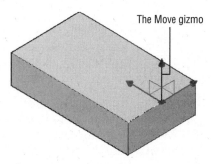

The Move gizmo

3. Point to the x-, y-, or z-axis of the Move gizmo but don't click it. As you hover over an axis, an axis vector appears indicating the direction your object will move if you click the axis, as shown in Figure 21.68.

**FIGURE 21.68**
An axis vector
appears when you
hover over an axis
of the gizmo.

Axis vector

4. Click an axis while the vector appears, and then enter a distance along the axis or click a point to complete the move.

Alternately, in step 3, you can hover over and click a plane indicator on the gizmo to restrain the motion along one of the planes defined by two of the axes (see Figure 21.69).

## Rotating an Object in 3D

The 3D Rotate command is another command that is like an extension of its 2D counterpart. With 3D Rotate, a Rotate gizmo appears that restrains the rotation about the x-, y-, or z-axis.

**FIGURE 21.69**
Hover over the plane indicator to restrain the motion along a plane.

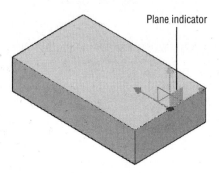

Plane indicator

Again, you don't need to perform these steps as an exercise. You can try the command on your own when you need to use it.

Here's how it works:

1. Click the 3D Rotate tool in the Home tab's Modify panel. You can also enter **3drotate↵**.

2. Select the object or objects you want to rotate and then press ↵. The Rotate gizmo appears on the object (see Figure 21.70).

**FIGURE 21.70**
The Rotate gizmo

3. At the `Specify a base point:` prompt, you can select a point about which the selected objects are to be rotated. The gizmo will move to the point you select.

4. Point to the colored circle that represents the axis of rotation for your objects. A vector appears, representing the axis of rotation. When you're happy with the selected axis, click.

5. At the `Specify angle start point or type an angle:` prompt, you can enter an angle value or click a point. You can use the Shift key or Ortho mode to restrain the direction to 90°.

6. If you click a point in step 5, you will see the `Specify angle end point:` prompt. Enter an angle value or click another point for the rotation angle.

You can also just select one of the circles in step 3 instead of selecting a base point. If you do this, then the selected object begins to rotate. You don't have to select a start and end angle.

> ### USING 3D MIRROR
>
> Two other tools, 3D Mirror and 3D Array, are available in the Home tab's Modify panel. They work in a way that's similar to how the standard Mirror and Array tools work, with a slight difference.
>
> 3D Mirror begins by asking you to select objects. Then you're asked to specify a mirror plane instead of a mirror axis. You can define a plane using the default three points, or you can use one of the seven other options: Object/Last/Zaxis/View/XY/YZ/ZX. By using a plane instead of an axis, you can mirror an object or set of objects anywhere in 3D space. One way to visualize this is to imagine holding a mirror up to your 3D model. The mirror is your 3D plane, and the reflected image is the mirrored version of the object. Imagine tilting the mirror to various angles to get a different mirror image. In the same way, you can tilt the plane in the 3D Mirror tool to mirror an object in any number of ways.

# The Bottom Line

**Master the User Coordinate System.**    The User Coordinate System (UCS) is a vital key to editing in 3D space. If you want to master 3D modeling, you should become familiar with this tool.

**Master It**    Name some of the predefined UCS planes.

**Understand the UCS options.**    You can set up the UCS orientation for any situation. It isn't limited to the predefined settings.

**Master It**    Briefly describe some of the ways you can set up a UCS.

**Use viewports to aid in 3D drawing.**    In some 3D modeling operations, it helps to have several different views of the model through the Viewports feature.

**Master It**    Name some of the predefined standard viewports offered in the Viewports dialog box.

**Use the array tools.**    The array tools—Rectangular, Path, and Polar Array—allow you to create 3D arrays dynamically.

**Master It**    What prompt in the Array command will allow you to have a 3D array?

**Create complex 3D surfaces.**    You aren't limited to straight, flat surfaces in AutoCAD. You can create just about any shape you want, including curved surfaces.

**Master It**    What tool did you use in this chapter's butterfly chair exercise to convert a surface into a solid?

**Create spiral forms.**    Spiral forms frequently occur in nature, so it's no wonder that we often use spirals in our own designs. Spirals are seen in screws, stairs, and ramps as well as in other man-made forms.

**Master It**    Name the commands used in the example in the section "Creating Spiral Forms," and name two elements that are needed to create a spiral.

**Create surface models.**   You can create a 3D surface by connecting a series of lines that define a surface contour. You can create anything from a 3D landscape to a car fender using this method.

**Master It**   What is the tool used to convert a series of lines into a 3D surface?

**Move objects in 3D space.**   You can move objects in 3D space using tools that are similar to those for 2D drafting. But when it comes to editing objects, 3D modeling is much more complex than 2D drafting.

**Master It**   What does the Rotate gizmo do?

## Chapter 22

# Editing and Visualizing 3D Solids

In the previous 3D chapters, you spent some time becoming familiar with the AutoCAD® software's 3D modeling features. In this chapter, you'll focus on 3D solids and how they're created and edited. You'll also learn how you can use some special visualization tools to show your 3D solid in a variety of ways.

You'll create a fictitious mechanical part to explore some of the ways you can shape 3D solids. This will also give you a chance to see how you can turn your 3D model into a standard 2D mechanical drawing. In addition, you'll learn about the 3D solid-editing tools that are available through the Solid Editing Ribbon panel.

In this chapter, you will learn to

- ◆ Understand solid modeling
- ◆ Create solid forms
- ◆ Create complex solids
- ◆ Edit solids
- ◆ Streamline the 2D drawing process
- ◆ Visualize solids

## Understanding Solid Modeling

Solid modeling is a way of defining 3D objects as solid forms. When you create a 3D model by using solid modeling, you start with the basic forms of your model—boxes, cones, and cylinders, for example. These basic solids are called *primitives*. Then, using more of these primitives, you begin to add to or subtract from your basic forms.

---

### 3D SOLIDS ARE NOT AVAILABLE IN AUTOCAD LT

Autodesk® AutoCAD LT® users don't have solid-modeling capabilities. However, you can take advantage of the region objects and their related editing commands described in the sidebar "Using 3D Solid Operations on 2D Drawings" later in this chapter.

---

For example, to create a model of a tube you first create two solid cylinders, one smaller in diameter than the other. You then align the two cylinders so that they're concentric and tell

AutoCAD to subtract the smaller cylinder from the larger one. The larger of the two cylinders becomes a tube whose inside diameter is that of the smaller cylinder, as shown in Figure 22.1. Several primitives are available for modeling solids in AutoCAD (see Figure 22.2).

**FIGURE 22.1**
Creating a tube by using solid modeling

Create two cylinder primitives, one for the outside diameter and one for the inside diameter.

Cylinder for inside diameter

Cylinder for outside diameter

Superimpose the cylinder for the inside diameter onto the cylinder for the outside diameter.

Use the Subtract command to subtract the inside diameter cylinder from the outside diameter cylinder.

**FIGURE 22.2**
The solid primitives

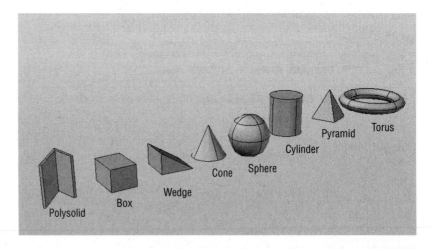

Polysolid

Box

Wedge

Cone

Sphere

Cylinder

Pyramid

Torus

You can join these shapes—polysolid, box, wedge, cone, sphere, cylinder, pyramid, and donut (or *torus*)—in one of four ways to produce secondary shapes. The first three, demonstrated in Figure 22.3 using a cube and a cylinder as examples, are called *Boolean operations.* (The name comes from the nineteenth-century mathematician George Boole.)

**FIGURE 22.3**

The intersection, subtraction, and union of a cube and a cylinder

A solid box and a solid cylinder are superimposed.

The intersection of the primitives creates a solid cylinder with the ends skewed.

The cylinder subtracted from the box creates a hole in the box.

The union of the two primitives creates a box with two round pegs.

The three Boolean operations are as follows:

**Intersection**   Uses only the intersecting volume of two objects to define a solid shape

**Subtraction**   Uses one object to cut out a shape in another

**Union**   Joins two primitives so that they act as one object

The fourth option, Interfere, lets you find exactly where two or more solids coincide in space—similar to the results of a union. The main difference between interference and union is that interference enables you to keep the original solid shapes, whereas union discards the original solids, leaving only their combined form. Interfere creates a temporary 3D solid of the coincident space. You can close the command or have AutoCAD create a solid based on the shape created. The selected objects will remain unchanged.

Joined primitives are called *composite solids.* You can join primitives to primitives, composite solids to primitives, and composite solids to other composite solids.

Now let's look at how you can use these concepts to create models in AutoCAD.

---

**EXERCISE EXAMPLES ARE "UNITLESS"**

To simplify the exercises in this chapter, the instructions don't specify inches or centimeters. This way, users of both the metric and Imperial measurement systems can use the exercises without having to read through duplicate information.

---

## Creating Solid Forms

In the following sections, you'll begin to draw the object shown later in the chapter in Figure 22.18. In the process, you'll explore the creation of solid models by creating primitives and then setting up special relationships between them.

Primitives are the basic building blocks of solid modeling. At first, it may seem limiting to have only eight primitives with which to work, but consider the varied forms you can create with just a few two-dimensional objects. Let's begin by creating the basic mass of your steel bracket.

First, prepare your drawing for the exercise:

1. Open the file called bracket.dwg. This file contains some objects that you'll use in the first half of this chapter to build a 3D solid shape.

2. If you aren't already in the 3D Modeling workspace, select 3D Modeling from the Workspace Switching tool or the Workspace drop-down list in the Quick Access toolbar.

3. Close the Materials Browser if it opens with the 3D Modeling workspace.

## Joining Primitives

In this section, you'll merge the two box objects. First you'll move the new box into place. Then you'll join the two boxes to form a single solid:

1. Start the Move command, pick the smaller of the two boxes, and then press ↵.

2. At the Specify base point or [Displacement] <Displacement>: prompt, use the Midpoint osnap override and pick the middle of the front edge of the smaller box, as shown in the top image in Figure 22.4.

3. At the Specify second point or <use first point as displacement>: prompt, use the Midpoint osnap to pick the middle of the bottom edge of the larger box, as shown in the bottom image in Figure 22.4.

4. Click the Solid, Union tool in the Home tab's Solid Editing panel, or type **UNI**↵.

5. At the Select objects: prompt, pick both boxes and press ↵. Your drawing now looks like Figure 22.5.

**FIGURE 22.4**
Moving the
smaller box

**FIGURE 22.5**
The two
boxes joined

As you can see in Figure 22.5, the form has joined to appear as one object. It also acts like one object when you select it. You now have a composite solid made up of two box primitives.

## Cutting Portions out of a Solid

Now let's place some holes in the bracket. In this next exercise, you'll discover how to create negative forms to cut portions out of a solid:

**1.** Turn on the layer called Cylinder. Two cylinder solids appear in the model, as shown in Figure 22.6. These cylinders are 1.5 units tall.

**FIGURE 22.6**
The cylinders appear when the Cylinder layer is turned on.

**2.** Select the Solid, Subtract tool from the Solid Editing panel, or type **SU**↵.

**3.** At the `Select solids, surfaces and regions to subtract from... Select objects:` prompt, pick the composite solid of the two boxes and press ↵.

**4.** At the `Select solids, surfaces and regions to subtract... Select objects:` prompt, pick the two cylinders and press ↵. The cylinders are subtracted from the bracket.

**5.** To view the solid, choose Hidden from the Visual Styles Control in the drawing area. You see a hidden-line view of the solid, as shown in Figure 22.7.

**FIGURE 22.7**
The bracket so far, with hidden lines removed

## USING 3D SOLID OPERATIONS ON 2D DRAWINGS

You can apply some of the features described in this chapter to 2D drafting by taking advantage of the AutoCAD region object. *Regions* are two-dimensional objects to which you can apply Boolean operations.

The following illustration shows how you can use regions to turn a set of closed polyline shapes quickly into a drawing of a wrench. First, you convert the shapes at the top of the figure into regions using the Region tool on the Draw panel. Next, you align the shapes, as shown in the middle of the image. Finally, you join the circles and rectangle with the Union command (type **UNI↵**); then, the hexagonal shapes are subtracted from the combined shape (type **SU↵**). You can use the Region.dwg sample file if you'd like to experiment.

Create closed polyline shapes and convert them to regions.

Move the shapes into position to lay out the object.

Use the Union and Subtract commands to create the final object.

You can use regions to generate complex surfaces that may include holes or unusual bends as in the image below. Keep in mind the following:

♦ Regions act like surfaces; when you remove hidden lines, objects behind the regions are hidden.

♦ You can explode regions to edit them. However, exploding a region causes the region to lose its surface-like quality, and objects no longer hide behind its surface(s).

♦ You can Ctrl+click the edge of a region to edit the region's shape.

♦ You can use the regional model to create complex 2D surfaces for use in 3D surface modeling, as in this image:

As you learned in the earlier chapters in Part 4, Wireframe views, such as the one in the previous exercise, are somewhat difficult to decipher. Until you use the Hidden visual style (step 5) or the Hide command, you can't be sure that the subtracted cylinders are in fact holes. Using the Hide command frequently will help you keep track of what's going on with your solid model.

You may also have noticed in step 4 that, even though the cylinders were taller than the opening they created, they worked fine to remove part of the rectangular solid. The cylinders were 1.5 units tall, not 1 unit, which is the thickness of the bracket. Having drawn the cylinders taller than needed, you saw that when AutoCAD performed the subtraction, it ignored the portion of the cylinders that didn't affect the bracket. AutoCAD always discards the portion of a primitive that isn't used in a subtract operation.

## Creating Complex Solids

As you learned earlier, you can convert a polyline into a solid by using the Extrude tool in the Modeling panel. This process lets you create more complex shapes than the built-in primitives. In addition to the simple straight extrusion you've already tried, you can extrude shapes into curved paths or you can taper an extrusion.

### Tapering an Extrusion

Let's look at how you can taper an extrusion to create a fairly complex solid with little effort:

1. Turn on the Taper layer. A rectangular polyline appears. This rectangle has its corners rounded to a radius of 0.5 using the Fillet command.

2. Click the Extrude tool in the Home tab's Modeling panel, or enter **EXT**↵ at the Command prompt.

3. At the Select objects to extrude or [MOde]: prompt, pick the polyline you just turned on from the Taper layer and press ↵. If you have Selection Cycling on, pick the polyline option from the list that appears.

4. At the Specify height of extrusion or [Direction/Path/Taper angle/ Expression]: prompt, enter **T**↵.

5. At the Specify angle of taper for extrusion or [Expression] <0>: prompt, enter **4**↵.

6. At the Specify height of extrusion or [Direction/Path/Taper angle/ Expression]: prompt, enter **3**↵. The extruded polyline looks like Figure 22.8.

**FIGURE 22.8**
The extruded polyline

7. Join the part you just created with the original solid. Select the Solid, Union tool from the Home tab's Solid Editing panel or type **UNI**↵.

8. Select the extruded part and the composite solid just below it. Press ↵ to complete your selection.

In step 5, you can indicate a taper for the extrusion. Specify a taper in terms of degrees from the z-axis, or enter a negative value to taper the extrusion outward. You can also press ↵ to accept the default of 0 to extrude the polyline without a taper.

---

**THE *ISOLINE* SYSTEM VARIABLE**

You may have noticed the message that reads as follows:

```
Current wire frame density: ISOLINES=4
```

This message tells you the current setting for the Isolines system variable. This variable controls the way curved objects, such as cylinders and holes, are displayed. A setting of 4 causes a cylinder to be represented by four lines with a circle at each end. You can see this in the holes that you created for the Bracket model in the previous exercise. You can change the Isolines setting by entering **Isolines**↲ at the Command prompt. You then enter a value for the number of lines to use to represent surfaces. This setting is also controlled by the Contour Lines Per Surface option in the Display tab of the Options dialog box.

---

## Sweeping a Shape on a Curved Path

As you'll see in the following exercise, the Sweep command lets you extrude virtually any polyline shape along a path defined by a polyline, an arc, or a 3D polyline. At this point, you've created the components needed to do the extrusion. Next you'll finish the extruded shape:

**1.** Turn on the Path layer. This layer contains the circle you'll extrude and the polyline path, which looks like an *S*, as shown in Figure 22.9.

**FIGURE 22.9**
Hidden-line view showing parts of the drawing you'll use to create a curved extrusion

The polyline path          The circle you will extrude

**2.** Click the Sweep tool from the Extrude flyout in the Home tab's Modeling panel, or type **Sweep**↲. Click the circle, and then press ↲.

**3.** At the Select sweep path or [Alignment/Base point/Scale/Twist]: prompt, click the polyline curve.

**4.** AutoCAD generates a solid tube that follows the path. The tube may not look like a tube because AutoCAD draws extruded solids such as this with four lines while using the wire-frame visual style. You can change the number of lines shown with the Isolines system variable as discussed earlier.

**5.** Click the Solid, Subtract tool in the Home tab's Solid Editing panel, or type **SU**↵ and then select the composite solid.

**6.** Press ↵. At the `Select objects:` prompt, click the curved solid and press ↵. The curved solid is subtracted from the square solid, and your drawing looks like Figure 22.10.

**FIGURE 22.10**
The solid after subtracting the curve

In this exercise, you used a curved polyline for the extrusion path, but you can use any type of 2D or 3D polyline, as well as a line or arc, for an extrusion path.

## Revolving a Polyline

When your goal is to draw a circular object, you can use the Revolve command on the Modeling panel to create a solid that is *revolved*, or swept in a circular path. Think of Revolve's action as being similar to a lathe that lets you carve a shape from an object on a spinning shaft. In this case, the object is a polyline and, rather than carve it, you define the profile and then revolve the profile around an axis.

In the following exercise, you'll draw a solid that will form a slot in the tapered solid. We've already created a 2D polyline that is the profile of the slot. You'll simply use cut and paste to bring the polyline into the bracket drawing:

**1.** In the Visual Styles Control, select 2D Wireframe.

**2.** Zoom in to the top of the tapered box so that you have a view similar to Figure 22.11.

**3.** Turn on the Revolve layer. This layer contains a closed polyline that you'll use to create a cylindrical shape.

**4.** Select the Revolve tool from the Extrude flyout in the Home tab's Modeling panel, or type **REV**↵ at the Command prompt.

**5.** At the `Select objects to revolve or [MOde]:` prompt, pick the polyline on the top of the tapered surface and press ↵.

**FIGURE 22.11**
An enlarged view
of the top of the
tapered box and
pasted polyline

6. When you see the prompt

```
Specify axis start point or define axis by [Object/X/Y/Z] <Object>:
```

use the Endpoint osnap override and pick the beginning corner endpoint of the polyline you just added, as shown in Figure 22.11.

7. At the Specify axis endpoint: prompt, pick the axis endpoint indicated in Figure 22.11.

8. At the Specify angle of revolution or [STart angle/Reverse/EXpression] <360>: prompt, press ↵ to sweep the polyline a full 360°. The revolved form appears as shown in Figure 22.12.

**FIGURE 22.12**
The revolved
polyline

You just created a revolved solid that will be subtracted from the tapered box to form a slot in the bracket. However, before you subtract it, you need to make a slight change in the orientation of the revolved solid:

**1.** Click the 3D Rotate tool in the Modify panel, or type **3drotate**↵. You see the following prompt:

```
Current positive angle in UCS:  ANGDIR=counterclockwise  ANGBASE=0
Select objects:
```

**2.** Select the revolved solid, and press ↵.

**3.** At the Specify base point: prompt, use the Midpoint osnap and click the right side edge of the top surface as shown in Figure 22.13.

**FIGURE 22.13**
Selecting the points to rotate the revolved solid in 3D space

Select this edge of the top surface for the 3D Rotate base point.

Point to the green circle for the rotation axis.

When you see the axis line, click the circle.

Point the cursor along the x-axis for the angle start point.

**4.** At the Pick a rotation axis: prompt, point to the green rotation grip tool. When you see a green line appear along the y-axis, click.

**5.** At the Specify angle start point or type an angle: prompt, enter –5↵ for a minus 5 degrees rotation. The solid rotates 5° about the y-axis.

**6.** Click the Solid, Subtract tool in the Solid Editing panel, or type **SU**↵. Click the tapered box, and then press ↵.

**7.** At the Select objects: prompt, click the revolved solid and press ↵. Your drawing looks like Figure 22.14.

**FIGURE 22.14**

The composite solid

# Editing Solids

Basic solid forms are fairly easy to create. Refining those forms requires some special tools. In the following sections, you'll learn how to use familiar 2D editing tools, as well as some new tools, to edit a solid. But first you'll be shown the Slice tool, which lets you cut a solid into two pieces.

## Splitting a Solid into Two Pieces

One of the more common solid-editing tools you'll use is the Slice tool. As you may guess from its name, Slice enables you to cut a solid into two pieces. The following exercise demonstrates how it works:

1. Click the Zoom All option to get an overall view of your work so far.

2. Click the Slice tool in the Home tab's Solid Editing panel, or type **Slice**↵.

3. At the Select objects to slice: prompt, click the part you've been working on and press ↵.

   Alternatively, you could select more than one solid. The Slice command would then slice all the solids through the plane that you'll indicate in steps 4 and 5.

4. At the prompt

   ```
   Specify start point of slicing plane or
   [planar Object/Surface/Zaxis/View/XY/YZ/ZX/
   3points] <3points>:
   ```

   type **XY**↵. This lets you indicate a slice plane parallel to the XY plane.

5. At the Specify a point on the XY-plane <0,0,0>: prompt, type **0,0,0.5**↵. This places the slice plane at the z-coordinate of 0.5 units. You can also use the Midpoint osnap and

pick any vertical edge of the rectangular base of the solid. If you want to delete one side of the sliced solid, you can indicate the side you want to keep by clicking it in step 6 instead of entering **B⏎**.

6. At the Specify a point on desired side or [keep Both sides]: prompt, type **B⏎** to keep both sides of the solid. AutoCAD divides the solid horizontally, one-half unit above the base of the part, as shown in Figure 22.15.

**FIGURE 22.15**
The solid sliced
through the base

In step 4, you saw a number of options for the Slice command. You may want to take note of those options for future reference. Table 22.1 provides a list of the options and their purposes.

**TABLE 22.1:** Slice command options

| OPTION | PURPOSE |
| --- | --- |
| planar Object | Lets you select an object to define the slice plane. |
| Surface | Lets you select a surface object to define the shape of a slice. |
| Zaxis | Lets you select two points defining the z-axis of the slice plane. The two points you pick are perpendicular to the slice plane. |
| View | Generates a slice plane that is perpendicular to your current view. You're prompted for the coordinate through which the slice plane must pass—usually a point on the object. |
| XY/YZ/ZX | Pick one of these to determine the slice plane based on the x-, y-, or z-axis. You're prompted to pick a point through which the slice plane must pass. |
| 3points | The default setting; lets you select three points defining the slice plane. Normally, you pick points on the solid. |

## Rounding Corners with the Fillet Tool

Your bracket has a few sharp corners that you may want to round in order to give it a more realistic appearance. You can use the Modify panel's Fillet and Chamfer tools to add these rounded corners to your solid model:

1. Click the Fillet tool in the Home tab's Modify panel or type **F**↵.

2. At the `Select first object or [Undo/Polyline/Radius/Trim/Multiple]:` prompt, pick the edge indicated in the first image in Figure 22.16.

**FIGURE 22.16**
Filleting solids

3. At the `Enter fillet radius or [Expression] <0.5000>:` prompt, type **0.2**↵.

4. At the `Select an edge or [Chain/Loop/Radius]:` prompt, type **C**↵ for the Chain option. Chain lets you select a series of solid edges to be filleted.

5. Select one of the other seven edges at the base of the tapered form and press ↵.

6. Type **Hide**↵ to get a quick look at your model in a hidden line view, as shown in the second image in Figure 22.16.

As you saw in step 4, Fillet acts a bit differently when you use it on solids. The Chain option lets you select a set of edges instead of just two adjoining objects.

## Chamfering Corners with the Chamfer Tool

Now let's try chamfering a corner. To practice using Chamfer, you'll add a countersink to the cylindrical hole you created in the first solid:

1. Type **Regen.↵** to return to a Wireframe view of your model.

2. Click the Chamfer tool on the Modify panel (click the Fillet flyout if you don't see Chamfer; see Figure 22.17) or type **CHA↵**.

**FIGURE 22.17**
Click the
Chamfer tool.

Flyout arrowhead ⌐

3. At the prompt

   ```
   Select first line or
     [Undo/Polyline/Distance/Angle/Trim/mEthod/Multiple]:
   ```

   pick the edge of the hole, as shown in Figure 22.18. Notice that the top surface of the solid is highlighted and that the prompt changes to Enter surface selection option [Next/OK (current)] <OK>:. The highlighting indicates the base surface, which will be used as a reference in step 5. (You could also type **N↵** to choose the other adjoining surface, the inside of the hole, as the base surface.)

4. Press ↵ to accept the current highlighted face.

5. At the Specify base surface chamfer distance or [Expression] <0.1250>: prompt, type **0.125↵**. This indicates that you want the chamfer to have a width of 0.125 across the highlighted surface.

6. At the Specify other surface chamfer distance <0.2000>: prompt, type **0.2↵**.

7. At the Select an edge or [Loop]: prompt, click the top edges of both holes and then press ↵. When the Chamfer command has completed its work, your drawing looks like Figure 22.19.

8. After reviewing the work you've done here, save the bracket.dwg file.

The Loop option in step 7 lets you chamfer the entire circumference of an object. You don't need to use it here because the edge forms a circle. The Loop option is used when you have a rectangular or other polygonal edge you want to chamfer.

**FIGURE 22.18**
Picking the edge
to chamfer

Select the edge of this hole.

**FIGURE 22.19**
The chamfered
edges

## Using the Solid-Editing Tools

You've added some refinements to the Bracket model by using standard AutoCAD editing tools. There is a set of tools that is specifically geared toward editing solids. You already used the Union and Subtract tools found in the Solid Editing panel. In the following sections, you'll explore some of the other tools in that panel.

You don't have to perform the following exercises, but reviewing them will show you what's available. When you're more comfortable working in 3D, you may want to come back and experiment with the file called solidedit.dwg shown in the figures in the following sections.

---

### PARALLEL PROJECTION NEEDED FOR SOME FEATURES

Many of the features discussed in these sections work only in a parallel-projection view. You can switch to a parallel-projection view by choosing the 2D Wireframe visual style or, if you have the ViewCube® turned on, right-click it and select Parallel.

---

### FINDING TOOLS IN THE SOLID EDITING PANEL

Many of the tools in the Solid Editing panel are in flyouts. This makes it a bit difficult to describe their location because the default tool changes depending on the last flyout tool that was selected. To help you easily find the tools described in these sections, Figure 22.20 shows the flyouts in their open position with each tool labeled. You can use this figure for reference when you are ready to use a tool.

**FIGURE 22.20**

The flyouts in the Home tab's Solid Editing panel

### MOVING A SURFACE

You can move any flat surface of a 3D solid using the Move Faces tool from the Faces flyout on the Solid Editing panel. When you click this tool, you're prompted to select faces. Because you can select only the edge of two joining faces, you must select an edge and then use the Remove option to remove one of the two selected faces from the selection set (see Figure 22.21). After you've made your selection, press ↵. You can then specify a distance for the move.

**FIGURE 22.21**

To select the vertical surface to the far right of the model, click the edge and then use the Remove option to remove the top surface from the selection.

Click here to select a surface to move.

Click here to remove a surface from the selection set.

After you've selected the surface you want to move, the Move Faces tool acts just like the Move command: You select a base point and a displacement. Notice how the curved side of the model extends its curve to meet the new location of the surface. This shows you that AutoCAD attempts to maintain the geometry of the model when you make changes to the faces.

Move Faces also lets you move entire features, such as the hole in the model. In Figure 22.22, one of the holes has been moved so that it's no longer in line with the other three. This was done by selecting the countersink and the hole while using the Move Faces tool.

**FIGURE 22.22**
Selecting a surface
to offset

Click on the solid here.

If a solid's History setting is set to record, you can Ctrl+click on its surface to expose the surface's grip. You can then use the grip at the center of the surface to move the surface.

### OFFSETTING A SURFACE

Suppose you want to decrease the radius of the arc in the right corner of the model and you also want to thicken the model by the same amount as the decrease in the arc radius. To do this, you can use the Offset Faces tool. The Offset Faces tool and the Offset command you used earlier in this book perform similar functions. The difference is that the Offset Faces tool in the Faces flyout on the Solid Editing panel affects 3D solids.

When you select the Offset Faces tool from the Faces flyout on the Solid Editing panel, you're prompted to select faces. As with the Move tool, you must select an edge that will select two faces. If you want to offset only one face, you must use the Remove option to remove one of the faces. In Figure 22.22, an edge is selected. Figure 22.23 shows the effect of the Offset Faces tool when both faces are offset.

### DELETING A SURFACE

Now suppose you've decided to eliminate the curved part of the model. You can delete a surface by using the Delete Faces tool. Once again, you're prompted to select faces. Typically, you'll want to delete only one face, such as the curved surface in the example model. If you select more than one face to delete, use the remove option in the command to remove faces from your selection set.

When you attempt to delete surfaces, keep in mind that the surface you delete must be recoverable by other surfaces in the model. For example, you can't remove the top surface of a cube, expecting it to turn into a pyramid. That would require the sides to change their orientation, which isn't allowed in this operation. You can, on the other hand, remove the top of a box with tapered sides. Then, when you remove the top, the sides converge to form a pyramid.

**FIGURE 22.23**
The model after offsetting the curved and bottom surfaces

## ROTATING A SURFACE

All the surfaces of the model are parallel or perpendicular to each other. Imagine that your design requires two sides to be at an angle. You can change the angle of a surface by using the Rotate Faces tool.

As with the prior solid-editing tools, you're prompted to select faces. You must then specify an axis of rotation. You can either select a point or use the default of selecting two points to define an axis of rotation, as shown in Figure 22.24. Once the axis is determined, you can specify a rotation angle. Figure 22.25 shows the result of rotating the two front-facing surfaces 4°.

**FIGURE 22.24**
Defining the axis of rotation

First select this edge.

Then select this bottom corner.

Finally select this top corner.

## TAPERING A SURFACE

In an earlier exercise, you saw how to create a new tapered solid by using the Extrude command. But what if you want to taper an existing solid? Here's what you can do.

The Taper Faces tool from the Faces flyout on the Solid Editing panel prompts you to select faces. You can select faces, as described for the previously discussed solid-editing tools, using the Remove or Add option (see Figure 22.26). Press ↵ when you finish your selection, and then indicate the axis from which the taper is to occur. In the model example in Figure 22.26, select two corners defining a vertical axis. Finally, enter the taper angle. Figure 22.27 shows the model tapered at a 4° angle.

**FIGURE 22.25**

The model after rotating two surfaces

### EXTRUDING A SURFACE

You've used the Extrude tool to create two of the solids in the Bracket model. The Extrude tool requires a closed polyline as a basis for the extrusion. As an alternative, the Solid Editing panel offers the Extrude Faces tool, which extrudes a surface of an existing solid.

When you select the Extrude Faces tool from the Faces flyout on the Solid Editing panel or type **Solidedit↵F↵E↵**, you see the `Select faces or [Undo/Remove]:` prompt. Select an edge or a set of edges or use the Remove or Add option to select the faces you want to extrude. Press ↵ when you've finished your selection, and then specify a height and taper angle. Figure 22.28 shows the sample model with the front surface extruded and tapered at a 45° angle. You can extrude multiple surfaces simultaneously if you need to by selecting them.

Aside from those features, the Extrude Faces tool works just like the Extrude command.

**FIGURE 22.26**

Selecting the surfaces to taper and indicating the direction of the taper

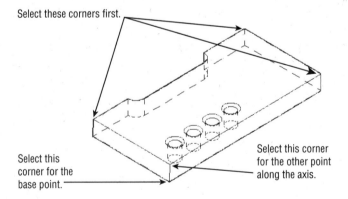

Select these corners first.

Select this corner for the base point.

Select this corner for the other point along the axis.

### TURNING A SOLID INTO A SHELL

In many situations, you'll want your 3D model to be a hollow mass rather than a solid mass. The Shell tool lets you convert a solid into a shell.

**FIGURE 22.27**
The model after
tapering the sides

**FIGURE 22.28**
The model with a
surface extruded
and tapered

When you select the Shell tool from the Separate/Clean/Shell/Check flyout on the Solid Editing panel or type **Solidedit↵B↵S↵**, you're prompted to select a 3D solid. You're then prompted to remove faces. At this point, you can select an edge of the solid to indicate the surface you want removed. The surface you select is completely removed from the model, exposing the interior of the shell. For example, if you select the front edge of the sample model shown in Figure 22.29, the top and front surfaces are removed from the model, revealing the interior of the solid, as shown in Figure 22.30. After selecting the surfaces to remove, you can enter a shell offset distance.

**FIGURE 22.29**
Selecting the edge
to be removed

Select this edge.

The shell thickness is added to the outside surface of the solid. When you're constructing your solid with the intention of creating a shell, you need to take this into account.

**FIGURE 22.30**
The solid model
after using the
Shell tool

### Copying Faces and Edges

At times, you may want to create a copy of a surface of a solid to analyze its area or to produce another part that mates to that surface. The Copy Faces tool (found in the Extrude Faces flyout) creates a copy of any surface on your model. The copy it produces is a type of object called a *region*.

The copies of the surfaces are opaque and can hide objects behind them when you perform a hidden-line removal (type **Hide↵**).

Another tool that is similar to Copy Faces is Copy Edges (found in the Extract Edges flyout). Instead of selecting surfaces as in the Copy Faces tool, you select all the edges you want to copy. The result is a series of simple lines representing the edges of your model. This tool can be useful if you want to convert a solid into a set of 3D faces. The Copy Edges tool creates a framework onto which you can add 3D faces.

### Adding Surface Features

If you need to add a feature to a flat surface, you can do so with the Imprint tool. An added surface feature can then be colored using the Color Faces tool or extruded using the Presspull tool. This feature is a little more complicated than some of the other solid-editing tools, so you may want to try the following exercise to see firsthand how it works.

You'll start by inserting an object that will be the source of the imprint. You'll then imprint the main solid model with the object's profile:

1. Back in the saved bracket.dwg, click the Insert tool in the Insert tab's Block panel; then click More Options to open the Insert dialog box, or type **I↵**.

2. Click Browse, and then locate the imprint.dwg sample file and select it.

3. In the Insert dialog box, make sure the Explode check box is selected and remove the check mark from the Specify On-Screen check box in the Insertion Point group.

4. Click OK. The block appears in the middle of the solid.

5. Select the Imprint tool from the Edges flyout on the Home tab's Solid Editing panel or type **Imprint↵**.

6. Click the main solid model.

7. Click the inserted solid.

8. At the `Delete the source object [Yes/No]<N>:` prompt, enter **Y↵↵**.

You now have an outline of the intersection between the two solids imprinted on the top surface of your model. The imprint is really a set of edges that have been added to the surface of the solid. To help the imprint stand out, try the following steps to change its color:

1. Click the Color Faces tool from the Edges flyout on the Solid Editing panel, or type **Solidedit↵F↵L↵**.

2. Click the imprint from the previous exercise. The imprint and the entire top surface are highlighted.

3. At the `Select faces or [Undo/Remove/ALL]:` prompt, type **R↵**; then click the outer edge of the top surface to remove it from the selection set.

4. Press ↵ to open the Select Color dialog box.

5. Click the red color sample in the dialog box, and then click OK. The imprint is now red.

6. Press ↵ twice to exit the command.

7. To see the full effect of the Color Faces tool, choose the Conceptual or Realistic visual style from the Visual Styles Control in the drawing screen.

If you want to remove an imprint from a surface, Ctrl+click the imprint and press the Delete key.

## SEPARATING A DIVIDED SOLID

While editing solids, you can end up with two separate solid forms that were created from one solid, as shown in Figure 22.31. Even though the two solids appear separated, they act like a single object. In these situations, AutoCAD offers the Separate tool from the Separate/Clean/Shell/Check flyout on the Solid Editing panel. To use it, click the Separate tool or type **Solidedit↵B↵P↵** and select the solid that has been separated into two forms.

Figure 22.31 is included in the sample files under the name `Separate example.dwg`. You can try the Separate tool in this file on your own.

**FIGURE 22.31**
When the tall, thin solid is subtracted from the larger solid, the result is two separate forms, yet they still behave as a single object.

Subtract the tall, thin solid from the flat solid.

The result is two forms that act like a single object when selected.

Separate will separate the two forms into two distinct solids.

Through some simple examples, you've seen how each of the solid-editing tools works. You aren't limited to using these tools in the way they were demonstrated in this chapter, and this book can't anticipate every situation you might encounter as you create solid models. These examples are intended as an introduction to these tools, so feel free to experiment with them. You can always use the Undo option to backtrack in case you don't get the results you expect.

This concludes your tour of the Solid Editing panel. Next you'll learn how to use 3D solid models to generate 2D working drawings quickly.

### FINDING THE PROPERTIES OF A SOLID

All this effort to create a solid model isn't designed just to create a pretty picture. After your model is drawn and built, you can obtain information about its physical properties.

You can find the volume, the moment of inertia, and other physical properties of your model by using the Massprop command. These properties can also be recorded as a file on disk, so you can modify your model without worrying about losing track of its original properties.

To find the mass properties of a solid, enter **Massprop**↵, and then follow the prompts. AutoCAD LT users can use the Massprop command described here to find the properties of solids that are part of an existing drawing.

### USING THE COMMAND LINE FOR SOLID EDITING

The solid-editing tools are options of a single AutoCAD command called Solidedit. If you prefer to use the keyboard, here are some tips on using the Solidedit command. When you first enter **Solidedit**↵ at the Command prompt, you see the following prompt:

```
Enter a solids editing option [Face/Edge/Body/Undo/eXit] <eXit>:
```

You can select the Face, Edge, or Body option to edit the various parts of a solid. If you select Face, you see the following prompt:

```
[Extrude/Move/Rotate/Offset/Taper/Delete/Copy/coLor/mAterial/Undo/eXit] <eXit>:
```

The options from this prompt produce the same results as their counterparts on the Solid Editing panel.

If you select Edge at the first prompt, you see the following prompt:

```
Enter an edge editing option [Copy/coLor/Undo/eXit] <eXit>:
```

The Copy option lets you copy a surface, and the coLor option lets you add color to a surface.

If you select Body from the first prompt, you see the following prompt:

```
[Imprint/seParate solids/Shell/cLean/Check/Undo/eXit] <eXit>:
```

These options also perform the same functions as their counterparts on the Solid Editing panel. As you work with this command, you can use the Undo option to undo the last Solidedit option you used without exiting the command.

# Streamlining the 2D Drawing Process

CERT
OBJECTIVE

Using solids to model a part—such as with the bracket and Solidedit examples in this chapter—may seem a bit exotic, but there are definite advantages to modeling in 3D, even if you only want to show the part in 2D as a page in a set of manufacturing specs.

The exercises in the following sections show you how to generate a typical mechanical drawing from your 3D model quickly by using paper space and the Solid Editing panel. You'll also examine techniques for dimensioning and including hidden lines.

---

### ARCHITECTURAL ELEVATIONS FROM 3D SOLIDS

If your application is architectural and you've created a 3D model of a building by using solids, you can use the tools described in the following sections to generate 2D elevation drawings from your 3D solid model.

We've used solid models in the past to generate 2D line drawings of elevations. Such line drawings can be "rendered" in a 2D drawing program like Adobe Photoshop or Illustrator. Be aware that such drawings will not be as accurate as those drawn from scratch, but they are fine for the early stages of a design project.

---

## Drawing Standard Top, Front, and Right-Side Views

One of the more common types of mechanical drawings is the *orthogonal projection*. This style of drawing shows separate top, front, and right-side views of an object. Sometimes a 3D image is added for clarity. You can derive such a drawing in a few minutes using the Flatshot tool described in Chapter 20, "Creating 3D Drawings" (see "Turning a 3D View into a 2D AutoCAD Drawing" in that chapter).

With Flatshot, you can generate the standard top, front, and right-side orthogonal projection views, which you can further enhance with dimensions, hatch patterns, and other 2D drawing features. Follow these steps:

1. In the bracket.dwg file, open the 3D Navigation drop-down list in the View Controls, and then click on an orthogonal projection view from the list, such as Top, Left, or Right (see Figure 22.32). You can also use the 3D Navigation flyout in the Visualize tab's Views panel or use the ViewCube to select an orthogonal view. See Chapter 20 for more on the ViewCube.

2. Click the Flatshot tool on the Home tab's expanded Section panel, or type **Flatshot**↵.

3. In the Flatshot dialog box, select the options you want and click Create (see Figure 22.33). See Table 20.1 in Chapter 20 for the Flatshot options.

If you select Insert As New Block in the Flatshot dialog box, you're prompted to select an insertion point to insert the block that is the 2D orthogonal view of your model. By default, the view is placed in the same plane as your current view, as shown in Figure 22.34. After you've created all your views, you can move them to a different location in your drawing so that you can create a set of layout views to your 2D orthogonal views, as shown in Figure 22.35. You can also place the orthogonal view blocks on a separate layer and then, for each layout viewport, freeze the layer of the 3D model so that only the 2D views are displayed.

**FIGURE 22.32**
The 3D Navigation
drop-down list

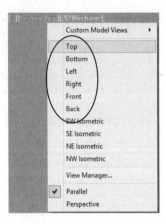

---

**SET UP STANDARD VIEWS IN A LAYOUT VIEWPORT**

To set up a layout viewport to display a view, like a top or right-side view of a 3D model, select a view from the 3D Navigation drop-down list in the Home tab's View panel and then click on the viewport border. To set the scale of a viewport, click the viewport border and then select a scale from the VP Scale drop-down list on the status bar. If you'd like to refresh your memory on layouts in general, refer to Chapter 15, "Laying Out Your Printer Output."

---

**FIGURE 22.33**
The Flatshot
dialog box

If your model changes and you need to update the orthogonal views, you can repeat the steps listed here. However, instead of selecting Insert As New Block in the Flatshot dialog box, select Replace Existing Block to update the original orthogonal view blocks. If you want, you can include an isometric view to help communicate your design more clearly.

## Creating 2D Drawings with the Base View Command

You saw how 2D views of a 3D model can be made using the Flatshot command. The Base View command also creates 2D views, but in a different way. Follow these steps for a demonstration:

1. In the bracket.dwg file, go to paper space and activate the Layout tab in the Ribbon (see Figure 22.36). The Create View panel contains the Base View command.

2. Start the Base command and choose the From Model Space option.

   You can also import an Autodesk® Inventor® file if you have one available.

**FIGURE 22.34**
The 2D orthogonal views shown in relation to the 3D model

3. A preview of your model will be shown. Pick a place in your drawing to insert your first view.

   If you aren't happy with the location, you can always move the view later with the Move command or by using the move grip edit. Views are objects that can be moved, deleted, and so on, just like any other object.

4. When the view is placed, you have several options (see Figure 22.37). You can control the orientation and set the visibility of hidden lines and the scale of the view. The visibility setting provides further control of how your model's edges will be displayed. When all is set, click Exit.

**FIGURE 22.35**
You can use a layout
to arrange a set of
views created by
Flatshot. Dimen-
sions, notes, and a
title block can be
added to complete
the layout.

**FIGURE 22.36**
The Base View com-
mand in the Layout
tab of the Ribbon

**FIGURE 22.37**
After you place the
parent base view,
this menu displays
the options you
can set.

The Base View command is still running and is ready for you to insert additional views.

**5.** Move the cursor around the first view you inserted. The appropriate views—left, right, and isometric views—will be previewed, as shown in Figure 22.38. When you have inserted all of the views you want, press Enter.

You can now perform basic manipulations on the inserted views. Specifically, you can add or remove views at any time. Any view can be selected. The grip control lets you quickly change to a view's scale. Each child view inherits the Scale setting, as well as all other settings, from the parent (or first) view. You can change each view's settings independently of each other or leave them the way they are.

**FIGURE 22.38**
The Base View command can quickly create projection views of your 3D model.

To change the settings on your views, select one. This will activate a contextual Ribbon tab called Drawing View (Figure 22.39), bringing up the tools you need to edit your selected view. Use the Projected command to create new projections from the selected view. The Section command will create a cross-section view. Detail will create a detail view. Edit View allows you to make changes to the hidden lines, scale, and visibility settings.

**FIGURE 22.39**
Selecting a view will activate the contextual Drawing View Ribbon tab.

## CREATING SECTION VIEWS

The Section command can create several types of cross sections, but they all work in a similar way. You can create full, half, offset, or aligned sections. You can also create a section based on an object. The Section button in the Ribbon has a flyout that will display these commands, but you can always just click the Section command itself (see Figure 22.40). This will start the Aligned Section command, which should fill most of your needs:

1. Click the Section command and select a view. In drafting, a cross section is defined by the section callout arrows. Cross sections in the Section command work the same way.

2. Pick a place for your first section arrow, and then pick the second. This creates the section plane. These arrows can always be changed, and the section will then automatically update itself to reflect the new section arrow placement.

3. Continue to add more points in your section plane if you want.

4. After you have picked all of the points needed, press Enter and pick a direction for the arrows to point. You will also see a preview of what the section will look like.

**FIGURE 22.40**

Select the Section command or choose a specific type of section to create.

A section has display settings similar to those for the base views but with a few more elements you have to define. Two of the more obvious additional items are the label and the hatching. The Annotation setting controls the label and callouts. The first section of a drawing is typically labeled as A-A. As you insert new sections, AutoCAD will continue down the alphabet automatically for you. The second section created will be labeled B, then C, and so on. Of course, you can change any of these at any time.

As illustrated in Figure 22.41, the section will be labeled. It will be called Section and will display the scale. These items are text fields and can be changed too, or you can turn them off. The label is an Mtext object and can be manipulated just as any other text object. Double-click the label to open the text editor. The hatching in the section is a hatch object and can be edited with the hatch editor. It, too, can be turned off.

To change the display features of the section, you can click the Edit View command in the Ribbon and select the section view. (In fact, you can use the Edit View command to make changes to any type of view that you have created.) A contextual Ribbon tab appears. You can change how the section is displayed in the Appearance panel, change the method by which the section is generated in the Method panel, alter the label in the Annotation panel, and toggle the hatch on or off in the Hatch panel.

You can create section styles, similar to dimension styles, by typing **viewsectionstyle** at the command line. If you have worked with dimension styles, discussed in Chapter 11, "Using Dimensions," the following process will be second nature:

1. In the Section View Style Manager dialog box, click the New button.

2. Name your new style, and then click Continue to open the New Section View Style dialog box.

3. The first tab, Identifiers And Arrows, lets you specify the appearance and placement of the section identifiers and arrowheads. Select the text style, color, and size of your identifiers.

   You can make similar adjustments to the arrowheads. Change the type of symbol, its size, color, and so on.

4. Select the Arrangement tab and specify how the identifiers are positioned and aligned.

   The remaining tabs allow you to define the section cutting plane lines and end lines (linetype, color), the view label content and appearance, and the hatch settings. You can create styles that have different labels, use different arrowheads, or have different hatch patterns.

**FIGURE 22.41**
Section views are edited in the same way as all other view types. They also contain hatch objects and annotation labels.

## CREATING DETAIL VIEWS

The Detail command, located in the Create View panel in the Layout tab in the Ribbon, creates an enlarged detail view, either circular or rectangular, of a specific area of your model. Follow these steps:

1. To choose which type of detail view you want to create, use the Arrow command's pull-down menu. If you click the Detail button, the command will default to the detail type last used.

2. Select the view you want to display, and then define the area you want detailed.

3. Pick a center point for the detail and then pick an outer edge.

4. A preview of the detail appears and prompts you to select a location. Click where you want the detail placed.

Detail views have settings similar to the settings for the other views, with a few that are unique. Figure 22.42 illustrates the detail view contextual Ribbon tab. The Boundary setting controls whether the detail is a rectangle or circle. The Model Edge setting controls the boundary around the detail; it can be jagged, smooth, smooth with a border, or smooth with a connection line. The remaining settings are the same as for other view types. Views typically inherit the scale from the parent view. Detail views will be "zoomed in" so you can see the details more clearly.

**FIGURE 22.42**
While you're creating a detail view, a contextual Ribbon appears that will provide access to the detail view settings.

When you have created your views (see Figure 22.43 for a finished set of views), you can always remove them or add more. If the model changes, you can update the views by using the Update View command in the Update panel of the Layout tab. Toggle on the Auto Update setting (also in the Update panel), and whenever the model is changed, the views will automatically update.

**FIGURE 22.43**
The Base View command along with the section and detail views can make creating 2D drawings from a 3D model a simple and quick process.

## Adding Dimensions and Notes in a Layout

Although we don't recommend adding dimensions in paper space for architectural drawings, doing so may be a good idea for mechanical drawings such as the one in this chapter. By maintaining the dimensions and notes separate from the actual model, you keep these elements from getting in the way of your work on the solid model. You also avoid the confusion of having to scale the text and dimension features properly to ensure that they will plot at the correct size. See Chapter 9, "Adding Text to Drawings," and Chapter 11 for a more detailed discussion of notes and dimensions.

As long as you set up your paper space work area to be equivalent to the final plot size, you can set the dimension and text to the sizes you want at plot time. If you want text ¼" high, you set your text styles to be ¼" high.

To include dimensions, make sure you're in a layout view and then use the dimension commands in the normal way. However, you must make sure full associative dimensioning is turned on. Choose Options from the Application menu to open the Options dialog box, and then click the User Preferences tab. In the Associative Dimensioning group, make sure the Make New Dimensions Associative check box is selected. With associative dimensioning turned on, dimensions in a layout view display the true dimension of the object being dimensioned regardless of the scale setting of the viewport.

If you don't have the associative dimensioning option turned on and your viewports are set to a scale other than 1 to 1, you have another option: You can set the Annotation Units option in the Dimension Style dialog box to a proper value. The following steps show you how:

1. Back in the `bracket.dwg` drawing, select the Model tool in the status bar, and then select the Annotate tab in the ribbon ➤ Dimensions Panel ➤ Dimension Style to open the Dimension Style Manager.

2. Make sure you've selected the style you want to use, and then click Modify to open the Modify Dimension Style dialog box.

3. Click the Primary Units tab.

4. In the Scale Factor box in the Measurement Scale group, enter the value by which you want your paper space dimensions multiplied. For example, if your paper space views are scaled at one-half the actual size of your model, enter **2** in this box to multiply your dimensions' values by 2.

5. Click the Apply To Layout Dimensions Only check box. This ensures that your dimension is scaled only while you're adding dimensions in paper space. Dimensions added in model space aren't affected.

6. Click OK to close the Modify Dimension Style dialog box, and then click Close in the Dimension Style Manager.

You've had to complete a lot of steps to get the final drawing, but compared with drawing these views by hand, you undoubtedly saved a great deal of time. In addition, as you'll see later in this chapter, what you have is more than just a 2D drafted image. With what you created, further refinements are now easy.

## Using Visual Styles with a Viewport

In Chapter 20, you saw how you can view your 3D model using visual styles. A visual style can give you a more realistic representation of your 3D model, and it can show off more of the details, especially on rounded surfaces. You can also view and plot a visual style in a layout view. To do so, you make a viewport active and then turn on the visual style you want to use for that viewport. The following exercise gives you a firsthand look at how this is done:

1. Continuing in the `bracket.dwg` drawing, click the Layout1 Paper Space tab at the bottom of the screen.

2. Double-click inside the viewport with the isometric view of the model to switch to Floating Model Space.

3. Select Conceptual from the Visual Styles drop-down list in the Visualize tab's Visual Styles panel or the Home tab's View panel (see Figure 22.44).

   The view may appear a bit dark because of the black color setting for the object. You can change the color to a lighter one, such as cyan or blue, to get a better look.

4. Double-click outside the isometric viewport to return to paper space.

**FIGURE 22.44**
The Visual Styles panel and the View panel

If you have multiple viewports in a layout, you can change the visual style of one viewport without affecting the other viewports. This can help others visualize your 3D model more clearly.

You'll also want to know how to control the hard-copy output of a shaded view. For this you use the context menu:

1. Click the isometric view's viewport border to select it.

2. Right-click to open the context menu, and select the Shade Plot option to display a set of Shade Plot options (see Figure 22.45).

3. Take a moment to study the menu, and then click As Displayed.

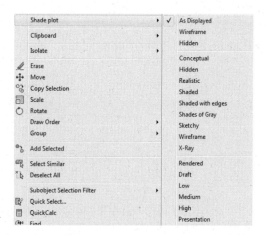

**FIGURE 22.45**
The Shade Plot options

The As Displayed option plots the viewport as it appears in the AutoCAD window. You use this option to plot the currently displayed visual style. Wireframe plots the viewport as a Wireframe view. Hidden plots the viewport as a hidden-line view similar to the view you see when you use the Hide command. Below the Hidden option in the context menu is a list of the available visual styles. At the bottom of the menu is the Rendered option, which plots the view by using the Render feature, described in the online bonus chapter "Rendering 3D Drawings," available at www.omura.com/chapters. You can use the Rendered option to plot raytraced renderings of your 3D models.

Remember these options on the context menu as you work on your drawings and when you plot. They can be helpful in communicating your ideas, but they can also get lost in the array of tools that AutoCAD offers.

## Visualizing Solids

If you're designing a complex object, sometimes it helps to be able to see it in ways that you couldn't in the real world. AutoCAD offers two visualization tools that can help others understand your design ideas.

If you want to show off the internal workings of a part or an assembly, you can use X-Ray Effect, which you can find in the Visualize tab's Visual Styles panel.

Figure 22.46 shows an isometric view of the bracket using the Realistic visual style and with X-Ray Effect turned on. The color of the bracket has also been changed to a light gray to help visibility. You can see the internal elements as if the object were semitransparent. X-Ray Effect works with any visual style, although it works best with a style that shows some of the surface features (such as the Conceptual or Realistic visual style).

Another tool to help you visualize the internal workings of a design is the Section Plane command. This command creates a plane that defines the location of a cross section. A section plane can also do more than just show a cross section. Try the following exercise to see how it works:

1. In the bracket.dwg file, click the Model tab at the bottom of the drawing area and then change the color of layer 0 to a light gray so that you can see the bracket more clearly when using the Realistic visual style.

2. Select Realistic from the Visual Styles Control drop-down list in the drawing screen.

**FIGURE 22.46**
The bracket displayed using a Realistic visual style and X-Ray Effect

3. Make sure the Object Snap and Object Snap Tracking tools are turned off in the status bar. This will allow you to point to surfaces on the model while using the Sectionplane command.

4. Adjust your view so that it looks similar to Figure 22.47.

**FIGURE 22.47**
Adding the section plane to your bracket

5. In the Home tab's Section panel, click the Section Plane tool. You can also enter **sectionplane**↵ at the Command prompt. You'll see the following prompt:

```
Select face or any point to locate
section line or [Draw section/Orthographic]:
```

6. Select the front face of the bracket to place the section plane as shown in Figure 22.47. A plane appears on that surface.

You can move the section plane object along the solid to get a real-time view of the section it traverses. To do this, you need to turn on the Live Section feature. To check whether Live Section is turned on, do the following:

1. Click the section plane, and then right-click. If you see a check mark by the Activate Live Sectioning option, then you know it's on. If you don't see a check mark, then choose Activate Live Sectioning to turn it on.

2. Click the red axis on the gizmo, as shown in Figure 22.48. The axis turns yellow to indicate that it is active and you see a red vector appear.

**FIGURE 22.48**

Moving the surface plane across the bracket

Click this arrow.

3. Move the cursor slowly toward the back of the bracket. As you do this, the bracket becomes lighter in the foreground.

4. When the section plane is roughly in the middle of the tapered portion of the bracket, click to fix the plane in place. You should have a view similar to Figure 22.49.

Now you see only a portion of the bracket behind the section plane plus the cross section of the plane, as shown in Figure 22.49. You can have the section plane display the front portion as a ghosted image by doing the following:

1. With the section plane selected (you should still see its Move gizmo), right-click and choose Show Cut-Away Geometry. The front portion of the bracket appears (see Figure 22.50).

2. Press the Esc key to end the command. The section plane and the cut-away geometry remain in view.

You can double-click on the section plane to toggle between a solid view and a cut-away view of the geometry. This toggles the Active Live Sectioning option.

You can also add a jog in the section plane to create a more complex section cut. Here's how it's done:

1. Select the section plane, right-click, and select Show Cut-Away Geometry to turn this feature off. There should be no check mark by this feature name in the menu. This is necessary in order to gain access to the section plane Jog features.

2. Right-click, and choose Add Jog To Section.

3. At the `Specify a point on the section line to add jog:` prompt, use the Nearest object snap to select a point on the section plane line (see Figure 22.51).

**4.** Click the grip on the back portion of the section plane, as shown in the center image of Figure 22.51, and drag it toward the right so that the jog looks similar to the third panel in the figure.

**5.** Press the Esc key to end the command.

**FIGURE 22.49**
The surface plane fixed at a location

**FIGURE 22.50**
The front portion of the bracket is displayed with the Show Cut-Away Geometry option turned on.

As you can see from this example, you can adjust the section using the grips on the section plane line. You can use the Nearest osnap to select a point anywhere along the section line to a jog. Click and drag the endpoint grips to rotate the section plane to an angle.

You may have also noticed another arrow in the section plane (see Figure 22.52).

When you click the down-pointing arrow, you see three options for visualizing the section boundary: Section Plane, Section Boundary, and Section Volume.

By using these other settings, you can start to include sections through the sides, back, top, or bottom of the solid. For example, if you click the Section Boundary option, another boundary line appears with grips (see Figure 22.53). To see it clearly, you may have to press Esc and then select the section plane again. You can then manipulate these grips to show section cuts along those boundaries.

**FIGURE 22.51**

Moving the jog in the section plane

Use the Nearest osnap, and click the section line here to create the jog.

Click this grip to move the back portion of the section plane.

Move the plane to this location.

The Section Volume option displays the boundary of a volume along with grips at the top and bottom of the volume (see Figure 22.54). These grips allow you to create a cut plane from the top or bottom of the solid.

Finally, you can get a copy of the solid that is behind or in front of the section plane. Right-click the section plane and choose Generate 2D/3D Section to open the Generate Section/Elevation dialog box. Click the Show Details button to expand the dialog box and display more options (see Figure 22.55).

If you select 2D Section/Elevation, a 2D image of the section plane is inserted in the drawing in a manner similar to the insertion of a block. You're asked for an insertion point, an X and Y scale, and a rotation angle.

The 3D Section option creates a copy of the portion of the solid that is bounded by the section plane or planes, as shown in Figure 22.56.

**FIGURE 22.52**
The arrow presents additional options for the section plane.

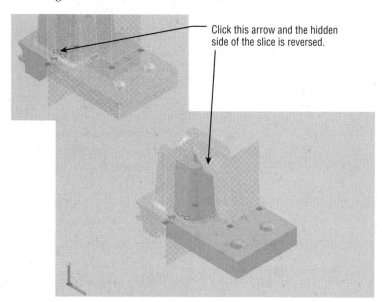

Click this arrow and the hidden side of the slice is reversed.

**FIGURE 22.53**
Another boundary line appears with grips when you click the Section Boundary option.

**USING A SECTION PLANE IN AN ARCHITECTURAL MODEL**

If your application is architectural, you can use a section plane and the 2D Section/Elevation option to get an accurate elevation drawing. Instead of placing the section plane inside the solid, move it away from the solid model and use the 2D Section/Elevation context menu option.

**FIGURE 22.54**
The boundaries shown using the Section Volume option

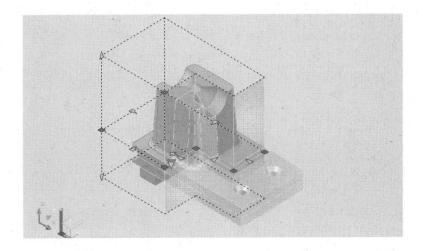

**FIGURE 22.55**
The Generate Section/Elevation dialog box.

Click this button to expand the dialog box

You can access more detailed settings for the 2D Section/Elevation, 3D Section, and Live Section Settings options by clicking the Section Settings button at the bottom of the Generate Section/Elevation dialog box. This button opens the Section Settings dialog box (see Figure 22.57), which lists the settings for the section feature.

**FIGURE 22.56**
A copy of the solid minus the section area is created using the 3D Section option of the Generate Section/Elevation dialog box.

**FIGURE 22.57**
The Section Settings dialog box

If you create a set of orthogonal views in a layout, the work you do to find a section is also reflected in the layout views (see Figure 22.58).

## TAKING ADVANTAGE OF STEREOLITHOGRAPHY

A discussion of solid modeling wouldn't be complete without mentioning stereolithography. This is one of the most interesting technological wonders that has appeared as a by-product of 3D computer modeling. *Stereolithography* is a process that generates physical reproductions of 3D computer solid models. Special equipment converts your AutoCAD-generated files into a physical model.

This process offers the mechanical designer a method for rapidly prototyping designs directly from AutoCAD drawings, though applications don't have to be limited to mechanical design. Architects can take advantage of this process too. This author's interest in Tibetan art led him to create a 3D AutoCAD model of a type of statue called a Zola, shown here. He sent this model to a service to have it reproduced in resin.

AutoCAD supports stereolithography through the 3dprint and Stlout commands. These commands generate an STL file, which can be used with a *Stereolithography Apparatus (SLA)* to generate a model. You must first create a 3D solid model in AutoCAD. Then you can use the Export Data dialog box to export your drawing in the STL format. Choose Export To Another File Format from the Application menu, and make sure the Files Of Type drop-down list shows Lithography (*.stl) before you click the Save button. You can also choose Send To 3D Print Service from the Output tab's 3D Print panel.

The AutoCAD 3D solids are translated into a set of triangular-faceted meshes in the STL file. You can use the Rendered Object Smoothness setting in the Display tab of the Options dialog box to control the fineness of these meshes. See Chapter 23, "Exploring 3D Mesh and Surface Modeling," for more information on this setting.

When you use Send To 3D Print Service, which can also be found in the Application menu's Publish options, you will see a message box asking if you want to learn more about preparing a 3D model for printing. If you are unfamiliar with stereolithography and 3D printing, it is a good idea to select the Learn About Preparing A 3D Model For Printing option so that you don't make some of the common mistakes.

**FIGURE 22.58**
A set of orthogonal
views in a layout

# The Bottom Line

**Understand solid modeling.** Solid modeling lets you build 3D models by creating and joining 3D shapes called solids. There are several built-in solid shapes called primitives, and you can create others using the Extrude tool.

**Master It** Name some of the built-in solid primitives available in AutoCAD.

**Create solid forms.** You can use Boolean operations to sculpt 3D solids into the shape you want. Two solids can be joined to form a more complex one, or you can remove one solid from another.

**Master It** Name the three Boolean operations you can use on solids.

**Create complex solids.** Besides the primitives, you can create your own shapes based on 2D polylines.

**Master It** Name three tools that let you convert closed polylines and circles into 3D solids.

**Edit solids.** After you've created a solid, you can make changes to it using the solid-editing tools offered on the Solid Editing panel.

**Master It** Name at least four of the tools found on the Solid Editing panel.

**Streamline the 2D drawing process.** You can create 3D orthogonal views of your 3D model to create standard 2D mechanical drawings.

**Master It** What is the name of the tool in the expanded Section panel that lets you create a 2D drawing of a 3D model?

**Visualize solids.** In addition to viewing your 3D model in a number of different orientations, you can view it as if it were transparent or cut in half.

**Master It** What is the name of the command that lets you create a cut view of your 3D model?

# Chapter 23

# Exploring 3D Mesh and Surface Modeling

Autodesk® AutoCAD® software has always offered tools that allow users to construct fairly complex 3D models. With the introduction of the latest solid modeling tools, you can even model some very organic forms. But some forms require a type of modeling known as *mesh modeling*. Mesh modeling lets you create smooth, curved volumes by manipulating faces that make up an object's surface.

With mesh modeling, you can quickly create curved shapes that are difficult or even impossible to create by other means. With AutoCAD you can also convert a mesh model into a 3D solid so that you can perform Boolean operations.

In addition, AutoCAD has a set of 3D surface modeling tools that extend its ability to produce and edit curved, organic forms. In this chapter, you'll get a chance to explore many of the current features of mesh modeling through a series of exercises, and you'll be introduced to the surface modeling tools. You'll also learn how you can convert a mesh or 3D surface into a solid. You'll start by creating a simple shape as an introduction, and then you'll move on to a more complex form.

In this chapter, you will learn to

♦ Create a simple 3D mesh

♦ Edit faces and edges

♦ Create mesh surfaces

♦ Convert meshes to solids

♦ Understand 3D surfaces

♦ Edit 3D surfaces

## Creating a Simple 3D Mesh

As an introduction to the mesh modeling features in AutoCAD, you'll draw a simple box and then smooth the box. This first exercise will show you some of the basic mesh modeling tools and what types of control you can exert on a model.

First, you'll make sure you are in the 3D Modeling workspace and that you have a blank drawing set up for the mesh. Follow these steps:

1. Click the New tool on the Quick Access toolbar.

2. In the Select Template dialog box, select the acad3D.dwt template and then click Open.

3. Click the Workspace pop-up list in the status bar and select 3D Modeling, as shown in Figure 23.1.

**FIGURE 23.1**
The 3D Modeling workspace

4. Choose the Shaded With Edges visual style from the Visual Styles drop-down list on the drawing screen. This will give you a close approximation of the appearance of the meshes you'll see in the illustrations in this book.

## Creating a Mesh Primitive

Meshes are similar to solids in that they start from a *primitive*. You may recall that 3D solid primitives are predetermined shapes from which you can form more complex shapes. The mesh primitives are similar to the 3D solid primitives you learned about in Chapter 20, "Creating 3D Drawings," and Chapter 22, "Editing and Visualizing 3D Solids." You can see the different mesh primitives that are available by clicking the Mesh flyout in the Primitives panel (see Figure 23.2).

**FIGURE 23.2**
The primitives in the Mesh flyout of the Primitives panel

In the next exercise, you'll use the Mesh Box primitive to start your cushion:

1. In the Mesh tab's Primitives panel, click the Mesh Box tool, or type **Mesh↵B↵**.

2. At the Specify first corner or [Center]: prompt, enter **0,0↵** to start the mesh at the drawing origin.

3. You'll want a mesh that is 21 units in the x-axis by 32 units in the y-axis, so at the Specify other corner or [Cube/Length]: prompt, enter **21,32↵**.

**4.** At the Specify height or [2Point]: prompt, place your cursor anywhere above the base of the mesh and enter 4↵ for a 4 unit height. You now have a basic shape for your mesh (see Figure 23.3).

**FIGURE 23.3**
The Mesh Box primitive

You've just created a mesh box, but you have several other mesh primitives at your disposal. If you click the Mesh flyout on the Primitives panel, you'll see the cone, cylinder, pyramid, sphere, wedge, and torus primitives. When creating your model, consider which of these primitives will best suit your needs.

## Understanding the Parts of a Mesh

Before you go any further, you'll want to understand the structure of a mesh. Notice that each side is divided into nine panels, or *faces*, as they are called in AutoCAD. You can edit these faces to change the shape and contour of your mesh. You can control the number of faces of a mesh through an options dialog box that you'll learn about later.

Figure 23.4 shows the names of the different parts of a simple mesh: the vertex, the edge, and the face. These three parts are called *subobjects* of the mesh, and you can move their position in the mesh to modify a mesh's shape.

**FIGURE 23.4**
The subobjects of a mesh

To help you select different subobjects on a mesh, the Selection panel offers the Filter flyout, which shows the No Filter tool by default. You'll get to use this flyout in many of the exercises in this chapter.

## Smoothing a Mesh

One of the main features of a mesh is its ability to become a smooth, curved object. Right now your cushion has sharp edges, but you can round the corners using the Smooth tools.

Try modifying the mesh to smooth its corners:

1. Click the rectangular mesh to select it.

2. Click the Smooth More tool in the Mesh panel or the Smooth panel, or type **Meshsmoothmore.**↵. The edges of the mesh become faceted and smoother in appearance.

3. Click Smooth More again. The mesh becomes smoother still (see Figure 23.5).

**FIGURE 23.5**
The mesh after applying the Smooth More tool twice

4. Now click Smooth Less, or type **Meshsmoothless.**↵. The mesh becomes less smooth.

5. Press Esc to clear the selection.

As you can see from this exercise, you can smooth a mesh using the Smooth More tool. The more times you apply it to a mesh, the smoother your mesh becomes. The number of faces of the mesh determines how the Smooth More tool affects the mesh. The fewer the faces, the broader the application of smoothness.

When you apply the Smooth More tool to a mesh, the faces of the mesh become faceted. This simulates the smooth appearance. If you look closely at a mesh that has only one or two levels of smoothing applied, you can see the facets.

## Editing Faces and Edges

The shape you created earlier demonstrates one of the main features of meshes. In this section, you'll create a model of a surfboard to see how you can push and pull the subobjects of a mesh to create a form.

---

**KNOW THE VIEWCUBE**

Throughout the following exercise, you'll make heavy use of the ViewCube®. Be sure you are familiar with how it works. If you need a refresher, go to Chapter 20.

---

You'll start with the same form, a box shape, but this time you'll modify some of the parameters that define the box's structure. You can control the number of faces that a mesh primitive will have before it is created. The following exercise introduces you to the tools and methods used to edit meshes.

Start by creating a new drawing and setting up the parameters for the mesh:

1. Click the New tool in the Quick Access toolbar, select acad3D.dwt, and then click Open.

2. In the Mesh tab, click the Mesh Primitives Options tool in the Primitives panel title bar. The Mesh Primitive Options dialog box appears (see Figure 23.6).

**FIGURE 23.6**
The Mesh Primitive Options dialog box

3. In the Tessellation Divisions rollout in the Mesh group, change the Length and Width values to **4** and the Height value to **1**. Click OK when you've finished making the changes.

4. In the Home tab's View panel, choose the Shaded With Edges visual style from the Visual Styles drop-down list.

The parameters you change alter the number of faces on mesh primitives that you create, including the box primitive that you will create in the next exercise. You'll see the results after following the next set of steps:

1. Click the Mesh Box tool found on the Mesh tab in the Primitives panel.

2. At the Specify first corner or [Center]: prompt, type **0,0↵** to start the corner at the origin of the drawing.

3. At the Specify other corner or [Cube/Length]: prompt, enter **50,30↵** to create a 50×30 unit base for the box.

4. At the Specify height or [2Point] prompt, point the cursor in the positive Z direction and then enter **3.5↵** for a 3.5 unit thickness.

5. Center the box in your view. Your model should look similar to Figure 23.7.

**FIGURE 23.7**
The mesh box

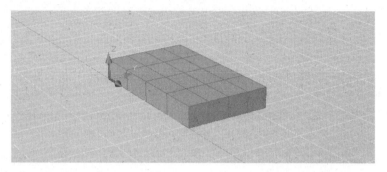

6. Click the box to select it. Then, in the Mesh panel, click the Smooth More tool twice. The edges of the mesh become more rounded.

---

#### WHAT DOES THE SMOOTH OBJECT TOOL DO?

It's hard not to notice the very large Smooth Object tool in the Mesh panel. Your first reaction might be to try to use this tool on a mesh, but it is not intended to work on meshes. Instead, it converts 3D objects other than meshes into mesh objects. You can convert a solid into a mesh, for example, using this tool. 3D surfaces can also be converted, and it even works on region objects that are technically not 3D objects.

You might be tempted to convert a mesh to a solid, edit it, and then turn it back into a mesh. Although this can be done, we don't recommend it. You'll find that your model becomes too unwieldy to work with.

---

### Stretching Faces

CERT
OBJECTIVE

You now have the basis for the surfboard, though it might seem like an odd shape for a surfboard. Next you'll start to form the surfboard by manipulating the faces and edges of the mesh. Start by pulling two sides of the mesh to give it a shape more like a surfboard:

1. Use the ViewCube and Pan tools to adjust your view so that it looks similar to Figure 23.8. This view will allow you to easily select and "pull" some of the faces that will become the front and back of the surfboard.

2. In the Selection panel, select Face from the Filter flyout (see Figure 23.9).

**FIGURE 23.8**
Hold down the
Ctrl key, and place
a crossing selection
window as
shown here.

Crossing selection window

**FIGURE 23.9**
Select the
Face filter.

3. Hold down the Ctrl key, and then click and drag a crossing selection window over the middle faces at the front edge of the box, as shown in Figure 23.8. The faces are highlighted, and you see the XYZ gizmo.

4. Place your cursor on the red x-axis of the gizmo.

5. When the red axis vector line appears, click and drag the gizmo downward in a positive X direction. The mesh begins to elongate.

6. When your mesh looks similar to Figure 23.10, release your mouse button.

7. Press Esc to remove the faces from the current selection.

**FIGURE 23.10**
Click and drag the gizmo when you see the red axis vector.

The portion of the mesh you "pull" out will become the front. Next do the same for the back of the surfboard:

1. Use the Pan tool to adjust your view so that it looks similar to Figure 23.11. This view will allow you to easily select and "pull" some of the faces that will become the back of the surfboard.

**FIGURE 23.11**
Place a crossing selection window as shown here. Be sure to press and hold the Ctrl key in order to make the proper selection.

2. Click on the box mesh to expose its mesh lines again.

3. Hold down the Ctrl key, and then place a crossing selection window over the middle faces at the back edge of the box, as shown in Figure 23.11. The faces are highlighted, and you see the XYZ gizmo.

4. Place your cursor on the red x-axis of the gizmo, and when the red axis vector line appears, click and drag the gizmo upward in a negative X direction.

**5.** When your mesh looks similar to Figure 23.12, release your mouse button.

**FIGURE 23.12**
Adjust the mesh
to look similar to
this one.

**6.** Press Esc to remove the faces from the current selection.

**7.** Click the Home tool on the ViewCube to get a better view of your mesh at this point (see Figure 23.13).

**FIGURE 23.13**
The mesh so far

## Moving an Edge

The surfboard needs a sharper point at the front. Instead of moving the faces as you've already done, you can move an edge to give the front a more pointed shape. The next set of steps will show you how to do this:

**1.** Using the ViewCube, adjust your view so that you have a close-up of the front tip of the surfboard, as shown in Figure 23.14.

**2.** In the Selection panel, select Edge from the Filter flyout.

Edge

**3.** Hover over the front edge until you see the edge line, and then click the edge, as shown in Figure 23.14. The Move gizmo appears.

**FIGURE 23.14**
Click the front-center edge shown here.

Click this edge

**4.** Hover over the x-axis of the gizmo, and when the red vector line appears, click and drag the x-axis downward along the positive X direction.

**5.** When it looks similar to Figure 23.15, release the mouse button.

**FIGURE 23.15**
Pull the front edge so that the mesh looks similar to this image.

Next, give the front of the mesh a slight curve by adjusting the z-axis of the front edge:

**1.** Hover over the z-axis of the gizmo, and when the blue axis vector line appears, click and drag the z-axis downward in the negative Z direction.

**2.** When it looks similar to Figure 23.16, release the mouse button.

**3.** Press the Esc key twice to clear your edge selection.

**4.** Click the Home tool in the ViewCube to return to the home view.

We asked you to adjust the edge downward because you'll want to have a bottom view of your surfboard. This will enable you to add fins to the board without having to flip the mesh over.

## FINE-TUNE THE MESH

You might notice that the surfboard has a slight trough down the middle after you move the front edge downward. You can remove that trough and add some additional curvature to the board by moving the two edges on the side of the mesh toward the front.

Select these edges.

You can Ctrl+click these edges with the Edge subobject filter selected. After you have these edges selected, use the z-axis on the gizmo to move them down to eliminate the trough.

**FIGURE 23.16**
Move the front edge downward in the z-axis.

## Adding More Faces

The surfboard is still missing some fins. You could model some fins as separate meshes and then later join them to the surfboard. You can also use the Refine Mesh tool to add more edges and then use those edges as the basis for your fins. The following exercise will show how this is done:

**1.** Adjust your view so that it looks similar to the top image in Figure 23.17.

**FIGURE 23.17**
Select the faces to refine.

Ctrl+click these two faces. ─────

2. From the View tab's Visual Styles panel, open the Visual Styles drop-down list and select Shaded With Edges. This will allow you to see the edge lines of the mesh as you work through the following steps.

3. Click the mesh, and then from the Mesh tab's Mesh panel, click Smooth More. This will increase the number of edges that are generated in the next step.

4. Press the Esc key to clear your selection.

5. On the Selection panel, select Face from the Filter flyout.

6. Ctrl+click the two faces shown in the top image of Figure 23.17.

7. Click the Refine Mesh tool on the Mesh panel, or type **Meshrefine**⏎. The selected faces will be subdivided into smaller faces and edges, as shown in the bottom image of Figure 23.17.

---

**UNDERSTANDING HOW REFINE MESH WORKS**

You have some control over the number of faces that Refine Mesh creates, through the level of smoothness applied to a mesh. If you reduce the smoothness of a mesh, the Refine Mesh tool will produce fewer faces. If you increase the smoothness, Refine Mesh will produce more faces—four more per facet, to be precise.

To understand how this works, you have to take a closer look at how the Smooth More tool works. Each time you apply the Smooth More tool to a mesh, every face of the mesh is divided into four facets. These facets aren't actually faces, but they divide a face in such a way as to simulate a rounded surface. The Refine Mesh tool further divides each of these facets into four faces. You can see this division clearly if you apply Refine Mesh to a face in a mesh that has only one level of smoothness applied.

---

The next step in creating the fins is to edit some of the newly created edges:

1. Zoom into the surfboard so that your view looks similar to Figure 23.18.

**FIGURE 23.18**
Select the edges for the fins.

Ctrl+Click these two edges.

Edge

2. On the Selection panel, select Edge from the Filter flyout.

3. Click the edges shown in Figure 23.18.

4. Hover over the z-axis on the gizmo so that the axis vector appears, and then click and drag the z-axis upward in the positive Z direction. If you run out of room at the top of the window, you can move the z-axis as far as you can with one click and drag and then repeat the move.

5. Adjust the edges so that they look similar to those in Figure 23.19, and then release the mouse button.

**FIGURE 23.19**
Adjust the edges to create the fins.

6. Adjust the x-axis of the gizmo toward the back of the surfboard so that the fins look similar to Figure 23.20.

**FIGURE 23.20**
Adjust the fins toward the back of the surfboard.

7. Press the Esc key to clear your selection of mesh edges.

## Rotating an Edge

The fins aren't quite the right shape. They are a bit too broad at the base. The next exercise shows you how to rotate an edge to adjust the shape of the fins further:

1. With the Edge subobject filter still selected, click the back edge of the fins, as shown in Figure 23.21.

**FIGURE 23.21**

Click and drag the green circle on the Rotate gizmo.

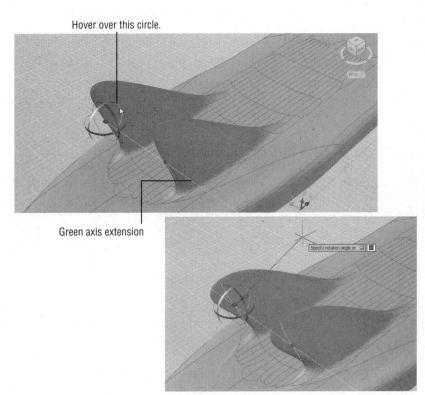

2. In the Selection panel, select the Rotate Gizmo tool from the Gizmo flyout (see Figure 23.22).

**FIGURE 23.22**

Select the Rotate Gizmo tool.

**3.** Hover over the green circle of the Rotate gizmo in the location shown in the top panel of Figure 23.21 until you see the green axis vector, and then click and drag to rotate the edge. Adjust the rotation of the edge so that the fins look similar to those in the lower panel of Figure 23.21, and then release the mouse button.

**4.** Press the Esc key to clear your selection.

**5.** Use the Home tool on the ViewCube to get an overall view of the surfboard (see Figure 23.23).

**FIGURE 23.23**
The finished surfboard

In this exercise, you switched from the Move gizmo to the Rotate gizmo. You can also use the Scale gizmo to scale a face or edge.

This may not be the most accurate rendition of a surfboard (our apologies if you are a surfer), but the general shape of the surfboard has given you a chance to explore many of the features of the Mesh toolset.

---

**CHANGING THE GIZMO ON THE FLY**

Instead of using the Gizmo flyout on the Selection panel, you can right-click the gizmo to change it. You can also set the orientation of the gizmo through the context menu, which will allow you to move subobjects in directions other than perpendicular to the face or edge. You can orient the gizmo to the WCS, the current UCS, or a face on a mesh through the Align Gizmo With right-click option.

---

## Adding a Crease

You'll want to know about one more tool that can help you fine-tune your mesh shapes. The Add Crease tool on the Mesh panel does exactly what it says. It can introduce a crease in your otherwise smooth mesh shape. Add Crease does this in two ways: It can flatten a face or remove the smoothing around an edge.

In the following exercises, you'll use the surfboard one more time to experiment with the Add Crease tool. First you'll see how you can add a sharp point to the surfboard:

1. Adjust your view of the surfboard so that you can see the front point, as shown in Figure 23.24. Turn off the grid so that you can see the shape clearly.

**FIGURE 23.24**
Set up your view. Select the front edge of the surfboard.

Select the front edge.

2. From the Mesh tab's Selection panel, select the Move Gizmo tool from the Gizmo flyout.

3. Click the Add Crease tool in the Mesh panel.

4. At the Select Mesh Subobjects to Crease prompt, click the front edge of the surfboard, as shown in Figure 23.24.

5. Press ↵. At the `Specify Crease Value [Always] <Always>:` prompt, press ↵.

6. The point of the surfboard becomes much sharper.

You can see from this exercise that the front edge of the surfboard is now quite sharp since it no longer has any smoothness.

Now try applying the Add Crease tool to a face:

1. From the Selection panel, select Face from the Filter flyout.

2. Click the Add Crease tool and, at the `Select Mesh Subobjects to Crease:` prompt, click the two faces on either side of the front edge, as shown in Figure 23.25, and press ↵.

3. At the `Specify Crease Value [Always] <Always>:` prompt, press ↵.

   The faces are flattened and the point of the surfboard becomes even sharper, as shown in Figure 23.26.

4. Save your drawing.

The surfboard is grossly deformed, but you can see how the side faces have now become flat and the edges of the face form a crease. You could use the Add Crease tool to sharpen the edge of the fins. This would also have the effect of making the fins thinner. We didn't use that example for this exercise because the effects would have been too subtle to see clearly.

**FIGURE 23.25**
Click these faces to flatten them.

Click these two faces.

Select mesh subobjects to crease:

**FIGURE 23.26**
The surfboard after applying Add Crease to the side faces on the front

## Splitting and Extruding a Mesh Face

Before we move on to the next topic, there are two more tools that can be a great aid in editing your meshes. The Split Face tool does just what its name says. It will split a face into two faces. The Extrude Face tool behaves like the Extrude Face tool you have seen for 3D solids. Both of these tools are a bit tricky to use, so they bear a closer look.

To use the Split Face tool, you first select a mesh face, and then select two points, one on each side of the face. The following exercise shows how it works:

**1.** Open the SplitMesh.dwg sample file from the Chapter 23 folder. This file contains a simple mesh box that has been smoothed.

**2.** In the Mesh tab's Mesh Edit panel, click the Split Mesh Face tool, or type **Meshsplit↵**.

**3.** Make sure the Face filter tool is selected in the Selection panel.

**4.** Click the face shown in the top panel of Figure 23.27.

**FIGURE 23.27**
Selecting the points
for the split

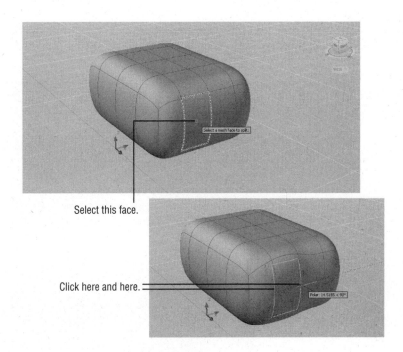

Select this face.

Click here and here.

5. Move the cursor to the left edge of the face until you see a knife icon appear next to the cursor.

6. Click roughly in the middle of the edge.

7. Move the cursor along the right edge of the face. You'll see some temporary lines, giving you a preview of the location of the split (see Figure 23.27).

8. Move the cursor roughly in the middle of the right edge. The face changes temporarily to show you how it will look when it is divided into two faces.

9. Click. The shape of the mesh changes to accommodate the new face.

As you can see, Split Face is not a precision tool, but if you don't like the location of the split, you can move the newly created edge using one of the gizmos.

Next let's look at the Extrude Face tool. At first, you might think that the Extrude Face tool is redundant since you can use the Move gizmo to move a face in a direction away from the mesh, as you saw in an earlier exercise. Using the Extrude Face tool is different from moving a face because it isolates the movement to the selected face as much as possible. To see how this works, try the following:

1. With the Face filter selected in the Selection panel, Ctrl+click the face indicated in Figure 23.28.

2. Click and drag the z-axis in the positive direction. When the mesh looks similar to the upper panel of Figure 23.29, click to finish the move. The smoothness of the side is maintained as you pull the face.

**FIGURE 23.28**
Select this face.

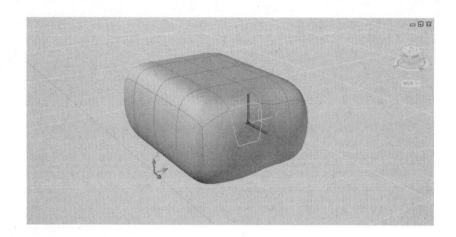

**FIGURE 23.29**
A moved face and
an extruded face

3. Press the Esc key and click Undo to revert back to the mesh as it was before you moved the face.

4. Click the Extrude Face tool in the Mesh Edit panel.

5. Click the same face you selected before, and then press ↵.

6. Move the cursor along the z-axis in the positive direction. The face is extruded, leaving the faces around it unmoved except for a slight curvature at the base (the lower panel of Figure 23.29).

You can see from this example that the Extrude Face tool confines the deformation of the mesh to only the face you select. Note that you can select multiple faces for the extrusion.

 **Real World Scenario**

### USING SPLIT MESH FACE AND ADD CREASE TOGETHER

In a usability study conducted by Autodesk, the product designers gave an example of how to add a crease to the top surface of a computer mouse model. In the example, the Split Face and Add Crease tools were used together. First a new edge was created using the Split Face tool, and then the Add Crease tool was applied to the newly created edge to form the crease. Using these two tools together in this way, you can add a crease just about anywhere on a mesh.

## Creating Mesh Surfaces

So far, you've been working with mesh volumes, but the Primitives panel of the Mesh tab offers four tools that let you create a variety of surface meshes. These are the *revolved, edge, ruled,* and *tabulated surfaces.* If you're an old hand at working with 3D in AutoCAD software, then these tools should be familiar. They are the latest incarnation of some of the earliest 3D tools offered by AutoCAD, and they work exactly like the old features they replace. But just like the mesh volumes you've been working with, the mesh surfaces can be quickly smoothed and their subobjects can be edited using the gizmos you learned about in this and earlier chapters. The following sections give a little more detail about these tools and how they are used. The figures used in these sections are taken directly from the cue cards for each tool.

### TRY OUT THESE TOOLS ON A SAMPLE FILE

The following instructions are for your reference only, and you are not required to do them as exercises. But if you like, you can try them out on the `SurfaceMeshSamples.dwg` file provided with the sample drawings for this chapter.

### Revolved Surface

To create a revolved surface, you need a profile to revolve and a line that acts as an axis of revolution (see Figure 23.30). The profile can be any object, but a polyline or spline is usually used.

To create a revolved surface, follow these steps:

1. Click the Modeling, Meshes, Revolved Surface tool in the Primitives panel, or type **Revsurf**↵.

2. Select the profile object, and then select the axis object.

**FIGURE 23.30**
The Revolved Surface tool's cue card

3. At the Specify start angle <0>: prompt, enter a start angle, or just press ↵ to accept the default angle of 0.

4. At the Specify included angle (+=ccw, -=cw) <360>: prompt, enter the angle of rotation for the surface, or just press ↵ to accept the default angle of 360 degrees. As you might infer from the prompt, you can create a revolved surface that is not completely closed.

---

**GETTING SMOOTHER SURFACES**

The mesh surfaces will appear faceted when you first create them. Typically, the revolved, ruled, and tabulated surfaces will have six faces. The edge surface will have an array of 36 faces. You can increase the number of faces that are generated by these tools by changing the Surftab1 and Surftab2 settings. Surftab1 will increase the faces generated by the revolved, ruled, and tabulated surface tools. Surftab1 and Surftab2 can be used to increase the faces of an edge surface.

To use the Surftab settings, type **Surftab1**↵ or **Surftab2**↵ and enter a numeric value. The value you enter will be the number of faces generated by these surface mesh tools. Don't get carried away because an increase in the number of faces will also increase the size of your file. Besides, you can always use the Smooth More tool to smooth out the appearance of these surface objects up to the maximum smoothness level allowed.

Surftab1 and Surftab2 are set to 6.        Surftab1 is set to 12 and Surftab2 is set to 24.

## Edge Surface

In Chapter 21, "Using Advanced 3D Features," you learned how to use the Loft tool to draw a butterfly chair that has the shape of a draped fabric seat. Other 3D modeling tools have been introduced into AutoCAD in recent releases that you could use to create the seat. One tool to use in the butterfly chair example is the Edge Surface tool (see Figure 23.31). This tool is a bit trickier to use only because the objects defining the surface must be selected in sequential order. In other words, you can't randomly select the objects.

**FIGURE 23.31**

The Edge Surface cue card

Modeling, Meshes, Edge Surface

Creates a mesh between four contiguous edges or curves

Select four adjoining edges that define the mesh. The edges can be lines, arcs, splines, or open polylines. The edges must touch at their endpoints to form a single, closed loop.

EDGESURF

Press F1 for more help

Here's how it works:

1. On the Mesh tab's Primitives panel, click the Modeling, Meshes, Edge Surface tool, or type **Edgesurf**↵.

2. Select the four objects that are the edges of the surface you want to create. Make sure you select the objects in clockwise or counterclockwise order. Don't select them "crosswise."

## Ruled Surface

The Ruled Mesh tool creates a surface mesh from two 2D objects such as lines, arcs, polylines, or splines. This is perhaps the simplest mesh tool to use since you have to click only two objects to form a mesh (see Figure 23.32). But like Edge Mesh, it has a tricky side. The location where you click will affect the way the mesh is generated. You'll want to click the same side of each object unless you want the surface to twist, as shown in Figure 23.33.

To create a ruled mesh, follow these steps:

1. On the Mesh tab's Primitives panel, click the Modeling, Meshes, Ruled Surface tool, or type **Rulesurf**↵.

2. Click two objects that are not on the same XY plane. The mesh is created between the objects.

**FIGURE 23.32**
The Ruled Surface
cue card

**FIGURE 23.33**
Where you click an
object affects the
outcome.

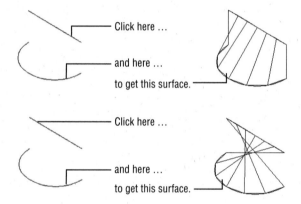

## Tabulated Surface

The Tabulated Mesh tool is like an extrude tool for surfaces (see Figure 23.34). Chapter 20 showed you how you can use the Extrude tool to create a 3D solid from a closed polygon. The Extrude tool will also work on open polygons, lines, and arcs, but it will extrude the object in only a perpendicular direction. The Tabulated Surface tool lets you "extrude" an object in a direction you control with a line. The line can point in any direction in space.

Here's how to use it:

1. On the Mesh tab's Primitives panel, click the Modeling, Meshes, Tabulated Surface tool in the Primitives panel, or enter **Tabsurf**.↵

2. Select the object that defines the profile of your mesh.

3. Click the object that defines the direction for the surface.

As with the other surface mesh tools, the point at which you select objects will affect the way the object is generated. For the tabulated mesh, the direction of the mesh depends on where you click the line that defines the surface direction.

**FIGURE 23.34**
The Tabulated Surface cue card

Modeling, Meshes, Tabulated Surface

Creates a mesh from a line or curve that is swept along a straight path

Select a line, arc, circle, ellipse, or polyline to sweep in a straight path. Then select a line or polyline to determine the first and last points of a vector that indicates the direction and length of the polygon mesh.

TABSURF

Press F1 for more help

# Converting Meshes to Solids

We mentioned earlier that you can convert a mesh to a solid. In doing so, you can take advantage of the many solid-editing tools available in AutoCAD. The Boolean tools can be especially useful in editing meshes that have been turned into solids.

Conversion is a fairly simple process using the tools in the Convert Mesh panel of the Mesh tab. Just click the Convert To Solid tool, or type **Convtosolid**↵, and then select the mesh or meshes you want to convert. Press ↵ to complete the process. The Convert To Surface tool (**Convtosurface**↵) works in much the same way, but it creates a surface object instead of a solid.

When you convert a mesh to a solid, you have the option to apply more or less smoothing to the conversion process. The Smoothed, Optimized flyout in the Convert Mesh panel gives you four options. You can select one of these options before you use the Convert To Solid or Convert To Surface tool to get a different smoothing effect during the conversion. Table 23.1 describes these options and how they affect the conversion of meshes.

**TABLE 23.1:**    Options on the Convert Mesh panel's flyout

| OPTION | EFFECT ON MESH |
| --- | --- |
| Smoothed, Optimized | The mesh is smoothed and the faces are merged. |
| Smoothed, Not Optimized | The mesh is smoothed but maintains the same number of faces as the original. |
| Faceted, Optimized | The facets are maintained, and the smoothing remains the same but planar faces are merged. |
| Faceted, Not Optimized | The facets are maintained, the smoothing remains the same, and the number of faces also remains the same. |

---

**WHY CONTROL FACES IN THE CONVERSION?**

The mesh-to-solid conversion options shown in Table 23.1 may seem like overkill, but there is a good reason for offering these settings. Many of the solid-editing tools in the Home tab's Solid Editing panel are designed to work on solid faces. You can apply many of these tools to the faces of a converted mesh. Having control over the way faces are converted from a mesh to a solid will give you some control over how you are able to edit the solid later. See Chapter 22 for more on the solid-editing tools.

---

# Understanding 3D Surfaces

So far in this book you've worked with 3D solids and meshes. A third type of 3D object called a surface completes the AutoCAD set of 3D modeling tools to make it a complete 3D modeling application in its own right.

Click the Surface tab, and you'll see the Surface panels that offer the tools you'll need to work with surface modeling (see Figure 23.35).

**FIGURE 23.35**
The Surface tab and Ribbon panels

In the Create panel, you see a different set of tools from the Mesh and Solid tabs, but a handful should look familiar. The Loft, Sweep, Extrude, and Revolve tools at the far left of the Create panel are tools you've seen in previous chapters. These surface creation tools work in the same way as the tools of the same name in the Solid tab. In fact, they are essentially the same tools. They just use a different command option to create a surface instead of a solid. The big difference is that to create a solid, you need to start with a closed polyline. With the surface version of the Loft, Sweep, Extrude, and Revolve tools, you can start with an open spline, polyline, or other object. And even if you do use a closed object such as a circle or closed polyline, you will still get a 3D surface instead of a solid (see Figure 23.36).

---

**DRAWING 2D CURVES WITH THE CURVES PANEL**

Since 3D surfaces are derived from 2D objects, the Surface tab has the convenient Curves panel that offers most of the 2D drawing tools you'll need to build your surfaces from scratch. The Spline flyout even features the Spline Freehand tool, which will let you draw a curve "freehand" with a click and drag of your mouse. Experienced users will recognize this Spline Freehand tool as an updated version of the Sketch command.

---

**FIGURE 23.36**
A circle extruded
using the solid
Extrude and the
surface Extrude

3D Surface

3D Solid

Two other surface-creation tools that are unique to the Surface tab of the Ribbon are the
Network Surface and Planar Surface tools. Here's a brief description of each:

 **Network Surface Tool**  The Network Surface tool lets you create a surface from several
curves. The cue card for the Network Surface tool gives you a good idea of how this tool
works (see Figure 23.37).

**FIGURE 23.37**
The cue card
description of
the Network
Surface tool

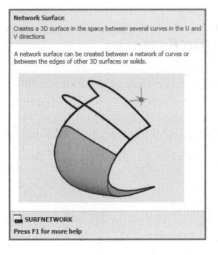

> **Network Surface**
> Creates a 3D surface in the space between several curves in the U and
> V directions
>
> A network surface can be created between a network of curves or
> between the edges of other 3D surfaces or solids.
>
> SURFNETWORK
> **Press F1 for more help**

 **Planar Surface Tool**  The Planar Surface tool creates a flat surface either by selecting two
points to indicate a rectangular surface or by selecting a closed 2D object to create a flat surface
with an irregular boundary (see Figure 23.38).

**FIGURE 23.38**

Creating a planar surface

Click the Planar Surface tool and click two points to create a rectangular surface.

Click the Planar Surface tool and press ⏎, and then select a closed 2D shape like a circle or polyline.

---

### LEARNING FROM ANIMATED CUE CARDS

Animated cue cards show you how many of the tools on the Surface Ribbon tab work. These animated cue cards can help get you up and running with surface modeling. Just hover over a tool for a moment after the tool tip appears. For tools that have animated cue cards, you will see the message "Video is loading" in the lower-right corner of the tool tip.

---

## Editing Surfaces

Once created, surface objects have a unique set of editing tools that allow you to create fairly detailed models. Some tools, like Surface Fillet and Surface Trim, offer the same function as their 2D drawing counterparts. The following list includes a description of each tool:

**Surface Fillet**  With the Surface Fillet tool, you can join one surface to another with an intermediate rounded surface (see Figure 23.39).

**FIGURE 23.39**

Using the Surface Fillet and Surface Trim tools

**Surface Trim**  The Surface Trim tool lets you trim one or several surfaces to other surfaces.

**Surface Untrim**  Surface Untrim does exactly what it says. It reverses a trim operation.

**Surface Extend**  The Surface Extend tool simply enables you to extend the edge of a surface beyond its current location. Unlike its 2D equivalent, it does not extend a surface to another surface object, though you could extend beyond a surface and then use the Trim tool.

**Surface Sculpt**   The Surface Sculpt tool is like a super trim. You can align several surfaces to enclose a volume completely (the left image in Figure 23.40), and then use the Sculpt tool to trim all of the surfaces at once into a completely closed 3D shape (the right image in Figure 23.40). By default, the new object is a solid.

**FIGURE 23.40**
The Surface Sculpt tool creates a container-like shape from several surfaces.

The Create panel also offers three other tools that could be considered editing tools. Blend, Patch, and Offset need existing surfaces to do their job, so they may seem a bit like editing tools. Here's a description of each:

**Surface Blend**   Surface Blend will connect two surfaces with an intermediate surface.

**Surface Patch**   The Surface Patch tool will close an open surface like the end of a tube. Surface Patch also lets you control whether the closing "patch" is flat or curved, as shown in Figure 23.41.

**FIGURE 23.41**
The Surface Patch tool can create a flat or rounded patch over an open surface.

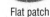
Open surface            Flat patch            Curved patch

**Surface Offset**   Surface Offset, like the Surface Trim tool, mimics its 2D counterpart. It will create a new surface that is parallel to the original. When you start the Surface Offset tool from the Create panel and select a surface, you'll see arrows indicating the direction of the offset. You can type **F↵** to flip the direction of the offset. Enter a distance for the offset, and press ↵ to create the offset surface (see Figure 23.42).

## Using Extrude, Surface Trim, and Surface Fillet

Now that you have an overview of the basic surface modeling tools, try the following set of exercises to see how they work.

**FIGURE 23.42**
Using the Create panel's Surface Offset tool

Select the surface.    Determine the direction of the offset.    Enter a distance for the offset.

## USING THE EXTRUDE TOOL

Start with the Extrude tool on two basic shapes:

1. Open the Surfaces1.dwg file from the sample folder.

2. Choose Extrude from the Surface tab's Create panel.

3. Click the circle in the drawing, and then press ↵. A surface appears and its length changes as you move the cursor.

4. Adjust the surface height to 5 units so that it looks similar to Figure 23.43 on the left.

5. Click Extrude again and extrude the arc horizontally 5 units while your cursor is left of the arc so that it looks similar to the extrusion on the right side of Figure 23.43.

**FIGURE 23.43**
Extrude the circle and arc (left image) 5 units to look like the image on the right.

As you can see, the Extrude tool is similar to the Extrude tool in the Solid tab in how it works, but the objects created are surfaces.

### USING THE SURFACE TRIM TOOL

The Surface Trim tool is similar to the 2D Trim tool except that there is an additional step at the beginning, where you select the object you intend to trim. At first this step seems redundant, but after you use the tool for a while, it begins to make more sense. Also notice that the original arc you used to extrude the arc surface is still there. You'll use that a little later in this chapter.

Next try out the Surface Trim tool:

**Trim**

1. Click Surface Trim in the Surface tab's Edit panel.

2. Click both the cylinder and the extruded arc surface, and then press ↵. This first step selects the objects to trim.

3. Click both objects again, and then press ↵. This time you're selecting the objects to trim to. You want to trim the top of the cylinder to the arc and the arc to the cylinder.

4. Finally, click the cylinder near the top edge to indicate what part you want to trim. Also click the extruded arc surface anywhere outside of the cylinder. Press ↵ to end the command. Your surfaces should look like the right-side image in Figure 23.44.

**FIGURE 23.44**

Trimming the surfaces

Click the top edge of the cylinder.  Click the extruded arc anywhere outside the cylinder.

### USING THE SURFACE FILLET TOOL

Now try out the Surface Fillet tool:

**Fillet**

1. Click the Surface Fillet tool in the Surface tab's Edit panel.

2. Click the top surface, and then click the cylinder. The two surfaces are "filleted," as shown in Figure 23.45.

3. The following prompt appears: Press Enter to accept the fillet surface or [Radius/Trim surfaces]. Type **R**↵ to enter a different radius.

4. Type **0.5**↵. The radius changes. You still have the opportunity to change the radius again.

**FIGURE 23.45**
Using the Surface
Fillet tool

**5.** Type **R↵**, and then type **0.2↵**. The radius changes again.

**6.** Press ↵ to finish the fillet.

In this case we created a fillet all of the way around the top of the cylinder. While you're creating surface fillets, you'll see a preview of what the new surface will look like. You don't have to stick with that fillet until you fully finish the command; you are free to make changes to the fillet until then.

## Using Surface Blend, Patch, and Offset

As mentioned earlier, a few of the tools on the Create panel are a bit like editing tools. Surface Blend, Surface Patch, and Surface Offset create new surfaces that use existing surfaces as their basis. Surface Blend is a bit like the Surface Fillet tool in that it will join two surfaces with an intermediate surface. Surface Offset creates a new surface that is parallel to an existing one and is similar to the 2D offset command. Surface Patch will create a surface that closes an open-ended surface.

To get a better idea of how these three tools work, try the following set of exercises. Start by creating a parallel copy of an existing surface using the Offset tool:

**1.** Open the Patch1.dwg sample file from the Chapter 23 sample folder.

**2.** Click the Surface Offset tool from the Surface tab's Create panel.

Offset

**3.** Click the surface in the drawing, and then press ↵. You see a set of arrows appear as shown in the left image of Figure 23.46.

**FIGURE 23.46**
Using the Surface
Offset tool

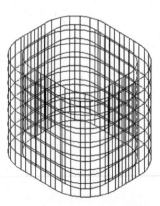

4. Type **F↵**. The arrows now point in the opposite direction.

5. Type **F↵** again to return the arrows to their previous direction facing outward.

6. Enter **0.5↵** for the offset distance. The offset surface appears around the original surface, as shown on the right in Figure 23.46.

Here you see how the Surface Offset tool differs from the 2D Offset tool that you've seen in Chapter 18, "Drawing Curves." The arrows play an important role in helping you visualize the result of your offset, so instead of picking a direction, you adjust the direction of the arrows.

### USING THE SURFACE BLEND TOOL

Now try the Surface Blend tool:

1. Use the Move command to move the outer surface vertically in the z-axis roughly 5 units. Remember that you can hold down the Shift key to restrain the cursor to the z-axis. If you see the Surface Associativity message, click Continue. You'll learn more about associativity later in this chapter.

2. Adjust your view so that you can see both surfaces, and then click the Surface Blend tool in the Surface tab's Create panel.

3. Select the eight edges along the top of the lower surface, as shown in Figure 23.47. When you're sure you've selected all of the edges, press ↵. You can also select the Chain option, which will find all edges that are connected.

4. Select the eight edges along the bottom of the upper surface, as shown in Figure 23.47. When you're sure you've selected all of the edges, press ↵. A new, preview surface appears that joins the upper and lower surfaces.

5. You might notice a couple of grip arrowheads that appear along the top and bottom edge of the new blend surface. Click one of them, and a menu appears offering three options: Position, Tangent, and Curvature (see Figure 23.48).

**FIGURE 23.47**
Selecting the edges
for the Surface
Blend tool

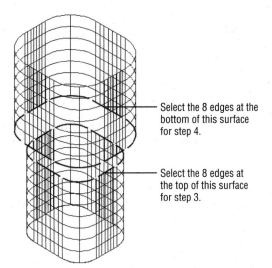

Select the 8 edges at the
bottom of this surface
for step 4.

Select the 8 edges at
the top of this surface
for step 3.

**FIGURE 23.48**
Using the grip
arrowhead to adjust
the blend surface

**6.** Click Curvature, and then press ↵ to place the blend surface.

The Surface Blend tool offers a number of options that control the shape of the blend surface. You saw three options available from the grip arrowhead. The options are available even after you have placed the surface. You can click on the surface to expose the grip arrowheads.

In addition, the Surface Blend tool offers two command options: CONtinuity and Bulge Magnitude. Table 23.2 in the next section describes these features and their functions.

## USING THE SURFACE PATCH TOOL

Now let's take a look at the Surface Patch tool. This tool lets you close the end of a surface with another surface. You can add a flat or curved surface, as you'll see in the next exercise.

Try adding a patch surface to the top of the upper surface in the Patch1.dwg model:

**1.** Pan your view so that you can clearly see the top of the surface model, as shown in the left image in Figure 23.49.

**2.** Click the Surface Patch tool in the Surface tab's Create panel.

**3.** Select the edges of the surface, as shown in Figure 23.49.

**4.** Press ↵ when you are sure you've selected all of the edges. The patch surface appears.

**5.** Click the grip arrowhead that appears along the edge of the patch and select Tangent. The surface is now curved.

**6.** Press ↵ to finish the patch surface.

**7.** To get a better view of the surface, select the Shaded With Edges option from the Visual Styles drop-down list in the View tab's Visual Styles panel. Your model should resemble the right side of Figure 23.49.

**FIGURE 23.49**
Adding the patch
surface to the end
of the model

Select the top edges.

You may have noticed that the grip arrowhead options in step 5 were similar to the grip options you saw for the Surface Blend tool. The Surface Patch tool offers an additional command option called CONStrain Geometry. Table 23.2 describes these options.

**TABLE 23.2:**      The Blend and Patch options

| FEATURE OPTION | FUNCTION |
| --- | --- |
| Position (G0) | Causes the surface to connect without any blending curvature. |
| Tangent (G1) | Causes the surface to blend with direction. |
| Curvature (G2) | Causes the surface to blend with direction and similar curvature or similar rate of change in the surface direction. |
| **COMMAND OPTION** | **FUNCTION** |
| CONtinuity | Controls how smoothly the surfaces flow into each other. |
| Bulge Magnitude | Allows you to adjust the amount of bulge or curvature in the blend surface. Values can be between 0 and 1. |
| CONStrain Geometry (Surfpatch command) | Offers additional guide curves to control the patch surface. |

## Understanding Associativity

You may have noticed the Surface Associativity icon in the Create panel. This is feature is on by default, and its function is similar to the Associative feature of hatches (see Chapter 7, "Mastering Viewing Tools, Hatches, and External References," for more on hatches). You may recall that when you create a 2D hatch pattern with the hatch associative feature turned on, the hatch's shape will conform to any changes made to the boundary used to enclose the hatch pattern.

The Associativity feature in surface modeling works in a similar way, only instead of a hatch pattern conforming to changes in a boundary, the surface conforms to changes in the shapes that are used to create them. For example, if you were to make changes to the arc that you used to extrude the arc surface, the arc surface and the trimmed cylinder would also follow the changes.

## USING ASSOCIATIVITY TO EDIT A SURFACE MODEL

This concept is a bit tricky to explain. Try the following exercise to see how associativity works firsthand:

1. Return to the Surfaces1.dwg file, and click the arc to expose its grips.

2. Click the square grip at the arc's left endpoint and drag it downward along the z-axis. When it is roughly in the position shown in Figure 23.50, click again to fix the grip's location. The shape of the surface model changes to conform to the new shape of the arc.

**FIGURE 23.50**
Adjusting the shape
of the arc

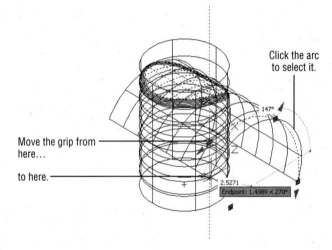

3. Zoom into the top of the surface model so that you have a view similar to Figure 23.51.

4. Click the filleted portion of the surface. An arrowhead grip appears.

5. Click the arrowhead grip. Another arrowhead grip appears.

6. Click this arrowhead grip, and slowly drag it toward the center of the cylinder. Notice that the radius of the fillet changes as you move the grip.

7. Click to fix the fillet radius to its new size.

8. Press the Esc key to clear your selection.

**FIGURE 23.51**
Adjusting the
fillet radius

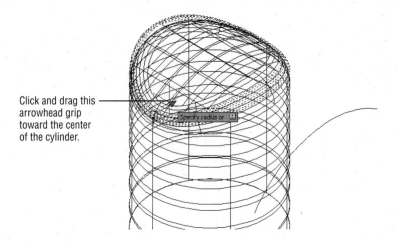

Click and drag this
arrowhead grip
toward the center
of the cylinder.

Specify radius or

## USING ARROWHEAD GRIPS TO EDIT A SURFACE

You've just seen the Associativity feature in action. You can also change the shape of the circle used to extrude the cylinder to modify the surface model's diameter. Additional hidden grips are available that allow you to adjust the shape of the surfaces directly. For example, you can modify the taper of the cylinder using an arrowhead grip that you can turn on using the Properties palette, as shown in these steps:

1. Click the cylindrical part of the surface model.

2. Right-click and select Properties.

3. Scroll down to the bottom of the Properties palette to the Surface Associativity panel.

4. Click the Show Associativity option, and select Yes.

5. Close the Properties palette.

6. At the top of the cylinder, click and drag the right-pointing arrowhead grip to the right. As you do this, you see the dynamic display showing you an angle (see the image on the left in Figure 23.52).

7. Position the arrowhead grip so that the angle shows 6, and then click to fix the grip in place. The cylinder is now tapered and the top surface conforms to the new shape, as shown in the image on the right in Figure 23.52.

Surface Associativity can be very useful, but in order to take full advantage of this feature, you will want to plan your model construction carefully. In addition, the Associativity feature can limit some editing and creation functions. For example, the Surface Fillet tool may not work on a complex surface model with associativity turned on but will work when the associativity is turned off for the objects involved.

**FIGURE 23.52**
Changing the taper
of the cylinder

Click and drag this
arrowhead grip.

## TURNING OFF OR REMOVING ASSOCIATIVITY

You can turn off or remove associativity for an object through the Properties palette. Select the object, and then right-click and select Properties. In the Properties palette, scroll down the palette to the Surface Associativity group (see Figure 23.53). This group offers two options: Maintain associativity and Show associativity. The Maintain associativity option offers Yes, Remove, and None.

**FIGURE 23.53**
The Surface Asso-
ciativity group
in the Properties
palette

Show associativity
Maintain associativity

You can select Remove to remove associativity altogether or None to limit the associativity to the set of objects currently associated with the surface model. After you change this setting, you can't return to a previous setting except with the Undo command.

### CONSTRAINTS, SURFACES, AND ASSOCIATIVITY

In Chapter 16, "Making 'Smart' Drawings with Parametric Tools," you learned that you can add constraints to objects to control their behavior. With Surface Associativity turned on, you can extrude constrained objects and the resulting surface will also follow the constraints of the source 2D objects. But remember that if you use constraints with 3D surfaces in this way, you need to plan the way you build your model carefully to make efficient use of the constraints.

## Editing with Control Vertices

So far you've been creating what are called *procedural surfaces*, which are surfaces that allow you to take advantage of associativity. AutoCAD also allows you to create NURBS surfaces. You may recall that splines are also NURBS, so you might think of a NURBS surface as a kind of 3D surface spline. Splines allow you to move, add, or subtract control vertices (CVs), and you can control the way the CVs "pull" on the curve of the spline. Likewise, NURBS surfaces allow you to add or remove CVs and adjust the direction and force of the CVs.

There are two ways to create a NURBS surface. You can turn on the NURBS Creation option in the Surface tab's Create panel and then go about creating your 3D surfaces. Any 3D surface you create with this option turned on will be a NURBS surface. Or you can convert an existing surface to a NURBS surface.

### CONVERTING A SURFACE TO A NURBS SURFACE

You can convert an existing surface to a NURBS surface by using the Convert To NURBS tool on the Surface tab's Control Vertices panel. This tool also converts 3D solids and meshes. To use it, follow these steps:

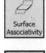

1. Open the CVedit1.dwg sample file.

2. Turn off Surface Associativity in the Surface tab's Create panel.

3. Turn on NURBS Creation in the Surface tab's Create panel.

4. Click the Extrude tool in the Surface tab's Create panel.

5. Click the spline and press ↵.

6. Point the cursor upward, and type 6↵ to make the extruded surface 6 units in the z-axis.

If you want to create NURBS objects, be sure to turn on NURBS Creation. It's easier to create objects as NURBS than to have to go through the extra step of converting them later.

### EXPOSING CVS TO EDIT A NURBS SURFACE

You've just created a NURBS surface. You can expose the CVs for the surface using the Show CV tool. Try the following to view and edit the CVs:

1. Click the Surface CV – Show tool in the Control Vertices panel.

2. Click the surface you just created and press ↵. The CVs appear for the surface.

3. Click the surface to select it, and then click the CV, as shown in Figure 23.54.

4. Move the CV in the y-axis, and notice how the surface deforms. The top edge moves with the CV, whereas the bottom edge maintains its shape.

5. Press the Esc key twice to clear your selection.

In this exercise, you saw how you can gain access to the CVs of a NURBS surface to make changes to the shape. Right now, the CVs are located only at the top and bottom of the surface, but you can add more CVs to give you more control over the shape of the surface.

**FIGURE 23.54**
Exposing the CVs

Click and drag this CV along the y-axis.

## ADDING CVs TO A NURBS SURFACE

The next exercise shows you how you can add additional CVs through the Rebuild option:

**1.** Click the Surface – Rebuild tool in the Control Vertices panel, and then click the surface. Or you can click the surface to select it and then right-click and select NURBS Editing ➢ Rebuild. The Rebuild Surface dialog box appears (see Figure 23.55).

**FIGURE 23.55**
The Rebuild Surface
dialog box

**2.** In the Control Vertices Count group of the Rebuild Surface dialog box, make sure the In U Direction option is set to 8 and the In V Direction option is set to 7. You'll see what these settings do in a moment.

**3.** Click OK. Now you see that many more CVs are available.

In step 2 you specified the number of CVs you want in the U and V directions. The U direction is along the horizontal curve, and the V direction is along the straight, vertical direction. If you count the CVs in each row or column, you'll see that they match the values you entered in step 2.

Now if you were to move a CV, the surface is able to deform along the z-axis, whereas it remained a straight line before.

---

### WHAT ARE THE U AND V DIRECTIONS?

While working in 3D, you'll see references to the U and V directions. You can think of these as the x- and y-axes of a 3D surface. There is also a W direction, which corresponds to the z-axis, or the normal direction of a surface.

---

The Rebuild Surface dialog box offers a number of other options you'll want to know about. Table 23.3 gives you a rundown.

**TABLE 23.3:**     The Rebuild Surface dialog box

| SECTION/OPTION | EFFECT |
| --- | --- |
| **Control Vertices Count** | |
| Sets the number of CVs in the U direction | In U Direction |
| Sets the number of CVs in the V direction | In V Direction |
| **Degree** | |
| In U Direction | Sets the number of CVs available per span in the U direction |
| In V Direction | Sets the number of CVs available per span in the V direction |
| **Options** | |
| Determines whether the original geometry is retained | Delete Original Geometry |
| Determines whether trimmed surfaces are retained from the original surface | Retrim Previously Trimmed Surfaces |
| Displays the maximum deviation between the original and rebuilt surface | Maximum Deviation |

Two other tools just below the Surface Rebuild tool allow you to either add or remove a set of CVs. The Surface CV – Add tool lets you place a row of CVs. The Surface CV – Remove tool will remove a row of CVs. Both options allow you to toggle between the U and V directions for the row addition or removal by typing **D**↵.

The Surface CV Add and Remove tools can be useful when you want to fine-tune the curvature of a surface. Where you want a "tighter" curve, you can add more CVs to an area of the surface. You can then move the CVs in the selected area to increase the curvature. To smooth out the curvature of an area, remove the CVs.

## Editing with the CV Edit Bar

You've seen how a NURBS surface can be set up to add additional CVs, which in turn allow you to adjust the shape of the surface. But the CVs by themselves allow you to adjust their pull on the surface only by moving them closer or farther away from the surface.

The CV Edit bar gives you more control over the behavior of individual CVs. With the CV Edit bar, you can change the strength and direction of the "pull" exerted by a CV.

Try the following exercise to see how the CV Edit bar works:

CV Edit Bar

1. Click the Surface CV Edit Bar tool in the Control Vertices panel.

2. Select the surface. Now as you move the cursor across the surface, you see two red lines that follow the U and V directions of the surface (see Figure 23.56).

**FIGURE 23.56**
The CV Edit bar's U and V directions are shown by two red lines.

3. Click the point shown in Figure 23.56. A Move gizmo appears along with two other features called the magnitude handle and the expansion grip (see Figure 23.57).

The Move gizmo gives you a bit more control over the location of the CV since it allows you to isolate movement in the X, Y, or Z direction. The expansion grip lets you change the tangency of the CV, whereas the magnitude grip lets you control the strength of the CV.

Try the following steps to see how these two features work:

1. Click the expansion grip and select the Tangent Direction option. Notice that the Move gizmo switches to the location of the expansion grip.

2. Hover over the green y-axis of the gizmo, and when you see the green y-axis vector, click and drag the mouse. Notice how the surface warps as you move the mouse. If you look carefully at the CV Edit bar, you see that it pivots around the new location of the expansion grip, the CV location.

3. Press the Esc key to release the y-axis, and then click the expansion grip and choose the Move Point option. The Move gizmo returns to its original location at the CV.

4. Now click the magnitude handle, and move it horizontally. You see that the surface is "pulled" in both directions of the U direction of the surface.

5. Press the Esc key to release the magnitude handle.

6. Right-click the CV Edit bar and select V Tangent Direction. Notice that the magnitude handle changes its orientation so that it is aligned to the V direction of the surface.

7. Click and drag the magnitude handle to see how it affects the surface.

8. Press the Esc key twice to exit the CV Edit bar.

**FIGURE 23.57**
The magnitude handle and expansion grips.

Magnitude handle          Expansion grip

As you can see from this exercise, the CV Edit bar gives you much more control over a CV than you would have otherwise. You also saw the context menu for the CV Edit bar in step 6 (see Figure 23.58). The context menu allows you to change the direction of the magnitude grip, but it also lets you switch the position of the Move gizmo and the expansion grip with the Move Point Location and Move Tangent Direction options. The Relocate option lets you move to a different CV location. Table 23.4 includes descriptions of these options.

**FIGURE 23.58**
The CV Edit bar's context menu

**TABLE 23.4:**    The CV Edit bar's right-click options

| OPTION | PURPOSE |
| --- | --- |
| Move Point Location | Places the Move gizmo at the CV location |
| Move Tangent Direction | Places the Move gizmo at the expansion grip location to allow adjustment to the tangent direction of the CV |
| U Tangent Direction | Aligns the magnitude grip to the surface's U direction |
| V Tangent Direction | Aligns the magnitude grip to the surface's V direction |
| Normal Tangent Direction | Aligns the magnitude grip to a direction that is normal (perpendicular) to the surface |
| Set Constraint | Constrains changes to the tangency in a specific direction such as X, Y, or Z or in a plane defined by a pair of axes |
| Relocate Base Point | Moves the CV Edit bar to a different location on the surface |
| Align Gizmo With | Aligns the gizmo with the world or current UCS or with a face on the surface |

## Making Holes in a Surface with the Project Geometry Panel

Eventually, you'll need to place an opening in a surface, so AutoCAD offers the Project Geometry panel. This panel contains several tools that allow you to project a closed 2D object's shape onto a 3D surface. For example, if you want to place a circular hole in the surface you edited in the previous exercise, you would draw a circle parallel to that surface and then use the Surface Projection UCS tool.

Try the following exercise to see how the Project Geometry feature works:

**1.** Select the Layer Properties tool from the Layers panel of the Home tab.

**2.** Turn on the Circle layer. A circle appears in the drawing.

**3.** Type **UCS↵**, and then type **OB↵**. This lets you align the UCS to an object.

**4.** Click the circle to align the UCS to it.

**5.** In the Surface tab's Project Geometry panel, click the Surface Auto Trim tool to turn it on.

**6.** Click the Surface Projection UCS tool in the Project Geometry panel.

**7.** Click the circle and press ↵.

**8.** Click the surface. The circle is projected onto the surface and the area inside the projected circle is trimmed (see Figure 23.59).

In this exercise, you aligned the UCS to the circle. The Surface Projection UCS tool you used in step 6 projected the circle in the z-axis of this new UCS that is aligned with the circle.

**FIGURE 23.59**
The circle projected
onto the surface

The other two Project Geometry tools use different criteria to project geometry. The Surface Projection View projects geometry along the line of sight. If you had used this tool in the previous exercise, the projected circle and opening would appear directly behind the circle in your current view. The Surface Projection Vector projects geometry along a vector that you indicate with two points. You can use the 3D object snaps to select points on the geometry and the surface.

## Visualizing Curvature: Understanding the Analysis Panel

In addition to the surface editing tools, AutoCAD offers several surface analysis options. These options offer some visual aids to help you see the curvature of your surface models more clearly. They can be found in the Analysis panel of the Surface tab and are called Analysis Zebra, Analysis Curvature, and Analysis Draft.

Analysis Zebra displays stripes that let you better visualize how the curvatures of surfaces blend (see Figure 23.60). The smoother the stripes, the better the transition between surfaces.

**FIGURE 23.60**
The cue card
description for
Analysis Zebra

Analysis Curvature displays colors to indicate the direction and amount of curvature in a surface (see Figure 23.61). As the cue card describes, a negative curvature is a saddle shape and displays a blue color. A positive curvature, or bowl shape, displays in red.

Analysis Draft displays colors to help you determine draft angles (see Figure 23.62). Draft angles are often used in the design of objects that are to be cast from a mold, and they are important in allowing the cast object to be removed easily from the mold.

The Analysis Options tool opens the Analysis Options dialog box, where you can control the way the different analysis tools are displayed. Note that graphics hardware acceleration must be turned on before you can use these tools. You must also use a visual style other than Wireframe.

To turn on graphics hardware acceleration, right-click the Hardware Acceleration tool in the right portion of the status bar and select Hardware Acceleration.

**FIGURE 23.61**

The cue card description for Analysis Curvature

**FIGURE 23.62**

The cue card description for Analysis Draft

---

### USING THE 3D OBJECT SNAPS

You may have noticed the 3D Object Snap tool in the status bar:

It might not be turned on. Click the Customization button on the far right of the status bar to bring up a list of possible status bar icons. Click the 3D Object Snap option to turn it on. This tool works in a way similar to the Object Snap tool you've used in earlier chapters. When the 3D Object Snap tool is on, you can snap to geometry on 3D objects. If you right-click this tool, you'll see the list of locations to which you can snap:

You can think of the 3D Object Snap tool as an extension of the standard set of object snaps that allow you to pick locations on 3D solids, meshes, and surfaces. Right-click the 3D Object Snap tool and select Settings and you will see the Drafting Settings dialog box open to the 3D Object Snap tab. There you can choose which 3D object snap you want to appear as the default when this tool is turned on.

---

## The Bottom Line

**Create a simple 3D mesh.** Mesh modeling allows you to create more organic 3D forms by giving you unique smoothing and editing tools. You can start your mesh model by creating a basic shape using the mesh primitives.

**Master It** Name the seven mesh primitives available on the Primitives panel of the Mesh Modeling tab.

**Edit faces and edges.** The ability to edit faces and edges is essential to creating complex shapes with mesh objects.

**Master It** Name the tool that is used to divide a face into multiple faces.

**Create mesh surfaces.** The Mesh primitives let you create shapes that enclose a volume. If you just want to model a smooth, curved surface in 3D, you might find the surface mesh tools helpful.

**Master It** How many objects are needed to use the Edge Surface tool?

**Convert meshes to solids.** You can convert a mesh into a 3D solid to take advantage of many of the solid-editing tools available.

**Master It** Name at least two tools you can use on a solid that you cannot use on a mesh.

**Understand 3D surfaces.** 3D surfaces can be created using some of the same tools you use to create 3D solids.

**Master It** Name at least two tools you can use to create both 3D solids and 3D surfaces.

**Edit 3D surfaces.** AutoCAD offers a wide range of tools that are unique to 3D surfaces.

**Master It** Name at least four tools devoted to CV editing.

# Part 5

# Customization and Integration

# Chapter 24

# Customizing Toolbars, Menus, Linetypes, and Hatch Patterns

AutoCAD® 2015 software offers a high degree of flexibility and customization, enabling you to tailor the software's look and feel to your requirements. In this chapter, you'll see how to customize AutoCAD so that it integrates more smoothly into your workgroup and office environment.

The first part of the chapter shows how to adapt AutoCAD to fit your particular needs. You'll learn how to customize AutoCAD by modifying its menus, and you'll learn how to create custom macros for commands that your workgroup uses frequently.

In this chapter, you will learn to

♦ Use workspaces

♦ Customize the user interface

♦ Create macros in tools and menus

♦ Edit keyboard shortcuts

♦ Save, load, and unload your customizations

♦ Understand the Diesel macro language

♦ Create custom linetypes

♦ Create hatch patterns

## Using Workspaces

When you're comfortable with AutoCAD, you may find that you like a certain arrangement of Ribbon panels, toolbars, and palettes or that you have several sets of panels and toolbars that you like to use, depending on your type of work. You've already worked with two of the workspaces AutoCAD offers out of the box: Drafting & Annotation and 3D Modeling. You can also set up your own custom panel and toolbar arrangements and then save those arrangements for later retrieval using the Workspace feature. Let's take a closer look at how you can create a custom workspace.

The Workspace Switching tool and its menu are shown in Figure 24.1. In the "Getting to Know the 3D Modeling Workspace" section in Chapter 20, "Creating 3D Drawings," you saw how you can use a similar tool, the Workspace drop-down list, to switch to a 3D modeling workspace. You can save several arrangements of panels, toolbars, and palettes and then recall them easily by selecting them from the Workspace Switching tool in the status bar or Workspace drop-down list in the Quick Access toolbar.

**FIGURE 24.1**

The Workspace Switching tool

Click the Workspace Switching tool on the status bar and select Workspace Settings to open the Workspace Settings dialog box, shown in Figure 24.2. You can also select Workspace Settings from the Workspace drop-down list in the Quick Access toolbar or type **Wssettings.**↵

**FIGURE 24.2**

The Workspace Settings dialog box

With the Workspace Settings dialog box open, you can see the Drafting & Annotation, 3D Basics, and 3D Modeling options. If you've used the Initial Setup Wizard to create an industry-specific workspace, you'll see the Initial Setup Workspace option here as well. From here, you can control the behavior of the settings.

The check box next to each setting lets you control whether the item appears in the Workspace Switching tool menu. For example, if you remove the check mark from the 3D Basics setting, you'll see only Drafting & Annotation and 3D Modeling in the Workspace Switching tool menu.

The My Workspace drop-down list lets you select which workspace setting is activated when you click the My Workspace tool on the Workspace toolbar. You can use this option for your most frequently used workspace settings.

The options in the When Switching Workspaces group at the bottom of the Workspace Settings dialog box let you determine whether workspace changes are saved automatically. For example, if you select Automatically Save Workspace Changes, then the next time you switch to a different workspace setting, AutoCAD will save any changes you've made to the current workspace.

The Workspace Switching tool is the easiest customization feature you'll find in AutoCAD, and it can go a long way toward helping you stay organized. But workspaces are just the tip of the iceberg when it comes to customizing AutoCAD. Next, you'll delve into the Customize User Interface (CUI) feature to see how you can customize the AutoCAD menus, panels, and toolbars directly.

**ARE YOU IN THE RIGHT WORKSPACE?**

The exercises in this chapter assume that you are in the Drafting & Annotation workspace.

# Customizing the User Interface

Out of the box, AutoCAD offers a generic arrangement of Ribbon panels, tools, and palettes that works fine for most applications. But the more you use AutoCAD, the more you may find that you tend to use tools that are scattered over several Ribbon panels. You'll probably feel that your work would go more easily if you could create a custom set of panels and menus to consolidate those tools. If you're at the point of creating custom macros, you may want a way to have easy access to them.

The *Customize User Interface (CUI)* dialog box is a one-stop location that gives you nearly total control over the menus, panels, and toolbars in AutoCAD. With the CUI feature, you can mold the AutoCAD interface to your liking. The main entry point to the CUI is the Customize User Interface dialog box.

The following section introduces you to the CUI by showing you how to add a tool to the Draw Ribbon panel. You'll also get a chance to see how to create an entirely new panel and custom tools.

## Taking a Quick Customization Tour

The most direct way to adapt AutoCAD to your way of working is to customize the Ribbon. AutoCAD offers new users an easy route to customization through the Customize User Interface dialog box. With this dialog box, you can create new Ribbon panels and toolbars, customize tools, and even create new icons. You can also create keyboard shortcuts.

To get your feet wet, try adding a tool to the Draw panel:

1. If it's still open, close the Workspace Settings dialog box.

2. Click the User Interface tool in the Manage tab's Customization panel to open the Customize User Interface dialog box, shown in Figure 24.3. You can also type **CUI**↵. You see three groups in this dialog box: Customizations In All Files, Command List, and Properties.

3. In the Customizations In All Files group, expand the Ribbon option and then expand the Panels option that appears just below. Scroll down the list and expand the Home 2D – Draw option. You see a set of options labeled Row 1, Row 2, and so on.

4. Click the Home 2D – Draw option. A view of the Draw Ribbon panel appears in the Panel Preview area (see Figure 24.4).

5. Expand the Row 3 item under the Home 2D – Draw option. You'll see the names of the three tools that appear at the very bottom of the Draw panel. These tools are 3D Polyline, Helix, and Donut.

6. In the Command List group, select Dimension from the Filter The Command List By Category drop-down list (see Figure 24.5).

**FIGURE 24.3**
The Customize User
Interface dialog box

**FIGURE 24.4**
The Draw Ribbon
panel appears.

**FIGURE 24.5**

Choose the Dimension category.

7. In the bottom panel of the Command List group, scroll down the list and then locate and select Dimension, Linear. This is the Linear Dimension command. When you select Linear, the Properties group displays the properties of the Linear command. The Panel Preview area changes to show the Button Image group, and you see the Linear Dimension icon, as shown in Figure 24.6.

8. Carefully click and drag the Dimension, Linear item from the Command List group into the Customizations In All Files group, but don't release the mouse button yet. As you drag the item over the tool names in the Customizations In All Files group, a bar tells you where your dragged item will appear (see Figure 24.6). If you pause over an option, you'll see an arrowhead appear next to the option. The arrowhead also indicates where the dragged command will be placed. The list may automatically scroll up or down depending on where you place the bar. This is to allow you to place the bar in an area of the list that isn't currently displayed.

9. Place the bar just above 3D Polyline, and release the mouse button. Dimension, Linear appears above 3D Polyline in the list (see Figure 24.7), and while it may be difficult to see, the Dimension Linear icon appears in the Panel Preview area.

10. Click OK. The next time you check, you'll see the Dimension, Linear tool appear in the expanded Draw panel just to the left of the 3D Polyline tool (see Figure 24.8).

**FIGURE 24.6**
The Panel Preview area changes when you select an element from the Command List group or the Customizations In All Files group.

The bar tells you where the command will be placed.

**FIGURE 24.7**
After positioning the Dimension icon

**FIGURE 24.8**

The tool is in place.

You've just added a command to the Draw panel. You can follow the previous steps to add any command to any Ribbon panel, toolbar, or menu bar menu. Now suppose you change your mind and you decide to remove Dimension, Linear from the Draw panel. Here's how it's done:

1. Click User Interface in the Manage tab's Customization panel, or type **CUI**↵.

2. In the Customizations In All Files group of the Customize User Interface dialog box, expand the Ribbon option and Panels option and then continue to expand options as you did before to get to the Dimension, Linear command you added earlier.

3. Click Dimension, Linear, and then right-click and choose Remove from the context menu. You'll see a warning message asking if you "really want to delete this element."

4. Click Yes. The Dimension, Linear command is removed.

5. Click OK to close the dialog box.

Dimension, Linear has been removed from the Draw panel. As you've just seen, adding tools to a panel is a matter of clicking and dragging the appropriate item from one list to another. To remove tools, right-click the tool and select Remove.

Before you go too much further, you may want to know a little more about the Customize User Interface dialog box and how it works. You saw briefly how each group displayed different elements of the AutoCAD interface, from a listing of panel tools to an individual tool's icon. Let's look at each group independently to see how it's organized.

## Understanding the Customizations In All Files Panel

In the previous exercise, where you placed the Dimension, Linear command in the Draw panel, you saw an arrowhead appear when you hovered over an option. The arrowhead indicates where the command will be placed when you release the mouse button. If the arrowhead points to a command, the new command will be placed after the item indicated by the arrowhead. If the item is a folder icon, the new command will be placed inside that folder.

You may see items called *Sub-Panel* options. These allow you to mix single tools and rows like the Line tool and the three rows you see to the right of the Line tool at the top of the Draw panel. Finally, the <SLIDEOUT> item you see in the list indicates the division between the main part of the panel and the expanded panel. Figure 24.9 shows how the list in the Customizations In All Files group relates to the Ribbon panel components.

**FIGURE 24.9**
The Customizations In All Files list compared to the Ribbon panel preview

Notice that the Line, Polyline, Circle, and Arc tools straddle the two rows in the expanded Draw panel and are at the same level as the Sub-Panel 1 options of Rectangle, Ellipse, and Hatch. This is done by placing the Line, Polyline, Circle, and Arc commands at the same level as the Sub-Panel 1 option. The Sub-Panel 1 option is further divided into rows. Figure 24.10 shows how the rows appear when they are expanded. Flyouts on the Ribbon panel appear as Drop-down options in the Customizations In All Files group.

If you expand a Drop-down option, you'll see the tools that appear in the flyouts of the tool in the panel (see Figure 24.11).

You can add new panels, rows, subpanels, and drop-downs (flyouts) by right-clicking an item in the list and selecting the appropriate option from the context menu (see Figure 24.12). These types of interface elements are called *containers* in the Customize User Interface dialog box.

If you understand the structure of these lists, you'll find that it is quite easy to customize the Ribbon panels to your liking.

## Getting the Overall View

When you first opened the Customize User Interface dialog box by right-clicking the Ribbon, you saw a listing of the AutoCAD interface elements in the Customizations In All Files group. Just as you saw with the Ribbon panels, each of the other interface elements in the list can be expanded to get to its individual commands. If you expand the Toolbars list, for example, all the AutoCAD toolbars are available. Expand a toolbar and the commands contained in the toolbar are displayed. As you saw earlier, you can expand the Ribbon Panels list to gain access to the Ribbon panels. Table 24.1 lists all the interface elements in the Customizations In All Files group with a brief explanation of their contents.

**FIGURE 24.10**
The Sub-Panel 1 option contains the rows that in turn contain flyouts labeled as "Drop-down" options.

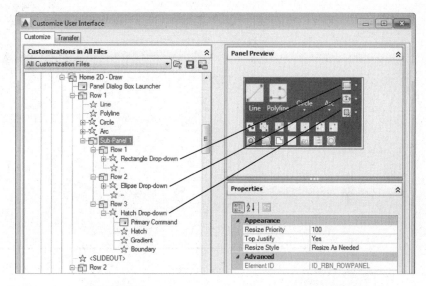

**FIGURE 24.11**
The tools in the Customizations In All Files panel's Drop-Down list appear in the appropriate flyout.

**FIGURE 24.12**
Create new containers via the context menu.

**TABLE 24.1:** Main headings in the Customizations In All Files group

| ITEM | WHAT IT CONTAINS |
| --- | --- |
| Workspaces | Workspaces that are currently available |
| Quick Access Toolbars | Quick Access toolbars |
| Ribbon | The Ribbon tabs, panels, and contextual tab states |
| Toolbars | Toolbars |
| Menus | Menu bar menus |
| Quick Properties | Options on the Quick Properties palette |
| Rollover Tooltips | Rollover tooltip settings |
| Shortcut Menus | Menus shown with right-clicks |
| Keyboard Shortcuts | Current keyboard shortcuts, such as Ctrl+C and Ctrl+V |
| Double-Click Actions | Object-dependent double-click actions |
| Mouse Buttons | Mouse button options, such as Shift+click and Ctrl+click |
| LISP Files | Any custom LISP files that are used with your CUI |
| Legacy | Any legacy custom items you use, such as table or screen menus |
| Partial Customization Files | Custom CUI files that have been included in the main CUI file |

You can customize any of the interface elements. For example, if you want to create new keyboard shortcuts, you can expand the Keyboard Shortcuts listing and add new shortcuts or edit existing ones. Right-click any item to add or delete options. If you click an item, its properties appear in the Properties group, where you can modify the item's function. Just as you added the Dimension, Linear command to the Draw panel, you can click and drag a command into one of the menus under the Menus listing to add a command there.

You also see some options in the Customizations In All Files title bar. These options give you control over what is displayed in this group. You can also load and save CUI files from here.

Load Partial Customization File

Save All Current Customization Files

Image Manager

You'll learn more about these options later in this chapter.

---

**ADD A PANEL TITLE BAR COMMAND WITH THE PANEL DIALOG BOX LAUNCHER**

You may have noticed the Panel Dialog Box Launcher item that appears just below a panel name (when expanded) in the Customize User Interface dialog box. With this placeholder you can add a command that will launch when you click an arrow icon in the right side of the panel title bar. You can see an example of such an icon in the Insert tab's Reference panel or the Annotate tab's Text and Dimensions panels. These arrow icons typically open dialog boxes that control the main features presented in the panel. For example, the one in the Annotate tab's Text panel opens the Text Style dialog box.

To add a command to the Panel Dialog Box Launcher item, click and drag a command from the Command List area to the Panel Dialog Box Launcher item. To remove a command, right-click the Panel Dialog Box Launcher item and select Remove Command. Click Yes to confirm the removal.

The Panel Dialog Box Launcher item is included automatically whenever you create a new panel.

---

## Finding Commands in the Command List

You've already seen how the Command List group contains all the commands in AutoCAD. You also saw that you can click and drag these items into options in the Customizations In All Files group. This list also contains predefined macros, icons used for tools, and *control elements* (called combo boxes in the Ribbon panels), which are the drop-down lists you see in panels and toolbars. The layer drop-down lists in the Layers panel and the lists in the Home tab's Properties panel are examples of control elements. When you select an item in the Command List group, you see its properties in the Properties group or its icon in the Button Image group, or both. The control elements are the exception to this because they have no editable features.

## Opening Preview, Button Image, and Shortcuts

You've already seen how you can get a preview of a Ribbon panel by selecting the panel from the Customizations In All Files group. If you click a Ribbon panel from the list, you'll see the Panel Preview group, which shows you how the selected panel will appear. Previews aren't editable and are there for your reference.

If you click a tool listing—or *element* in AutoCAD nomenclature—in the Customizations In All Files group, you see the Button Image group. You can open this group by clicking the double arrowhead to the right of the Button Image group title bar. You may also need to adjust the bottom border of the Button Image group downward so you can see more of the group. This group lets you select an icon for that tool by clicking a list of icons (see Figure 24.13), or you can edit an existing icon or create an entirely new icon. You'll get a chance to see this firsthand later in this chapter.

**FIGURE 24.13**
The Button
Image group

The Keyboard Shortcuts area in the Customizations In All Files group shows the Shortcuts group, which lists the existing keyboard shortcuts.

## Getting to the Core of Customization in the Properties Group

Finally, when you're ready to do some serious customizing, you'll work with the Properties group. You see the Properties group in the lower half of the right side of the Customize User Interface dialog box when you select a command from the left side of the dialog box.

The Properties group is set up just like the Properties palette, and it works the same way. On the left side, you see a listing of options. To the right of each option is a description or a text box where you can make changes (see Figure 24.14).

If you go to the Customizations In All Files group and select the Line tool under the Home 2D – Draw option that you worked on earlier (Ribbon ➤ Panels ➤ Home 2D – Draw ➤ Row 1 ➤ Line), you see the properties for that tool in the Properties group, as shown in Figure 24.14. You'll have to close the Button Image group to get a complete view of the Properties group. You can close any group by clicking the double arrow on the right side of the group's title bar.

In the Command category, you see the Line tool's name in the Command Name listing. You also see the description that is displayed in the tool tip for the Line tool. You can change this description here in the Properties group, and the description will change in the status bar.

**FIGURE 24.14**

The Properties group showing the properties for the Line tool

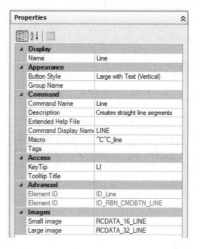

In the Macro listing, you see the command as it would be entered through the keyboard. The ^C^C that precedes the actual line command input is equivalent to pressing the Esc key twice. If you scroll down, you'll see the Advanced category, which offers information regarding the ID of this particular tool. Finally, the Images category lists the name of the image files used for the Line tool icon. Two icons are listed: one for the large icon version and one for the small icon version of the tool.

You'll get a chance to work with the Properties group later in this chapter. Next you'll try your hand at creating your own custom toolbar.

## Creating Your Own Ribbon Panels and Menus

Earlier, we mentioned that you can collect your most frequently used tools into a custom Ribbon panel or toolbar. Now that you've familiarized yourself with the Customize User Interface dialog box, you can try the following exercise to create your own Ribbon panel:

1. If the Customize User Interface dialog box isn't open, click User Interface in the Manage tab's Customization panel.

2. In the Customizations In All Files group, expand the Ribbon option and then right-click Panels and choose New Panel. The list expands and you see a new panel called Panel1 at the bottom of the Panels list. The name Panel1 is highlighted and ready to be edited.

3. Replace Panel1 by typing **My Panel** to give your panel a distinct name (see Figure 24.15). As you type, the name changes. If you decide to change a panel name later, right-click a panel listing and then choose Rename.

**FIGURE 24.15**

The new Panel1 name changed to My Panel

You now have a custom Ribbon panel. You'll want to start to populate your panel with some commands. You've already seen how this works, but to review try adding a few commands:

1. Select Draw from the Filter The Command List By Category drop-down list. It's the list that is below the Search box under Command List.

2. In the Command List group, locate the command you want to add. In this instance, locate the Line tool.

3. Click and drag the Line command to your new panel so that you see an arrowhead pointing to the Row 1 option (see Figure 24.16).

**FIGURE 24.16**

Point to the Row 1 option, and you'll see the arrowhead appear.

4. Release the mouse button. The Line tool appears below Row 1.

5. Repeat steps 2, 3, and 4 to add more commands to your panel.

6. To add another row, right-click My Panel and select New Row. You can add more tools to your second row.

You can add several more rows to your panel, but after the first row, additional rows will be placed below <SLIDEOUT>, in the expanded portion of the panel.

---

**DELETING A CUSTOM TOOL OR PANEL**

You can delete any tool from your custom panel by right-clicking the tool and choosing Remove while in the Customizations In All Files group of the Customize User Interface dialog box. You can also delete your entire panel using this method. Take care not to delete any of the panels you want to keep.

---

## Customizing Ribbon Panel Tools

Let's move on to more serious customization. Suppose you want to create an entirely new button with its own functions. For example, you might want to create a set of buttons that insert your favorite symbols. Or you might want to create a Ribbon panel containing a set of tools that open some of the other toolbars that are normally put away.

### CREATING A CUSTOM TOOL

Follow these steps to create a custom tool:

1. Open the Customize User Interface dialog box, expand the Ribbon Panels list, and then expand the My Panel list.

2. In the Command List panel title bar, click the Create A New Command tool. A new command called Command1 appears in the list of commands (see Figure 24.17).

**FIGURE 24.17**
Click the Create
A New Command
tool and a new
command appears
in the list.

3. Right-click the Command1 item, select Rename from the context menu, and change the name to **Door**.

4. In the Properties group to the right, change Description to **Insert a 36" door**.

5. Change the Macro option to the following:

```
^C^C-insert door;\36;;
```

6. Click and drag the Door element from the Command List panel into Row 1 of your My Panel item in the Customizations In All Files group. If you look at the Panel Preview group, you see that the Door tool you just added appears as a blank tool. This happens when no icon has been assigned to the tool.

The series of keystrokes you entered for the macro in step 5 are the same as those you would use to insert the door with the addition of a few special characters. The semicolons are equivalent to ↵, and the backward slash (\) is a special macro code that tells AutoCAD to pause the macro for user input. In this case, the pause allows you to select the insertion point for the door. The Properties group should look similar to Figure 24.18.

**FIGURE 24.18**

The Properties group for your new custom tool that inserts a door block

---

**LOCATE FILES SO AUTOCAD CAN FIND THEM**

A misplaced file is a common problem you have to troubleshoot when you're supporting an office full of AutoCAD users. AutoCAD likes to place files in a lot of different places. When it can't find a file it needs, it will give you an error message, or worse, it just won't work. It helps to know where AutoCAD looks for files so that you can place the resources for your custom tools in the right places.

In the Door example, the door drawing used in your macro must be in the default folder, My Documents, or in the acad search path before the door will be inserted. For easy access, copy the Door.dwg file from the Chapter 4 project folder to the My Documents folder.

---

You've created your panel, but it will not appear anywhere in the AutoCAD interface until you add it to a Ribbon tab group. Here's how this is done:

1. Under your My Panel listing in the Customizations In All Files group, click the My Panel panel option you just created and then right-click and select Copy.

2. In the Customizations In All Files group, scroll up to the top of the list and expand the Tabs option.

3. Right-click Home – 2D just below Ribbon ➢ Tabs, and then select Paste from the context menu. Your My Panel panel appears at the bottom of the Home – 2D list.

4. Click OK in the Customize User Interface dialog box to close it. Your panel appears in the Home tab of the Ribbon.

Next try the custom tool to make sure it works:

1. Put a copy of the Door.dwg file in your My Documents folder.

2. Point to the Door tool in your My Panel panel in the Home tab. You see the Door tool tip.

**3.** Click the Door tool. The door appears in the drawing area at the cursor. It may appear very small because initially it's being inserted at its default size of 1 unit.

**4.** Click a location to place the door, and then click a point to set the door rotation. The door appears in the drawing.

In this example, you created a custom tool that inserts the door block. Later in this chapter, you'll learn more about creating macros for menus and tools. Next you'll learn how to add a custom icon for your custom tool.

### CREATING A CUSTOM ICON

You have all the essential parts of the button defined. Now you just need to create a custom icon to go with your Door button:

**1.** Open the Customize User Interface dialog box.

**2.** Expand the Customizations In All Files Ribbon list to your My Panel option (Ribbon ➢ Panels ➢ My Panel).

**3.** Expand the Row1 list, and select Door.

**4.** Open the Button Image group, and click any icon image. The icon appears in the Panel Preview group, replacing the blank image for your Door tool.

**5.** In the Button Image group, click the Edit button to open the Button Editor. The Button Editor is like a simple drawing program. Across the top are the tools to draw lines, circles, and points as well as an eraser. Along the left side is a color toolbar from which you can choose colors for your icon. At the upper right, you see a preview of your button.

---

**YOU CAN USE THE EXISTING ICONS**

If you prefer, you can use any of the predefined icons in the scroll box to the right of the Button Image group in the Customize User Interface dialog box. Click the icon you want to use, and then click Apply.

---

**6.** Before you do anything else, click the Clear button. This clears the current image.

**7.** Draw the door icon shown in Figure 24.19. Don't worry if it's not perfect; you can always go back and fix it.

**8.** Click Save, and then at the Save Image dialog box, enter **Door36** for the name. The door icon is saved in the AutoCAD CUI file that stores all of the interface data.

**9.** Click OK, and then click Close at the Button Editor dialog box.

**10.** Click OK to close the Customize User Interface dialog box. You see your custom icon for the Door tool.

**FIGURE 24.19**
Draw this door icon.

The Button Editor behaves like a simplified image editing tool, and it is fairly straightforward to use. The only part that may be confusing is that you have to clear the image and save any new image under a new name.

You can continue to add more buttons to build a panel of symbols. Of course, you're not limited to a symbols library. You can also incorporate your favorite macros or even AutoLISP® routines that you accumulate as you work with AutoCAD. The possibilities are endless.

## Creating Macros in Tools and Menus

Combining existing commands into new panels or toolbars can be useful, but you'll get even more benefit from the CUI by creating your own macros. *Macros* are predefined sets of responses to commands that can help automate your most frequently used processes.

Early on, you saw how a macro was included in a tool to insert a door. You added a special set of instructions in the Macro option of the Properties group to perform the door insertion and scale. You also saw how the Line command was formatted as part of a tool.

Let's take a closer look at how macros are built. Start by looking at the existing Line tool and how it's formatted.

The Macro option for the Line tool starts with two ^C elements, which are equivalent to pressing the Esc key twice. This cancels any command that is currently operative. The Line command follows, written just as it would be entered through the keyboard. Two Cancels are issued in case you're in a command that has two levels, such as the Edit Vertex option of the Pedit command.

The underscore character (_) that precedes the Line command tells AutoCAD that you're using the English-language version of this command. This feature lets you program non-English versions of AutoCAD by using the English-language command names.

---

**WHAT IS THE HYPHEN FOR?**

In the previous door macro example, you used a hyphen in front of the Insert command. The hyphen causes the Insert command to run in the command line instead of using a dialog box, where the macro keyboard input will not work. Many commands will run in the command line when preceded with a hyphen.

---

You may also notice that there is no space between the second ^C and the Line command. A space in the line would be the same as ↵. If there were a space between these two elements, ↵ would be entered between the last ^C and the Line command, causing the command sequence to misstep. Another way to indicate ↵ is by using the semicolon, as in the following example:

```
^C^C_Line;;
```

---

**HELP MAKE YOUR MACRO READABLE**

If a menu macro contains multiple instances of ↵, using semicolons instead of spaces can help make your macro more readable.

---

In this sample menu option, the Line command is issued and then an additional ↵ is added. The effect of choosing this option is a line that continues from the last line entered into your drawing. The two semicolons following Line tell AutoCAD to start the Line command and then issue ↵ twice; the first ↵ starts the Line command, and then the second ↵ tells AutoCAD to begin a line from the endpoint of the last line entered. (AutoCAD automatically issues a single ↵ at the end of a menu line. In this case, however, you want two instances of ↵, so they must be represented as semicolons.)

## Pausing for User Input

Another symbol used in the Macro option is the backslash (\); it's used when a pause is required for user input. For example, the following sample macro starts the Arc command and then pauses for your input:

```
^C^C_arc \_e \_d
```

The space between ^C^C_arc and the backslash (\) represents pressing the spacebar. The backslash indicates a pause to enable you to select the starting endpoint for the arc. The _e represents the selection of the Endpoint option under the Arc command after you've picked a point. A second backslash allows another point selection. Finally, the _d represents the selection of the Direction option. Figure 24.20 illustrates this. If you want the last character in a menu item to be a backslash, you must follow the backslash with a semicolon.

## Opening an Expanded Text Box for the Macro Option

As you become more expert at creating macros, you may find the line provided in the Macro option too small for your needs. Fortunately, you can open an expanded text box in which to write longer macros. For example, suppose you want to include the following macro in a tool:

```
(defun c:breakat ()
(command "break" pause "f" pause "@")
)
breakat
```

**FIGURE 24.20**
The execution of the
Arc menu item

This example shows the Breakat AutoLISP macro. Everything in this segment is entered just as it would be from the keyboard at the Command prompt. You may find it a bit cumbersome to try to enter this macro in the text box provided by the Macro option in the Properties group of the Customize User Interface dialog box, but if you click the Macro text box, a Browse button appears to the right (see Figure 24.21).

**FIGURE 24.21**
The Browse button
in the Macro option

Click the Browse button to open the Long String Editor. You can then enter the macro and see it clearly. The following shows how it would be entered:

```
^C^C(defun c:breakat ()+
(command "break" pause "f" pause "@")+
);breakat
```

It starts with the usual ^C^C to clear any current commands. The plus sign at the end of lines 1 and 2 tells AutoCAD that the macro continues in the next line without actually breaking it. The break is there to help make the macro easier to read as you enter it. It's okay to break an AutoLISP macro into smaller lines. Doing so can help you read and understand the program more easily.

---

**LOADING AUTOLISP MACROS**

As you become a more advanced AutoCAD user, you may want many of your own AutoLISP macros to load with your custom interface. You can make them do that by combining all your AutoLISP macros into a single file. Give this file the same name as your menu file but with the `.mnl` filename extension. Such a file automatically loads with its menu counterpart. For example, say you have a file called `Mymenu.mnl` containing the `Breakat` AutoLISP macro. Whenever you load `Mymenu.cui`, `Mymenu.mnl` is automatically loaded along with it, giving you access to the `Breakat` macro. This is a good way to manage and organize any AutoLISP program code you want to include with a menu.

To learn more about the AutoLISP language, see the online bonus chapter "Exploring AutoLISP," available at `www.omura.com/chapters`.

---

## Editing Keyboard Shortcuts

Another area of customization that can be useful is the keyboard shortcut. You probably already know about the standard Ctrl+C and Ctrl+V, which are shortcuts for the Windows Copy and Paste functions. In AutoCAD, Shift+Ctrl+A toggles groups on and off, and Ctrl+1 opens the Properties palette.

You can edit existing keyboard shortcuts or create new ones by opening the Keyboard Shortcuts list in the Customizations In All Files group of the Customize User Interface dialog box. If you expand this list, you see Shortcut Keys and Temporary Override Keys. These can be expanded to reveal their elements. Select an element to display its properties in the Properties group.

You can click and drag a command from the Command List group into the Shortcut Keys group and then edit its properties to set the shortcut keys you want to use for the command. For example, if you click and drag the 3D Free Orbit command from the Command List group into the Shortcut Keys list and then select it from that list, you see its properties in the Properties group (see Figure 24.22).

**FIGURE 24.22**

The Properties group

Click the Key(s) option in the Properties group, and then click the Browse button that appears to the far right of the Keys option to open the Shortcut Keys dialog box.

Click in the Press The New Shortcut Key text box, and then press the shortcut key you want to use for this command. For example, if you press Shift+Ctrl+Z, that sequence appears in the text box. If the shortcut you selected is already assigned to another command, you see a message that says so just below the text box. Click OK when you're done.

## RECORD AND PLAY BACK ACTIONS

If AutoLISP seems a bit too intimidating but you still need a way to automate certain tasks, the Action Recorder is a feature you'll want to explore. The Action Recorder enables you to record a series of actions in AutoCAD and store them as *action macros*. You can play back your action macros at any time. This is a great time-saver when you are performing repetitive tasks, something that you may find yourself doing frequently in AutoCAD.

An entire panel is devoted to the Action Recorder in the Manage tab:

To use the Action Recorder, click the Record button. The Record button changes to a Stop button, and a red dot appears next to the cursor to remind you that you are recording your activity. You'll also see the Action Tree appear just below the recorder.

Continue working as you normally would in AutoCAD. As you work, your activity is displayed in the Action Tree. When you've completed the activity that you want to record, click the Stop button. The Action Macro dialog box appears, where you can give the recorded activity a name and description.

After you've closed the Action Macro dialog box, you can play back your recorded action macro at any time. From the Action Recorder panel, select the macro name from the Available Action Macro drop-down list and then click Play.

The Action Tree enables you to include some interactivity in your macro. You can right-click an individual action in the Action Tree to modify its behavior to allow user input. Perhaps the most common modification you'll want to make is to allow different selections or to change coordinate input and point selections. To do this, right-click an action and select Pause For User Input.

Upon selecting this option, you will be prompted for input when this particular action comes up in the macro. You can also use the Insert User Message option to have a message display while the macro is running. Messages can be helpful for users who are unfamiliar with your macro.

# Saving, Loading, and Unloading Your Customizations

You may want to save the custom menus, panels, and toolbars you create with the Customize User Interface dialog box so that you can carry them with you to other computers and load them for ready access. To save your customization work, you need to use the Transfer tab of the Customize User Interface dialog box. Here's how it works:

1. Open the Customize User Interface dialog box.

2. Click the Transfer tab. This tab contains two panels: The left panel shows the Customizations In Main File group, and the right panel shows a similar group called Customizations In New File.

3. In the left panel, locate your custom component, such as a menu, a Ribbon panel, or a toolbar.

4. Click and drag it to the appropriate item in the right panel. For example, click and drag a custom panel from the Ribbon panel list of the left group to the Ribbon panel section in the right group.

5. Repeat step 4 for each custom component you've created.

6. When you've copied everything from the left group to the right, click the drop-down list in the Customizations In New File title bar and select Save As.

7. In the Save As dialog box, enter a name for your customization file and select a location.

8. Click Save to complete the process.

---

### SYNCHRONIZE YOUR CUSTOM SETTINGS WITH AUTODESK 360

When you use Autodesk® 360 and the Sync My Settings Through The Cloud option, you can always have your custom settings available no matter where you are. To use this option, log into Autodesk 360 (see the section "Getting Started with Autodesk 360" in Chapter 25, "Managing and Sharing Your Drawings"). Then make sure the Sync My Settings Through The Cloud option is checked in the InfoCenter's Autodesk 360 drop-down menu. AutoCAD will automatically store your custom settings in the Autodesk 360 cloud service. If you start an AutoCAD 2015 session at another location and log into Autodesk 360, your custom settings will be synchronized with the settings stored in the cloud.

You can control which settings are synced by using the Online tab of the Options dialog box. Click the Autodesk 360 drop-down list from the InfoCenter, and then select Online Options. Doing so opens the Online tab of the Options dialog box. Click the Choose Which Settings Are Synced button to open a dialog box that lets you select which settings to sync.

---

Your customization is saved with the .cuix filename extension. After it's saved as a file, you can load it into another copy of AutoCAD by doing the following:

1. Open the Customize User Interface dialog box.

2. Click the Load Partial Customization File tool in the Customizations In All Files group toolbar.

3. In the Open dialog box, locate and select your CUI file and then click Open.

4. Back in the Customize User Interface dialog box, click OK.

5. If your CUI file contains menus, enter **Workspace** ↵↵ at the Command prompt. Or select a workspace from the Workspace Switching tool in the status bar. If it contains toolbars, right-click in a blank area next to an existing docked toolbar, and then select the name of your CUI file and the toolbar.

As an alternative to using the Customize User Interface dialog box, you can use the CUIload command. Enter **Cuiload** ↵ at the Command prompt to open the Load/Unload Customizations dialog box.

Click the Browse button to locate and select your CUI file. After you've done this, the name of your file appears in the File Name text box. You can then click the Load button to import it into your AutoCAD session.

Finally, if you want to unload a CUI file, do the following:

1. Open the Customize User Interface dialog box.

2. Scroll down to the bottom of the list in the Customizations In All Files group, and expand the Partial Customization Files item.

3. Right-click the partial CUI file you want to unload, and select Unload *name*.cuix.

4. Close the dialog box by clicking OK.

## CUSTOMIZING THE AUTOCOMPLETE COMMAND ENTRY FEATURE

AutoComplete provides a way to speed up your keyboard entry by offering command and system variable name suggestions as you type. For example, if you want to start the polygon command but you're not sure of the command name, you can type **poly** and AutoComplete will fill in the rest of the name for you.

AutoComplete offers a few options in the way it presents command and system variable name suggestions. To get to these options, right-click in the command-line interface and then select Input Settings. You will see a list of options that you can toggle on or off. These options are AutoComplete, AutoCorrect, Search System Variables, Search Content, Mid-string Search, and Delay Time.

The AutoComplete option lets you enable or disable the AutoComplete feature. The AutoCorrect option will correct for misspelled entries. Search System Variables will include system variables when looking for AutoComplete suggestions. Search Content will search for names of objects in the drawing. Mid-string Search will suggest names that start with or contain the letters you type. Delay Time lets you control the delay between the time you start to type and when AutoComplete offers a suggestion.

Besides these selections, you can also make more detailed setting modifications through the Input Search Options dialog box.

This dialog box offers some additional control over how the AutoComplete feature works. To open this dialog box, right-click in the Command window and select Input Search Options in the context menu.

# Understanding the Diesel Macro Language

Diesel is one of many macro languages AutoCAD supports, and you can use it to perform simple operations and add some automation to menus. As with AutoLISP, parentheses are used to enclose program code.

In the following sections, you'll look at the different ways to use the Diesel macro language. You'll start by using Diesel directly from the command line. This section will show you how a Diesel macro is formatted, and it will give you a chance to see Diesel in action. Then you'll go on to see how Diesel can be used as part of a menu option to test the current state of AutoCAD. In the third section, you'll see how Diesel can be used as part of the menu label to control what is shown in the menu. Finally, you'll learn how to use Diesel with field objects to control text in your drawing.

## Using Diesel at the Command Line

You can use Diesel at the AutoCAD command line by using a command called Modemacro. The Modemacro command sends information to the status bar. Diesel can be used with Modemacro to perform simple tasks.

Try the following exercise to experiment with Diesel:

**1.** Open a drawing, and then at the Command prompt, type **Modemacro**↵.

**2.** At the `Enter new value for MODEMACRO, or .for none <" ">:` prompt, enter **$(/,25,2)**↵. The answer to the equation appears at the left end of the status bar icons.

The answer to the equation appears here.

**3.** To clear the status bar, enter **Modemacro** ↵.

**4.** At the `Enter new value for MODEMACRO, or . for none <" ">:` prompt, enter . (a period). The status will then clear.

The equation you entered in step 2 is referred to as an *expression*. The structure of Diesel expressions is similar to that of AutoLISP expressions. The dollar sign tells AutoCAD that the information that follows is a Diesel expression.

A Diesel expression must include an operator of some sort, followed by the items to be operated on. An *operator* is an instruction to take a specific action, such as adding two numbers or dividing one number by another. Examples of mathematical operators include the plus sign (+) for addition and the forward slash (/) for division.

The operator is often referred to as a *function* and the items to be operated on are referred to as the *arguments* to the function, or simply the arguments. In the expression (/,25,2), the / is the function and 25 and 2 are the arguments. All Diesel expressions, no matter what size, follow this structure and are enclosed by parentheses.

Parentheses are important elements of an expression. All parentheses must be balanced; for each left parenthesis, there must be a right parenthesis.

You can do other things with Diesel besides performing calculations. The getvar function is an AutoLISP function that you can use to obtain the drawing prefix and name. Try the following to see how Diesel uses getvar:

1. Type **Modemacro**↵ again.

2. Type **$(getvar,dwgprefix)**↵. The location of the current drawing appears in the status bar.

3. Press ↵ to reissue the Modemacro command; then type **$(getvar,dwgname)**↵. The name of the drawing appears in the status bar.

In this example, the getvar function extracts the drawing prefix and name and displays it in the status bar. You can use getvar to extract any system variable you want. If you've been working through the tutorials in this book, you've seen that virtually all AutoCAD settings are also controlled through system variables. (The Help section of the Autodesk Exchange window contains a list of all the system variables. See Chapter 2, "Creating Your First Drawing," for more on Autodesk Exchange.) This can be a great tool when you're creating custom menus because with getvar, you can poll AutoCAD to determine the state of a given system variable. For example, you can find out what command is currently being used. Try the following exercise to see how this works:

1. Click the Line tool on the Draw panel.

2. Type **'Modemacro**↵. The apostrophe at the beginning of Modemacro lets you use the command while in another command.

3. Type **$(getvar,cmdnames)**↵. The word *LINE* appears in the status bar, indicating that the current command is the Line command.

This information can be useful in building a menu when you want an option to perform a specific task depending on which command is currently active.

---

**AUTOCAD LT USERS CAN USE DIESEL**

Users of AutoCAD LT® software can't use AutoLISP to find the location of AutoCAD resource files. However, you can use the Diesel macro language. For example, to find the log file path, enter **Modemacro**↵ and then **$(getvar,logfilepath)**. The path is displayed in the status bar. To get the status bar tools back, enter **Modemacro**↵ and then enter a period.

---

## Using Diesel in a Custom Menu Macro

So far, you've been experimenting with Diesel through the Modemacro command. Using Diesel in a menu macro requires a slightly different format. You still use the same Diesel format of a dollar sign followed by the expression, but you don't use the Modemacro command to access Diesel. Instead, you use $M=. You can think of $M= as an abbreviation for Modemacro.

Here's a Diesel expression that you can use in a menu macro:

```
^C^C_Blipmode;$M=$(-,1,$(getvar,Blipmode))
```

This menu option turns Blipmode on or off depending on Blipmode's current state. Blipmode is a feature that displays point selections in the drawing area as tiny crosses. These tiny crosses, or *blips*, don't print and can be cleared from the screen with a redraw. They can be helpful when you need to track your point selections.

In this example, the Blipmode command is invoked, and then the $M= tells AutoCAD that a Diesel expression follows. The expression

```
$(-,1,$(getvar,Blipmode))
```

returns either 1 or a 0, which is applied to the Blipmode command to turn it either on or off. This expression shows that you can nest expressions. The most deeply nested expression is evaluated first, so AutoCAD begins by evaluating

```
$(getvar,Blipmode)
```

This returns either 1 or a 0, depending on whether Blipmode is on or off. AutoCAD then evaluates the next level in the expression

```
$(-,1,getvar_resultgetvar_result)
```

in which *getvar_result* is either 1 or a 0. If *getvar_result* is 1, the expression looks like

```
$(-,1,1)
```

which returns 0. If *getvar_result* is 0, the expression looks like

```
$(-,1,0)
```

which returns 1. In either case, the end result is that the Blipmode command is assigned a value that is the opposite of the current Blipmode setting.

## Using Diesel as a Menu Bar Option Label

In the previous example, you saw how to use Diesel in a menu macro to read the status of a command and then return a numeric value to alter that status. You can also use Diesel as part of the menu bar option name so that the text it displays depends on certain conditions. The following expression shows how to write a menu option name to display the current setting for Blipmode. It includes Diesel code as the menu option label:

```
$(eval,Blipmode = $(getvar,blipmode))
```

Normally, you would just have a menu name, but here you see some Diesel instructions. These instructions tell AutoCAD to display the message Blipmode = 1 or Blipmode = 0 in the menu, depending on the current Blipmode setting. You would place this code in the Properties group for the Blipmode custom command in the Customize User Interface dialog box. It goes in the Display/Name text box.

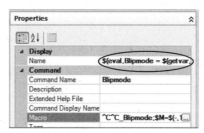

Here's how it works. You see the familiar $(getvar,blipmode) expression, this time embedded in a different expression. You know that $(getvar,blipmode) returns either 1 or a 0, depending on whether Blipmode is on or off. The outer expression

```
$(eval,Blipmode = getvar_result)
```

displays Blipmode = and then combines this with *getvar_result*, which, as you've learned, will be either 1 or 0. The eval function evaluates any text that follows it and returns its contents. The end result is the appearance of Blipmode = 1 or Blipmode = 0 in the menu, depending on the status of Blipmode. Here's how the properties look as a menu bar option under the Tools list of the Menus option in the Customizations In All Files panel:

You can get even fancier and set up the menu option label to read Blipmode On or Blipmode Off by using the if Diesel function. Here's that same menu listing with additional Diesel code to accomplish this:

```
$(eval,Blipmode = $(if,$(getvar,blipmode),Off,On))
```

In this example, the simple $(getvar,blipmode) expression is expanded to include the if function. The if function reads the result of $(getvar,blipmode) and then returns the Off or On value depending on whether $(getvar,blipmode) returns 0 or a 1. Here's a simpler look at the expression:

```
$(if, getvar_result, Off, On)
```

If *getvar_result* returns 1, the if function returns the first of the two options listed after *getvar_result*, which is Off. If *getvar_result* returns 0, the if function returns On. The second of the two options is optional. Here's how the fancier Blipmode option appears in a menu:

You've just skimmed the surface of what Diesel can do. To get a more detailed description of how Diesel works, press the F1 function key to open the Autodesk Exchange website. Click the Contents tab, expand the Customization Guide listing, and click the DIESEL listing that appears.

Table 24.2 shows some of the commonly used Diesel functions. Check the AutoCAD Help dialog box for a more detailed list.

**TABLE 24.2:** Sample of Diesel functions

| CODE | FUNCTION | EXAMPLE | RESULT | COMMENTS |
|------|----------|---------|--------|----------|
| + | Add | `$(+,202,144)` | 346 | |
| – | Subtract | `$(-,202,144)` | 58 | |
| * | Multiply | `$(*,202,144)` | 29,088 | |
| / | Divide | `$(/,202,144)` | 1.4028 | |
| = | Equal to | `$(=,202,144)` | 0 | If numbers are equal, 1 is returned. |
| < | Less than | `$(<,202,144)` | 0 | If the first number is less than the second, 1 is returned. |
| > | Greater than | `$(>,202,144)` | 1 | If the first number is greater than the second, 1 is returned; otherwise, 0 is returned. |
| ! | Not equal to | `$(!,202,144)` | 1 | If the numbers are equal, 0 is returned. |
| <= | Less than or equal to | `$(<=,202,144)` | 0 | If the first number is less than or equal to the second, 1 is returned. |
| >= | Greater than or equal to | `$(>=,202,144)` | 1 | If the first number is greater than or equal to the second, 1 is returned; otherwise, 0 is returned. |
| eq | Equal string | `$(eq,Yes, No)` | 0 | If both text strings are the same, 1 is returned. |
| eval | Evaluate text | `$(eval,Here I Am)` | Here I Am | Returns the text that follows. |
| getvar | Get system variable value | `$(getvar,ltscale)` | Current linetype scale | Returns the value of the system variable. |
| if | If/Then | `$(if,1,Yes,No)` | Yes | The second argument is returned if the first argument evaluates to 1. Otherwise, the third argument is returned. The third argument is optional. |

*Note: To indicate true or false, Diesel uses 1 or 0.*

## Using Diesel and Fields to Generate Text

Using Diesel expressions in the status bar or in a menu can be helpful to gather information or to create a more interactive interface, but what if you want the results of a Diesel expression to become part of the drawing? You can employ field objects to do just that.

For example, suppose you want to create a note that shows the scale of a drawing based on the dimension scale. Further, you want the scale in the note to be updated automatically whenever the dimension scale changes. You can add a field object and associate it with a Diesel expression that displays the dimension scale as it relates to the drawing scale. Try the following steps to see how it's done:

1. In the Annotate tab, click the Multiline Text tool and select two points to indicate the text location. The Text Editor Ribbon tab and text editor appear.

2. Right-click in the text editor, and select Insert Field to open the Field dialog box.

3. In the Field Category drop-down list, select Other; then, in the Field Names list box, select DieselExpression.

4. Add the following text in the Diesel Expression box to the right. If you need to expand the width of the dialog box, click and drag its right edge:

```
$(eval,Dimension Scale: 1/)$(/,$(getvar, dimscale),12)
$(eval, inch = 1 foot)
```

5. Click OK in the Field dialog box, and then click Close Text Editor in the Text Editor Ribbon tab. The following text is displayed in the drawing:

```
Dimension Scale: 1/0.08333333 inch = 1 foot
```

The resulting text may not make sense until you change the dimension scale to a value that represents a scale other than 1-to-1. Here's how to do that:

1. Enter **Dimscale**↵ at the Command prompt.

2. At the Enter new value for DIMSCALE <1.0000>: prompt, enter **96**↵. This is the value for a ⅛″ scale drawing.

3. Type **RE**↵. The text changes to read

```
Dimension Scale: 1/8 inch = 1 foot
```

In this example, several Diesel operations were used. The beginning of the expression uses the eval operation to tell AutoCAD to display a string of text:

```
$(eval Dimension Scale: 1/)
```

The next part tells AutoCAD to get the current value of the Dimscale system variable and divide it by 12:

```
$(/,$(getvar, dimscale),12)
```

Notice that this is a nested expression: $(getvar,dimscale) obtains the value of the Dimscale system variable, which is then divided by 12. The end of the expression adds the final part to the text:

$(eval, inch = 1 foot)

When it's all put together, you get the text that shows the dimension scale as an architectural scale. Because it's an AutoCAD text object, this text is part of the drawing.

# Creating Custom Linetypes

As your drawing needs expand, the standard linetypes may not be adequate for your application. Fortunately, you can create your own. The following sections explain how to do so.

You'll get an in-depth view of the process of creating linetypes. You'll also learn how to create complex linetypes that can't be created by using the Make Linetype Express tool.

## Viewing Available Linetypes

Although AutoCAD provides the linetypes most commonly used in drafting (see Figure 24.23), the dashes and dots may not be spaced the way you would like, or you may want an entirely new linetype.

**FIGURE 24.23**

The lines in this partial list of standard linetypes were generated with the underscore key (_), the period (.), and other symbols and are only rough representations of the actual lines.

WHERE ARE THE LINETYPES STORED?

AutoCAD stores the linetypes in a file called acad.lin, which is in ASCII format. When you create a new linetype, you add information to this file. Or, if you create a new file containing your own linetype definitions, it too will have the extension .lin at the end of its name. You can edit linetypes as described here, or you can edit them directly in these files.

To create a custom linetype, use the -Linetype command. Let's see how this handy command works by first listing the available linetypes:

1. Open a new AutoCAD file.

2. At the Command prompt, enter **-Linetype**↵. (Don't forget the hyphen at the beginning.)

3. At the Enter an option [?/Create/Load/Set]: prompt, enter **?**↵.

4. In the dialog box, locate and double-click acad.lin in the listing of available linetype files. You get a list that shows the linetypes available in the acad.lin file along with a simple description of each line.

5. A message at the bottom says Press ENTER to continue:. Do so until you see the Command prompt.

## Creating a New Linetype

Next, let's try creating a new linetype:

1. Enter **-Linetype**↵ again.

2. At the [?/Create/Load/Set]: prompt, enter **C**↵.

3. At the Enter name of linetype to create: prompt, enter **Custom**↵ as the name of your new linetype.

4. The dialog box you see next is named Create Or Append Linetype File. You need to enter the name of the linetype file you want to create or add to. If you select the default linetype file, acad, your new linetype is added to the acad.lin (acadiso.lin for metric users) file. If you choose to create a new linetype file, AutoCAD opens a file containing the linetype you create and adds .lin to the filename you supply.

5. Let's assume you want to start a new linetype file. Enter **Newline**↵ in the File Name text box.

---

**NEW OR EXISTING LINETYPE FILE**

If you accept the default linetype file, acad, the prompt in step 4 is Wait, checking if linetype already defined. This protects you from inadvertently overwriting an existing linetype you want to keep.

---

6. At the Descriptive text: prompt, enter a text description of your linetype. You can use any keyboard character as part of your description, but the actual linetype can be composed of only a series of lines, points, and blank spaces. For this exercise, enter the following, using the underscore key (_) to simulate the appearance of your line:

```
Custom - My own center line _____ _ _____  ↵
```

**7.** At the `Enter linetype pattern (on next line):` prompt, enter the following numbers, known as the *linetype code* (after the A, which appears automatically):

`A,1.0,-.125,.25,-.125↵`

---

### YOU CAN SET THE DEFAULT LINETYPE

If you use the Set option of the -Linetype command to set a new default linetype, you'll get that linetype no matter what layer you're on.

---

**8.** At the `New linetype definition saved to file. Enter an option [?/Create/Load/Set]:` prompt, press ↵ to exit the -Linetype command.

Remember, after you've created a linetype, you must load it in order to use it, as discussed in Chapter 5, "Keeping Track of Layers and Blocks."

---

### ADD LINETYPES DIRECTLY TO THE *ACAD.LIN* FILE

You can also open the `acad.lin` or other LIN file in Windows Notepad and add the descriptive text and linetype code directly to the end of the file.

---

## Understanding the Linetype Code

In step 7 of the previous exercise, you entered a series of numbers separated by commas. This is the linetype code, representing the lengths of the components that make up the linetype. The separate elements of the linetype code are as follows:

◆ The `1.0` following the A is the length of the first part of the line. (The A that begins the linetype definition is a code that is applied to all linetypes.)

◆ The first `-.125` is the blank or broken part of the line. The minus sign tells AutoCAD that the line is *not* to be drawn for the specified length, which is 0.125 units in this example.

◆ Next comes the positive value `0.25`. This tells AutoCAD to draw a line segment 0.25 units long after the blank part of the line.

◆ The last negative value, `-.125`, again tells AutoCAD to skip drawing the line for the distance of 0.125 units.

This series of numbers represents the one segment that is repeated to form the line (see Figure 24.24). You can also create a complex linetype that looks like a random broken line, as shown in Figure 24.25.

**FIGURE 24.24**

Linetype description with plotted line

**FIGURE 24.25**

Random broken line

You may be wondering what purpose the A serves at the beginning of the linetype code. A linetype is composed of a series of line segments and points. The A, which is supplied by AutoCAD automatically, is a code that forces the linetype to start and end on a line segment rather than on a blank space in the series of lines. At times, AutoCAD stretches the last line segment to force this condition, as shown in Figure 24.26.

**FIGURE 24.26**

AutoCAD stretches the beginning and the end of the line as necessary.

---

**LINE SEGMENT LENGTHS AND SCALE**

The values you enter for the line segment lengths are multiplied by the Ltscale factor, so be sure to enter values for the plotted lengths.

---

As mentioned earlier, you can also create linetypes outside of AutoCAD by using a word processor or text editor such as Windows Notepad. The standard acad.lin file looks like Figure 24.23 with the addition of the code used by AutoCAD to determine the line segment lengths.

Normally, to use a linetype you've created you have to load it through either the Layer Properties Manager or the Linetype Manager dialog box (choose Other from the Linetype drop-down list in the Home tab's Properties panel). If you use one of your own linetypes frequently, you may want to create a button macro so that it will be available as an option on a menu.

## Creating Complex Linetypes

A *complex linetype* is one that incorporates text or special graphics. For example, if you want to show an underground gas line in a site plan, you normally show a line with the intermittent word *GAS*, as in Figure 24.27. Fences are often shown with an intermittent circle, square, or X.

For the graphics needed to compose complex linetypes, use any of the symbols in the AutoCAD font files discussed in Chapter 9, "Adding Text to Drawings." Create a text style by using these symbol fonts, and then specify the appropriate symbol by using its corresponding letter in the linetype description.

**FIGURE 24.27**

Samples of complex linetypes

| | |
|---|---|
| Fenceline1 | |
| Fenceline2 | |
| Tracks | |
| Batting | |
| Hot_water_supply | HW — HW — HW — HW — HW |
| Gas_line | GAS — GAS — GAS — GAS — GAS |
| Zigzag | |

To create a linetype that includes text, use the same linetype code described earlier but add the necessary font file information in brackets. For example, say you want to create the linetype for the underground gas line mentioned previously by using just the letter *G*. You add the following to your acad.lin file:

```
*Gas_line, -G-G-G-
A,1.0,-0.25,["G",STANDARD,S=.2,R=0,X=-.1,Y=-.1],-0.25
```

The first line serves as a description for anyone looking at this linetype code. The next line is the code itself. Note that the code should not contain spaces.

The information in the square brackets describes the characteristics of the text. The actual text that you want to appear in the line is surrounded by quotation marks. Next are the text style, scale, rotation angle, X displacement, and Y displacement.

---

### EDIT THE *ACAD.LIN* FILE TO CREATE COMPLEX LINETYPES

You can't use the -Linetype command to define complex linetypes. Instead, you must open the acad.lin file by using a text editor, such as Notepad, and add the linetype information to the end of the file. Make sure you don't duplicate the name of an existing linetype.

---

You can substitute A for the rotation angle (the R value), as in the following example:

```
A,1.0,-0.25,["G",standard,S=.2,A=0,X=-.1,Y=-.1],-0.25
```

This has the effect of keeping the text at the same angle regardless of the line's direction. Notice that in this sample, the X and Y values are -.1; this will center the *G*s on the line. The scale value of .2 will cause the text to be 0.2 units high, so .1 is half the height.

In addition to fonts, you can specify shapes for linetype definitions. Instead of letters, shapes display symbols. Shapes are stored not as drawings but as definition files, similar to text font files. Shape files have the same .shx filename extension as font files and are also defined similarly. Figure 24.28 shows some symbols from sample shape files. The names of the files are shown at the top of each column.

**FIGURE 24.28**

Samples of shapes

| ST.SHX | ES.SHX | PC.SHX | LTYPESHP.SHX |
|---|---|---|---|
| opt-x | con1 | dip14 | track1 |
| obl-x | cap | dip18 | |
| pro-x | pnp | dip24 | box |
| opt-m | mark | dip8 | bat |
| bol-m | jump | dip16 | zig |
| pro-m | zener | dip20 | circ1 |
| opt-c | nor | | |
| obl-c | and | dip40 | |
| pro-c | buffer | | |
| opt-r | box | | |
| obl-r | res | | |
| pro-r | diode | | |
| opt-p | npn | | |
| obl-p | arrow | | |
| pro-p | con2 | | |
| opt-perp | or | | |
| obl-perp | xor | | |
| pro-perp | nand | | |
| opt-parallel | inverter | | |
| obl-parallel | neg | | |
| pro-parallel | feedthru | | |

To use a shape in a linetype code, you use the same format as shown previously for text. However, instead of using a letter and style name, you use the shape name and the shape file-name as in the following example:

```
*Capline, ====
a,1.0,-0.25,[CAP,ES.SHX,S=.5,R=0,X=-.1,Y=-.1],-0.25
```

This example uses the CAP symbol from the Es.shx shape file. The symbol is scaled to 0.5 units with 0 rotation and an X and Y displacement of –0.1.

Here is another example, this one using the arrow shape:

```
*Arrowline, -|-|-|-
a,1.0,-0.25,[ARROW,ES.SHX,S=.5,R=90,X=-.1,Y=-.1],-0.25
```

Just as with the Capline example, the ARROW symbol in this example is scaled to 0.5 units with 0 rotation and an X and Y displacement of –0.1. Figure 24.29 shows what the Arrowline linetype looks like when used with a spline.

**FIGURE 24.29**

The Arrowline linetype used with a spline

In this example, the Ltype generation option is turned on for the polyline. Note that the arrow from the Es.shx sample shape file is used for the arrow in this linetype.

# Creating Hatch Patterns

AutoCAD provides several predefined hatch patterns from which you can choose, but you can also create your own. This section demonstrates the basic elements of pattern definition.

Unlike linetypes, hatch patterns can't be created while you're in an AutoCAD file. The pattern definitions are contained in an external file named acad.pat. You can open and edit this file with a text editor that can handle ASCII files, such as Notepad. Here is one hatch pattern definition from that file:

```
*SQUARE,Small aligned squares
0, 0,0, 0,.125, .125,-.125
90, 0,0, 0,.125, .125,-.125
```

You can see some similarities between pattern descriptions and linetype descriptions. They both start with a line of descriptive text and then give numeric values defining the pattern. However, the numbers in pattern descriptions have a different meaning. This example shows two lines of information. Each line represents a line in the pattern. The first line determines the horizontal line component of the pattern, and the second line represents the vertical component (see the image to the far right in Figure 24.30). A pattern is made up of line groups. A *line group* is like a linetype that is arrayed a specified distance to fill the area to be hatched. A line group is defined by a line of code, much as a linetype is defined. In the square pattern, for instance, two lines—one horizontal and one vertical—are used. Each of these lines is duplicated in a fashion that makes the lines appear as boxes when they're combined. Figure 24.30 illustrates this point.

**FIGURE 24.30**

The individual and combined line groups

Vertical line group      Horizontal line group      Groups merged to form pattern

Look at the first line in the definition:

```
0, 0,0, 0,.125, .125,-.125
```

This example shows a series of numbers separated by commas. It represents one line group. It contains four sets of information separated by blank spaces:

♦ The first component is the 0 at the beginning. This value indicates the angle of the line group, as determined by the line's orientation. In this case, it's 0 for a horizontal line that runs from left to right.

♦ The next component is the origin of the line group, 0,0. This doesn't mean the line begins at the drawing origin (see Figure 24.31). It gives you a reference point to determine the location of other line groups involved in generating the pattern.

**FIGURE 24.31**

The origin of the patterns

◆ The next component is 0,.125. This determines the distance and direction for arraying the line as illustrated in Figure 24.32. This value is like a relative coordinate indicating X and Y distances for a rectangular array. It isn't based on the drawing coordinates, but on a coordinate system relative to the orientation of the line. For a line oriented at a 0° angle, the code 0,.125 indicates a precisely vertical direction. For a line oriented at a 45° angle, the code 0,.125 represents a 135° direction. Remember that the very first number in the line definition determines the angle of the line. In this example, the duplication occurs 90° in relation to the line group, because the X value is 0. Figure 24.33 illustrates this point.

**FIGURE 24.32**

The distance and direction of duplication

**FIGURE 24.33**
How the direction
of the line group
copy is determined

The X and Y coordinate values given for the array distance are based on
the orientation of the line group.

◆ The last component is the description of the line pattern. This value is equivalent to the value given when you create a linetype. Positive values are line segments, and negative values are blank segments. This part of the line group definition works exactly as in the linetype definitions you studied in the previous section.

This system of defining hatch patterns may seem somewhat limiting, but you can do a lot with it. Autodesk managed to come up with 69 patterns—and that was only scratching the surface.

---

**ADDING THICK LINES TO HATCH PATTERN LINETYPES**

If you want to include thick lines in your hatch patterns, you have to build up line widths with multiple linetype definitions.

---

## The Bottom Line

**Use workspaces.** Often with AutoCAD you find that you have different sets of panels or toolbars open to perform specific tasks. You might have one set of Ribbon panels for editing text and dimensions, whereas another set is more useful for design. Using workspaces is a great way to organize your different editing modes.

**Master It**   Where do you find the Customize option for workspaces?

**Customize the user interface.** In addition to using workspaces to organize tools and Ribbon panels, you can customize the AutoCAD interface to make it fit the way you like to work. You can add tools to Ribbon panels or even create your own tools for operations you perform frequently.

**Master It**   What does the Customizations In All Files group display?

**Create macros in tools and menus.**   A macro is a set of instructions that performs more complex operations than single commands. Macros are often built on commands with additional predefined responses to help speed data input.

**Master It**   What does the ^C do in a macro?

**Edit keyboard shortcuts.**   Keyboard shortcuts can help improve your speed when drawing in AutoCAD. They can reduce several clicks of the mouse to a simple keystroke. AutoCAD lets you create custom shortcuts for your favorite commands.

**Master It**   What is the name of the feature that lets you record and play back actions?

**Save, load, and unload your customizations.**   To keep your customizations organized, you can save new toolbars, menus, and Ribbons as files that you can load on demand. When you save your custom elements as a file, you can move them to other computers. In addition, you can use the cloud to synchronize your custom settings with other computers.

**Master It**   Name the feature that lets you synchronize your custom settings from a cloud source.

**Understand the Diesel macro language.**   If you're adventurous, you may want to try your hand at creating more complex macros. The Diesel macro language is an easy introduction to AutoCAD macro customization and is most useful in controlling the behavior in menu options.

**Master It**   What does the expression $(getvar, blipmode) do?

**Create custom linetypes.**   AutoCAD offers a number of noncontinuous linetypes, and you may find them adequate for most of your work. But every now and then, you may need a specific linetype that isn't available. Creating custom linetypes is easy when you understand the process.

**Master It**   What is the purpose of a negative value in the linetype code?

**Create hatch patterns.**   Like linetypes, the hatch patterns provided by AutoCAD will probably fill most of your needs. But every now and then you may need to produce a specific pattern.

**Master It**   How are a hatch pattern code and a linetype code similar?

# Chapter 25

# Managing and Sharing Your Drawings

Whether you're a one-person operation working out of your home or one of several hundred Autodesk® AutoCAD® software users in a large company, file sharing and file maintenance can become the focus of much of your time. In our interconnected world, the volume of messages and files crossing our paths seems to be increasing exponentially. In addition, the Internet has enabled us to be more mobile, adding yet more complexity to file management and data sharing tasks.

In this chapter, you'll learn about some of the tools AutoCAD offers to help you manage your files and the files you share with others. You'll also examine some general issues that arise while using AutoCAD in a workgroup environment. You may find help with problems you've encountered when using AutoCAD.

In this chapter, you will learn to:

♦ Share drawings online

♦ ePublish your drawings

♦ Get started with Autodesk® 360

♦ Manage your drawings with DesignCenter and the tool palettes

♦ Search your drawing library with Content Explorer

♦ Establish office standards

♦ Convert multiple layer settings

## Sharing Drawings Online

Through AutoCAD you can use tools to post drawings on the Internet that others can view and download. In the architecture, engineering, and construction (AEC) industry in particular, this can mean easier access to documents needed by contractors, engineers, cost estimators, and others involved in the design, bidding, and construction of building projects. Suppliers of products can post symbol libraries of their products or even 3D solid models.

In the following sections, you'll learn about the tools AutoCAD provides for publishing and accessing drawings over the Internet (and on any local or wide area network). You'll start by looking at one of the most common uses of the Internet: file transmission.

## Sharing Project Files with eTransmit

Whether you're a one-person office or a member of a 50-person firm, you'll eventually have to share your work with others outside your building. Before eTransmit existed as a feature in AutoCAD, you had to carefully examine what you were sending to make sure you included all the ancillary files needed to view or work on your drawings. Xref, font, and custom linetype files all had to be included with the drawings that you sent to consultants or partners in a project, and often one of these items was omitted from the transmission.

By using eTransmit, you can quickly collect all your project drawings into a single archive file, or you can store the files in a separate folder for later processing. This collection of files is included with a report file as a transmittal. Try the following to see how eTransmit works:

1. In AutoCAD, open a file you intend to send to someone and then choose Publish ➤ eTransmit from the Application menu to open the Create Transmittal dialog box (see Figure 25.1). If you've edited the file before choosing eTransmit, you will see a message telling you that you must save the drawing before continuing.

**FIGURE 25.1**

Creating a transmittal

2. In the dialog box, a tree structure lists the files that are included in the transmittal. If you need to add more files to the transmittal than are shown in the list, you can click the Add File button to open the Add File To Transmittal dialog box. To remove files, expand the listed item and remove the check mark that appears next to the file you want to exclude. You can also use the Files Table tab to view the files as a simple list.

3. Click in the Enter Notes To Include With This Transmittal Package box, and enter a description or other note.

4. In the Select A Transmittal Setup group, click the Transmittal Setups button to open the Transmittal Setups dialog box (see Figure 25.2). Here, you can create a new transmittal or rename or modify an existing one.

**FIGURE 25.2**
Choose whether to create from scratch or edit an existing transmittal.

5. Click the Modify button to open the Modify Transmittal Setup dialog box (see Figure 25.3).

**FIGURE 25.3**
Set your transmittal options.

6. In the Transmittal Package Type drop-down list, select the format for your collection of files. You can create a Zip archive or you can save the files in a folder.

You can tell AutoCAD where to place the files by using the Browse button to the right of the Transmittal File Folder drop-down list. For this exercise, choose the Folder option in the Transmittal Package Type list.

7. Click the Browse button next to the Transmittal File Folder drop-down list to open the Specify Location Folder dialog box. This is a typical AutoCAD file open dialog box that you can use to select a location for your files.

   You can use the Create New Folder tool to create a new folder for your files. You'll want to keep your transmittal files separate from other files. After you select a location, click Open to return to the Modify Transmittal Setup dialog box.

8. After you've set up your transmittal, click OK. Then click Close in the Transmittal Setups dialog box.

9. Preview the report file by clicking the View Report button in the Create Transmittal dialog box. This report gives you a detailed description of the types of files included in the transmittal. It also alerts you to files that AutoCAD was unable to find but that are required for the drawing.

10. Close the report. After you've set up the eTransmit options, click OK in the Create Transmittal dialog box.

11. If you selected the Zip option in step 6, you see the Specify Zip File dialog box. You can then send the files over the Internet or put them on a removable disk for manual transport.

You probably noticed that you can create additional transmittal setup options in the Transmittal Setups dialog box. That way, you can have multiple transmittal options on hand that you don't have to set up each time a different situation arises. For example, you might have the Standard setup configured to create a Zip file and another setup configured to copy the files into a folder. A third setup might be created with a password.

Several options are available for configuring the transmittal setup. Table 25.1 gives a rundown of those options.

**TABLE 25.1:**　　　Modify Transmittal Setup dialog box options

| OPTION | PURPOSE |
| --- | --- |
| Transmittal Package Type | Lets you select Folder or Zip. |
| File Format | Lets you select 2013, 2010, 2007, 2004, or 2000 file formats in case your recipient requires an earlier version. |
| Maintain Visual Fidelity For Annotative Objects | Maintains visual fidelity for annotative objects when drawings are viewed in AutoCAD 2007 and earlier. |
| Transmittal File Folder | Lets you determine the location for your transmittal package. |
| Transmittal File Name | Not available if you select Folder as the transmittal package type. Options are Prompt For A Filename, Overwrite If Necessary, and Increment File Name If Necessary. |

| OPTION | PURPOSE |
| --- | --- |
| Use Organized Folder Structure | Preserves the folder structure for the files in the transmittal. This can be important when Xref and other files are located across several folder locations. |
| Place All Files In One Folder | Self-explanatory. |
| Keep Files And Folders As Is | Preserves the entire folder structure for the files in the transmittal. |
| Include Fonts | Tells AutoCAD to include the font files in the transmittal. |
| Include Textures From Materials | Lets you include bitmap files that are part of a file's material settings. |
| Include Files From Data Links | Lets you include external data-link files for tables. |
| Include Photometric Web Files | Lets you include photometric web files for 3D lighting models. |
| Include Unloaded File References | Lets you include references for unloaded Xref files. |
| Send E-Mail With Transmittal | Lets you send an email with the files included as an attachment. |
| Set Default Plotter To 'None' | Removes any reference to printers or plotters that you've set up for the drawing. (The type of printer you've set up for your files is stored with the drawing file.) |
| Bind External References | Lets you bind external references to the drawings that contain them if it isn't important for the recipient to maintain the external references as separate drawings. |
| Purge Drawings | Purges drawings of unused elements. |
| Transmittal Setup Description | Lets you add a description to the transmittal file. |

eTransmit gives you a quick way to package a set of files to be sent to others working on the same project. But you may need to offer a wider distribution of your files. You might want to let others view and plot your drawings from a website without exposing your drawing database to anyone who might visit your site. If you need this approach, you'll want to know about the AutoCAD DWF file format, which lets anyone view AutoCAD files whether or not they own the program. You'll learn more about the DWF file format in the section "ePublishing Your Drawings" later in this chapter.

---

**AUTOCAD AND MOBILE DEVICES**

If you've been hoping to work with AutoCAD files on mobile devices, such as smartphones or tablets using Apple iOS and Android operating systems, you're in luck. Autodesk 360 lets you view and perform basic editing on AutoCAD files that have been uploaded to the Autodesk 360 website. In addition, any PC can be used to view and edit drawings on the Autodesk 360 website, whether or not you have AutoCAD installed.

The site is account-based, but it's free, and even if you're not using a mobile device, you might consider using the Autodesk 360 website to share files with others. If you have AutoCAD installed on your PC, an AutoCAD plug-in lets you seamlessly open, edit, and upload drawings to your AutoCAD® 360 account. If you're on a PC that doesn't have AutoCAD, you can upload, download, and edit a drawing using the basic editor that runs in your browser. To start an account, just go to https://360.autodesk.com or www.autocad360.com and sign up.

---

## Protecting AutoCAD Drawing Files

Because AutoCAD drawings specify the methods and materials used to produce an object or a building, they are frequently treated like legal documents. After an AutoCAD drawing is issued, it's often archived and guarded as a legal record of a design. For this reason, many AutoCAD users are concerned about possible tampering with drawings that are sent to third parties. Even minor unauthorized changes to a drawing can have major repercussions on the integrity of a design.

AutoCAD offers password protection for individual files as well as a digital signature feature that helps protect both the author of a drawing and the recipient in the event of file tampering.

### ADDING PASSWORD PROTECTION TO FILES

The basic type of file protection is password protection of individual files. AutoCAD offers password protection through the Save Drawing As dialog box and the Options dialog box.

To add a password to a drawing when you save it, do the following:

1. Choose Save As from the Application menu to open the Save Drawing As dialog box.

2. Choose Tools ➢ Security Options in the upper-right corner of the dialog box.

3. In the Password tab of the Security Options dialog box, enter a password or phrase in the text box.

4. Click OK. You're prompted to enter the password again.

5. Enter the password again, and click OK to return to the Save Drawing As dialog box.

6. Enter the name and location of your file, and then click Save.

In addition to adding password protection through the Save Drawing As dialog box, you can use the Options dialog box:

1. Choose Options from the Application menu to open the Options dialog box, and then click the Open And Save tab.

**2.** Click the Security Options button in the File Safety Precautions group to open the Security Options dialog box.

**3.** Enter your password, select other options as necessary, and then click OK. You may have to enter your password a second time to confirm.

As a third option, you can enter **Securityoptions**↵ at the Command prompt to go directly to the Security Options dialog box.

After you've added a password, anyone attempting to open the file will be asked to provide the password. This includes any attempt to use the file as an Xref or a file insertion.

---

### AutoCAD Remembers That You've Opened a File

After you give the password and open a password-protected file, you can open and close the file repeatedly during that AutoCAD session without having to reenter the password. If you close and reopen AutoCAD, however, the program will prompt you for a password the next time you attempt to open the password-protected file.

---

### USING A DIGITAL SIGNATURE

In addition to password protection, you can use a digital signature to authenticate files. A digital signature can't prevent someone from tampering with a file, but it offers a way to validate whether a file has been modified after it has been saved. This protects you in the event that your file is unofficially altered. It also protects the recipient of your file by verifying the file's authenticity and by verifying that it was not altered from the time it left your computer.

The first time you attempt to use the digital signature feature, you see a message telling you that you need a digital ID. AutoCAD uses a digital ID issued by any certificate authority, such as VeriSign, a company that specializes in Internet security. The VeriSign digital ID service is fee based, with prices ranging from about $90 for a basic one-year enrollment to nearly $700 for a professional-level ID. A free 60-day trial is also offered. The following steps show how to acquire a digital ID:

**1.** From the Windows Taskbar, choose Start ➢ (All) Programs ➢ Autodesk ➢ AutoCAD 2015 ➢ Attach Digital Signatures. Or, from AutoCAD, enter **Securityoptions**↵ to open the Security Options dialog box and then click the Digital Signature tab. The Digital Signatures – Digital ID Not Available warning dialog box appears.

**2.** Click the Obtain ID button. Your web browser opens at the Symantec VeriSign page.

**3.** Select the security services you want, and follow the rest of the instructions.

After you've obtained a digital ID, the signature resides in the Registry on your computer. You can then access the digital ID from AutoCAD by using the Digital Signature tab of the Security Options dialog box. Here are the steps:

**1.** Open the drawing to which you want to attach the digital signature, and then open the Security Options dialog box by entering **Securityoptions**↵ at the Command prompt.

**2.** Click the Digital Signature tab (see Figure 25.4).

**FIGURE 25.4**

Attach a signature.

**3.** Select the Attach Digital Signature After Saving Drawing option. The Signature Information options become available. You can add a date stamp and a brief description.

**4.** Click OK to exit the dialog box.

The next time you save the file, depending on the level of security you chose during the digital ID setup, you may be prompted for a password. After you enter the password, the file is saved.

The next time the file is opened, you'll see the Digital Signature Contents dialog box (see Figure 25.5), which verifies that no one has tampered with the drawing.

**FIGURE 25.5**

The signature is verified when the file opens.

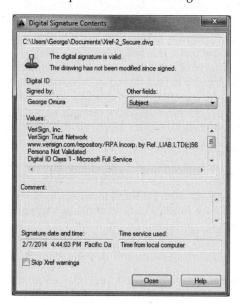

You'll also see a stamp icon in the lower-right corner of the AutoCAD window. You can click this icon at any time to view the file's digital signature status. You can also issue the SigValidate command to view the status.

A file containing a digital signature displays a warning when the user attempts to save the file after making modifications (see Figure 25.6). If the user continues to save the file, the signature is detached and no longer displays the Digital Signature Contents dialog box when opened.

**FIGURE 25.6**

Checking signature status

If you need to update a drawing that contains your digital signature, you can do so and then use the Security Options dialog box to reissue the digital signature.

### ADDING YOUR DIGITAL SIGNATURE TO MULTIPLE FILES

If you have multiple files to which you'd like to attach your digital signature, you should use the Attach Digital Signatures utility. This program runs outside AutoCAD, and it provides a convenient way to attach your digital signature to a set of drawings. Here's how it works:

1. From the Windows Taskbar, choose Start ➢ All Programs ➢ Autodesk ➢ AutoCAD 2015 ➢ Attach Digital Signatures to open the Attach Digital Signatures dialog box (see Figure 25.7).

**FIGURE 25.7**

Signing multiple files

2. Click the Add Files button to locate and select files. You can also search for files in a particular folder by clicking the Search Folders button. The files you add appear in the Files To Be Signed list box.

3. If you decide to remove a file from the list box, highlight it and then click Remove. You can also remove all the files from the list by clicking Clear List.

---

**A DIGITAL ID IS REQUIRED**

If you haven't obtained a digital ID, you see a message telling you that no valid digital ID is available on your system. To proceed, you'll have to obtain a digital ID from a certificate authority such as VeriSign, as described earlier in "Using a Digital Signature."

---

4. The rest of the dialog box is the same as the Digital Signature tab of the Security Options dialog box. You can enter the date and time and a comment for the files you've selected.

5. Click Sign Files when you're sure you've selected the correct files and entered an appropriate comment.

If you exchange AutoCAD drawings regularly with clients and consultants, you'll want to obtain a digital ID and use the digital signature feature. Be aware, however, that because this feature was new in AutoCAD 2004, it works only if you exchange files with others using AutoCAD 2004 or later. In fact, a quick way to remove a digital signature from a file is to save the file in the AutoCAD 2000 or Release 14 file format.

If you intend to use the password feature in conjunction with your digital signature, you must add the signature first before adding the password.

---

**DIGITAL IDs AND PDFs**

In today's offices, PDFs are being used often for submittals, which are common documents used during the construction phase of a project. In the past, paper submittals were stamped to validate their review by an architect. PDF submittals can be "stamped" using digital IDs that are unique to the individual who is reviewing the submittal. If you've obtained a digital ID from VeriSign and you have the full version of Adobe Acrobat, you can use the Acrobat Advanced Security and stamp features to apply an ID to any PDF document. Acrobat will also generate its own digital ID. Unfortunately, the ID from Acrobat cannot be used with AutoCAD.

---

# ePublishing Your Drawings

The features discussed so far are intended mostly for exchanging files with others who need to work directly with your AutoCAD files. However, there are always associates and clients who need to see only your final drawings and don't care whether they get AutoCAD files. Alternatively, you might be working with people who don't have AutoCAD but still need to view and print your drawings. For those non-AutoCAD end users, AutoCAD offers the DWF file format.

You can think of the DWF file format as a kind of Adobe Acrobat file for AutoCAD drawings. DWF offers a way to get your plans and design ideas in the hands of more people more easily.

With the help of the free Autodesk® DWF™ Viewer—equivalent to the Adobe Reader for Acrobat PDF documents—users can view DWF files using the same types of pan and zoom tools available in AutoCAD, which lets you present greater detail in your drawings. In addition, you can embed URL links that can open other documents with a single mouse click. These links can be attached to objects or areas in the drawing.

You can also print DWF files using your Windows system printer or plotter, all without having AutoCAD installed. A single DWF file can contain multiple drawing sheets, so you can combine a complete set of drawings into one DWF file. By default, AutoCAD saves DWF files in the DWFx format that is compatible with the Windows 8, Windows 7, and Windows Vista XPS formats.

## Exchanging Drawing Sets

Imagine that you're working on a skylight addition to a house and you need to send your drawings to your client for review. In addition to the skylight plans, you want to include some alternate floor plans that your client has asked you to generate. In this exercise, you'll put together a set of drawings that will become a single DWF file that you'll send as an email attachment to your client:

1. Open the Sample house.dwg file, which can be found in the Chapter 25 folder of the sample files. The file has several layout views, each representing a separate drawing sheet.

2. Click the Save tool in the Quick Access toolbar. If you don't do this, the Publish tool you use later will ask you to do it.

3. Choose Publish from the Application menu to open the Publish dialog box (see Figure 25.8). You can also type **Publish**↵. The dialog box lists all the layouts in its main list box, including the Model layout, which is equivalent to the Model Space tab. (See Chapter 8, "Introducing Printing, Plotting, and Layouts," for more on layouts.)

**FIGURE 25.8**

Choosing the layouts to publish

**4.** In the list box, Ctrl+click Sample House-Model, Sample House-Foundation Details, and Sample House-Skylite Details to select them. You don't want to include these layouts in your DWF file.

**5.** Right-click any of the selected files and choose Remove, or click the Remove Sheets button just above the list of sheets. The items you selected are removed from the list.

At this point, you could go ahead and create a DWF file. However, suppose you want to include layouts from a file that isn't currently open? The following steps show you how to accomplish this:

**1.** Right-click and choose Add Sheets or click the Add Sheets button to open the Select Drawings dialog box.

**2.** Locate and select the `sample house alt.dwg` file, which can be found in the `Chapter 25` folder of the sample files. You see two new items, Sample House Alt-Model and Sample House Alt-Alternate Plan, in the list box. These are the layout and model views contained in the `sample house alt.dwg` file.

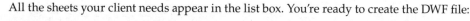

> **AUTOMATICALLY EXCLUDING LAYOUTS**
>
> In step 2 of the previous exercise, the Model tab was imported. You can prevent Model tabs from being included in the sheets list by turning off the Include Model When Adding Sheets option. This option is located in the context menu when you right-click in the Sheets list.

All the sheets your client needs appear in the list box. You're ready to create the DWF file:

**1.** Save the current list in case you want to reproduce it later. Click the Save Sheet List button. The Save List As dialog box, which is a standard file dialog box, appears.

**2.** Select a location and name for the sheet list and click Save.

**3.** Back in the Publish dialog box, in the Publish To drop-down list near the top of the dialog box, make sure that the DWF option is selected. Notice that you can also select Plotter Named In Page Setup, DWFx, and PDF.

**4.** Turn off the Publish In Background option. By turning off this feature, you'll get your results faster.

**5.** Click the Publish button. The Specify DWF File dialog box appears. This is a standard file dialog box in which you can find a location for your DWF file and also name it. Select a name and location for the DWF file. By default, AutoCAD uses the same name as the current file and the folder location of the current file. You can also set up a default location in the Publish Setup dialog box.

**6.** When AutoCAD is finished publishing your drawings, you may see a message stating that you do not have a DWF viewing application installed. You can view the DWF file using the free Autodesk® Design Review program available on the Autodesk website.

**7.** Go back to AutoCAD, and click the Plot And Publish Details Report icon in the right side of the status bar. The Plot And Publish Details dialog box appears, offering detailed information about the sheets you published. You can then click the Copy To Clipboard button to export the list to a file as a record. If you want to recall this dialog box later, you can do so by choosing Print ➤ View Plot And Publish Details from the Application menu.

You may notice that when you click the Publish button in the previous exercise, AutoCAD behaves as if it's printing the layouts in your list—and that is exactly what it's doing. AutoCAD uses its own DWF printer driver to "print" your drawings to a DWF file. AutoCAD uses the layout settings from the Plot dialog box for each layout to produce the DWF pages.

## Exploring Other Publish Options

A few more options are available when you use the Publish feature. Let's take a moment to review some of the options in the Publish dialog box toolbar:

♦ The Preview tool lets you preview a sheet based on the current settings.

♦ The Add Sheets tool lets you add sheets to the list. The Remove Sheets tool removes a selected item from the list.

♦ The Move Sheet Up and Move Sheet Down tools let you move an item in the list up and down. These are important options because the order of drawings in the list determines the order in which the drawings will appear in the Autodesk DWF Viewer. The item at the top of the list appears first, the next one on the list is second, and so on.

♦ The Load Sheet List and Save Sheet List tools let you load and save the list you've compiled, respectively. It's a good idea to save your list in case you need to reproduce the DWF file at some future date.

♦ You can use the Plot Stamp Settings tool to specify the data you want to include in the plot stamp. This tool opens the Plot Stamp dialog box. (See the bonus chapter "Hardware and Software Tips," available at www.omura.com/chapters, for more on the Plot Stamp dialog box.)

### CONTEXT MENU OPTIONS

If you right-click an item or a set of items in the Publish dialog box list box, you see a menu with the standard options mentioned earlier plus some additional options. You'll want to know about a few of these options.

---

#### VIEWING DWF FILES

The Autodesk Design Review program offers a fast and simple way to view DWF files, and as we mentioned earlier, it's free.

If the person receiving your DWF file doesn't have a copy of the Autodesk DWF Viewer, send them to the Products page of the Autodesk website (www.autodesk.com) to download their own copy. The download file is relatively small, and it is easily downloaded. If they are using Windows 7, Windows 8, or Windows Vista, they won't need the viewer since the default DWF file format (DWFx) is XPS compatible.

---

By default, AutoCAD applies the existing layout settings for each layout when it produces the DWF file. These are the settings found in the Plot Or Page Setup dialog box and include the sheet size, scale, and page orientation. The Change Page Setup option lets you use a different set of layout settings for a selected layout in the list. To use this option, you must have saved a page setup in the file's Page Setup or Plot dialog box. (See Chapter 8 for more on the Page Setup dialog box and its options.) You can import a page setup from a different AutoCAD file, or you can assign a page setup to a sheet. Do this by clicking the sheet name and selecting a page setup from the list box that appears in the Page Setup column.

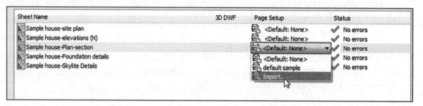

To change the page setup for multiple sheets, select the sheets from the list first and then select the setup from the list box.

If you happen to have two layouts with the same name, right-click a layout name, and then select the Rename Sheet option on the context menu to rename a layout. The Copy Selected Sheets option adds copies of selected layouts to the list. The copies have the word *copy* appended to their names. The last two items in the context menu let you control what is displayed in the list box. Include Layouts When Adding Sheets controls whether layouts are automatically imported from a drawing into the list box. Include Model When Adding Sheets controls whether Model Space views are automatically imported from a drawing into the list box.

## THE PUBLISH OPTIONS DIALOG BOX

You can set up additional options by clicking the Publish Options button in the Publish dialog box. You'll then see the Publish Options dialog box (see Figure 25.9).

**FIGURE 25.9**
Publish Options
dialog box

This dialog box offers options for the location and type of output. The Default Output Location group lets you select the location for DWF files. The General DWF/PDF Options group lets you choose between a multisheet DWF file, which combines multiple sheets into one file, and single-sheet DWF files, which create a file for each sheet. If you choose the multisheet file option, you have the added option to specify a default name for your DWF files or to have AutoCAD prompt you for a name each time you create a DWF file. The DWF Data Options group lets you add password protection to the DWF file by using the Password option. If your drawing contains 3D information, you can use the options in the 3D DWF Options group, which control Xref hierarchy and materials.

## Creating a DWF File by Using the Plot Dialog Box

Another way to create DWF files is through the Plot dialog box. If you need to create a DWF file of only a single sheet, you may want to use the Plot dialog box because it's a simple and familiar procedure.

1. Open the file that you want to convert to DWF, and then proceed as if you're going to plot the drawing.

2. In the Plot dialog box, select DWFx ePlot (XPS Compatible).pc3 or DWF6 ePlot.pc3 from the Name drop-down list in the Printer/Plotter area. The DWFx ePlot (XPS Compatible).pc3 option creates a file that is readable in Windows 8, Windows 7, or Windows Vista without the need for any special viewing program.

3. Proceed with the plot the normal way. When AutoCAD would normally send the drawing to the printer, you'll see a dialog box asking you to enter a name for your plot file and finish with the rest of the plot. You can control the DWF plot as you would any plot.

In addition to using the settings available in the Plot dialog box, you can make some special configuration adjustments to the DWF plotter configuration file. Here is where to find those configuration settings:

1. Select a layout tab to make it current, and then right-click the tab and select Page Setup Manager to open the Page Setup Manager dialog box. Select a setup from the Page Setups list, and then click Modify to open the Page Setup dialog box.

2. Make sure the DWFx ePlot (XPS Compatible).pc3 configuration file is listed in the Name list box of the Printer/Plotter group. Although you may see an incorrect paper size message, you can continue.

3. Click the Properties button to the right of the Name drop-down list to open the Plotter Configuration Editor dialog box.

4. Make sure the Device And Document Settings tab is selected, and then click Custom Properties in the list box (see Figure 25.10).

5. Click the Custom Properties button that appears in the lower half of the dialog box to open the DWFx ePlot (XPS Compatible).pc3 Properties dialog box. Here you can set the resolution, format, background color, and paper boundary for your DWF file. You can also specify whether to include layer and font information.

**FIGURE 25.10**

Controlling the plotter configuration file

6. Click OK after selecting your settings. The Plotter Configuration Editor dialog box reappears. After you've set the custom properties, you can save any new settings in the DWFx ePlot (XPS Compatible).pc3 file, or you can create a new DWFx ePlot (XPS Compatible).pc3 plot-configuration file. To save any setting changes, click the Save As button and select the PC3 file in which you want to save the settings. For more information about PC3 plot configuration files, see "Fine-Tuning the Appearance of Output" in the bonus chapter "Hardware and Software Tips," available at www.omura.com/chapters.

7. Click OK in the Plotter Configuration Editor dialog box to return to the Page Setup dialog box.

8. Click OK to exit the Page Setup dialog box, and then close the Page Setup Manager.

After you select your custom configuration settings in step 5, you needn't open the Plotter Configuration Editor dialog box again the next time you plot a DWF file. If you save your new settings as a new PC3 file, you can select it from the File drop-down list in the Plotter Configuration group. You don't have to reenter the custom settings.

You can either use the Publish feature described in the previous section to create single or multiple DWF files or create DWF files directly through the Plot dialog box. You can post the output from either method to a website to offer a wide distribution of your drawings. Just create a link to the DWF file from your web page. Be aware that persons attempting to view your DWF file from a web browser will need a copy of the free Autodesk DWF Viewer program that lets them view AutoCAD DWF files. The Autodesk DWF Viewer is automatically installed with AutoCAD 2015.

# Sharing Files with Autodesk 360

Whether you share native AutoCAD DWG files or share files using the DWF format, you have a number of ways to convey the files to those who need them. Downloading from websites, transferring via FTP, and exchanging through email are all common methods for sharing files, but they are limited and can leave a user wanting more flexibility.

Autodesk offers the free Autodesk 360 service, where you can share files in a much more open and organized fashion. With Autodesk 360, you can make files available to others in a way similar to how you would make files available on an FTP site or a website, with the addition of more easily controlled access. You can track the shared history of a document or set of documents and organize files to suit nearly any project requirement.

---

**UPGRADE TO THE LATEST BROWSER**

The Autodesk 360 website works best when viewed using Internet Explorer 10, Apple Safari v5.1, Mozilla Firefox v19, Google Chrome v33, or later versions. If you are not using one of these versions of your browser, you may want to upgrade before proceeding with the exercises. Some features may not work or appear properly under earlier versions.

---

## Getting Started with Autodesk 360

To appreciate what Autodesk 360 can do for you, you'll want to try out some of its features. The entry point to the cloud service is the Autodesk 360 Sign In option in the InfoCenter. Try the following to get started:

1. Click Sign In from the drop-down list in the InfoCenter and select Sign In To Autodesk 360 (Figure 25.11). If you are not signed in with your Autodesk ID already, the Autodesk – Sign In dialog box appears first.

**FIGURE 25.11**
The Sign In To Autodesk 360 menu option and the Autodesk 360 welcome window

If you haven't already set up an Autodesk ID, click the Need An Autodesk ID link at the bottom of the Sign In window; otherwise enter your sign-in information.

After you log in, the Autodesk 360 welcome window appears. This window only appears the first time you log in to Autodesk 360.

**2.** After you've signed into your Autodesk account, the InfoCenter Sign In drop-down list offers a new set of options (Figure 25.12).

**FIGURE 25.12**

The InfoCenter Sign In drop-down list with new options

**3.** Click the Sign In drop-down list and select Autodesk 360. Your default browser opens and the Autodesk 360 site appears.

**4.** Click the Close icon in the upper-right corner of the Welcome panel, which occupies the top of the page just below the title bar.

**5.** Click the Documents tab in the upper-left corner of the page to open the Documents page. Figure 25.13 shows this page with a few files to give you an idea of how they appear. You can switch between a thumbnail view and a list view by using the icons to the right of the Sort By drop-down list.

**FIGURE 25.13**

The Autodesk 360 Documents page showing several documents

The Autodesk 360 Documents page has three main parts. The largest area is a file view panel, where your files appear. Across the top is the menu bar that offers a set of actions you can apply to your files. To the left is a column of display filters that help you keep your drawings organized.

Let's take a look at the menu bar. You can click the Upload option to upload files. This option opens the Upload Documents dialog box. You can then click and drag files into the Drag And Drop Here panel. The filename appears in the list box below (Figure 25.14). You can also just click and drag files into the blank file area to open the Upload Documents dialog box.

**FIGURE 25.14**
The Upload Documents dialog box

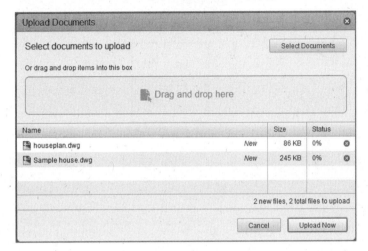

The New Folder option creates new folders in the current file view panel. To the right of the New Folder option are two icons: Actions and Categories. To use these icons, you first need to select a file or set of files from the file view panel, which you can do by clicking the check box next to the filename. The Actions icon displays a menu that offers options to download, share, move, rename, or delete your files.

The Categories icon displays a menu that lets you assign your files to a category that you create. You can create categories in the panel to the left by clicking the arrowhead to the right of the Categories title. A file can be assigned to multiple categories.

The Actions and Categories icons appear in several places in the Autodesk 360 site so that no matter where you are, you always have the Actions or Categories icons available. For example, if you hover over a file in the file view panel, you will see the icons along with a magnifying glass icon you can click to display an enlarged view of the thumbnail and a comments icon that enables you to add a text comment to the file.

## Sharing Files

When you select a file by placing a check in the file's check box and clicking Actions ➤ Share, you'll see two options: Private Sharing and Public Sharing. If you want to share a drawing with another Autodesk 360 user, you can select the Private Sharing option. You are then asked to supply the email address of the person with whom you want to share your drawing. After you complete this step, the file will appear in the file panel of the person you are sharing with.

With the Public Sharing option you can share drawings with people who do not have an Autodesk ID account. Before you can share publicly, you will first have to turn on Public Sharing for the file. To do this, click the file to go to the Document Details/View page and then click the Document Details option in the menu bar (Figure 25.15).

**FIGURE 25.15**
The Document Details view

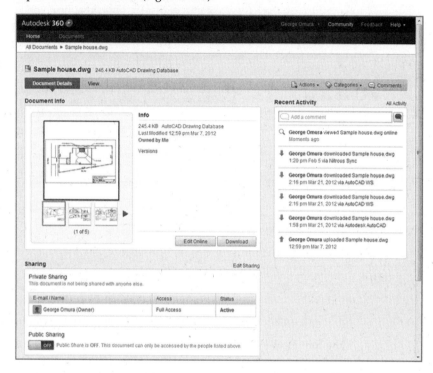

Scroll down to the bottom of the view to the Sharing panel. At the bottom of the Sharing panel, click the Off button to change the Public Sharing status to On (Figure 25.16).

**FIGURE 25.16**
The Public Sharing option

Finally, click the E-Mail button. If you are logged into your email client, an email window appears with the subject filled in and a link to your shared drawing already included in the body of the email text. You only need to fill in the recipient information and send the email off. When the recipient receives the email, they can go to the link in the email to view or download the drawing.

If you want to see what your recipient sees in the link, you can click the Preview button in the Sharing panel of the Document Details view. Their view is similar to your Document Details view without the Sharing and Recent Activity information.

---

**INSERTED DRAWINGS NOT TO SCALE?**

If you're sharing files that have the potential for being inserted as blocks or Xrefs, you'll want to know about a little setting that can have a big effect on your work. The Insertion Scale setting in the Units dialog box controls how DWG files are scaled when they are inserted into a drawing. To get to the Insertion Scale setting, open the Application menu and select Drawing Utilities ➤ Units or type **Units**↵. The Insertion Scale drop-down list is in the middle of the dialog box, as shown here:

Suppose your drawing is in centimeters and you anticipate that someone will be inserting your drawing into another one that is using millimeters. You would set the Insertion Scale in your drawing to Centimeters. When the person receiving your drawing inserts it in their millimeter drawing, your drawing will be automatically scaled to the appropriate size. Likewise, if you receive a drawing that does not scale properly when inserted in your drawing, check the Insertion Scale value of both your drawing and the inserted drawing and adjust the settings so that the inserted drawing appears at the appropriate scale. Drawings that use the Architectural unit type should always be set to Inches, but drawings set to the Decimal unit type can have any Insertion Scale setting.

---

## Editing Drawings Online

Autodesk 360 is intended as a tool for collaboration, so it includes some basic editing features. The specific features depend on the type of file you have available in your file panel.

If you look back at Figure 25.15, you will notice the Edit Online button. Click this button and the Autodesk 360 editor, a web-based AutoCAD drawing editor, opens the file (Figure 25.17.)

**FIGURE 25.17**
Autodesk
360 editor

Notice that the Autodesk 360 editor offers many of the tools you've already seen in AutoCAD. Autodesk 360 offers the most common editing tools so that users can make minor changes to a drawing.

A set of toolbars in the lower-left corner offers features similar to the status and Navigation bars. You can control properties and layers by using the panels to the right. For collaborative work, the Design Feed panel appears in the lower-right corner of the Autodesk 360 page. To view layouts, click the Design flyout arrowhead located in the Autodesk 360 menu bar. You can plot your drawing to a PDF or DWF file using the Output icon in the menu bar. If you want to create a new file, click the plus icon to the far left of the menu bar.

You can store other types of files, such as PDF and DWF files, in Autodesk 360. You can annotate and get a closer view of these types of files using the AutoCAD 360 editor. Open the document in Autodesk 360 and select Actions > Edit Online in AutoCAD 360 from the menubar to switch to the editor (Figure 25.18).

## Controlling File Access

When you privately share a drawing, you can also control the level of access you give to the person you are sharing with. For example, you may want to allow only one person to view a file, whereas another person may require enough access to edit the file online.

After you've shared a file, you can control the access level through the Share Document dialog box (Figure 25.19). To open this dialog box, click the Edit Sharing link to the right of the Sharing panel on the Document Details view (shown in Figure 25.15 earlier).

**FIGURE 25.18**
Editing a DWF file
in AutoCAD 360

**FIGURE 25.19**
The Share Document dialog box

You can change the access level by clicking in the Access column of the dialog box. A list opens offering three levels of access: View DWG, View & Download DWG, and View, Download & Update DWG. When you hover over one of these options, a description of what the collaborator can and cannot do is listed to the right.

## Tracking File Versions

A unique feature of Autodesk 360 is its ability to track different versions of the same file. For example, you can upload a file, and then have a collaborator make changes to that file online using the AutoCAD 360 editor. You can then click the Actions icon to check the version dates of the file (Figure 25.20).

**FIGURE 25.20**
The Document
Versions dialog box

| Document Versions | | ⊗ |
|---|---|---|
| Sample house.dwg | | ⬆ Upload New Version |
| Version Date | Uploaded By | Actions |
| **2:57 pm Jan 31** * | Me (Owner) | ⬇ |
| 2:23 pm Jan 31 | Alan Wakeman | ⬇ 🕐 |
| 2:16 pm Jan 30 | Me (Owner) | ⬇ 🕐 |

In addition, you can download any version using the down arrow in the Actions column or, as the owner of the file, revert to a prior version by clicking the clock icon. Even if you revert the file, the Document Versions dialog box will still display all of the versions of the file that have been uploaded or edited online.

As you can see from this brief tour of Autodesk 360, sharing files and collaborating with others is becoming much easier. You may want to spend some time on your own experimenting with the settings and features of Autodesk 360 now that you've gotten your feet wet.

## Collaborating with Others Using Design Feed

Besides sharing and editing files, you can add comments and images to files shared on Autodesk 360 through the Design Feed feature. Design Feed gives you a way to communicate ideas through your drawings by letting you post messages and images directly onto your AutoCAD files. You can find Design Feed on the Autodesk 360 tab in the AutoCAD Online panel (see Figure 25.21).

**FIGURE 25.21**
Clicking the Design
Feed tool

Click the Design Feed tool and the Design Feed palette opens (see Figure 25.22). If the drawing has not been saved to the Autodesk 360 site, you will see a message at the top of the Design Feed panel asking you to save to Autodesk 360. When this is done, you can start to add comments to the drawing that others can view and respond to. The comments will appear in the middle portion of the panel.

There are four tools just below the Create A New Post box:

♦ Associate This Post To An Area In The Drawing

♦ Associate This Post To A Point In The Drawing

♦ Tag In This Post

♦ Attach Image(s) To This Post

**FIGURE 25.22**
Design Feed panel

**FIGURE 25.22**
Design Feed panel

Associate this post to an area in the drawing
Associate this post to a point in the drawing

Attach image(s) to this post
Tag in this post

To use the area or point tool, click the tool icon and then click in the drawing to indicate the post's location. Next, enter a message in the Create A New Post box. Click the Create Post button when you're done. With the Tag tool you can alert the recipient to your post via an email. The Attach Image tool will open a file dialog box where you can locate an image file to include with your post. Figure 25.23 shows a drawing with a post attached to an area.

**FIGURE 25.23**
A drawing with a post attached to an area

When a recipient of your post views the drawing in Autodesk 360, they will see a post as a numbered icon. They can click the icon and the post associated with it will be highlighted in the Design Feed panel. They can then add their comments and replies to the post.

# Adding Hyperlinks to Drawings

AutoCAD offers the Hyperlink tool, which enables you to link any document to an AutoCAD object. Then, with a few clicks of your mouse, you can follow the links to view other drawings, text files, spreadsheets, or web pages. Hyperlinks persist even after you've exported your drawing to a PDF file. You can then post that PDF file on a web page where others can gain access to those links.

## Creating Hyperlinks

The following steps show you how to add links to a sample floor plan:

1. In AutoCAD, open the file houseplan.dwg.

2. In the Insert tab's Data panel, click the Hyperlink tool.

3. At the Select objects: prompt, click the hexagonal door symbol, as shown in Figure 25.24.

**FIGURE 25.24**
The door symbol in the houseplan .dwg file

Click this symbol.

4. When you're done, press ↵. The Insert Hyperlink dialog box opens (see Figure 25.25).

5. Click the File button on the right side of the dialog box to open the Browse The Web – Select Hyperlink dialog box. It's a typical file dialog box.

6. Locate the doorsch.pdf file and select it.

**FIGURE 25.25**
The Insert Hyperlink dialog box

7. Click Open. The Insert Hyperlink dialog box reappears. Notice that `doorsch.pdf` appears in the list box at the top of the dialog box in the Type The File Or Web Page Name box.

8. Make sure the Use Relative Path For Hyperlink option isn't selected, and then click OK.

The link you just created is stored with the drawing file. You can create a PDF file from this drawing, and the link will be preserved in the PDF file.

Now let's see how you can use the link from within the AutoCAD file:

1. Move your cursor over the hexagonal door symbol. Notice that the cursor changes to the hyperlink icon when it's placed on the symbol. It also shows the name of the file to which the object is linked. This tells you that the object is linked to another document somewhere on your system, on your network, or on the Internet (see Figure 25.26).

**FIGURE 25.26**
The hyperlink icon and tool tip

2. Click the hexagonal door symbol to select it.

3. Right-click in a blank area of the drawing. In the context menu, choose Hyperlink ➢ Open ".\doorsch.pdf" to choose the link to the `doorsch.dwf` file. You can also Ctrl+click the door symbol.

The Autodesk Design Review program opens and displays the file doorsch.pdf. If you installed the sample figures on another drive or folder location, the Hyperlink menu option will reflect that location.

You've used the doorsch.pdf file as an example in these exercises, but this could have been a text file, a spreadsheet, a database, or even another AutoCAD file. AutoCAD will start the application associated with the linked file and open the file.

### Editing and Deleting Hyperlinks

You can edit or delete a hyperlink by doing the following:

1. Select and right-click the object whose link you want to edit, and then choose Hyperlink ➤ Edit Hyperlink from the context menu. Doing so opens the Edit Hyperlink dialog box, which offers the same options as the Insert Hyperlink dialog box (see Figure 25.25, earlier in this chapter), with the addition of the Remove Link button.

2. You can now change the link, or you can click the Remove Link button in the lower-left corner of the dialog box to delete the link.

### Taking a Closer Look at the Hyperlink Options

You were introduced to the Insert Hyperlink dialog box, shown in Figure 25.25, in the previous exercises. Let's take a moment to study this dialog box in a little more detail.

To specify a file or a website to link to, you can enter either a filename or a website URL in the Type The File Or Web Page Name box or use the Or Select From List area, which offers a list box and three button options. When you select one of the buttons, the list box changes to offer additional related options:

**Recent Files**  Displays a list of recently edited AutoCAD files, as illustrated in Figure 25.25. You can then link the object to a file in the list by clicking the filename.

**Browsed Pages**  Displays a list of websites that you recently visited using your web browser.

**Inserted Links**  Displays a list of recently inserted links, including files or websites.

You can also use the three buttons to the right of the list box to locate specific files (the File button), websites (the Web Page button), or saved views (the Target button) in the current drawing.

As you saw in the exercise, the File button opens the Browse The Web – Select Hyperlink dialog box, which lets you locate and select a file from Autodesk 360, from your computer, from your local area network, or even from an FTP site. This is a typical AutoCAD open file dialog box with some additional features.

The Web Page button on the right opens a simplified web browser that lets you locate a web page for linking. You can use the standard methods for accessing web pages, such as using the Look In drop-down list to select recently visited pages or entering a URL in the Name Or URL box. The page is then displayed in the main window of the dialog box.

If the selected hyperlink file is an AutoCAD DWG file, the Target button in the Insert Hyperlink dialog box opens the Select Place In Document dialog box, which lists the saved views in the drawing.

Views are subdivided by layout tabs. At the top is the Model Space tab listing, and below that are other layout tab listings. If the current drawing contains saved views, you see a plus sign next to the layout tab name. Click the plus sign to display a listing of the views in that layout.

At the top of the Insert Hyperlink and Edit Hyperlink dialog boxes is a box labeled Text To Display. When a hyperlink is added to an object in AutoCAD, AutoCAD will display a hyperlink icon whenever the cursor passes over the object. You can also include descriptive text that will display along with the icon by entering the description in the Text To Display box.

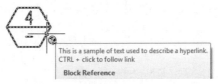

By default, the text is the name of the hyperlinked item that you select. You can change the text to provide a better description of the link.

The Insert Hyperlink dialog box contains a column of options at the far left labeled Link To. The top button, Existing File Or Web Page, displays the options discussed so far in this section. The other two buttons change the appearance of the Insert Hyperlink dialog box to offer different but familiar options:

**View Of This Drawing** This button changes the display to show just the views that are available in the current drawing. This option performs the same function as the Target button described earlier.

**E-Mail Address** This button changes the Insert Hyperlink dialog box to enable you to link an email address to an object. Clicking the object will then open your default email application, letting you send a message to the address.

## Managing Your Drawings with DesignCenter and the Tool Palettes

As you start to build a library of drawings, you'll find that you reuse many components of existing drawing files. Most of the time, you'll probably be producing similar types of drawings with some variation, so you'll reuse drawing components such as layer settings, dimension styles, and layouts. It can be a major task to keep track of all the projects on which you've worked. It's especially frustrating when you remember setting up a past drawing in a way that you know would be useful in a current project but you can't remember that file's name or location.

AutoCAD offers DesignCenter™ to help you keep track of the documents you use in your projects. You can think of DesignCenter as a kind of super Windows Explorer that is focused on AutoCAD files. DesignCenter lets you keep track of your favorite files and helps you locate files, blocks, and other drawing components. In addition, you can import blocks and other drawing components from one drawing to another by using a simple click and drag. If you've been diligent about setting a unit format for each of your drawings, you can use DesignCenter to import symbols and drawings of different unit formats into a drawing and the symbols will maintain their proper size. For example, a 90 cm door symbol from a metric drawing can be imported into a drawing in Imperial units and DesignCenter will translate the 90 cm metric door size to a 35.43" door.

## Getting Familiar with DesignCenter

At first glance, DesignCenter looks a bit mysterious. But it takes only a few mouse clicks to reveal a tool that looks much like Windows Explorer. Try the following steps to get familiar with DesignCenter:

1. Open AutoCAD to a new file, and then click the DesignCenter tool in the View tab's Palettes panel.

   DesignCenter opens as a floating palette (see Figure 25.27).

**FIGURE 25.27**
DesignCenter opens as a floating palette.

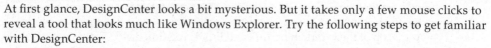

---

**OPENING THE TREE VIEW**

If your DesignCenter view doesn't look like Figure 25.27, with the DesignCenter window divided into two parts, click the Tree View Toggle tool on the DesignCenter toolbar. The Tree view opens on the left side of the DesignCenter window. Click the Home tool to display the contents of the `C:\Program Files\Autodesk\AutoCAD 2015\Sample\DesignCenter` folder.

---

2. Click the Favorites tool on the DesignCenter toolbar.

   DesignCenter displays a listing of the `Favorites` folder. You're actually looking at a view of the `C:\Users\`*User Name*`\Favorites\Autodesk` folder, where *User Name* is your login name. Unless you've already added items to the `\Favorites\Autodesk` folder, you see a blank view in the right panel. You can add shortcuts to this folder as you work with DesignCenter. You may also see a view showing the tree structure of the files you have open in AutoCAD.

3. Place your cursor in the lower-right corner of the DesignCenter window so that a double-headed diagonal arrow shows. Then click and drag the corner out so that you have an enlarged DesignCenter window that looks similar to Figure 25.28. The view on the right, containing the `Favorites` folder, is called the Palette view. The view on the left is called the Tree view.

**FIGURE 25.28**

The components of the DesignCenter palette

Tree view · Palette view · Preview panel · Description panel

4. Place your cursor on the border between the Tree view and the Palette view until you see a double-headed cursor. Then click and drag the border to the right to enlarge the Tree view until it covers about one-third of the window.

5. Use the scroll bar at the bottom to adjust your view of the Tree view so that you can easily read its contents.

---

**AUTO-HIDE DESIGNCENTER**

Like the tool palettes and the Properties palette, DesignCenter has an Auto-Hide feature. To use it, click the double-headed arrow icon near the bottom of the DesignCenter title bar. DesignCenter will disappear except for the title bar. You can quickly open DesignCenter by placing the cursor on the title bar.

---

After you have it set up like this, you can see the similarities between DesignCenter and Windows Explorer. You can navigate your computer or network by using the Tree view, just as you would in Windows Explorer. There are a few differences, however, as you'll see in the following exercise:

1. Click the Home tool on the DesignCenter toolbar. The Palette view changes to display the contents of the Sample folder under the Program Files\Autodesk\AutoCAD 2015\ folder.

2. Double-click en-us to open the en-us folder, and then double click the DesignCenter folder.

Instead of the usual list of files, you see a sample image of each file. These are called *preview icons* (see Figure 25.29).

**FIGURE 25.29**
The DesignCenter
display

3. Click the Views tool on the DesignCenter toolbar and choose Details from the menu. The Palette view changes to show a detailed list of the files in the DesignCenter folder.

4. Click the Views tool again, and choose Large Icons to return to the previous view. The Views tool is similar to the various View options in Windows Explorer.

5. Click the Basic Electronics.dwg file to select it. You see a preview of the selected file in the Preview panel of DesignCenter. You can adjust the vertical size of the Preview panel by clicking and dragging its top or bottom border.

You can also open and close the Preview panel by clicking the Preview tool in the DesignCenter toolbar. The preview can be helpful if you prefer viewing files and drawing components as a list in the main part of the Palette view.

Below the Preview panel is the Description panel. This panel displays any text information included with the drawing or drawing element selected in the Palette view. To add a description to a drawing that will be visible here, choose Drawing Utilities ➤ Drawing Properties from the Application menu; to add a description to a block, use the Summary tab in the Block Definition dialog box.

You can open and close this panel by clicking the Description tool on the DesignCenter toolbar. Because the Basic Electronics.dwg file doesn't have a description attached, the Description panel shows the message Last saved by: Autodesk.

Both the Preview and Description panels can offer help in identifying files for which you may be looking. After you find a file, you can click and drag it into a folder in the Tree view to organize your files into separate folders.

You can also add files to the Favorites folder by right-clicking and then choosing Add To Favorites. The file itself isn't moved to the Favorites folder; instead, a shortcut to the file is created in the Favorites folder. If you want to work on organizing your Favorites folder, you can open a window to the Favorites folder by right-clicking a file in the Palette view and choosing Organize Favorites. A window to the Favorites folder appears.

Because you'll be working with the sample drawings, go ahead and add the Projects folder to the Favorites folder:

1. Locate the Projects folder (the one created when you installed the sample files) in the left panel Tree view, and right-click it.

2. Choose Add To Favorites from the context menu.

3. To go directly to the Favorites folder, click the Favorites tool on the DesignCenter toolbar. The Projects folder appears in the right panel in the Palette view.

4. Double-click the Projects shortcut in the Palette view. You see the contents of the Projects folder.

You can go beyond just looking at file listings. You can also look inside files to view their components:

1. In the Palette view, locate the file named 15-unit.dwg in the Chapter 15 folder and double-click it. You see a listing of its components in the Palette view. The Tree view also shows the file highlighted.

2. Double-click the Blocks listing in the Palette view. Now you see a listing of all the blocks in 15-unit.dwg.

---

**WHAT IS AUTODESK SEEK?**

You might notice the Autodesk® Seek banner in the upper-right corner of the DesignCenter palette. If you click this banner, your web browser opens to the Autodesk Seek home page, where you will find a rich resource for drawings and models from manufacturers and users. There are 2D and 3D files available in a number of formats, including DWG, DWF, and PDF.

If you prefer to use your web browser to explore the Autodesk Seek site without opening AutoCAD, the website address is http://seek.autodesk.com.

---

Here, you can import any of the drawing components from the DesignCenter palette into an open drawing in AutoCAD. But before you try that, let's look at a few other features of DesignCenter.

## Opening and Inserting Files with DesignCenter

**CERT OBJECTIVE**

By using DesignCenter, you can more easily locate the files you're seeking because you can view thumbnail preview icons. But often that isn't enough. For example, you might want to locate all the files that contain the name of a particular manufacturer in an attribute of a drawing. This can be accomplished using the search feature of DesignCenter, which you'll learn about later in the chapter.

After you've found the file you're seeking, you can load it into AutoCAD by right-clicking the filename in the Palette view and then choosing Open In Window. Try it with the following exercise:

1. Click the Up tool in the DesignCenter toolbar three times. This takes you up two levels in the Palette view, from the view of the drawing blocks to the list of filenames.

2. In the Tree view, select the Chapter 11 folder. Then, in the Palette view of DesignCenter, locate the 11c-unit.dwg sample.

3. Right-click the 11c-unit.dwg file, and select Open In Application Window. The drawing appears in the AutoCAD window.

If you want to insert a file into another drawing as a block, you can do so by clicking and dragging the file from the DesignCenter Palette view into an open drawing window. You can also right-click and select Insert As Block. You're then prompted for the insertion point, scale, and rotation angle. If you prefer to use the Insert dialog box to insert a drawing from DesignCenter, right-click the filename in the Palette view and then choose Insert As Block. The Insert dialog box opens, offering you the full set of Insert options, as described in Chapter 4, "Organizing Objects with Blocks and Groups."

Finally, you can attach a drawing as an Xref by right-clicking a file in the Palette view of DesignCenter and choosing Attach As Xref. The Attach External Reference dialog box opens, offering the insertion point, scale, and rotation options similar to the options in the Insert dialog box. This is the same dialog box described in Chapter 7, "Mastering Viewing Tools, Hatches, and External References."

## Finding and Extracting the Contents of a Drawing

Aside from the convenience of being able to see thumbnail views of your drawing, DesignCenter may not seem like much of an improvement over Windows Explorer. But DesignCenter goes beyond Windows Explorer in many ways. One of the main features of DesignCenter is that it enables you to locate and extract components of a drawing.

Imagine that you want to find a specific block in a drawing. You remember the name of the block, but you don't remember the drawing into which you put it. You can search the contents of drawings by using DesignCenter's Search dialog box. In the following exercise, you'll search for a block named Kitchen2-metric among a set of files:

1. In the DesignCenter toolbar, click the Search tool to open the Search dialog box. It looks similar to the Search tool that comes with Windows.

2. Select the drive that contains your `Projects` folder from the In drop-down list. Make sure that the Search Subfolders option is checked.

3. Select Blocks from the Look For drop-down list. As you can see from the list, you can look for a variety of drawing component types (see Figure 25.30).

**FIGURE 25.30**
Select Blocks from the Look For drop-down list.

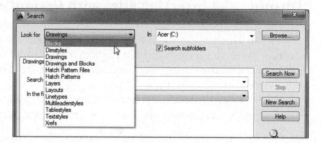

4. Enter **Kitchen2-metric.⤶** in the Search For The Name box, and then click the Search Now button to start the search. The magnifying glass icon in the lower-right corner moves in a circular pattern, telling you that the Search function is working. After a minute or two, the name of the block appears in the window at the bottom of the dialog box.

5. Double-click the block name. DesignCenter displays the block in the Palette view and the file that contains the block in the Tree view.

### EXPLORING THE SEARCH OPTIONS

As you saw from the previous example, the Search dialog box can be helpful in finding items that are buried in a set of drawings. In the exercise, you searched for a block, but you can search for any named drawing component, including attribute data and text. For example, if you want to find all attributes that contain the name *ABC Manufacturing Company* in your drawings, you can do so with the DesignCenter Search dialog box. Table 25.2 shows a summary of its features. When you select Drawings from the Look For drop-down list, you see a set of additional tabs in the Search dialog box, as described in Table 25.3.

**TABLE 25.2:**  DesignCenter Search dialog box options

| OPTION | PURPOSE |
| --- | --- |
| In | Lets you select the drive you want to search. |
| Look For options | Lets you select the type of item to search for. The options are Blocks, Dimstyles, Drawings, Drawings And Blocks, Hatch Pattern Files, Hatch Patterns, Layers, Layouts, Linetypes, Multileaderstyles, Tablestyles, Textstyles, and Xrefs. |
| Browse | Lets you locate a specific folder to search. |
| Search Subfolders | Lets you determine whether Search searches subfolders in the drive and folder you specify. |
| Search Now | Starts the search process. |
| Stop | Cancels the current search. |
| New Search | Clears all the settings for the current search so you can start fresh on a new search. |
| Help | Opens the AutoCAD help system to the Search topic. |

**TABLE 25.3:**  DesignCenter Search dialog box tab options when Drawings is selected from the Look For drop-down list

| TAB OPTION | PURPOSE |
| --- | --- |
| **Drawings Tab** | |
| Search For The Word(s) | Lets you specify the text to search for in the Drawing Properties fields. |
| In The Field(s) | Lets you specify the field of the Drawing Properties dialog box to search through, including Filename, Title, Subject, Author, and Keywords. These are the fields you see in the Summary tab of the Drawing Properties dialog box, which can be opened by choosing Drawing Utilities ➤ Drawing Properties from the Application menu. |

**TABLE 25.3:**   DesignCenter Search dialog box tab options when Drawings is selected from the Look For drop-down list   *(continued)*

| TAB OPTION | PURPOSE |
| --- | --- |
| **Date Modified tab** | |
| Radio buttons | Let you limit search criteria based on dates. |
| **Advanced tab** | |
| Containing | Lets you select from a list of data to search for, including block name, block and drawing description, attribute tag, and attribute value. |
| Containing Text | Lets you specify the text to search for in the types of data you select from the Containing option. |
| Size Is | Lets you restrict the search to files larger than or smaller than the size you specify. |

## AUTOMATICALLY SCALING BLOCKS AT INSERTION

After you've found a block by using DesignCenter, you can click and drag the block into your open drawing. In the following exercise, you'll do that but with a slight twist. The block you've found is drawn in centimeters, but you'll insert the Kitchen2-metric block into a drawing named 11c-unit.dwg, which was created in the Imperial measurement system. If you were to insert the Kitchen2-metric block into 11c-unit.dwg, the kitchen would be exactly 2.54 times as large as it should be for 11c-unit.dwg. But as you'll see, DesignCenter takes care of scaling for you. Follow these steps:

1. If you haven't done so already, open the 11c-unit.dwg sample drawing in AutoCAD. You can temporarily close DesignCenter to do this.

2. Back in DesignCenter, click and drag the Kitchen2-metric block from the Palette view into the 11c-unit.dwg window in AutoCAD. The kitchen appears at the appropriate scale.

3. To confirm that DesignCenter did indeed adjust the scale, select the Kitchen2-metric block, right-click, and select Properties.

4. Check the Unit factor value under the Misc category. Notice the value shows 3⁄8″. This is the value at which the Kitchen2-metric block has been scaled. If no scaling is applied, this value would be 1.

5. After reviewing the Properties palette, close it.

You may recall from Chapter 3, "Setting Up and Using the Drafting Tools," that you can specify the type of units for which the drawing is set up in the Drawing Units dialog box under the Insertion Scale group. DesignCenter uses this information when you drag and drop blocks from DesignCenter into an open drawing. This is how DesignCenter is able to correctly scale a block drawn in metric to a drawing that is drawn in the Imperial format. The same option is offered in the Block Definition dialog box.

Blocks aren't the only type of drawing component you can click and drag from the Palette view. Linetypes, layouts, dimension styles, and text styles can all be imported from files on your computer or network through DesignCenter's Palette view.

## Exchanging Data between Open Files

You've seen how you can extract a block from a file stored on your hard disk and place it into an open drawing, but what if you want to copy a block from one open drawing to another open drawing? You change the way the Tree view displays data so that it shows only the files that are loaded in AutoCAD. The following exercise demonstrates how this works:

1. In AutoCAD, make sure that 11c-unit.dwg is still open, and then open the 11b-unit-metric.dwg file.

2. In DesignCenter, click the Open Drawings tab above the Tree view. The Tree view changes to display only the drawings that are open.

3. Click the plus sign (+) to the left of the 11c-unit.dwg filename in the Tree view. The list expands to show the components in 11c-unit.dwg.

4. Click Blocks in the Tree view. The Palette view changes to show a list of blocks available in 11c-unit.dwg.

5. Locate the Kitchen block in the Palette view.

6. Click and drag Kitchen from the Palette view into the open 11b-unit-metric.dwg drawing in AutoCAD. The block moves with the cursor. Once again, DesignCenter has automatically scaled the block to the appropriate size, this time from Imperial to metric.

7. Release anywhere in the drawing to place the Kitchen block.

In this example, you inserted a block from one open drawing into another drawing. If you prefer to use the Insert dialog box, you can right-click the block name in step 6 and choose Insert Block. The Insert dialog box opens, enabling you to set the Insertion Point, Scale, and Rotation options.

Just as with drawings, you can see a preview and descriptive text for blocks below the Palette view. In Chapter 4, you had the option to save a preview image with the block when you first created a block. This is where that preview icon can be really helpful. The preview icon gives you a chance to see what the block looks like when you use DesignCenter to browse through your drawing files. If you don't save a preview icon, you'll see the same block icon that was displayed in the previous Palette view.

You can also add the text description at the time you create the block. Before saving the block, enter a description in the Description box of the Block Definition dialog box.

If you're updating older drawing files to be used with DesignCenter, you can add text descriptions to blocks by using the Create tool in the Home tab's Block panel or the Create Block tool in the Insert tab's Block Definition panel. Click the Create tool and then, in the Block Definition dialog box, select the name of a block from the Name drop-down list. Enter the description you want for this block in the Description box toward the bottom of the Block Definition dialog box. When you're finished, click OK.

## Loading Specific Files into DesignCenter

You've seen how you can locate files through the Tree view and Palette view. If you already know the name and location of the file with which you want to work, you can use a file dialog box to open files in DesignCenter. Instead of choosing the Open tool on the Quick Access toolbar, you use the Load tool on the DesignCenter toolbar to open the Load dialog box. This is a standard file dialog box that lets you search for files on your computer or network.

If you want to open a file in DesignCenter that you've recently opened, you can use the History tab just above the Tree view. The Tree view closes, and you see a list of the files you've worked on most recently.

## Customizing the Tool Palettes with DesignCenter

CERT
OBJECTIVE

Many AutoCAD users have built their own custom library of symbols. In Chapter 1, "Exploring the Interface," you saw how easy it is to drag and drop a symbol, known as a tool, from the tool palettes. At first glance, there is no obvious way to add your own tools to the palettes, but adding tools and additional palettes to the tool palettes is fairly simple once you're familiar with DesignCenter. The following exercise shows you how it's done:

Tool
Palettes

1. If tool palettes aren't open already, click the Tool Palettes tool in the View tab's Palettes panel.

2. Right-click in the tool palettes title bar, and then choose New Palette from the context menu.

3. Enter **My Tool Palette**↵. A new, blank tab is added to the tool palettes.

4. Go back to DesignCenter, make sure the Folders tab is selected, click the Home tool, and select en-us ➤ DesignCenter.

5. In the Palette view to the right, double-click the Landscaping.dwg file and then double-click the Blocks icon that appears in the Palette view.

6. Make sure the tool palettes are visible behind DesignCenter, and then Ctrl+click Clump Of Trees Or Bushes – Plan and North Arrow.

7. Click and drag the selection to the tool palettes.

---

### BE CAREFUL CLICKING IN THE TOOL PALETTE

If you click a tool in a tool palette, it's inserted in the current drawing, so take care when clicking around in the tool palettes.

You've just created a tool palette and added two symbols. You can continue to add symbols from other drawings to your custom tool palette. Or, if you have a drawing that contains all the blocks you need for a tool palette, you can quickly create a tool palette directly from a file. Here's how that's done:

1. In DesignCenter, go up two folder levels so you can select the Landscaping.dwg file.

2. Right-click Landscaping.dwg, and then choose Create Tool Palette. After a few moments, a new tool palette called Landscaping appears in the tool palettes. This new palette contains all the blocks found in the Landscaping.dwg file.

This exercise showed that you can quickly create a palette of all the blocks from a file. You can do the same thing with entire folders of drawings, although you may want to make sure such folders don't contain too many files.

But what if you don't want some of the items in your custom palette? You can remove items easily by using the context menu:

1. In the Landscaping palette, select the top three symbols by right-clicking the tool that is third from the top and then Shift+clicking the top tool. This is a little different from the typical Windows method for selecting items from a list.

2. Right-click and choose Delete from the context menu. Click OK to confirm the deletion.

You may have noticed the Cut and Copy options in the context menu in step 2. You can use these options to move symbols from one palette to another. For example, instead of deleting the three symbols in step 2, you can choose Cut from the context menu, open another palette, right-click, and choose Paste. The symbols move to the new palette location. In the next section, you'll see how you can use the Copy and Paste context menu options to make a copy of a tool in the same palette.

## CUSTOMIZING A TOOL

Other context menu options let you delete entire palettes or rename tools or palettes. You can also edit the properties of symbols in a palette. The following exercise shows how to use the context menu options to create two scale versions of the same tool:

1. In the Landscaping tab of the tool palettes, right-click the North Arrow tool and choose Copy from the context menu.

2. Right-click in a blank area of the palette and choose Paste. A copy of the North Arrow tool appears at the bottom of the palette.

3. Right-click the copy of the North Arrow tool, choose Rename from the context menu, and then enter **North Arrow Copy**↵.

4. Right-click the North Arrow Copy tool and choose Properties to open the Tool Properties dialog box (see Figure 25.31).

5. Click 1 to the right of the Scale listing, and change the value to **4**.

6. Click OK, and then click and drag the North Arrow Copy tool into the drawing.

7. Click and drag the original North Arrow tool into the drawing. Notice that the original North Arrow is smaller than the North Arrow Copy, whose scale you changed to 4.

**FIGURE 25.31**
The Tool Properties dialog box

This exercise demonstrated that you can have multiple versions of a tool at different scales. You can then use the tool that's appropriate to the scale of your drawing. As you can see from the Tool Properties dialog box, you can also modify other tool properties, such as color and layer assignments. You can use this feature to create sets of tools for different-scale drawings. For example, you can create a palette of architectural reference symbols for ¼"-scale drawings, and you can create another palette for ⅛"-scale drawings.

### ADDING HATCH PATTERNS AND SOLID FILLS

You've seen how you can turn blocks into tool palette tools, but what about solid fills? In Chapter 1, you learned that sample hatch patterns and solid fills are available in the tool palettes. Here's how you can add your own:

1. In DesignCenter, use the Tree view to locate the AutoCAD 2015 Support folder. In Windows 8, Windows 7, or Windows Vista, it's typically in C:\Users\*User Name*\ AppData\Roaming\Autodesk\AutoCAD 2015\R20.0\enu\Support (*User Name* is your Windows login name).

2. Double-click the acad.pat file shown in the Palette view. AutoCAD builds a list of the patterns and displays the list in the Palette view.

3. You can now click and drag a pattern into any tool palette. You can also click and drag an entire PAT file into the tool palette to create a palette of all the patterns in a hatch pattern file.

**LOCATING SUPPORT AND HIDDEN FILES**

To find out exactly where support files are located, choose Options from the Application menu to open the Options dialog box. Click the Files tab. Expand the Support File Search Path item at the top of the list, and then place the cursor on the item just below Support File Search Path. You see the path to the Support folder. You can also enter **(findfile 'acad.pat')** at the Command prompt as a shortcut to find the support file search path. If you use this shortcut, note that the directory names are separated with double hash marks (\\). This is an artifact of AutoLISP®. User support files are in a hidden folder. See "Finding Folders That Contain AutoCAD Files" in Appendix B, "Installing and Setting Up AutoCAD," for information on how to unhide hidden folders.

In this exercise, you used the standard hatch patterns that come with AutoCAD. You can also create your own custom hatch patterns and import them to the tool palettes by using the method described here. See Chapter 24, "Customizing Toolbars, Menus, Linetypes, and Hatch Patterns," for more information on creating custom hatch patterns.

If you want to set up a set of solid fill colors, you can do the following:

1. Click and drag the SOLID pattern from the acad.pat file into the tool palette.

2. Click the new solid fill tool, choose Properties from the context menu, and select a color from the Color drop-down list in the Tool Properties dialog box.

You can select any color, including colors from the True Color or Color Books tab in the Select Color dialog box that you learned about in Chapter 5, "Keeping Track of Layers and Blocks." You can also cut and paste an existing solid fill tool to make copies. You can then modify the color property for each copy to get a set of custom solid fill colors.

## MANAGING THE TOOL PALETTES

You can perform other types of tool palette maintenance operations by using the Customize dialog box. For example, you can change the order of the tool palette tabs, or you can group tabs into categories that can be turned on or off. The following steps offer a glimpse of what you can do by showing you how to group palettes:

1. To open the Customize dialog box (see Figure 25.32), right-click the tool palettes and choose Customize Palettes from the context menu.

2. Right-click in a blank area of the Palette Groups panel, and choose New Group.

3. Enter **My Group** for the new group name.

4. Click and drag My Group to a position just above another group; that way, My Group is its own group instead of a subgroup.

5. Click and drag Landscaping from the left panel to the right panel just below My Group. A black bar appears below My Group. Release the mouse button.

6. Click and drag My Tool Palette from the left panel to the right, just below Landscaping.

**FIGURE 25.32**

Customize dialog
box for tool palettes

You've just created a new palette group and moved the two new palettes. You can view the palettes separately or all together:

**1.** Click Close to close the Customize dialog box. The tool palette still displays all the tabs.

**2.** To display only the new tabs, click the Properties button at the top of the palette title bar.

**3.** Select My Group. Now the tool palette shows only the two tabs you just created.

You may have noticed that in the Properties menu, you also have the option to show just the new groups or all the palettes. This feature lets you keep the tabs in the tool palettes organized.

The list on the left side of the Customize dialog box also lets you change the order of the tabs by clicking and dragging the tab names up or down in the left panel. If you select a palette in the left panel and right-click, you can rename, delete, import, or export a palette.

DesignCenter and tool palettes offer great features that will prove invaluable to AutoCAD users. Although these examples show you how to use DesignCenter on a stand-alone computer, you can just as easily perform the same functions across a network or even across the Internet.

---

**DON'T FORGET THE SOURCE FILES WHEN EXPORTING**

If you use the Export or Import option to move a palette from one computer to another, be aware that you must also import or export the drawings that are the source files for the palette tools.

---

This ends our exploration of DesignCenter and tool palettes. In the next section, you'll look at an AutoCAD feature that lets you perform detailed searches in your hard drive for files and drawing elements.

# Searching Your Drawing Library with Content Explorer

DesignCenter works well as a drawing management tool as long as you know where to look for your files. It's great for current projects where you are editing and creating files daily. But what if you need to find drawings, blocks, hatch patterns, and other drawing elements from a long-forgotten past project? This is where Content Explorer™ can be a lifesaver.

Content Explorer has many features that overlap with DesignCenter, but Content Explorer places an emphasis on searching for data rather than relying on the user's own file organization. But before you can begin to use Content Explorer, you'll have to do a little setting up.

## Indexing Your Files

Before you can put Content Explorer to use, you have to give it the location of your drawing files. After you do that, it will look at the drawing files and catalog and index the data that it finds. If you have an extensive library of files, creating this index can take some time, but it occurs in the background so you don't have to stop working. The index is stored as a database file, so when you perform a query, you don't have to wait for a lengthy search to take place. If you've ever used a file-indexing program like Google Desktop, you'll be familiar with how Content Explorer works.

To start Content Explorer and index a drive or folder, do the following:

1. Click the Explore tool in the Add-ins tab's Content panel. Content Explorer appears (Figure 25.33).

**FIGURE 25.33**
The Explore tool and Content Explorer

2. Click the Add Watched Folder bar at the bottom of Content Explorer.

3. Use the Select Watched Folder dialog box (see Figure 25.34) to locate the folder or drive that contains your drawing library, and then click OK. In this exercise, locate the `Projects` folder for the *Mastering AutoCAD 2015* sample files. The folder appears in Content Explorer.

**FIGURE 25.34**
The Select Watched
Folder dialog box

You'll see a clock icon on the folder when you first add it to Content Explorer. This tells you that it is being indexed. As with DesignCenter, you can double-click the folder to view its contents. If a file is displayed, you can double-click the file to view the elements that are available within it.

## Searching Your Files

The most powerful feature of Content Explorer is its ability to find an AutoCAD drawing or element by name. For example, suppose you remember that you created a block last year but you've forgotten the name and location of the drawing where the block was placed. Without Content Explorer, you'd have to make a best guess at the file location and just start hunting. This search could take hours. With Content Explorer's search feature, you could find the block in minutes. Try the following to see firsthand how this can work. Note that you'll have to wait until the indexing has finished from the previous exercise before the following exercise will work properly:

1. Suppose you want to find a block named gate. Enter **gate**↵ in the Search box at the top of Content Explorer. Content Explorer returns a list of files that contain the word *gate* as part of a block, linetype, layer, or other element (see Figure 25.35).

2. Double-click the gate block reference in the list. AutoCAD opens the drawing.

You can also click and drag the gate block into an open drawing or right-click the block reference and select Go To Folder to open the folder containing the drawing. Other context menu commands include Explore, Open, Insert, Attach, and Properties.

If the item in the list is a drawing, you can double-click the drawing and its drawing elements will be listed in a way similar to the DesignCenter display.

## Controlling Content Explorer's Display

Content Explorer offers a few display options that are similar to the display options in Windows Explorer. Click the Change View Options arrowhead next to the Toggle Icon Size tool at the bottom of Content Explorer and you'll see a list of options (see Figure 25.36). As you can see from the figure, you can select from a variety of sizes for the icons as well as the type of display.

**FIGURE 25.35**

The results of the gate search

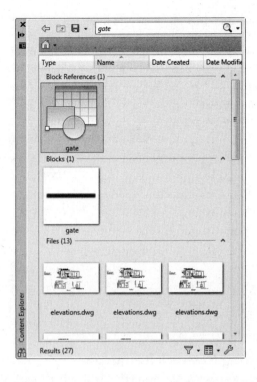

**FIGURE 25.36**

The Toggle Icon Size display options

With the Configure Filtering tool you can filter the contents of the display based on the type of drawing element you want to find. Click the Configure Filtering tool to open the Configure Filters dialog box (see Figure 25.37). In this dialog box, you can select the types of files and drawing objects to filter. For example, if you want to view only the blocks that a Content Explorer search has turned up, you can click the Object Types tab and then deselect all the types except for Block Definition and Block Reference. Content Explorer will display only blocks. You can also filter by date by selecting the Date tab at the top.

**FIGURE 25.37**
Configure Filtering icon (left) and the Configure Filters dialog box (right)

## Adding Network Resources

If you use AutoCAD in an office with other AutoCAD users, you'll want to install Content Explorer on your server where the AutoCAD drawings reside. You don't have to install a full version of AutoCAD on the server. The part of Content Explorer that creates and maintains the index (the Content Service) can be installed on the server. The AutoCAD workstations will then be able to connect to the index that is created and maintained on the server.

To install the Content Service, start the AutoCAD installation on the server where your drawing files reside. At the main installation screen, select the Install Tools And Utilities option. In the Tools And Utilities window, make sure there is a check mark by the Autodesk Content Service option and deselect the other options. When you click Install, the Content Service will be installed.

You still need to make some additional setting changes after the Content Service is installed. From the Windows Desktop, choose Start ➤ All Programs ➤ Autodesk ➤ Content Service ➤ Content Service Console. In the Autodesk Content Service – Administration Console dialog box, click Add Watch Folder to add a folder to include in the indexing. The folder you wish to add must be a network shared folder.

To connect to the Content Service index from a workstation, do the following:

1. Open Content Explorer.

2. Click the Configure Settings tool in the lower-right corner of Content Explorer.

3. In the Autodesk Content Explorer – Configuration Console dialog box, click Add Content Provider in the lower-left corner (see Figure 25.38) and select Autodesk Content Service.

**FIGURE 25.38**

The Content Explorer – Configuration Console dialog box

4. In the Add New Content Provider dialog box, enter the name of the server or its IP address, and then click OK.

5. Click Close at the Autodesk Content Explorer – Configuration Console dialog box.

Besides searching network resources, you can use Content Explorer to search the Autodesk Seek site. Autodesk Seek is a website where you can find prebuilt drawing files and other resources. To search the site, click the arrowhead next to the Home icon in the upper-left corner of the Content Explorer window and select Autodesk Seek. The Home icon will change to the Seek icon to indicate that your searches will take place there.

# Establishing Office Standards

Communication is especially important when you're one of many people working on the same project on separate computers. A well-developed set of standards and procedures helps to minimize problems that may be caused by miscommunication. In this section, you'll find some suggestions for setting up these standards.

## Establishing Layering and Text Conventions

The issue of CAD standards has always been difficult to resolve. Standardizing layers, dimensions, and text can go a long way toward making file exchange more seamless between different trades, and standards can also make files easier to understand. When everyone follows a standard, the structure of a drawing is more easily understood, and those who have to edit or interpret your work can do so without having to ask a lot of questions.

You've seen how layers can be a useful tool. But they can easily get out of hand when you have free rein over their creation and naming. Users may become confused while attempting to isolate or identify objects and layers in a drawing they're not familiar with. Inconsistent layer naming can also inhibit the use of timesaving tools like the Layer Translator (covered later in this chapter), AutoLISP routines, and script files that might otherwise be able to automate many repetitive tasks. With an appropriate layer-naming convention, you can minimize this type of problem (although you may not eliminate it entirely). A too-rigid naming convention can cause as many problems as no convention at all, so it's best to give general guidelines rather than force everyone to stay within narrow limits. As mentioned in Chapter 5, you can create layer names in a way that enables you to group them by using wildcards. AutoCAD allows up to 255 characters in a layer name, so you can use descriptive names.

Lineweights should be standardized along with colors. If you intend to use a reprographics service for your plotting, check with them first; they may require that you conform to their color and lineweight standards.

---

### Know the Standards

If you're an architect or an engineer or in the construction business, check out some of the CAD layering standards set forth by the American Institute of Architects (AIA) and the Construction Specifications Institute (CSI). The AIA's website is located at www.aia.org, and the CSI's website can be found at www.csinet.org. The most popular framework for drawing standards remains the National CAD Standard (NCS) from the National Institute of Building Sciences, and it includes the AIA layering guidelines. See www.nationalcadstandard.org for more information.

---

## Checking Office Standards

AutoCAD offers an open-ended environment that lends itself to easy customization, but this also leaves the door wide open for on-the-fly creation of layer names, dimension styles, and other drawing format options. It's easy to stray from standards, especially when you're under pressure to get a project out on a deadline. To help you and your office maintain a level of conformity to office or industry standards, AutoCAD includes the Standards command.

The Standards command lets you quickly compare a drawing against a set of standard layer names, dimension style settings, linetypes, and text styles. A dialog box displays any item that doesn't conform to the standards you selected. You can then adjust the file to make it conform to your standards.

You can create several sets of standards for different types of files, and you can assign the standards directly to a file so that anyone editing that file can make periodic checks against your office standards while the drawing is being edited.

The Standards command discussed here isn't available in the Autodesk® AutoCAD LT® software.

### Setting Up Standards Files

The first step in using the Standards command is to set up a file to which other drawing files can be compared. This *standards file* will be an AutoCAD drawing file with a .dws filename extension. Here are the steps to create a new DWS standards file:

1. Open AutoCAD, and click New from the Quick Access toolbar to create a new file.

2. Set up the file with the layers, linetypes, dimension styles, and text styles you want as your standards.

3. Choose Save As from the Application menu.

4. In the Save Drawing As dialog box, choose AutoCAD Drawing Standards (*.dws) from the Files Of Type drop-down list.

5. Choose a convenient folder for the location of your standards file and click Save.

As an alternative to creating a new file, you can open an existing file that contains all the typical settings you'll want to use on your projects. You can then delete all the graphics in the file and purge all its blocks and shapes. After you've done this, you can begin at step 3 of the previous exercise to save the file as a DWS standards file.

You can set up as many DWS files as you need for your office. Often, a single set of standards is too limiting if your office is involved in a diverse range of projects, so you may want to set up DWS files on a project basis, drawing on a core of generic DWS files.

## USING THE STANDARDS COMMAND TO ASSOCIATE STANDARDS

After you've created your DWS standards files, you can begin to check other files for conformity. The next task is to assign your DWS file to the drawing file that you want to check:

1. In AutoCAD, open the file you want to check for standards conformity.

2. Click Configure on the Manage tab's CAD Standards panel to open the Configure Standards dialog box. The Standards tab of this dialog box contains a list box and a description area. A row of buttons appears vertically between the list box and description.

3. Click the Add Standards File (F3) button in the middle column of the dialog box.

4. The Select Standards File dialog box opens. This is a typical AutoCAD file dialog box. Notice that the Files Of Type drop-down list shows the Standards (*.dws) file type.

5. Locate and select the standards file that you want to use to check the current file and click Open. After a moment, the name of the file you select appears in the list box (see Figure 25.39). On the right side of the dialog box you see a description of the standards file.

6. Check the current file against the DWS standards file. Click the Check Standards button in the lower-left corner of the Configure Standards dialog box. AutoCAD pauses while it checks the current file, and then you see the Check Standards dialog box.

If AutoCAD finds a discrepancy between the standards file and the current file, a description of the problem appears at the top of the dialog box. For example, if the name of a dimension style that isn't in the standards file appears in the current file, a message appears indicating that a nonstandard dimension style exists in the current drawing. If this happens, take the following steps:

1. Below the problem statement is the Replace With list box, which contains options related to the nonstandard item. You can replace the nonstandard item in your file with an option in the Replace With list box by selecting the option and clicking the Fix button in the lower half of the dialog box. Or you can leave the problem alone for now.

2. Click the Next button in the lower-right corner of the Check Standards dialog box to move to the next problem.

3. Repeat steps 1 and 2 until you see the statement `Checking is complete` in the Problem list box and the Checking Complete dialog box opens to display a summary of the checking results.

**FIGURE 25.39**
Associating a
set of standards
with a file

You can check Mark This Problem As Ignored if you want the Check Standards dialog box to ignore the problem in future standards-checking sessions.

In this example, you entered the Check Standards dialog box directly from the Configure Standards dialog box. After you've used the Check Standards dialog box on a file, the DWS standards file is associated with the checked file. You can go directly to the Check Standards dialog box by choosing Manage ➢ CAD Standards ➢ Check during any subsequent editing session.

---

**DON'T LOSE THE DWS**

After you've assigned a DWS standards file to a drawing, you'll need to save the drawing or its association with the DWS file will be lost.

---

### CHECKING STANDARDS FOR MULTIPLE DRAWINGS

The Standards and Check Standards commands are great for checking individual files, but eventually you'll want a method to batch-check a set of files. AutoCAD 2015 provides a utility that does just that. The Batch Standards Checker is a stand-alone utility that audits a set of drawing files and checks them against their associated DWS files. The Batch Standards Checker can also check a set of drawings against a single DWS file of your choice. It then generates an audit report showing any problems it encounters.

Here's how it works:

1. From the Windows Desktop, choose Start ➢ All Programs ➢ Autodesk ➢ AutoCAD 2015 ➢ Batch Standards Checker to open the Batch Standards Checker dialog box (see Figure 25.40).

2. Click the plus button in the middle of the dialog box to open the Batch Standards Checker – File Open dialog box. This is a typical AutoCAD file dialog box.

**FIGURE 25.40**

The Batch Standards Checker dialog box

3. Locate and select the drawings you want to check. You return to the Batch Standards Checker dialog box, and after a moment, a list of the drawings you selected appears in the Drawings To Check list box.

4. Click the Standards tab (see Figure 25.41). This is where you can select the standards file against which your selection will be checked.

If the drawings you selected in step 3 already have a standards file associated with them, you can use the Check Each Drawing Using Its Associated Standards Files option to check each file. You can then skip to step 7.

**FIGURE 25.41**

Choose the files you want to check.

5. If you select the Check All Drawings Using The Following Standards Files option, click the plus sign in the middle of the dialog box to open the file dialog box.

6. Locate and select a DWS standards file. The file then appears in the Standards Used For Checking All Drawings list box on the left of the Standards tab in the Batch Standards Checker dialog box.

7. Click the Save button at the top of the Batch Standards Checker dialog box.

   The Batch Standards Checker's file save dialog box opens to enable you to specify a standards check filename and location. This file has a .chx filename extension.

8. After you've specified the location and name of a check file, click the Start Check button.

---

**WHAT IS A CHX FILE?**

The Batch Standards Checker file is an audit file that stores the drawing list and the list of standards files in the current session. It also stores the results of the audit. The CHX file is an XML-based file. XML is a file format designed to allow data exchange over the Internet.

---

AutoCAD proceeds to check each file listed in the Drawings tab list box. The progress is shown in the Progress tab of the Batch Standards Checker dialog box. If you decide to cancel the audit, you can click the Stop Check button, which cancels the audit currently in progress. When files are being checked, the Stop Check button turns red.

When all the files have been checked, the data from the audit is automatically saved in the check file you created in step 7. Then the audit file is opened in your web browser and you see the results of the audit.

The audit report file displays a number of options in a set of radio buttons:

**Overview** Displays a simplified view of the problems encountered by the audit. It lists the drawings audited and the number of problems encountered.

**Plug-Ins** Shows the standard plug-ins used to audit the drawings. Autodesk supplies these standard plug-ins, which test for layers, dimension styles, linetypes, and text styles. Third-party developers can create other plug-ins to check for additional problems.

**Standards** Lists the DWS standards files used for the audit.

**Problems** Displays a detailed description of the problems encountered in the audit. It gives the drawing name and the name of the specific item that is a problem. For example, if the audit discovers a nonstandard layer name, the layer name is listed under the drawing name as a nonstandard layer name.

**Ignored Problems** Displays problems that have previously been flagged as problems to ignore. You can flag problems to be ignored by using the Check Standards command in AutoCAD. (See the section "Using the Standards Command to Associate Standards" earlier in this chapter.)

**All** Displays all the audit information.

### REVIEWING PREVIOUSLY SAVED STANDARDS AUDITS

After you've created a check file and completed a standards audit, you can always return to the audit by opening the Batch Standards Checker utility and clicking the Open tool in the toolbar.

This opens the Batch Standards Checker file open dialog box, where you can locate and open a previously saved standards check file with the .chx filename extension. In this file, you see a list of the files that were checked in the Drawings tab and the DWS standards file used in the Standards tab.

You can then view the results of the audit by clicking the View Report tool in the toolbar. This opens a web browser and displays the audit results contained in the standards check file.

## Converting Multiple Layer Settings

As AutoCAD files flow in and out of your office, you're likely to find yourself working with layering standards from another system. You might, for example, receive files from an architect who uses the CSI standard for layer names, whereas your office prefers the AIA standard. If your job involves extensive reworking of such files, you'll want to change the layering system to one with which you're most familiar. But converting layer settings is a painstaking and time-consuming process, especially if several files need conversion.

Fortunately, AutoCAD offers a tool that can make layer conversion from one standard to another much easier. The Layer Translator lets you map nonstandard layers (that is, those using a system different from your own) to your own set of standards. It can then convert those layers to match your office standards. After you've mapped a set of layers between two files, you can save the map settings in a drawing file. Then any other files you receive that contain the same nonstandard layer settings can be converted to your own layer standards quickly. Let's take a closer look at how the Layer Translator works.

When using the Layer Translator, you must initially match the layers of your incoming file with those of a file whose layers are set up the way you want. Here are the steps to do this:

1. Open the file whose layers you want to convert in AutoCAD. Select the Layer Translator tool from the Manage tab's CAD Standards panel to open the Layer Translator dialog box, which lists the layers from the current file in the Translate From list box.

2. Click the Load button in the Translate To group to open the Select Drawing File dialog box. Locate and select a file that contains the layer settings you want to use for this project. The file can be a standard DWG file, or it can be a DWS standards file or a DWT template file. After you've opened a file, its layer names appear in the Translate To list box.

3. Select a layer name in the Translate From list, and then select the layer with the settings you want to use from the Translate To list box. After you've made your two selections, click the Map button in the middle of the dialog box. An item in the Layer Translation Mappings group shows you the old and new layer names and the layer settings for the conversion (see Figure 25.42).

4. Repeat step 3 for all the layers you want to convert. You can map several layers from the Translate From list to a single layer in the Translate To list if you need to do so.

5. If there are matching layers in the Translate From and Translate To list boxes, the Map Same button in the middle of the dialog box becomes active. You can then click this button to automatically map layers that have the same names in both the Translate From and the Translate To lists.

**FIGURE 25.42**
The Layer Translator dialog box

After you've completed your layer mapping, you can save the mapping for future use:

1. While still in the Layer Translator dialog box, click the Save button in the Layer Translation Mappings group to open the Save Layer Mappings dialog box. This is a typical AutoCAD file dialog box.

2. Enter a name for your saved settings and click Save. You can save the layer map settings as either a DWS standards file or a DWG file.

3. Click the Translate button and AutoCAD will proceed to translate the mapped layers.

After you've saved the layer mapping in step 2, you can load the saved layer map settings into the Layer Translator dialog box in future layer translations. This saves you the effort of mapping each layer individually each time you want to perform a translation. This will work for incoming files that use the same layer settings, but you'll have to create another layer map settings file for each different layer system you encounter.

To use a saved layer map, click the Load button in the Translate To group of the Layer Translator dialog box and then select the layer map file you saved in step 2. You can have several layer map files for each project involving files with nonstandard layer settings.

## Exploring Other Layer Translator Options

You'll often come across situations in which the layers in the Translate From list don't correspond directly to those in the Translate To list. For these situations, the Layer Translator offers a few additional options.

If you have difficulty finding a match for layers in the Translate From list, you can create a new layer by clicking the New button in the Translate To group. This opens the New Layer dialog box (see Figure 25.43) in which you can enter the properties for your new layer. After you create a new layer with this dialog box, it appears in the Translate To list box, enabling you to map Translate From layers to your new layer.

Another option you'll find useful is the Edit button in the Layer Translation Mappings group. You may find that after you've mapped a Translate From layer to a Translate To layer, the

Translate To layer isn't exactly what you want. You can highlight the mapped layer in the Layer Translation Mappings group list box and then click Edit to open the Edit Layer dialog box (see Figure 25.44). From here, you can modify the new layer's settings from their original values.

**FIGURE 25.43**

Creating a new layer

**FIGURE 25.44**

Changing a layer's properties

Finally, the Layer Translator offers a set of options that give you some control over the way translations are performed. For example, you can control whether layer colors and linetypes are forced to the ByLayer setting or whether layer assignments for objects in blocks are translated. You can access these options by clicking the Settings button in the lower-left corner of the Layer Translator dialog box. Figure 25.45 shows the Settings dialog box. The options are self-explanatory.

**FIGURE 25.45**

The Layer Translator and its Settings dialog box

## The Bottom Line

**Share drawings online.**    As a drafter or designer, you'll likely be involved in collaborative efforts, which means that you'll have to share your work with others. The Internet has made it much easier to do this.

**Master It**    Why is eTransmit important for sending AutoCAD drawings over the Internet?

**ePublish your drawings.**    Autodesk offers the DWF drawing format, which lets non-CAD users view and add comments to simplified versions of your drawings. You can use the Publish feature to create a single DWF file from several drawings.

**Master It**    True or false: The Publish feature can be used to plot multiple drawings in the background.

**Get started with Autodesk 360.**    Autodesk 360 makes sharing files and exchanging design ideas much easier.

**Master It**    Name the feature that lets you revert a revised drawing to its prior state.

**Manage your drawings with DesignCenter and the tool palettes.**    DesignCenter is a great tool for managing your drawings' resources, like blocks, custom linetypes, and other elements.

**Master It**    True or false: DesignCenter has the capacity to scale a block automatically to the correct size when moving from metric to Imperial drawings.

**Search your drawing library with Content Explorer.**    If you need to find a drawing or drawing elements fast, Content Explorer is the tool to use.

**Master It**    True or false: The Content Service enables users to search folders on a server.

**Establish office standards.**    AutoCAD allows for a wide range of settings in a drawing. For this reason, it's a good idea to create standards for the way drawings are set up.

**Master It**    Name the filename extension for an AutoCAD drawing standards file.

**Convert multiple layer settings.**    If you exchange files with another office, you may find that their layer scheme is different than yours. AutoCAD offers the Layer Translator to help you translate layer names from an unfamiliar drawing to names with which you're more comfortable.

**Master It**    Name the filename extensions of the types of files that you can use as a template for layer name translations.

# Appendices

# Appendix A

# The Bottom Line

Each of The Bottom Line sections in the chapters suggest exercises to deepen skills and understanding. Sometimes there is only one possible solution, but often you are encouraged to use your skills and creativity to create something that builds on what you know and lets you explore one of many possible solutions.

## Chapter 1: Exploring the Interface

**Use the AutoCAD window.** AutoCAD® is a typical Windows graphics program that makes use of menus, toolbars, Ribbon panels, and palettes. If you've used other graphics programs, you'll see at least a few familiar tools.

**Master It** Name the components of the AutoCAD window you can use to select a function.

**Solution** AutoCAD offers the Quick Access toolbar, the Application menu, Ribbon panels, the Navigation bar, and the status bar to give you access to the most common functions.

**Get a closer look with the Zoom command.** One of the first things you'll want to learn is how to manipulate your views. The Zoom command is a common tool in graphics programs.

**Master It** Name at least two ways of zooming into a view.

**Solution** Choose options from the Zoom flyout in the View tab's Navigate panel. You can also right-click and select Zoom from the shortcut menu and select Zoom options from the Navigation bar's Zoom flyout.

**Save a file as you work.** Nothing is more frustrating than having a power failure that causes you to lose hours of work. It's a good idea to save your work frequently. AutoCAD offers an Automatic Save feature that can be a lifesaver if you happen to forget to save your files.

**Master It** How often does the AutoCAD Automatic Save feature save your drawing?

**Solution** Automatic Save saves a copy of a drawing every 10 minutes by default. This interval can be modified by the user.

**Make changes and open multiple files.** As with other Windows programs, you can have multiple files open and exchange data between them.

**Master It** With two drawings open, how can you copy parts of one drawing into the other?

**Solution** Use Windows Copy and Paste. Select the parts you want to copy, right-click, and select Clipboard and then Copy. Go to the other drawing and then right-click in the drawing area and select Clipboard and then Paste.

# Chapter 2: Creating Your First Drawing

**Specify distances with coordinates.**    One of the most basic skills you need to learn is how to indicate exact distances through the keyboard. AutoCAD uses a simple annotation system to indicate distance and direction.

**Master It**    What would you type to indicate a relative distance of 14 units at a 45° angle?

**Solution**    @14<45.

**Interpret the cursor modes and understand prompts.**    The AutoCAD cursor changes its shape depending on the command that is currently active. These different cursor modes can give you a clue regarding what you should be doing.

**Master It**    Describe the Point Selection cursor and the Pickbox cursor.

**Solution**    The Point Selection cursor is a simple crosshair. The Pickbox cursor is a small square, or pickbox.

**Select objects and edit with grips.**    Grips are small squares or arrowheads that appear at key points on the object when they're selected. They offer a powerful way to edit objects.

**Master It**    How do you select multiple grips?

**Solution**    Hold down the Shift key while clicking the grips.

**Understand the AutoCAD Cursor.**    The cursor changes in appearance depending on the tool or command that is being used.

**Master It**    What does the cursor badge look like when using the Erase tool?

**Solution**    A red X.

**Display data in a text window.**    AutoCAD offers the AutoCAD Text Window, which keeps a running account of the commands you use. This can be helpful in retrieving input that you've entered when constructing your drawing.

**Master It**    Name a command that displays its results in the AutoCAD Text Window.

**Solution**    The List command.

**Display the properties of an object.**    The Properties palette is one of the most useful sources for drawing information. Not only does it list the properties of an object, it also lets you change the shape, color, and other properties of objects.

**Master It**    How do you open the Properties palette for a particular object?

**Solution**    Select the object whose properties you want to view. Right-click the object and select Properties.

**Get help.**    The AutoCAD Autodesk Exchange website is thorough in its coverage of AutoCAD features. New and experienced users alike can often find answers to their questions through the Help window, so it pays to become familiar with it.

**Master It**    What keyboard key do you press for context-sensitive help?

**Solution**    For help you'd press the F1 key.

## Chapter 3: Setting Up and Using the Drafting Tools

**Set up a work area.** A blank AutoCAD drawing offers few clues about the size of the area with which you're working, but you can get a rough idea of the area shown in the AutoCAD window.

**Master It** Name two ways to set up the area of your work.

**Solution** You can use the Limits command to define the work area, otherwise known as the limits of the drawing. You can also draw a rectangle that is the size of your work area.

**Explore the drawing process.** To use AutoCAD effectively, you'll want to know how the different tools work together to achieve an effect. The drawing process often involves many cycles of adding objects and then editing them.

**Master It** Name the tool that causes the cursor to point in an exact horizontal or vertical direction.

**Solution** Polar Tracking. Ortho mode can also perform this function.

**Plan and lay out a drawing.** If you've ever had to draw a precise sketch with just a pencil and pad, you've probably used a set of lightly drawn guidelines to lay out your drawing first. You do the same thing in AutoCAD, but instead of lightly drawn guidelines, you can use any object you want. In AutoCAD, objects are easily modified or deleted, so you don't have to be as careful when adding guidelines.

**Master It** What is the name of the feature that lets you select exact locations on objects?

**Solution** Object Snap, or Osnap.

**Use the AutoCAD modes as drafting tools.** The main reason for using AutoCAD is to produce precision technical drawings. AutoCAD offers many tools to help you produce a drawing with the precision you need.

**Master It** What dialog box lets you set both the grid and snap spacing?

**Solution** The Drafting Settings dialog box.

## Chapter 4: Organizing Objects with Blocks and Groups

**Create and insert a symbol.** If you have a symbol that you use often in a drawing, you can draw it once and then turn it into an AutoCAD block. A block can be placed in a drawing multiple times in any location, like a rubber stamp. A block is stored in a drawing as a block definition, which can be called up at any time.

**Master It** Name the dialog box used to create a block from objects in a drawing, and also name the tool used to open this dialog box.

**Solution** The Block Definition dialog box can be opened using the Create tool.

**Modify a block.** Once you've created a block, it isn't set in stone. One of the features of a block is that you can change the block definition and all the copies of the block are updated to the new definition.

**Master It** What is the name of the tool used to "unblock" a block?

**Solution** You can use the Explode tool to break a block down to its component objects. Once this is done, you can modify the objects and then redefine the block.

**Understand the annotation scale.** In some cases, you'll want to create a block that is dependent on the drawing scale. You can create a block that adjusts itself to the scale of your drawing through the annotation scale feature. When the annotation scale feature is turned on for a block, the block can be set to appear at the correct size depending on the scale of your drawing.

**Master It** What setting in the Block Definition dialog box turns on the annotation scale feature, and how do you set the annotation scale of a block?

**Solution** The Annotative option in the Block Definition dialog box turns on the annotation scale feature. You can set the scales for a block by selecting the block, right-clicking, and selecting Object Scale ➢ Add/Delete Scales.

**Group objects.** Blocks can be used as a tool to group objects together, but blocks can be too rigid for some grouping applications. AutoCAD offers groups, which are collections of objects that are similar to blocks but aren't as rigidly defined.

**Master It** How are groups different from blocks?

**Solution** You can easily edit objects in a group by turning groups off with a Shift+Ctrl+A keystroke. Also, unlike blocks, groups don't have a single definition that's stored in the drawing and that defines the group's appearance. You can copy a group, but each copy is independent of the other groups.

# Chapter 5: Keeping Track of Layers and Blocks

**Organize information with layers.** Layers are perhaps the most powerful feature in AutoCAD. They help to keep drawings well organized, and they give you control over the visibility of objects. They also let you control the appearance of your drawing by setting colors, lineweights, and linetypes.

**Master It** Describe the process of creating a layer.

**Solution** First, click the Layer Properties Manager tool in the Home tab's Layers panel. Second, click the New Layer button at the top of the palette. Finally, type the name for your new layer.

**Control layer visibility.** When a drawing becomes dense with information, it can be difficult to edit. If you've organized your drawing using layers, you can reduce its complexity by turning off layers that aren't important to your current session.

**Master It** Describe two methods for hiding a layer.

**Solution** Open the Layer Properties Manager, select a layer, and click the Freeze icon for the layer. You can also open the layer drop-down list in the Home tab's Layers panel and click the Freeze icon for the layer you want to hide.

**Keep track of blocks and layers.** At times, you may want a record of the layers or blocks in your drawing. You can create a list of layers using the log-file feature in AutoCAD.

**Master It** Where do you go to turn on the log-file feature?

**Solution** You can open the Options dialog box or use the Logfilemode system variable.

# Chapter 6: Editing and Reusing Data to Work Efficiently

**Create and use templates.**   If you find that you're using the same settings when you create a new drawing file, you can set up an existing file the way you like and save it as a template. You can then use your saved template for any new drawings you create.

**Master It**   Describe the method for saving a file as a template.

**Solution**   After setting up a blank drawing with the settings you use most frequently, choose Save As from the Application menu. In the Save Drawing As dialog box, choose AutoCAD Drawing Template (*.dwt) from the Files Of Type drop-down list, give the file a name, and click Save. In the Template Options dialog box, enter a description, and click OK to save the template.

**Copy an object multiple times.**   Many tools in AutoCAD allow you to create multiple copies. The Array command offers a way to create circular copies, row and column copies, and copies that follow a path.

**Master It**   What names are given to the three types of arrays offered in the Modify panel?

**Solution**   Rectangular, polar, and path.

**Develop your drawing.**   When laying down simple line work, you'll use a few tools frequently. The exercises in the early part of this book showed you some of these commonly used tools.

**Master It**   What tool can you use to join two lines end to end?

**Solution**   Fillet.

**Find an exact distance along a curve.**   AutoCAD offers some tools that allow you to find an exact distance along a curve.

**Master It**   Name the two tools you can use to mark off exact distances along a curve.

**Solution**   Measure and Divide.

**Change the length of objects.**   You can accurately adjust the length of a line or arc in AutoCAD using a single command.

**Master It**   What is the keyboard alias for the command that changes the length of objects?

**Solution**   The command is Lengthen. You may also use len.

**Create a new drawing by using parts from another drawing.**   You can save a lot of time by reusing parts of drawings. The Export command can help.

**Master It**   True or false: The Export command saves only blocks as drawing files.

**Solution**   False. You can use Export on any type of object or set of objects in a drawing.

# Chapter 7: Mastering Viewing Tools, Hatches, and External References

**Assemble the parts.**   Technical drawings are often made up of repetitive parts that are drawn over and over. AutoCAD makes quick work of repetitive elements in a drawing, as shown in the first part of this chapter.

**Master It** What is the object used as the basic building block for the unit plan drawing in the beginning of this chapter?

**Solution** Blocks of a typical unit plan are used to build a floor plan of an apartment building.

**Take control of the AutoCAD display.** Understanding the way the AutoCAD display works can save you time, especially in a complex drawing.

**Master It** Name the dialog box used to save views in AutoCAD. Describe how to recall a saved view.

**Solution** The View Manager dialog box allows you to save views. You can recall views by selecting them from the Views flyout on the View tab's Views panel.

**Use hatch patterns in your drawings.** Patterns can convey a lot of information at a glance. You can show the material of an object or you can indicate a type of view, like a cross section, by applying hatch patterns.

**Master It** How do you open the Hatch And Gradient dialog box?

**Solution** Choose Hatch from the Home tab's Draw panel, and then click the Hatch Settings tool in the Hatch Creation tab's Options panel title bar.

**Understand the boundary hatch options.** The hatch options give you control over the way hatch patterns fill an enclosed area.

**Master It** Describe an island as it relates to boundary hatch patterns.

**Solution** An island is an enclosed object that is found in an area to be hatched.

**Use external references.** External references are drawing files that you've attached to the current drawing to include as part of the drawing. Because external references aren't part of the current file, they can be worked on at the same time as the referencing file.

**Master It** Describe how drawing files are attached as external references.

**Solution** Open the External References palette, click the Attach DWG tool at the upper left, and then locate and select the file you want to attach.

# Chapter 8: Introducing Printing, Plotting, and Layouts

**Understand the plotter settings.** Unlike other types of documents, AutoCAD drawings can end up on nearly any size sheet of paper. To accommodate the range of paper sizes, the AutoCAD plotter settings are fairly extensive and give you a high level of control over your output.

**Master It** Name a few of the settings available in the Plot dialog box.

**Solution** Paper Size, Plot Area, Plot Scale, and Printer/Plotter Name are a few of the settings available in the Plot dialog box.

**Use layout views to control how your plots look.** The Layout tabs in AutoCAD offer a way to let you set up how a drawing will be plotted. You can think of the layout views as paste-up areas for your drawings.

**Master It** Name some of the items that you see in a layout view.

**Solution**   Layout views show the paper orientation, plotter margins, and the location of your drawing on the final plotted output.

**Add an output device.**   Typically, AutoCAD will use the Windows system printer as an output device, but often you will find that the printer you use is a dedicated plotter that is not connected to Windows in the usual way. AutoCAD lets you add custom plotters and printers through the Add-A-Plotter Wizard.

**Master It**   How do you start the Add-A-Plotter Wizard?

**Solution**   Click the Plotter Manager tool on the Output tab's Plot panel, and double-click the Add-A-Plotter Wizard application in the Plotters window.

**Store a page setup.**   Most of the time, you will use the same plotter settings for your drawings. You can save plotter settings using the Page Setup feature.

**Master It**   Describe a way to create a page setup. Describe how to retrieve a setup.

**Solution**   Click the Page Setup Manager tool in the Output tab's Plot panel; then click New in the Page Setup Manager dialog box. Enter a name for your page setup in the New Page Setup dialog box, and then click OK. When you plot your drawing, you can retrieve a page setup by selecting it from the Page Setup drop-down list in the Plot dialog box.

# Chapter 9: Adding Text to Drawings

**Prepare a drawing for text.**   AutoCAD offers an extensive set of features for adding text to a drawing, but you need to do a little prep work before you dive in.

**Master It**   Name two things you need to do to prepare a drawing for text.

**Solution**   Set up a layer for your text. Create a text style for your drawing.

**Set the annotation scale and add text.**   Before you start to add text, you should set the annotation scale for your drawing. Once this is done, you can begin to add text.

**Master It**   In a sentence or two, briefly describe the purpose of the annotation scale feature. Name the tool you use to add text to a drawing.

**Solution**   The annotation scale feature converts your text size to the proper height for the scale of your drawing. To add text to a drawing, use the Mtext tool.

**Explore text formatting in AutoCAD.**   Because text styles contain font and text-size settings, you can usually set up a text style and then begin to add text to your drawing. For those special cases where you need to vary text height and font or other text features, you can use the Formatting panel of the Text Editor tab.

**Master It**   What text formatting tool can you use to change text to boldface type?

**Solution**   The Bold button.

**Add simple single-line text objects.**   In many situations, you need only a single word or a short string of text. AutoCAD offers the single-line text object for these instances.

**Master It**   Describe the methods for starting the single-line text command.

**Solution**   Click the Single Line tool in the Text panel. Enter **DT.⏎** at the Command prompt.

**Use the Check Spelling feature.** It isn't uncommon for a drawing to contain the equivalent of several pages of text, and the likelihood of having misspelled words can be high. AutoCAD offers the Check Spelling feature to help you keep your spelling under control.

**Master It** What option do you select in the Check Spelling dialog box when it finds a misspelled word and you want to accept the suggestion it offers?

**Solution** Change.

**Find and replace text.** A common activity when editing technical drawings is finding and replacing a word throughout a drawing.

**Master It** True or false: The Find And Replace feature in AutoCAD works very differently from the find-and-replace feature in other programs.

**Solution** False.

# Chapter 10: Using Fields and Tables

**Use fields to associate text with drawing properties.** Fields are a special type of text object that can be linked to object properties. They can help to automate certain text-related tasks.

**Master It** Name two uses for fields that you learned about in the first part of this chapter.

**Solution** Fields can be used to update text that labels a block. They can also be used to update text and report the area enclosed by a polyline.

**Add tables to your drawing.** The Tables feature can help you make quick work of schedules and other tabular data that you want to include in a drawing.

**Master It** What is the name of the dialog box that appears when you click the Table tool in the Annotate tab's Tables panel?

**Solution** Insert Table.

**Edit the table line work.** Because tables include line work to delineate their different cells, AutoCAD gives you control over table borders and lines.

**Master It** How do you get to the Cell Border Properties dialog box?

**Solution** Select the cell or cells in the table, right-click, and choose Borders.

**Add formulas to cells.** Tables can also function like a spreadsheet by allowing you to add formulas to cells.

**Master It** What type of text object lets you add formulas to cells?

**Solution** Field.

**Import and export tables.** The Table feature allows you to import Microsoft Excel spreadsheets into AutoCAD.

**Master It** Describe how to import a spreadsheet from Excel into AutoCAD.

**Solution** Open the spreadsheet and select the cells you want to import. Right-click and select Copy to copy the spreadsheet data into the Clipboard. In AutoCAD, choose Paste Special from the Paste flyout of the Home tab's Clipboard panel. In the Paste Special dialog box, select AutoCAD Entities, and click OK.

**Create table styles.** Table styles can save time by enabling you to set up preformatted tables with a title, column headings, and other data.

**Master It** Name the four groups in the New Table Style dialog box.

**Solution** Starting Table, General, Cell Styles, and Cell Style Preview.

# Chapter 11: Using Dimensions

**Understand the components of a dimension.** Before you start to dimension with AutoCAD, become familiar with the different parts of a dimension. Doing so will help you set up your dimensions to fit the style you need.

**Master It** Name a few of the dimension components.

**Solution** Dimension line, dimension text, extension line, and arrow.

**Create a dimension style.** As you become more familiar with technical drawing and drafting, you'll learn that there are standard formats for drawing dimensions. Arrows, text size, and even the way dimension lines are drawn are all subject to a standard format. Fortunately, AutoCAD offers dimension styles that let you set up your dimension format once and then call up that format whenever you need it.

**Master It** What is the name of the dialog box that lets you manage dimension styles, and how do you open it?

**Solution** The Dimension Style Manager is the name of the dialog box. You can open it by clicking the Dimension Style tool in the Annotate tab's Dimensions panel title bar.

**Draw linear dimensions.** The most common dimension that you'll use is the linear dimension. Knowing how to place a linear dimension is a big first step in learning how to dimension in AutoCAD.

**Master It** Name the three locations you are asked for when placing a linear dimension.

**Solution** First extension line origin, second extension line origin, and dimension line location.

**Edit dimensions.** Dimensions often change in the course of a project, so you should know how to make changes to dimension text or other parts of a dimension.

**Master It** How do you start the command to edit dimension text?

**Solution** Enter **ED**↵ at the Command prompt.

**Dimension nonorthogonal objects.** Not everything you dimension will use linear dimensions. AutoCAD offers a set of dimension tools for dimensioning objects that aren't made up of straight lines.

**Master It** Name some of the types of objects for which a linear dimension isn't appropriate.

**Solution** Arc and angle between two lines. Linear dimensions can be used for circles in certain situations.

**Add a note with a leader arrow.** In addition to dimensions, you'll probably add lots of notes with arrows pointing to features in a design. AutoCAD offers the multileader for this purpose.

**Master It** What two types of objects does the multileader combine?

**Solution** Leader lines (arrowhead and line) and text.

**Apply ordinate dimensions.** When accuracy counts, ordinate dimensions are often used because they measure distances that are similar to coordinates from a single feature.

**Master It** What AutoCAD feature do you use for ordinate dimensions that isn't strictly associated with dimensions?

**Solution** UCS.

**Add tolerance notation.** Mechanical drafting often requires the use of special notation to describe tolerances. AutoCAD offers some predefined symbols that address the need to include tolerance notation in a drawing.

**Master It** How do you open the Geometric Tolerance dialog box?

**Solution** Click the Tolerance tool in the Dimensions panel.

# Chapter 12: Using Attributes

**Create attributes.** Attributes are a great tool for storing data with drawn objects. You can include as little or as much data as you like in an AutoCAD block.

**Master It** What is the name of the object you must include in a block to store data?

**Solution** Attribute definition.

**Edit attributes.** The data you include in a block is easily changed. You may have several copies of a block, each of which must contain its own unique set of data.

**Master It** What is the simplest way to gain access to a block's attribute data?

**Solution** Double-click the block to open the Enhanced Attribute Editor.

**Extract and export attribute information.** Attribute data can be extracted in a number of ways so that you can keep track of the data in a drawing.

**Master It** How do you start the data-extraction process?

**Solution** Click the Extract Data tool in the Insert tab's Linking & Extraction panel to open the Data Extraction Wizard.

# Chapter 13: Copying Existing Drawings from Other Sources

**Convert paper drawings into AutoCAD files.** AutoCAD gives you some great tools that let you convert your paper drawings into AutoCAD files. Several options are available. Depending on your needs, you'll find at least one solution that will allow you to convert your drawings quickly.

**Master It** Describe the different methods available in AutoCAD for converting paper drawings into CAD files.

**Solution** The methods are scaling directly from a drawing, scanning and converting with a third-party program, and scanning to a raster file that can then be imported into AutoCAD to be traced over.

**Import a raster image.** You can use bitmap raster images as backgrounds for your CAD drawings or as underlay drawings that you can trace over.

**Master It** Import a raster image of your choice, and use the AutoCAD drawing tools to trace over your image.

**Solution** Click Attach from the Insert tab's Reference panel or type **Attach.⌐** to open the Select Reference File dialog box. Locate and select the raster image file you want to import. Click Open to open the Attach Image dialog box, and then click OK. Specify an insertion point and scale factor.

**Work with a raster image.** Once imported, raster images can be adjusted for size, brightness, contrast, and transparency.

**Master It** Import a raster image of your choice, and fade the image so that it appears to blend into the background with less contrast.

**Solution** Click a raster image's border to expose the Image tab. Click and drag the Fade slider to the right so that it's near the middle of the slider scale, or enter **50** in the Fade box to the right of the slider. Click OK. The raster image appears faded.

**Work with PDF files.** AutoCAD allows you to import and control the display of PDF files. This is significant since the PDF file format is so prevalent in the business world.

**Master It** In a PDF that includes layers, how do you gain access to the layer settings?

**Solution** Click the imported PDF drawing, and then click the Edit Layers tool that appears in the PDF Underlay tab. You can then control layer visibility through the Underlay Layers dialog box.

**Use a geolocation map.** You can include a correctly scaled background aerial view or road map of a site in your drawing to help you better coordinate your design with site conditions.

**Master It** Name three types of information you can use to find a site in the Geographic Location dialog box.

**Solution** You can enter latitude/longitude, street addresses, or the name of a site.

# Chapter 14: Advanced Editing and Organizing

**Use external references (Xrefs).** You've seen how you can use Xrefs to quickly build variations of a floor plan that contain repetitive elements. This isn't necessarily the only way to use Xrefs, but the basic idea of how to use Xrefs is presented in the early exercises.

**Master It** Try putting together another floor plan that contains nothing but the Unit2 plan.

**Solution** Replace the eight studio units in the Common.dwg file with four of the Unit2 plans.

**Manage layers.** Once you start to edit complex drawings, you'll find that you'll want to save the On/Off or Freeze/Thaw layer states so you can access parts of a drawing more easily. The Layer States Manager lets you save as many layer conditions as you may need in the course of a project.

**Master It** What part of the Layer States Manager dialog box lets you control the layer properties that are affected by a saved layer state?

**Solution** The Layer Properties To Restore group in the expanded view of the Layer States Manager.

**Use advanced tools: Filter and Quick Select.** The Filter and Quick Select tools are great for isolating objects in a crowded drawing. You can select objects by their color or layer assignment. You can select all instances of a specific block.

**Master It** True or false: The Quick Select tool lets you select a set of objects to limit your selections.

**Solution** True.

**Use the QuickCalc calculator.** The QuickCalc calculator offers many standard calculator tools plus a few that you may not see in other calculators.

**Master It** Name a few of the more unusual features offered by the QuickCalc calculator.

**Solution** Add feet and inch lengths; find percentages of lengths; obtain coordinates, lengths, and angles graphically from a drawing.

# Chapter 15: Laying Out Your Printer Output

**Understand model space and paper space.** AutoCAD offers two viewing modes for viewing and printing your drawings. Model space is where you do most of your work; it's the view you see when you create a new file. Layouts, also called paper space, are views that let you arrange the layout of your drawing, similar to the way you would in a page-layout program.

**Master It** What are three ways of moving from model space to paper space?

**Solution** You can hover over the drawing tab above the drawing area to display the Model and Layout preview panels, or you can use the Model and Layout tabs in the lower-left corner of the drawing area. Finally, you can use the keyboard shortcuts Ctrl+PgUp or PgDn.

**Work with paper space viewports.** While in paper space, you can create views in your drawing using viewports. You can have several viewports, each showing a different part of your drawing.

**Master It** Name some of the ways you can enlarge a view in a viewport.

**Solution** You can double-click inside a viewport and then use the Zoom tools to enlarge the view. You can also use the Viewport Scale tool in the status bar to set the scale of the view.

**Create odd-shaped viewports.** Most of the time, you'll probably use rectangular viewports, but you have the option to create a viewport of any shape.

**Master It** Describe the process for creating a circular viewport.

**Solution** In paper space, draw a circle. Next, click Object from the Viewport flyout in the Layout tab's Layout Viewports panel, and then follow the prompts.

**Understand lineweights, linetypes, and dimensions in paper space.** You can get an accurate view of how your drawing will look on paper by making a few adjustments to AutoCAD. Your layout view will reflect how your drawing will look when plotted.

**Master It** Name the two dialog boxes you must use to display lineweights in a layout view.

**Solution** You use the Layer Properties Manager (to set up lineweights) and the Lineweight Settings dialog box.

# Chapter 16: Making "Smart" Drawings with Parametric Tools

**Use parametric drawing tools.** Parametric drawing tools enable you to create an assembly of objects that are linked to each other based on geometric or dimensional properties. With the parametric drawing tools, you can create a drawing that automatically adjusts the size of all of its components when you change a single dimension.

**Master It** Name two examples given in the beginning of the chapter of a mechanical assembly that can be shown using parametric drawing tools.

**Solution** The examples are a crankshaft and piston and a Luxo lamp.

**Connect objects with geometric constraints.** You can link objects together so that they maintain a particular orientation to each other.

**Master It** Name at least six of the geometric constraints available in AutoCAD.

**Solution** The constraints are coincident, collinear, concentric, fix, parallel, perpendicular, horizontal, vertical, tangent, smooth, symmetric, and equal.

**Control sizes with dimensional constraints.** Dimensional constraints, in conjunction with geometric constraints, let you apply dimensions to an assembly of objects to control the size of the assembly.

**Master It** Name at least four dimensional constraints.

**Solution** The dimensional constraints are linear, horizontal, vertical, aligned, radius, diameter, and angular. In addition, a tool allows you to convert a normal dimension into a dimensional constraint.

**Use formulas to control dimensions.** Dimensional constraints allow you to link dimensions of objects so that if one dimension changes, another dimension follows.

**Master It** What example was used to show how formulas could be used with dimensional constraints?

**Solution** A circle's diameter was linked to the width dimension of a drawing of a simple part.

**Put constraints to use.** Constraints can be used in a variety of ways to simulate the behavior of real objects.

**Master It** Name at least three geometric or dimensional constraints used in the `piston.dwg` sample file to help simulate the motion of a piston and crankshaft.

**Solution** The geometric constraints used were horizontal, parallel, fix, and coincident. The dimensional constraints used were horizontal, vertical, aligned, and diameter.

# Chapter 17: Using Dynamic Blocks

**Work with the Block Editor.**   To create dynamic blocks, you need to become familiar with the Block Editor. You can use the Block Editor to modify existing blocks in your drawing.

**Master It**   What does the Edit Block Definition dialog box allow you to do?

**Solution**   The Edit Block Definition dialog box lets you select the block you want to edit from a list of blocks in the drawing.

**Create a dynamic block.**   A dynamic block is a block you add grips to so you can modify the block in a number of ways.

**Master It**   Name some of the features of the Block Editor that let you add additional grip editing functions to a block.

**Solution**   Geometric constraints, dimensional constraints, parameters, and actions.

**Add Scale and Stretch actions to a parameter.**   You can set up a dynamic block to perform multiple operations with a single grip.

**Master It**   What do you need to do to have one grip perform two functions?

**Solution**   Use a single parameter to control two actions.

**Add more than one parameter for multiple grip functions.**   In addition to having one grip perform multiple operations, you can add as many grips as you need to make your block even more customizable.

**Master It**   What feature do you use to set up a list of options for a block?

**Solution**   The Block Table.

**Create multiple shapes in one block.**   Many of the dynamic block functions let you adjust the shape of the original block. Another feature lets you choose completely different shapes for the block.

**Master It**   When a block uses the Visibility parameter to set up different shapes, how do you select a different block shape in the drawing?

**Solution**   Click the block, and then click the Visibility grip. A list appears showing the different shapes that are available.

**Rotate objects in unison.**   Blocks can be set up so that the action of one set of objects affects another set. This chapter gives the example of rotating objects in unison.

**Master It**   Name the dimensional constraint that was used in the object rotation example in this chapter.

**Solution**   Angular.

**Fill in a space automatically with objects.**   A dynamic block can help you automate the addition of repetitive elements to your drawing.

**Master It**   What is the name of the action used to produce an array of an object in a block when the block is stretched?

**Solution**   The Array action.

# Chapter 18: Drawing Curves

**Create and edit polylines.**   Polylines are extremely versatile. You can use them in just about any situation where you need to draw line work that is continuous. For this reason, you'll want to master polylines early in your AutoCAD training.

**Master It**   Draw the part shown here.

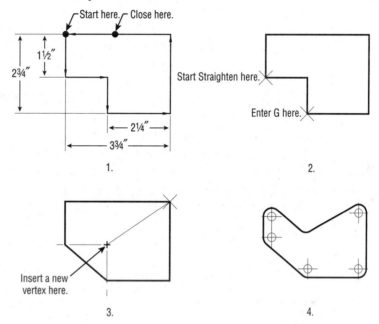

**Solution**   There are many ways to create this drawing, including using the following instructions:

1.  Open a new file called PART14 using the acad.dwt template. Set the Snap spacing to **0.25**, and be sure Snap mode is on. Use the Pline command to draw the object shown just before this step. Start at the upper-left corner, and draw in the direction indicated by the arrows. Use the Close option to add the last line segment.

2.  Start the Edit Polyline tool, select the polyline, and then type **E**⏎ to issue the Edit Vertex option. Press ⏎ until the X mark moves to the corner labeled "Start Straighten here." Enter **S**⏎ for the Straighten option.

3.  At the Enter an option prompt, press ⏎ twice to move the X to the other corner labeled "Enter G here." in step 2 of the drawing. Press **G**⏎ for Go to straighten the polyline between the two selected corners.

4.  Press ⏎ three times to move the X to the upper-right corner, and then enter **I**⏎ for Insert. Pick a point as shown in step 3 of the drawing. The polyline changes to reflect the new vertex. Enter **X**⏎ to exit the Edit Vertex option, and then press ⏎ to exit the Pedit command.

5. Start the Fillet command, use the Radius option to set the fillet radius to 0.30, and then use the Polyline option and pick the polyline you just edited. All the corners become rounded to the 0.30 radius. Add the 0.15 radius circles as shown in step 4 of the drawing, and exit and save the file.

**Create a polyline spline curve.** Polylines can be used to draw fairly accurate renditions of spline curves. This feature of polylines makes them very useful AutoCAD objects.

**Master It** Try drawing the outline of an object that contains no or few straight lines as shown in the file lowerfairing.jpg, which is included in the Chapter 18 sample files. You can use the methods described in Chapter 13, "Copying Existing Drawings from Other Sources," to import a raster image of your object and then trace over the image using polyline splines.

**Solution** Import a raster image by using the Attach tool in the Insert tab's Reference panel. Use the Polyline tool to trace over the image. Use short, straight polyline segments while you trace. After you place the polyline, double-click it and select the Spline option. After you change the polyline to a spline curve, it may shift away from the original line over which you traced. Click the polyline, and then adjust the grips so that the line fits over the raster image.

**Create and edit true spline curves.** If you need an accurate spline curve, you'll want to use the Spline tool. Spline objects offer many more fine-tuning options that you won't find with polylines.

**Master It** Try tracing over the same image from the previous Master It section, but this time use the Spline tool.

**Solution** Import a raster image by using the Attach tool in the Insert tab's Reference panel. Use the Spline tool to trace over the image. As you draw the spline, select control points that are close together for tighter curves. The closer the control points, the tighter you can make the curve. Notice that, unlike using a polyline spline, with this method you don't have to readjust the curve after it's been placed.

**Mark divisions on curves.** The Divide and Measure tools offer a quick way to mark off distances on a curved object. This can be a powerful resource in AutoCAD that you may find yourself using often.

**Master It** Mark off 12 equal divisions of the spline curve you drew in the previous Master It exercise.

**Solution** Choose Divide from the expanded Draw panel, click the spline, and then enter 12↵. If you don't see the points that mark off the divisions, type **DDPTYPE**↵, select the X point style, and click OK.

# Chapter 19: Getting and Exchanging Data from Drawings

**Find the area of closed boundaries.** There are a number of ways to find the area of a closed boundary. The easiest way is also perhaps the least obvious.

**Master It** Which AutoCAD feature would you use to find the area of an irregular shape quickly, such as a pond or lake?

**Solution** Hatch.

**Get general information.**    A lot of information that is stored in AutoCAD drawings can tell you about the files. You can find out how much memory a file uses as well as the amount of time that has been spent editing the file.

**Master It**    What feature lets you store your own searchable information about a drawing file, and how do you get to this feature?

**Solution**    The Drawing Properties dialog box. You can open it by choosing Drawing Utilities ➤ Drawing Properties from the Application menu.

**Use the DXF file format to exchange CAD data with other programs.**    Autodesk created the DXF file format as a means of sharing vector drawings with other programs.

**Master It**    Name some of the versions of AutoCAD you can export to using the Save As option.

**Solution**    2013, 2010, 2007, 2004, 2000, and R12.

**Use AutoCAD drawings in page layout programs.**    AutoCAD drawings find their way into all types of documents, including brochures and technical manuals. Users are often asked to convert their CAD drawings into formats that can be read by page layout software.

**Master It**    Name some file formats, by filename extension or type, that page layout programs can accept.

**Solution**    PDF (.pdf), WMF (.wmf), EPS (.eps), and a wide variety of bitmap image files.

**Use OLE to import data.**    You can import data into AutoCAD from a variety of sources. Most sources, such as bitmap images and text, can be imported as native AutoCAD objects. Other sources may need to be imported as OLE objects.

**Master It**    To link imported data to a source program through OLE, what dialog box would you use?

**Solution**    Paste Special.

# Chapter 20: Creating 3D Drawings

**Know the 3D Modeling workspace.**    When you work in 3D, you need a different set of tools from those for 2D drafting. AutoCAD offers the 3D Modeling workspace, which provides the tools you need to create 3D models.

**Master It**    Name some of the Ribbon panels that are unique to the 3D Modeling workspace.

**Solution**    Modeling, Solid Editing, Visual Styles, Edge Effects, Lights, Sun & Location, Materials, Palettes, Animations, and Render.

**Draw in 3D using solids.**    AutoCAD offers a type of object called a 3D solid that lets you quickly create and edit shapes.

**Master It**    What does the Presspull command do?

**Solution**    Presspull lets you press or pull a 3D solid shape from another 3D solid. It can also be used to press or pull a closed 2D object drawn on the surface of a solid.

**Create 3D forms from 2D shapes.**    The Modeling panel offers a set of basic 3D shapes, but other tools enable you to create virtually any shape you want from 2D drawings.

**Master It**    Name the command that lets you change a closed 2D polyline into a 3D solid.

**Solution**    Extrude.

**Isolate coordinates with point filters.**    When you're working in 3D, selecting points can be a complicated task. AutoCAD offers point filters or coordinates to let you specify the individual x-, y-, and z-coordinates of a location in space.

**Master It**    What does the .XY point filter do?

**Solution**    The .XY point filter lets you select an x-y-coordinate, after which you can specify a z-coordinate as a separate value.

**Move around your model.**    Getting the view you want in a 3D model can be tricky.

**Master It**    Where is the drop-down list that lets you select a view from a list of pre-defined 3D views?

**Solution**    The Home tab's View panel contains a drop-down list that offers predefined 3D views.

**Get a visual effect.**    At certain points in your model making, you'll want to view your 3D model with surface colors and even material assignments. AutoCAD offers several ways to do this.

**Master It**    What are the steps to take to change the view from Wireframe to Conceptual?

**Solution**    Click the Visual Styles drop-down list, and select Conceptual.

**Turn a 3D view into a 2D AutoCAD drawing.**    Sometimes, it's helpful to convert a 3D model view into a 2D AutoCAD drawing. AutoCAD offers the Flatshot tool, which quickly converts a 3D view into a 2D line drawing.

**Master It**    What type of object does Flatshot create?

**Solution**    A block or drawing file.

## Chapter 21: Using Advanced 3D Features

**Master the User Coordinate System.**    The User Coordinate System (UCS) is a vital key to editing in 3D space. If you want to master 3D modeling, you should become familiar with this tool.

**Master It**    Name some of the predefined UCS planes.

**Solution**    Front, Back, Left, Right, Top, Bottom.

**Understand the UCS options.**    You can set up the UCS orientation for any situation. It isn't limited to the predefined settings.

**Master It**    Briefly describe some of the ways you can set up a UCS.

**Solution**    Object orientation, selection of three points, rotation about an axis, selection of a z-axis direction, and selection of the view plane.

**Use viewports to aid in 3D drawing.**   In some 3D modeling operations, it helps to have several different views of the model through the Viewports feature.

**Master It**   Name some of the predefined standard viewports offered in the Viewports dialog box.

**Solution**   Two: Vertical, Two: Horizontal, Three: Right, Three: Left, Three: Above, Three: Below, Three: Vertical, Three: Horizontal, Four: Equal, Four: Right, and Four: Left.

**Use the array tools.**   The array tools—Rectangular, Path, and Polar Array—allow you to create 3D arrays dynamically.

**Master It**   What prompt in the Array command will allow you to have a 3D array?

**Solution**   When you specify Rows, the prompt that will put the array in a 3D plane is Specify the incrementing elevation between Rows.

**Create complex 3D surfaces.**   You aren't limited to straight, flat surfaces in AutoCAD. You can create just about any shape you want, including curved surfaces.

**Master It**   What tool did you use in this chapter's butterfly chair exercise to convert a surface into a solid?

**Solution**   The Thicken tool.

**Create spiral forms.**   Spiral forms frequently occur in nature, so it's no wonder that we often use spirals in our own designs. Spirals are seen in screws, stairs, and ramps as well as in other man-made forms.

**Master It**   Name the commands used in the example in the section "Creating Spiral Forms," and name two elements that are needed to create a spiral.

**Solution**   The commands are Helix and Sweep. A helix and a profile are needed.

**Create surface models.**   You can create a 3D surface by connecting a series of lines that define a surface contour. You can create anything from a 3D landscape to a car fender using this method.

**Master It**   What is the tool used to convert a series of lines into a 3D surface?

**Solution**   Loft.

**Move objects in 3D space.**   You can move objects in 3D space using tools that are similar to those for 2D drafting. But when it comes to editing objects, 3D modeling is much more complex than 2D drafting.

**Master It**   What does the Rotate gizmo do?

**Solution**   It lets you graphically determine the axis of rotation for an object being rotated.

# Chapter 22: Editing and Visualizing 3D Solids

**Understand solid modeling.**   Solid modeling lets you build 3D models by creating and joining 3D shapes called solids. There are several built-in solid shapes called primitives, and you can create others using the Extrude tool.

**Master It**   Name some of the built-in solid primitives available in AutoCAD.

**Solution**   Box, wedge, cone, sphere, cylinder, pyramid, torus, and polysolid.

**Create solid forms.** You can use Boolean operations to sculpt 3D solids into the shape you want. Two solids can be joined to form a more complex one, or you can remove one solid from another.

**Master It** Name the three Boolean operations you can use on solids.

**Solution** Intersection, subtraction, and union.

**Create complex solids.** Besides the primitives, you can create your own shapes based on 2D polylines.

**Master It** Name three tools that let you convert closed polylines and circles into 3D solids.

**Solution** Extrude, Revolve, and Sweep.

**Edit solids.** After you've created a solid, you can make changes to it using the solid-editing tools offered on the Solid Editing panel.

**Master It** Name at least four of the tools found on the Solid Editing panel.

**Solution** The tools found on the Solid Editing panel are Union, Subtract, Intersect, Interfere, Slice, Thicken, tools on the Edges flyout, tools on the Faces flyout, tools on the Separate flyout, Convert To Solid, and Convert To Surface.

**Streamline the 2D drawing process.** You can create 3D orthogonal views of your 3D model to create standard 2D mechanical drawings.

**Master It** What is the name of the tool in the expanded Section panel that lets you create a 2D drawing of a 3D model?

**Solution** Flatshot.

**Visualize solids.** In addition to viewing your 3D model in a number of different orientations, you can view it as if it were transparent or cut in half.

**Master It** What is the name of the command that lets you create a cut view of your 3D model?

**Solution** Sectionplane or Viewsection.

# Chapter 23: Exploring 3D Mesh and Surface Modeling

**Create a simple 3D mesh.** Mesh modeling allows you to create more organic 3D forms by giving you unique smoothing and editing tools. You can start your mesh model by creating a basic shape using the mesh primitives.

**Master It** Name the seven mesh primitives available on the Primitives panel of the Mesh Modeling tab.

**Solution** The mesh primitives are box, cylinder, cone, sphere, pyramid, wedge, and torus.

**Edit faces and edges.** The ability to edit faces and edges is essential to creating complex shapes with mesh objects.

**Master It** Name the tool that is used to divide a face into multiple faces.

**Solution** The Refine Mesh tool.

**Create mesh surfaces.** The Mesh primitives let you create shapes that enclose a volume. If you just want to model a smooth, curved surface in 3D, you might find the surface mesh tools helpful.

**Master It** How many objects are needed to use the Edge Surface tool?

**Solution** Four.

**Convert meshes to solids.** You can convert a mesh into a 3D solid to take advantage of many of the solid-editing tools available.

**Master It** Name at least two tools you can use on a solid that you cannot use on a mesh.

**Solution** Union, Subtract, Intersect, Interfere, and any of the edge or face editing tools on the Solid Editing panel of the Home tab.

**Understand 3D surfaces.** 3D surfaces can be created using some of the same tools you use to create 3D solids.

**Master It** Name at least two tools you can use to create both 3D solids and 3D surfaces.

**Solution** Any of the following: Loft, Sweep, Extrude, and Revolve.

**Edit 3D surfaces.** AutoCAD offers a wide range of tools that are unique to 3D surfaces.

**Master It** Name at least four tools devoted to CV editing.

**Solution** Any of the following: CV Edit bar, Convert To NURBS, Show CV, Hide CV, Surface Rebuild (Rebuild), Surface CV – Add (or just CV Add), and Surface CV – Remove (or just CV Remove).

# Chapter 24: Customizing Toolbars, Menus, Linetypes, and Hatch Patterns

**Use workspaces.** Often with AutoCAD you find that you have different sets of panels or toolbars open to perform specific tasks. You might have one set of Ribbon panels for editing text and dimensions, whereas another set is more useful for design. Using workspaces is a great way to organize your different editing modes.

**Master It** Where do you find the Customize option for workspaces?

**Solution** The Workspace drop-down menu or the Workspace Switching tool.

**Customize the user interface.** In addition to using workspaces to organize tools and Ribbon panels, you can customize the AutoCAD interface to make it fit the way you like to work. You can add tools to Ribbon panels or even create your own tools for operations you perform frequently.

**Master It** What does the Customizations In All Files group display?

**Solution** Interface elements like toolbars, menus, Ribbon panels, and so on.

**Create macros in tools and menus.** A macro is a set of instructions that performs more complex operations than single commands. Macros are often built on commands with additional predefined responses to help speed data input.

**Master It** What does the ^C do in a macro?

**Solution** The ^C is equivalent to pressing the Esc key.

**Edit keyboard shortcuts.** Keyboard shortcuts can help improve your speed when drawing in AutoCAD. They can reduce several clicks of the mouse to a simple keystroke. AutoCAD lets you create custom shortcuts for your favorite commands.

**Master It** What is the name of the feature that lets you record and play back actions?

**Solution** Action Recorder.

**Save, load, and unload your customizations.** To keep your customizations organized, you can save new toolbars, menus, and Ribbons as files that you can load on demand. When you save your custom elements as a file, you can move them to other computers. In addition, you can use the cloud to synchronize your custom settings with other computers.

**Master It** Name the feature that lets you synchronize your custom settings from a cloud source.

**Solution** Autodesk® 360.

**Understand the Diesel macro language.** If you're adventurous, you may want to try your hand at creating more complex macros. The Diesel macro language is an easy introduction to AutoCAD macro customization and is most useful in controlling the behavior in menu options.

**Master It** What does the expression $(getvar, blipmode) do?

**Solution** It returns 1 or 0 depending on the current state of the Blipmode system variable.

**Create custom linetypes.** AutoCAD offers a number of noncontinuous linetypes, and you may find them adequate for most of your work. But every now and then, you may need a specific linetype that isn't available. Creating custom linetypes is easy when you understand the process.

**Master It** What is the purpose of a negative value in the linetype code?

**Solution** A blank or break in the line.

**Create hatch patterns.** Like linetypes, the hatch patterns provided by AutoCAD will probably fill most of your needs. But every now and then you may need to produce a specific pattern.

**Master It** How are a hatch pattern code and a linetype code similar?

**Solution** They both use numeric values to describe lines.

# Chapter 25: Managing and Sharing Your Drawings

**Share drawings online.** As a drafter or designer, you'll likely be involved in collaborative efforts, which means that you'll have to share your work with others. The Internet has made it much easier to do this.

**Master It** Why is eTransmit important for sending AutoCAD drawings over the Internet?

**Solution** An AutoCAD drawing can have many different external files associated with it, such as fonts, Xrefs, and image files. eTransmit offers a quick way to gather these files into one place or into a single archive file.

**ePublish your drawings.** Autodesk offers the DWF drawing format, which lets non-CAD users view and add comments to simplified versions of your drawings. You can use the Publish feature to create a single DWF file from several drawings.

**Master It** True or false: The Publish feature can be used to plot multiple drawings in the background.

**Solution** True.

**Get started with Autodesk 360.** Autodesk 360 makes sharing files and exchanging design ideas much easier.

**Master It** Name the feature that lets you revert a revised drawing to its prior state.

**Solution** Versions.

**Manage your drawings with DesignCenter and the tool palettes.** DesignCenter is a great tool for managing your drawings' resources, like blocks, custom linetypes, and other elements.

**Master It** True or false: DesignCenter has the capacity to scale a block automatically to the correct size when moving from metric to Imperial drawings.

**Solution** True.

**Search your drawing library with Content Explorer.** If you need to find a drawing or drawing elements fast, Content Explorer is the tool to use.

**Master It** True or false: The Content Service enables users to search folders on a server.

**Solution** True.

**Establish office standards.** AutoCAD allows for a wide range of settings in a drawing. For this reason, it's a good idea to create standards for the way drawings are set up.

**Master It** Name the filename extension for an AutoCAD drawing standards file.

**Solution** .dws.

**Convert multiple layer settings.** If you exchange files with another office, you may find that their layer scheme is different than yours. AutoCAD offers the Layer Translator to help you translate layer names from an unfamiliar drawing to names with which you're more comfortable.

**Master It** Name the filename extensions of the types of files that you can use as a template for layer name translations.

**Solution** .dwg, .dws, and .dwt.

# Appendix B

# Installing and Setting Up AutoCAD

This appendix gives you information about installing Autodesk® AutoCAD® 2015 software on your system and describes the system parameters you should set to configure AutoCAD to meet the needs of your operating environment. Throughout this appendix, the system variable associated with a setting, when available, is included at the end of an option description, enclosed in brackets. System variables are settings that enable you to control the behavior of AutoCAD when you're using commands and features. You'll find a detailed description of the AutoCAD system variables on the AutoCAD 2015 Help website.

## Before Installing AutoCAD

Before you begin the installation process, be sure you have at least 6 GB of free disk space. You should also have at least an additional 100 MB of free disk space for AutoCAD temporary files and swap files, plus another 20 MB for the tutorial files you'll create. AutoCAD will work with Microsoft Windows 7 or 8. AutoCAD also works with Internet Explorer 10.

For 2D work, you'll also need a dual-core processor with at least 2 GB of RAM and a video card that supports at least 1024×768 resolution and True Color.

For serious 3D work, Autodesk recommends at least 4 GB of RAM, 6 GB of free disk space (not including the AutoCAD installation), and a 128 MB or greater Direct3D-capable workstation-class graphics card. Autodesk has a list of certified graphics cards for 3D modeling. This list is always being updated, so check the Autodesk website for the latest information.

Single-user systems have a 30-day grace period, so you can install and use AutoCAD without entering an authorization code right away. You can authorize your installation over the Internet at any time within the 30-day grace period as indicated when you first start AutoCAD. The trial software available on the Autodesk website can't be authorized unless you purchase a license, so be sure you have a good block of free time to study AutoCAD before you install it.

## Proceeding with the Installation

AutoCAD 2015 installs like most other Windows programs, but you should know a few things before you start.

Installing AutoCAD is straightforward. AutoCAD uses an installation wizard like most other Windows programs. Here are some guidelines to follow during the installation process:

◆ Before you start, make sure you have enough disk space, and also make sure no other programs are running. If you purchased a license, you'll need your AutoCAD serial number and product key, which are usually on the package label. If you're installing the trial version from the Autodesk website, select the "I want to try this product for 30 days" option on the Product Information page of the installation wizard.

◆ Typically, the AutoCAD installation program starts automatically when you double-click on the installation file. After the program launches, follow the directions in the installation wizard.

If you have an earlier release of AutoCAD installed on your PC, you will see the Migrate Custom Settings dialog box when you first start up AutoCAD 2015. This dialog box enables you to selectively import custom settings from your prior AutoCAD release. If you do not want to import settings, you can click the Cancel button in the dialog box.

## Configuring AutoCAD

In the following sections, you'll learn how to configure AutoCAD to work the way you want it to function. You can configure AutoCAD at any time during an AutoCAD session by using the Options dialog box.

The exercises in this book assume that you're using the default Options settings. As you become more familiar with the workings of AutoCAD, you may want to adjust the way AutoCAD works by using the Options dialog box. You can also set many of the options in the Options dialog box through system variables.

Choose Options from the Application menu, or type **options**↵ at the Command prompt to open the Options dialog box, which has the tabs and settings described in the following sections.

Many of the options in the Options dialog box show an AutoCAD file icon. This icon indicates that the option's setting is saved with individual files instead of being saved as part of the default AutoCAD settings. Other options, such as the User Profiles and command alias settings, can be exported or imported using the Migrate Custom Settings feature. This feature can be found in the Windows Start menu under All Programs ➢ Autodesk ➢ AutoCAD 2015 ➢ Migrate Custom Settings.

### The Files Tab

You use the options on the Files tab (see Figure B.1) to tell AutoCAD where to place or find the files it needs to operate. It uses a hierarchical list, similar to the one presented by Windows Explorer. You first see the general topics in the Search Paths, File Names, And File Locations list box. You can expand any item in the list by clicking its plus sign.

The following are descriptions of each item in the list box. Chances are that you won't have to use most of them, but you may change others occasionally.

When available, the related system variable is shown in brackets at the end of the description.

**Support File Search Path** AutoCAD relies on external files for many of its functions. Menus, text fonts, linetypes, and hatch patterns are a few examples of features that rely on external files. The Support File Search Path item tells AutoCAD where to look for these files. You can add folder paths to this listing by selecting it, clicking the Add button, and entering a new path, or you can select it and use the Browse button. It's probably not a good idea to delete any of the existing items under this heading unless you really know what you're doing.

**FIGURE B.1**
The Files tab

If you're familiar with using environment variables, you can include them in the search paths.

**Working Support File Search Path**   The Working Support File Search Path item contains a read-only list of the support file search paths for the current session, together with any special settings that may be included with command switches and environment settings.

**Trusted Locations**   Data security has become an increasingly important feature for Autodesk software. The Trusted Locations option lets you set a location on your system where you keep files that contain trusted executable code. See the Security group under the System tab for related information.

**Device Driver File Search Path**   The Device Driver File Search Path item locates the device drivers for AutoCAD. Device drivers are applications that enable AutoCAD to communicate directly with printers, plotters, and input devices. In most cases, you don't have to do anything with this setting.

**Project Files Search Path**   Eventually, a consultant or other AutoCAD user will provide you with files that rely on Xrefs or raster images. Often, such files expect the Xref or raster image to be in a particular folder. When they are moved to another location with a different folder system, Xref-dependent files won't be able to find their Xrefs. The Project Files Search Path item enables you to specify a folder where Xrefs or other dependent files are stored. If AutoCAD is unable to find an Xref or other file, it will look in the folder you specify in this listing.

To specify this folder, highlight Project Files Search Path and then click the Add button. AutoCAD suggests `Project1` as the folder name. You can change the name if you prefer. Click the plus sign next to `Project1`, and then click Browse to select a location for your project file search path. The project file search path is stored in a system variable called `Projectname`.

**Customization Files**   If you're customizing AutoCAD with your own menu files and icons, you can use this setting to locate your files. This option makes it convenient to keep your customization files in a place that is separate from the built-in AutoCAD files. You can specify a location for the main customization files like your CUI menu files, enterprise customization files for files you want to share, and your custom icons.

**Help And Miscellaneous File Names**   This item lets you set the location of a variety of support files, including menu, help, automatic save, log, and configuration files. If you have a network installation, you can also set the License Manager location on your network.

**Text Editor, Dictionary, And Font File Names**   Use this item to set the location of the text editor [`Mtexted`], custom and main dictionaries [`Dctmain, Dctust`], and the alternate font and font-mapping files [`Fontalt`]. Chapter 9, "Adding Text to Drawings," describes these tools in more detail.

**Print File, Spooler, And Prolog Section Names**   You can specify a print filename other than the default that is supplied by AutoCAD whenever you plot to a file. The Spooler option lets you specify an application intended to read and plot a plot file. The Prolog option is intended for PostScript export. It lets you specify the Prolog section from the `acad.psf` file that you want AutoCAD to include with exported Encapsulated PostScript (EPS) files [`Psprolog`].

**Printer Support File Path**   Several support files are associated with the AutoCAD printing and plotting system. This item enables you to indicate where you want AutoCAD to look for these files.

**Automatic Save File Location**   You can indicate the location for the Automatic Save file in AutoCAD by using this item [`Savefilepath`].

**Color Book Locations**   This item lets you specify the locations for the PANTONE color books. This is an optional installation item, so if the PANTONE color books aren't installed, you can install them through your AutoCAD 2015 Installation DVD.

**Data Sources Location**   This item lets you specify the location for Open Database Connectivity (ODBC) data-link files for linking AutoCAD drawings to database files.

**Template Settings**   When you select the Use A Template option in the Create New Drawing dialog box, AutoCAD looks at this setting for the location of template files. You can modify this setting, but chances are you won't need to.

**Tool Palettes File Locations**   This item lets you specify a location for the resource files for your custom tool palettes. When you create custom palettes, AutoCAD stores its data regarding those palettes in this location.

**Authoring Palette File Locations**   If you're creating custom dynamic blocks, you can designate a folder location where you keep your custom block settings and files.

**Log File Location**   With this item, you can indicate where log files are to be placed [`Logfilepath`].

**Action Recorder Settings**   The Action Recorder saves action macros as files on your computer. You can specify the location of those saved macros in this option.

**Plot And Publish Log File Location**   With this item, you can indicate where plot and publish log files are to be placed [Logfilepath].

**Temporary Drawing File Location**   AutoCAD creates temporary files to store portions of your drawings as you work on them. You usually don't have to think about these temporary files unless they start crowding your hard disk or unless you're working on a particularly large file on a system with little memory. This item lets you set the location for temporary files. The default location is the C:\Users\*User Name*\appdata\local\temp\ folder (*User Name* is your login name). If you have a hard disk that has lots of room and is very fast, you may want to change this setting to a location on that drive to improve performance [Tempprefix, read-only].

**Temporary External Reference File Location**   If you're on a network and you foresee a situation where another user will want to open an Xref of a file on which you're working, you can set the Demand Load Xrefs setting in the Open And Save tab to Enabled With Copy. This causes AutoCAD to make and use a copy of any Xref that is currently loaded. This way, others can open the original file. The Temporary External Reference File Location item lets you specify the folder where AutoCAD stores this copy of an Xref [Xloadpath].

**Texture Maps Search Path**   This item specifies the location for AutoCAD Render texture maps. In most cases, you won't have to change this setting. You can, however, add a folder name to this item for your own texture maps as you acquire or create them.

**Web File Search Path**   Although you may think this is for Internet files, it's really for photometric web files that are used to control the way lights behave in 3D models. These files have an .ies filename extension. See the online bonus chapter "Rendering 3D Drawings," available at www.omura.com/chapters, for more about using these files.

**i-drop Associated File Location**   This is where you specify the location of files imported to your computer through the i-drop function in AutoCAD. By default, no location is specified, so the i-drop imported DWG file is placed in the same folder location as the current drawing.

**DGN Mapping Setup Locations**   You can specify the location for the DGNsetup.ini file, which is a file used for DGN commands. Using these commands you can import or export DGN files. You can also control the translation of layers, linetypes, lineweights, and color between the AutoCAD DWG file format and the DGN file format.

While in AutoCAD, you may want to quickly find the location of a resource file, such as a log file or the Automatic Save file. You can do so by using the system variable associated with the resource. For example, to find the location of the log file path quickly, enter **logfilepath**↵ at the Command prompt. For the Automatic Save file, enter **savefilepath**↵. Autodesk® AutoCAD LT® users can employ the Modemacro command as in **Modemacro↵$(getvar,logfilepath)**↵ or **Mode macro↵$(getvar,savefilepath)**↵. See Chapter 24, "Customizing Toolbars, Menus, Linetypes, and Hatch Patterns," for more on Modemacro.

## The Display Tab

The settings on this tab (see Figure B.2) let you control the appearance of AutoCAD. You can make AutoCAD look completely different with these settings if you choose. Scroll bars, fonts, and colors are all up for grabs.

## THE WINDOW ELEMENTS GROUP

These options control the general settings for AutoCAD windows:

**Color Scheme**   Lets you select between a dark or light color scheme for the AutoCAD interface, including toolbars, Ribbon panels, and dialog boxes.

**Display Scroll Bars In Drawing Window**   Lets you turn the scroll bars on and off. If you have a small monitor with low resolution, you may want to turn off the scroll bars for a larger drawing area.

**Use Large Buttons For Toolbars**   Controls whether large icon buttons are used in toolbars.

**Resize Ribbon Icons To Standard Sizes**   When Ribbon icons do not match the standard sizes, they can be scaled to match the small (16×16) or large (32×32) default pixel size.

**Show ToolTips**   Controls whether tool tips are shown when you hover the mouse over tools [Tooltips].

**Show Shortcut Keys In ToolTips**   Controls whether shortcut keys are displayed in tool tips.

**Show Extended ToolTips**   Controls whether extended tool tips are displayed. Also allows the users to specify the duration of time before the extended tool tip is displayed in the Number Of Seconds To Delay text box.

**Show Rollover ToolTips**   Controls whether rollover tool tips are displayed [Rollovertips].

**Display File Tabs**   Displays (or hides when unchecked) the drawing file tabs at the top of the drawing.

**areaColors**   Opens a dialog box that lets you set the color for the various components of the AutoCAD window. This is where you can change the background color of the drawing area if you find that black doesn't work for you.

**Fonts**   Opens a dialog box that lets you set the fonts of the AutoCAD window. You can select from the standard set of Windows fonts available in your system.

**FIGURE B.2**
The Display tab

## THE DISPLAY RESOLUTION GROUP

These options control the way objects are displayed in AutoCAD. You can choose between display accuracy and speed:

**Arc And Circle Smoothness**   Controls the appearance of arcs and circles, particularly when you zoom in on them. In some instances, arcs and circles appear to be octagons even though they plot as smooth arcs and circles. If you want arcs and circles to appear smoother, you can increase this setting. An increase also increases memory use [Viewres].

**Segments In A Polyline Curve**   Controls the smoothness of polyline curves. Increase the value to make curved polylines appear smoother and less segmented. Decrease the value for improved display performance [Splinesegs].

**Rendered Object Smoothness**   Controls the smoothness of curved solids when they're rendered or shaded. Values can range from 0.01 to 10 [Facetres].

**Contour Lines Per Surface**   Lets you set the number of contour lines used to represent solid, curved surfaces. Values can range from 0 to 2047 [Isolines].

## THE LAYOUT ELEMENTS GROUP

These options control the display of elements in the Paper Space Layout tabs. See Chapter 8, "Introducing Printing, Plotting, and Layouts," and Chapter 15, "Laying Out Your Printer Output," for more information. Most of these options are self-explanatory. The Show Page Setup Manager For New Layouts option opens the Page Setup Manager dialog box whenever a layout is first opened. The Create Viewport In New Layouts option automatically creates a viewport in a layout when it's first opened.

## THE DISPLAY PERFORMANCE GROUP

You can adjust a variety of display-related settings in this group:

**Pan And Zoom With Raster & OLE**   Controls the way raster images react to real-time pans and zooms. If this option is selected, raster images move with the cursor. Turn off this option for better performance [Rtdisplay].

**Highlight Raster Image Frame Only**   Determines how raster images appear when selected. Turn on this option for better performance [Imagehlt].

**Apply Solid Fill**   Controls the display of filled objects such as wide polylines and areas filled with the solid hatch pattern. This option is also controlled by the Fillmode system variable. Turn off this option for better performance.

**Show Text Boundary Frame Only**   Controls the way text is displayed. Turn on this option to display text as rectangular boundaries [Qtextmode].

**Draw True Silhouettes For Solids And Surfaces**   Controls whether surface meshes for solid models are displayed. Turn off this option for better performance [Dispsilh].

## THE CROSSHAIR SIZE GROUP

This slider controls the size of the crosshair cursor. You can set this to 100 percent to simulate the full-screen crosshair cursor of earlier versions of AutoCAD [Cursorsize].

### THE FADE CONTROL GROUP

These two sliders control the fade effect on external references. The Xref Display option sets the overall fade effect [Xdwgfadectl]. The In-Place Edit And Annotative Representations option controls the display of nonselected objects during in-place reference editing. See Chapter 7, "Mastering Viewing Tools, Hatches, and External References," for more information on in-place reference editing [Xfadectl].

## The Open And Save Tab

The Open And Save tab (see Figure B.3) offers general file-related options such as the frequency of the automatic save and the default file version for the Save and Save As options.

**FIGURE B.3**

The Open And Save tab

### THE FILE SAVE GROUP

You can control how AutoCAD saves files by using the options in this group:

**Save As**    Lets you set the default file type for the Save and the Save As Application menu options. If you're working in an environment that requires Release 14 files as the standard file type, for example, you can use this option to select Release 14 as the default file type. You can also set up AutoCAD to save DXF files by default.

**Maintain Visual Fidelity For Annotative Objects**    Ensures that annotative scale is preserved in layouts when you save drawings to earlier versions of AutoCAD. If you work primarily in Model Space, leave this setting off [Savefidelity].

**Maintain Drawing Size Compatibility**   AutoCAD 2015 has no restrictions on object size. This option ensures that restrictions are applied in case you want to save your file to an earlier version [Largeobjectsupport].

**Thumbnail Preview Settings**   Lets you determine whether a preview image is saved with a drawing. Preview images are used in the AutoCAD file dialog box and in DesignCenter™ to let you preview a file before opening it [Rasterpreview]. You can also control the display of the sheet set preview [Updatethumbnail].

**Incremental Save Percentage**   Controls the degree to which the Incremental Save feature is applied when a file is saved. An incremental save improves the time required to save a file to disk, but it also makes the file size larger. If you have limited disk space, you can set this value to 25. A value of 0 turns off Incremental Save altogether but reduces AutoCAD performance [Isavepercent].

## THE FILE SAFETY PRECAUTIONS GROUP

These options control the automatic backup features in AutoCAD:

**Automatic Save**   Offers control over the Automatic Save features. You can turn it on or off by using the check box or set the frequency at which files are saved by using the Minutes Between Saves box. You can set the location for the Automatic Save files by using the Automatic Save File Location item in the Files tab of the Options dialog box. You can also set the frequency of automatic saves through the Savetime system variable [Savefilepath, Savefile].

**Create Backup Copy With Each Save**   Lets you determine whether a BAK file is saved along with every save you perform. You can turn off this option to conserve disk space [Isavebak, Tempprefix].

**Full-Time CRC Validation**   Controls the cyclic redundancy check feature, which checks for file errors whenever AutoCAD reads a file. This feature is helpful in troubleshooting hardware problems in your system.

**Maintain A Log File**   Lets you record the data in the AutoCAD Text Window. See Chapter 19, "Getting and Exchanging Data from Drawings," for more on this feature. You can set the location for log files in the Files tab of the Options dialog box [Logfilemode, Logfilename].

**File Extension For Temporary Files**   Lets you set the filename extension for AutoCAD temporary files. These are files AutoCAD uses to store drawing data temporarily as you work on a file. If you're working on a network where temporary files from multiple users may be stored in the same folder, you may want to change this setting to identify your temporary files.

**Security Options**   Opens the Security Options dialog box, in which you can either password-protect a file or add a digital signature. See Chapter 25, "Managing and Sharing Your Drawings," for more on these features.

**Display Digital Signature Information**   When a file containing a digital signature is opened, this option will display a warning message alerting you to the presence of the signature [Sigwarn]. See Chapter 25 for more on the digital signature feature.

### THE FILE OPEN GROUP

You can control how AutoCAD displays filenames in the File menu or the drawing title bar:

**Number Of Recently-Used Files**   Lets you specify the number of files listed in the File menu history list. The default is 9, but you can enter a value from 0 to 50.

**Display Full Path In Title**   Controls whether the full path is included in the title bar with a drawing's name.

### THE APPLICATION MENU GROUP

This option controls the number of recently used files that are displayed in the Application menu.

### THE EXTERNAL REFERENCES (XREFS) GROUP

These options let you control memory and layer features of Xrefs:

**Demand Load Xrefs**   Lets you turn on the Demand Load feature of Xrefs. Demand Load helps to improve the performance of files that use Xrefs by loading only those portions of an Xref drawing that are required for the current open drawing. This option has a drop-down list with three choices: Disabled turns off demand loading, Enabled turns on demand loading, and Enabled With Copy turns on demand loading by using a copy of the Xref source file. This last option enables others on a network to edit the Xref source file while you're working on a file that also uses it [Xloadctl].

**Retain Changes To Xref Layers**   Lets you save layer settings of Xref files in the current drawing. This doesn't affect the source Xref file. With this setting turned off, the current file imports the layer settings of the Xref file when it loads that file [Visretain].

**Allow Other Users To Refedit Current Drawing**   Lets you specify whether others can simultaneously edit a file that you're editing. This option is intended to enable others to use the Xref And Block Editing option (the Refedit command or the Edit Reference tool found on the Insert tab's expanded Reference panel) on files you currently have loaded in AutoCAD [Xedit].

### THE OBJECTARX APPLICATIONS GROUP

AutoCAD allows users and third-party developers to create a custom object that usually requires the presence of a custom ObjectARX application to support it. These options control the way AutoCAD treats custom objects and their related ObjectARX applications:

**Demand Load ObjectARX Apps**   Controls when a supporting third-party application is loaded if a custom object is present in a file. This option offers several settings that you can select from a drop-down list. The available settings are Disable Load On Demand, Custom Object Detect, Command Invoke, and Object Detect And Command Invoke. Disable Load On Demand prevents AutoCAD from loading third-party applications when a custom object is present. Some standard AutoCAD commands won't work if you select Disable Load On Demand because AutoCAD itself uses ObjectARX applications. Custom Object Detect causes AutoCAD to load an ARX application automatically if a custom object is present. Command Invoke loads a custom application when you invoke a command from that application. The Object Detect And Command Invoke option loads an ARX application when either a custom object is present or you invoke a command from that application [Demandload].

**Proxy Images For Custom Objects**   Offers a drop-down list with three settings that control the display of custom objects when the objects supporting ARX applications aren't present on your system. Do Not Show Proxy Graphics turns off the display of custom objects. Show Proxy Graphics displays the custom objects. Show Proxy Bounding Box shows a bounding box in place of a custom object [Proxyshow].

**Show Proxy Information Dialog Box**   Lets you determine whether the Show Proxy Information warning dialog box is used. When this option is selected, the Show Proxy Information warning appears when a drawing with custom objects is opened but AutoCAD can't find the objects' associated ARX application [Proxynotice].

## The Plot and Publish Tab

The Plot And Publish tab in the Options dialog box offers settings related to printing and plotting. See Chapter 8 for a description of these options.

## The System Tab

The options in the System tab (see Figure B.4) offer control over some of the general AutoCAD interface settings, such as settings for display drivers and pointing devices.

**FIGURE B.4**

The System tab

### THE HARDWARE ACCELERATION GROUP

Clicking the Performance Settings button in this group displays a variety of settings to help you fine-tune the performance of your 3D graphics. When you click this option, the Graphics Performance dialog box opens. See the section "Adjusting the AutoCAD 3D Graphics System" later in this appendix.

### THE CURRENT POINTING DEVICE GROUP

You can choose the type of pointing device you want to use with AutoCAD through the options in this group. The drop-down list offers Current System Pointing Device and Wintab Compatible Digitizer ADI 4.2 – By Autodesk. If you want to use the default Windows pointing device, choose Current System Pointing Device. If you have a digitizer that uses the Wintab driver, you can select Wintab Compatible Digitizer.

You can further limit AutoCAD to use only the Wintab Compatible Digitizer by selecting the Digitizer Only radio button. If you select the Digitizer And Mouse radio button, AutoCAD will accept input from both devices.

### THE TOUCH EXPERIENCE GROUP

If you are using a touch-enabled PC such as a Windows 8 tablet or Ultrabook, the Display touch mode Ribbon panel option will display the Touch Ribbon panel. This panel offers the Select Mode tool, which enables you to cancel the current command.

### THE LAYOUT REGEN OPTIONS GROUP

With this set of radio buttons you can specify how regens are applied when you are working with layout tabs:

**Regen When Switching Layouts**    Causes AutoCAD to force a regen when you select a layout tab or the Model tab. Use this option when your computer is limited in RAM.

**Cache Model Tab And Last Layout**    Causes AutoCAD to suppress regens when you switch to the Model tab or the most recently opened layout tab. Other layouts will regen when selected.

**Cache Model Tab And All Layouts**    Causes AutoCAD to suppress regens when you select any layout tab or the Model tab.

### THE GENERAL OPTIONS GROUP

This set of check boxes lets you set options related to the general operation of AutoCAD:

**Hidden Messages Settings**    A number of dialog boxes offer the "Do not show me again" option. If you select it and later find that you would like to see the dialog box again, you can use this button to view the message.

**Display OLE Text Size Dialog**    Lets you control the display of the OLE Text Size dialog box, which normally appears when you insert OLE text objects into an AutoCAD drawing by choosing Paste from the Paste flyout in the Home tab's Clipboard panel.

**Beep On Error In User Input**    Turns on an alarm beep that sounds whenever there is an input error.

**Allow Long Symbol Names**    Enables you to use long names for items such as layers, blocks, linetypes, and text styles. With this option turned on, you can enter as many as 255 characters for names [Extnames].

### THE HELP AND WELCOME SCREEN GROUP

AutoCAD uses a web-based help system. If for some reason you do not have web access, you can install help files using the AutoCAD 2015 installation tools. The Access Online Content When Available option should be deselected after help files have been installed.

### THE INFOCENTER GROUP

This group contains just one button: Balloon Notifications. This button opens the InfoCenter Settings dialog box, which gives you control over the behavior of the InfoCenter feature, including balloon notifications, the Live Update channel, the Product Support information channel, and the Did You Know messages.

### THE SECURITY GROUP

The Executable File Settings in this group opens the Executable File Settings dialog box, where you can set restrictions on how executable files are loaded.

### THE dbCONNECT OPTIONS GROUP

The check boxes in this group offer controls over the dbConnect feature:

**Store Links Index In Drawing File**   Lets you specify where database link data is stored. If this check box is selected, link data is stored in the drawing that is linked to a database. This increases file size and file-loading time.

**Open Tables In Read-Only Mode**   Lets you limit access to database files.

## The User Preferences Tab

The options in the User Preferences tab (see Figure B.5) enable you to adjust the way AutoCAD reacts to user input.

### THE WINDOWS STANDARD BEHAVIOR GROUP

These settings let you control how AutoCAD reacts to keyboard accelerators and mouse right-clicks:

**Double Click Editing**   Controls whether a double-click on an object automatically starts an editing command for the object. If this option is turned off, double-clicking objects has no effect [Dblclkedit].

**Shortcut Menus In Drawing Area**   Lets you see the context menu when you right-click. When this check box isn't selected, AutoCAD responds to a right-click with a ↵ [Shortcutmenu].

**Right-Click Customization**   Opens the Right-Click Customization dialog box (see Figure B.6), which offers further options for the behavior of the right-click in AutoCAD. The Turn On Time-Sensitive Right-Click option causes AutoCAD to respond differently depending on whether you right-click quickly or hold the right mouse button down momentarily. With this option, a rapid right-click issues an ↵—as if you pressed the Enter key. If you hold down the right mouse button, the context menu appears. You can further adjust the time required to hold down the mouse button by adjusting this setting.

**FIGURE B.5**

The User Preferences tab

**FIGURE B.6**

The Right-Click Customization dialog box

## THE INSERTION SCALE GROUP

These settings control how DesignCenter or the i-drop feature determines the scale of blocks when blocks are given a unitless setting for their DesignCenter unit type. Each drop-down list offers the standard set of unit types that are available in the Block Definition dialog box under the Insert Units drop-down list. See Chapter 4, "Organizing Objects with Blocks and Groups," for more information on blocks and Chapter 25 for information on DesignCenter [Insunits, Insunitsdefsource, Insunitsdeftarget].

### THE HYPERLINK GROUP

The one option in this group turns on or off the display of the hyperlink cursor, tool tip, and context menu [Hyperlinkoptions].

### THE FIELDS GROUP

These settings offer control over the display of fields and how they refresh. Display Background Of Fields lets you control the display of the gray background on fields. This background lets you see at a glance which text object in a drawing is a field. The background doesn't print. Clicking the Field Update Settings button opens a dialog box that lets you select the action that updates fields [Fielddisplay, Fieldeval].

### THE PRIORITY FOR COORDINATE DATA ENTRY GROUP

These options control the way AutoCAD responds to coordinate input:

**Running Object Snap**   Forces AutoCAD to use running osnaps at all times [Osnapcoord].

**Keyboard Entry**   Lets you use keyboard entry for coordinate input [Osnapcoord].

**Keyboard Entry Except Scripts**   Lets you use keyboard entry for coordinate input for everything but scripts [Osnapcoord].

### THE ASSOCIATIVE DIMENSIONING GROUP

This area has one option, Make New Dimensions Associative, which you can toggle on or off. This option lets you control whether AutoCAD uses the Associative Dimensioning feature. With true associative dimensioning, a dimension follows changes to an object whenever the object is edited. In the old method, you have to include a dimension definition point during the editing process to have the dimension follow changes in an object [Dimassoc].

### THE UNDO/REDO GROUP

These options control how Undo and Redo react with the Zoom, Pan, and Layer Properties Manager commands.

### BLOCK EDITOR SETTINGS

Click the Block Editor Settings button to open the Block Editor Settings dialog box. This dialog box allows you to control the appearance of objects and features in the Block Editor.

### LINEWEIGHT SETTINGS

Click the Lineweight Settings button to open the Lineweight Settings dialog box. See Chapter 15 in this book as well as the online bonus chapter "Understanding Plot Styles," available at www.omura.com/chapters, for more information about the Lineweight Settings dialog box.

### DEFAULT SCALE LIST

Click the Default Scale List button to open the Default Scale List dialog box. You can add your own custom scales for use with viewports and layouts and while plotting.

## The Drafting Tab

The Drafting tab (see Figure B.7) offers settings that relate to the drawing cursor, including the AutoSnap and AutoTrack features.

**FIGURE B.7**
The Drafting tab

### THE AUTOSNAP SETTINGS GROUP

The options in this group control the AutoSnap features that are engaged when you use osnaps:

**Marker**   Turns on the small, square graphic that appears on the osnap location. If you prefer not to see this marker, clear this check box [Autosnap].

**Magnet**   Causes the Osnap cursor to jump to an osnap location as it moves close to that location [Autosnap].

**Display AutoSnap Tooltip**   Controls the display of the osnap tool tip [Autosnap].

**Display AutoSnap Aperture Box**   Displays a square over the cursor whenever osnaps are active. If you're familiar with earlier versions of AutoCAD, you'll recognize the aperture box as the graphic used to indicate osnaps before the AutoSnap feature was introduced [Apbox].

**Colors**   Opens the Drawing Window Colors dialog box. Lets you determine the color for the AutoSnap marker and other interface elements.

### THE AUTOSNAP MARKER SIZE GROUP

Move the slider to control the size of the AutoSnap marker.

### THE OBJECT SNAP OPTIONS GROUP

This group offers four settings. When Ignore Hatch Objects is turned off, osnaps attempt to snap to geometry in hatch patterns. When Ignore dimension extension lines is turned on, osnaps will ignore dimension extension lines. Ignore Negative Z Object Snaps For Dynamic UCS causes osnaps to ignore locations with negative Z values while you're using the Dynamic UCS feature [Osoptions]. When turned on, Replace Z Value With Current Elevation causes AutoCAD to use the current UCS default Z value instead of the Z value of the selected point.

### THE AUTOTRACK SETTINGS GROUP

These options offer control over the tracking vector used for Polar Tracking and Osnap Tracking:

**Display Polar Tracking Vector**   Turns the Polar Tracking vector on or off [Trackpath].

**Display Full-Screen Tracking Vector**   Lets you control whether the tracking vector appears across the full width of the drawing window or stops at the cursor location or the intersection of two tracking vectors [Trackpath].

**Display AutoTrack Tooltip**   Turns the Osnap Tracking tool tip on or off [Autosnap].

### THE ALIGNMENT POINT ACQUISITION GROUP

These options let you determine the method for acquiring Osnap Tracking alignment points.

### THE APERTURE SIZE GROUP

Move the slider to set the size of the osnap aperture pickbox [Aperture].

### DRAFTING TOOLTIP SETTINGS

Click the Drafting Tooltip Settings button to control the color, size, and transparency of tool tips.

### LIGHTS GLYPH SETTINGS

Click the Lights Glyph Settings button to control the color and size of the spot and point light glyphs.

### CAMERAS GLYPH SETTINGS

Click the Cameras Glyph Settings button to control the color and size of the cameras glyph.

## The 3D Modeling Tab

The options on this tab (see Figure B.8) control the behavior and display of your drawing when you're working in 3D modes. You can adjust the appearance of the crosshair and the UCS icon. You can specify the default method for displaying 3D objects, and you can specify the default settings for Walk And Fly and Animation features.

The 3D
Modeling tab

## THE 3D CROSSHAIRS GROUP

These settings control the behavior and appearance of the crosshair cursor when you're viewing your drawing in 3D:

**Show Z-Axis In Crosshairs**    Displays the z-axis in the crosshair.

**Label Axes In Standard Crosshairs**    Displays the x-, y-, and z-axes' labels on the crosshair.

**Show Labels For Dynamic UCS**    Displays axis labels during the use of Dynamic UCS regardless of the Label Axes In Standard Crosshairs setting.

**Crosshair Labels**    Lets you select from three label styles: Use X, Y, Z; Use N, E, Z; or Use Custom Labels. If you select Use Custom Labels, you can enter the labels you want to display for the x-, y-, and z-axes in the boxes provided.

## THE DISPLAY TOOLS IN VIEWPORT GROUP

These three options pretty much explain themselves. Each option determines when the ViewCube®, UCS icon, and Viewport Controls are displayed. By default, they're all turned on and are always displayed.

### THE 3D OBJECTS GROUP

These settings affect the display of 3D objects. Visual Style While Creating 3D Objects is self-explanatory. Deletion Control While Creating 3D Objects lets you determine whether objects AutoCAD uses to create 3D objects are saved or deleted.

The U and V isoline settings let you set the number of isolines on 3D solids and surface meshes. Isolines are the lines you see on a mesh or solid that help you visualize their shape. You see them in wireframe and realistic visual styles [Surfu, Surfv].

The Maximum point cloud points per drawing control lets you set a limit to the number of point cloud points so they don't overwhelm your computer.

The Tessellation button opens the Mesh Tessellation Options dialog box where you can set how the Meshsmooth command affects objects. The Mesh Primitives button opens the Mesh Primitive Options dialog box where you adjust the default mesh primitive settings. The Surface Analysis button lets you make adjustments to the way the surface analysis tools behave.

### THE 3D NAVIGATION GROUP

If you want to adjust the way AutoCAD behaves when you're navigating a 3D view, these settings will help. Reverse Mouse Wheel Zoom is self-explanatory [Zoomwheel]. The remaining four buttons give you control over the behavior of the Walk And Fly feature, the Animation settings, the ViewCube display and behavior, and the SteeringWheels™ display and behavior:

**Walk And Fly**   Click this button to open the Walk And Fly Settings dialog box (see Figure B.9). When you first start the 3DWalk or 3DFly feature, you see an instructional window that tells you how to use it. You use the options in the Settings group of the Walk And Fly Settings dialog box to specify when that instructional window appears. After using these features a few times, you may find the instructional window annoying and turn it off. You can turn it back on in this dialog box. You can also set the Position Locator window to appear or not appear automatically.

**FIGURE B.9**
The Walk And Fly
Settings dialog box

The Current Drawing Settings group lets you set the step size and steps per second when you're "walking" or "flying" through your model. These are the same settings you see in the Navigate control panel for Step Size and Steps Per Second [Stepsize, Stepspersec].

**ViewCube** Click this button to open the ViewCube Settings dialog box (see Figure B.10). These settings allow you to control the behavior and appearance of the ViewCube [Navvcubelocation, Navvcubeopacity, Navvcubeorient, Northdirection].

**Animation** Click this button to open the Animation Settings dialog box (see Figure B.11). Here you can control the default visual style, resolution, frame rate, and animation file format when using the Motion Path Animation (Anipath) feature.

**FIGURE B.10**

The ViewCube Set-
tings dialog box

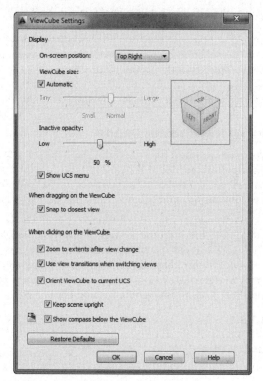

**FIGURE B.11**

The Animation
Settings dialog box

**SteeringWheels** Click this button to open the SteeringWheels Settings dialog box (see Figure B.12). Here you can set the appearance and behavior of the SteeringWheels feature [Navwheelsizemini, Navwheelopacitymini].

**FIGURE B.12**
The SteeringWheels
Settings dialog box

### The Dynamic Input Group

When turned on, the Show Z Field For Pointer Input option offers a z-coordinate for input when Dynamic Input mode is used.

## The Selection Tab

The options in the Selection tab of the Options dialog box (see Figure B.13) control the way you select objects in AutoCAD. You can also make adjustments to the Grips feature.

### The Pickbox Size Group

This slider control lets you adjust the size of the pickbox [Pickbox].

### The Selection Modes Group

These options let you control the degree to which AutoCAD conforms to standard graphical user interface (GUI) methods of operation:

**Noun/Verb Selection**   Makes AutoCAD work more like other Windows programs by letting you select objects before you choose an action or command [Pickfirst].

**Use Shift To Add To Selection**   Lets you use the standard GUI method of holding down the Shift key to select multiple objects. When the Shift key isn't held down, only the single object picked or the group of objects indicated with a window will be selected. Previously selected objects are deselected unless the Shift key is held down during selection. To turn on this feature by using system variables, set Pickadd to 0.

**FIGURE B.13**
The Selection tab

**FIGURE B.13**

The Selection tab

**Object Grouping**   Lets you select groups as single objects [`Pickstyle`].

**Associative Hatch**   Lets you select both a hatch pattern and its associated boundary by using a single pick [`Pickstyle`].

**Implied Windowing**   Causes a window or crossing window to start automatically if no object is picked at the `Select objects:` prompt. This setting has no effect on the Noun/Verb setting. In the system variables, set `Pickauto` to 1 for this option.

**Allow Press And Drag On Object**   Lets you use the standard GUI method for placing window selections. When this option is selected, you click and hold down the Pick button on the first corner of the window. Then, while holding down the Pick button, drag the other corner of the window into position. When the other corner is in place, you let go of the Pick button to finish the window. This setting applies to both Verb/Noun and Noun/Verb operations. In the system variables, set `Pickdrag` to 1 for this option.

**Allow Press And Drag For Lasso**   Enables the Lasso selection feature that lets you create a free-form selection area. When this option is selected, you click and hold the left mouse button while drawing a "free-hand" selection area. A counterclockwise direction creates a "crossing" lasso selection area, and a clockwise direction creates a standard lasso selection area.

**Window Selection Method**   Lets you determine how window selections work. There are three options offered in a drop-down list: Click And Click, Press And Drag, and Both – Automatic Detection. Click And Click places a window by clicking the first corner and then the second. Press And Drag places a window with a press and drag motion of the mouse. Both – Automatic

Detection lets you use both Click And Click and Press And Drag depending on whether you click and hold your mouse on the first click [Pickdrag].

**Object Limit For Properties Palette**   Lets you set the limit for the number of objects that can be edited using the Properties palette at one time. The Value range is 0 to 32,767 [Propobjlimit].

### THE RIBBON OPTIONS GROUP

The Contextual Tab States button in the Ribbon Options group opens the Ribbon Contextual Tab State Options dialog box. This dialog box lets you set the conditions under which the Ribbon contextual tabs are displayed. Contextual tabs are Ribbon tabs that offer tools to edit certain types of objects such as Xrefs or 3D meshes [Ribbonselectmode, Ribboncontextsellim].

### THE GRIP SIZE GROUP

This slider control lets you adjust the size of grips [Gripsize].

### THE GRIPS GROUP

These options control the Grips feature:

**Grip Colors**   Lets you select a color for grips in their various states, such as unselected, selected, hovered, and contour [Gripcolor].

**Show Grips**   Controls the display of grips [Grips].

**Show Grips Within Blocks**   Turns on the display of grips in blocks. Although you can't edit grips in blocks, you can use grips in blocks as selection points [Gripblock].

**Show Grip Tips**   Controls the display of grip tool tips [Griptips].

**Show Dynamic Grip Menu**   Displays a dynamic menu when you're hovering over a multi-function grip [Gripmultifunctional].

**Allow Ctrl+Cycling Behavior**   Turns on Ctrl+cycling behavior for multifunction grips [Gripmultifunctional].

**Show Single Grip On Groups**   Displays a single grip on groups. When this option is not selected, all of the grips in the set of objects in a group are displayed [Groupdisplaymode].

**Show Bounding Box On Groups**   Displays a bounding box around a selected group [Groupdisplaymode].

**Object Selection Limit For Display Of Grips**   Controls the display of grips based on the number of objects selected. If this is set to 1, grips aren't displayed if more than one object is selected. You can select a range from 1 to 32,767. The default is 100 [Gripobjlimit].

### THE PREVIEW GROUP

These options let you control the behavior of the selection preview when you hover over objects or when you are using a command. Click the Visual Effect Settings button to fine-tune the visual effects of the object selection, including the color and pattern of Autoselect windows and which entities to exclude [Selectionpreview]. The Command preview toggle determines whether the result of a command is displayed before you commit to the command. The Property Preview toggle determines whether you see a live view of property changes when rolling over drop-down lists and galleries.

## The Profiles Tab

In Windows, a user profile is saved for each login name. Depending on the login name you use, you can have a different Windows setup. The Profiles tab (see Figure B.14) offers a similar function for AutoCAD users. You can store different settings from the Options dialog box in a profile and recall them at any time. You can also save them to a file with the .arg filename extension and then take that file to another system. It's a bit like being able to take your Options settings with you wherever you go.

**FIGURE B.14**

The Profiles tab

The main part of the Profiles tab displays a list of available profiles. The default profile is shown as <<Unnamed Profile>>. As you add more profiles, they appear in the list.

To create a new profile, highlight a profile name from the list that will be the template for the new profile, and then click Add To List. The Add Profile dialog box opens, where you can enter a profile name and a description of the profile. The description appears in the box below the list on the Profiles tab whenever that profile is selected.

After you've created a new profile, you can modify the settings on the other tabs of the Options dialog box and the new settings will be associated with the new profile. Profiles store the way menus are set up, so you can use them as an aid to managing both your own custom schemes and third-party software. Here is a brief description of the options on the Profiles tab:

**Set Current**   Installs the settings from the selected profile.

**Add To List**   Creates a new profile.

**Rename**  Lets you rename a profile and change its description.

**Delete**  Removes the selected profile from the list.

**Export**  Lets you save a profile to a file.

**Import**  Imports a profile that has been saved to a file.

**Reset**  Resets the values for a selected profile to its default settings.

## The Online Tab

Autodesk® 360 is a feature that allows you to store drawings and AutoCAD settings in a secure, online location. The Online tab enables you to determine the level to which you intend to use Autodesk 360. This tab doesn't show any options until you sign in to your Autodesk 360 account using the Sign In option in the AutoCAD InfoCenter. Once signed in, you will see the options in the Online tab, shown in Figure B.15.

**FIGURE B.15**
The Online tab

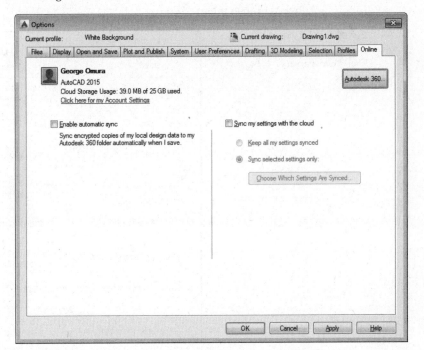

There are two main settings on the Online tab: Enable Automatic Sync and Sync My Settings With The Cloud. With Enable Automatic Sync turned on, you can have AutoCAD automatically save documents to the cloud.

With the Sync My Settings With The Cloud option turned on, you can have all of your AutoCAD settings saved to the cloud or you can select a set of options to be saved.

If you'd like to learn more about Autodesk 360, see "Sharing Files with Autodesk 360" in Chapter 25.

## Configuring the Tablet Menu Area

If you own a digitizing tablet and you would like to use it with a Tablet menu template, you must configure your Tablet menu. Install your Tablet menu into AutoCAD using the Menuload command, and then do the following:

1. Securely fasten your Tablet menu template to the tablet. Be sure the area covered by the template is completely within the tablet's active drawing area.

2. Type **Tablet↵Cfg↵**. The following prompt appears:

```
Enter number of tablet menus desired (0-4) <0>:
```

Enter the number of tablet areas your menu uses and then press ↵. For the next series of prompts, you'll be locating the Tablet menu areas, starting with Menu Area 1. Figure B.16 shows an example of how to locate the Tablet menu areas for the legacy AutoCAD Tablet menu.

**FIGURE B.16**
How to locate the Tablet menu areas

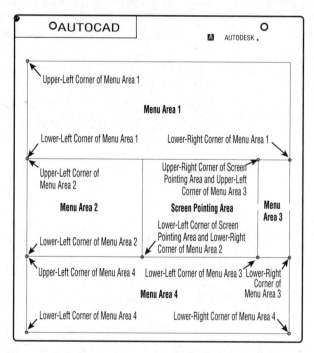

3. Follow the instructions provided by the command-line interface.

4. When you're asked if you want to respecify the fixed screen pointing area, enter **Y↵** and then select the corners of the pointing area as indicated by the prompts.

## Turning On the Noun/Verb Selection Method

If for some reason the Noun/Verb Selection method isn't available, follow these steps to turn it on:

1. Choose Options from the Application menu. Then, in the Options dialog box, click the Selection tab.

2. In the Selection Modes group, click the Noun/Verb Selection check box.

3. Click OK.

You should now see a small square at the intersection of the crosshair cursor. This square is an object selection cursor superimposed on the point selection cursor. It tells you that you can select objects, even while the Command prompt appears at the bottom of the screen and no command is currently active. As you saw earlier, the square momentarily disappears when you're in a command that asks you to select points.

You can also turn on the Noun/Verb Selection method by entering **'Pickfirst**⏎ at the Type a command prompt. At the Enter new value for PICKFIRST <0>: prompt, enter **1**⏎. (Entering 0 turns off the Pickfirst function.) The Pickfirst system variable is stored in the AutoCAD configuration file.

## Turning On the Grips Feature

If for some reason the Grips feature isn't available, follow these steps to turn it on:

1. Choose Options from the Application menu. Then, in the Options dialog box, click the Selection tab.

2. In the Grips group, click the Show Grips check box.

3. Click OK and you're ready to proceed.

The Selection tab of the Options dialog box also lets you specify whether grips appear on objects that compose a block (see Chapter 4 for more on blocks) as well as set the grip color and size. You can also set these options by using the system variables.

You can also turn the Grips feature on and off by entering **'Grips**⏎. At the Enter new value for GRIPS <0>: prompt, enter **1** or **2** to turn grips on or **0** to turn grips off. The 2 option turns on grips and displays additional midpoint grips on polyline line segments. The Grips system variable is stored in the AutoCAD configuration file.

## Setting Up the Tracking Vector Feature

If AutoCAD doesn't display a tracking vector as described in the early chapters of this book, or if the tracking vector doesn't behave as described, chances are this feature has been turned off or altered. Take the following steps to configure the tracking vector so that it behaves as described in this book:

1. Open the Options dialog box by choosing Options from the Application menu.

2. Click the Drafting tab.

**3.** Click all three options in the AutoTrack Settings group.

**4.** Make sure the Marker, Magnet, and Display AutoSnap Tooltip check boxes are selected in the AutoSnap Settings group.

**5.** Make sure the Automatic radio button in the Alignment Point Acquisition group is selected.

**6.** Click OK to exit the dialog box.

## Adjusting the AutoCAD 3D Graphics System

You can adjust the performance of the 2D and 3D graphics system in AutoCAD using the Graphics Performance dialog box (see Figure B.17). To open this dialog box, click the System tab in the Options dialog box and then click the Graphics Performance button in the Hardware Acceleration group.

**FIGURE B.17**
Tuning graphics performance

This dialog box lets you turn on hardware acceleration for your graphic display. If you find that the AutoCAD display is not working properly, you can turn off hardware acceleration. This dialog box also offers control over the way AutoCAD displays 3D modeling features.

## Finding Folders That Contain AutoCAD Files

Many AutoCAD features rely on external files to store settings and other resources. Many of these files reside in folders that are difficult to find. These folders are as follows:

```
C:\Users\User Name\AppData\Local\Autodesk\AutoCAD 2015\R20.0\enu
C:\Users\User Name\AppData\Roaming\Autodesk\AutoCAD 2015\R20.0\enu
```

When you've located these folders, you may want to create a shortcut to them (right-click the folder and choose Create Shortcut). Place the shortcut on your desktop or other convenient location. That way, you can get to them without having to navigate through several layers of folders.

## Setting Up AutoCAD with a White Background

As mentioned in the beginning of Chapter 2, "Creating Your First Drawing," the 2D screen shots in this book are shown with a white background instead of the default dark gray. This is intended to help keep the figures legible in the printed version of this book. You can easily set up your AutoCAD to display the 2D drawing area in the same way by taking the following steps:

1. Open the Application menu and select Options near the bottom of the menu. You can also type **Options.⏎** in the Command window.

2. Select the Display tab in the Options dialog box.

3. Click the Colors button in the Windows Elements group.

4. In the Drawing Window Colors dialog box, make sure 3D parallel projection is selected in the Context settings and that Uniform background is selected in the Interface elements settings.

5. In the Color drop-down list, select white.

6. Select Grid Major Lines in the Interface element list.

7. In the Color drop-down list, click the Select Color option. In the Select Color dialog box, click the Index Color tab and enter **253** in the Color box. Click OK.

8. Select Grid Minor Lines in the Interface element list.

9. In the Color drop-down list, click the Select Color option. In the Select Color dialog box, click the Index Color tab and enter **254** in the Color box. Click OK.

10. Click Apply & Close in the Drawing Window Colors dialog box, and then click OK in the Options dialog box.

# Appendix C

# The Autodesk AutoCAD 2015 Certification

Autodesk certifications are industry-recognized credentials that can help you succeed in your design career, providing benefits to both you and your employer. Getting certified is a reliable validation of skills and knowledge, and it can lead to accelerated professional development, improved productivity, and enhanced credibility.

This Autodesk® Official Press guide can be an effective component of your exam preparation. Autodesk highly recommends (and we agree!) that you schedule regular time to prepare, review the most current exam preparation road map available at www.autodesk.com/certification, use Autodesk Official Press guide, take a class at an Authorized Training Center (find ATCs near you here: www.autodesk.com/atc), and use a variety of resources to prepare for your certification—including plenty of actual hands-on experience.

**CERT OBJECTIVE**

To help you focus your studies on the skills you'll need for these exams, the following tables show objectives that could potentially appear on an exam and in which chapter you can find information on the corresponding topic—and when you go to that chapter, you'll find certification icons like the one in the margin here.

Table C.1 is for the Autodesk Certified User Exam and lists the section, exam objectives, and chapter where the information is found. Table C.2 is for the Autodesk Certified Professional Exam. The sections and exam objectives listed in the table are from the Autodesk Certification Exam Guide.

These Autodesk exam objectives were accurate at press time; please refer to www.autodesk.com/certification for the most current exam road map and objectives.

Good luck preparing for your certification!

**TABLE C.1:** Certified User Exam sections and objectives

| TOPIC | LEARNING OBJECTIVE | CHAPTER |
|---|---|---|
| User Interface: UI Navigation/Interaction | Access various tools on the application menu to create, open, and publish a file. | Chapters 1, 2, 8, and 25 |
| | Identify and state the purpose of the main interface elements: Ribbon ➢ panels ➢ tabs, context (right-click) menus, menus. | Chapter 1 |
| | Demonstrate the use of the tools on the Quick Access toolbar. | Chapters 1 and 2 |
| | Define and set the workspace. | Chapter 24 |

**TABLE C.1:**     Certified User Exam sections and objectives   *(continued)*

| TOPIC | LEARNING OBJECTIVE | CHAPTER |
|---|---|---|
| | Describe the functions of InfoCenter. | Chapter 2 |
| | Use the Application menu or Quick Access toolbar to open an existing file. | Chapter 1 |
| | Describe the two primary spaces in AutoCAD. | Chapters 1, 8, and 15 |
| | Use the Zoom and Pan commands to view different areas of the drawing. | Chapters 1, 2, 6, and 7 |
| Creating Drawings: Coordinate Entry | Describe the two coordinate systems. | Chapter 2 |
| | Use dynamic input, direct distance, and shortcut menus. | Chapters 1 and 2 |
| Creating Drawings: Draw Tools and Settings | Use the Line, Circle, Arc, Erase, Rectangle, and Polygon commands to create and erase geometry in the drawing. | Chapters 1 and 2 |
| | Use object snaps to accurately place and create objects in the drawing. | Chapter 3 |
| | Activate and use the Polar Tracking and PolarSnap modes to more accurately create geometry at different angles in the drawing. | Chapter 3 |
| | Explain, enable, and use object snap tracking to position geometry in the drawing. | Chapter 3 |
| | Describe the process of setting length and angle units. | Chapter 3 |
| | Describe the Snap and Grid, Polar Tracking, and Object Snap settings. | Chapter 3 |
| Manipulating Objects: Grips | Use grip modes to stretch, move, scale, rotate, or mirror an object. | Chapter 2 |
| Manipulating Objects: Object Selection | Use single clicks to add and remove objects from a selection set. | Chapter 2 |
| | Use a window to select only objects that are entirely enclosed by the rectangular area. | Chapter 2 |
| | Use a window to select objects that the rectangular window encloses or crosses. | Chapter 2 |

| TOPIC | LEARNING OBJECTIVE | CHAPTER |
|---|---|---|
| Manipulating Objects: Move Objects | Use coordinates, grid snap, object snaps, and other tools to move objects with precision. | Chapters 2 and 3 |
| Drawing Organization and Inquiry Commands: Layers | Use layers and the Layer Properties Manager to organize objects in your drawing. | Chapter 5 |
| Drawing Organization and Inquiry Commands: Object Properties | Use the Quick Properties palette to display and change the most commonly used properties. | Chapter 5 |
| | Use the Properties palette to display and change the properties of the selected object or set of objects. | Chapters 2, 5, 7, 12, and online bonus chapter "Understanding Plot Styles" |
| | Use the Match Properties command to apply the properties from a source object to destination objects. | Chapter 7 |
| Drawing Organization and Inquiry Commands: Linetypes | Use linetypes to distinguish objects in the drawing. | Chapter 5 |
| Drawing Organization and Inquiry Commands: Inquiry | Use the Inquiry commands (Distance, Radius, Angle, Area, List, and ID) to obtain geometric information. | Chapters 2, 5, and 19 |
| Altering Objects: Modify Tools | Change the length of objects using the Trim and Extend commands. | Chapters 3 and 6 |
| | Create parallel and offset geometry in your drawing by using the Offset command. | Chapters 3 and 18 |
| | Use the Join command to combine multiple objects into a single object. | Chapters 3, 6, and 18 |
| | Break objects into two or more independent objects. | Chapters 5 and 6 |
| | Apply a radius corner to two objects in the drawing. | Chapters 3, 6, and 18 |
| | Apply an angled corner to two objects in the drawing. | Chapter 6 and 24 |
| | Use the Stretch command to alter the shape of objects in the drawing. | Chapters 2 and 11 |

**TABLE C.1:**     Certified User Exam sections and objectives   *(continued)*

| TOPIC | LEARNING OBJECTIVE | CHAPTER |
|---|---|---|
| Working with Layouts: Layouts and Viewports | Identify the environments in which you can plot data and create a new layout. | Chapters 1, 8, and 15 |
| | Create and manipulate viewports. | Chapter 15 |
| Annotating the Drawing | Use the Mtext command to create multi-line text. | Chapter 9 |
| | Create single-line text. | Chapter 9 |
| | Use different methods to edit text. | Chapter 9 |
| | Create text styles to manage text. | Chapter 9 |
| Dimensioning | Create dimensions using different options: Linear, Angular, Aligned, Radius, Diameter, and Center Mark. | Chapter 11 and online bonus chapter "System Variables and Dimension Styles" |
| | Use dimension styles to manage dimensions. | Chapter 11 and online bonus chapter "System Variables and Dimension Styles" |
| | Create and edit multileader styles and multileaders. | Chapter 11 |
| | Use different commands and methods to edit dimensions. | Chapter 11 |
| Hatching Objects | Add a hatch pattern to a defined boundary. | Chapter 7 |
| Hatching Objects: Fills and Gradients | Add a fill pattern or gradient to a defined boundary. | Chapter 7 |
| Hatching Objects: Edit Hatch Patterns and Fills | Modify an existing hatch or fill. | Chapter 7 |
| Working with Reusable Content: Blocks | Define and name a block. | Chapters 4 and 17 |
| | Specify the name and position of a block or drawing to insert in a drawing. | Chapter 4 |
| Working with Reusable Content: DesignCenter | Use DesignCenter™ to reuse the data in a drawing. | Chapter 25 |
| Working with Reusable Content: Tool Palettes | Access tool palettes and use their tools. | Chapters 1 and 25 |

| TOPIC | LEARNING OBJECTIVE | CHAPTER |
|---|---|---|
| Creating Additional Drawing Objects: Shapes | Create and edit polylines with the Polyline command. | Chapter 18 |
| | Create smooth curves with the Spline command. | Chapter 18 |
| | Create ellipses and elliptical arcs with the Ellipse command. | Chapter 3 |
| Plotting Your Drawing: Output | Create and activate page setups. | Chapter 8 |
| | Plot design geometry from model space or from a layout. | Chapters 8 and 22 |

**TABLE C.2:**   Certified Professional Exam sections and objectives

| TOPIC | LEARNING OBJECTIVE | CHAPTER |
|---|---|---|
| Apply Basic Drawing Skills | Draw lines and rectangles. | Chapters 1, 2, and 3 |
| | Use coordinate systems. | Chapters 2, 3, and 21 |
| | Draw circles, arcs, and polygons. | Chapters 2, 6, and 18 |
| | Fillet and chamfer lines. | Chapters 3 and 6 |
| Use Drawing Aids | Work with Grid and Snap. | Chapter 6 |
| | Use Ortho and Polar Tracking. | Chapter 3 |
| | Use Polar Snap. | Chapter 3 |
| | Use running object snaps. | Chapters 2, 3, and 11 |
| | Use object snap tracking. | Chapters 2, 3, and 6 |
| Edit Entities | Create selection sets. | Chapter 2 |
| | Use Move and Copy. | Chapter 2 |
| | Use Rotate and Scale. | Chapter 2 |
| | Create and use arrays. | Chapters 6 and 21 |
| | Use Trim and Extend. | Chapter 3 |

**TABLE C.2:** Certified Professional Exam sections and objectives *(continued)*

| TOPIC | LEARNING OBJECTIVE | CHAPTER |
|---|---|---|
| | Use Offset and Mirror. | Chapters 3 and 18 |
| | Use grip editing. | Chapter 2 |
| Work with Curves | Draw and edit curved polylines. | Chapter 18 |
| | Blend between objects with splines. | Chapters 6 and 18 |
| Control Object Visibility and Appearance | Change object properties. | Chapter 2 |
| | Alter layer assignments for objects. | Chapter 5 |
| | Manage layer properties. | Chapter 5 |
| Use Blocks and Xrefs | Define blocks. | Chapters 4 and 17 |
| | Work with global blocks. | Chapter 4 |
| | Reference external drawings and images. | Chapters 7 and 14 |
| Use Hatching and Gradients | Apply hatch patterns. | Chapter 7 |
| Create and Edit Text | Create text styles. | Chapter 9 |
| | Write lines of text. | Chapter 9 |
| Dimensioning | Create and apply dimension styles. | Chapter 11 |
| | Use multileaders. | Chapter 11 |
| Layouts and Annotative Objects | Create annotative styles and objects. | Chapters 4, 9, and 11 |
| | Create layouts. | Chapters 8 and 15 |
| | Use viewports. | Chapters 8 and 15 |
| Printing and Plottings | Set printing and plotting options. | Chapter 8 |

# Index

**Note to the Reader:** Throughout this index **boldfaced** page numbers indicate primary discussions of a topic. *Italicized* page numbers indicate illustrations.